Tenth Edit

POLITICS AND CHANGE IN THE MIDDLE EAST

Roy R. Andersen

Robert F. Seibert

Jon G. Wagner

All of Knox College

Longman

Boston   Columbus   Indianapolis   New York   San Francisco   Upper Saddle River
Amsterdam   Cape Town   Dubai   London   Madrid   Milan   Munich   Paris   Montreal   Toronto
Delhi   Mexico City   Sao Paulo   Sydney   Hong Kong   Seoul   Singapore   Taipei   Tokyo

Senior Acquisitions Editor: Vikram Mukhija
Editorial Assistant: Beverly Fong
Senior Marketing Manager: Lindsey Prudhomme
Production Project Manager: Clara Bartunek
Project Coordination, Text Design, and Electronic
   Page Makeup: George Jacob / Integra Software Services Pvt. Ltd.
Cover Design Manager: Jayne Conte
Cover Designer: Karen Noferi
Cover Illustration/Photo: Getty Images / Amir Sadeghi
Manufacturing Buyer: Clara Bartunek
Printer and Binder: STP Courier / Stoughton
Cover Printer: STP Courier / Stoughton

Credits and acknowledgements borrowed from other sources and reproduced, with permission, in this textbook appear on appropriate page within text.

Library of Congress Cataloging-in-Publication Data
Andersen, Roy.
   Politics and change in the Middle East : sources of conflict and accommodation / Roy R. Andersen,
   Robert F. Seibert, Jon G. Wagner.—10th ed.
      p. cm.
   ISBN-13: 978-0-205-08239-1 (alk. paper)
   ISBN-10: 0-205-08239-4 (alk. paper)
   1. Middle East—Politics and government.   I. Seibert, Robert F.   II.   Wagner, Jon G.   III. Title.
DS62.8.A5 2012
956—dc22
                                                                                2010047707

1 2 3 4 5 6 7 8 9 10—CRS—14 13 12 11

Longman
is an imprint of

PEARSON

www.pearsonhighered.com

ISBN-13: 978-0-205-08239-1
ISBN-10:   0-205-08239-4

To Our Children and Grandchildren
Brynn, Eric, Kyla, Nicholas, Joanna and Seth
and Our Wives
Corine, Jan and Marna

BRIEF CONTENTS

DETAILED CONTENTS

PREFACE

As we begin the revisions necessary to our tenth edition, we are struck as authors by the range and intensity of changes that have occurred in the Middle East and the outside world during the 30 years since the publication of our first edition. Changes since 2008 require this new edition—changes that have been dramatic, often violent, and certainly fraught with future consequences.

We are also struck by how different the challenges in 2010 are from the changes that required our ninth edition. The single-most important event necessitating this new edition is the election in November 2008 of Barack Obama as president of the United States. Obama's election signaled a sea-change in the philosophy and conduct of U.S. foreign policy generally and toward the Middle East specifically. Obama replaced the neoconservative unilateralism of the Bush Administration with a realist multilateralism. The specific changes in policy are substantive and in many cases dramatic. We address the implications of this change throughout the portions of the text dealing with contemporary issues.

The old bipolar world is definitely gone. It has been replaced by a more fluid international system with a less than dominant superpower. The same observation also applies to the Middle East itself, where tensions between neighbors continue to color political relationships. Syria's abrupt withdrawal from its 30-year occupation of Lebanon has created complications of its own. Syria's neighbor to the south, Iraq, complains that jihadists routinely cross the Syrian border into Iraq. Israel sees Iran as a real danger to its security, and Iran, under the leadership of its president, Ahmad Amadinejad, threatens Israel with destruction. Jordan, Egypt, and Saudi Arabia have been the targets of serious terrorist attacks. The list goes on and on.

NEW TO THIS EDITION

As we look at the Middle East in 2010, we are confronted with a different series of challenges, some of them specific to the Middle East; others clearly are more global in character. Among the substantive political challenges for the tenth edition, we note:

- An important series of elections, beginning with the late 2008 U.S. presidential election
- The Obama Administration's change in the conduct of U.S. foreign policy
- The 2009 parliamentary elections in Israel, which brought an unprecedented right-of-center coalition into power, with contingent changes in foreign policy
- The 2009 Iranian presidential elections, which reversed Iran's previous accomplishments at electoral democracy
- The continued presidency of Mahmoud Ahmadinezad, the controversial and erratic leader of Iran
- Iran's continued movement toward nuclear capability
- The Iraqi parliamentary elections of spring 2010, which had failed months after the election to organize a new government, adding measurably to the ethnic volatility of the country
- All of this in the context of a global economic crisis of epic proportions

All of these changes, mind you, occurred during the normal course of political events in the countries and cultures of the Middle East. Therefore, we have embarked on a tenth edition, marking over 30 years of political change. Any smaller combination of these events would argue for a new edition; taken together, they require it.

FEATURES

Fortunately, not all of these changes, as important and dramatic as they are, compel us to abandon all previous lines of research and analysis. Our original paradigm of political conflict and accommodation, combined with the **thematic analyses** of the area (**culture, history, economics, social systems, religion,** and, of course, **politics**), has proved sufficiently flexible. We emphasize here that our thematic approach to analysis differs dramatically from the more common and conventional "country studies" that treat these issues in a fragmented and piecemeal way.

An important feature added to this new edition is a Glossary appearing at the back of the book. This tool will help the reader in reviewing the various key terms and words used in the countries of the Middle East.

We have directed our writing to an undergraduate audience not specifically acquainted with the Middle East. In addition, we have made every effort to avoid disciplinary jargon, arcane theoretical concepts, or other devices that would necessitate a sophisticated background in any of the social sciences. This is not to say that we do not introduce any special concepts or terms, but we do so only as necessary, and we do it as painlessly as possible.

Our thematic pedagogy is apparent in the organization of the book and in the particular sequence of chapters. We begin with a series of chapters designed to acquaint the student with the necessary fundamentals regarding the history and cultures of the area. We remind everyone here that the subject matter of these chapters is opaque and distant to most readers seeking an introduction to the area. It is important that a thematic treatment of the Middle East begin with this information. The particular introductory chapters are featured here:

Chapter 1: Traditional Cultures of the Middle East.
This chapter introduces the area and argues for its importance in the development of world civilization.

Chapter 2: The Foundations of Islam.
Islam is possibly the single-most influential factor in the ancient and modern Middle East. A basic familiarity with the history and tenets of this major monotheistic religion is very important to an understanding of salient issues in the contemporary Middle East system.

Chapter 3: The Political Legacy of Islam.
This chapter reviews important themes and events in the development of the various political institutions of Islam, including the classic caliphate, the collapse of the classic empires, the development of shariah law, the divide between Sunni and Shi'a communities, the role of Sufism; and the rise of radically Islamist movements.

Chapter 4: Western Imperialism, 1800 to 1914.
The intrusion of the European west into the political and social life of the Middle East is examined and explained. Much of the resentment toward Western power in the late twentieth and early twenty-first centuries is derived from this important historical experience.

Chapter 5: The Rise of the State System.
This chapter examines the establishment during colonial rule of the basic national institutions of the colonial state. This period is of great importance to the following analysis of the efforts by Middle Eastern peoples to shake off the effects of European imperialism.

Chapter 6: The Drive for Self-Determination.
This chapter brings us analytically into the modern era and the politics of petroleum, nationalism, and the rise of Israel and the accompanying Palestinian resistance.

Chapters 7 through 15 examine specific issues important to an understanding of contemporary Middle Eastern politics, up to and including events in the twenty-first century. They are:

Chapter 7: Turning Points.
Chapter 7 presents a survey of current events and

issues specific to the Middle East, including the topics of globalization, Arab nationalism, economic development, and efforts to resolve the Israeli–Palestinian conflict.

Chapter 8: The Politics of Religion, Culture, and Social Life. In this chapter, we examine the situation "on the ground" as it pertains to the contemporary cultural politics of the region, including analysis of the questions of gender, the importance of the Iranian revolution, and a look at the important question of the role of religion in economic and political development.

Chapter 9: Political Elites. Here, we examine and analyze the configuration of political elites across the region. Elites are categorized as traditional, transitional, and technically modernizing.

Chapter 10: Political Leadership in the Contemporary Middle East. This chapter focuses on the leadership of traditional, charismatic, and modernizing configurations. The styles and consequences of particular leaders are given as examples, such as the leadership experience of Egypt under Nasser and Sadat, of Iran under Ayatollah Khomeini and the Shah, and Israel under Sharon and Netanyahu.

Chapter 11: The Economic Setting. The important questions of economics in the region—including sections on the economics of land, water, oil, and population—are addressed. The history of area economies are examined and the role of Islamic banking is appraised. The important questions of globalization and economic liberalization are examined.

Chapter 12: International Relations in the Middle East, 1945–1990. This chapter sets the stage for a continuing discussion and analysis of international relations in the region. Issues include the great power system, the specific foreign policies of the United States, Russia, Britain, France, China, and Japan.

Chapter 13: International Relations in the Middle East, 1945–1990: The Regional Actors. Chapter 13 begins with an analysis of the Palestinian effort to resist Israel's control, and the specific policy regimes of Egypt, Saudi Arabia, Iran, and Israel. OPEC is analyzed and evaluated.

Chapter 14: The Middle East and the Changing International Order. This chapter examines the foreign policy environment in the Middle East beginning with the decline of Soviet power, the changing configuration of power within the region, up to the end of the twentieth century.

Chapter 15: Did 9/11 Change Everything? The concluding chapter examines the international politics of the region in the twenty-first century, It begins with the catastrophic attacks on the World Trade Center and the Pentagon, the resulting transformation of U.S. foreign policy under President Bush, the second war with Iraq and the subsequent occupation of Iraq, and ends with the changing dimensions of U.S. foreign policy under President Obama.

U.S. foreign policy in the area has been problematic and complicated since World War II and remains so. The Obama Administration brings new assumptions and new personnel to the conduct of U.S. foreign policy generally, and in the Middle East specifically. Among the apparent changes in foreign policy is an effort to reach out to the Muslim world, an effort to engage problems and opportunities multilaterally. This contrasts strongly with the "muscular unilateralism" of the George W. Bush Administration and in the short run shows some promise for broader coalitions, the most recent example being the coalition of states and international organizations now cooperating in the sanctions regime against Iran. The long-term effects of the U.S. policy toward Iraq have yet to play out fully; but at this time, the United States finds itself in the very definition of a quagmire, as a fair and open election has produced political stasis in Iraq, at the time in which the U.S. is committed to ending its combat role in Iraq and to reducing its forces there to less than 50,000 troops. All of this occurred as the war in Afghanistan achieved the dubious honor of being the longest war in U.S. history.

No major contemporary issue demonstrates that complexity as strongly as the **Iranian nuclear crisis,** fomented by Iran's pursuit of a nuclear power capability, and by the corresponding fact that such an industrial capability also could provide Iran with the components for a basic nuclear weapons capability. The United Nations, the International Atomic Energy Agency, the United States, France, Russia, and China all are involved in attempts to resolve the problem. Russia, more sympathetic to Iran than Israel or the Western European powers, has offered to perform the uranium enrichment for Iran in Russia. Israel has threatened direct military action, and the United States has threatened "progressive sanctions." The problem is real, the consequences are important, and the policy process is ongoing.

For these reasons and more, we have embarked on a tenth edition of this book. This book grew directly out of the authors' conviction that a proper understanding of present events in the Middle East requires knowledge of the cultural, historical, social, economic, and political background of these events. It is, more specifically, an outgrowth of the authors' attempts to develop an undergraduate course sequence aimed at such understanding. We found that, despite the abundance of excellent scholarship on the Middle East, there was a paucity of works that brought together the diverse disciplinary perspectives in a way suitable to our pedagogic aims. It is our belief that this book, with its combination of historical and contemporary materials and its integrated perspective, provides something of value that is not available elsewhere to the undergraduate student or educator.

We also acknowledge here some important organizational changes at Pearson Publications. First, there is the reorganization of Pearson's academic publications. Titles of a technical nature will now be the preserve of Prentice-Hall, our publisher for the last 30 years. Academic publications will now be part of the Longman list, of which we are now proud members. With the shift to Longman, a number of pedagogical changes have been made.

One of the characteristic problems in writing about another culture involves the use of language. The words used by Arabs, Turks, and Persians to describe institutions and concepts fundamental to their civilization usually have no direct equivalent in English. We are faced with the dilemma of whether to translate them (which introduces our own cultural bias) or to use "native" terms (which places on the reader the burden of learning a new vocabulary). Compounding this problem is the more technical matter of how to transliterate Arabic or other languages into the medium of the English alphabet. Our solution has been one of compromise; we have used foreign words when there is no English equivalent or when the nearest English equivalent would be awkward or misleading. Despite our efforts to minimize the use of foreign words, the text has unavoidably made use of many of them—especially Arabic terms. All of these are explained in the text, and whenever possible the explanation accompanies the first appearance of a term, which is indicated by the use of italics. As an extra aid to the student, we also have included important terms in a glossary. The terms explained in the glossary are in boldface type the first time they appear in the text. As for the spelling of Arabic and other foreign words, we have omitted the diacritical marks that scholars use to render their transliterations technically correct. We do so on the assumption that the limited number of terms we use can, for the reader's purposes, be determined without these marks. Nearly all Arabic terms appear in several different English forms in the literature;

we have tried to hold to those forms that reflect the most frequent current usage among informed scholars who write for a general audience. In personal names especially, we have often departed from the technically correct forms and employed instead the forms used in English for news reportage and popular historical writing.

One further matter that deserves mention here is the definition of the Middle East itself. The term *Middle East* raises some problems, for it originates in recent Western military usage and uses present national boundaries that cut across historically significant cultural and geographic divisions. The reference to the region as part of the "East" reveals a European bias; from the larger perspective of the whole civilized area stretching from Western Europe to East Asia, the so-called Middle East is located toward the West and has close cultural ties with the Mediterranean region as a whole. Despite these problems, we shall follow the (more or less) established convention and define the *Middle East* as the region bounded on the northwest by Turkey, on the southwest by Egypt, on the southeast by the Arabian Peninsula, and on the northeast by Iran. It must be remembered that this division is arbitrary, and that bordering regions such as Afghanistan, the Sudan, and North Africa have much in common with their "Middle Eastern" neighbors. For this reason, we shall include them in our discussions whenever appropriate.

The authorship of this book is genuinely a joint affair; there is no "senior" author. The order of our names on the title page was randomly chosen. One of the authors is an economist with a long-standing interest in economic development, one is a political scientist specializing in political development in the third world, and the third is a cultural anthropologist specializing in religion and culture change. Each chapter was largely the work of a single author, but each reflects a dialogue that began long before the book was conceived and has continued throughout its preparation and revision.

SUPPLEMENTS

Longman is pleased to offer several resources to qualified adopters of *Politics and Change in the Middle East* and their students that will make teaching and learning from this book even more effective and enjoyable.

PASSPORT FOR COMPARATIVE POLITICS   With Passport, choose the resources you want from MyPoliSciKit and links to them into your course management system. If there is assessment associated with those resources, it also can be uploaded, allowing the results to feed directly into your course management system's gradebook. With over 150 MyPoliSciKit assets such as video case studies, mapping exercises, comparative exercises, simulations, podcasts, *Financial Times* newsfeeds, current events quizzes, politics blog, and much more, Passport is available for any Pearson introductory or upper-level political science book. Use ISBN 0-205-00296-X to order Passport with this book. To learn more, please contact your Pearson representative.

MYSEARCHLAB   Need help with a paper? MySearchLab saves time and improves results by offering start-to-finish guidance on the research/writing process and full-text access to academic journals and periodicals. Use ISBN 0-205-09565-8 to order MySearchLab with this book. To learn more, please visit www.mysearchlab.com or contact your Pearson representative.

THE ECONOMIST   Every week, *The Economist* analyzes the important happenings around the globe. From business to politics, to the arts and science, its coverage connects seemingly unrelated events in unexpected ways. Use ISBN 0-205-00288-9 to order a 15-week subscription with this book for a small additional charge. To learn more, please contact your Pearson representative.

THE FINANCIAL TIMES   Featuring international news and analysis from journalists in more than

50 countries, *The Financial Times* provides insights and perspectives on political and economic developments around the world. Use ISBN 0-205-0747-X to order a 15-week subscription with this book for a small additional charge. To learn more, please contact your Pearson representative.

ACKNOWLEDGMENTS

We cannot hope to name all the people and institutions that have made important contributions to this writing. We wish to thank Knox College for its material and moral support, and particularly for maintaining an atmosphere that nourishes interdisciplinary collaboration and teaching. We are indebted to the U.S. Office of Education, which made it possible for us to observe. first hand, the phenomena of social and political change in two Muslim countries, Egypt and Malaysia, during 1976 and 1977. We also thank Dr. John Duke Anthony, founder, director, and driving force of the National Council on U.S.–Arab Relations, under whose sponsorship we have collectively traveled to Bahrain, Iraq, Jordan, Kuwait, Saudi Arabia, Syria, the United Arab Emirates, and Israel and the Palestinian territories it occupies. There are scores of individuals in each of these countries who gave generously of their precious time and considerable talents so that we could better appreciate some nuances of highly complex situations. We also owe thanks to Professor John Woods and the Center for Middle Eastern Studies at the University of Chicago.

The staff at Longman, especially Vikram Mukhija and Beverly Fong, has been supportive and professional. We would also like to thank the reviewers for the last edition, including Zohair Husain, University of South Alabama; Paul Rowe, Trinity Western University; Sanford Silverburg, Catawba College; and Anca Turcu, University of Central Florida. Finally, we thank our students at Knox, whose interest in the Middle East, energy, and enthusiasm give us continued motivation for this work.

Above all, we take this opportunity to express our appreciation to our wives and children for suffering bravely through what is, as every author knows, the seemingly endless task of transforming a set of ideas into a finished book.

Roy R. Andersen

Robert F. Seibert

Jon G. Wagner

INTRODUCTION

Events in the Middle East have been capturing worldwide attention since the 1970s. Hefty increases in petroleum prices brought about by the efforts of the Organization of Petroleum Exporting Countries (OPEC), the spectacular rise of the Islamic Republic of Iran, the Iran–Iraq war, and conflicts in Lebanon, the West Bank, and the Persian (Arabian) Gulf have riveted the attention of the regional actors and the world as a whole. Only a couple of decades earlier, many outside the region saw the problems of the Middle East as largely local affairs that rarely affected the world political arena. Today, the Middle East is properly regarded as crucial to world events, and it will continue to be so regarded in the foreseeable future.

The Middle East's geographic position alone, at the junction of Africa, Asia, and Europe, is ample reason for it to command the world's attention. A sign in the Cairo airport proclaims it the "Crossroads of the World," a slogan that rings true for several reasons. Three great monotheistic religions—Judaism, Christianity, and Islam—arose from the same society and culture; the Western and Muslim intellectual heritages have much more in common than is generally recognized. Although some major strands of Western thought can be traced to Greece, much of Greek philosophy and science were preserved and transmitted to the West through the writings of Muslim scholars. The Middle East served as a repository of Greek thought while Europe languished in the Dark Ages. Also during this time, a great intellectual and cultural florescence occurred in the Islamic world. The development of algebra (in Arabic, *al-jabr*), fundamental advances in the sciences of optics and medicine, and many other intellectual achievements originated in the Middle East. Concepts from the Far East were melded into Middle Eastern intellectual and cultural patterns. "Arabic" numerals, the decimal system, and the use of zero—all brought to the Middle East from India—paved the way for profound advances in quantitative thinking. The role of the Middle East in trade and conquest, no less than its intellectual activity, made it a crossroads in every way. The Middle East is not a desert devoid of high culture and rich history; the religion of its peoples is not characterized by wild-eyed fanaticism. The Middle East should not be viewed as an exotic area of intellectual inquiry, but rather as integral to our understanding of the world.

A serious study of the relationship of the Middle East to the rest of the world must introduce a broad array of facts, assumptions, hypotheses, and theories—all of which might threaten to overwhelm the beginning student. Although Egypt, Saudi Arabia, Iran, Lebanon, and other Middle Eastern states share a common heritage, particular historic, geographic, and economic influences have produced substantial regional diversity. The Middle East cannot be viewed as a monolithic entity; its constituent regions and entities must be studied carefully to identify points of commonality and divergence. The welter of information generated by these complexities can create more confusion than understanding, more tedium than excitement. We have selected two themes— conflict (and its resolution) and social change—to make the task more manageable for the beginning student. Although we focus on political systems in the Middle East, we carry our themes across disciplinary lines into other social sciences. We have not attempted, however, a systematic coverage of Islamic art, literature, science, and theology, even though such coverage would lend richness and subtlety to the topics covered in the text. We encourage the student to explore these topics.

POLITICS AND CONFLICT

The first theme of our text centers on the definition of politics employed: the study of conflicts between groups of people and how those conflicts are resolved in human institutions. Conflict is present in all societies and is caused by competing demands for limited resources. The demand for resources embraces a wide variety of valued things; it may include ordinary things, such as money, land, and water, or more abstract things, such as deference, prestige, or even claims on cultural and religious symbols of legitimacy. The propensity of humans to demand such things in greater quantity than the supply allows leads to conflict over distribution or consumption. When formal organizations make socially binding decisions regarding such things, they are engaging in the political resolution of social conflict. To sum up, *conflict* arises out of the inevitable competition for scarce resources; *politics* involves the resolution of these conflicts through the formal and informal processes and institutions that constitute government. We consequently equate politics with the formation and resolution of conflict in social life. Although there are many alternate definitions of politics that could be employed, the one given here is widely used and fits into the major plan of this book.

Conflict and conflict resolution occur at various levels of social organization. Conflict over water resources can occur at the local level (Which fields are to receive how much water?), at the regional level (Should a dam be constructed in region A or region B?), or at the national level (Should a country rely on its existing water sources or explore the feasibility of desalination of ocean water?). Although all of these decisions involve the provision and allocation of scarce resources, the people, institutions, and style of decision making vary from one level to another. Conflict resolution involving personal discussion among those affected is more likely to occur at the local level than at the regional or national level. The political

processes employed depend on the level and arena of conflict.

In this text, we discuss political conflict in terms of the applicable arenas. In a discussion of the elite structure of a given government, we distinguish between the qualities and styles of national and local elites. This is a convenient way of analyzing a nation's political system. However, no nation consists of neatly layered conflict arenas; any given arena interacts with other arenas that are potentially higher, lower, or equal in level. The arenas of conflict in a nation resemble the composition of a multiflavored marble cake in which various colors and flavors dip and swirl irregularly.

As an example, the complex interaction of arenas can be seen in the decisions that led to the construction and operation of the Aswan High Dam in Egypt. Egypt is, as Herodotus said more than 2,000 years ago, the "gift of the Nile." Almost all its arable land lies in the Nile Valley and Delta. Over thousands of years, the cultivators of the land have adapted their agricultural techniques and timing to the annual flooding of the river. Regulating the flow of the Nile through the construction of a large dam, it was theorized, would free the farmers from dependence on the caprice of the river, minimize flood damage, and maximize agricultural production.

The project brought to light many unanticipated conflicts—some of which had been simmering below the surface of day-to-day events, and some of which were created by the construction and operation of the dam. The major themes of conflict were as follows:

1. The financing and construction of the dam involved superpower interests. The United States had first agreed to finance the project, but backed out of the agreement; the U.S.S.R. then stepped in to fill the breach.
2. The determination of water rights between Egypt and the Sudan had to be resolved because the lake formed by the

dam crossed the border dividing the two countries.

3. Thousands of families had to be relocated from the lake site into existing or new villages and towns.
4. A system for allocating irrigation water to Nile Delta farmers had to be developed.
5. Drainage problems induced by the operation of the dam required individual, village, provincial, national, and finally World Bank intervention.

The relationships among various groups involved had to be reworked, sometimes drastically. The Aswan High Dam was—and is—the focal point of conflict in several arenas; it is an example of the tendency for solutions in one arena to generate new problems in another, in a complex cycle of cause and effect.

APPROACHES TO SOCIAL CHANGE

Human social life is changing with increasing speed. Certain trends set in motion only a few centuries ago have accelerated and spread until they have profoundly affected most of the world's societies and have drawn nations into an unprecedented degree of interdependence. Westerners, who have benefited in particular from many of these changes, sometimes take them for granted as part of the natural course of human "progress," without much attempt at a deeper critical understanding. Even the social sciences may be subtly influenced by ethnocentric assumptions. For the Western reader to grasp the essence of these changes and to understand their causes without falling into the trap of cultural chauvinism (or its negative counterpart, cultural self-deprecation) is no easy task.

Many Westerners naively assume that the West has been in the forefront of cultural development for thousands of years This view is enhanced by grafting European history onto that of the Greeks while placing the Middle East in the vague category of "Oriental" or "Asian" cultures. By any objective standards, Western Europe could not be called a leader in world cultural development until very late in history. Even after the Renaissance, Europe was on no more than an equal footing with the older centers of civilization, and it was only in the eighteenth century that it decisively surpassed the Middle East in technology and commercial power.

What is the nature of the unique change that originated in Western society and subsequently influenced the emerging world order, and why did it occur in Europe rather than in the older centers of civilization? Marshall G. S. Hodgson, in his remarkably insightful work. *The Venture of Islam,* has characterized this change as one toward "technicalization."[1] A technicalized society is one in which the interplay of specialized technical considerations tends to take precedence over esthetic, traditional, interpersonal, religious, or other nontechnical concerns—in short, a society structured by the demands of specialized technical efficiency. This is not to imply that nontechnicalistic societies have no interest in technical efficiency or that technicalistic societies care for nothing else, but only that the unprecedented emphasis on specialized technical considerations has played a key role in the development of modern cultures. The process of technicalization and its ramifications can be seen as central to many of the cultural changes that are taking place in contemporary countries, from the poorest to the most affluent. Some of these changes tend to occur repeatedly in different countries because they are directly related to the process of technicalization; others, such as style of clothing or taste in entertainment, are communicated as part of a growing international cosmopolitan culture. Some changes are predictable, whereas others are not, and some may be fundamental to the technicalization process, whereas others are only incidental to it.

---

[1]Marshall G. S. Hodgson, *The Venture of Islam,* Vol. 3 (Chicago: University of Chicago Press, 1974), pp. 186–196.

Perhaps the most fundamental elements are economic and technological in nature. The rise of technicalism in Europe was accompanied by certain changes that still seem inseparable from it, and central among these is the institutionalization of technical innovation. The ability to adopt efficient technical innovations was the key to success among the competing private business enterprises of seventeenth-century and eighteenth-century Europe, and for that reason traditional European social forces that impeded free scientific inquiry gradually gave way before a cultural outlook that took for granted continuous inquiry and innovation. Such an outlook has had far-reaching consequences in noneconomic realms, but its effect on the technoeconomic order has been most immediate. It has led to a rapid development of industrial production, the use of fossil fuels, complex machines, standardized mass production, a highly specialized division of labor and knowledge, and a substantial reinvestment of profits in the machinery of production. This pattern of production has been accompanied by a growth of regional interdependence so that even nonindustrialized regions tend to become part of a growing network for the exchange of raw materials and manufactured items. This integration may or may not occur on such terms as to facilitate an increase in economic independence and material well-being for a given society; there is nothing in the creation of a world economic system that ensures justice, equality, or a universal advance in well-being.

In addition to its material aspects, the technicalizing trend has had many social and cultural consequences. In society in general, there has been a greater tendency for roles and social status to be achieved rather than ascribed on the basis of gender, age, kinship, or circumstances of birth. The criterion of technical efficiency is applied in politics, where technical competence gradually displaces the more traditional criteria for choosing leaders, while the public becomes increasingly informed and competent in political matters. Mass communication has brought about the possibility of mass public support for political leaders and programs, ushering in a new era of participatory politics (or active repression of burgeoning popular movements). The institutionalization of change, together with the notion of holding customs and institutions accountable to criteria of technical efficiency, also brings about new attitudes toward societal rules, which are less likely to be seen as absolute and eternal. Finally, increased communication and interdependence have helped to create a much more cosmopolitan outlook in which an increasing number of people see themselves, if not as "citizens" of the whole world, at least as actors in it.

The historical reasons for the technicalization of the West are difficult to unravel, but they may include some geographic and ecological components. Some of the ecological conditions that retarded European civilization in earlier history may have aided its more recent rise. Among the most significant factors in the rise of technicalism in the West were the unprecedented importance of capital reinvestment and technological innovation, both of which were being built into the commercial institutions of eighteenth-century Europe. It is possible that entrepreneurial capitalism, which supported this competition for technical efficiency, was discouraged in the older civilizations where irrigation-based agriculture promoted the consolidation of a more centralized governmental control. Europe, by contrast, had an economy based on rainfall agriculture that provided less of a basis for centralized control of the economy; monarchs and central bureaucracies were less able to thwart and exploit would-be capitalists. The West's economic potential in the eighteenth century may have been bolstered by the fact that it, in contrast to the land-depleted Middle East, still had virgin countryside into which agricultural production could expand. Whatever the historical reasons for the priority of Europe in making the transition, the West's institutionalization of technical efficiency and technological innovation has done much to determine not only the character of the West itself, but also of the world order.

The West did not set out to conquer the world; rather, each European nation sought to extend its political and economic interests and to protect them, not only from local threats but also from other European powers. Whatever their nationality, Europeans invariably saw themselves as a progressive people ruling and tutoring the backward segments of humankind, and they were able to support this attitude with a technically efficient military force. Sometimes European domination took the form of direct occupation and political rule; even when it did not, the pattern of domination remained similar. The European powers intervened as necessary to ensure that local governments kept sufficient order to protect European interests, but not enough power to pose any challenge to European hegemony. Typically, the economic production of the dominated countries was structured to provide a limited range of the raw materials most needed by the dominant power.

In some respects, European cultural domination was just as far-reaching as its political, military, and economic domination. Middle Easterners were classified along with the various Asian peoples as "Orientals," and it was widely held that such people were given to inscrutable peculiarities of thought, blind obedience to tradition, and insensitivity to suffering. Even Middle Eastern nationalism sometimes has been influenced by Western biases in subtle ways; many Middle Easterners have tacitly accepted the classification of themselves as "Orientals," a category that has little meaning except as an expression of European ethnocentrism.

One of the lingering and pervasive effects of Western ethnocentrism is the tendency to confuse "progress" with westernization and to hold up middle-class Europe and America as a

universal model of "modernity." It is intellectually and morally indefensible to assume that everything non-Western is backward, especially when much of Western culture comes from a time when Western civilization was less developed than that of the Middle and Far East. Yet it is often tempting, even for a non-Westerner, to equate change with westernization. The political and economic dominance of the West during the past few centuries has made westernization a companion of most other changes, so that Westerners and non-Westerners alike sometimes find different types of changes difficult to distinguish from westernization.

In keeping with the prejudice that Western society sets the course for universal human progress, some Westerners—including certain social theorists—have pictured non-Western societies as stagnant and mired in an unreflective obedience to "tradition." A theoretical view widely accepted 40 years ago contrasted the purportedly inflexible and unimaginative conservatism of the "traditional" Middle Easterner with the open-minded, resourceful, optimistic, and empathetic outlook of the "modernized" person. According to this view, the key to progress and affluence in the third world is a fundamental change in psychological outlook that comes from exposure to more liberated ways of thinking that originate in the West. Critics of this now-outdated view have pointed out, with some justice, that it is more self-congratulatory than illuminating. It ignores the great diversity of outlooks that exist within the "traditional" world and the particular historical conditions that have given rise to them. It also overlooks the possibility that cultural attitudes may be understandable responses to political, economic, or ecological realities that cannot be waved away by a change in attitude—realities that include the Western presence itself.

Perhaps the chief oversight of the "modernization" theory, in the context of this book, is its failure to appreciate the political dimensions of human choice in "traditional" settings. Conflict, political strategy, and calculated choice are found in all human societies, even when they result in the reproduction of a relatively stable system—and few if any societies are ever completely stable. Although the Western observer may be tempted by the romantic notion that every "exotic" custom or idea dates from time immemorial, a closer look at cultural history (especially that of the Middle East) reveals a continuous state of flux. The origin and spread of Islam is one example of the speed and magnitude of change, even in basic beliefs, that can occur in a traditional society. Although people everywhere are inclined to accept the beliefs and perspectives with which they were reared, they are everywhere capable of revising and criticizing these traditions when they no longer seem to fill their needs.

Although it is true that a "modern" or technicalized setting may present people with a greater range of possibilities than was previously known, it is important not to underestimate the degree to which rational calculation enters into decision making even when "traditional" values are invoked. Some of the supposed differences between "traditional" and "modern" outlooks may be largely a matter of rhetorical style. A political leader planning the invasion of a neighboring country may seek to justify it in a variety of ways: He may use a rationalistic rhetoric that stresses its benefits ("This invasion will bring peace, security, and good government to all concerned"); he may use a traditionalistic rhetoric that looks to the authority of the past ("These people have always been our subjects"); or he may use religious rhetoric ("God will look kindly on us for subduing the infidel"). All these styles of rhetoric have been used throughout history, but the rationalistic style is relatively fashionable in technicalized societies. The use of such rhetoric does not in itself make one's actions particularly reasonable, any more than the use of a religious rhetoric means that one's actions are divinely guided, or a traditionalist rhetoric proves that a given practice is genuinely traditional. It is a mistake to conclude simply from these differences in public rhetoric that one society's motives and actions are more rational than another's.

The perspective of distance almost always makes other cultures look flat, arbitrary, and deterministic compared with our own. Whether we are getting married or getting dressed in the morning, we see our own actions as guided by reason, filled with subtle meaning, and tempered by personal freedom. The corresponding behavior in another culture seems to us simple, stereotyped, and unreflective. "We" put on neckties because we think, and "they" put on turbans because they don't—or so it seems. Yet close studies of traditional peoples have shown them to be more critically aware of circumstances and choices than is commonly assumed. Often behavior that seems motivated by blind conservatism turns out instead to be based on a realistic assessment of the alternatives; many people are capable of grasping the significance of changing circumstances and are able to adapt to them accordingly. Such choices must always be made, however, within the framework of existing institutions and guided by existing values and assumptions about the nature and purpose of human existence. These values and assumptions are deeply rooted in the cultural heritage of a people; this is as true of the West as it is of the Middle East, and it helps account for the continuing role of religion in both settings. For that reason we have adopted two basic strategies in presenting the material. First, we shall emphasize the historical forces that have shaped the Middle East. To understand what the Middle East is and what it might be requires that one know what it was. The chapters dealing with the history of past centuries are best viewed as part of the present landscape and not as a separate story. Second, because the politics of the Middle East are woven together with general social and economic forces, we shall adopt a multidisciplinary approach—an approach facilitated by the diversity of the authors' academic training in political science, economics, and cultural anthropology.

Political affairs in the Middle East are treated here as the product of the interaction among social organization, secular values, religion, and the control and allocation of authority and resources at all levels. Although the variables sometimes must be isolated for analysis, to remove them permanently from their context is to invite misunderstanding.

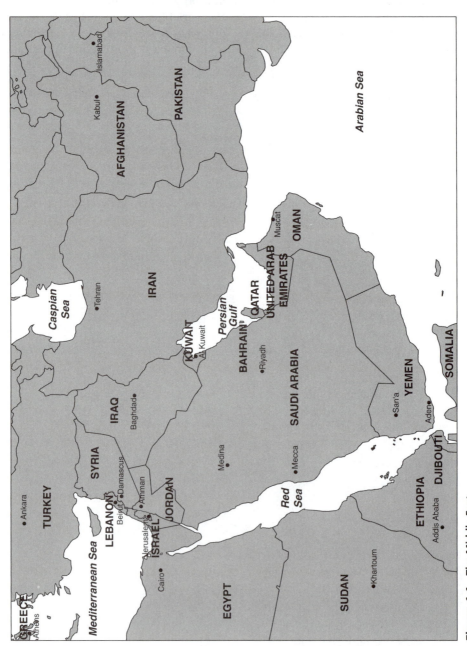

Figure 1.1 The Middle East

1

TRADITIONAL CULTURES OF THE MIDDLE EAST

The Cradle of Civilization and Politics

In dealing with "exotic" peoples and cultures, we often form stereotypical images, based on some grain of truth but containing enough distortion and error to make them useless and often even harmful. Popular images of the Middle East are a case in point.

The Middle East is no stranger to the Western imagination. It is the setting of the Jewish and Christian Holy Scriptures. We derive our images of the Middle East partly from these Scriptures and Hollywood images spun around them and partly from news reports of current events. The Middle East is often seen as the primeval wilderness from which Western civilization sprang—a wilderness that has since lapsed into timeless stagnation. In the popular imagination, the Middle East is inhabited mainly by fierce desert nomads who, driven by a childlike attachment to tradition and the fiery narrowness of the barbaric "Mohammedan" faith, spend most of their time menacing each other and impeding peace and progress. With alarming regularity, the "Arab" is depicted in film and on television as regressive, sex-crazed, violent, and sinister. News coverage highlights "terrorism," oil profiteering, and other supposed threats, casting Middle Easterners as odious but ineffectual enemies. Thus, Westerners form a composite picture of the Arab (and all native Middle Easterners are commonly thought to be Arabs) as an evil buffoon. However, the popular notion of the Middle East as a geographic and cultural backwater inhabited by ignorant fanatics is incompatible with even the most elementary knowledge of Middle Eastern culture and history.

Besides the need to dispel these common prejudices, there are other reasons why a look at traditional Middle Eastern culture is useful. First, it provides a backdrop against which to understand the historical development of innovative social, religious, and political institutions in the region. Second, it allows us to understand better the aspects of contemporary Middle Eastern life that still retain substantial continuity with past traditions. The Middle East today, like any region of the world, has constructed its modern institutions on a base of traditional social arrangements, values, philosophical assumptions, and everyday practices that are deeply rooted in a cultural heritage. In contrast to most of the Western world, the Middle East contains regions, or aspects of social life, whose continuity with the lifestyle of two or three centuries ago is in some respects more apparent than are the more recent influences of a cosmopolitan, "technicalized" cultural milieu. One must be careful, however, not to fall into the common Eurocentric bias of thinking that all non-Western practices are ancient and lacking in developmental change— a habit of thought encouraged by referring to "tradition" as though it represented some time-less eternality. Except when it is otherwise clear from the context, in this book the term *traditional* will be used to refer generally to patterns of social and cultural life that prevailed in the few centuries before the massive incur-sion of European influence and technicalizing changes. As we shall see, however, such cultural features are in many respects part and parcel of historical patterns that reach further back and further forward in time.

Contrary to the previously mentioned Western stereotypes about the region, the most significant historical features of the Middle East were not marginality and simplicity, but centrality and diversity. The centrality of the Middle East in history was partly the product of its strategic loca-tion at the junction of the three continents of Africa, Asia, and Europe and its consequent pivotal role in trade, conquest, communication, and migration. Middle Eastern cultural diversity has been aided by local geography and by the complexities of cultural adaptation in the region.

The geographic diversity of the Middle East, which depends largely on the relative availability of water, is striking. Although the "desert" image is correct in that the region is predominantly arid, there are sharp contrasts. The Nile Valley and the "Fertile Crescent" of the Tigris–Euphrates region and Mediterranean coast were the sites of the first-known farming civilizations and the sources of the images of Eden and of the "Land of Milk and Honey." These geographic contrasts have led to diverse but interlocking ways of life suited to different strategies of survival and adaptation.

Another factor contributing to diversity in the Middle East is the region's long and com-plex cultural evolution. Before about 10,000 B.C.E., all the world's peoples were gatherers of wild foods; the domestication of plants and animals—which set human culture on its path of increasing complexity—originated in the Middle East at about that time. During the ensuing 12 millennia, the Middle East has ranked in the vanguard of social and technolog-ical evolution more consistently than any other region of the world. From the Middle East, Europe received not only its basic agricultural crops and techniques but also all the most fundamental social and cultural elements we associate with "civilization," including literacy, urban life, and occupational specialization.

It is especially interesting, in view of this book's political theme, that the Middle East was the site of the earliest states and formal govern-ments. Partly because of the organizational requirements of irrigation systems, the independ-ent villages of the region were soon encom-passed in regional forms of political organization, in which the village-dwelling farmers became "peasants" dominated by a nonfarming urban ruling class. This ruler–producer split was the foundation of the state because it facilitated, through various forms of taxation, a substantial amount of *surplus production*—that is, produc-tion that exceeded the subsistence needs of the farming population. This surplus subsidized the power of the state and ultimately allowed the existence of an urban population engaged in various occupations not directly associated with agricultural production, a necessary condition for the specialized accomplishments of "civilized" peoples. The necessity of enforcing peasant taxation and protecting the prerogatives of the ruling classes, regulating trade and exchange, and generally mediating social relationships in an increasingly complicated society gave rise to what we now take for granted as the political apparatus of the state: legal codes, police and military forces, courts, and other instruments of "law and order."

The role of the Middle East in political innovation did not end with the early civiliza-tions; the region was also the birthplace of three world religions, each involving unique contributions to social thought. Yet despite the leadership of the Middle East in political and social development, the region has long been characterized by social conservatism. The everyday lives of most peasants, nomads, and townspeople have until more recently been little affected by intellectual and organizational advances in the larger society; instead, these lifestyles have been woven into the fabric of an increasingly complicated plural society.

FOUNDATIONS OF SOCIAL DIVERSITY

The American "melting pot" ideology views cultural diversity as an accidental and temporary byproduct of history, whereas such diversity has been an enduring and valued part of life in the Middle East. Middle Eastern culture is characterized not only by diversity but also by *pluralism*—the maintenance of diversity as a significant aspect of the social system. The use of cultural diversity, or pluralism, as a structuring principle in society has led some writers to characterize social life in this region as a "mosaic." This mosaic character is particularly difficult to describe because it follows no simple pigeon-hole scheme but includes many dimensions, levels, and criteria of variation that often cut across one another. These include six important dimensions of variability and identity that together have shaped much of the character of traditional life in the Middle East: (1) ecological pluralism, (2) regional and local ethnic pluralism, (3) religion, (4) family and tribe, (5) occupational groups, and (6) class distinctions. Although it is sometimes useful to discuss these criteria separately, the reader should remember that in practice they are partly dependent on one another.

Ecological Diversity

Of the many elements that contribute to social diversity in the Middle East, one of the most basic is the relation of people to the land. The vicissitudes of wind patterns, rainfall, and river courses, combined with the effects of irrigation systems, often lead to stark contrasts in the land and its potential uses. In parts of Egypt, a railroad track divides a verdant field producing two or three crops a year from a desert so barren as to discourage even Bedouin herders. Although the arable regions constitute less than 10 percent of the land in the Middle East, their role in the economic and social order of the region has been crucial since prehistoric times. For several thousand years, since the beginnings of the state and its associated intensive agricultural techniques, a large portion of Middle Eastern farmland and an even larger portion of the farming population and agricultural produce have depended on irrigation systems.

The nonagricultural lands that constitute the bulk of the Middle East are by no means uniform in character. Some of these lands are forested mountain slopes; others are arid steppes capable of supporting nomads with their herds of camels, sheep, or goats; still other regions, such as the "empty quarter" of Arabia or Egypt's Western Desert, support virtually no human populations at all. Water is the crucial resource in all these regions. The utility of a territory inhabited by a group of camel nomads may change from year to year, day to day, and mile to mile according to variations in rainfall or groundwater. The importance of water is illustrated by the fact that a permanent well, hardly worth noticing in more watered parts of the world, determined the location of the early Arab trading settlement of Mecca, later to become the birthplace of Islam and the spiritual homeland of Muslims around the world.

The geographic division between the desert and the arable lands is a recurrent phenomenon throughout the Middle East, and it has been accompanied by a threefold social division that also spanned the entire region—the division between peasants, nomads, and townspeople. Peasants, who composed three-quarters of the population, were engaged directly in agricultural production and lived in the small, simple villages that dotted the cultivable countryside. Nomads also were engaged in primary economic production, based on the husbandry of camels, sheep, goats, or cattle, usually in regions incapable of supporting agricultural production. Urbanites were engaged not in primary food production but in other, more specialized occupations traditionally ranging from government, scholarship, or priestly functions to crafts, peddling, and begging and more recently including modern industrial, service, and other business pursuits.

Nomads

Nomadic herders captivate the imaginations of Middle Easterner and foreigner alike and often tend to be seen by both (and by nomads themselves) as the "purest" expression of the region's cultural tradition. The nomads have been economically and politically marginal throughout most of history and are becoming more so today. Although nomads traditionally have been the sole inhabitants of the region's nonarable land, their population has never been more than a small fraction of the total for the region (in recent times probably less than 15 percent of the population). Nomadic herding was not practiced in the intensive farming regions, and in transitional regions it was combined with village farming. The forms of nomadism varied according to the capacity of the land, which depended on water. Semiarid steppes supported cattle, sheep, and goats, whereas the true desert sustained only camel nomads, such as the **Bedouins** of Arabia. The camel nomads, for all their aristocratic airs, were confined to the most marginal lands, those unusable to anyone else. Their place in politics has been a complex one. They traditionally have been admired for their independence, virility, and simple virtue, and the fourteenth-century Arab sociologist Ibn Khaldoun took note of their role in periodically taking over and revitalizing the leadership of Islamic states, drawing on their qualities of military discipline and tribal solidarity. It is also true, however, that the political influence of nomads was only sporadic, and that much of the time they were peripheral to the sources of state

power. In recent decades, national governments have tried to control nomads by promoting their settlement in sedentary communities.

The ruggedness and apparent simplicity of nomadic life have led to the widespread misconception that it was the oldest and most primitive lifestyle of the Middle East, and that it involved complete independence from the more settled and sophisticated life of the cities and villages. This was not strictly true, for nomadic herders traditionally depended on settled communities for manufactured items and agricultural products, which they obtained by trading their animal products and, before the control of the modern state, by raiding the villages. When drought made herding less feasible, some nomads were able to shift temporarily or permanently to a more settled life in the city or village. The camel nomadism of the desert has existed only since the introduction of the camel in about 2000 B.C.E.; even the herding of sheep and goats, which originated much earlier, depended to some extent on the existence of settled populations and probably did not predate them as a general stage of development.

Of all the nomads in the Middle East, the Arab Bedouin has occupied a position of special significance. The Bedouins are Arabian camel nomads who constitute only one of the many nomadic groups in the Middle East, but they have played a unique role in the cultural consciousness of the region. Before the birth of the Prophet Muhammad, the Arabs (that is, the original speakers of Arabic) were a group of tribes occupying central Arabia. Many were camel nomads, and the others were sailors, caravanners, and townspeople who traced descent from nomadic herders. Islam facilitated the spread of Arabic as the daily language of much of the Middle East and the holy language of all Muslims, and with it came some measure of identification with the Arab Bedouin heritage. Despite the ambivalence that urbanites and villagers have often felt toward the fierce and "lawless" inhabitants of the desert, the Bedouins were at the same time acknowledged as the "truest" Arabs. (In Arabic, the term *Arab* refers, in the strictest usage, only to the Bedouin.) A Cairo shopkeeper might underscore his business integrity by referring to his (literal or figurative) Bedouin heritage, and the desert outside modern Riyadh is periodically dotted with the tents of Saudi urbanites celebrating their recent Bedouin past with weekend campouts.

Peasants and Urbanites

Despite the common perception of pastoral nomadism as the primeval Middle Eastern lifestyle, peasants and traditional city dwellers carried on an equally old and well-established pattern of life, one with roots in the early civilizations of Egypt and Mesopotamia. The historical relationship between village-dwelling peasants and urbanites depended on a political organization that taxed the village-dwelling farmers, subsidizing the ruling class in particular and the nonfarming urban populations in general. The development of the state entailed two divergent ways of life, the urban and the rural, each of which existed as a result of the other. (In this context, "city" and "urban" refer to permanent settlements of any size whose populace consists primarily of nonfarmers—as opposed to a rural peasant "village" whose inhabitants walk daily to their farms.) From the perspective of the traditional Middle Eastern state, the peasant village existed for the purpose of delivering its tax quota in the form of agricultural produce, money, labor, or some combination of these. For their taxes, the villagers rarely, if ever, received such government services as police protection, education, or public works. As long as the village headman delivered the taxes, the village was left to govern itself. Internally, the village was relatively homogeneous, consisting of peasants who exercised little influence on the politics of the state that governed their lives and who had few, if any, opportunities for social mobility.

Although modern Middle Eastern states are generally committed to changing these conditions, life in peasant villages retains a continuity with the past. Many villagers are still small landholders, sharecroppers, or landless laborers. Each village is divided into families and blocks of related families and is headed by a patriarch of the most influential family, whose authority is shared with other village elders. Similar to the nomads, the peasants have been led by the conditions of their lives to a distinctive worldview. In contrast to the nomads, whose traditional values emphasized militant independence, peasants were typically fearful of authority, distrustful of the world outside the village (and often of their own neighbors), and pessimistic with regard to social change. The unenviable position of peasants led traditional urbanites and nomads alike to despise them as "slaves of the soil," while continuing to depend on them for the production of basic foodstuffs.

If popular conceptions of the Middle East give undue attention to the nomads because of their romantic image, "historical" treatments of the region tend to place great emphasis on the towns and cities as the locus of rulers and their "high" culture, the source of written documents on which historical scholarship largely depends. Traditional urban life in the Middle East does not lend itself easily to general description because urbanites were involved in a great variety of occupations and modes of living. The traditional Middle Eastern cities were, among other things, seats of local and regional government. As such, they were home to political elites and their retinue, including military commanders, civil and legal authorities, government bureaucrats, and religious leaders. In addition to individuals involved in government, traditional urban life also involved a middle class of merchants, artisans, professionals, and petty officials. The least affluent and least prestigious urbanites were peddlers, laborers, and sometimes beggars. In addition to its role in political and religious leadership, the city traditionally has been a center of crafts and trade, with the **suq**, or bazaar, serving as a distribution point for manufactured wares and for the products of the farmers and nomads. Many traditional cities also became producers of wealth in their own right by virtue of their profitable involvement in the trade between Europe, Asia, and Africa.

Although many aspects of traditional Middle Eastern urban life were as ancient as the lifestyles of the village and desert, *ancient* does not imply *simple*. Life in Middle Eastern towns and cities reached a high degree of sophistication and complexity millennia ago. Some urban centers, such as Jericho and Damascus, were already ancient in biblical times. Others, such as Baghdad and Cairo, were founded more than a thousand years ago as seats of government and represent landmark achievements in urban planning. Today, Middle Eastern cities are also hubs of modern industrial and commercial activity; yet in many ways the old continues to exist alongside the new.

Ethnic and Religious Diversity

The ecological pluralism of nomads, peasants, and townspeople was only one dimension of traditional cultural diversity, the others being ethnic, religious, familial, occupational, and social class distinctions. Ethnic differences, or differences in historical descent and cultural heritage, have existed between and within regions. Vast regions of the Middle East are set apart from others by their distinctive language and culture, the most prominent example being the division between the speakers of Turkish, Persian, and Arabic. Each of these groups occupies a major contiguous portion of the Middle East, and each correctly conceives of itself as having distinct cultural roots. The extent of their historical divergence is suggested by the languages themselves, which are classified into different families and differ from one another more than English does from Persian. These regional groups also have exhibited major differences in values, outlook, details of social organization, and, to some extent, religion.

The ethnic diversity of the Middle East would be relatively easy to discuss if it were confined to regional divisions, but the vicissitudes of history have brought about a more complex situation, as migrations have created much cultural diversity within regions. It is difficult to say whether the Middle East has seen more migrations than other regions or whether these are simply better documented because of the region's long tradition of literacy. Waterways and seafaring, land trade, the nomadic ways of some of the inhabitants, and the existence of organized states bent on conquest have all contributed to the physical mobility of peoples. The Sumerians appeared suddenly more than 6,000 years ago in the lower Mesopotamian region, creating the world's first literate civilization, then fading from the scene to be displaced and eclipsed by peoples of other backgrounds. The Jews historically occupied several parts of the Middle East, including Egypt and Palestine, then many dispersed from the region only to return in the twentieth century. During the long career of the Islamic state, Arab ruling classes spread their influence from Spain to Persia; Egyptians were ruled by resident Turks; and much of the region found itself under the sword of Asian Mongols, while the ethnically diverse elites of the Islamic world sought refuge in Muslim India. Although such migration resulted in a considerable amount of cultural assimilation, it also gave rise to multiple ethnic communities within regions.

What is especially striking about local ethnic diversity, from the viewpoint of the outsider, is that these ethnic differences have been institutionalized as a stable feature of traditional Middle Eastern life. One reason for this is that ethnic distinctions have often been reinforced by other kinds of traditional diversity, such as religion, occupation, and social status.

Descent, Occupation, and Social Stratification

The traditional importance of family, kinship, and common descent in the Middle East is difficult for a Westerner to appreciate. Although a European or American considers the individual to be the basic functioning unit of society, the individual has had relatively little autonomous importance in the traditional Middle East or for that matter in most traditional societies. Instead, the individual's status, privileges, obligations, identity, and morality were inextricably tied to the descent group. Traditionally, the minimal descent unit was the extended family, whose structure will be discussed in the following section. The extended family was part of a larger group of related families, the lineage (in Arabic, *hamula*). The families of a nomadic hamula pitched their tents together, and among sedentary villagers the hamula was (and is) likely to be represented by a clustering of residences. The hamula has served, among other things, as a political unit that resolved internal disputes between families and represented their interests to the outside world. Sometimes the lineages were further united into a "tribe." Each of these units was based on the notion of shared ancestry from some patrilineal founder. The idea of common descent remains important in the contemporary Middle East, and as in the past it extends to larger groupings: All Arabs consider themselves as having a common descent; the Jews, Christians, and Muslim Arabs together are thought to share common ancestors in the biblical patriarchs. The more specific and immediate the common descent, the more relevant it is to one's personal obligations and identity. It is hardly surprising, in view of the practical importance of descent, that ethnic groups within a particular region are in no hurry to obliterate their distinctive ancestry.

Another important factor in maintaining ethnic distinctions has been their connection with occupation. In the traditional Middle East, one's occupation was often determined by one's family background. The matter of occupation was relatively simple for the child of a Bedouin or peasant family, but it was scarcely less so for the son of an urban artisan. Membership in organizations that controlled crafts and trades was frequently passed from father to son, as was the requisite training. Because occupation was largely ascribed rather than achieved, certain trades frequently became associated with specific ethnic groups. The continuing relationship of descent to occupation was dramatized in practical terms when, after the formation of Israel, the exodus of the Jewish population of Yemen left the country virtually bereft of blacksmiths, bricklayers, and practitioners of certain other trades traditionally followed by this ethnic group.

As the previous example shows, ethnic differences have often been associated with religious affiliation, reflecting differences within and between the three major religions of the Middle East. Whole regions may be characterized by a predominant religion, as in the concentrations of **Shia** Islam in Iran and parts of Iraq. Many minority religions also are concentrated in specific regions, as with the Christian Copts of Egypt. The integrity of the non-Muslim groups has been reinforced on the local level by the traditional Muslim practice of allowing minority religious communities protection and self-government in return for their recognition of Muslim hegemony.

A final type of social diversity is the division of socioeconomic classes. Since the origin of the earliest states, Middle Eastern society has been stratified into classes that enjoy varying degrees of privilege and wealth. These distinctions are relatively subdued in the countryside, but are quite apparent in the cities, where lifestyles span the extremes from poverty to opulence. Distinctions of class are tied in various complex ways to family background, ethnicity, occupation, and ecological situation.

The Patchwork of Pluralism: Two Historical Examples

Traditional Middle Eastern society was a complex tapestry in which ecological, ethnic, family, tribal, occupational, and class factors were interwoven. The complex way in which these dimensions intertwined can be seen in two different examples of traditional life: the city of Mecca in Muhammad's day and the Bedouin camp.

The city of Mecca, as Muhammad knew it in about 600 C.E., forms the backdrop of major historical events that will be discussed in Chapter 2. It had been founded two centuries earlier by a tribe of Bedouins who had shifted from nomadism to trading and had located their settlement at the site of a permanent water supply and the junction of two major trade routes. Their social organization and worldview still bore the stamp of Bedouin life, yet even this budding town had begun to manifest a more urban sort of complexity. The formerly egalitarian founding tribe had differentiated into richer and poorer divisions, and the more favored displayed the trappings of aristocracy. Some families of this tribe had begun to control and monopolize religious worship, a practice in which shrines played a large role. Attached to the ruling tribe were subordinate "client" groups, and below them were slaves. The range of occupations was considerable, and many were interwoven with specific ethnic backgrounds. One author makes reference to "Syrian caravan leaders; travelling monks and curers; Syrian merchants; foreign smiths and healers; Copt carpenters; Negro idol sculptors; Christian doctors, surgeons, dentists and scribes; Abyssinian sailors and mercenaries."[1] Mecca was at this time a relatively new and modest-sized trade settlement, a mere upstart compared with the more established seats of Middle Eastern government.

Even the traditional Bedouin camp was hardly the simple affair one might expect. Such a camp was likely to include representatives of half a dozen non-Bedouin groups, each performing a separate function as defined by various criteria of descent and cultural tradition. The Bedouin extended family owned the livestock, but the camel herders themselves might have come from another, less "noble" group that lent its services as a form of tribute to the Bedouins, who took the responsibility of fighting to protect the herds from other Bedouin raiders. Members of another ethnic group, the Sulaba, whom some anthropologists recognize as the most ancient inhabitants of the desert, served as desert guides, coppersmiths, and leatherworkers, and in various other specified functions. The Sunna, members of a group said to be of partly African origin, served as blacksmiths. African slaves also were part of an affluent Bedouin household; well dressed and well fed, they were reputed to be fierce fighters in defense of their masters' herds. Two sorts of traders were also likely to be found in the Bedouin camp. One of these was the Kubaisi, an ambulatory shopkeeper who supplied the camp with a variety of merchandise; the name is derived from a town on the Euphrates from which at least some such merchants traditionally came. Finally, the 'Aqaili, usually a member of the tribe of 'Aquil, bought camels on behalf of urban firms in return for cash and rifles. In this complex scheme, the Bedouins served primarily as soldiers and protectors, engaging in raids against other Bedouins, defending the group against such raids, and granting safe conduct across their territory.[2]

UNITY IN DIVERSITY

The cultural pluralism of the traditional Middle East was set in a context of unity and integration. The ties that bound diverse segments of society into an integrated whole were based on two principles: the functional interdependence and the complementarity of unlike parts and certain overarching similarities of culture, social organization, and religion.

Traditional nomads, peasants, and urbanites were by no means autonomous groups, and they were not necessarily set apart by

[1]Eric R. Wolf, "Social Organization of Mecca and the Origins of Islam," *Southwestern Journal of Anthropology,* VII (1951): 336–337.

[2]Carleton S. Coon, *Caravan: The Story of the Middle East* (Huntington, NY: Robert E. Krieger Co., 1976), 191–210.

competition, although conflicts of interest certainly have occurred between them. Bedouins have depended on peasants for agricultural products and on townspeople for manufactured goods. In the past, they often exacted tribute from peasant villages, sold protection to caravans, and acted as middlemen in trade. The existence of cities and villages was a further convenience when climate or other factors forced Bedouins into settled life, just as the opposite movement often occurred when conditions were reversed. Although before the twentieth century the Bedouins were rarely subject to the sort of constraint and taxation the state would have liked to impose, neither were they entirely exempt from state control. Peasants were always under direct state rule, which set the conditions that governed their lives. Despite internal village self-government, peasants were expected not only to fill their tax quotas but also to obey all laws of the state, over which they had little say. As previously noted, the peasants were also subject to raiding and tribute demands from nomads. It is difficult to say in what ways the peasants benefited from others because exchanges between them and urbanites or Bedouins were typically out of their control and in their disfavor. The towns did provide manufactured items and markets where certain of the peasants' needs could be provided for, and the state provided, in principle, military protection.

Because they were not engaged directly in food production, urbanites were in a sense the most dependent of all. Like all urban populations, they ultimately depended on the rural production of food and raw materials directed into the towns through taxation and trade. In the Middle East, the situation was complicated by the presence of the Bedouins because the urban marketplace served as an intermediary between two modes of rural production. The divisions among occupational specialties, similar to those among ecological niches, have been characterized by economic interdependence and complementarity.

The Middle East possesses overarching cultural similarities that in some measure unite all its people. If one's identity as an Arab implies separation from Persians, Turks, Berbers, and Kurds, it also implies a unity of outlook and identity with many millions of other Arabs. Cultural similarity transcends, however, even these broad regional and ethnic groupings; significant features of culture and social organization traditionally have united all Middle Easterners. A list of these features would be long and would range from the threefold ecological system to particulars of material culture, such as the use of the black hair tent among nomads throughout the region. Most significant, however, are similarities in traditional social organization and cultural values that underlie the region's diverse social types.

Family, Kinship, and Marriage

Throughout the Middle East, the traditional family has had a similar structure and function. It was patrilineal—that is, it traced descent principally through the male line. Wives were expected to take up residence with their husbands after marriage. The traditional family was strongly patriarchal, remaining intact until the death of the father, at which time each of the sons became a family head. Typically, such a family consisted of three generations of men and their wives and any unmarried daughters or sisters. The traditionally preferred form of marriage among Muslims is between a man and his father's brother's daughter. Although there are conflicting reports on the actual frequency of such cousin marriages, Muslim marriages do tend to favor patrilineal relatives. The Middle Eastern family has long served as the basic unit for holding property in the form of farmland, herds, or smaller business enterprises; it thus acquired a fundamental economic significance.

The importance of kinship in traditional society did not end with the family. Peasant villagers, townspeople, and nomads all recognized larger kin groupings among related families. Among the nomads and their recent descendants, these groupings have often been extended to a tribal organization. Tribes varied in size from a single band to a powerful and influential group encompassing numerous bands. Relationships among the men of each tribe were relatively egalitarian, leadership being based on the "first among equals" principle. Frequently, however, there were marked differences of social standing, or "nobility," among tribes, to the extent that marriage to members of lesser tribes was sometimes forbidden. Today, as in the past, in the nomad and nomad-derived groups and their tribal organizations, one finds the strongest development of blood feuds, collective responsibility, group honor or "face" (Arabic **wajh**), and strict rules governing hospitality and sanctuary. (These are discussed further in Chapter 2.)

Traditional marriage and sex mores have shown considerable persistence in much of the Middle East. Despite more recent trends to the contrary, marriage is still often arranged by parents, being seen more as a relationship between kin groups than one between individuals. An effort was usually made to match mates in terms of social prestige and background. The traditional position of women was, on the whole, one of subordination to men. Compared with the West, a greater emphasis is still placed on female chastity, purity, modesty, and even complete seclusion and veiling. As in the past (but now for different reasons), veiling and seclusion tend to be practiced most often among urban elites. The conduct of women generally has been thought to reflect on the honor of the patrilineal family, and men are vulnerable to dishonor by the conduct of their daughters, sisters, or wives. Muslim law permits four wives, but although multiple marriages are a sign of affluence, they have

always been infrequent in actual practice. Traditionally, Muslim men could initiate divorce more easily than women could. Despite the patriarchal bias that it shares with other Middle Eastern religions, Islamic law has allowed remarriage of divorced women, ensured women a share in the inheritance of property, and protected their right to own property separately from their husbands. Today, traditional ideas about marriage, the family, and the position of women are being modified in some quarters in response to new interpretations of Islam and secular ideas of individualism, women's rights, and romantic love.

Religion

Of all the factors that unify Middle Eastern culture, none is so fundamental as religion. The Middle East is the birthplace of the three major monotheistic religions: Judaism, Christianity, and Islam. Most Middle Easterners today are Muslims, or adherents of Islam. This is significant not only because of the unifying influence of one ubiquitous religion but also because that religion has a remarkably pervasive influence on social and cultural life. Islam permeates the daily life and social norms of most of the Middle Eastern Muslim population. It is a religion whose stated aim at the time of its inception in the early seventh century was the unity of all people into a single social and spiritual community, and it succeeded to a noteworthy degree. Islam brought unprecedented political, intellectual, and spiritual unity to the Middle East and made the region a hub of world power for a thousand years. How and why this happened is the subject of Chapter 2.

Key Terms

Bedouins	*4*	
Suq	*5*	
Shia	7	
wajh	*10*	

2 | THE FOUNDATIONS OF ISLAM

Through the dusty streets of a middle-class residential neighborhood in Cairo echo the sounds of dawn: The first vendors are calling their wares, their chants accompanied by the clopping of hooves and the rattling of cart wheels. Blended with these is a more haunting but equally familiar sound, a singsong of Arabic from the loudspeakers on the minaret of a small local **mosque**:

> God is most great.
>
> I testify there is no deity but God.
>
> I testify that Muhammad is the Messenger of God.
>
> Come to Prayer;
>
> Come to Salvation . . .

The same message five times daily has called the faithful to prayer in Cairo and its predecessors for more than 1,300 years. That same message, in the same Arabic, emanates from mosques as far away as West Africa and Indonesia, calling one-fifth of the world's population (only a minority of whom are Middle Easterners or Arabs) to pray toward their spiritual homeland in Mecca. The religion of Islam, signified by this call to prayer, is central to an understanding of the Middle East's most salient features—its historical and contemporary influence on other parts of the world; the unity of belief and commitment that counteracts some of its bitterest political divisions; and the religious vitality that infuses every aspect of its social, cultural, and political life.

Ninety-five percent of all Middle Easterners are Muslims, followers of the faith of Islam. For them, religion is not a matter separable from daily life or confined to certain times and places; it is the foundation of all ethics, morality, and family life—ultimately, the blueprint for a righteous and satisfying life. Dismayed by the secularism of the capitalist and the communist ideologies, Muslims see Islam as an essential element that gives direction to their social aspirations and saves them from the dissipation and immorality they see in the West. They also are keenly aware of Islam's success as a world religion—a religion that has always aimed at the social unity of the entire community of believers, that has led the Middle East to a position of considerable historical influence, and that provided the foundations of a civilization that for many centuries surpassed that of Europe.

CENTRAL BELIEFS OF ISLAM

For the Muslim, Islam is at its root the complete acceptance of God and submission to His will. The word *Islam* means "submission," and *Muslim* means "one who submits." The most important step toward this submission is the recognition that there is only one God, the God of Abraham and Moses, of Christians and Jews as well as of Muslims, whose name in Arabic is *Allah*. Muslims believe that they alone have accepted God completely, and that all their beliefs follow from this acceptance. According to the teachings of Islam, a complete accept-ance of God entails recognition of His absolute oneness; a Muslim must reject not only other gods but also all alleged "associates" of God, including offspring and other semidivine personages. Christians, they feel, have compro-mised their monotheism by mistaking one of God's prophets for the "son" of God. The acceptance of God also requires belief in all of God's messages through all His appointed messengers, including not only Jesus and the Old Testament prophets, but also—and most significantly—the seventh-century Arab Prophet Muhammad. It is through Muhammad, the "seal of the prophets," that God has sent His final and most comprehensive revelations, placed on the lips of Muhammad by God and recorded in the Holy Scripture, the Koran. Because true belief in God means acceptance of His final revelations, the Muslim declaration of faith (the **shahada**) testifies that "There is no God but Allah, and Muhammad is His prophet." Such a declaration is sufficient to make a person a Muslim, but the conscientious pursuit of the faith demands much more.

The Five Pillars of Islam

Muslims recognize five fundamental ritual obli-gations, which constitute the "pillars" of their religion. The first and most important of these is the declaration of faith. The second is prayer, which ought to be performed five times a day (before dawn, at noon, in late afternoon, just after sunset, and in mid-evening), facing in the direction of the **Kaaba**, the holy shrine in Mecca. Prayer may be performed anywhere, but the preferred situation is with other Muslims in a special place of worship, the mosque. Prayer involves a complex series of preparations, prescribed movements, and phrases. The most important prayer time is Friday noon, when Muslims participate in a formal service under the direction of a prayer leader (**imam**), who reads from the Koran and may deliver a sermon and discuss matters of public interest.

The third pillar of Islam is the giving of alms, either in the form of **zakat**, a fixed amount used to meet the needs of the religious community and provide for the welfare of its members, or as a voluntary contribution (**sadaqa**), which brings religious merit to the donor. The fourth pillar of Islam is fasting during the daylight hours of the month of **Ramadan**. Although Islam is not an ascetic religion, Muslims view the abstention from food, liquids, smoking, and sexual relations as a celebration of moral commitment, healthy self-discipline, and religious atonement. Because Ramadan is a lunar month, it rotates through the seasons; the abstention from food or water from dawn to dusk of a summer day is no small sacrifice. At the same time, it is typical of Islam's relatively practical orientation that the very young, the elderly, the sick, and travel-ers are exempted, at least temporarily, from this obligation.

The fifth and final ritual obligation of Islam, the pilgrimage to Mecca, falls only on members of a Muslim community whose health and resources permit them to fulfill it. It is a great honor to make the **hajj**, or pilgrimage, and individuals who have done so carry the honorific title of **hajji**. The center of the pilgrimage is a shrine in Mecca said to have been founded by Abraham. The pilgrimage draws together, physically and spiritually, individuals from various national and cultural backgrounds who represent the farthest reaches of Islam. During the pilgrimage, however, all participants shed the marks of their nationality and social position and don the plain white cloak that signifies the equality of every Muslim before God.

The Koran and the Hadith

The ritual obligations of Islam, important as they are, are only the outward expressions of the system of belief that underlies Muslim life. When Muslims accept the oneness of God and the validity of Muhammad's revelations as the word of God, they also accept certain sources of authority for religious truth. Foremost among these is the written record of Muhammad's revelations, the **Koran**. The Koran is said to be the exact word, and even the exact language, of God. Approximately as long as the New Testament, the Koran is composed of a series of chapters, or **suras**, of varying length. If we were to compare it with the literary forms familiar to U.S. readers, it more closely resembles a book of poetry than a narrative or a continuous essay. The Koran in the original Arabic (the form in which Muslims of all nations know it) is regarded as a masterpiece of poetic literature. Its subject matter ranges from terse warnings about the Day of Judgment to long discourses on marriage, inheritance, the treatment of non-Muslim minorities, and the duties of each Muslim in spreading the faith. More is said of the Koran's message on these points later in this chapter.

A second source of divine authority is the collection of sayings and practices attributed to the Prophet. The Prophet's personal utterances were not, like the Koran, a direct recitation of God's words, but they are thought to have been informed by the Prophet's divine inspiration. Muslim religious scholars recognize that not all these reports (**hadith**) about the Prophet are equally reliable, and much effort has been devoted to tracing their sources and evaluating their accuracy. Even so, there exist various hadith that can, similar to the holy texts of other religions, be used to support widely

differing positions on many issues. Several recognized schools of Muslim law differ on the degree to which analogy, scholarly interpretation, social consensus, and established custom might be used to supplement the Koran and the hadith, but all agree that these two sources together form the basis of the Muslim social and legal code (**Sharia**). In principle, they apply to every life situation that a believer might encounter and provide a guide for every sort of decision.

The Ulema

Because Islam teaches the equality of every believer before God, there are, at least in orthodox **Sunni** Islam, no clergy to act as intercessors with the divine. The emphasis on written texts has given rise, however, to an important class of religious scholars, the **ulema**, who collectively advise the community and its political rulers according to God's word. To the extent that most traditional education in Muslim societies is religious in nature, the ulema have filled the role of academics and teachers; to the extent that Islam recognizes no ultimate division of religion and state, the ulema have been not only legal and political thinkers but also a political force in their own right. This is true in the contemporary Muslim world, where Cairo's Al-Azhar, the center of Muslim high scholarship, is also an international forum for the discussion of contemporary issues of Muslim politics and social values.

In contrast to most Far Eastern religions, which generally try to divorce themselves from the flow of historical events, Islam resembles Judaism and Christianity in its explicit involvement with society and history. Although it is the ultimate concern of individual Muslims to prepare themselves for the Day of Judgment, that preparation takes worldly form in the pursuit of a just and righteous social life. Perhaps even more than Judaism and Christianity, Islam is intimately concerned with specific social relations and institutions. Our discussion of Islam will take the form of a historical account. Islam arose in a particular social setting, and it directly addressed social problems related to that setting. One of the paradoxes of Islam is that although it goes beyond most other religions in specific references to the cultural institutions of its original setting, it has spread to encompass an astonishing variety of peoples and cultures without sacrificing the relevance of its original precepts. In so doing, it has followed a remarkable path of adaptiveness balanced with continuity, operating in some contexts as a revolutionary force and in others as a source of stability and cohesion, or, when its practitioners have seen fit to use it so, as a source of deep conservatism. None of these uses is inherent in the religion itself, but each is the outcome of particular human communities applying Islam to particular historical situations. Because Western readers are likely to see Islam as an essentially conservative ideology, let us consider the radical transformations that Islam brought to its original social setting.

PRE-ISLAMIC ARAB ETHICS

In contrast to people who lived in the Persian, Byzantine, and other empires that were the heirs of thousands of years of urbanization and central government, the Arab urbanites of Muhammad's time were in a process of transition to settled life, and their society was still organized on the ethical principles that had served their nomadic Bedouin forebears. This traditional Arab ethic, or rather the conflict between it and urban life, provided the backdrop for Muhammad's teachings. Islam at its inception constituted a revitalization and a radical reform of the old ethic. For these reasons, it is worthwhile to take a closer look at traditional Bedouin society.

As is usually the case with nomadic peoples, the Bedouins did not have a centralized government or political authority. Such authority would have been impossible to maintain, not only because no centralized power can easily

impose itself on peoples of such mobility but also because there was no economic foundation to support one. Yet Bedouins were by no means isolated in the desert wastes; they were in frequent contact with other Bedouin and non-Bedouin groups and had need of some measure of political order to regulate cooperation and resolve conflict. In such situations, political organization tended to be built from the bottom up—that is, groups were arranged in a hierarchy of levels that acted to deal with whatever conflicts or common interests were at hand.

There is a saying attributed to the Arabs: "I against my brother; my brother and I against my cousin; my brother and cousins and I against the outsider." The saying signifies a hierarchy of loyalties based on closeness of kinship that ran from the nuclear family through the lineage, the tribe, and even, in principle at least, to an entire ethnic or linguistic group (which was believed to have a kinship basis). Disputes were settled, interests were pursued, and justice and order were maintained by means of this organizational framework, according to an ethic of self-help and collective responsibility. If a member of one nuclear family was injured or offended by a member of another family, it was the right and obligation of all members of the injured family to settle the score. If the disputants were members of different lineages, all members of both lineages became involved (in varying degrees, depending on closeness to the offended and offending parties). In the same way, a whole tribe or alliance of tribes might have been moved to defend its interests against another group. The collective duty to take up the disputes of a kinsman also meant that someone might legitimately be killed in atonement for the crimes of a relative. An "even score" might take the form of a life for a life or a theft for a theft, or it might be sought in a negotiated settlement. An inherent weakness in the system emerged, however, when the disputing sides were unable to agree on what constituted an even score, and the situation developed into a blood feud that involved whole tribes and their allies and lasted for generations.

The revenge ethic was not the unbridled play of impulse, but a system designed to keep a modicum of order in a society without centralized legal authority. Because the individual's kin group answered collectively for his transgressions, it exercised considerable power of restraint over impulsive acts. Restraint was required even in revenge, which if excessive could initiate a new cycle of offense and counter-revenge. As already noted, revenge could be mitigated through an arbitrated settlement that preserved the system of order and the honor of the disputants, while keeping violence to a minimum. In the end, it was the ever-present threat of violent reprisal that acted as the chief deterrent against crime.

Every form of social organization requires a particular kind of value commitment, and the central value of the Bedouin ethic was (and still is) the honor and integrity of the various groups, or rather of the concentric circle of groupings, with which the individual identified. Group honor was often referred to as "face" (*wajb*), the maintenance of which was a central concern of every member of a given group. (It is, incidentally, the enduring concern for the purity of the group through its patrilineal kin line, and the belief that sexual misconduct of its women is one of the greatest blows to a family's honor, that contributes today to the seclusion of Arab women.) The other side of the Bedouin's fierce unity against outsiders was his hospitality toward those who entered his domain with permission and were under his protection. Hospitality, as much as revenge, was the measure of a group's willingness and ability to protect its interests and those of its allies and was a reflection on its honor.

Despite its harshness, the Bedouin ethic also had its benign side. Not only was hospitality highly valued in Bedouin society, but generosity also was valued. Arab traditions point to the existence, from pre-Islamic times to the present, of a strong belief in the virtue of generosity and sharing, even with strangers. Generosity to outsiders was a gesture of hospitality that reflected

favorably on the strength and honor of the group. The sharing of wealth within the kin group provided for the needy, reinforced the sense of general equality and cooperation essential to the members' mutual commitment, and supported the leader's prestige by emphasizing his benevolence.

Although the Bedouin Arab's system of law and politics was based on the patrilineal kin group, it could be extended in various ways to adapt to varying circumstances. Alliances could be established between tribes, and genealogies might consciously or unconsciously be altered to reflect the new relationships. In pre-Islamic times, other pseudo-kin relations were established through adoption. Through the payment of tribute and obedience, one group could become the protected client of another, a status that connoted social inferiority and was undertaken only when necessary. Slavery, a widespread practice throughout the ancient Mediterranean and Middle East, provided another set of human relationships that supplemented the family and tribe, and that carried its own set of customary regulations.

The Bedouin system of political and legal organization centered on kin groups and their dependents. Ultimately, it depended not on authority imposed from the top, but on the individual's sense of honor, which was invested in an ever-widening series of kinship groupings. Although such a system was well adapted to the needs of a decentralized society, it resulted in a relativistic morality, which placed loyalty to the group above all abstract standards guiding human conduct. A deed was evaluated in terms of kin loyalties rather than absolute ethical merit; even the deities were often tied to territories and groups and provided no means for moral transcendence. The outlook created has sometimes been called "amoral familism" because it equated ethics with family interests; it might be better thought of, however, as a coherent moral system centered on kinship, a system that was functional in certain circumstances but carried with it some severe limitations in uniting people under a more inclusive morality.

We have examined the pre-Islamic Bedouin social ethic in detail for several reasons. It is important to realize that the organizational and moral aspects of the system have persisted not only among Bedouins but also to some extent among settled Arabs to the present time, and that this ethic has influenced Muslim society in many ways. It is even more important to realize that the ministry of Muhammad revolutionized the Arab society of its time by subordinating the old familistic ethic to a transcendent system of morality, facilitating a moral and political transformation in Arabia and beyond.

THE SOCIAL SETTING OF MECCA

At the time of Muhammad's birth in about 570 C.E., Arabic-speaking peoples occupied the central Arabian Peninsula; they were subject to the influences of several powerful empires. Most Arabs were either Bedouin nomads or their settled descendants who occupied themselves with trade and agriculture. Agriculture in the area did not compare with that of the more fertile regions of the Tigris–Euphrates region and Mediterranean coast to the northwest or of the Yemen[1] to the southeast. Consequently, neither the wealth nor the political organization of the Arabs matched that of their neighbors. At that time, Syria (the traditional name for the fertile part of the Middle East bordering the eastern Mediterranean) was under the control of the Byzantine Empire, whereas the Iraq (the farming region along the Tigris and Euphrates) was controlled by Byzantium's principal antagonist, the Sassanian Empire with its ties to the Iranian highland. The Yemen, home of an urban agricultural and trading civilization, was losing its former power and was under the threat of domination by the Christian Abyssinian Empire in Africa, which had already intervened in the

region on one occasion. Placed in a delicate situation between several more powerful forces, the Arabs were gradually developing their own urban economy and their own political strategies. Arab groups near the areas of Byzantine, Sassanian, and Yemen influence benefited from an arrangement in which the empires sponsored and subsidized them as "kingdoms" in return for military protection of their borders against the rival empires and their Arab clients. Away from these "buffer" Arab kingdoms, equidistant from the contemporary superpowers, most Arabs remained nomadic, while some others were beginning to develop a different source of strength.

Located astride some of the most important trade routes that connected Europe, Africa, and Asia, Arabia moved much of the world's long-distance trade. For several centuries before Muhammad's time, Arabs had been assuming an increasingly active part in the trade that crossed their region. The Arab tribe of **Quraish** had founded the trade settlement of Mecca in the **Hijaz** (the mountainous region of Arabia's Red Sea coast) at the juncture of several major trade routes.

Although the Meccans were relatively sophisticated urbanites who were several generations separated from Bedouin life, their society was essentially structured by the Bedouin ethic, with some modifications. The backbone of Meccan organization was the Quraish tribe and its constituent lineages, which had managed to avoid blood feuds only by emphasizing tribal loyalties over more divisive ones. The leadership of the community was vested in the tribal elders, who, as among the Bedouins, had limited powers of enforcement. To ensure the much-needed security of the regions through which their trade passed, it was necessary to enter into alliances with surrounding desert tribes—alliances that obliged them to take part in costly disputes with their allies' respective enemies. Meccan trade was sanctified and protected by pagan religious practices, particularly by the Meccan holy

---

[1]The terms *the* Yemen and *the* Iraq distinguish the historically recognized regions from the modern nations of the same name, Yemen and Iraq.

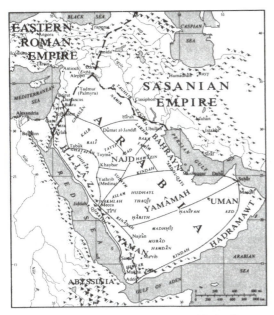

FIGURE 2.1 Towns and Tribes in Arabia in the Time of Muhammad.

Source: Marshall G. H. Hodgson, *The Venture of Islam*, Vol. 1 (Chicago: University of Chicago Press, 1974).

shrine of the Kaaba, which drew pilgrims from much of Arabia. By establishing times and places of truce connected with religious observances, the Meccans were able to protect trade from the threat of feuds among the tribes. Through the selective use and modification of Bedouin organization, the Meccans established a viable urban-mercantile economy. The system brought considerable affluence to the Meccans and allowed them to win influence and respect among other urbanites and merchants in the Yemen and Syria and the Hijaz.

The Bedouin ethic as applied to an urbanized mercantile society was beginning to show its limitations in Muhammad's time, with accompanying strains on Meccan life. Economic inequality had increased between the various lineages of the Quraish, leading to a conflict of interests and a growing social stratification that was difficult to reconcile with familial unity. Non-Quraish minorities

who had become clients of the Quraish were now reduced to little more than debt slaves. The town of Mecca held a wide range of occupations practiced by several resident ethnic groups, including Copts, Syrians, Africans, and Jews; these also did not fit comfortably into a social structure based primarily on kinship, pseudo-kinship, and slavery. In addition to the problems of inequality and diversity, the Meccans were faced with the ever-present threat of feuding should the unity of the Quraish become disturbed; there was no binding, authoritative central leadership. Located between warring empires and in the midst of feuding tribes, the Meccans lacked convincing assurances that their military strength could always be concentrated against outside threats rather than internal squabbles. In adapting the Bedouin social ethic to their needs, the Meccans were straining it to its limits.

The Confessional Religions

The religious and social life of Mecca were hovering on the brink of significant change. The previous centuries had seen the rise, in an area extending from Asia to Europe, of a variety of religious traditions that, in contrast to their more ancient counterparts, "looked to *individual* personal adherence to ('confession of') an explicit and often self-sufficient body of moral and cosmological *belief* . . . which was embodied in a corpus of sacred *Scriptures*, claiming *universal* validity for all men and promising a comprehensive solution to human problems in terms which involved *a world beyond death*" (emphasis added).[2]

Although these "confessional religions" included such widely divergent traditions as Christianity and Buddhism, the forms native to the Middle East exhibited some general similarities. The Zoroastrianism of Persia resembled

---

[2]Marshall G. S. Hodgson, *The Venture of Islam*, Vol. 1 (Chicago: University of Chicago Press, 1974), p. 125.

the major Semitic religions, Christianity and Judaism, in its belief in the oneness of God and of transcendent truth, a single universal standard for righteous conduct, a historical struggle between good and evil, the necessity of practical social action and individual responsibility, and a final divine judgment that holds every person accountable for the actions of his or her lifetime. The implications of such religions are quite different from those of a pluralistic, relativistic, kinship-centered paganism.

These confessional religions had political implications as well as spiritual and intellectual influences. The major political entities of the time were associated with confessional religions—the Persian Sassanian Empire with Zoroastrianism, the Byzantines and Abyssinians with Christianity, and the Yemen with Christianity and Judaism. These last two religions in particular had been making inroads in central Arabia, and some Arab groups already had converted to them. The cohesiveness that these religions offered was an attractive alternative to pagan pluralism, and it might have seemed in 600 C.E., that many more Arabs eventually would become Jews or Christians.

Inner developments as well as outer pressures were moving the Meccans toward religious change. The Meccans had found it expedient to promote the centralization of worship in pilgrimages such as that of the Kaaba, and that change carried with it the seeds of a more fundamental religious transformation. In Arab tradition, the minor deities of places and social groupings had been the most important forces in daily life. Allah, the God presiding over relations between tribes—and over intertribal pilgrimages, shrines, and truces—began to assume a greater importance as the intertribal character of worship developed. In Muhammad's time, the Kaaba was associated primarily with Allah, but the Meccans still recognized a plurality of gods, rites, and cults that separated

them from the monotheistic religions by a wide gulf.

MUHAMMAD'S MINISTRY

Muhammad was born into a minor but respectable branch of the Quraish. His father died shortly before his birth, and in keeping with the custom of some Meccan families, Muhammad spent the first few years of his life in the desert under the care of a Bedouin wet nurse. Muhammad's mother died when he was 6 years old, after which he was placed in the care of his uncle, Abu Talib. The young Muhammad tended sheep and sold goods in the marketplace, and by the time he reached adulthood he had gained a reputation as a capable businessman and a person of good character (in Mecca he was known as al-Amin, "the trustworthy"). At the age of 25, he married Khadija, a wealthy widow 15 years his senior, for whom he had been managing business accounts. She remained his only wife until her death some 25 years later. During their marriage she bore him three sons, all of whom died before reaching adulthood, and four daughters.

Had Muhammad been an ordinary man, he might have settled into a life of secure prosperity, but he was extraordinarily preoccupied with the moral and religious problems of his time. Like many of his contemporaries, Muhammad was dissatisfied with the religious climate around him. He often retreated to a cave on the outskirts of town, where he meditated. It was during one of these retreats that he received the first of a series of visions in which the Angel Gabriel called on him to become the Apostle of God. According to his biographers, Muhammad at first doubted the visions, but he accepted his calling after Khadija and a Christian relative of hers pronounced them genuine. These first visions came in about 610 C.E., but it was several years before he began his public preaching. Khadija became his first convert; she was quickly followed by Ali, a younger cousin being raised in his household, and by Zayd, a former slave of Khadija. During the first few years of his ministry, Muhammad's converts were to span the social scale from slaves and tribeless individuals to wealthy merchants; for the most part, however, they tended to be young men occupying less-favored positions within more respected families.

When Muhammad began his public preaching, his revelations were simple and direct: There is but one God, Allah the Creator, and those who ungratefully turn away from Him to the pleasures of this world will be held accountable on the Day of Judgment. Wealth and social position will count for nothing in the Final Judgment, but justice, piety, and righteousness will count for everything. Every person is equal before God, and righteousness is a matter between the individual and God, not a striving for power and position among kin groups. Pride, the mainspring of the Bedouin ethic, was a vice to be replaced by humility before the Creator. It seems that another central theme in the earliest revelations was the Meccans' excessive pride in wealth and their unwillingness to share with those in need. Through Muhammad, God accused the Meccans:

> You honor not the orphan, and you
> urge not the feeding of the needy,
> and you devour the inheritance
> greedily, and you love wealth with
> an ardent love. (Koran, 89:18–21)

There is no evidence that Muhammad supported a communistic system in which all wealth was to be made public, but only that he advocated more compassion and sharing, and less stinginess and pride, than was common among the Quraish. In this, evidently one of the earliest ethical messages in Muhammad's preaching, there is considerable continuity with the Bedouin ethic. The most favored Meccan families had succeeded in cornering a growing portion of the community's wealth and privilege, and they had all but abandoned the traditional obligations of sharing. By attacking the Meccans' greed and calling on them to share their wealth,

Muhammad was reasserting a moral principle recognized in the Bedouin tradition, but now in a new context and with new ramifications. In a mercantile society where success depended more on opportunism than kinship, the power of the kin group over the individual was often too weak to enforce such sharing. But in the Koran, these obligations came to be represented as sacred duties for which the individual would answer to an all-powerful God on Judgment Day. In this way, Muhammad's reassertion of a traditional value had a radical twist.

In some respects, the revelations of Muhammad were perfectly in tune with the developmental course of Meccan society. As previously pointed out, the Meccans were in need of a unifying moral–religious system not only to serve their need for internal cohesion but also to meet the challenge of the other monotheistic religions and the political forces with which they were associated. Yet in other ways, the teachings of the Prophet ran against the grain of the prevailing cultural beliefs and the vested power interests in Mecca. In particular, the Quraish saw in Muhammad's budding sect a challenge to the values that legitimized their own power and a denunciation of the religious observances that they had so carefully structured to serve their political and economic interests. The Prophet himself, as God's appointed leader of the righteous, seemed to be making a personal bid for power that might encroach on the power of the Quraish. Not surprisingly, the Quraish led the way in persecuting Muhammad and his followers to the extent that part of the Muslim community (but not the Prophet) sought temporary asylum in Abyssinia. Relations between Muslims and non-Muslims were tense in Mecca and became more so as the Muslims made it increasingly clear that they sought the conversion of all Meccans. The tide seemed to turn against Muhammad in 619 C.E., when his wife Khadija, his most intimate personal supporter, and his uncle Abu Talib, who had ensured the support of his lineage against the rest of the Quraish, both died.

The Hijira

Muhammad's followers were saved from an increasingly threatened existence in Mecca by what was to become a turning point in the growth of Islam. In 620 C.E., the Prophet was approached by a handful of converts from the town of Yathrib, 200 miles to the north of Mecca. Yathrib had been founded (or revived) as a farming oasis by several Arab Jewish clans, who had later been joined by other families of pagan Arabs. The problems of family ethics in the city had eventually reached a level of crisis, in which blood feuding was so widespread that the community had little peace. The Muslims and others at Yathrib saw in Muhammad an arbitrator whose religious commitments and sense of justice would serve them well; they promised obedience to Muhammad and safety to the Muslims if the Prophet would agree to relocate in their city. After negotiating during the two following years with a growing delegation of Muslims from Yathrib, the Muslim community emigrated in 622 C.E. The year of the migration, or **hijira**, subsequently became the first year of the Muslim holy calendar, and the city of Yathrib thereafter became known as Medinat al-Nabi ("city of the Prophet") or simply Medina ("the city").

There is more than a ritual meaning to the hijira date as a demarcation. In Medina, the Muslims, cut off from previous kinship ties, established their independent political existence based on the principles of Islam. Also in Medina, Muhammad was presented with the opportunity to construct a new Islamic social order among his followers. If Mecca was the birthplace of Islam as a religion, Medina was its birthplace of Islam as a state and a way of life.

The Koran's Social Regulations

The social problems of Medina had some parallels to those of Mecca, but the differences were considerable. Medina depended on farming rather than trade, and the kinship groups there were still relatively strong. Unlike Mecca, where the domination of the Quraish had given some measure of unity and had helped avert blood feuding, Medina was torn by violent strife among its many kinship groups. The predominantly Arab population of Medina was not entirely pagan, but included a substantial and influential Jewish faction, a fact that was to complicate Muhammad's ministry there. Although some of the most basic ideas of Islam—including the oneness of God, Final Judgment, humility, and generosity—were preached at Mecca, the longer suras containing the most detailed social regulations came to Muhammad while he was judge-arbiter at Medina and were first addressed to the people of that city.

For the most part, the social regulations of the Koran do not define political institutions as such (even the leadership of the Muslims after the Prophet's death was left unprovided for). They do, however, emphasize the moral responsibility, autonomy, and dignity of the individual by providing detailed rules by which the righteous can guide their daily lives with a minimum of dependence on the old sources of authority, particularly the tribe and lineage. The required abstention from pork, wine, and gambling was a matter to which any individual believer could adhere without outside support or resources, placing himself in the community of believers and setting himself apart from tradition by these simple and personal acts of choice. The blood feud, one of the most sacred duties of the old order, was outlawed; in its place equal penalties were set for specified crimes, regardless of the social status of the parties involved. Similarly, the zakat, the alms tax collected by the Muslim community on behalf of the needy, transferred certain duties and powers from the lineage and tribe to the religious leadership and at the same time gave the powerless a more secure status independent of their kin groups.

Many of the Koran's social regulations concern marriage and the family, and the tendency was to favor the rights of the individual and the immediate family over those of tribe and lineage. Numerous forms of marriage prevailed in Arabia before Islam; some of them were nothing more than casual relationships in which each partner remained under the control of his or her respective family, whereas others made wives little more than slaves. The status of marriages and their participants was determined more by family connections, power, and social position than by any universal rules. The Koran universalized marriage forms and family obligations; it discouraged casual forms of quasi-marriage and gave equal status in law to all marriages between free persons. The Koran limited the number of wives a man might take to four and counseled that all wives must be treated equally. Inheritance remained within the immediate family rather than becoming diffused into the larger kin group. The rights of the husband-father (including the right to divorce) were strengthened, not so much at the expense of the wife (who had never enjoyed much power) as at the expense of his and his wife's lineages. The husband's rights included the ultimate custody of children after divorce.

In tune with the theme of personal autonomy and responsibility, the Koran showed its recognition of individual rights in other ways. The right to life was affirmed in the prohibition of infanticide, a practice that had often been used to eliminate female infants. The Koran spoke strongly for individual property rights, urging respect for the property of even the most vulnerable members of society, including women and orphans. The bride wealth that was traditionally paid by a husband to the wife's family was to become her personal property, and a woman's property was protected from the husband during marriage and retained for the wife in the event of divorce.

Slavery was a firmly entrenched practice in the Middle East (and until more recently, in many other places where economic factors favored it). Nevertheless, the Koran allowed slaves greater rights than those granted in the United States in the nineteenth century and

taught that it is meritorious to free a slave. Muhammad set an example by freeing his own slave, who later became a prominent Muslim.

It has been suggested by some writers that the conception of fairness, individualism, and equality implied in Koranic teachings is derived more from the cultural outlook of the marketplace than from the temple or the palace. If this is true, it may be more than coincidence that such an innovation originated not in the older and more civilized centers of power, but in the new mercantile communities of the Hijaz. In any case, it is difficult to deny that Islam was, in the context where it originated, a major step toward the forms of morality most widely recognized in the modern world.

The Spread of Islam

Although Muhammad's position in Medina was that of judge-arbiter and did not depend on the conversion of the populace, the pagan Arab population of the city increasingly became Muslim. The pressure to convert came from several sources, including not only the attractiveness of the teachings and the prospect of inclusion in a cohesive social entity but also an increasingly aggressive self-identification on the part of the Muslim community.

A central concept in the Koran is that of the **Umma**. Originally, the term referred to the people to whom a prophet is sent, but it soon came to refer to the believers in Islam as a community in themselves. It was to this community that a Muslim's social responsibilities were ultimately directed, and loyalty to the Umma came to be seen as inseparable from loyalty to God. The idea of the Umma expresses Islam's radical departure from the past in a most fundamental way because membership in this community of believers cut across all traditional distinctions of family, class, and ethnicity. In principle, a Muslim owed allegiance unconditionally to another Muslim, even a foreigner or an individual without social standing, and against a sibling or a parent if he or she was an unbeliever.

It does not seem that Muhammad at first had in mind the creation of a new religious community to oppose Judaism and Christianity. Rather, he saw himself as a reformer of those religions, who in the tradition of previous prophets would lead Jews, Christians, and pagan Arabs out of error and revitalize the religion of Abraham. Muhammad at first prayed in the direction of Jerusalem and observed the fast of the Jewish Day of Atonement. He was soon to be disappointed, however, by the unwillingness of most Medinese Christians and Jews to convert to Islam. During the Medina period, the religion of Islam came to be defined in a manner increasingly distinct from the other monotheistic religions. Muslim prayer was reoriented in the direction of Mecca, where the Kaaba was eventually to become the central shrine of Islam. The fast of the Day of Atonement was replaced by the month of Ramadan. The Koranic revelations outlined a general policy toward the other religions in Arabia that later came to be applied in other contexts as well. If the message of the Prophet is God's holy word, it applies equally to all who accept it. Because of Islam's emphasis on the creation of a divinely guided community whose religion is expressed in ethics and justice, the dedicated Muslim cannot rest content with personal enlightenment or salvation.

Jihad and the Djimmi System

The extension of the faith is a holy duty and a struggle from which a conscientious Muslim should never retire. The struggle is represented in the concept of **jihad**, or holy war. What is entailed in the Koran's support of jihad has always been subject to various interpretations by Muslims, but the Koran did make it clear that Christians and Jews were "People of the Book" who, though in error, ought not to be converted against their will. As long as they did not oppose the hegemony of the Muslim community in Arabia, they were accorded the status of a protected community, or **djimmi**. Following the Arab traditions of client–patron

relationships, these communities were expected to pay a tribute tax and to show deference to the Muslims, but they were protected from harsh treatment, exploitation, and attack by outsiders and Muslims. The pagan Arabs were a different case: Muhammad was above all a prophet sent to them, for they had strayed the farthest from God. The conversion of all pagan Arabs, including not only most Meccans but also most Bedouin tribes, was so important that it was to be implemented by whatever use of force proved necessary.

The conversion of the Arabs proceeded swiftly during the Medina years. After the hijira, Muhammad and his followers began to attack the Meccan caravan trade and to clash in a series of skirmishes and battles with Meccan forces. The success of some of these early engagements, sometimes against unfavorable odds, was widely interpreted in Arabia as evidence of divine favor toward the Muslims. Muhammad offered all converts a share in the booty of war, and the Muslims began to gather a following of Arab tribes that posed a growing threat to the Meccans and their own Arab allies. Under Islam, much of the amorphous realm of the Arabs was crystallizing into a community united by a divine purpose and a sense of community.

The Meccans had been obliged to make so many concessions to the growing power of the Muslims that when the Prophet's army reentered the city, some eight years after the forced emigration, it encountered only token resistance. Muhammad was a benign conqueror, so much so that his veteran followers complained of the material rewards granted to the Quraish in return for their support. Mecca became a Muslim city almost overnight. The Kaaba, following the destruction of pagan idols and its "restoration" to Allah as Abraham's temple, became the focal point of Muslim prayer and pilgrimage.

Two years later, in 632 C.E., Muhammad, the messenger of God, died. In contrast to most prophets, he had lived to see the basic fulfillment of his mission. The word of God had been delivered and heard, and the pagan tribes of Arabia had at least nominally converted to Islam. The religion of Muhammad's childhood had become virtually extinct. Islam was established as a coherent set of beliefs, ritual practices, and social ethics that had swept much of the world known to Muhammad. This in itself is a remarkable enough accomplishment, and it is unlikely that Muhammad could have anticipated that Islam was to spread its influence farther and more deeply than did the Roman Empire, or that within four generations people from Spain to western China would be praying toward Mecca.

FIVE POPULAR MISCONCEPTIONS ABOUT ISLAM

According to popular notions widespread in the West, Islam is an exotic religion of the desert nomad, a religion characterized by fanatical intolerance of the "infidel," spread "by the sword," and dedicated to an ultraconservative view of human social existence. Such a picture is founded on misconceptions about the nature of Islam and of its historical role in Middle Eastern society.

Islam as an Exotic Religion

Viewed from the perspective of Jews and Christians, Islam is by no means an exotic religion. Each of these three religions embodies many of the same notions of society, history, divine will, and personal responsibility—especially compared with the nonhistorical, otherworldly orientation of many Eastern religions. Each recognizes the same God, the same early patriarchs, and most of the same prophets; each originated among Semitic-speaking peoples of the Middle East. Although there are differences in the perspective of cultural history, the three religions must be seen as closely related. In some respects, the Muslim might see more continuity among the three religions than does the Jew or the Christian because Muhammad's prophecies are believed to be merely an

outgrowth of the same tradition that encompasses Jesus and the Old Testament prophets. Muhammad had come into contact with Jews and Christians and was familiar with their verbal renditions of their Scriptures. Although there is no direct written connection between Judeo-Christian and Muslim Scriptures (Muhammad was said to have been illiterate), and certain scriptural events are rendered differently in the Koran, Islam unquestionably views itself as the culmination of the Judeo-Christian religious tradition.

Insofar as Muhammad was an apostle to the Arabs, and the Arabs identify ultimately with their Bedouin heritage, there is some truth to the picture of Islam as a "religion of the desert." Islam draws selectively on certain ancient Bedouin values, such as sharing wealth and caring for those in need. Nevertheless, at its core Islam is an urban and cosmopolitan religion that in its day undermined the tribal system of ethics and religion and replaced it with a rationalized, universal set of beliefs. Its main thrust is at one with the other confessional religions and not with "primitive" religions centered on nature and the family. To represent Islam as merely an extension of the Bedouin outlook, as is so often done, is fundamentally false.

Islam as a Militant Religion

One often encounters the assertion, even among some historians, that Islam is a particularly militant and intolerant religion, and that it was spread mainly through the use of force—or as the phrase goes, "by the sword." Historically, Islam no more deserves such a reputation than does Christianity. It is true that the Scriptures of Islam do not advise believers to turn the other cheek, and that the Koran actually praises those who go to war in defense of the faith. The concept of jihad, the holy struggle against the unbeliever, seems to the Westerner to suggest a program of ruthless suppression of other religions. The concept of jihad is a complex one for Muslims, however, and the idea of struggle can be interpreted and implemented in various ways. In some sense, the duty of spreading the faith and the idea of universal brotherhood and equality before God are two sides of the same coin. If the message of God is good for all people, one does humankind a disservice by leaving the infidels to their disbelief. This does not mean, however, and never has meant that the Muslim community sanctions random acts of aggression against non-Muslims. On the contrary, the djimmi system protected the rights of religious communities that rejected Islam entirely.

As for conversion by the sword, this Western accusation against Islam has an exceedingly weak foundation. The Koranic stand on forced conversion is ambiguous, and one can find hadith that seem to forbid it and those that seem to support it. Muhammad took a hard stand toward pagans, the nonmonotheistic Arab tribes, but opposed the forced conversion of adherents of the confessional religions in Arabia. In later times other communities, including the Hindus in India, were extended formal protection as djimmis. As we shall see in Chapter 3, the millions who converted to Islam did so for a variety of reasons. The pagan Arabs probably converted more often for the sake of various material, social, and spiritual advantages than out of fear. The Muslims of the Far East, whose population today rivals that of the Muslim Middle East, were generally converted through the influence of peaceful merchants. Despite the teachings of Jesus, Christianity was spread at the point of a sword in much of Europe and the Western Hemisphere. If the historical record were examined carefully, it probably would show that the spread of Islam depended no more consistently on the use of force than did the spread of Christianity.

Islam as an Intolerant Religion

As for religious intolerance, it is instructive to compare the attitudes of Christians and Muslims toward the Jews, who were a religious minority in the Muslim and Christian worlds. Tensions have often existed between Jewish communities and the politically dominant Muslims or Christians. One reason for this tension lies in the nature of Jewish existence as a religious and cultural minority, with all the conflicting loyalties, suspicions, and persecutions that frequently accompany minority status. In addition, the presence of an unconverted population seems to thwart the universalistic claims of Islam and Christianity. Finally, the historical connections of Christianity and Islam with Judaism have given rise to more specific allegations against the Jews: Christians traditionally have blamed them for betraying Christ, and Muslims have accused them of spurning Muhammad's ministry. Tension between Muslims and Jews became severe even at Medina, where early attempts to convert the Jewish Arabs of that city came to nothing. The Prophet eventually expelled two of the major Jewish clans and sanctioned a blood bath against the third for their alleged intrigues against him. During this period, the Koranic revelations upbraided the Jews for their supposed errors and their lack of faith in God's prophet.

Despite the ever-present potential for conflict, the actual history of Jewish minorities in Christian and Muslim worlds has been variable, and it would be difficult to portray the differences in terms of Christian love versus Muslim intolerance. Although interethnic relations in both contexts had their ups and downs, the Christian and Jewish minorities under Islam ultimately enjoyed the status of protected communities as defined in the Koran. This djimmi status carried obligations of civil obedience, special taxation, and limitation of political independence, but it also exempted minorities from the requirements of jihad and zakat. It can be argued that Jewish minorities in Christendom labored under equally severe restrictions and held a less secure legal status. When the Muslims were expelled from Spain in the twelfth to fifteenth centuries, the Jewish communities that had previously thrived under Muslim rule were subjected by the conquering Christians to persecution, forced conversion, and banishment. Putting aside the ecumenical spirit that has more recently appeared in the Christian world, there is little in the historical record to support the Western image of Islam as an essentially fanatical and intolerant religion compared with traditional Christianity. Similarly, there is little support for the idea that active enmity between Muslims and Jews (or Christians) is inevitable.

Islam as an Ultraconservative Religion

Many Westerners believe that Islam is a more socially conservative religion than is Judaism or Christianity. Some have even referred to the more recent revival of religious commitment in Muslim countries as a "return to the seventh century" (as though, in contrast to Christians and Jews, a Muslim must choose between religion and modern life). Islam's Scriptures are notable for their detailed pronouncements on the conduct of social life, a fact that poses a special challenge to the Islamic modernist. Judaism and Christianity are by no means lacking in specific social rules, however, and the Scriptures of these religions date to an even earlier period than the Koran. The social ideas presented in the Koran were in many respects radical departures from the prevailing customs of the time and must be seen in their historical context as innovative.

Throughout history and into the present, Islam, similar to other religions, has been invoked to justify a wide variety of social agendas ranging from the restoration of an idealized past to the pursuit of progressive programs of social reform. In the end, it is difficult to make the judgment that Islam, any more than other world religions, is inherently opposed to changes that would allow for a satisfying and effective life in the modern world. Because Islam's position on women's rights has sometimes been used as an example of Muslim

conservatism and is often used in demeaning portrayals of Muslim life, let us examine this subject further as a case in point.

Islam as a Sexist Religion

Similar to Judaism and Christianity, Islam reflects the patriarchal character of Middle Eastern society at the time of its origin. Many of its social regulations presuppose a family in which the man is the chief authority and economic provider and a descent system traced through the husband and father. We therefore find a variety of sexually differentiated rules: Men but not women may take more than one spouse, a woman receives only half a man's share of an inheritance, and divorce is easier for a man than for a woman to initiate. In each of these matters, however, Islam may not be as conservative as it first appears. Plural marriage was permissible among pagans, Jews, and Christians until long after Muhammad's day, and the effect of Islam was not to originate plural marriage but to regulate it, to set limits on it, and to define the rights and obligations of each partner. Under Islam, a man is allowed no more than four wives, and he is permitted only one if he is unable to treat several wives equally. Men are counseled to treat their wives with kindness, and hadith even criticize men who behave selfishly in sexual intercourse. The Koran advises individuals with marital difficulties to seek arbitration by representatives of the wife's and the husband's families, indicating not only that the preservation of a marriage is desirable but also that a woman's grievances ought to be taken seriously. As for property and inheritance, the most significant innovations of Islam were in securing for women the right to inherit property and to receive the bride wealth previously paid to the bride's family by the husband, and in protecting her full rights of property ownership even in marriage and divorce. This right of a woman to control her own property after marriage, established by the Koran in the seventh century, is still being sought by women in some parts of the Western world.

The veiling and seclusion of women, for which Islam is often criticized, is more a matter of folk practice than an intrinsic part of Islam. Although the Koran advocates sexual modesty on the part of women, it makes the same requirement of men. The social custom of keeping women veiled or behind closed doors is not specifically Muslim, but reflects traditional Middle Eastern concerns. The purity of the women in a family guaranteed its honor and ensured the integrity of the male line. The impracticality of keeping women in extreme seclusion has caused the practice to be concentrated in, and symbolic of, the traditional urban upper classes (including many Jews and Christians). Traditional public opinion in favor of female seclusion, contrary to the practice of Muhammad and the early Muslims, has kept women out of the mosques and away from active religious practice. Over the past century, many Muslim intellectuals have objected to the seclusion of women on the grounds that it is contrary to the tenets of Islam.

The Koran echoes the sentiments of traditional Middle Eastern society and of Judeo-Christian thought in saying that "men are the managers of the affairs of women, for that God hath preferred in bounty one of them over the other" (4:5–52). Islamic Scriptures do not go as far as the Christian Scriptures, however, in asserting the moral inequality of women and men. We do not find in the Koran anything corresponding to Paul's pronouncement about the "shame" of women for having brought sin into the world (in the Koran, Adam and Eve are tempted equally) or to the Christian idea that man is the image and "glory of God," whereas woman is "created for man." If anything, the Koran goes out of its way to emphasize the moral (as distinct from social) equality of the sexes. Repeatedly it makes clear that its pronouncements stand alike for every believer "be you male or female."

If we can separate the essential religious teachings from social customs that have grown up around them, we find in Islam no more basis for sexist attitudes than is present in the Scriptures of Judaism and Christianity. It is true that a relatively large proportion of Muslims retain close ties with the customs of a premodern age, whereas many Christians and Jews living in the West have all but forgotten some of the more conservative social customs upheld in their Scriptures. Nevertheless, there is no reason to assume that Islam is inherently less compatible with modern life and change than its sister religions. Many Muslim modernists view Islam as an essentially progressive religion with regard to sex roles and other social issues, and they chide conservative Muslims for allowing custom and prejudice to distract them from the true principles of their faith. We shall have more to say on this subject in a later chapter.

CONCLUSION

In this chapter, we have endeavored to portray Islam as a religious faith and as a product of human history. In so doing, we have introduced the reader to the interplay between religion and society. At any given point in history, the relationship between religious thought and social practice is likely to be a complex one, with religion acting as a conservative force and an invitation to social change. As a society develops through time, that relationship is subject to constant revision and reinterpretation, sometimes in differing ways by different members of society. Although every religion has fundamental themes and values that ultimately guide its development, the range of possible circumstances, applications, and interpretations is often astonishing.

A fundamental challenge to any religion is to address the universal problems of human existence in a way that transcends the narrow limits of time and place, while retaining enough particularity to give its message substance and social relevance. Islam originally addressed the problems of a very specific society in an exceptionally particular and detailed way, and yet it has subsequently presided over a dozen centuries of cultural development among peoples spanning three continents. Although readers should be sensitive to the unifying features of Islam, they also should keep in mind the many contradictions and conflicting interpretations that have occurred within other religious traditions as they adapted to varying circumstances and interests and expect no more consistency from Islam than from any other living religion.

Key Terms

mosque *11*	hajj *12*	ulema *13*
shahada *12*	hajji *12*	Quraish *16*
Kaaba *12*	Koran *13*	Hijaz *16*
imam *12*	suras *13*	hijira 20
zakat *12*	hadith *13*	Umma *21*
sadaqa *12*	Sharia *13*	jihad *22*
Ramadan *12*	Sunni *13*	djimmi *22*

3 | THE POLITICAL LEGACY OF ISLAM, *632–1800* C.E.

Accustomed as Westerners are to the ideal of separating politics from religion, they can easily overlook the extent to which political thought and action throughout history have been expressed in religious terms. In traditional Christianity, no less than in Islam, questions of justice, public obligation, class privilege, and even revolution have been inseparable from religious issues. Some writers see this as evidence that until more recently humankind was driven by religious urges at the expense of practical considerations; others have concluded that the religious impulse is nothing more than a cloak for self-interest. A more moderate interpretation, which the author prefers, is that religion has provided the concepts and the language by which humans have pursued their immediate interests and defined their ultimate values. For this reason, a religious outlook never remains static. It is a continuous dialogue; the form of that dialogue bears the stamp of general human concerns, the changing circumstances of history, and the special qualities of vision that characterize the particular tradition.

Although the social thought of Islam is in itself neither more nor less important than that of other world religions, it is especially significant for the study of Middle Eastern politics. Islam has had a decisive influence on state politics throughout the region since the death of Muhammad, and today the Islamic heritage is present in new ways. Islam is not immune to the influence of contemporary events, and its current political role is different from the one it played in previous centuries. Nevertheless, Islam has a personal and social significance that most contemporary Middle Easterners take seriously, and there is no doubt that the present restructuring of Middle Eastern societies and their interrelations will continue to be based on a common Islamic cultural heritage. Even people who wish to minimize the role of religion in politics must pursue their programs with an acute consciousness of the Islamic milieu.

The revelations of Muhammad introduced a new framework within which to work out the problems of social life. Yet, no matter how consistent a statement one makes about the human condition, the attempt to apply it to actual conditions will always lead to contradictions and conflicts and to resolutions that raise new problems. The difficulties are compounded further as a religious tradition encounters cultural variation and historical change. As human communities over the past

13 centuries have explored the implications of the Islamic vision, they have uncovered numerous conflicts and paths of resolution. No simple generalization can do justice to this rich heritage of thought, and it is not possible to catalogue fully the many outlooks that have developed under the auspices of Islam. It is possible, however, to sample some of the issues that Muslims have most often raised and to indicate the characteristic ways in which these issues have been approached within that tradition.

The ministry of Muhammad had a dual character that arose from his role as a civic leader and a religious visionary. Muhammad made it clear that Islam can be realized only by the creation of a religiously guided community, the Umma. At the same time, such a community exists only insofar as it is defined by Islam. Neither the religion nor the Umma can exist except in terms of the other. Islam requires, by its very nature, a social order that is politically sound and divinely guided. However, the requirements of political efficacy and divine guidance are not always easy to reconcile, at least in the short run, and the problems arising from this contradiction have stimulated much of the political dialogue in Islamic thought. This problem of mediating the demands of faith and politics has manifested itself in more specific conflicts, such as power versus justice, privilege versus equality, guidance by the community versus the conscience of the individual, and the need for adaptive innovation versus the enduring vision of Muhammad's model community.

THE ESTABLISHMENT OF THE ISLAMIC STATE

The teachings of Muhammad, concentrating as they did on individual obligations, left unanswered many questions vital to the future of his community. Most pressing was that of leadership, for which Muhammad had made no provisions. After the Prophet's death, the community at Medina made preparations to choose its own leadership and expected the Meccans to do the same. Many Bedouin "converts" considered themselves to be personal clients of Muhammad and believed that their obligations ended with his death. At this critical moment in history, the initiative was seized by Abu Bakr and Umar, two of Muhammad's closest associates who were to become the first two **caliphs**, or representatives, of the Prophet. Under their strong leadership, the unity of the Muslim community was aggressively asserted. They declared that there would be no prophets after Muhammad, and that the Umma must unite under a single authority. Bedouins slipping away from the Islamic fold were brought back by force in the **Riddah Wars** ("Wars of Apostasy"); even as these campaigns were being completed, the energies of the newly united Arab armies were turned against the faltering empires of Persia and Byzantium, launching Islam on its fateful course.

The Muslim campaigns against the neighboring empires were phenomenally successful. Weakened by decades of indecisive warfare against one another and by internal strains, the exhausted, stalemated Sassanian and Byzantine empires encountered the greatest threat where they had least expected it. The old Arab buffer states, no longer subsidized by the empires, joined with the Muslim Arab conquerors; other local populations, often religious minorities long persecuted by the established state religions, were less than enthusiastic in defending the hegemony of their old masters. Under Umar's guidance (634–644 C.E.), the terms of conquest were lenient, even attractive. Establishing a pattern for subsequent conquests, Umar allowed life to go on, protected and undisturbed in the cities that submitted willingly; they were subject only to a tax. These taxes, along with revenues from lands won in battle and one-fifth of all other loot, went to the Muslim state, which distributed much of it to its soldiers. Under Umar's leadership, Egypt, the Fertile Crescent, and much of Iran came under Muslim domination; the

Sassanian Empire was toppled, and the Byzantines were driven back into Anatolia.

The Muslim Empire, as it took form in the early period, was an Arab military state. Using Bedouin military experience and turning its energies from internal raiding and feuding toward fighting the infidel, the Muslim state rapidly gained power. Under capable administrative leadership, the Arab conquerors instituted an orderly process for collecting revenue and for distributing it by means of the army register, or **diwan**. Conquered people were guaranteed their civil and religious freedom as djimmis in return for their submission to Muslim rule and taxation (often a more attractive arrangement than the older empires had afforded). The Arabs themselves lived in garrison towns segregated from the conquered populace; they had no intention either of blending into the local life or of inviting their new subjects to become like them. Forced conversion of the djimmis was rarely an issue because the Muslims considered their religion, their Arab background, and their privileged status as conquerors and tax recipients to be inextricably connected. To promote religious unity and to safeguard against any possible deviations from the faith, Umar did much to establish the forms of worship and to promulgate knowledge of the Koran in the garrison towns. The center of social life in such towns became the mosque, and the military leader himself emphasized the religious character of the community by personally leading the people in prayer.

The Caliph Uthman (644–656 C.E.) continued Umar's policies, but with less success, for the Muslim community was now confronting some of the social and moral problems arising from the transition of a religious movement into an organized state. Many malcontents saw Uthman as a symbol of what they thought was wrong with the community: a turning from faith to secular power. For them it was particularly galling that Uthman's kinsmen, the **Umayyads**—who unlike Uthman himself had long opposed Muhammad—were now being favored in administrative appointments. Opposition to Uthman was particularly strong in the Iraq at Kufah and in Egypt. In 656 C.E., Uthman was murdered by a group of his opponents from the Egyptian garrison, and the Prophet's cousin and son-in-law Ali was immediately proclaimed caliph. The rebels, who supported Ali's accession, claimed that Uthman had betrayed Islam and that his murder was justified; Uthman's supporters and others horrified by the killing accused Ali of condoning it and demanded that he punish those responsible. The situation quickly developed into civil war, with Ali's supporters in the Iraq pitted against Muawiya, the Umayyad governor of Syria. After initial successes, some of Ali's men persuaded him to submit to arbitration as demanded by Muawiya, whereupon a faction of Ali's army, the **Kharijites**, turned against him for abandoning the cause. His supporters' loyalties were split, the arbitration was damaging to his position, and Ali's fortunes declined until his death at the hands of a Kharijite in 661 C.E.

The death of Ali was a turning point for Islam. The last of the Prophet's close personal followers was now gone. The initial unity of Islam was forever shattered, and the issue was raised—an issue that was to continue to trouble Islam up to the present—of whether civil order within the Umma is more important than the divinely mandated legitimacy of its leadership. The accession of Muawiya established a dynasty of rulers whose ultimate recourse was to secular power, and the religious idealists took on the function, which they have generally had ever since, of a moralistic oppositional force.

THE GOLDEN AGE OF THE CALIPHATE

If Islam had lost some of its purity in the eyes of its more idealistic adherents, it was also coming into its own as a civilization and an empire. Under the Umayyads (661–750 C.E.), Islam spread across North Africa to Spain; in the east, it spread to the Indus Valley (see Figure 3.1,

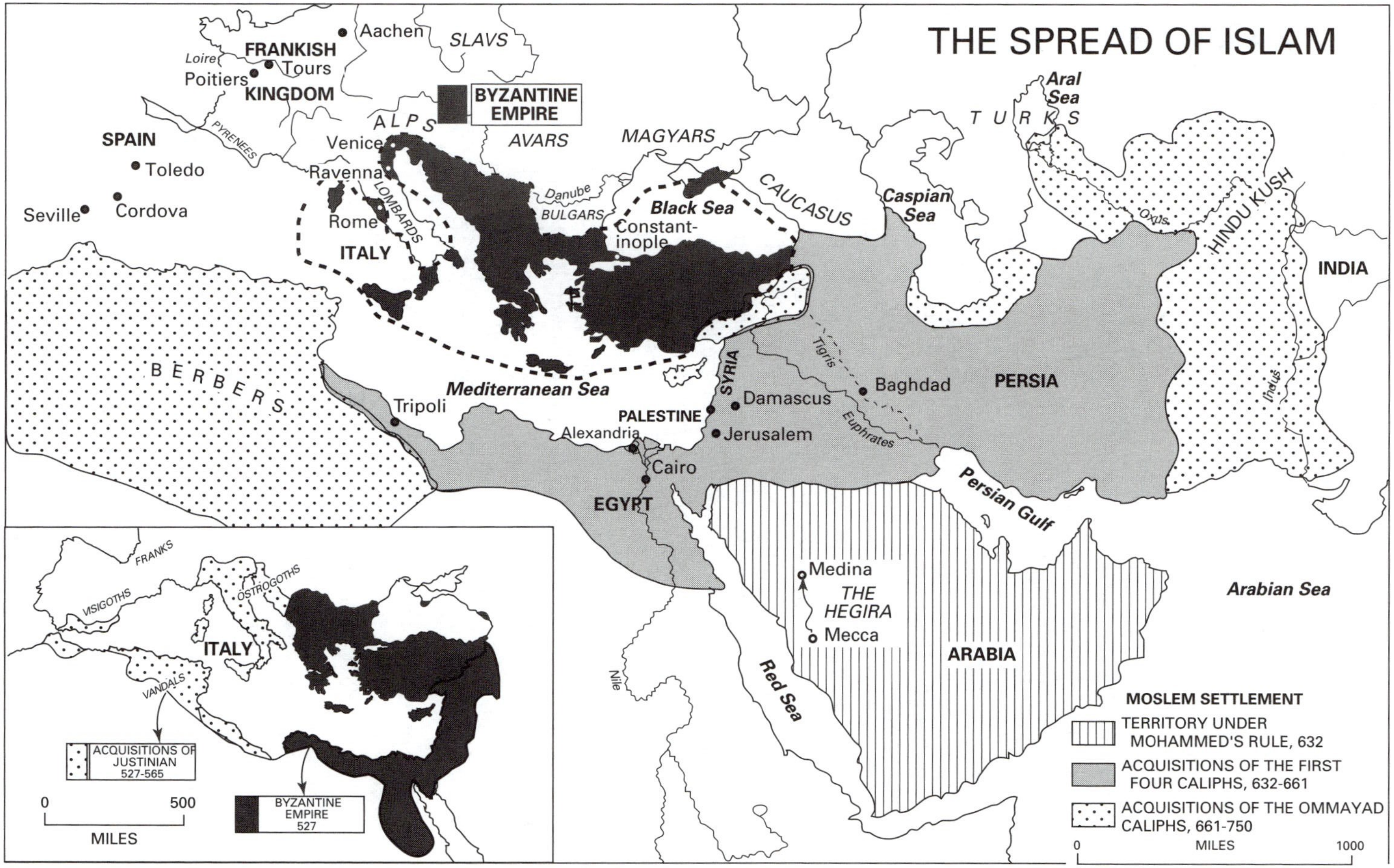
THE SPREAD OF ISLAM
Aachen
SLAVS
FRANKISH
KINGDOM
Loire
Tours
Poitiers
BYZANTINE EMPIRE
SPAIN
Toledo
Cordova
Seville
PYRENEES
ALPS
Venice
Ravenna
Rome
LOMBARDS
ITALY
AVARS
MAGYARS
Danube
BULGARS
Constant-inople
Black Sea
CAUCASUS
Caspian Sea
Aral Sea
TURKS
Oxus
HINDU KUSH
INDIA
Indus
BERBERS
Mediterranean Sea
Tripoli
Alexandria
Cairo
EGYPT
PALESTINE
SYRIA
Damascus
Jerusalem
Tigris
Euphrates
Baghdad
PERSIA
Persian Gulf
Arabian Sea
Medina
THE HEGIRA
Mecca
ARABIA
Red Sea
Nile
MOSLEM SETTLEMENT
TERRITORY UNDER MOHAMMED'S RULE, 632
ACQUISITIONS OF THE FIRST FOUR CALIPHS, 632-661
ACQUISITIONS OF THE OMMAYAD CALIPHS, 661-750
0 MILES 1000
FRANKS
VISIGOTHS
OSTROGOTHS
ITALY
VANDALS
ACQUISITIONS OF JUSTINIAN 527-565
BYZANTINE EMPIRE 527
0 500
MILES

FIGURE 3.1 The Spread of Islam

The Spread of Islam.) The structure of the empire remained essentially that of an Arab conquest state, in which Islam remained primarily the religion of a segregated Arab elite. Other trends were beginning to appear, however.

Despite the ethnic biases of the Arabs, the universalistic, cosmopolitan facets of Islam were beginning to surface as the empire embraced highly sophisticated peoples who were willing and able to take an active part in Muslim civilization. At first, non-Arab converts to Islam were given only marginal status as *Mawalis*, or clients, of influential Arab families. Their existence posed economic problems because the empire was set up on the assumption that Arab Muslims would collect taxes from their subjects on the basis of religious affiliation. In practice, non-Arab converts to Islam often found themselves excluded from Muslim economic privileges despite their conversion. But the forces of change were at work. The Arabs with their Bedouin and mercantile backgrounds were now heirs to the traditions of the centralized agrarian state, and the conditions associated with agrarian life came to have more and more influence over them. The Arab ruling class increasingly began to look like any other local gentry, and the caliphs took on the aspect of semidivine emperors ruling at their court in Damascus.

Throughout the period of Umayyad rule, a variety of gathering factions promoted a growing antigovernment spirit. Some factions disliked the favoring of Syrians over other Arabs; some opposed the distinction of Arabs from other Muslim converts; and some disliked the centralized control over the distribution of revenues, which they thought worked to their disadvantage. Many Arabs despised the pretensions of the caliphs and chafed under the spirit of imperial rule, so incompatible with traditional Arab values. Whatever the specific sources of discontent, the criticisms tended to converge on the accusation that the government was impious, that it had made irreligious "innovations" instead of following the way of the

Prophet, and that it had forgotten its communal obligations in favor of material advantages for the few. What was needed, they agreed, was true Islamic guidance for the community. In the 740s C.E., a coalition of interest groups and sects, including the Shia (the "party" of Ali, which still bore a grudge against the Umayyads), launched a civil war that ended with the establishment of the **Abbasid** dynasty in 750 C.E.

Many who had supported the overthrow of the Umayyads were soon to be disappointed. The bases of the empire were considerably broadened by the change, for the new order with its capital at Baghdad was much more open to the participation and influence of the Iraqi Arabs and especially the non-Arab Persians. Some writers have even gone so far as to characterize the change as one from Arab to Persian domination because of the decisive participation of Persians at the highest levels of government and the increasing influence of Persian language, literature, and culture. Yet, in these changes lay the seeds of bitter disappointment for the old opposition. Far from returning to charismatic rule by Ali's inspired descendants, as the Shia had hoped, or even a return to a purer life modeled on the early Umma, as others had advocated, the caliphate continued on its evolution toward agrarian absolutism. Under the Abbasid caliphs, the power of the court reached its peak, with the caliph exercising his own law at his whim, which was enforced on the spot by his ever-present executioner.

The city of Baghdad, which the Abbasids built for their capital, symbolized the trends in government. In contrast to the Arab garrison towns located on the edge of the desert, Baghdad was built on the Tigris River on a site that commanded key agricultural land in the Iraq and principal trade routes. It was laid out in a circle, and instead of emphasizing Arab tribal divisions, as the garrison towns had done, the entire city was oriented toward the government complex and the caliph's huge palace. The court of the caliph was the center of an aristocratic high culture marked by strong Persian influences, and Baghdad came to play a dominant economic, political, and cultural role reminiscent of the older Persian and Mesopotamian seats of government.

Although absolute despotism was as repugnant to the Bedouin and the ulema as it is to modern taste, it by no means hindered Abbasid civilization itself. Such a monarchy protected the powerless—especially the peasants—against the more grotesque abuses frequently visited on them by decentralized oligarchies and competing petty rulers, and it brought a degree of order that set the stage for unprecedented material prosperity in the Muslim world. Trade and agriculture flourished, banking and communications were effectively organized across the empire, and government was carefully regulated under a *vizier* (comparable to a prime minister) and an established bureaucracy.

This was the golden age of Muslim civilization, to which Muslims in later times would look for inspiration. Muslim power was unparalleled anywhere in the world, and Islamic art, architecture, literature, and poetry—drawing on Arabic, Persian, Greek, Indic, and other traditions and supported by the courtly high culture—reached their peak of development. Arabic works from this period in mathematics (*algebra* and *logarithm* are Arabic-derived words), chemistry, optics, and medicine put these sciences at such a high state of development that Europeans were still consulting the Arabic sources 500 years later. The Crusaders who entered the Middle East at the end of the eleventh century, after the decline of the Abbasid caliphate, were seen with some justice as uncultivated barbarians.

Ironically, the golden age of Islamic civilization also signaled the beginning of the decline of the caliphate. For reasons not altogether clear, the Abbasid caliphs began to lose their hold on the vast empire after their first century of rule. In an attempt to bolster their own power against competing factional loyalties, the caliphs by 850 C.E. had begun to use private armies. These guards were usually slaves obtained from the Turkic-speaking nomadic tribes of the Eurasian steppes; they were kept totally dependent on the caliph and were loyal, presumably, only to him. The caliphs, however, soon found themselves at the mercy of their own palace guards; by the middle to late ninth century, most caliphs were puppets of a Turkish soldier class that was in one form or another to dominate most of Islam for the next thousand years. In the ninth century, some provinces started to assert their independence, and the empire began to devolve into a decentralized civilization with the caliph as figurehead.

Under various dynasties, multiple centers of power developed, and their political control decreased with distance; in some areas, there was little more than local civic government. Yet the social unity of the Umma and the norms that governed Muslim life did not depend on a central government and did not decline with the caliphate. Instead, the political disintegration of Islam was accompanied by the continued development of a common, international pattern of Muslim social life that was based on Islamic Sharia law and was overseen by the formally educated ulema.

MONGOL DESTRUCTION AND THE REBIRTH OF THE EMPIRE

The period from the mid-tenth to the mid-thirteenth centuries saw the militarization of political power. This tendency was brought to an extreme by the Mongol conquests and afterward in the period of the Ottoman Empire and other late empires. Before the thirteenth century, the overall tendency toward decentralized rule by local emirs was reversed only a few times—as in the case of the Seljuk Turks during the eleventh century. The Mongols, however, were able to consolidate pure military power on an unprecedented level. The Mongol invasions were joint efforts involving Turkic-speaking armies recruited among the nomadic tribes of the Eurasian steppes and a Mongol military elite originating in Asia. As a result of a complex of historical and techno-logical factors, during the thirteenth and fourteenth centuries, the Mongols and their armies were able to conquer most of the civi-lized world from China to Eastern Europe and place it under the centralized administration of military chieftains. With the fall of Baghdad in 1258 and the execution of the last Abbasid figurehead caliph, political control passed into purely military hands. Although non-Muslim in origin, the Mongols and their Turkish forces converted to Islam; subsequently, some of the severest Mongol campaigns under Timur (Tamerlane) were fought in the name of Islamic purity. Destructive as their terrorist techniques were, once established, the Mongols became patrons of Islamic high culture and rebuilders of public works. One of their most enduring influences was the establishment of efficient, highly organized states based on the army. In these states, ultimate control was in the hands of a supreme military ruler whose succession was determined by armed contest within the ruling dynasty; the army organization included not only combat troops but also the entire governmental apparatus. So centered on the army were these empires that their capitals were wherever the army and its supreme leader happened to be, and government records were carried into the field on campaigns.

Eventually, the effects of Mongol con-quest gave way to more home-grown military empires, which in some respects benefited from the destruction of the old order and from the Mongol military system. Equally important in these new empires was the use of gunpow-der, which favored the technically advanced urban populations over the Eurasian nomads and allowed greater concentrations of power to develop. The most important post-Mongol concentrations of power in the Middle East were the Safavid Empire, centered approxi-mately in what is now Iran, and the **Ottoman Empire**, originating in what is now Turkey.

Each arose and achieved much of its glory during the sixteenth century, and each was dominated by a Turkic military elite but used Persian or Turkish as a literary language and Arabic as the religious language. Each followed similar paths of development, but the Ottoman state is of the greater interest here, partly because it most directly confronted the grow-ing power of Europe, and partly because it continued as an active force in world politics until the twentieth century.

The Ottoman Empire

The Ottoman Empire, named after its original ruling family of Osman Turks, had its roots in Anatolia during the pre-Mongol period. Located on the frontier of the Byzantine Empire, the Ottoman state had long been asso-ciated with the continuing struggle against the infidel; accordingly, it held a prestigious posi-tion within Islam and attracted many would-be **ghazis**, or defenders of the faith. A turning point for the Ottomans came with the long-sought conquest of Constantinople in 1453, which they renamed Istanbul and made their capital. Ottoman power grew rapidly as Islamic territories expanded into Hungary and even to the gates of Vienna, which the Ottomans unsuccessfully besieged in 1541 and again in 1683. To the south, Ottoman power encompassed the Levant, Syria, the Iraq, the Hijaz, and Muslim North Africa as far west as Algeria. Rivalry between the Ottomans and Safavids took on religious overtones as the Safavids became more militantly Shia and the Ottomans increasingly Sunni, a conflict that has left the Middle East religiously divided to this day along former Ottoman–Safavid bound-ary lines, as Figure 3.2, The Ottoman and Safavid Empires, amply illustrates.

Similar to other Muslim empires before it, the Ottoman Empire developed features of an agrarian state with its social stratification and its absolute monarchy, but the Ottoman form remained distinctive. A military ruling

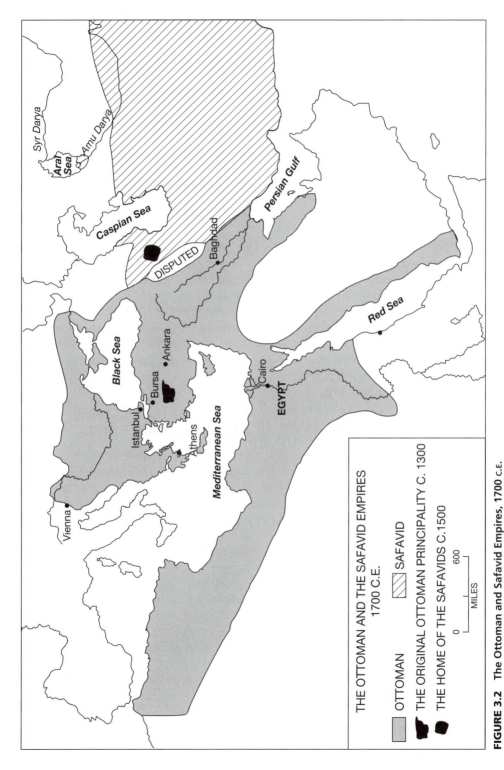

FIGURE 3.2 **The Ottoman and Safavid Empires, 1700 c.e.**

Source: Yahya Armajani, *Middle East Past and Present*, © 1970, p. 161. Reprinted by permission of Prentice Hall, Upper Saddle River, N.J.

THE OTTOMAN AND THE SAFAVID EMPIRES
1700 C.E.

OTTOMAN

SAFAVID

THE ORIGINAL OTTOMAN PRINCIPALITY C. 1300

THE HOME OF THE SAFAVIDS C.1500

0   600

MILES

Syr Darya

Amu Darya

Aral Sea

Caspian Sea

Black Sea

Baghdad

DISPUTED

Persian Gulf

Red Sea

Ankara

Bursa

Istanbul

Athens

Mediterranean Sea

Cairo

EGYPT

Vienna

family presided over a vast army of **Janissaries**, recruited as slaves and loyal only to the rulers. These slaves were obtained as children from non-Muslim populations, often Christian, and were brought up and trained as Muslims. They formed a class that composed not only the military component of the state but also the bureaucracy. At first they were not allowed to marry. When marriage was permitted, the offspring of slaves were freeborn and disqualified from government service, and so there was little opportunity for the formation of privileged classes or loyalties at odds with Ottoman interests.

The machinery of Ottoman government was remarkably efficient. The Ottomans accomplished what few Muslim governing powers had done before them: They successfully allied themselves with the ulema. Ottoman success with the ulema was related to the empire's origin as a ghazi state and its devotion to defending the faith against not only the Christian powers but also the Shia Safavids. A career as a religious scholar was one of the few paths of prestige open to the freeborn sons of the military-bureaucratic slave class. Under the Ottoman system, the ulema relinquished much of their traditional oppositional role with regard to the ruling powers and came instead to identify with those powers. In return, the government supported the ulema's authority and that of Sharia law and submitted to some token checks on its power; for example, the ulema in theory could depose the Ottoman sultan if they judged him unfaithful to Islam.

A certain amount of pluralism was built into the Ottoman system. The djimmi communities, or **millets**, were allowed military protection, religious freedom, and self-government under their own chosen leaders, subject as always to a kind of second-class citizenship in the Muslim state. Ottoman provinces relatively distant from Istanbul, such as the Hijaz and North Africa, also were allowed some degree of self-government. The **Mameluks** of Egypt, a Turkish slave class that had ruled Egypt from

1250 until their defeat by the Ottomans in 1517, were allowed to continue in power under minimal Ottoman supervision.

By the eighteenth century, the empire had long since stopped increasing its territories and was beginning to take note of the rapidly growing European threat. Some attempts were made to modernize the Ottoman army, but these were thwarted by more sweeping problems that plagued the empire. The military ruling class had gradually become civilianized, had suffered a loss of discipline, and had begun to lose even its former structural integrity (for example, army bureaucrats began to pass their status on to their children). Corruption and demoralization became widespread in government, a condition that many Western observers of the time assumed to be a universal trait of "Oriental" governments. When the Western powers began in earnest to move in on the Middle East around the turn of the nineteenth century, they found the Ottoman Empire ill-prepared to resist them.

GROWTH AND DECLINE IN THE ISLAMIC STATE

Many observers have noted that Muslim civilization and Muslim political power seem to have gone through an early period of phenomenal growth and vitality that was followed by a long era of "decline," or "stagnation," ending finally in Western dominance. Often, the rapid growth is attributed to military force driven by religious fanaticism, whereas the decadence that followed is said to reveal the defects either of the "Oriental mind" or of Islam itself, both of which are often accused of authoritarianism and resistance to innovation. Such a view is misleading not only because there is no such thing as an Oriental mind but also because the problem of growth and decline is much too complex to lend itself to such easy generalizations. The Muslim world, similar to any civilization that endures for centuries or millennia, experienced many different kinds of growth and decline. What is decline from one point of view may be growth from another—for example, the decline of centralized government was accompanied by a strengthening of Muslim law that reached across political boundaries. Decline in one local region may be offset by growth in another.

The original growth of Islamic civilization involved two processes that reinforced one another: the spread of Islam as a religion and the extension of Muslim political rule (or ties with the centers of Muslim power). The reasons for the spread of Islamic influence varied with the circumstances. In Medina, conversion to Islam was a matter of civic convenience and personal conviction. Among the Bedouins of the Arabian Peninsula, political advantage and later the threat of force encouraged conversion. The subjects of the Sassanian and Byzantine empires yielded to a well-organized conquering army, but at the same time they were attracted by the promise of being better off as djimmi communities than as Sassanian or Byzantine subjects. Under the Umayyads, non-Arabs converted despite Arab discouragement to benefit from the advantages of Muslim social status. In India, political conquest preceded conversion, and conversion itself resulted more often from the attractiveness of Muslim institutions and the personal appeal of **Sufism** (Muslim mysticism) than from the threat of force. In Southeast Asia, which now includes a large segment of the world's Muslim population, Islam spread peacefully as part of an international mercantile culture, also aided by the appeal of Sufism.

The difficulties encountered by the various Muslim political powers after their establishment were due to a variety of causes, but none of these involved turning away from Islam as such. The Middle East may have been suffering some long-term adverse effects on its ecology, as a result of the ancient and intensive agricultural exploitation of the land. Many Islamic governments followed a policy of assigning "tax farms" as rewards to the military.

These temporary revenue assignments were often exploited with little regard for the welfare of the peasants or the condition of the land and irrigation works, contributing to the decline of productivity. Coupled with the Mongol invasions and the plague (Black Death) during the thirteenth and fourteenth centuries, these trends may have reduced the vitality of agriculture, urban life, and even trade. There is some indication that population may have declined, and that nomadism may have increased during the age of the Muslim empires.

In addition to the economic factors, certain political processes seem to involve an inherent dynamic of growth and decline. In agrarian societies, an existing order tends to accumulate vested interests, tax exemptions, and special privileges to the detriment of the overall functioning of the polity, until at last the weakened governmental power is overthrown, and the accumulated commitments are wiped away (as happened in the Arab conquest of Byzantine and Sassanian domains). This and other political processes may have contributed to cycles of political disintegration and revitalization before and during the age of Muslim power.

As for intellectual development, the creative exploration of new ideas seemed to reach a peak during the Abbasid caliphate; afterward, the legal, moral, and theological conceptions of the ulema prevailed and became increasingly hostile to innovation, especially after the ulema were integrated into the Ottoman order. Although some writers see this as further evidence of the stagnation of "Oriental" civilizations, one could just as easily see it as the natural consequence of the refinement of the Sharia, and particularly of its institutionalization in the **madrasah** schools where the ulema were trained—features that provided much of the resiliency of Islamic law. The spirit of conservatism that prevailed after the collapse of the caliphate did not in itself cause political decline, and it was not very different from the conservatism that prevailed in Europe before the eighteenth century. The pattern of peaks and valleys in political power and social strength has been common to both regions throughout most of history.

LEGITIMACY IN GOVERNMENT

As stated earlier, the teachings of Muhammad stressed the righteous community that was structured to realize the demands of justice and piety. Since the early caliphate, a central problem in Islam has been to reconcile the demands of political reality and the demands of faith. The champions of Islamic values needed a workable government in theory, but rarely approved of what they found in practice. The Islamic governments needed the approval of Islam to make them legitimate; although the Muslim rulers were devout men, they were willing to make only limited concessions to Islamic ideals in government.

In some respects, the first caliphs were able to avoid many of the inherent difficulties of legitimizing Islamic political power. They were personal followers of the Prophet and were intimately acquainted with his words and deeds. The Prophet ruled largely by virtue of that knowledge. Similar to traditional Arab leaders, they also depended largely on their own personal qualities and reputation and on their close acquaintance with the community (that is, with the core of Muhammad's following). They also acquired much legitimacy through their military leadership (Umar preferred to be called the "commander of the faithful" rather than caliph), a role that was well established in Arab tradition and that carried with it the notion of leadership among men who were essentially equals.

The Political Role of the Ulema

Under Uthman, a gap began to develop (or become apparent) between Islamic ideals and the realities of political power and privilege. The issue of Uthman's murder and Ali's accession became symbolic for Muslims of the conflict between communal loyalty and religious purity. Although the Umayyads won on behalf of political solidarity, they had to face renewed challenges first from Ali's sons and later from a coalition of factions that wished to see Islamic government guided by uncompromising religious ideals. When this coalition failed to reverse the tendency toward secular power, Muslims were obliged to choose between remaining loyal to the protest against government or to the powers that governed Islam, regardless of their faults. Although the Shia took the former course, the bulk of the community, later called Sunni, chose in favor of the political unity of the Umma.

As the pious, learned men of the Islamic world began to form into a coherent body of ulema, this body became a kind of loyal opposition, aloof from and critical of the government but not overtly disloyal to it. The ulema generally recognized the legitimacy of the caliphs, even while criticizing their ways. As the caliphs became powerless, they were still invested with theoretical legitimacy as the arbiters of any affairs concerning all Islam, and as the source of authority to the various *emirs*, or local rulers. After the fall of the caliphate, the ulema were inclined to grant at least some legitimacy to the emirs on the grounds that they provided the political order necessary to the community. This trend culminated in the Ottoman theory that whoever can rule the Muslim community according to the Sharia is entitled to be considered the caliph. The Ottoman interpretation completes the transition from the original theory, in which secular power is derived from religious legitimation, to one in which religious legitimation is derived from secular power.

The unique political role of the ulema in Islam deserves special comment. Many traditional agrarian societies had a priesthood, a privileged group of religious practitioners who mediated ritually between the common people and the supernatural, and who tended to be intimately connected with—and supportive of—the political ruling class. The Muslim ulema are scholars rather than priests, however, and their training in subsidized institutions has been open, in theory, to anyone showing promise. Under the protection of Islam, the ulema traditionally have presented a voice of opposition that attempted to hold political figures accountable to the principles of Islam—principles opposed to privilege and self-indulgence. Even today, this heritage influences the relations between the Muslim religious leadership and the politicians. The ulema in Saudi Arabia retain the right to declare a king unfit to govern, and they exercised this right in 1964 when they approved the deposing of King Saud.

THE SHARIA LAW

The Koran did not provide a complete guide for social life, and after the death of Muhammad, the question arose as to how it was to be interpreted and how Muslims should deal with problems it did not directly anticipate. It soon became evident that the secular values of the conquered agrarian states, not to mention the old Arab ways, might reassert themselves unless Islam provided more detailed codes. By gradual steps, religious scholars developed a complex, cumulative set of guiding rules for Muslims that came to be known as the *Sharia*. At the core of the Sharia is the Koran, but it was necessary to supplement the Koran with reports (hadith) about the sayings and practices of the Prophet and his community. Later, as Sharia thinking attacked more complex problems, the Koran and the hadith were extended by means of the principle of analogy, by reference to the consensus of the Umma (or, more specifically, its recognized religious leaders), and by reference to the welfare of the Umma. The relative importance of these various avenues of **fiqh**, or understanding, was debated by leading scholars, and by the ninth century, several major schools of legal thinking had developed. Each of these was accorded equal validity, and although they differed in the methods of arriving at legal

codes, their results were similar. Muslims were expected to adhere consistently to one or another of these schools, usually according to the common practice of the locality. Today, there are four such recognized schools in Sunni Islam.

Formal training in Sharia law became institutionalized in the madrasahs, Islamic schools supported by privately endowed religious foundations (**waqf**, plural *awqaf*) where any capable individual could study free of charge. Such schools helped to determine who was qualified to interpret the tradition and to standardize the Sharia against indiscriminate reinterpretation. They also made it possible to broaden the Sharia beyond the strict limits of the Koran and hadith without sacrificing its coherence or throwing it open to uncontrolled change. The Sharia, thus broadened and codified, provided a universal law that applied to every Muslim and to diverse aspects of life ranging from the settlement of political and business disputes to the regulation of family life. The application of this code and the qualifications of its administrators were valid in all Muslim nations regardless of political boundaries, which allowed Islam to prosper as an international social order even in times of political decentralization.

Based on the mercantile and Arab values of Mecca and Medina, the Sharia embodied a social philosophy that was opposed to social class or other privilege; it tended to support individual rights and individual social mobility and to protect the weak against the strong. Along with an uncompromising concern for Islamic principles of social justice, however, was a distrust of innovation and of the deviant or the outsider—an inclination that became more and more established in the madrasahs after the fourteenth century. In the madrasahs, the methods of teaching became extremely conservative and were aimed at discouraging innovation. Any question that had once been decided on and accepted by the ulema was no longer open for discussion, and new issues were to be resolved insofar as possible in exact accordance with previous decisions. Even the number of errors was determined—there were six dozen false sects of Islam, and every new heresy could be classified with those already known. Yet without this careful regulation, the Sharia probably could not have served its vital function in Muslim life.

The influence of the Sharia was never absolute. Because monarchs often found the Sharia incomplete, irrelevant to certain questions, or excessively "soft" on criminals, they typically established their own courts and legal codes. The peasants and townspeople sometimes found it in their interest to follow customary law, even (as in the case of some inheritance rules) when it contradicted the Sharia. Despite these auxiliary legal systems, however, the Sharia stood as the supreme expression of legitimacy. It was the core of Islamic social life, to which every Muslim ultimately owed allegiance. Safe from random innovation, local cultural influence, and the tampering of political interest groups, the Sharia provided a means of integrating an international civilization.

THE SHIA

The conflicting demands of political unity and religious purity, which became apparent so early in Islamic history, gave rise to the great sectarian split within Islam—that of the Sunnis and the Shia. Although most Muslims are Sunnis, who place loyalty to the established order of the Umma above religious disputation, the Shia, a substantial minority, believe that only a divinely inspired political leadership is worthy of a Muslim's loyalty. The historical split between the two groups is difficult to discuss because the key events of the past have been imbued over the years with complex symbolic significance. At the time of his death, Ali stood for the protest against the supposed corruptions of Uthman's rule, and his defeat was viewed by many Muslims—particularly those in the Iraq—as an unfortunate triumph of worldly

power over true Islamic piety. Those loyal to Ali and to what he stood for came to be known as the Shia (party) of Ali.

A turning point in the history of the Shia was an insurrection in 680 c.e., against the Umayyads under Ali's son Husayn, in which Husayn, abandoned by the bulk of his supporters, was killed. With the rise of the Abbasids in 750 c.e., Shia hopes that the new political unrest would lead to a reinstatement of Ali's line were dashed, and the Shia assumed the posture of a minority opposition to the political establishment.

Under the Abbasids, the division between the Shia and the Sunnis became more distinct. The Sunni position, even among those who sympathized with Ali's protest and despised Uthman and the fallen Umayyad dynasty, was that devotion to the solidarity of the Umma and obedience to its recognized leadership should transcend religious dissension. By the tenth century, the Shia had developed into a distinct and influential group that proposed, in opposition to the Sunni view, that Muslims should follow only the authorities who were rightly guided. In the Shia view, this gift of divine guidance (what sociologists call "charisma") was possessed only by a few elect, descendants of the Prophet through his daughter Fatima and his son-in-law Ali. Although Husayn was the last of these to make an open bid for power, the Shia believed that secret knowledge and divine inspiration had passed through Ali's line to a succession of rightful leaders.

The Shia movement eventually split over differing interpretations of this line of succession. The largest faction was the "Twelvers," who believed that the twelfth Imam in the succession had gone into hiding from the wicked world, where he would remain until his eventual return as the **Mahdi**, or Muslim messiah. In Twelver Shiism, which predominates in Iran, it has occasionally been possible for religious leaders to claim sweeping powers as representatives of this "Hidden Imam." Another major faction, the **Ismailis**, parted with the Twelver line in disputing the identity of the seventh Imam. They came to emphasize the esoteric knowledge of a secret religious elite, a knowledge revealed to the pious individuals only by degrees as they ascend in the religious hierarchy. Ismaili Islam reached the peak of its influence in the Fatimid dynasty in Egypt (969–1171 c.e.), which was renowned for its achievements in government, commerce, art, and learning.

The Shia came to see most Muslims as betrayers of their faith, and temporal power as essentially illegitimate. In this atmosphere of resistance, they developed the practice of denying their true beliefs in public when necessary and the idea that the inward truth of the Koran (as opposed to its outward or superficial meaning) is unknown to the community at large and must be interpreted by the Imams or their agents. (The use of the term *imam* can be confusing because it can refer to a variety of roles ranging from a leader of Muslim prayer to—in Shia thought—a leader of all Islam. Generally, we have capitalized Imam only when it refers to the latter or to a specific historical personage, such as the Imam Ayatollah Khomeini.) Another strong current in Shia thought is the tragic view of the fate of the righteous man in an unrighteous society, and a deep sense of guilt over the betrayal and martyrdom of Husayn. Once a year, during the month of **Muharram**, Husayn's martyrdom is commemorated in an outpouring of grief, self-flagellation, and resentment toward the Sunnis. If the ulema of Sunni Islam looked askance at the political establishment, the Shia simply regarded it as illegitimate, to be tolerated only for the time being. Despite the differences in outlook, Sunni and Shia Islam actually developed remarkably parallel institutions, parallel Sharia codes, and even parallel debates over similar issues. Mystical Sufism, which was largely a Sunni phenomenon, developed its Shia counterpart in a particularly inward-turning brand of personal devotion to Ali and Husayn.

Even in Ali's day, Iraq was a center of proto Shia resistance. It remained so under the Umayyads as part of the protest against Syrian power; and even after the fall of the Umayyads, Shiism remained strong in the old Sassanian domains—so much that some historians characterize Shiism as a Persian movement against Arabism. Shiism was even more radically localized, however, during the rivalry between the Sunni Ottomans and the Shia Safavids, when nonconforming minorities in each domain were persecuted or driven out. Today, Shiism is largely confined to the Middle East, where more than a fourth of the Muslims are Shia, most of whom live in Iraq or Iran.

SUFISM

If the Sharia was uncompromisingly oriented toward history, justice, and practical responsibility, other elements of Islam addressed different facets of religious life. Mysticism, that brand of religious awareness that emphasizes the clarifying and enlightening inward experience over conventionalized and verbally communicated ideas, is pervasive in human cultures and was well established in the Middle East before the rise of Islam. Similar to Christianity and Judaism, Islam has developed its own distinct tradition of mysticism. In early times, the mystically inclined Muslims, or Sufis, were a small minority hardly distinguishable from other Muslims, but after 1100 they became more prominent and influential. The Muslim philosopher-theologian Ghazali (d. 1111), although not a Sufi himself, aided the rise of Sufism by arguing that it was not only consistent with the Sharia but was also a valuable complement to it.

Sufi mystics used classic techniques of posture, breathing, meditation, music, and dance to induce states of extraordinary awareness that they regarded as closeness to God. In their philosophical writings, they emphasized love and cosmic unity, even posing Jesus as the ideal Sufi. Like the Sharia, Sufism was populistic—it took little notice of traditional lines of privilege and was open to all who would pursue it. Unlike the ulema, who were oriented strongly toward the Sharia, the mystics tended to be tolerant of local cultures and customs, of human weakness, and of different levels of understanding. They viewed the Islamic concept of jihad, often translated in English as holy war, as an inward struggle for enlightenment.

Even so, Sufism had its outward, institutional side. After the tenth century, Sufis began to organize themselves into separate orders, or **tariqahs**. Each of these recognized a different line of communication of mystical knowledge, beginning with the private communications of Muhammad to certain followers, and going through a known line of teachers (**pirs**). One could become a pir only by studying under another recognized pir so that the body of knowledge within each order was preserved and controlled. These Sufi orders had social and political uses, for they often became the organizational core of guilds, young men's military clubs, or even some governmental organizations. One ambitious caliph, shortly before the Mongol invasions, even sought to restore the power of the caliphate through the judicious use of Sufi tariqahs.

Because of Sufism's tolerance, its association in folk religion with local "saints" and their tombs, and its abuse by wandering charlatans or extremists who considered themselves outside the Sharia, the ulema often took a dim view of Sufism. Despite occasional outbursts of anti-Sufi reaction, as in the thirteenth century, Sufism was established as legitimate by the Sharia principle of consensus. Some ulema scholars were Sufi pirs themselves, and Sufism came to dominate the inward side of religious life in Islam, especially among the Sunnis. The personal appeal of Sufism supplemented the social appeal of the Sharia and contributed greatly to Islam's spread as a religion and indirectly to the political sway of Islam. Sufism remained another potential counterbalance to the outward authority of any "Islamic" government.

ISLAM AND RADICAL POLITICS

Muhammad's ideal of religiously based law and government contained the seeds of religious support for the establishment and of religious opposition to it. The tradition of religious opposition is represented in one way by the ulema and in quite another by the many radical movements in Islam's history. It is not possible to mention all the major movements that have arisen in Islam, but a few examples suffice for illustration: the Kharijites, the Ismailis, the Sudanese Mahdi, Twelver Shiism, and the Muwahiddun movement.

The Kharijites

Islam's first civil war began with an insurrection of Egyptian soldiers who murdered the caliph Uthman and justified the act with the accusation that he had departed from Islam and was a usurper. Ali's supporters accepted this line of reasoning, whereas his opponents accused him of condoning the murder of a believer and of attempting to disrupt the community. When Ali agreed to submit the issue to arbitration, his most extreme supporters turned against him to become Kharijites ("seceders"). The Kharijites embodied a radically anarchistic interpretation of Islam, in which personal piety was held to be not only the sole measure of a person's right to lead the community, but the only criterion for membership in the Umma itself. The impious Uthman was not only a false caliph but he was also an unbeliever falsely professing Islam; it was the duty of a believer to kill him. In Kharijite eyes, anyone who had committed a "grave" sin was excluded from the Umma, and the most extreme Kharijites did not hesitate to kill non-Kharijites indiscriminately when the occasion presented itself. Even among the Kharijites themselves, on principle no leader was to be trusted, and their "caliph" could be deposed for the slightest transgression. Ali found it necessary to suppress the Kharijites by force, and he was eventually assassinated by one of them. There were more than a score of

Kharijite rebellions during Ali's and Muawiya's reigns, and small Kharijite communities have continued to exist to the present. In their extreme approach to the issue of piety versus political order, the Kharijites severely crippled their own political strength and assured themselves a marginal role in Islamic society.

Ismailis and Qarmatians

The Shia went in a direction opposite to that of the Kharijites by elevating the charismatic leader to an exalted status, the Ismaili Shia going to the farthest extreme. Their central belief was that a highly esoteric knowledge of the all-important inner meaning of Muhammad's teachings was transmitted through secret communication from the Prophet to certain elect followers. The Ismailis gave rise to numerous movements, but none more fascinating than the **Qarmatians**. Originating in the desert between Syria and the Iraq in the late ninth century, the movement designated its leader as an emissary of God. The Qarmatians were dedicated to the overthrow of the wealthy and privileged, and the Bedouins and peasants who joined the sect apparently held all goods in common. After its suppression by the Abbasids, the movement reappeared in Bahrain, where it became established as an egalitarian, communistic state that lasted well into the eleventh century. It is said that the Qarmatians spurned the Sharia and orthodox forms of worship, and that one of their leaders who was thought to be the Mahdi, or Muslim messiah, set himself above Muhammad (this, however, may be hostile propaganda). In any case, the Qarmatians seem to have regarded other Muslims as unbelievers, and in 930 C.E. they succeeded in abducting temporarily the Black Stone from the shrine at Mecca, on the grounds that it was an object of idolatry.

The Mahdi

The Qarmatians were by no means the only Muslims to believe in a Mahdi. Running sporadically throughout Islam is a chiliastic orientation, which holds that the world eventually will be delivered from its wickedness into an age of justice and piety, and the wicked will suffer vengeance from the righteous. The idea of a deliverer, or Mahdi, appears repeatedly in this chiliastic thinking. Of the many individuals hailed as Mahdis, one of the most recent and striking examples is the Sudanese Mahdi of the late nineteenth century. Arising in opposition to the inroads of the modernizing Egyptian ruler Ismail, whose stated intention was to make Egypt part of Europe (and the Sudan part of Egypt), the Mahdi drove the Egyptians out of the Sudan and preached a program of Islamic moral reform, not only for the Sudan but for all Islam. The Mahdi appointed his own caliph. Publicized among pilgrims at Mecca, his program seemed to many Muslims an attractive alternative to the weakened and discredited Ottoman leadership until the British finally succeeded in crushing the movement in the 1890s.

Twelver Shiism

Of all the Shia movements, Iranian "Twelver" Shiism has the greatest contemporary relevance. Although it shares with the other forms of Shiism its basic emphasis on esoteric knowledge vouchsafed through the lineage of the Prophet, Twelver Shiism has shown itself to be a persistent factor in the political arenas of the Middle East, alternating between active and passive political activity. Although the Ismaili Shia held substantial power only during the Fatimid reign, the Twelver Shia held dynastic power many times, always in the area of Iran and Iraq.

As a consequence of its substantial dynastic experience, Twelver Shiism has developed elaborate doctrines regarding the relationship between faith and the state and between the ulema and the governor. These theories saw contemporary expression during the "Tobacco riot" protests against the Qajar dynasty near the turn of the twentieth century, during the nationalist protests against the shah of Iran in the immediate aftermath of World War II, and most recently in the successful movement against the shah and in the design and implementation of an Islamic republic in Iran. More recent scholarship indicates that a crucial turning point in the movement against the shah was Ayatollah Khomeini's successful invocation of the activist symbols of Twelver Shiism, effectively transforming Iranian Shia religious activity from quiet protest to political confrontation. In so doing, Ayatollah Khomeini of necessity invoked symbols and myths from the earliest days of Shiism, showing anew the relevance of the past to the present.

The Muwahhidun Movement

In Arabia during the late eighteenth century, a former Sufi teacher, Muhammad Ibn Abd-al-Wahhab, came under the influence of the conservative Hanbali school of Sunni Muslim thought, which rejected the role of ulema consensus in the interpretation of the Sharia. He called for the purification of Islam from the influence of evil innovations, which he believed were responsible for the decadence of the Ottoman world. With the aid of Ibn Saud, a local ruler who had converted to the movement, Ibn Abd al-Wahhab set about to promote an extremely puritanical reform of Islam, which opposed all forms of Sufism and pre-Islamic custom and denounced most Muslims as idolaters and infidels to be killed. Even after decades of Ottoman attempts to suppress the movement, Ibn Saud's grandson was able to seize Mecca and Medina, destroy many of Islam's holy shrines, and massacre the residents of these cities. The movement was temporarily suppressed in 1818, only to reappear in the twentieth century, again championed by members of the house of Saud. This "Unitarian" or **Muwahhidun** movement (a designation preferred by its followers over the more frequently encountered term, **Wahhabi**) was to become the foundation of the modern state of Saudi Arabia. Thus, the deep-lying conservatism of contemporary Saudi Arabia, far from being a

continuation of some ancient local heritage, as Westerners often assume, is actually the result of a relatively recent political–religious movement, which by usual Muslim standards can only be regarded as unusually conservative and puritanical.

As these examples show, Islamic political–religious movements have a long history and can take many forms. Like similar movements in Christianity, they tend to adopt a "restitutionist" outlook—that is, they see themselves as restoring the original purity of the religion. The exact nature of that restoration tends to be partly a projection of the values of the reformers. Despite their unswervingly religious tone, such movements tend to display an acute consciousness of social problems and to support political programs—some more practical than others—to remedy them. Some such movements bear significant political fruit, as in the case of Muwahhidun influence in Saudi Arabia. The sociology of religion shows that such religious movements often center on charismatic leaders who are thought to have special knowledge of transcendent order and purpose, and they often arise in times of cultural, social, political, and economic upheaval. It should not be surprising, then, if the future sees a succession of charismatic religious movements within Islam, propounding various avenues toward the revitalization of the faith and providing the vehicles for an assortment of social and political reforms. We will have more to say about Islamic revivalist movements in Chapter 7.

DIVERSITY IN ISLAMIC POLITICAL THOUGHT

The Ayatollah Ruhollah Khomeini, leader of Iran's 1979 revolution, was quoted as saying, "We Muslims are of one family even though we live under different governments and in various regions." Although the statement is an accurate reflection of the Muslim ideal of a united Umma, it should not be taken to mean that Islam represents a single, monolithic bloc with a fixed perspective on every significant issue. The more recent upsurge of Islamic revival can only be expected to revitalize discussion and controversy among Muslims on the many issues that have always occupied the dialectic of Islamic thought. It is not easy to say, once and for all, what constitutes the Islamic vision of society, law, and government. Almost from its beginning, Islam has had its factions, particularly the Sunnis and the Shia. It has manifested an inward, mystical side and an outward set of codes and institutions. Muslims have tried to mediate between the heritage of Middle Eastern civilization, with its despotism and social privilege, and the principles of social equality enunciated in the Koran.

Islamic civilization has been deeply influenced in various times and places by diverse cultural traditions, secular philosophies carried on from the Greeks, the aristocratic high culture of the royal courts, and the folk practices that preceded Islam and were independent of formal theology. Cosmopolitan and universalistic in its core outlook, Islam has had to deal with those who chose not to join the brotherhood of Islam. Each one of these conflicts has engendered not one but numerous solutions, depending on historical circumstance.

It would be misleading, despite the change and adaptability of Islam, to see it as entirely amorphous or plastic, lending itself indifferently to every possible interpretation. Throughout the Islamic dialogue run certain recurrent themes that have their roots in the fundamental principles laid out in Muhammad's ministry. One of these is the interdependence of religion and the sociopolitical order, which is built more deeply into Islam than into most world religions. It would be harder for a serious Muslim to accept the separation of church and state than for a traditional Christian, even though the possibility of such a separation was suggested by Egyptian President Sadat's admonition that there should be "no religion in politics, and no politics in religion." Muslim law involves a detailed pattern of everyday life that regulates such matters as alcohol consumption and marriage. Such personal moral regulations exist more informally in traditional Christianity, but in Islam they are part of a literate tradition that would be relatively difficult to change or to separate from political issues.

The Sharia is not easily circumvented; strictly speaking, it is open only to interpretation, not legislation. The forces that gave the Sharia and the ulema such independence in the past will probably continue to ensure Islam's role as an active challenge to the political status quo. Westerners observing the dialogue in contemporary Islamic political thought may mistakenly assume that Islam is "waking up" and examining these issues critically for the first time, but nothing could be further from the truth. Whatever the solutions toward which Muslims move, they can be expected to show the influence of previous dialogue within the tradition, a dialogue that will continue to allow for diverse possibilities.

Key Terms

caliphs *29*	Janissaries *36*	Ismailis *40*
Raddah Wars *29*	millets *36*	Muharram *41*
diwan *30*	Mameluks *36*	tariqah *42*
Umayyads *30*	Sufism *37*	pirs *42*
Kharijites *30*	madrasah *37*	Qarmatians *43*
Abbasid *32*	fiqh *39*	Muwahhidum *44*
Ottoman Empire *34*	waqf *39*	Wahhabi *44*
ghazis *34*	Mahdi *40*	

4 WESTERN IMPERIALISM, 1800–1914 C.E.

Imperialism is a familiar word that seems at first to have a clear and straightforward meaning, but on closer inspection it becomes blurred and indistinct. It may refer to any one of three relationships in which a relatively powerful country dominates the political, economic, or cultural affairs of a weaker one. In *political imperialism,* the powerful country controls the major governmental decision making of the weaker country, either directly or by proxy through pliant, cooperative officials of the weaker country. *Economic imperialism* denotes a situation in which a weaker country becomes dependent on stronger countries for income. *Cultural imperialism* refers to a situation in which a weaker country adopts the language, manners, and lifestyle of the stronger.

All three kinds of imperialism occurred in the Middle East in the nineteenth century. It is difficult to assess the full consequences of these relationships because many aspects of them have not yet been fully played out and are still active today, but most writers believe that the negative effects of imperialism outweigh the positive. The study of imperialism contains many difficulties, however, in concept, definition, and measurement, and a final assessment is uncertain. It is often difficult to say whether certain commercial transactions between weak countries and powerful ones benefit only the powerful, or whether they work to the mutual benefit of both. Although a weaker, less-developed country may chafe at being dependent on a stronger one, its dissatisfaction may spur it to make some positive reforms that it might not have made otherwise. The effects of imperialism on the weaker country may be shallow, or they may be deep. A country may survive a period of imperial stewardship and keep most of its social, cultural, and economic fabric intact. Imperial domination in such a case is only a kind of veneer. In other cases, imperial domination may deeply disrupt a country's social, economic, and political structures.

Nationalism, like imperialism, is another term that most people understand immediately, but on closer study find difficult to apply precisely. Nationalism is not just a matter of simple patriotism born of deep loyalty to an ethnic group, religion, homeland, leader, or set of institutions, although nationalist movements frequently contain a mixture of all these elements. Nationalistic movements give the appearance of solidity because they are often bound together by resentment toward the imperial power. When the imperial power is removed, the seemingly solid and cohesive nationalist movement often disintegrates into factional conflicts. We must study such root factions and forces if we are to gain a deeper understanding of a particular country or region. In this chapter, we shall examine how European imperialist powers penetrated the Middle East in the nineteenth century, just before the various nation-states in the region emerged. The Europeans penetrated the Middle East in a series of powerful, deep-reaching thrusts, and we shall examine how certain areas responded to such battering.

SETTING THE STAGE

For thousands of years, most areas of the world were fairly equal in technology and economic well-being. Major inventions and technological innovations occurred at irregular intervals and in widely separated regions. An innovation that arose at a certain time or in a certain region had little influence on a technology that was being developed in another place or time. It took centuries, even millennia, for ideas and innovations to become uniformly diffused over the large areas of Asia, Europe, and the Middle East. Regions that were late to adopt a particular innovation or bit of technology from abroad had a comfortably long time in which to achieve parity with other regions before the next innovation came along.

During the period from about 1400 to 1700 C.E., a set of institutions and cultural forms was developed in Europe that promoted and regularized the flow of innovations. The most important advances occurred in organization and administration, weaponry, and communications. The process by which these innovations were accepted and by which a continuing need for them was institutionalized is still not well understood. The result, however, is clear: Technical innovation became a continuous, irreversible, accelerating process. The time when regions could regain parity because of

slow diffusion was at an end; Western Europe achieved technological dominance over the rest of the world, and other regions had no time to catch up.

It is difficult to say just when the West began to penetrate the Middle East, or when it finally achieved political and economic dominance. One important date is 1498. In this year, the Portuguese navigator Vasco da Gama sailed around the southern tip of Africa to India, opening an important new trade route to the East. Although Europeans had gradually taken control of the Mediterranean Sea trade over the preceding 200 years, the opening of this new ocean route to India now assured them of total control over most of the world's maritime trade. The Middle Eastern overland trade routes began to decline. European control of the Mediterranean already had begun to shift the middleman functions from the Arabs to the Venetians and Genoese. Western technical and manufacturing innovations were resulting in the production of better goods. Consequently, Middle Eastern handicraft production, especially along the southern and eastern Mediterranean coasts, also began to decline.

These developments tore wide rents in the economic and social fabric of the region. Middle Eastern handicraft production was loosely organized in guilds—groups of craftsmen whose taxes provided a source of revenue for the various local governments, and whose presence contributed vitally to the social life of the area. Many of the ulema were guild members or were supported by guilds. A decline in the well-being and consequent leadership role of the religious establishment directly followed the decline in handicraft industries.

European dominance in commerce and production was accompanied by advances in military technology. European armies became powerful instruments of national will. After centuries of successful expansion, the Ottoman Empire began to lose territory to the Europeans.

Some writers claim that the Europeans' technological superiority also gave a sense of moral superiority. Although this may or may not be true, Europeans, in their quest for control of the Middle East, often clothed their political and economic motives in the vestments of religion. A belief in the inherent decadence and wickedness of Islam provided generations of Europeans with a strong rationale for imperialistic ventures in the Middle East, and this belief had a strong impact on the various cultures with which they associated.

THE OTTOMANS

By 1800, the decline of the Ottoman Empire was well under way; it would accelerate over the next 100 years. Western technology and military power were having an increasingly strong impact. The Ottoman elite, long used to thinking that Western knowledge was not worth having, realized that it no longer could maintain its sense of superiority. An early sign of this change of attitude is the so-called Tulip Period (1718–1730), during which the Ottoman elite succumbed to a fad for everything Western. It built French-style pleasure palaces, wore Western clothes, sat on Western chairs, and cultivated Western gardens. It developed a mania for tulips, sending the price of tulip bulbs to absurd heights, with high offices being sold for particularly exotic strains.

Aside from these extravagances, the period also saw the tentative beginnings of a new intellectual atmosphere; previously rejected reforms were now being seriously entertained. Most of these reforms were shallow and aimed only at making institutions in the existing framework—especially the military—more effective. Selim III (reigned 1789–1807) attempted more fundamental reforms; although most of these failed or were only partially successful, they did lay the groundwork for later reforms in the nineteenth century. When antireformist resistance was overcome, particularly that from the traditional military corps, the Janissaries, reform activity quickened. The Janissaries

represented the most important group in the nonmodernized army. They viewed the building of a modern army and bureaucracy as a threat to their power, and they were at the forefront of the coalition resisting reform. Sultan Mahmud II (reigned 1808–1839) cleverly built a new coalition loyal to him and in 1826 had the Janissaries killed when they rebelled. This event is called the "Auspicious Incident" because it allowed the sultan to initiate the period of significant reform known as the **Tanzimat** period.

Tanzimat Period (1839–1876)

The Tanzimat reforms were achieved with no clearly defined master plan other than a mostly unstated desire for greater government centralization. During previous centuries, the empire had expanded successfully by means of policies that favored extreme decentralization. By giving local governments large measures of autonomy, the millet system had kept the provinces reasonably satisfied. However, the military in remote areas had begun to look more to its own interests than to those of the empire. Within limits, local authorities had the power to tax the population as they saw fit, so long as they remitted a negotiated amount to the central government; the sultan consequently had little control over the size of the royal treasury. As the empire declined, and the spoils of conquest stopped flowing into the capital, the Ottoman sultans tried to make up the difference by increasing taxes. The provincial authorities, having become used to self-rule for several generations, felt no great loyalty to the sultans, however, and firmly resisted them. The sultans saw that it was crucial to reorganize the empire around a strong central authority.

The Tanzimat reforms were many and far-reaching. Ministries were established to impose uniform regulations all over the empire. The military was completely reorganized along Western lines, and its incentive system was restructured to create greater commitment to the empire. The tax collection system was streamlined to allow revenues to flow directly to the royal treasury; local government powers were reduced.

Although many Tanzimat reforms failed, and many others did not work out exactly as intended, they marked a turning point in Ottoman history. Although the empire continued to lose territory in the nineteenth century, the reforms were a sign of considerable lingering vitality. The Ottoman Empire was far from being the "sick man of Europe," as was said at the time and as was commonly believed well into the twentieth century. The empire was beset by internal and external difficulties of massive proportions, but there was also substantial positive change. The entrenched powers were understandably opposed to the reforms, but in time they were either accommodated or suppressed. Modern organizational forms and military technology spread to other areas, especially communications and education.

Although the impact of the reforms on cultural life was not a central concern during the early years of the Tanzimat period, they had a pervasive and enduring result. Many reforms required that administrators undergo specialized training and education. A new generation of technocrats arose who began to respect the West, for it was there that the needed knowledge was stored. Along with technical knowledge, this new class also absorbed the political philosophies of nationalism and democracy. The lack of qualified personnel within the empire and the increasing encroachments of European governments and commercial interests also brought an influx of powerful and active Europeans to the center of the empire.

The Tanzimat reforms occurred in an atmosphere of international intrigue. England, France, and Russia (and later Germany) had vital interests in the Middle East, which they tried to protect and enlarge. For most of the nineteenth century, the Ottoman Empire had to defend itself against European powers that were pushing and shoving among themselves for competitive advantage. Europe generally did not want to see the Ottoman Empire collapse; the scramble for spoils afterward would have ended in a bloodbath and much destruction. First one European power and then another supported the empire, but while the Europeans wished the Ottoman Empire a long life, they did not want to see it strong. They chipped away at its edges and blunted many of the effects of the Tanzimat reforms. There is no question that nineteenth-century Ottoman administration was corrupt and inept, but it is questionable whether a smoothly functioning modern organization would have done much better. The European powers had the empire pinioned. The Tanzimat reforms were a significant attempt to adapt to technological realities, and they represented a skillful attempt to resolve the empire's internal conflicts while playing off European interests. In the end, however, the Ottomans could not escape the debilitating entanglements imposed on them by Westerners.

As the European powers increased their leverage, responsible parties in the empire grew increasingly dissatisfied with the course taken by the sultan and his inner circle. Various changes of policy were demanded, the most important being representation in the legislative bodies, the adoption of a constitution, and the formation of an Ottoman ideology. Some parties favored a wholesale adoption of European ways; some sought a return to a past era of Islamic purity; some advocated a host of intermediate positions. The restive attitude of the new technocrats and the role of the Western powers presented the sultan with a problem common to most reforming autocrats—how to control the demands of a new class of people who possess the technical knowledge on which the regime depends. Because the military and commercial presence of the competing Europeans prevented any return to past ways, and because the Europeans could not be expelled, a long series of struggles and partial accommodations took place; this process resulted in the granting of a constitution in 1876 by the shrewd Sultan Abdulhamit (reigned 1876–1909). The constitution was suspended shortly thereafter, but was reinstated with significant changes in 1908.

The Young Turk revolution (1908), which prompted the sultan to reconvene the legislative body and activate the constitution, had its ideological roots in various sources of discontent. A significant pan-Islamic and then pan-Ottoman movement, supported by the sultan, arose during the last third of the nineteenth century. The pan-Islamic movement championed the rights of all Muslims. The pan-Ottoman movement was broader; it called for more or less equal rights for all (including non-Muslim) subjects of the empire. These movements contained many contradictions, however. Increasingly, waves of ethnic and geographic nationalism developed in reaction to Ottoman hegemony at the same time the sultan was reaffirming the equality of all his subjects. This situation led to discontent among the military forces, who were asked to support the call for equality, while being attacked by its supposed beneficiaries. The ideological reaction was pan-Turkism, the notion that the ethnic identity of the empire deserved first consideration. Turkish greatness and the virtues of the Turkish people were celebrated in numerous literary works.

The combination of the calls for a Turkish nation, military discontent, millet terrorism, and European pressures put Sultan Abdulhamit in an increasingly defensive position. He responded with many repressive measures. He paralyzed the bureaucracy by insisting on personally approving the smallest changes in policy. A financial crisis sparked a widespread revolt. The revolution of 1908 forced the sultan to agree to demands for a constitution and representation.

The period after World War I was devastating for the empire. The positive effects of some of the modernizing reforms had been undone by a series of crippling conflicts. The Ottoman Empire had aligned itself with the Central Powers during the war; when they were defeated, the empire was dismembered. The Allied forces divided the empire among themselves and imposed a particularly harsh rule on Turkey. The Turkish nationalist forces that had been successful in 1908 rose to defend the homeland. Led by Kemal Ataturk, they repelled the Europeans and established an independent Turkish state. A remarkable series of reforms followed that ultimately would transform and secularize Turkey.

EGYPT

Long-standing corruption and generally ineffective rule had led to centuries of decay in Egypt, but the power of this weak Ottoman province was to change markedly during the nineteenth century. For the Ottomans of the nineteenth century, Egypt was something to be feared and imitated.

In the last decade of the eighteenth century, the French were looking at Egypt with increased interest, largely because of their struggle with the British. Egypt could be France's granary, control Middle Eastern military and commercial traffic, and provide a base from which to threaten the British in India. With these aims in view, Napoleon invaded Egypt in July 1798 and with remarkable ease destroyed the Mameluk forces that ruled Egypt under loose Ottoman control. Napoleon presented himself to the Egyptians, and especially the ulema, as a liberator from foreign rule. His call for cooperation went unheeded, however, and he was forced to quell a rebellion in Cairo in October 1798.

As all rulers of Egypt knew, control of the Levant was vital to Egyptian security. Consequently, Napoleon invaded Palestine and Syria in 1799. He met with failure, however, as Ottoman forces halted the French advance, and the British navy attacked the French fleet.

Because the security of Egypt could not be maintained, Napoleon quickly reassessed his position and quit Egypt in August 1799. The last French forces withdrew by 1801.

The brief French presence in Egypt gave advance warning that European powers would be drawn into Middle Eastern affairs on a much larger scale than previously. It also served as a lesson to the Ottoman rulers and to the future Egyptian ruler, **Muhammad Ali (Mehemet Ali)**, that European organizational and technical skills were superior to those of the Ottoman Empire—so superior that the rulers would have to adapt quickly if the empire were to remain secure.

Muhammad Ali had fought against the French in Syria. Born in Albania, and serving in the Ottoman army, this "selfish, illiterate genius" slowly eliminated his Ottoman rivals in Egypt and assumed control in 1805. He ruled Egypt until his death in 1849. The lessons of French military superiority were not lost on him. He also realized that the key to building a similar kind of force was a fundamental reordering of the Egyptian economy; the material requirements of a strong military depended on an economy that could supply the needed goods. Although he was officially confirmed as governor in 1806, it was only after beating back a halfhearted British invasion in 1807 and massacring the last serious Mameluk rivals to power in 1811 that Muhammad Ali achieved a secure hold in Egypt. He then began in earnest to modernize Egypt's military. Egyptians were sent to France to learn modern military technology, and foreign advisers, particularly French, were brought to Egypt. Technical knowledge was diffused throughout Egypt by means of training institutes and translations of technical treatises.

Because a strong military was necessary for retaining and expanding power, much of the early effort was directed toward meeting the military's basic needs. An army of more than 100,000 men, if it was to be modern, needed munitions, communication systems,

clothing, and food. Because there was no established industrialist class in Egypt, the government financed and managed its own factories. European industrialists and financiers were invited to provide capital and expertise to supplement the effort. In addition, Egyptian soldiers—drafted into military service in 1823 for the first time in centuries—were required to learn technical skills. To guard against foreign domination of key positions, European factory managers and technical personnel were needed to train their Egyptian counterparts.

To mount this ambitious drive, the government needed a strong financial base. The 1811 massacre of the Mameluks gave the state control of their vast landholdings. The government subsumed all land rights, and the system of tax administration was altered. The traditional system had allowed local leaders to pay a sum to the government in return for the right to tax the **fellahin**; under the revised system, the government collected the taxes directly. The government also assumed control of most agricultural marketing, especially of export crops. These policies increased revenues, lessened the power of reactionary local leaders, and partially circumvented an Anglo-Ottoman treaty that limited import and export taxes to 3 percent.

Long-staple cotton was introduced to the Nile Delta in 1821. Although this superior strain of cotton stimulated local textile production, it also tied Egyptian economic fortunes to the vagaries of the international market. Cotton soon became Egypt's leading export, accounting for 75 percent of all receipts by 1860. The Delta, capable of producing a food surplus from a variety of crops, was transformed into a cotton monoculture designed to sustain the textile mills of England. Egyptian dependence on cotton earnings forced more and more land to be turned over to its production, and the country that Napoleon saw as a granary for France was now forced to import food.

Muhammad Ali grew increasingly independent of the Ottoman authorities. The empire saw little harm in this during the early years of his rule. Before Muhammad Ali, Egypt had been a corrupt and militarily weak entity and of little value beyond the taxes paid by Cairo. Under Muhammad Ali, Egypt seemed to be undergoing constructive change and developing a credible military force. Muhammad Ali's armies waged various campaigns under the Ottoman banner, the most important being the successful campaigns against the Wahhabis, the conservative expansionist tribal movement in Arabia.

Muhammad Ali's independent actions finally led to a crisis in 1832. Under the pretext of insufficient payment for Egyptian aid in the empire's unsuccessful attempts to stem the Greek rebellion, he invaded and occupied Syria—making Egypt an all but independent political and military force. In 1838, he declared his intention to become king of Egypt. The antiquated military force that the empire sent to displace the Egyptians from Syria was no match for Muhammad Ali's modern troops. After defeating the empire's forces, he toyed with the idea of invading Anatolia proper, but European interests, especially the British, defused the crisis. The British did not want to see Egypt, an ally of France, grow powerful, and they did not relish the possibility of Russia dominating a weakened Ottoman Empire. When the Ottoman sultan Mehmut II died in the midst of the crisis, it seemed that Russian influence in the imperial court would be expanded significantly. The admiral of the Ottoman navy sailed the fleet to Alexandria to be put in the service of Muhammad Ali rather than run the risk of being controlled by the infidel Russians. As it was, the empire weathered this "Russian threat."

British and Ottoman pressures effectively halted the reformist and expansionist actions of the Egyptian ruler. Muhammad Ali retained his role as governor of Egypt and was given the right to hereditary rule, but he lost much in the bargain. He relinquished the Ottoman fleet, pulled out of Syria, reduced the size of the army from 130,000 men to 18,000, and

accepted the 1838 Anglo-Ottoman Commercial Code. The 1838 Commercial Code enlarged the preferential treatment afforded to foreigners doing business in the Ottoman Empire and made state monopolies illegal. The aggressive economic policies of the preceding 30 years had changed the face of Egypt. Some ventures had been successful, but many operations were wasteful and inefficient. Although Egypt may not have been able to sustain these at such a pace, it was unquestionably shaking off its moribund status of the previous centuries. Acceptance of the 1838 Commercial Code sealed the fate of Egypt's economic experiment and ensured foreign control of most Egyptian commerce and industry.

The story behind the building of the Suez Canal under the direction of the remarkable Ferdinand de Lesseps illustrates European dominance in a spectacular fashion. The terms of the contract to build the canal (1854), the methods used to construct the canal, and subsequent European actions serve as a model of imperial deceit and connivance at its worst. Essentially, Egypt supplied all the labor, about 20,000 men, and gave the shrewd de Lesseps free access to the Egyptian treasury through various contract provisions, bribes, and bullying. In return, Egypt retained seven-sixteenths ownership, but surrendered most of its rights to the profits until the canal was completed (1869). Other smaller ventures proposed by Europeans and accepted by the weakened heirs to Muhammad Ali's governorship were similarly one-sided. The granting of concessions to Europeans ended in a financial crisis that opened the way to total European control.

The financial chaos that engulfed Egypt in the 1870s was not due exclusively to European chicanery. The Civil War in the United States brought a tripling of cotton prices and deprived English mills of cotton grown in the southern states. In an attempt to Europeanize Egypt, the Egyptian governor of this period, Ismail Pasha, constructed a large system of canals, railroads, bridges, harbors, and telegraph facilities and brought more than one million acres of land back into cultivation. He did much of this on the assumption that cotton prices would remain high. Many of the contracts with foreign construction firms were made on highly unfavorable terms, the Egyptian administration being very corrupt. The spending extravaganza, coupled with the end of the U.S. Civil War and the consequent dive of cotton prices, put Egypt in an impossible position. The external debt of Egypt had reached more than £70 million by the time the Suez Canal opened, as opposed to about £3 million six years earlier. An increasing proportion of the government's revenue went directly to foreign debt repayment—about 60 percent in 1875. In that year, the British government bought the Egyptian shares in the Suez Canal for £4 million, in what amounted to a liquidation sale. Egypt was now bankrupt and faced with foreign ownership of the Suez Canal. By 1876 British and French officials were overseeing Egyptian and Ottoman finances to protect European interests.

To improve Egypt's finances, the puppet governor Tawfiq imposed an austere fiscal policy that led to an army rebellion in 1882. This gave the British ample excuse for drastic action to protect their investments. At the "official request" of Tawfiq, British forces invaded Egypt, crushed the rebellion, and settled in for the next 75 years. The official British position in Egypt was awkward, however. Although they had been invited to enter at the governor's request, they nevertheless owned the Suez Canal, which was situated in a province of the Ottoman Empire. This ambiguous situation was to persist until Egypt was declared a British protectorate in 1914.

Britain had an excellent reason for wanting to control Egypt: The Suez Canal shortened the route between England and India by 4,000 miles. The occupation of Egypt burdened the English, however, with the usual geopolitical anxieties. The security of the Red Sea and the Arabian Peninsula became vital. The Levant and the Sudan also had to be dealt

with if security was to be assured. The latter two problems were solved by convincing the Ottoman sultan to cede the Sinai Peninsula to Egypt (1906) and by establishing a joint Anglo-Egyptian force to reimpose rule over the Sudan (1898). Britain entered the twentieth century with a firm foothold in Egypt.

THE LEVANT

Muhammad Ali's control of the Levant during the 1830s forms a watershed in the history of the area. The reforms introduced and the subsequent European penetration have been aptly called "the opening of South Lebanon." In the decades before the Egyptian incursion, the population of the interior, if not the coast, looked eastward when they were looking outside their immediate area at all. European trade had been on the decline, and Europeans were treated with a xenophobic hostility when they did manage to gain access to the area. The area had a relatively sparse population (about 1,300,000), rapacious Ottoman governors, and a highly insecure hinterland. However, the urban population, about half of the total, had learned to live with the situation by developing a relatively closed system of production and distribution.

The modernized, Western-oriented Egyptian army radically altered this situation. Security of travel was greatly enhanced; life in the cities became more secure; and, most important, a wave of European commercial interests quickly entered and soon dominated economic life. By the time of the Egyptian withdrawal, Syria was looking to the West for trade; the indigenous craftsmen had to shoulder the brunt of the change because their nonstandardized, low-quality, high-priced goods could no longer find a local market. The process continued after the Egyptian departure.

Western ascendancy was given a further boost in 1858 when the **Maronites** created a crisis in Lebanon by declaring it a republic. Under Ottoman rule, the **Druze**, Sunni Muslims, and Maronite Christians had achieved an uneasy balance. The Tanzimat declaration of equality for all non-Muslims in the empire had already aroused Muslim antipathy. In 1860, the situation worsened and erupted into large-scale religious massacres. Because they had long-standing interests there, the French landed troops under the pretext of giving aid to the Ottomans, and they calmed the situation. An autonomous Lebanon, limited to the mountains and not including the coastal areas, was established. A Catholic Christian governor was to administer the area and maintain a local militia. The Ottomans maintained only titular control and effectively abandoned the area. The French and a host of Christian missionaries gained a base of operations in the Middle East.

THE ARABIAN PENINSULA

In the history of the world's major religions, circumstances occasionally allow strong revivalist movements to form and flourish. The Middle East in the nineteenth century provided the right circumstances for Islam. The **Sanussi** movement in Libya, the rise of the Mahdists in the Sudan, and the Wahhabi movement in Arabia were three of the most important.

Muhammad ibn Abd-al-Wahhab (1691–1787) spread his message during the latter part of the eighteenth century. He was convinced that the strict, austere Hanbali law was superior to the other three sanctioned Sunni schools of law, and that Islam had deviated from its true path. He criticized especially the Sufi (and pre-Islamic) custom of venerating saints by worshiping at their tombs, which he thought to be idolatry. Abd-al-Wahhab spread his word throughout the **Najd** region of Arabia; in time, he converted a powerful tribal ruler, Ibn Saud, who spread the doctrine and his rule over great stretches of Arabia.

The Ottomans had long controlled the coastal Hijaz and the holy cities of Mecca and Medina. From there, Ottoman rule arched out over what is now Jordan and extended south to

the al-Hassa area of Arabia on the Persian Gulf. It is likely that the Wahhabis would have been left undisturbed in the great desert areas if their religious beliefs had allowed them to adhere to geopolitical boundaries, but this was not to be the case. They declared that people who practiced the idolatry of saint worship were infidels and, as such, deserved death. By 1803, the grandson of Ibn Saud controlled the Hijaz, including Mecca and Medina. The tombs were destroyed, and many worshipers were put to death. The Ottoman authorities could not tolerate a renegade force holding two of the most holy cities of Islam, but lacked the means to expel them. It was not until Muhammad Ali consolidated his strength in Egypt that an attempt was made to beat back the Wahhabi movement. The first Egyptian forces were dispatched to Arabia in 1811; however, the armies of Ibn Saud were not pushed deep into the interior until the Egyptian campaign of 1818–1820.

For the remainder of the nineteenth century, the interior of Arabia passed back and forth between the authority of the Ottoman-backed Rashids and the forces of the Saud family. Finally, in 1902, a small band of Saudi forces raided Riyadh, the seat of Rashid power, and began to assume control of most of what is now Saudi Arabia—with the exception of the Hijaz, which remained under Ottoman control. Saudi power was more or less consolidated by the beginning of World War I.

Nineteenth-century European interests in the Arabian Peninsula centered on trade and communications, so they concentrated on securing the safety of the coastal areas. The British were seeking greater control in the area to defend India from possible encroachments by the French, Russians, and Germans.

Napoleon's invasion of Egypt in 1798 brought a swift reaction. In addition to Nelson's destruction of the French fleet off Alexandria, the British took Perim Island (1799), which lies between Africa and Arabia in the narrow southern inlet to the Red Sea. Because they lacked supplies, especially water, they were quickly forced to abandon the island and withdraw to Aden, a port area long known and used by the British in their East India dealings. The British reluctantly made Aden a permanent outpost as event after event dictated their presence; they would retain control of Aden until 1967.

What Westerners call the Persian Gulf (and the Arabs call the Arabian Gulf) came under British control with the taking of the Strait of Hormuz in 1622. (A glance at a map reveals that whoever controls the Strait of Hormuz controls all traffic in and out of the Gulf. Because a substantial percentage of the world's petroleum passes through the strait, the area is vital.) To the British in the seventeenth century, the security of the Strait of Hormuz and the ability to ensure safe passage through the Gulf were important because they needed a quick line of communications to India. The route around the Cape of Good Hope was long and risky, and the Red Sea was under uncertain Ottoman control until the British intervened in Egypt in 1882. The next best route from India to England was to sail to what is now Kuwait and travel overland through Basra and Baghdad.

By the 1830s, the British had largely suppressed piracy in the Persian Gulf through military forays and treaties with the coastal powers. Later in the century, they thwarted other European trade schemes in the Middle East by entering into treaties with local rulers that prohibited trade or other dealings with any other foreigners without British approval. The most notable of these agreements was the one made with Kuwait in 1899.

In the nineteenth century, British Gulf policy changed from simply establishing a line of communications within the empire to defending it. British control of Egypt and the Suez Canal relieved them from having to penetrate the interior of Iraq to protect their communication lines. German influence in the Ottoman Empire gave them reason to go on the defensive. The Germans gained a concession in 1899 to build a railroad through Ottoman territories in the Middle East. By the beginning of World War I, the Constantinople–Baghdad portion of the line was complete. By 1900, however, the ruler of Kuwait, in accordance with the recent British treaty, had refused the Germans permission to build a terminal on the Gulf.

Events finally forced the British to push into Iraq. In 1907, petroleum was discovered in the Abadan area of Iran, and there was some evidence that nearby Iraq would hold equally important fields. Another chapter of Middle Eastern history was beginning to unfold.

IRAN

Although all of the nation-states in this area are special cases in many ways, Iran stands apart. Because of its political, social, and cultural differences, and because of its geographical position, Iran's relationship with the Middle East proper has waxed and waned over the centuries.

During the eighteenth and nineteenth centuries, Persia was subject to less European influence than Egypt or the Levant. European commercial interest had become well established during the preceding centuries, but the full-scale economic, military, and philosophical thrusts of the West had not yet penetrated to the heart of the Persian system. Yet Persia's nationalist sentiments—generally reactions against foreign domination expressed in mass movements—in some ways presaged those in other parts of the Middle East. This seeming contradiction is not yet fully understood, but it is clear that important aspects of Persian society included such elements as official social classes, power relationships designed to increase insecurity and mistrust, and the central place of the Shia clergy.

From Sassanian times on, the social structure of Iran consisted, with some exceptions, of four major groups: (1) the royal family, (2) the political and military bureaucracy, (3) the religious establishment, and (4) the masses. Although some outstanding individual cases helped promote a popular belief in easy social mobility, shifts from one class to another were relatively infrequent. Widespread belief in the possibility of upward mobility enabled the ruling class to promise the less fortunate a chance to enjoy a better life. In such a system, however, downward mobility is just as possible; favored positions were jealously protected. Individuals usually procured desirable posts by some form of money payment, or bribe, indicating that accumulated wealth was generally a prerequisite for entering and retaining a high position. Because the accumulation of wealth depended on having a good position, the system not only reduced mobility but it also promoted class tensions. The bureaucracy also suffered because considerations of individual merit were often set aside. The shah presided over a system that was full of class rivalry and predatory competition. The ruling class could move social inferiors about with relative ease and frequency, as if they were chess pieces, limiting any individual's or group's power and influence.

Iran had long had a Shia majority. Traditionally, the Shia had opposed any secular authority because of their belief that the betrayal of Ali had given rise to a series of illegitimate rulers. While waiting for the return of the Hidden Imam, who would set the world on the correct path again, the Shia believed that the clergy had an obligation to examine all secular actions and make them consistent with Islamic thought. Because interpreting the correct path of state and religious affairs depended on specialized scholarly wisdom and knowledge, a loose hierarchy of clerical authority developed in Iran that was lacking in Sunni Islam. Because most secular authorities are unwilling to submit to higher authorities, an understandable tension developed between government officials and clergy. Because the clergy had the ear of the masses, any secular ruler had to be careful and restrained in dealings with the clergy.

Bazaar merchants traditionally have been important sources of discontent and have led opposition movements in the Middle East, but in Persia they were subject to the same insecurities that shackled the bureaucrats and the military. The clergy, through their spokesmen, the **mujtahids** (learned religious leaders with successful ministries), were the only group not under the shah's direct control.

Qajar Dynasty

The Qajar dynasty (1779–1925) came to power about 50 years after the fall of the Safavid Empire. At first, the Qajars were extremely brutal in their attempts to consolidate power. After they had established a reasonable degree of control over the various tribes, they then had to face the emerging threat from the West. By the 1850s, two major Western players—England and Russia—had forced Persia into the arena of Western politics. The British feared that a Russian advance southward ultimately would threaten India. The Russians had long desired access to the Indian Ocean.

The Qajars seem to have seen the need for radical bureaucratic and military reforms, but their actions were no more than superficial palliatives. Shah Nasiruddin's rise to power (1848–1896) roughly marks the beginning of the reform movement; the Persian elite began to realize that the Western powers could not be banished but would have to be accommodated. The last half of the nineteenth century saw numerous intrigues between the British, the Russians, and occasionally the French, as they entered into agreements over their respective roles in Persia, broke the agreements, and then hammered out new ones. Meanwhile, the shah, to maintain Persian independence, was attempting to play off one power against the other and create a stalemate between them.

To accomplish this political stalemate, and to build up the treasury, the Qajar rulers during this period began to grant concessions to

Europeans. In essence, a European adventurer-entrepreneur would pay a sum of money to obtain a monopoly in some sphere of economic activity. The concessionaire would return home to sell shares in the new company to speculators and turn a profit. The rulers granting these concessions welcomed European money because it absolved them from having to impose heavier taxes on an already restive population. They also hoped that they could check European power by granting concessions to individuals of different nationalities, that the Europeans would see the need for political security and stability in Persia to protect profits, and that they would introduce some industrial development to boot. To be successful, such a policy called for a finely tuned balance of forces. The concessionaires often played fast and loose with contracts, however, and the ruling elite were increasingly concerned with shoring up royal revenues. The 1872 concession drawn up by the grand vizier for Baron Julius de Reuter, a British citizen, is a spectacular example of the sorry state of Qajar affairs. The concession gave de Reuter a monopoly over railways, mines (excepting precious metals and stones), irrigation construction, all future factories, telegraph lines, road construction, and, for 25 years, the proceeds of customs collections. In return, the royal purse was to be increased by a small flat payment and a share of the profits of the various ventures. In short, the country had been sold, and sold very cheaply. The reaction against this outrageous concession was swift in coming. Protests erupted from the Russians, members of the royal court, the clergy, and nationalistic groups. The combination of international pressure and internal discontent forced the shah to cancel the concession on a technicality.

Concession granting did not come to an end, however. The British continued to make inroads, the most significant being the right to form a national bank, the right to navigate the Karun River, and the granting of a tobacco monopoly. The tobacco concession (1890), following on the heels of the bank and river navigation concessions, was to be complete—from the growing of the tobacco to export sales. Russian reaction was strongly negative. Internal reactions led by a domestic coalition (which was to surface periodically throughout the twentieth century) signaled the beginnings of the drive for a constitution.

Under the inspiration of the remarkable Jemal al-Din **al-Afghani**, who was active all over the Middle East as a proponent of pan-Islamic policies, a coalition was formed of merchants, clergy, and intellectuals, many of the latter having a Western orientation. The intellectuals and mujtahids were able to set aside their fundamental disagreements in the face of their common hatred of what they viewed as the selling of Persia. The Russian government gave material and moral support to the coalition.

As the dissatisfaction grew into a country-wide protest—ironically coordinated through the use of the British telegraph system—and the country tottered on the brink of revolution, it became clear that the reaction against the tobacco concession was part of a larger hatred toward all foreign concessions and the policies of the Qajar regime. Facing the prospect of revolution, the shah canceled the tobacco concession in 1892.

The "tobacco riots" and the cancellation of the tobacco concession had far-reaching implications for the subsequent history of Persia. For the first time, a nationwide protest against the policies of the regime, spearheaded by the relatively independent and powerful clergy, had immobilized the government. After many years of quietude, the clergy took an active role. The internal coalition formed the backbone of the movements that later resulted in the granting of the 1906 constitution and the overthrow of the Pahlevi dynasty in 1978–1979. More immediate effects included a decade of Russian ascendancy in Persia, the slowing of concession granting to foreigners, and the beginnings of the same kind of disastrous debt policy that had brought so many woes to Egypt and the Ottoman Empire in previous decades.

The shah was forced to pay a sizable compensation to the tobacco concessioners. Because he lacked requisite funds, the British provided a loan. The Russians, fearing a reassertion of British influence, also provided loans, tightening the financial noose. In this respect, Persia was closing the gap between it and other Middle Eastern countries by the beginning of the twentieth century. Persia received little benefit from foreign intrusion, however, because of the conditions of the intervention; the corrupt, obsolete government structure; and the relationship between the various social classes.

Further British inroads were made with the award of a petroleum concession in 1901, the discovery of petroleum in 1908, and the British government's purchase of most of the shares in the resulting oil company a few months before the beginning of World War I. The weakness of the Qajar dynasty and growing fears of expansionist Germany also led the British and Russians to formalize an often-breached agreement that divided Persia into spheres of influence: The Russians were to have the north and the British the south, with a neutral strip in between.

The Qajar dynasty limped along until the conclusion of World War I, but its power rested on a weak base. Riots in 1905–1906, led again by the mujtahids with the support of modernizers and merchants, forced the granting of a constitution (1906) and the formation of a consultative assembly, the Majlis. Although the assembly initiated a series of reforms, intrigues by the rulers and international powers, internal dissension in the Majlis, and economic recession militated against a full-blown democratic and modernizing movement.

During World War I, the Allies viewed Persia as a vital conduit through which to supply material to Russia. As a result of the success of the Russian Revolution of 1917, the Bolsheviks renounced the tsarist claims in the 1907 Anglo-Russian agreement. The British moved northward and assumed almost total control of Persia. Shortly after this, they withdrew from the Caspian Sea area, and the Soviets invaded the port of Enzeli. The Iranian Soviet Socialist Republic of Gilan was formed in 1920, but the Soviet Union withdrew its support for it less than a year later, and the republic failed. In this chaotic swirl of events, Reza Shah came to power.

Reza Shah led the Russian-trained Cossack Brigade, one of the few effective military units in the Persian army, if not the only one. He assumed power on February 26, 1921, named himself commander in chief of the military, and appointed an intellectual ally as prime minister. As Reza Shah gathered more power, he dismissed the prime minister in 1923. In 1925, he ascended to the throne and took the ancient and kingly Persian name of Pahlevi.

Reza Shah was an extraordinary modernizer and autocrat who faced the formidable tasks of establishing internal order, lessening foreign domination, and establishing Iran as a modern nation. The Majlis continued to function under his rule. His taking of the Peacock Throne was confirmed by a vote of the Majlis and by an amendment to the constitution, but the Majlis failed to fulfill the hopes of those opposed to autocratic rule, in that it merely rubber-stamped Reza Shah's policies rather than evolving into an independent legislative body. The shah promoted divisiveness among those on the periphery of power, which created insecurity, fragmented the opposition, and convulsed the machinery of government. Acting along the lines of Muhammad Ali in Egypt a century earlier and his contemporary Ataturk, the shah developed a series of reforms to lessen the power of the clergy and increase his own. He also laid the foundation for a modern economy by constructing an improved communications network and instituting educational reforms.

Because of the shah's flirtation with Germany during the 1930s, culminating in his refusal to join the Allied cause at the outset of World War II, the 1907 Anglo-Russian accord was renewed, the British protecting their petroleum interests in the south and the Russians controlling the north. To save the throne, Reza Shah abdicated to his son, Mohammed Reza Pahlevi, in 1941.

CONCLUSION

Nineteenth-century Middle Eastern history was dominated by the tidal wave of European power that swamped and distorted every society it touched. Although the procedures and timing of European penetration differed in the specific countries, there were some common features.

First, most Western inroads were made with reference to European geopolitical rivalries. It was not until the twentieth century that the Europeans (and the United States) seriously considered the economic prizes to be gained from the Middle East. During the nineteenth century, the various European powers generally tried to avoid the financial and political headaches associated with direct rule; rather, they sought to establish client relationships.

Second, the general process of Western dominance had a certain inevitability because of the technical superiority and advanced organizational structure of the West. The technical revolution had been largely institutionalized in the West after centuries of cultural and scientific preparation. Military might was the most obvious manifestation of this superiority, but it was perhaps no more important than the organizational and cultural modifications that supported the technical revolution.

Third, European involvement in Middle Eastern affairs dramatically disrupted the area's society and culture. Some countries attempted to adopt Western ways; others rejected all Western influence. All countries generally recognized the technical superiority of the West and tried to avoid Western domination; however, they all failed. The peoples of the Middle East fought a rear-guard action; their policies and pronouncements tended to be protective, not affirmative. Much of the history of the Middle East in the twentieth century can be viewed as an unraveling of the consequences of nineteenth-century European domination.

Key Terms

Tanzimat *48*
Muhammad Ali
  (Mehemet Ali) *51*
fellahin *51*

Maronites *53*
Druze *53*
Sanussi *54*
Najd *54*

mujtahids *56*
al-Afghani *57*

5 | THE RISE OF THE STATE SYSTEM, 1914–1950

The period after World War I saw the decline of Western political hegemony in the Middle East. However, many events during the preceding decades paved the way. The defeat of the Russians by the Japanese in 1905 was greeted with much satisfaction in the non-European world. A Western power had been humiliated, at last, by an Asian power. The news of the Russian defeat, together with other events, provided a needed catalyst for action in the unsettled Middle East. In Persia, the revolts of 1905–1906 severely weakened the Qajar dynasty and resulted in the establishment of a consultative assembly. In Turkey, the Young Turk revolution of 1908 sealed the fate of the Ottoman rulers. In Egypt, an incident in 1906 sparked a nationalist movement.

Each change in Ottoman policy over the first decade of the twentieth century—from pan-Islam to pan-Turkism—had a strong impact on Arab lands. After 1908, the ethnic nationalism of the Turkish leaders became openly imperialistic. Under the *millet system,* an individual's nationality was not defined by geographic boundaries. An Ottoman Muslim could identify equally with all Muslims of the empire—members of his own millet. Ottoman Muslims did not consider themselves to be Turks, Iraqis, or Syrians; these words existed as historical terms or identified administrative districts. As pan-Ottomanism and then pan-Turkism weakened identification with the empire, and as Western influences filtered into the Middle East, the Arabs of the provinces began to search for a new set of symbols on which to base their identity. The Ottoman Middle East was in a state of political and intellectual flux at the onset of World War I.

The strong ties between Germany and the Ottoman Empire that had developed over the preceding quarter century led to an alliance in war. The Allies had good reason to fear Ottoman entry into the war. The Ottoman military forces were reasonably strong, and the truncated Ottoman Empire still posed a considerable threat to what the Allies, especially the British, perceived as their national interests. The Suez Canal and the petroleum fields of Persia were of particular importance.

Egypt was still nominally part of the Ottoman Empire until the outbreak of the war, although British forces had occupied the country since 1882. Egypt was made a British protectorate in 1914, after England declared war on the Ottoman Empire. There was little fear for the security of Egypt from the west and south. Libya (then Tripolitania and Cyrenaica) had been invaded by the Italians in 1911 and declared a possession of Italy. The Italians faced continual tribal resistance, however, especially after their entry into the war on the Allied side prompted the Central Powers to aid the Libyan guerrillas. When members of the Sanussi, a largely rural religious movement, were beaten back after moving to attack Egypt, the fractious Libyan resistance became ineffective. The Sudan had been administered by the joint Anglo-Egyptian condominium since 1898–1899 and caused little concern.

The Arab lands of the Hijaz and (Greater) Syria posed the most significant threat to the security of Egypt and the Persian Gulf. Two basic concerns faced the Allies: the Ottoman military threat and the closely related, but distinct, question of the attitudes of the local Arab leaders.

The military concern was realized early on the Egyptian and Persian Gulf fronts. By early 1915, Ottoman forces had reached the Suez Canal, and Ottoman supporters had disrupted the flow of petroleum from Persia. There followed a long and bitter struggle by the British to beat back the enemy. After sustaining heavy losses, the British entered Baghdad by March 1917. The British pushed through Palestine, taking Jerusalem in December 1917. An armistice was reached in October 1918. By then the British had pushed toward Homs and Aleppo. The "sick man of Europe" had waged a brave and tenacious battle.

With the military balance in doubt until the end of the war, the Allies sought aid from every available quarter. This situation led to a series of secret agreements and overt pledges that helped swing the outcome in their favor. These same pacts contained fundamental contradictions, some of which still have not been resolved.

THE McMAHON–HUSEIN CORRESPONDENCE

At the onset of the war, an immediate Allied concern was how the people in the Ottoman provinces would react to the coming call for a jihad by the sultan-caliph. An Arab revolt against the Ottomans would aid the Allied war effort in the Middle Eastern front. There were reasons to suppose that conditions were ripe for such a revolt. The key figure to be won over was Sherif Husein, sherif of Mecca and emir of the Hijaz. The British high commissioner in Egypt, Sir Arthur Henry McMahon, contacted Husein, hoping to persuade him to sever his already strained relationship with the Ottoman Empire.

The McMahon–Husein correspondence (July 14, 1915 to January 30, 1916) set the terms for an Arab revolt. In return for entering the war on the Allied side, Husein was assured that a large stretch of Ottoman-Arab territory would be made independent under his leadership at the conclusion of the war; it included the Hijaz and what is now Syria, Iraq, and Jordan. He had first demanded that other territories be included, but allowed his claims to lapse on what now is the non-Hijaz portion of Saudi Arabia, Lebanon, and areas extending northward into Turkey. The fate of Palestine was left ambiguous in the correspondence. After the war, the British seized on this ambiguity to press their claim that Palestine was not part of the agreement.

Husein's silence to the call for a jihad was transformed into a call for an Arab revolt. Although the revolt did not produce anything resembling a mass movement, it brought relief to the Allies. The crack Ottoman troops stationed in the Yemen were isolated in Medina and between the Hijaz and British-dominated Aden, and the people of Syria found cause to retaliate against the brutality of their Ottoman rulers.

The British also made an agreement with Ibn Saud, recognizing his rule in the non-Hijaz area of what is now Saudi Arabia; allowed for a formal recognition of Kuwait; and entered into agreements that essentially called for the Persian Gulf peoples to cooperate with the British without forcing them to take up arms in the actual conduct of the war. The success of the British in promoting the Arab revolt by promises of independence did not prevent them from completing negotiations with the French and the Russians (who repudiated their claims after the 1917 revolution), which created a new division of Western influence in the Middle East. The Sykes–Picot Agreement (1915–1916) gave the French control of the Levant coastal area and the right to oversee the interior of Syria. The British were to receive what is now most of Iraq and Jordan. Palestine was to become an international zone. The terms of this agreement were revealed to Husein by the Russians during the war, but the British managed to calm his fears by minimizing the document's importance. However, this agreement formed the basis of the postwar division of British and French areas of domination. The Allies entered into other agreements that defined areas of influence or rule throughout the rest of the region. As with the Sykes–Picot Agreement, the Allies were able to dictate terms that would expand their influence after the war. These agreements were to cause much frustration and bitterness (see Figure 5.1).

The Balfour Declaration

Although the disposition of Palestine was unclear under the McMahon–Husein Agreement, it seemed most likely that it would become an independent Arab state. The Sykes–Picot Agreement called for Palestine to become internationalized. After the British issued the famous Balfour Declaration on November 2, 1917, the fate of Palestine remained unclear. The declaration, sent by Lord Balfour to Lord Rothschild, must be quoted in full:

> I have much pleasure in conveying to you on behalf of His Majesty's Government the following declaration of sympathy with Jewish Zionist aspirations, which has been submitted and approved by the cabinet:
>
> His Majesty's Government view with favor the establishment in Palestine of a National Home for the Jewish People, and will use their

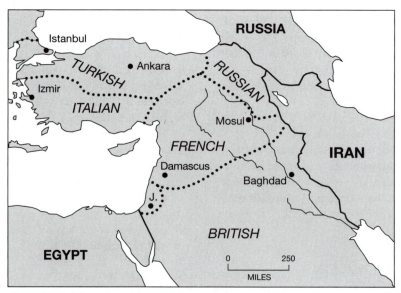

FIGURE 5.1   Secret Partition of Turkey and the Sykes–Picot Agreement, 1915–1917

Source: Yahya Armajani, *Middle East Past and Present,* © 1970, p. 304.
Reprinted by permission of Prentice Hall, Upper Saddle River, N.J.

best endeavors to facilitate the achievement of this object, it being clearly understood that nothing shall be done which may prejudice the civil and religious rights of existing non-Jewish communities in Palestine, or the rights and political status enjoyed by Jews in any other country.

I should be grateful if you would bring this declaration to the knowledge of the Zionist Federation.

The carefully constructed ambiguity of the statement was designed to elicit Jewish support for the Allies without alienating the Arabs. It succeeded in the former, but failed in the latter and added another layer of misunderstanding to the growing dilemma.

Palestine, the Holy Land of the Bible, had always had Jews among its population. But it was not until the last two decades of the nineteenth century that substantial numbers emigrated to Palestine from Europe. Many European Jews were motivated by the ethnic nationalism that had spread throughout Europe in the nineteenth century and was now beginning to take hold in other areas. But wherever they lived, the Jewish people were a small minority—a minority that had frequently endured extreme physical brutality and systematic social and economic discrimination. Although their situation was not always desperate in Christian Europe, it was always insecure.

Whether or not the Jews could or should be assimilated into their European countries of residence was a central question for Jewish leaders. Many of them began to believe that the Jews were entitled to self-determination. To enjoy this self-determination, however, the Jewish people would have to have their own political entity, a separate state. The trickle of Jews who settled in Palestine before the turn of the twentieth century came primarily from

Russia and Poland (most Jewish émigrés from these countries fled to Western Europe and the United States). The Jews who emigrated to Palestine did so for many reasons—religious, secular, socialistic, and personal. All, however, sought a better life.

World Zionist Organization

The idea of creating a special homeland for the Jewish people was popularized by Theodor Herzl (1860–1904). After covering the Dreyfus trial (1895) as a correspondent, Herzl became convinced that so long as they remained a minority people, Jews would always suffer periods of deprivation. His book, *The Jewish State* (1896), aroused enough interest to warrant calling the first World Zionist Congress, which was held in Basel, Switzerland, in 1897. The congress created the World Zionist Organization and called for the formation of a Jewish homeland in Palestine. The movement spread quickly throughout Europe. Palestine had not been a unified area under the Ottomans, however; it had been divided into two provinces, with the area around Jerusalem enjoying a special status.

During the nineteenth century, millions of Europeans were emigrating to new lands in various parts of the world; the Jewish call for a homeland in Palestine was not unique in that regard. Zionist leaders believed mistakenly, however, that hardly any local people would be displaced because most of Palestine was relatively empty. They believed that the people who were there were of such a low culture that they could only benefit from contact with sophisticated Europeans.

The World Zionist Organization financed and organized a substantial wave of immigration to Palestine in the decade before World War I. By 1914, about 85,000 Jews were living in Palestine, three times the number 30 years earlier; however, they constituted less than 15 percent of the total population. Jews were still a small minority even in Palestine, but they were a highly organized and growing minority. A settler's life was often difficult, and many settlements failed because of lack of farming experience, harsh agricultural conditions, and a host of other reasons. But the settlements generally succeeded. However loosely it was controlled, Palestine was still part of the Ottoman Empire, and the settlers were subject to Ottoman law and administration. Ottoman law did not always allow noncitizens to own land. A complex system of third-party land ownership had to be worked out. Also, Russian Jews were often singled out for harsh treatment because Russia was an Ottoman enemy.

With the beginning of World War I, the Ottomans imposed systematically harsh treatment on all Jews in Palestine. Wartime dislocations and a failed harvest compounded the woes of all residents—Muslim, Christian, and Jewish. By the time of the Balfour Declaration, the Jewish population had declined to about 55,000. Given these deteriorating conditions, Zionist leaders saw their vision of an independent Jewish state rapidly receding. The war posed difficult problems for them. Jewish leaders were not sure that supporting the Allied cause would improve the position of world Jewry or further the goal of creating a Jewish homeland. Germany had recently improved conditions for Jews and created a better environment for them than had any other country in Europe. Seeing that Jews would have a difficult time wherever they lived, and seeing widespread anti-Semitism in the Allied countries, the Zionist leaders gave the Allies only half-hearted support.

The Allied powers were facing enormous difficulties during the war and needed support. Dr. Chaim Weizmann, a Manchester University chemist with connections to high-ranking officials in England (owing to his war-related research) and a Zionist leader, pressed the Zionist cause with the British. Zionists in other Allied countries were doing the same. Finally, an agreement was reached that culminated in the Balfour Declaration.

THE MANDATES

The Allies were aware that the contradictory agreements made during World War I were going to be difficult to resolve. After the war, the Americans (with some British support) urged the formation of a commission to ascertain the wishes of the local populations. The French rejected the idea, however, and insisted that the Sykes–Picot Agreement be carried out. The British suspected the French of wanting to establish a firm foothold in the Middle East and tried to change the terms of the agreement. An understanding was reached in September 1919: Mosul would eventually be appended to Iraq rather than Syria, Palestine would come under British control, British troops would leave Syria, and the French would be compensated with a share of the Turkish Petroleum Company. And thus the Midle East was divided between Britain and France (see Figure 5.2).

Syria and Lebanon

A son of Husein, Faisal, led the Arab revolt against the Ottomans and helped capture Damascus near the end of the war. He correctly foresaw France's intentions in Syria, but underestimated the extent to which Palestinian nationalism had flowered during the war. He was more concerned with the French than with the Zionists. Consequently, he entered into negotiations with the Zionist leaders, seeking their aid in thwarting France; in return, he accepted the legitimacy of Zionist aspirations. The French accord with the British placed Faisal in an impossible position. Because his agreement with the Zionists was conditional on the granting of Syrian independence, he repudiated the pact and was declared by the Arab Congress to be king of Syria and Palestine in March 1920. The French protected their claim to Syria by seizing on Faisal's failure to reply to an ultimatum calling for the acceptance of the mandate; the French brought in troops from Lebanon and routed Faisal. Faisal had sent a telegram of capitulation to the French, but it did not stop the troops.

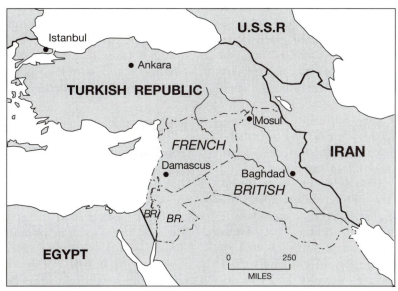

FIGURE 5.2 The Mandate System, 1920
Source: Yahya Armajani, *Middle East Past and Present*, © 1970, p. 304.
Reprinted by permission of Prentice Hall, Upper Saddle River, N.J.

The Syrians of the interior were hostile to the French invasion; France responded with firm political and military action. To win over the Lebanese elite, France quadrupled the area of Lebanon. To fragment the anti-French nationalistic movement, Syria was split into separate autonomous administrative districts. Although Syrian administration was centralized after about a year, the French found that this cosmetic remedy did not solve their problems. The hostility of the Syrian population required France to maintain a military presence and suppress all political activity. Damascus was shelled on several occasions. Direct French rule also was imposed on Lebanon. Although there was considerable opposition in Lebanon, it did not rival that in Syria. However, the new, enlarged Lebanon now included areas dominated by Muslim Arabs; the delicate balance of political, ethnic, and religious groups was upset, and tensions between the various indigenous groups occasionally erupted into violence.

Early in World War II, in 1941, British and Free French forces invaded Lebanon and

Syria to wrest them away from Vichy France. When it seemed that the French would renege on their promises of independence at the end of the war, the British forced them to withdraw. Lebanon and Syria finally achieved political independence.

Iraq and Transjordan

The expulsion of Faisal from Syria in 1920 left the British in a particularly delicate position. The wartime promises made to Faisal's father, along with Faisal's widespread (albeit thin) popular support, spelled increased instability and a loss of British influence. The British responded by engineering the election of Faisal as king of Iraq and by creating another area, Transjordan, where they installed Faisal's brother, Abdullah, as emir. The government of British India had supplied troops and administrators to Iraq during World War I. When the League of Nations gave Britain a mandate over Iraq instead of granting independence, widespread insurrection broke out. After a particularly bloody campaign to restore order, the British sought to install a friendly ruler and selected Faisal in July 1921. In 1922, Iraq was given a special status, and in 1932 it was granted nominal independence, with a continuing British military and administrative presence. The British retained their prominent position in Iraq, however, for another quarter century.

Transjordan had been carved out of the new British mandate of Palestine. Abdullah had been made emir to mollify Husein and to keep Abdullah from invading Syria in revenge for his brother's defeat. By splitting the mandate, the British hoped to defuse Palestinian nationalism. British policy won the enmity of Arabs and Zionists who were seeking control of Palestine. Transjordan was an extremely poor and sparsely populated country and did not have a strong current of nationalism. It attained formal independence in 1946, but remained dependent on British and U.S. aid. It was, in short, a client state.

Generally, Britain's policy of indirect rule in Iraq and Transjordan better prepared those countries for independence than France's direct rule in Syria. This is not to imply that British policy was particularly farsighted; although they were swayed by Wilsonian notions of self-determination, the British were weary of war and no longer wished to continue the heavy financial burden of direct rule. By staying in the background, the British allowed the area's indigenous people to educate themselves for self-government and to adapt to technological change. The French, ever fearful of increasing local power, kept their subjects politically and technologically ignorant.

A national consciousness determined by the boundaries drawn by Europeans began to form during the interwar years in Syria, Iraq, and Transjordan. People who for so long had traveled between Baghdad, Damascus, and Amman with no sense of being in foreign cities were now beginning to observe the new international borders. Passports were not the only things, however, that kept Iraqis, Syrians,

and Jordanians estranged from each other. Iraqis and Syrians learned different European languages, worked with incompatible technologies (the electrical system being a prime example), and started to perceive themselves as being of different nationalities.

EGYPT

The longtime (1883–1907) consul general of Egypt, Lord Cromer, brought financial order and economic progress to Egypt by establishing a highly effective administrative system and by major projects such as the first Aswan Dam. The nominal Egyptian rulers (and their even more nominal Ottoman rulers) were at the mercy of the British, but they had little reason to complain. Although the British controlled Egypt, they viewed their stay as temporary, brought order out of chaos, and prevented the nationalism of the urban intellectuals from gathering much steam. A 1906 incident in which British officers shot one villager and hanged three others touched off deep nationalist and anti-British feelings. The British began to make limited concessions to nationalist demands for political representation and participation. These all but stopped when Egypt became a British protectorate in 1914.

Immediately after World War I, Saad Zaghlul, a nationalist and a respected administrator, asked the British for permission to circulate a petition for Egyptian independence. After they refused, he organized an independence movement. The British arrested and deported him in 1919. Riots followed, and after a time the British began to relent on some issues. Because of the weakness of the official "puppet" government, and the considerable size of Zaghlul's following, the British decided to negotiate with him personally. Their concessions did not satisfy him or the other nationalists. After negotiations broke down, the British tried to maintain civil order by unilaterally declaring Egypt to be independent on February 28, 1922. The declaration, however, contained four "absolutely reserved" clauses in which the British retained control over areas they deemed vital to their interests: (1) the Sudan and with it, the Nile River; (2) all foreigners and minorities in Egypt; (3) the communications system; and (4) Egyptian defense.

After returning from a second British-imposed exile, Zaghlul saw his Wafd party win a sweeping victory in September 1923 in a parliament that had been recently declared by the king. Zaghlul was asked to form a new government. Because the British refused to back down on any of their four conditions, he saw no point in organizing a government. More riots followed. The assassination of a key British official, Sir Lee Stack, prompted fierce British reprisals, and the nationalist movement declined. By the late 1920s, the movement was in disarray. In 1936, the Egyptian government signed a treaty with Britain based on the 1922 declaration of independence and the revision of the four clauses: The British high commissioner would leave, British troops would be restricted to the Suez Canal Zone, and the capitulations (regarding the special status of foreigners) would eventually end. The 1936 agreement was prompted by British and Egyptian fears arising from Mussolini's invasion of Ethiopia (1935), the death of King Faud, the accession of King Farouk (a quiet and ambivalent nationalist sympathizer in those days), and the relatively quiescent state of the nationalist movement.

With the beginning of World War II, the British believed it necessary to reassert their control over Egypt. The country virtually became an Allied base for the duration of the war. Because many of the Egyptian political elite had pro-Axis leanings, the British intervened in Egyptian politics, especially in the selection of political leaders. The local Egyptian authorities were reluctant to take up arms against Britain's enemies; the British had humiliated the Egyptian nationalists, whereas the Germans and Italians had not. At the conclusion of World War I, Egyptian nationalism entered the post–World War II era with renewed vigor.

The Egyptian political struggles since 1882 had been three-sided and unevenly matched. Basically, the aspirants to political power, the nationalists, were strong enough not to be ignored, but weak enough to be manipulated between the British and the monarchy. The position of the king was delicate. On the one hand, he supported the nationalist cause to some degree to convince the British that the ruling elite would maintain civil order if power devolved to it after independence; on the other hand, he opposed the nationalist cause when it seemed to be getting strong enough to threaten the monarchy. The British discouraged nationalist causes that the king advocated, and approved the causes when the king seemed to be getting too much power. The nationalists made only modest gains, for several reasons: The nationalists advocated reform, not revolution; the nationalists were mostly members of the middle class; and various factions had been weakened by being played off against each other.

The first modern nationalist movement in Egypt had resulted in the 1882 British invasion. The nationalists had been jolted into action then by the financial collapse of the Egyptian government and the exploitative policies of Britain and France. Nationalists had gathered strength during the following decades, only to see their gains swept away by the British takeover during World War I. They again pressed their claims immediately after the war, gained some measure of self-rule, but then fell victim again to imperialist power. The trauma of World War II, another event that was basically a European affair, alerted the nationalists to the insufficiency of their past gains.

Wafd Party and Muslim Brotherhood

The nationalist groups in Egypt during the interwar period were of various persuasions, but they all saw the British as a common enemy.

The two most important movements were the Wafd party and the Muslim Brotherhood. The popular Wafd party of Zaghlul was a secular reformist movement, one that basically accepted British ideas of representative government and could accuse the British of perverting their own stated ideals. The Muslim Brotherhood, founded in 1928 by Hasan al-Bana, expressed its hatred of British domination by calling for a return to Islamic fundamentals, including the formation of an Islamic government. Its membership in the late 1930s was estimated to be around one million. The message of the Brotherhood was disarmingly clear: The wretched condition of the masses, the venal behavior of the elite, and the general degradation of their common heritage were a result of the acceptance of Western ways. The solution to the situation was equally clear: Get rid of the Westerners and their puppets, and establish an order that would make the Koran the constitution of the country.

Although the Wafd party had considerable influence with the middle-class voting population, the Brotherhood laid out a straightforward message that appealed to the masses. The Muslim Brotherhood's strident message was feared by the establishment. Because of this perceived threat, and because of occasional assassinations by zealots, it frequently had to operate in a clandestine way. An assassination attempt on Nasser in 1954 drove the group underground, and it was declared illegal. It remains a force, although the leadership of Egypt viewed it as a minor irritant until the assassination of President Sadat.

The Muslim Brotherhood represented an early twentieth century attempt to establish a new Islamic identity after two centuries of Western exploitation. The economy of Egypt was mangled, divisions among social classes were widening, and secularism was increasing. Many observers think that the ˈMuslim Brotherhood is naively fighting a rear-guard action that it will ultimately lose. Although these prognostications may yet prove true, it is now clear that the success of the Brotherhood in the 1930s helped similar political forces to coalesce in such far-flung countries as Syria, Libya, Iran, Pakistan, and Indonesia.

Egypt after World War II

After World War II, socialism gained widespread popularity in the Third World. Nationalists of all persuasions were quick to adopt current socialist slogans and formulate grandiose programs. Most socialist creeds were not based primarily on Marxism or any other intellectual system. Rather, they were more a reaction against the Western private enterprise system and commercial domination. Socialist programs called for an end to the gross income disparities in society. The misery of the masses was apparent enough, and the cause of their misery was held to be the selfishness of the local elites, who were allies of the imperialists. As young intellectuals and technical specialists absorbed these ideas, nationalist movements began to gather momentum. Broad-based nationalist parties attempted to draw in the masses, especially people in cities, who were more sophisticated than people in rural areas.

The situation in Egypt after World War II reflected these trends. When the British resisted the Egyptian government's demands for a troop withdrawal and a renegotiation of the 1936 treaty, popular sentiment erupted into major riots in Cairo. The situation was complicated by the desperate economic conditions and the failure of the Egyptian army to prevent the formation of the state of Israel, which many Egyptians regarded as another outpost of Western imperialism. On January 26, 1952, one month after 43 Egyptian policemen had been killed in a pitched battle with British troops in Ismailia, rampaging masses burned many Western-owned buildings in Cairo. Six months later, on July 23, 1952, a group of young army officers, including Gamal Abdel Nasser, Anwar Sadat, and Muhammud Neguib, staged an almost bloodless coup that forced King Farouk to abdicate and leave Egypt three days later. The monarchy was abolished the following June.

SAUDI ARABIA

After capturing the Rashid stronghold of Riyadh in 1902, Ibn Saud began to consolidate his rule over the interior of the Arabian Peninsula. He defeated the last Rashid forces in 1921. The British were divided as to what to do about this growing tribe of religious zealots. During World War I, it had looked as if Husein would not be able to control the important Hijaz region against the hostile Wahhabi forces of Ibn Saud. The British decided to back Husein and Ibn Saud on the condition that British financial support would be withdrawn from whatever side first attacked the other. The strategy worked through the war years but crumbled after the last Rashid power had been destroyed. It was then that Ibn Saud could turn his attention to the birthplace of Islam.

By 1924, Husein was in a particularly vulnerable position at home because of poor administration and abroad because he unilaterally declared himself caliph after Ataturk had abolished the title in Turkey in March 1924. Ibn Saud's forces struck and in short order forced Husein to abdicate in favor of his son Ali and established a protectorate of sorts over the Hijaz. In 1926, Ibn Saud was proclaimed king of the Nejd, the central area of Arabia, and in 1932 he was proclaimed king of Saudi Arabia (incorporating the Hijaz). A small band of Wahhabis, led by the Saud family, had spent the whole of the nineteenth century warring for temporary power in an "inhospitable and unimportant" area and had now achieved statehood. Given the region's chronic instability and poverty, one can forgive the British and others for their inability to see Ibn Saud's potential as a leader or the significance of the nation he created.

Saudi Arabian political stability was achieved through a combination of centralization and wise leadership. Ibn Saud extended the traditional system of Bedouin rule to the nation by demanding that all significant power

flow through him, by carefully adjudicating complaints, and by ensuring that people who came under his rule were treated with magnanimity. As power was consolidated, and the flow of petroleum started to transform life in Saudi Arabia, an essentially ad hoc system of government evolved. Although the line separating national from local power is still ambiguous, the council of ministers that was established in 1953 clarified the areas of responsibility and took over some of the powers of the king. The system has undergone continuous revision and adjustment, with the king and royal family incrementally losing power.

The evolution of Saudi Arabia's administrative system, however interesting, pales in importance compared with the history of its petroleum revenues. In the 1930s, Ibn Saud used the first trickles of oil money to subsidize and calm tribes that were reluctant to stay within the nation and to strengthen the weak financial base of the kingdom. After a time, the trickle of oil revenues became a torrent. The kingdom still had financial troubles, however, because there was no system of accountability. By 1962, an alarmed council of ministers (and other powerful notables) had convinced the weak King Saud, son and successor to Ibn Saud (who died in 1953), to submit the country's finances to modern budgetary procedures. By this time, the activities of some members of the royal family seemed to be based more on the visions of grandeur in *The Thousand and One Nights* than on the strict tenets of Wahhabi fundamentalism. Prince Faisal became king in 1964 when King Saud was forced from power by family pressures. The term *king* is misleading when applied to the leader of Saudi Arabia. He is better described as a leader chosen from and by the core elites of the country.

TURKEY AND IRAN

The two large non-Arab countries of the Middle East, Iran and Turkey, emerged from World War I in chaos. In each country, reforming autocrats came to power—Mustafa Kemal (later named Kemal Ataturk) in Turkey and Reza Shah (later Reza Shah Pahlevi) in Iran. Each gathered power and brought order to his respective country during the interwar period. Each instituted secular, nationalist, and developmental reforms. And each country became aligned with the West, especially the United States, after World War II. The two countries followed distinctively different paths, however: Turkey moved unsteadily and tentatively toward Western-style democracy, whereas Iran continued to be ruled by one family.

The policies of secularization—substantive and symbolic—had definite political aims: to lessen the power of the religious establishment and to create a new set of allegiances. In Turkey, the new allegiance was to the nation and democratic institutions. In Iran, the shah became the locus of power and the central symbol of the nation.

Turkey

Ataturk had a habit of ramming programs through the legislature and of not tolerating any significant opposition—a habit that conflicted with his populist ideal of involving the masses in political life. He encouraged opposition movements, but suppressed them as they gained strength. Because his reforms often involved "radical" secularization, they were sure to be opposed and cause populist ideals to be temporarily shelved. Ataturk considered the policies of his party—which controlled the Grand National Assembly—to be the only correct and permissible ones.

Ataturk was far more than a simple autocrat. He had a considerable influence on the development of democracy in Turkey. He set up democratic institutions, broke the power of the old ruling elite, patched up Turkey's international relations, brought a sense of nationhood to the country, and laid the groundwork for positive economic gains. In short, he lived up to the name bestowed on him—Ataturk, "father of the Turks."

When Ataturk died in 1938, Ismet Inonu, a longtime ally, was the natural choice of the Grand National Assembly to be the second president of the republic. With the autocratic Ataturk gone, a pent-up desire for reform gushed forth. The reformers had to bide their time, however, as Inonu negotiated Turkey through the years of World War II, declaring war on Germany only in 1945, when it was clear that the threat of a German invasion was practically nil. Turkey emerged from the war in near economic collapse and under the threat of Soviet expansion southward. Under the Truman Doctrine of 1947 and other pacts, the United States gave Turkey (and Greece) significant military and economic aid to thwart perceived Soviet intentions. U.S. aid also put Turkey firmly in the Western camp.

The clamor for reform after a quarter century of rule by the same political party proved too great for Inonu to overcome. The 1950 elections resulted in a stunning upset when the opposition party gained a legislative majority. The election marked a turning point in Turkish politics; a change of government had come about by popular vote.

Although the military had not intervened, it remained a formidable force in Turkish politics. The internal financial troubles that had beset rapidly developing Turkey brought a military takeover in 1960, but the military leaders respected the role of political parties in Turkish life. Their stated goal, which they carried out within a year, was to return Turkey to civilian rule after a reasonable degree of social and economic order was established. The military staged another coup in 1971; they promptly turned the reins of power back to the civilians after order was reestablished. As if running in 10-year cycles, the military reluctantly took power again in 1980. Civilian rule was partially in place two years later.

Iran

The 1950 elections and the later military coups in Turkey contrast sharply with events in Iran. In

1951, the Iranian prime minister, Dr. Mohammed Mossadegh, a longtime nationalist, led an unsuccessful battle to nationalize the British-owned petroleum company. The Iranian legislature, the Majlis, was dominated largely by individuals interested in maintaining the status quo and had gained considerable political power in the previous decade. In 1941, the Allies had forced Reza Shah Pahlevi to abdicate because of his flirtation with Germany and his refusal to accept Allied demands to redivide Iran into British and Soviet spheres of influence. His young son, Mohammed Reza Shah Pahlevi, ascended to the Peacock Throne. During the 1940s, the new shah had his hands full simply maintaining the throne as internal rivalries and Allied actions sheared power away from him and transferred it to the Majlis. Dr. Mossadegh convinced the members of the Majlis that it was in the national interest and their personal self-interest to vote for nationalization of the British-owned petroleum company.

Nationalization with due compensation was an established point of international law, but the Mossadegh-led Majlis met with British-led Western intransigence. The Western powers boycotted Iranian petroleum. World petroleum supplies were abundant enough to absorb the loss of Iranian production, especially as the region's other major producers did not support the Iranian nationalization and continued to sell their petroleum to the West. If they had cooperated, it is possible that Iran would have won the day, and the course of Middle Eastern history would have been changed.

As it was, the economic toll of the boycott mounted, and support from the Majlis dwindled; its members' nationalistic zeal fluctuated with the size of their purses. The Majlis's consequent rejection of Dr. Mossadegh's oil policy in the face of Western pressure reconciled it to the shah, for whom a nationalist victory would have meant a loss of power.

Dr. Mossadegh and his group of supporters became isolated. He could capitulate or take his case to the streets. He chose the latter course and won a short-term victory; the

outpouring of nationalization sentiment was strong enough to topple the throne. However, in 1953, with the active support of the U.S. Central Intelligence Agency, the military intervened, arrested Mossadegh, and restored power to the shah and the equally conservative Majlis. A revised agreement with the petroleum company was drawn up; this new agreement changed the terms of the previous agreement but allowed for continued Western ownership. People pressing for economic independence—the clergy, the communists, and a growing group of reformers—had lost the battle.

Within a year, Iran entered into a military pact with the United States and put itself firmly in the Western camp for the next quarter century. As Turkey struggled with a highly imperfect representative rule, Iran saw all its political and economic power become increasingly centered in the person of the shah.

By the early 1960s, the shah had promulgated the White Revolution, the goal of which was to hasten the industrialization of Iran and to better the lot of the peasants through a land reform program. It is no accident that the White Revolution shifted power away from the clergy and the restive urban technocrats and intellectuals. Although it promoted economic growth, the White Revolution also promoted insecurity among the opposition and concentrated more power in the hands of the ruling elite.

As the growing petroleum revenues enabled the shah to transform the Iranian economy, they also made his continued tight control of all political processes increasingly problematic. The same social forces that had coalesced in the 1890 tobacco riots were again finding a common bond. There is some irony in the fact that the shah's decisive support of the quadrupling of petroleum prices in 1973–1974 accelerated this process. As the shah immediately spent the riches that poured in, he began to lose control over the flow of events. The careful balancing of interests demanded by the informal Iranian political system degenerated into an indiscriminate bludgeoning of the opposition, as the SAVAK (the Iranian secret police) and its network of informants struggled against widespread resentment. The system was running amok.

FROM PALESTINE TO ISRAEL

By 1920, the forces that were to create the dilemma of Palestine for the remainder of the century were in place. The basic issue was, and remains, which group has the right to control the area.

The British were aware of the potential difficulties even before they were granted the mandate for Palestine. The Zionists clung to the idea of a national homeland as proclaimed in the Balfour Declaration. The Arabs demanded the same self-determination that had been promised to people living in other contiguous Arab lands. Over the next 25 years, British responses to the situation reflected the policy dilemma but did little to bring an acceptable resolution. The British issued periodic white papers that outlined the extremely low probability of a peacefully negotiated settlement, but formulated no coherent policy. They momentarily cooled the passions of first one side and then the other without resolving the source of the conflict.

Nationalism had infected the Arabs of Palestine and the Zionists by the end of World War I. Self-determination was the goal of each group. The British military administration and the civilian mandate government allowed Jewish immigration on a limited scale and made it easier for Jews to acquire property. Arabs and Jews were involved in several incidents in 1920, and in 1921, Arabs had made several significant attacks on Jewish settlements. The British promptly suspended immigration for one month until tempers subsided, then put the old policy back into force, temporarily acceding to violence and then continuing business as usual. They ignored the King-Crane Commission of 1919, which was organized by Woodrow Wilson, and British

committee reports that indicated that there was little room for compromise.

Winston Churchill, then colonial secretary, stated in 1922 that the phrase *national home* in the Balfour Declaration did not mean that all of Palestine was to become a Zionist nation, but that a national home for the Zionists could be created in Palestine. The British also separated Transjordan, first created in 1921, from the Palestinian mandate, shutting off Jewish settlements there. The Zionists viewed these policies as attempts to thwart their movement and abrogate the Balfour Declaration. Arab leaders saw the policy as working within the confines of the Balfour Declaration in that it simply redefined the specifics, and they rejected the "clarifications." For the next two decades, Arab policy was based on the premise of the illegitimacy of the Balfour Declaration. They could not acknowledge Britain's repeated attempts to modify the declaration. The Arabs rejected Britain's attempts to have Arabs and Jews sit on a joint consultative body in Palestine for the same reason; to sit in the same chamber would give legitimacy to the Balfour Declaration and to the Zionists.

Although the Zionist community was composed of several competing factions, its government was solidly organized and well structured, and it could depend on British support for its major concerns. The Arabs of Palestine stood in stark contrast. Although most politically aware Palestinian Arabs wanted self-determination, they had no effective political organization. Their rejection of the Arab-Zionist consultative bodies had its logic, but it was politically unwise because it deprived them of a forum in which to air their grievances.

The Arab Executive, a committee formed by the Third Arab Congress in December 1920, was the most important Palestinian Arab organization during the early 1920s. Because Syria had been occupied by the French earlier that year, the idea of Palestine becoming part of southern Syria had faded. The new Arab strategy was (1) to unify the Palestinians,

(2) to protest British moves that facilitated Zionist settlement in Palestine, and (3) to prohibit the League of Nations from forming a mandate on terms unfavorable to the Arabs.

Although the Arab Executive managed to hold the various Palestinian Arab groups together for a couple of years, it split apart in 1923. In September 1923, the League of Nations finished drawing up the provisions of the mandate. One of the major forces for unity was lost.

The Arab Executive was divided over what strategy to use. Should it lodge official protests and try to negotiate and persuade, or should it simply not cooperate at all? Some advocated not paying taxes, but landowners feared that this would lead to property confiscations. At the same time, some elite families revived their long-standing feuds.

The Sixth Arab Congress (1923) was the last for five years. The Palestinian voice became muted. Official negotiations ceased, and the Jewish and Arab (Muslim Arab and Christian Arab) communities became more isolated from one another. The Zionists prohibited Arabs from leasing or even working on land purchased by the Jewish National Fund. Histadrut, the General Federation of Jewish Labor, was insisting that Jewish-owned establishments hire only Jews. Outside of Jerusalem and Haifa, where Arabs and Jews lived side by side, the two groups lived and worked apart in an atmosphere of growing hostility.

Arab fears went beyond the fear of becoming a numerical minority in their own land. Most Zionists, after all, were Europeans, and however separated they had become from the mainstream of European society, they nevertheless were steeped in Western ways. In 1930, more than 90 percent of all Jewish men in Palestine were literate, as opposed to only 25 percent of all Arab men. About 75 percent of the Jews were urban residents, as opposed to 25 percent of the Arabs.

The relative calm that prevailed during the mid-1920s belied a growing sense of frustration

and bitterness. The Jews comprised about 10 percent of the total population of Palestine in 1922 (the remainder consisted of 10 percent Christians and 80 percent Muslims). Their numbers grew at a moderate rate through immigration except in 1925, when a relatively large number entered. As a result of a harsh recession, more Jews left Palestine in 1927 than entered. It seemed to the Arabs that the Zionist cause had lost its appeal, and that the Arabs would remain a firm majority. But 1927 proved to be an anomaly. By 1930 Jews comprised about 16 percent of the population. It was clear that Zionism was alive and vigorous.

The Seventh Arab Congress convened in 1928. Encouraged by the 1927 decline in Zionist immigration, the congress sought to present a united front to press Arab claims. The new Arab coalition sought legislative representation as a first step toward self-determination. Events were to weaken the coalition severely, however, and lead to its dissolution in 1934. A few months after the meeting of the Seventh Congress, Zionists demonstrated at the Wailing Wall by raising the Zionist flag and singing the Zionist anthem. There were clashes with Arabs. By August 1929, full-scale rioting broke out, resulting in 740 deaths (472 Jews and 268 Arabs). The cautious, elite-dominated Arab Executive was losing its grip on its base of power. Arab politics in the 1930s was fragmented at the top and radicalized at the bottom.

The British sent an investigating team to Palestine after the Permanent Mandate Commission of the League of Nations, in response to the 1929 riots, issued a report outlining Arab–Jewish tensions. The subsequent British white paper recognized the seriousness of the situation and called for an immediate temporary end to immigration. Arab satisfaction at the position taken in the Passfield white paper was short-lived. In England, the Zionist reaction was quick and vehement. An open letter from the British prime minister to Chaim Weizmann, the highly influential British Zionist, repudiated the latest immigration policy. This "black letter," as the Arabs referred to it, indicated to some Arab leaders that they could not hope to negotiate with Britain for independence. Britain was henceforth to be regarded as an enemy. An Arab boycott followed.

Although they succeeded in having immigration reinstated, the Zionists also were troubled by British actions. Although the British had acceded to Zionist pressures, it was clear that they had no clear commitment to the Zionists' ultimate goals. The British were faced with hostility from both camps.

The rise of Nazi Germany in 1932 produced a steady stream of Jewish immigration to Palestine. The Jewish population of Palestine increased fourfold from 1933 to 1936; by 1936, Jews numbered more than 27 percent of the total population. The Zionist resolve to accommodate Jews fleeing the horror of Nazi Germany aroused intense Arab bitterness. In April 1936, terrorist violence broke out between the two communities. The Arab leadership, united by the crisis, called for a general strike. Within a month the strike became a civil war. The dispatch of 20,000 British troops and mass arrests halted the general strike and the civil war by the end of October.

Another British investigating commission arrived in Palestine in 1936. The British accepted the report of the commission and issued another white paper calling for the partition of Palestine into Jewish and Arab sections with an international corridor extending from Jaffa to Jerusalem and beyond. The plan was rejected by significant (but not all) factions of both sides, and fighting broke out again in September 1937. At one point, the British had put several thousand Jews under arms to help quell Arab hostility. The arrangement broke down after the British hanged a convicted Jewish terrorist in June 1938, setting terrorist groups on a rampage of reprisals.

The adverse reaction to the 1936 white paper advocating partition prompted the appointment of a commission to reconsider the exact boundaries. Although the report of the commission, which was published in 1938, contained three potential partition plans, it also pointed out that the notion of partition was impractical.

A conference in London followed in 1939. The participants worked for a peaceful resolution, but they failed to gain acceptance from either side. The only interesting result was that the British government made the McMahon–Husein correspondence public for the first time. After the conference, the British decided unilaterally that within 10 years a united Palestine would receive a constitution that would guarantee Arab representation and protect Arab land rights. Jewish immigration was first to be reduced and then to cease after five years. Jews demonstrated their anger by burning and sacking government offices in Palestine and by launching terrorist attacks on the British.

During World War II, 8,000 Arabs and 21,000 Jews from Palestine served in the British armed forces. Hostility to the British in Palestine continued, however. The Jews were especially active because they considered the British policy to be a virtual death warrant for Jews fleeing the Holocaust. By 1946, the unofficial army of the Jewish Agency (to which the World Zionist Organization had changed its name in 1930), the Haganah, numbered 60,000. Various terrorist groups, most notably the Irgun (of which the later prime minister Menachem Begin was the leader) and the smaller Stern Gang, complemented this force.

The Zionists had taken the initiative in attacking the Arabs and the British. The weaker but numerically dominant Arabs attacked the Jews and the British. The war-weary British attempted to quell the violence, which was now out of control. As more survivors of the Holocaust illegally entered Palestine, the British desperately grabbed for a solution. In 1946, an Anglo-American committee devised a variant of the partition proposal that again was rejected; a 1947 British proposal calling for a five-year British trusteeship met with a similar fate. The British were totally frustrated and angry over

European and, especially U.S., support of Zionism; the United States, however, had refused to allow mass Jewish immigration to its shores. The British washed their hands of the affair and turned the problem over to the fledgling United Nations.

A subsequent United Nations commission found what all previous commissions had noted: The demands of each side were understandable, inflexible, and irreconcilable. In November 1947, the United Nations called for the partition of Palestine. The mandate was to end on May 1, 1948, and the two states were to be established on July 1, 1948. The Arab states began to rally their forces in support of the now disorganized Palestinians who had rejected all aspects of the plan, but it was too little too late. A Zionist offensive resulted in victories as the British pulled out. On May 14, 1948, David Ben-Gurion announced the formation of the state of Israel. The Zionists had Palestine, or at least a portion of it. Subsequently, Egypt administered Gaza militarily, and Transjordan announced the annexation of the West Bank of the Jordan River not under Israeli control (1950).

The formation of Israel did not give the Zionists complete security. The Arab population that had remained in Palestine, along with the sizable number who fled as the fighting became particularly vicious, viewed Israel as illegitimate and the Zionists as a foreign power. The Arab countries that had been defeated by the highly efficient Israeli army in the war after the declaration of independence suffered a deep humiliation. Although the Arab states surrounding Israel had a substantial numerical advantage, they were militarily weak. Their armies were ill-trained, badly equipped, and lacking in dynamic leadership.

According to the Arabs, Israel was just another outpost of Western hegemony. Various Arab leaders vowed that they would not rest until the state of Israel was destroyed. According to the Israelis, British vacillation, the Nazi Holocaust, and the refusal of the Western countries to accept large numbers of persecuted Jews proved Herzl's 1896 argument that only in their own sovereign state could Jews expect to be safe and secure. To the age-old Jewish dictum "Next Year in Jerusalem," was added the cry "Never Again."

There was no ground for accommodation on the issue of Palestinian rule. Both sides were desperate and bitter. The struggle had been waged for a third of a century, and almost every longtime resident knew someone who had been killed or attacked. The "freedom fighters" of one side were considered to be brutal "terrorists" by the other.

CONCLUSION

Most countries of the Middle East had achieved political independence by 1950. Few had achieved self-determination, however. The Western powers had substantial economic and strategic interests in the area that they were determined to protect.

The new alignment of Western powers into Soviet and American camps set the stage for renewed attempts to carve out spheres of influence. The American-led group sought to establish client relationships with the northern tier of nations—Turkey, Iraq, and Iran—to thwart Soviet aspirations. To the south, the United States sought to protect Gulf oil and the Suez Canal. Because overt outside control of local political systems was quickly becoming a relic of the past, the great powers tried to maintain their influence by other means. They gave economic and technical assistance and military aid to muffle revolutionary impulses. The primary aim of the United States and the Western powers was to stop Soviet expansion, not to develop independent economies and military forces. To strengthen Middle Eastern countries against revolution, the Western powers helped build a military and economic apparatus that was effective and resilient, but still depended on Western support.

The postwar economic and military position of most Middle Eastern countries was extremely weak. The political elite of these countries generally wanted to avoid fundamental reforms. In this, they had much in common with the United States: They both sought political stability. The extent of military and economic dependency was the major point in question. The growing militant nationalism in the Middle East complicated the matter, however.

The need to achieve economic independence and strengthen the indigenous cultures began to be appreciated by those concerned with self-determination: Political independence would not suffice. People who saw economic dependence as the major impediment to self-determination found socialism particularly attractive. It was, after all, Western private enterprise that had transfigured and dominated the economies of the Middle East. A restructuring of the local economies to meet local needs was going to be necessary, but this would be almost impossible in a system dominated by foreigners and serving foreign markets. If the foreign private enterprise system controlled the course of local economic events, it also could be blamed for the continuing misery of the masses. (Leaders of private enterprise systems seldom have been noted for placing at the top of their political agenda concerns for a more equitable distribution of income; socialists generally do.) Not all modernizers shared these thoughts, and their ideas were not set out in a neatly framed system. Rather, the sentiments more often than not arose from a sense of dissatisfaction—a growing awareness that a fundamental reordering of society had to occur before full self-determination could be achieved, and that the restructuring could not take place as long as foreigners remained dominant.

Another source of dissatisfaction came to the surface during this period. It appeared that continued Western domination was stripping away the cultural fabric of Arab (and especially Islamic) society. Calls for an indigenous cultural renaissance had been made throughout the twentieth century, but the pulse of the movement, led by disaffected religious leaders, gained momentum in the postwar era. The clergy also called for an end to the current order. They sought a return to Islamic fundamentals rather than a culture heavily laden with Western values, whatever form of economic independence was achieved.

Middle Eastern political leaders faced a difficult choice. Accepting Western aid would enhance their economic and military strength and possibly mute some of the discontent caused by the "revolution of rising expectations." But this alliance would meet with resistance by people who perceived continued Western economic or cultural domination as a barrier to self-determination. The situation was complicated for several Arab countries because the American-led bloc supported Israel, a country that the Arabs generally thought of as a Western colonial settler state.

6 | THE DRIVE FOR SELF-DETERMINATION, 1950–1990

Most of the major nations of the Middle East achieved independence by 1950. However, for some, independence was neither permanent nor even meaningful. Superpower, regional, and internal struggles were still in the process of shaping and being shaped in all countries. Although the postwar decline of direct European political control was bound to change Middle Eastern political relationships, it was an open question of whether those relationships and government institutions would be altered in a fundamental fashion. Amid this uncertainty came the growing recognition that attaining political independence was not the same as achieving self-determination. The latter was not likely to occur in a state if its economy depended on that of another or if the population looked to imperialist powers for cultural sustenance. Many false starts, program reversals, and policy contradictions occurred. There was no readily available blueprint for action—no clearly defined and agreed-on analysis of the problems and solutions. All parties were feeling their way through a minefield of political dangers.

The difficult task of building nations from states became more complicated after 1973. The petroleum price changes of the 1970s significantly changed many relationships between and within nations. The 1980s were dominated by another series of shocks—moral, societal, political, military, and economic. Finally, three fundamental events during 1988 to 1991 changed the playing field on which the game was being contested. These changes—the intifadah, the breakup of the U.S.S.R., and the Iraqi invasion of Kuwait, along with equally fundamental changes occurring around the turn of the twenty-first century—are the subject of Chapter 7. This chapter sets the stage.

The major sections in this chapter deal with the impact of an ideology, the effects of a change in economic well-being, and the analysis of a particular arena of conflict. The first section deals with the role of Egypt generally, and Gamal Abdel Nasser particularly, with respect to self-determination and Arab unity. Although the complexity of internal and regional politics denies a neat encapsulation of events and trends, it is clear that the visions held by Nasser were widely shared, that there was universal difficulty in effecting solutions, and that there was widespread disagreement on what package of policies would best serve as a vehicle to meet the goal. It could be argued that there is a connection between the decline of Arab unity as a symbol and the rise of "Political Islam." As Arab unity was becoming increasingly discredited through the years, especially after 1967, new paths were sought.

Gulf politics, including the general impact of petroleum prices, forms the basis for the second section. Organization of the Petroleum Exporting Countries (OPEC) initiated actions in 1973–1974 and 1979–1980 increased the nominal price of petroleum tenfold—to about $30 a barrel. In 1985–1986 prices crashed to $12. Prices soared to $40 in the immediate aftermath of Iraq's invasion of Kuwait and settled back to $20 a few months later. By 1998 the real (inflation-adjusted) price of petroleum hovered around pre-OPEC (1973) levels. Prices rebounded substantially in 1999. By 2006 petroleum prices were greater than $70 a barrel. The petroleum-exporting countries are in profoundly different places now than before the first wave of price increases. The resulting income disparities within and between countries are a potential source of instability. This rapid material change was accompanied by wars, the establishment of the Islamic Republic of Iran, and uneasy times for the monarchies of the Arabian Peninsula as they struggled with citizens' calls for greater political participation.

The third and longest section provides an analysis of Israel and Israeli-Palestinian-Arab state tensions. The reader should not infer from the length of this section that these issues dominate the Middle Eastern landscape. They are only dimensions of the larger scene, and most of the fundamental issues of conflict and accommodation would remain in force if the antagonists in this arena settled their differences. There are three major reasons why an extended discussion is in order. First, Israel has a unique place in the Middle East. The heritage of its people and the origins of its statehood differ in significant ways from other nations of the region. Second, the Israeli-Palestinian-Arab state issues have had a high degree of international visibility that often has been translated into simplistic notions of "good guys and bad

guys." Although it is difficult not to get passionate when millions of lives hang in the balance, it would be foolhardy to ignore the complex reality and throw reason to the wind. Third, this arena serves as an enduring example of the difficulties involved in conflict resolution.

ARAB NATIONALISM

The 1952 Free Officers' coup in Egypt is a good example of a transition in the Middle East. The leaders of the coup represented a new force in Egypt particularly and in the Middle East generally. Typically (but not exclusively) they were from nonelite families and had been among the first generation of their class allowed to rise in the ranks of the military. They viewed traditional regimes as preserving the status quo and maintaining the division between the haves and the have-nots. Their revolution was based on the belief that a continuation of the existing political order would consign most of the population to permanent impoverishment. They also thought that widespread political corruption and indifference to national needs were responsible for Egypt's humiliating defeat by the Israelis in 1948. The Free Officers had no clear plan for their new postrevolutionary society; rather, they saw the new society rising like a phoenix from the ashes of the old regime.

Gamal Abdel Nasser emerged in 1954 as the leader of the Revolutionary Command Council (RCC), the name adopted by the Free Officers after taking power. Three years after the revolution, he wrote of his disillusionment with the notion that a new social order based on equality and justice would evolve naturally. It became clear to him that the various groups competing to influence the reordering of Egypt generally were concerned with enhancing their own well-being without much regard for truly national concerns. Nasser perceived them as attempting to change the actors in the political and economic hierarchy without changing the structure. He believed that Egypt needed a transition phase between the old order and the new; he called this transition "guided democracy," and the RCC was to be its guide. Nasser and his associates believed that individual competition had to be channeled if it was to result in positive change. In practice, this meant that a just and democratic society could be attained only by temporarily limiting democratic action. With no clear definition of ultimate objectives and means, and given the day-to-day pressures of political life, Nasser and the RCC developed policy through experience and perceived necessity.

The Arab League was formed in 1945 in recognition of the power of collective action. It did not provide much more than a forum for debate during the first decade of its existence, but events centering around Egypt during 1955–1956 highlighted the need for cooperative action and provided an impetus to engage in fresh efforts to attain it. The historic Bandung Conference of 1955 brought together for the first time a large group of third-world leaders who wished to develop a nonaligned status. They expressed their desire to be free of U.S. and Soviet entanglements, the presumption being that the superpowers were unreliable allies who would manipulate third-world countries for their own interests. The superpowers generally discouraged notions of nonalignment and sought to exploit situations that at least would keep the nonaligned countries from being wooed by the other side. Nasser emerged from the conference as a leader of the movement. The United States was particularly alarmed by what it saw as Egypt's drift away from the Western bloc; it reasoned that if the Soviets vaulted the northern tier of U.S. allies—Turkey, Iraq, and Iran—its vital interests would be challenged.

Suez Canal Crisis and the Israeli War (1956)

The United States decided to deny military assistance to Egypt on the grounds that such assistance would promote an arms race in the Middle East (regardless of U.S. arms sales to Israel). This decision provided the impetus for the decade-long Soviet ascendancy in Egypt. Nasser purchased arms from the Soviet bloc in 1954–1955 in return for promised future deliveries of Egyptian cotton. When the United States countered in 1956 by withdrawing proposed financial assistance for the construction of the massive Aswan High Dam, Nasser nationalized the Suez Canal. Egypt and Britain had negotiated an agreement in 1954 that called for the end of British military presence in the canal but allowed Britain to use the military installations in time of crisis. Nasser's nationalization action weakened Britain's position. Nationalization itself was not contrary to international law so long as just compensation was paid to the owners of the property. Military actions took place, however, before issues of compensation could be settled. About three months after the nationalization, Israel invaded and captured the Sinai Peninsula and the Gaza Strip, stopping short of the Suez Canal. Israel claimed it needed to disrupt Egyptian-based guerrilla raids into Israel; that Egypt's blockade of the Straits of Tiran severely compromised its vital interests; and that a three-day-old Egyptian-Jordanian-Syrian defense pact, accompanied by verbal declarations to destroy Israel, constituted an immediate threat to its security. A couple of days after the Israeli invasion, British and French forces attempted to capture the Suez Canal. Their objective failed, a cease-fire was quickly arranged through the United Nations, and all three invaders subsequently quit Egyptian territory. President Eisenhower led vigorous U.S. efforts leading up to the end of the crisis. United Nations troops were placed in Gaza and at the head of the Gulf of Aqaba. The Soviet Union offered to provide financial assistance for the high dam at Aswan. The United States now had more reason than ever to believe that the Soviets were jumping the northern tier. However, Nasser's policy of nonalignment prevented Egypt from joining the Soviet camp.

Nasser emerged from the Suez Canal crisis as an Arab hero, and Egypt's long history of leadership in the Arab world was reaffirmed. Along with the status accorded Nasser was a recognition that Arab unity could help meet major Arab goals, victory over Israel being high on the list. Nasser and the RCC had realized that it was worthwhile to cooperate with other "progressive" Arab states on some matters and with all Arab states against Israel, but Arab unity now began to assume a new meaning. Instead of an end in itself, it came to be seen as a means to Arab victory in Palestine. Events in Syria were to provide Egypt with its first opportunity to exercise leadership under the banner of pan-Arabism.

Syria

In contrast to the relative ethnic and religious homogeneity of Egypt, Syrian society is characterized by considerable heterogeneity. Sunni Muslims constitute most of the population and are in an economically preferred position. Minorities play vital roles, however. Particularly important are numerous relatively prosperous Christian merchants and landholders, a large number of relatively poor Shia, and the Druze and the Alawites. The last-mentioned dominate the senior ranks of the military, partly as a result of the successful preindependence French policy of fragmenting power and the unwillingness of the Sunni elite to encourage their sons to enter the military as a career. Syria spent its first three years of independence, from 1946 to 1949, under ineffective civilian rule; a coup in 1949 ushered in the first of many military governments.

In 1954 the Arab Socialist Resurrection Party, or **Baath**, gained considerable influence in the government—influence that it held through 1958, which figured prominently in the 1958 drive to form a political union with Egypt. Baath ideology combines socialist thought with visions of past Arab unity. The Baathists argue that the unity of the Arab peoples will evolve

naturally as the individual states move along a socialist path. Baathist influence in Syria in the 1950s, however, was far from being uncontested. From the right, Baathists faced the growing hostility of conservative elements that saw Baathist policies of income redistribution and nationalization as simple expropriation. On the left, the relatively strong Communist Party was seeking closer ties with the Soviet Union, a country that the Baathists considered to be imperialist. The threat of a communist takeover of Syria occurred at a time when the Baathists were suffering a loss of prestige and power; the Baathists felt compelled to act forcefully to lessen the chance of Syria falling under Soviet hegemony. Nasser's immense popularity as an anti-imperialist and his growing enchantment with broad socialist principles helped promote the union between Egypt and Syria. Such a union fit neatly into the Baathist ideology of Arab unity, and it offered the Baathists a hope of maintaining their own position in Syria.

The United Arab Republic

The United Arab Republic (UAR) was formed in 1958 after a relatively brief period of negotiation and a hasty working through of the mechanics of formal acceptance in each country. As opposed to Muhammad Ali's expansionist motives in the capture of Ottoman Syria in 1832, Nasser's aims were limited and were more a result of Syrian persuasion than of any enthusiasm within Egypt. Although the union undercut communist influence in Syria, Egypt's growing control of the Syrian bureaucracy and its sometimes heavy-handed implementation of previously legislated but largely ignored income-leveling policies led to Syrian dissatisfaction with the union. Because the Baathists were the driving force behind the union, they suffered a corresponding loss of prestige. The experiment ended when the Syrian army forced the Egyptian high command to leave the country in September 1961. Nasser accepted the decision rather than engage

Syrian forces. A nonsocialist government was formed in Syria, but it was ousted from power in early 1962. A military Baathist group staged a coup in 1963; the Baathists had managed to regain a share of power.

The next round of power shifts resulted from a split within the Baathist party into a moderate faction led by people with political experience in Syria and a progressive faction led by younger men, generally army officers, who represented the minorities. Animosities between the two groups culminated in a 1966 coup in which Alawite officers played a prominent part. In 1970, another coup occurred, and the Alawite position became more firmly established under the leadership of Hafez Al-Assad. He led Syria until his death in 2000. This long continuous rule was accomplished through the establishment of tight organizational control of the armed forces and bureaucracy and suppression of local opposition. Although there is little argument that the rule of Hafez Al-Assad brought a measure of domestic stability and prosperity to Syria, there were times when elements of the population were restive. Especially noteworthy are the actions against civilian uprisings in Aleppo (1980) and Hamma (1982). It was necessary to dispatch regular forces to quell the disturbances, and much blood was spilled.

Syria assumed an increasingly important role as regional powerbroker. Especially important was the role it played in Lebanon, a country that holds immense strategic value to Syria. Besides having troops in Lebanon since the mid-1970s, President Assad positioned Syria as the only national body that could guide, but not direct, affairs in Lebanon.

Syria's role in Lebanon specifically and the Middle East generally was enhanced during and after their participation in the coalition that expelled Iraq from Kuwait. The Syrian economy suffered during the 1980s because of inefficient state-run enterprises; a cumbersome system of economic controls; heavy defense expenditures; an extended severe drought;

and significant cutbacks in Soviet bloc military, economic, and educational aid. During the last years of the 1980s, Syria worked hard at satisfying the major demands of the United States by being more supportive of private enterprise and free trade and more flexible toward convening a peace conference with Israel and dealing with the nettlesome issue of "state-sponsored terrorism." Although they made some progress repairing relations with the United States, they were still in a delicate position until the Iraqi invasion of Kuwait (1990–1991) and the subsequent need of the United States to build an alliance that included important Arab nations. Syria received substantial benefits from joining the alliance. They received tacit permission to rid Lebanon of (Christian) General Aoun, who had rejected a peace formula for Lebanon agreed to by most other participants. Syria's intervention helped bring peace of sorts to Lebanon, while enhancing Syrian power and prestige—some would say hegemony. Syria also received substantial financial aid from the Gulf States. Finally, increased U.S. pressure was put on Israel to join a peace conference.

Jordan, Lebanon, and Iraq

The 1958 formation of the UAR helped trigger significant events in Jordan, Iraq, and Lebanon. Jordan and Iraq were still ruled under separate Hashemite kings who had been installed by the British after World War I. However, the monarch in each country—King Hussein in Jordan and King Faisal II in Iraq—was in considerable difficulty by the time the UAR was formed.

JORDAN.   Jordan was a client state of Britain. It depended on Britain for military assistance and subsidies to prop up its weak economy. The nationalists of Jordan saw British aid in particular and Western actions in general as part of a new imperialism. They viewed Britain's 1954 Suez agreement with Egypt as a dangerous compromise because it allowed for reoccupation whenever British national interests were at stake. In 1955, Britain formed the Baghdad Pact with Turkey, Pakistan, Iraq, and Iran. Jordan was pressed to join, but nationalist reactions led to rioting in January 1956. King Hussein, then 20 years old, responded to the crisis by expelling the British military command from the country, including General Glubb, who had been in Jordan for 25 years. This popular move brought temporary respite to the monarch, but elections in October brought a pro-Nasserist and socialist majority to parliament. The British-French-Israeli invasion of Egypt a month later led the Jordanian government to sever ties with Britain, ending the subsidy. Hussein began to receive financial support from the United States in 1957, but he faced considerable political opposition even though he had suspended the parliament.

When Egypt and Syria formed the UAR, there was much local popular sentiment for Jordan to join. To counter this, and with advice from the United States, Jordan and Iraq hastily established an Arab Union. In July 1958, a revolution in Iraq ended Hashemite rule there and brought an end to the short-lived Arab Union. Hussein then was granted his request for 2,000 British troops to be stationed in Jordan to help save the throne. Military and economic aid also was given by the United States to help the young king. Contrary to the expectations of most informed observers, the dynasty survived not only that scrape but also several other crises through the decades. King Hussein was regarded as a much stronger leader than most observers would have imagined possible only a few years earlier. He made significant initiatives with respect to Israeli/Palestinian issues and partially patched up long-standing contentious relations with Iraq.

LEBANON. The rise of pan-Arab sentiments from 1956 to 1958 also had far-reaching consequences in Lebanon. The National Pact, an understanding rather than a formal document,

went into effect in 1943 and guided Lebanese political life for 30 years. The pact formally recognized the religious and cultural heterogeneity of Lebanon and divided the major governmental posts among the different groups who were to share power. It also stipulated that the Christians would not look to France for support, and that the other Lebanese Arabs would abandon their hopes of affiliation with Syria. The formula for political rule was based on the results of the 1932 census, which indicated that no single group constituted a majority of the population. Of the three largest groups, the Christian Maronites constituted 29 percent; the Sunnis, 21 percent; and the Shia, 18.5 percent. Because the Muslim birthrate exceeded the Christian birthrate, the Sunni–Shia Muslim population gained majority status in the ensuing decades, and the Shia became the largest group. However, because all parties doubted that a new pact could be worked out, the population ratios from 1932 remained in force; no subsequent census was taken in Lebanon. The story of Lebanon during the last half of the twentieth century is a case history for the need for careful analysis. For decades, outsiders marveled over the Lebanese talent for political compromise. It seemed as though they were building a solid nation, but as was to become painfully apparent, many Lebanese held deeper loyalties to their ethnic / religious group.

The government that came to power in 1943 lasted until 1952, when the president, Bishara Al-Khoury, became isolated by a coalition of disaffected politicians of different religious affiliations. The government collapsed when the army refused to follow a presidential order to break up a protest demonstration. This change of government, called the Rosewater Revolution, brought Camille Chamoun to power. The Social National Front, the coalition that brought the government down and elected Chamoun, started to split into factions as soon as its source of unity—opposition to the former government—was removed.

The carefully managed balance of religious forces tended to support the status quo; any fundamental reordering of the system ran the risk of upsetting the balance in unpredictable ways. The Christian leadership had an added incentive to resist change because Christians held more economic power than non-Christian citizens. There were also forces calling for significant changes, however. The Druze leader Kamal Jumblatt supported a package of reforms aimed at liberalizing the political structure and equalizing the income distribution. The Muslim population saw Chamoun leaning toward France as pan-Arab sentiments swelled. When Chamoun did not take a forthright stand against the 1956 attack on Egypt, his image as a pro-European was reinforced. Discontent became more widespread and seemingly more dangerous for the Christian leadership as Muslims were swept into the pan-Arab movement.

By the time of his 1958 visit to Dam... in conjunction with the formation of... Nasser was more than a popu... many people he symbolized the dr... self-determination. Muslims from... flocked to Damascus to hear him sp... event catalyzed Lebanese discontent. called for a new census to rid the country... fictitious Christian majority; some sugge... that Lebanon join Syria in the UAR. Presi... Chamoun responded to this slow but ine... orable wave of discontent by imposing piecemeal controls on political expression.

Lebanon was on the brink of civil war from May to October of 1958. A massive demonstration and general strike took place in May in response to overall conditions; it had been triggered by the assassination of a pan-Arab publicist. The pan-Arab Muslims were joined by a loosely organized group headed by the Druze leader Kamal Jumblatt and several prominent Christian leaders who saw Chamoun's policies leading to failure and a victory for the pan-Arab forces. In mid-July Hashemite rule in Iraq ended by revolution. As King Hussein of Jordan

received British troops, President Chamoun called on the United States to send help under the Eisenhower Doctrine. Troops from the United States landed on the beaches of Lebanon before the end of the month. It is difficult to say what effect these troops had. Their presence probably cooled passions sufficiently to allow the Lebanese to forge a compromise out of an intractable situation. Although Chamoun was replaced by the end of July, fighting along communal lines continued on a sporadic basis. A cabinet that would endure was pieced together in October; it contained equal numbers of Muslims and Christians, partially recognizing the changed demography. U.S. troops left Lebanon by the end of the year.

Although the Lebanese managed to avoid full-scale civil disorder until 1975, maintaining the fragile peace became increasingly di...ult. First, calls for Arab unity and later for ...lamic unity were met with sympathy by ...icant portion of the Arab population, ...the system under direct attack. ...he Western bias of its free market ...t Lebanon out of step with most ...ations and drew corresponding ...l, there were periodic incidents ...anon managed to avoid con-...rael during the 1956, 1967, and ...wars without being completely ostra-...ized by the Arab community of nations. However, border problems with Israel led to the civil war of 1975, the entry of Syrian troops into Lebanon, a deepening schism between the religious communities, and the Israeli invasion of 1982.

The Palestinians who were living in Lebanon did not pose a serious problem for the government until the mid-1960s. Having more than 200,000 Palestinians in loosely supervised camps administered by the United Nations caused much worry, but it was not until the rise in power and popularity of the Palestinian Liberation Organization (PLO) that the situation threatened to get out of hand. As Palestinian forces struck Israel, Lebanon suffered reprisal raids. The Lebanese government was in a difficult position. To suppress the PLO would anger the sizable and passionate anti-Israeli groups in the country and most probably lead to civil war. To allow the Palestinians to operate freely would result in further crippling reprisal raids.

By late 1969, an agreement between the Palestinian and Lebanese leaderships was reached with the help of President Nasser. Essentially it gave the Palestinians the right to rule the refugee camps and to move freely through the country in return for a promise of cooperation with the Lebanese government. After King Hussein of Jordan defeated a PLO army in Jordan in September 1970, the situation started to deteriorate; Lebanon became the only base from which the Palestinians could mount attacks on Israel. During the first few years of the 1970s, attacks on Israel increased, and Israel responded with reprisal attacks.

Civil war broke out in April 1975. A peace was hastily constructed, but it fell apart in August, and fighting raged again. The army of Lebanon intervened during the first few months of 1976, but some units joined the forces favoring the Palestinian position. Things had irrevocably fallen apart.

It would be inaccurate to characterize the Lebanese civil war as divided strictly along communal lines. Although communal divisions were present, many Christian Arabs supported the Palestinian cause. In any case, the Palestinians and their allies gained the upper hand and threatened the largely Christian strongholds. Israel announced that it would decisively counter the present danger. When the Syrian army sent forces to Lebanon to bring some order to the situation, Syrian president Assad was put in an extremely delicate position. The overriding immediate aim of Syrian policy was to defuse an explosive situation. The Palestinians and their supporters had to be held in check, but this meant that the Syrians would have to support the Christians. The irony was made complete by the open secret that the Christians also were supported by Israel.

The conflict, which eventually claimed at least 60,000 lives, gradually subsided as the Syrians stabilized the Christian areas. A coalition of Arab nations originally led by Saudi Arabia hammered out an agreement with the parties and installed an Arab Deterrent Force in Lebanon. The force was predominantly Syrian; it consisted of about 22,000 Syrian troops and about 5,000 from the other participating nations. Lebanon limped through the remainder of the 1970s with a largely powerless government, the Syrian army controlling the countryside, a growing Christian army, better armed private militias, a restive Palestinian population, the economy in shambles, and the future uncertain.

Understanding events in Lebanon always demanded an unusual attention to detail: The coalitions essential for order were based on intricate intersections of many forces. A change in the position of one group necessitated adjustments by all others if political coherence was to be maintained. Although it is apparent that the (1975) civil war started the unraveling of the delicate political web that held the country together for one-third of a century, the aftermath of the 1982 Israeli invasion made it clear that a reconstruction of the old web was impossible. A new order had to be established.

On June 6, 1982, Israeli forces invaded Lebanon. Israel had been ever more frustrated by PLO actions. An assassination attempt on the Israeli ambassador to Britain served as the official reason for the invasion. Israel's stated goal was to establish a 40-kilometer *cordon sanitaire* so as to blunt terrorist attacks on northern Israel. Another primary goal, unstated at the time, was the destruction of the PLO. In short order, Israel destroyed the Syrian air force located in east-central Lebanon and had Syria accept a cease-fire. This allowed Israeli troops to move up the coast directly to Beirut to do battle against PLO forces concentrated in several large "camps." Aerial bombardment of the camps preceded the troops.

Two months later, an arrangement was made whereby PLO forces in and around

Beirut would quit Lebanon. The removal to several different locations was supervised by a multinational force that included a relatively large contingent of U.S. troops. The multinational force left Lebanon by September 10, shortly after the evacuation. In the midst of this, Bashir Gemayel was elected president of Lebanon. He was assassinated one month later (September 14, 1982). Two days later, Israeli forces allowed Christian militia to enter the Palestinian camps of Sabra and Shatila. During the next three days many hundreds of Palestinians were massacred. A few days later Amin Gemayel, brother of Bashir, was chosen to be president, and shortly thereafter the multinational force returned to Beirut. Amin Gemayel remained in office until his term expired in 1988. The presidency remained vacant until 1991.

By 1983 the situation in Lebanon had changed dramatically. Syrian forces remained in large parts of eastern Lebanon, the army of Israel occupied the western part of the country north to Beirut, and the PLO was in disarray as a result of the exit of 8,000 of its troops from Beirut. In addition, the superpowers moved ever closer to direct involvement. The Soviet Union poured a massive amount of military aid into Syria to replace and upgrade the equipment destroyed by Israel. Soviet technical advisers were on hand to assist the Syrians. U.S. Marines, part of the multinational force, were in barracks at the Beirut airport. Their stated task was to assist the regular Lebanese army. Because no significant militia recognized the legitimacy of the government, the goal of U.S. forces lost meaning.

Internal security deteriorated markedly through the next two years. There were numerous battles between the various militias and between the militias and the Israelis. U.S. forces and mountain-entrenched militia exchanged artillery fire. In addition, urban terrorism increased. It became commonplace to have a bomb-laden vehicle explode in this or that quarter of the city, killing scores at a time.

Selected foreigners, especially Americans, were killed or kidnapped. The most spectacular action against Americans, who were generally perceived as allies of Israel or the Christian-dominated government or both, was the bombing of the airport barracks, killing 241 Marines and prompting the United States to leave Lebanon shortly thereafter (February 1984). The bombing seems to have been a direct response to a U.S.-brokered (and subsequently forgotten) peace agreement (May 17, 1983) between Lebanon and Israel.

In late 1983, rejectionist PLO units forced a second evacuation of forces loyal to Yasir Arafat, this time from the northern port city of Tripoli. The rebel units, initially aided by Syria, acted because of their distaste for a conciliatory attitude Arafat was taking toward a proposal to establish a Palestinian "entity associated" with Jordan. Israel finally quit most of Lebanon in mid-1985, although its forces continued to control the southern portions of the country indirectly.

While the Christian leadership was unwilling to yield its position of preeminence, the Shia plurality was "awakened" and found political voice. This awakening of the Lebanese Shia is a complex social phenomenon; however, a few convenient benchmarks can be mentioned. First, the appearance, success, and mysterious disappearance of a prominent and charismatic religious leader, Musa Al-Sadr, served as a focal point. During the 1970s, Al-Sadr organized the Shia of southern Lebanon and guided the formation of AMAL, a political and later military force that bypassed traditional Shia leadership. Second, the success of the Iranian revolution gave inspiration and material aid to many of these self-described "disinherited." Third, the successive dislocations of the local population of southern Lebanon by the Israeli-supported Christian militia, the Palestinians, and the Israeli army in the aftermath of the 1982 invasion increased the pressure to act.

AMAL advocated a Lebanon free of confessional politics, a policy that would strip power from the Christians in favor of the Shia. AMAL was not ideological, in that it did not call for the complete overhaul of the organization of Lebanese society. It merely sought a larger share of the pie in a peaceful Lebanon. It was in substantial, if unstated, agreement with the apparent goal of Israel and Syria. The leadership of AMAL reflected this "reformist" attitude in that it was largely middle class.

AMAL had to contend with another potential champion of the Shia, **Hizbollah** (Party of God). Hizbollah was led largely by clerics, financed by Iran, and strongly ideological in that it advocated the formation of an Islamic republic. It seems that grass-roots loyalties to each group were ephemeral, depending on particular and immediate material conditions rather than deep-seated ideological beliefs. The popularity of Hizbollah has been linked to the desperate state of the Shia of Lebanon and the perceived inability of AMAL to effect a solution. The spectacular rash of hostage taking in the 1980s often was alleged to have direct links to Hizbollah or some associated group.

The formal Lebanese government and its army were powerless as the various communities became more insular and desperate. Each of the major confessional groups, with the exception of the Druze, splintered into smaller factions and retreated into a vicious and fluid communal bloodletting. Lebanon was less a country than a tribal battlefield. Yet it continued to survive.

Amin Gemayel's presidential term was to end in September 1988. Efforts to find a new power-sharing arrangement and a new presidential candidate failed. The United States and Syria (generally in opposition to each other) were involved in the searches (and the vetos). The presidency fell vacant, and Gemayel appointed (Christian) General Aoun to head a caretaker military government. General Aoun refused to recognize a proposed government headed by (Sunni) Prime Minister Hoss, and an Arab League attempt at compromise failed.

General Aoun, supplied with weapons by an Iraq wanting to curb Syrian power, tried to wrest power through the ouster of Syria. Finally, an Arab League–initiated effort resulted in the Taif accords (November 1989). The Lebanese parliament (elected in 1972) was convened in Taif, Saudi Arabia. They agreed to a new power-sharing agreement. The number of seats in the parliament was to be expanded (to 108), equally divided between Christians and Muslims (instead of the old 6:5 Christian majority). The powers of the (Christian) president were trimmed, and the powers of the (Sunni) prime minister were enhanced. The Lebanese "special relationship" with Syria allowed Syrian troops to remain in Lebanon to help the government disarm the various militias. The clear winners were the Lebanese Sunni and the Syrians.

General Aoun rejected the government. He finally was removed from power in October 1990, under the fire of Syrian forces—and at a time when the United States needed Syrian participation in the coalition against Iraq and so gave a diplomatic "green light" to Syrian plans. As the new government assumed more control, and as the various militia were disarmed (of their large weapons), the average Lebanese citizen enjoyed more peace than in the preceding 15 years.

Lebanon remained in a difficult position, however. The Syrians held sway in large parts of the country. The Israelis and their Christian clients occupied the south. The Bekka valley had several thousand Iranian militia. The Palestinians remained. The Lebanese themselves were still seeking common ground. That common ground seemed to be emerging during the 1990s as Lebanon continued its tentative march toward political and economic reconstruction. Still, the Israelis and Syrians continued to cast large shadows over Lebanon even though Israeli forces left Lebanon by 2000. It is highly probable that Lebanon will continue to have foreign forces on its soil until a peace agreement is reached between Syria and Israel.

IRAQ. The July 1958 revolution in Iraq, led by General Abdul Karem Kassim, brought death to many of the country's traditional rulers, including King Faisal II and the veteran prime minister Nuri Al-Said. The coup originally was supported by an assortment of nationalist and leftist groups. The alliance began to unravel, however, soon after the revolution. The Iraqi Baathists urged joining the UAR, but in contrast to the Syrian Baathists, those in Iraq were not sufficiently powerful to force the decision. Rather, Kassim played off the pan-Arab Baathists against the communists. The nationalist group, the National Democrats, gained early favor with Kassim but lost most of their influence within a year. A highly turbulent five years followed; the communists tended to gain in power as a group, but individuals had to remain vigilant because of Kassim's frequent purges of top government leaders. Kassim was killed in a 1963 coup. General Abdel Salam Aref came to power. Aref had been an original member of the 1958 group that destroyed the monarchy and he had been purged in 1958. Aref brought Baathists into the government, but they were purged again within a year. When General Aref died in a helicopter accident in 1966, he was succeeded by his brother, Abdel Rahman Aref, the prime minister at the time, who held office until the 1968 coup, which brought General Ahmed Hassan Al-Bakr to power. Again the Baathists returned to a position of prominence, but it was a Baathist party stripped of its pro-Nasserist fervor. By 1968 the pro-Nasserist and communist elements were widely distrusted in Iraq. Part of the strength of General Hassan Al-Bakr's rule stemmed from the fact that many of his associates came from the same area in Iraq (many came from the same village). When illness caused him to resign in 1979, Saddam Hussein took power. As vice president for a decade, Saddam Hussein assumed an ever-greater proportion of strictly presidential roles for the aged and ailing Al-Bakr.

The decade of the 1970s in Iraq can be characterized as one of economic growth, fueled by petroleum price increases, and political consolidation of power through brutal repression and genuine progress in forging broad-based alliances with some major Kurdish and Shia groups. The 1980s were dominated by the horrifically bloody war with Iran (1981–1988). Iraq was able to continue quick economic growth through loans and grants given by the Arab Gulf states and credits extended by a variety of Western creditors. Baghdad had enough money to have about two million foreigners working in the economy as Iraqi men fought and died at the front. Although generally not mentioned, the war with Iran also had a potentially profound effect on the role of women. During the war, they filled jobs heretofore reserved for men, and after almost a decade of employment in a wide variety of posts, it was clear that the clock could not be turned back.

Iraq entered the 1990s with several pressing economic problems. First, the Gulf States stopped providing financial aid after the war with Iran was concluded, and the debt-servicing requirements of loans contracted during the decade were becoming a heavy burden. Second, petroleum prices were sagging. Third, Iraq's major port, Basra, was going to be closed for the indefinite future because the Shatt Al-Arab, the waterway from the Gulf to Basra, was filled with sunken ships and unexploded ordinance and had silted up. Beginning in the early months of 1990, official Baghdad articulated its grievances. They lost about $1 billion per year for every $1 per barrel decrease in the price of petroleum. They claimed that certain members of OPEC, notably Kuwait, were exceeding their quota, depriving Iraq of badly needed revenue. Kuwait's action was particularly galling because it had arguably the world's highest per capita income and was earning more from interest earnings on foreign investments than petroleum sales. Iraq also charged that Kuwait was cheating Iraq in that they were pumping more petroleum from a shared field than agreed to. Finally, Kuwait would not discuss yielding to Iraq two islands that were vital to protect Umm Qasr, Iraq's only sizable port after the closure of Basra.

Iraq also realized that the winds of change were blowing in the conservative monarchies of Arabia. Kuwaiti elections in April 1990 were roundly criticized as a sham and were effectively boycotted by groups of Kuwaitis calling for significant democratic reform. There did not seem to be a military counterforce in the area that would prevent an Iraqi takeover, and it was clear that most governments were not particularly sympathetic to Kuwait.

On a larger scale, the Iraqi leadership seems to have thought that it was poised to assume the mantle of leadership in the Arab world. One would have expected Iraq to be war weary in early 1990; it was not. Rather, it was aggressively proud that it had survived a war against an enemy with three times its population, that it had experienced economic growth through the period, and that the Kurds and especially the Shia did not heed Iran's calls to revolt. Words, actions, and visual symbols of the upbeat attitude abounded, one of the most startling being a billboard outside of partially reconstructed Babylon showing in profile Nebuchadnezzar and Saddam Hussein.

The invasion was the first in a series of Iraqi miscalculations. The United States quickly responded to a request from Saudi Arabia for protection. Iraq (10 percent) and Kuwait (10 percent) controlled about one-fifth of world petroleum exports. If Saudi Arabia were added, the figure exceeded 40 percent. After two months, the U.S. buildup was revised to include an offensive capability, this after the United States gathered European and Arab (especially Egyptian and Syrian) nations into a coalition against Iraq. On the international diplomatic front, the United Nations passed a series of resolutions against Iraq, and the Arab League condemned the invasion while seeking an all-Arab solution.

Although the Iraqi position became increasingly hopeless, they did not move. Finally, the coalition forces attacked in January 1991, killed many thousands of Iraqis (perhaps more than 100,000), devastated the infrastructure, and liberated Kuwait. Saddam Hussein remained in power as the coalition forces stopped short of a full-scale occupation. In the immediate aftermath of the defeat, the Shia and the Kurds were in open revolt. They were quickly crushed by the remnants of the army. The U.N.'s postwar sanctions against Iraq proved to be troublesome. The Iraqis were not forthcoming with United Nations' inspection teams charged with locating and destroying the nuclear, biological, and chemical military capabilities of Iraq. The sanctions brought suffering and death to thousands of average Iraqis who could not receive medicine, were denied spare parts to repair the water systems, and so on.

The difficulty of governing Iraq has been complicated by the pressure of communalism— the attempts of the various religious and ethnic communities to assert their power on the nation. Although Sunni Muslims are a minority, they have had a far greater hand in ruling the country than their numbers would indicate. The Shia Muslims in the southeast form the largest bloc of citizens, about 60 percent, but they had been largely excluded from power. Official Baghdad viewed with some concern revolutionary Iran's calls to the Iraqi Shia to overthrow the government; their numbers were large and they had some basis for discontent. The other large minority, composing nearly 20 percent of the population, is the Kurds. They are non-Arab Sunni Muslims with their own language and culture, and they have been extremely tenacious in their almost continuous struggle for autonomy against the governments where they are a sizable minority—Iraq, Syria, Turkey, and Iran.

Although the Treaty of Sèvres (1920) called for the establishment of an independent Kurdistan, this plan was not carried out. Kurdish leaders still seek an independent status, and the governments of Iraq, Iran, Syria, and Turkey have had long-standing difficulties trying to assimilate them. The Kurds have numbers large enough (maybe 25 million) to be a constant threat, but they are few enough in any one country that they never have had enough power to break away.

Generally, Kurdish fortunes take dramatic turns during times of regional conflict as the major actors selectively lend support to Kurdish resistance groups in the country of the antagonist. The shah of Iran supported Iraqi Kurds in their battle against Baghdad until a 1975 Iran–Iraq agreement was reached. In the early years of postrevolutionary Iran, the Kurds of Iran were supported by Iraq. By the mid-1980s, Iran had forged an alliance with some Iraqi Kurdish groups. The 1988 Iranian capture of a strategically important city in Iraq brought a particularly brutal Iraqi response: It dropped chemical weapons on the city, reportedly killing 5,000 (Iraqi) Kurdish noncombatants.

Although the fractious Kurdish resistance continued through the decades after World War I, partially as a result of aid delivered by one or more of the regional antagonists, the prospects for an independent Kurdish state remained dim because it was not in the interest of any nation to have the Kurdish movement become too successful. Regional cooperation on the issue started in 1984 when Iraq and Turkey agreed on joint action against Kurdish rebels. In 1987 Turkey and Syria agreed to "cooperate" on Kurdish security questions. After the 1988 cease-fire between Iraq and Iran, the Iraqi government launched a series of major attacks against the Kurds, driving many thousands to refugee camps in Turkey and Iran. On a more positive note, Turkey initiated a substantial economic development program in the Kurdish areas of Turkey in an attempt to woo Kurdish loyalties; however, Kurdish independence movements continued.

After the 1991 war, the prospects of the Kurds continued to follow this decades-long pattern, albeit in a more spectacular fashion.

The Kurds captured the attention of the world for a couple of weeks after the end of the war as television crews recorded poignant scenes of hundreds of thousands of civilian refugees walking through snowy mountain passes to escape the advancing Iraqi army, only to be met by Turkish border guards refusing sanctuary. By contrast, Iran accepted more than one million Iraqi Kurds. Concerted coalition action led to an arrangement where Iraqi troops would stay out of specified Kurdish areas. Major Kurdish leaders entered into negotiations with Baghdad concerning the form and extent of Kurdish autonomy within Iraq. As the talks dragged on without conclusion, the international media became bored, and the Kurds once more were forgotten by the larger world except for an occasional blurb showing their desperate condition. As the world stopped paying attention, the Iraqi military moved against the Kurds, only to be rebuffed by allied forces. The arrangement allowing the Kurds semiautonomous status continued, albeit with two long-standing Kurdish liberation parties and their respective armies dividing the area and engaging in bitter feuds. They did claim a unity of purpose, however, when the United States signaled that it would act to force a "regime change" in Iraq (in 2002). Although the Iraqi Kurds said that they wanted to remain part of Iraq after the regime change, most observers found it incredible that they would so suddenly abandon their goal of a Kurdish state.

IRAN, THE GULF STATES, AND PETROLEUM

A substantial percentage of world petroleum supplies come from the Gulf countries through the Straits of Hormuz or by pipelines in the Middle East. Because the industrial power of the West and Japan depends on Gulf petroleum exports, any threatened long-term disruption of supplies from the area invites intervention from the great powers and runs the risk of starting a global conflict.

The Iran–Iraq war was a central concern through the 1980s. As each of the antagonists attempted to disrupt the petroleum-exporting capabilities of the other, the remaining Gulf nations and the great powers nervously stood by. The stakes were raised in 1987 when the United States responded to a Kuwaiti request for protection of vessels from Iranian attack by "reflagging"—having ships sail under the U.S. flag—and offering safe passage to these tankers plying the Gulf. Within a year there were several limited engagements between U.S. and Iranian naval units. There also were a couple of disastrous mistakes, including an Iraqi air attack against a U.S. Navy vessel, killing 37 personnel, and a U.S. ship–based missile attack on an Iranian civilian airliner that killed 290 people.

Iraq's invasion of Kuwait brought renewed concerns over Gulf shipping safety. Environmental concerns became much more important during this episode. Massive amounts of petroleum were dumped into the Gulf during the conflict. Besides potentially disastrous effects on the fragile environment of the shallow Gulf, the slicks for a time threatened to foul desalination plants in Saudi Arabia and ruin significant fisheries.

Iranian Revolution

It is a somber irony that the Gulf's economic growth, which was made possible by the West's need for petroleum, generated instability. The checks and balances that the shah of Iran employed to discourage any gathering of power outside of his control became ineffective with economic growth. By the mid-1970s, the modified traditional Persian system of creating insecurity among the potentially powerful had broken down. The shah, especially through SAVAK, the large secret police organization, responded by applying more overtly repressive measures. It was as if the shah had traded his rapier for a meat axe. Much has been written about the heavy-handed role of SAVAK—originally trained

and supervised by the Central Intelligence Agency (CIA) of the United States and Mossad of Israel—and how popular reactions against it helped bring the downfall of the Pahlevi dynasty. However, it is important to understand why those in power thought that these actions were necessary. As the old system of controls was breaking down under the weight of its own complexity, the shah was faced with the choice of accepting a loss of power or redoubling his efforts to stamp out opposition. He chose the latter course and lost the gamble.

The apparent inability of the U.S. government to interpret the danger signals emanating from Iran during the shah's decline was dramatically illustrated when President Carter toasted the shah on New Year's Eve, 1977, with the remark that Iran was "an island of stability." The view from the palace was not the same, however, as the one from the streets of Tehran. By New Year's Eve, 1978, the U.S. government urged all of its citizens in Iran (approximately 40,000) to depart. The shah left Iran for a "vacation" on January 16, 1979. He died in an Egyptian military hospital a year and a half later, never having returned.

The young politically alienated urban technocrats joined the antigovernment movement in a manner surprisingly similar to the 1890–1892 tobacco riots. Again, the clergy led the revolt. They had two deep sources of disagreement with the shah. First, the policies of "modernization" introduced by the shah were unabashedly secular in design. Second, some policies (e.g., land reform) were designed partly to woo peasant support away from the religious authorities and over to the shah. Ayatollah Ruhollah Khomeini had been in exile in Iraq from 1963 until 1978, when he was expelled as part of the Iraqi–Iranian attempts to patch up their contentious relations. Iraq also had its own reasons for wanting the powerful leader out of the country. Shia Muslims constitute a majority of the Iraqi population and are concentrated in the southeast of Iraq. The Kurds, who are Sunni Muslims, but not Arabs, account for about 20 percent of the population and live in the north. The Sunni Arabs of central Iraq have controlled the government and have generally been in an economically advantageous position. The government of Iraq preferred not to harbor someone of Khomeini's stature and ideology. The banishment of Ayatollah Khomeini from Iraq did not lessen his influence against the shah. As the leaders of the tobacco riots used the telegraph to coordinate their actions, so Ayatollah Khomeini directed the Iranian revolution by telephone from Paris, until his return to Iran on February 1, 1979. The streets of Tehran ran with blood during 1978 as demonstrations, many of them peaceful, were repeatedly met with brutal force. By December 1978, it was apparent to most observers that the shah's time was limited.

Iranian Revolutionary Government

Khomeini's return to Iran brought a massive outpouring of popular approval. The last government appointed by the shah before he left Iran fell on February 11, 1979. Revolutionary Iran appointed a government headed by Mehdi Bazargan, but the civilian government was subject to the dictates of the Revolutionary Council headed by Ayatollah Khomeini and found it extremely difficult to conduct day-to-day business. Prime Minister Bazargan tendered his resignation several times before the Revolutionary Council accepted it (November 6). The Revolutionary Council ruled until the outlines of a new constitution could be drawn and a new president elected. Abolhassan Bani-Sadr was elected president in February 1980, and the new parliament, the Majlis, was elected in May 1980. The first Majlis of the new republic was dominated by the Islamic Republican Party—a group led by many of the country's most important religious leaders. The president, although closely aligned with this group when both were in opposition to the rule of the shah, was generally considered to have a more secular orientation than the clergy.

Although the particular twists and turns of events in postrevolutionary Iran were impossible to predict, the revolution followed a familiar pattern in that when the glue of common discontent toward the policies of the shah was removed, the fundamental differences between the various opposition groups surfaced. The enduring lessons are that successful revolutions are those that hold the important factions together after the old government has been removed, and that success or failure must be measured in terms of what has happened to the country decades after the seizure of political power.

Although the transition from one form of government to another is always problematic, Iran faced an unusual set of circumstances. First, it was attempting to establish an Islamic republic in a form apparently quite different from other governments adopting that label. A particularly difficult initial point involved the conflicts of authority between the president and the religious leaders. During the early days of Bani-Sadr's presidency, Ayatollah Khomeini directed the government to reverse its decisions on several occasions. It would have been difficult for the government even in the easiest of circumstances to decide on the limits of religious authority in matters not strictly religious, but the charismatic power of Khomeini was such that the issue was never in doubt. The government was forced to accede to his directives.

The crisis of authority deepened throughout the presidency of Bani-Sadr. In early June 1981, Ayatollah Khomeini stripped the president of his role as commander of the armed forces. The Majlis then declared Bani-Sadr politically incompetent, clearing the way for Ayatollah Khomeini to dismiss him as president on June 22. The role of president was to be filled by a three-person commission until a new president was elected. The three individuals, all members of the Islamic Republican Party, were the chief justice, the speaker of the Majlis, and the prime minister. Violence between the country's various political factions had been increasing in the months preceding the ouster of Bani-Sadr. The strife intensified, culminating in an explosion in Islamic Republican Party headquarters in Tehran, killing 74, including the chief justice (Ayatollah Beheshti), several cabinet ministers and subministers, 20 members of the Majlis, and other party leaders. The course of the Iranian revolution became highly problematic: Bani-Sadr was in hiding and being sought by the government, the political leadership was in disarray, and groups again were taking to the streets. The crisis of political authority was only one of the major issues faced by the new government. There was considerable diversity of opinion concerning the economic role of the state, the proper extent of limitations to be placed on private enterprise, and the ideologically correct nature of contracts.

The revolutionary government survived the near chaos of these years through a consolidation of formal political power by the clerics, systematic suppression of some important opposition forces such as the Tudeh (communist) Party, and the reestablishment of a functioning bureaucracy. The new government also had pressing international problems, especially with respect to the United States. It was commonly believed that the U.S. CIA had brought the shah back to power in 1952. Would the United States attempt to do it again? The leaders of the revolution knew that they were in a stronger position than the 1952 nationalists, but they also knew that thousands of SAVAK and military personnel loyal to the shah would take up arms at the bidding of the United States. Although the U.S. government tried to distance itself from the shah, its messages to Iran were mixed and were received with skepticism. As a positive step, the United States announced on October 5, 1979, that it would resume the shipment of some military replacement parts to Iran. Most of Iran's immense arsenal of military hardware had come from the United States, and

the United States had been supplying parts roughly on an "as needed" basis. Without an adequate supply of spare parts, Iranian military capability would be at a disadvantage. The promised parts were not shipped, however, because of events during the next month.

On October 22, 1979, the deposed shah entered the United States to receive medical treatment for cancer. The U.S. government had been told repeatedly that the entry of the shah into the United States would only inflame Iranian passions, increase suspicions about the United States, and endanger U.S. citizens still in Iran. On November 4, the U.S. Embassy in Tehran was occupied by individuals identified only as "students." About 60 embassy personnel were taken as hostages. In the following weeks, many furious words were hurled about without much action. However, some points seemed clear: Those holding the hostages were following the dictates of Ayatollah Khomeini, and the United States would refuse to meet Iranian demands to return the shah to Iran.

The U.S. government worked to bring diplomatic sanctions against Iran in the United Nations; it also imposed economic sanctions of its own and encouraged its allies to do the same. It used intermediaries not generally thought of as being in its camp to try to negotiate the release of the hostages. These U.S. actions did little to cool Iranian hostility. It is questionable, however, whether a conciliatory tone would have made a difference because Iran was full of conflict and contradiction. In April 1980, President Carter ordered military units to attempt a rescue of the hostages, but the mission was aborted when several problems made it impossible for the attack force to advance beyond a desert landing point south of Tehran. Given the apparent high odds against success, the fact that it was attempted at all indicates the president's overpowering need to end the crisis. The United States was forced to take a more patient stance. The hostages were released in January 1981. But the war with Iraq had started a couple of months earlier.

Iraq–Iran War: 1980–1988

The new republic faced the nettlesome problem of dealing with the minorities in Iran. The Kurds of the north, a Sunni group, had begun to agitate for independence. The Iraqi government supported Iranian Kurds in their efforts, just as the shah had supported Iraqi Kurds before a 1975 agreement with Baghdad. The government also faced challenges from the Baluchis of the southeast and the Azerbaijanis of the northwest. For its part, Iranian radio was exhorting the Iraqi Shia to overthrow their government. Other Gulf countries, all with sizable Shia populations, were understandably nervous. Even Saudi Arabia had cause for worry; its relatively small Shia population was located in the petroleum-rich northeast and was receiving the same message that was being sent to its Iraqi counterparts.

Iraq revoked its 1975 agreement with Iran that had ended Iranian support of the Kurds in Iraq in return for the settlement of a long-disputed border in the Gulf area in Iran's favor. The agreement had set the border between the two countries along the Shatt Al-Arab thalweg, Iraq's only major route to the Gulf and the only sea route for imports and exports from their port city of Basra. Iraq apparently wanted to regain control of the entire waterway—the pre-1975 (disputed) convention gave Iraq rights of the Shatt Al-Arab to the Iranian shore. The initial Iraqi assaults were verbal and attempted to foment trouble among the substantial Arab population in Iran's petroleum-rich Khuzistan area. Open warfare broke out on September 22, 1980. Iraq scored initial victories by taking some Iranian territory along the Shatt Al-Arab and by damaging the important port and refinery city of Abadan. Iran responded by bombing Baghdad several times and by making a considerable effort to hold Abadan.

The war droned on. There were times of relative quiet, furious offensives, deliberate bombings of civilians, the use of poison gas (by Iraq), and attempts to widen the war. There was little movement toward resolution, militarily or diplomatically. Official Tehran said several times that there could not be peace as long as the government of Saddam Hussein held power. The war may have strengthened the power of the Iraqi government in ways it did not perceive when it initiated the conflict. The government found it worthwhile to work to placate the country's Shia majority to counter messages from Iran calling for a Shia revolt. Also, the receipt of Gulf financial aid and the use of Jordanian transport routes served to strengthen ties with a couple of important Arab neighbors. Finally, at the close of 1984 the United States resumed diplomatic relations with Iraq, ending a 17-year break. The benefit to Iran was nil except for the possible internal unity gained from having such an active external threat.

A cease-fire was arranged in mid-1988. Earlier in the year, each side had terrorized the population of the enemy's capital city by lobbing missiles into civilian areas—a phase of the conflict dubbed "the War of the Cities." Then Iraq scored a series of major battlefield victories. Both countries were war weary.

The fact that Iran accepted a cease-fire pointed to changes in the course of the revolution. Early in the conflict, Iranian leaders proclaimed that a theological imperative directed their efforts; Iran would not yield until the "infidel" government in Baghdad fell. The world stood by nervously during Iran's "moment of enthusiasm" in the immediate post-coup years. Calls for the export of the revolution gave pause to conservative governments of the area. Although the cease-fire did not quiet all fears, it did signal that revolutionary fervor was lagging in an Iran increasingly ready to be guided in its internal and international affairs with the cold calculations of the pragmatist rather than the passion of the ideologue.

After Khomeini's death in 1989, the pragmatists strengthened their position. Khomeini was succeeded in the faqih-ship by Hojatoislami Ali Khamenei, a prominent cleric and ally of speaker Rafsanjani, the leader of the pragmatists. Rafsanjani was elected to an enhanced presidency later in 1989. Iran stood aloof from the Iraq–Kuwait affair in 1990–1991 and apparently was instrumental in the piecemeal freeing of all of the U.S. hostages held in Lebanon—the last being released in December 1991.

The subsequent elevation of title of Hojatoislami Ali Khamenei to Grand Ayatollah in 1991 signaled another vector of the power of the "pragmatists." Khamenei's new title met with substantial displeasure by more than 100 members of the Majlis. They stated that Khamenei did not have the theological background to assume the role of successor to Ayatollah Khomeini. The semiofficial conservative press summarily dismissed the complaints. It is interesting that they did not champion Khomeini's son, Ahmad, as a worthy alternative. This further hints that the revolution was becoming institutionalized, and that dynastic succession was not to be the rule. Elections to the Majlis in 1992 further strengthened the hand of the pragmatists. However, this trend toward increasing pragmatism moved slowly thereafter. One important consequence of the lack of a clear vision of the correct path to be taken was that the economy continued to perform poorly. This led to further recriminations and more policy stasis. Iran was not fully accepted in the international community and received differentially harsher treatment by the United States. Closer to home, the Gulf States continued to view Iran as a potential source of difficulty.

Saudi Arabia's Political Stability

On November 20, 1979, the day after "extremists," whose motivations initially were unclear to the outside world, took over the Grand Mosque in Mecca, the United States came under attack in widely scattered parts of the Islamic world. The attacks seem to have been sparked by a radio broadcast in which Khomeini implicated the United States in the Grand Mosque seizure. U.S. embassies were attacked in Calcutta, Dacca, Istanbul, Manila, Rawalpindi, and Lahore. The U.S. embassy in Islamabad, Pakistan, was burned down; two Americans were killed, and several others narrowly escaped death after waiting hours for the local authorities to intervene.

Until the attack on the Grand Mosque, Saudi Arabia's political stability had been shaken only slightly. When King Faisal was murdered by a nephew in 1975, there was some speculation that it was a political act, but the assassin seems to have been mentally unstable. Faisal was succeeded in orderly fashion by King Khalid. Partially because of his weak health, he was to yield many major state responsibilities to Prince Fahd. Fahd assumed the throne on the death of Khalid (1982). Because Saudi Arabia's massive petroleum output and low population had allowed it to accumulate enormous financial reserves, the West was particularly fearful of political instability in Saudi Arabia. Its petroleum was essential, and it could severely disrupt world financial markets by moving its reserves from country to country. The monarchy was politically cautious and conservative, however, and the Western countries viewed it as a moderate, "sensible" nation. Likewise, Saudi Arabia's adherence to strict Islamic ideals blunted criticisms of its monarchical form of government by most "progressive" Arab nations. Given this position and the desire to assume a greater leadership role in the Arab world, the Saudis promoted and developed a reputation as conciliators.

Saudi Arabia's public image of tranquility and stability concealed as much as it revealed. Saudi society was undergoing massive and rapid change. Its per capita income was one of the highest in the world, it was one of the world's leading financial powers, and it had begun countless expensive construction projects. Only a few decades earlier, central

Arabia had been one of the poorest areas of the world. Social change has not yet occurred on as dramatic a scale as the change in income. However, the tens of thousands of Saudis who have studied in the United States and Britain are not likely to completely accept their country's traditional political culture, nor its Islamic austerities. The seizure of the Grand Mosque in Mecca may have been an isolated event, but it is possible that such disturbances will begin to occur more regularly as the popular desire for more political participation increases.

The Iraqi invasion of Kuwait and the military action that followed shook Saudi Arabia to its core. It was clear that the Saudi military could not stop Iraq if Iraq's ultimate intentions were to overrun them. The first question they had to answer was, Should we take the chance that they will not cross the border? No, they decided. Then they had to determine the proper response. Although the Arab world generally opposed the invasion, many called for an "Arab solution" to the problem. But they were not ready to defend Saudi Arabia—at least not quickly—and time was not on the Saudi side. They knew that the West thought well of them, if for no other reason than that they supplied vital petroleum on a regular basis. Requesting the West, specifically the United States, to intervene would run counter to a host of important considerations. The Arab governments would not view Western intervention favorably; worldwide Muslim sentiment would not favor the keepers of the holy places of Mecca and Medina allowing infidels on their soil; and the influx of Western forces could upset the delicate interplay between religious austerity and material wealth. In the end, the Saudis had more than half a million allied forces in their country. Although they weathered the crisis, it is difficult to imagine that Saudi Arabians were not changed in the process. One such manifestation was the 1992 announcement of the intent to form a consultative assembly (appointed).

The collapse of petroleum prices in the mid-1980s gave rise to a different set of tensions faced by the Saudi government. In the early 1980s, Saudi Arabia earned more than $100 billion per year through petroleum sales. This figure fell to less than $20 billion by the last years of the decade. At first the government ran deficits financed from previous earnings; then it was forced into the politically unpopular act of slashing expenditures.

Another potential cause of instability concerned the "awakening of the Shia." In December 1981, Bahrain authorities arrested and subsequently convicted 73 individuals for plotting a coup. Bahrain charged that the coup was to be part of a larger effort, one that was to bring the fall of Saudi Arabia, and that the plotters had direct ties with Iran. During the Hajj of 1987, Saudi authorities clashed with demonstrating Iranian pilgrims in Mecca. More than 400 Iranians were killed. Shortly thereafter, the Saudi embassy in Tehran was overrun by Iranians. Relations between the two countries reached an all-time low, although diplomatic relations were quickly restored.

The Shia population in the Gulf is substantial. The particulars of the population are unknown, which tend to give it potential influence beyond that predicted simply by the strength of numbers. Shia in Saudi Arabia represent less than 10 percent of the population, but are concentrated in the petroleum-rich northeastern part of the country. The Shia in Oman represent less than 5 percent of the population, but they are concentrated in specific businesses. The Shia of Bahrain are the poorest and least educated of that country. Many of these Shia have ethnic ties to Iran. The governments of the Gulf countries, all ruled by Sunni elites, have to be especially sensitive to this issue.

Yemen

North and South Yemen effected a surprisingly quick and smooth unification ratified in May 1990. As opposed to several ill-fated attempts at unification in the Arab world, there was a strong logic to this move. During the prior several decades, North Yemen (actually, largely to the east of South Yemen) was evolving away from its 1,000-year-old theocratic and xenophobic state. Meanwhile, South Yemen was losing its radical zeal.

The Peoples Democratic Republic of Yemen, generally called South Yemen, attained independence in 1967 when the British pulled out of Aden. In 1970 it became a Marxist state. As the only long-standing nonconservative government in the area, South Yemen was involved in many political battles in the Arabian Peninsula. It received aid from the Soviet Union, East Germany, and China. Although any state in this volatile region must be taken seriously, it was tempting to regard South Yemen as the neighborhood's bad boy. It was continually in somebody else's backyard, but when dealt with sternly was dissuaded from doing much damage. However, this analogy does not illustrate its potential importance in the region (Ethiopia, Djibouti, and Somalia are all in the strategically important Horn of Africa across the Gulf of Aden), its past involvement with rebels in Oman, and its support of Iraq during the Iraq–Kuwait war. There were several impulses for unification, including a civil war in South Yemen in 1986, the collapse of the Soviet bloc, and the discovery of significant petroleum reserves in both countries.

Gulf Cooperation Council

The Gulf Cooperation Council (GCC) was formed in 1981 by the conservative Gulf States—Saudi Arabia, Kuwait, Bahrain, Qatar, the United Arab Emirates, and Oman—partially in response to the perceived threat from revolutionary Iran and partially in recognition of some of the more obvious economies of scale to be garnered through cooperation. The council proceeded slowly with respect to the establishment of joint security arrangements. The GCC made more progress on the economic front. Customs duties were eliminated on a wide range of products manufactured or grown in the member countries, and skilled labor was allowed freedom to take employment in any of the states.

The GCC also tried to build a common educational system. The most ambitious of these was the establishment of the campus for the Gulf University in Bahrain. The campus has no students, however. The squeeze on petroleum-based budgets in the late 1980s directly led to a forced fiscal austerity of the GCC.

Although the accomplishments of the GCC have been modest, it remains an important body in that it has provided a forum for collective political and economic ventures. This became obvious during the 1991 threat from Iraq. Cooperation and coordination were much smoother than they otherwise would have been. Formidable problems remain, however; for example, a customs union first proposed to come to fruition around 2000 was formally delayed several years as the deadline approached.

ISRAEL

The Jews of Palestine were not able to bask in the glory of victory after the state of Israel was formed in 1948. Their turbulent history has been dominated by war and the threat of war. It was not until President Anwar Sadat of Egypt set foot on Israeli soil in November 1977 that any Arab leader officially recognized that Israel was a permanent entity in the Middle East. Even then, President Sadat's act isolated Egypt in the Arab world for several years.

More than most nations of the world, much of Israel's daily life is directly, consciously, and openly affected by international events. Virtually every long-time citizen of Israel has known someone killed in war. The Israeli "siege mentality" has been born of experience and is firmly based in reality. Israel has been under siege since its inception. It has heard numerous calls for its destruction over the years, it has lost many of its sons and daughters in military action, and it has witnessed its enemies' tremendous growth in financial power and military capability. This is not to say that all Israelis agree on how to resolve Israel's almost continual crisis. On the contrary, Israeli public opinion on most vital issues reflects the considerable heterogeneity of Israeli society.

Political Setting

Israel's prime minister is the de facto head of government: The position of president is largely ceremonial. Until 1996, the prime minister was chosen from the members of parliament, the Knesset, and instructed to put together a cabinet; since then, the prime minister is directly elected. Members of the Knesset are elected through countrywide proportional representation. The voters choose between "lists," each list representing a political party or coalition of parties. The 120 Knesset seats are divided between the lists according to the percentage of the national vote garnered; a list gaining 10 percent of the vote receives 12 seats. Any single list must gain a minimum of 2 percent of the vote to be eligible for a seat. If the government is to function effectively, it must maintain the support of a legislative majority on at least the key issues of the day. This point is essential for an understanding of Israeli politics; coalition politics has dominated the system because no single party has ever gained a clear legislative majority.

Although Israeli citizens have been presented with a wide range of lists in each general election, they generally select from three prominent groups: the labor-dominated left-center, the right-center, and the religious parties. The Labor list formed the governments from 1949 to 1977. The right-center put together the ninth and tenth Knessets (1977 to 1984). The religious parties generally have gained 10 to 20 percent of the vote and have been the group that the other two have turned to in order to form a legislative majority. They have had an influence beyond their voting strength. The fact

that Israel defines itself as a Jewish state gives the message of the religious parties a particularly strong resonance among the population.

The Labor list itself is a coalition of several distinct parties that unite for election purposes. Generally, these parties have espoused a socialist ideal in domestic affairs. The most powerful Labor group, the Mapai, held the loyalties of many Israelis through its control of the Histradut, the pervasive Labor organization. Because the Mapai drew its leadership primarily from the Histradut, it has become identified by many as the group that in the past provided temporary relief to immigrants, helped them secure housing, and gave them employment. Other major Labor groups were more strident in their socialism, more willing to subsume nationalist aspirations and identify with the working classes of all nationalities. The Labor parties were able to garner a plurality of Knesset seats until 1977; they constructed their legislative majority by taking the religious parties into the fold. The religious parties, as the name suggests, are concerned primarily with religious issues— for example, the notion that Israeli Jews have the right to settle in all biblical lands regardless of existing political boundaries.

The Labor alliance started to lose power during the 1960s, partially and ironically because of its past success. Because it could not manage to win a majority of Knesset seats, and because the Labor bloc itself was an amalgam of parties and viewpoints, it had to broaden its political position to accommodate more of the electorate. In so doing, the political focus became blurred, and dissension within the bloc grew. A host of other factors contributed to its inability to gain a majority, including the changing profile of the voters (rural to urban, older to younger) and voter disillusion with incumbents who had failed to ensure peace and security.

The performance of governments based on coalitions is always problematic. The Labor bloc was large enough to prevent a quick succession of governments, but it had to depend on other parties and found it difficult to move away from the status quo. The status quo, however, meant insecure national borders and a large military budget.

Although there had been defections of important figures from Mapai during the 1960s, it was only after the 1973 war that the coalition began to face serious challenges to its premier position. The war resulted in heavy Israeli casualties, no military victory, and a psychological shock. In June 1974, the government of Prime Minister Golda Meir was forced to step down in favor of another set of Labor bloc leaders headed by Itzhak Rabin. However, the new government also faced a rocky road. Israel was becoming more and more isolated internationally, the military budget grew larger and more burdensome, and the economy faced high rates of inflation. Because the Rabin government was forced to adopt the amorphous policies of its predecessors, it had difficulty in resolving vital issues. Finally, in 1977, a series of financial scandals involving Rabin and some cabinet ministers eliminated the government's remaining strength.

The Democratic Movement for Change (DMC) emerged as an important new coalition party. It was a single-issue party that advocated changing Israeli electoral laws to rid the Knesset of debilitating factionalism. The leadership of the DMC was drawn from a wide ideological spectrum, although much of the platform resembled that of the Labor bloc. Their apparent aim was to gain enough seats in the Knesset to help form a majority in return for a promise of electoral reform. The results of the election dashed their hopes.

The Labor alignment had its number of Knesset seats reduced from 51 in 1973 to 32 in 1977. Because the National Religious Party, holding 12 seats in 1977, no longer desired to unite with the Labor alignment, it proved impossible for the alignment and the DMC (15 seats), along with the other smaller parties, to form a majority in the Knesset. The big winner in the 1977 elections was the Likud bloc, which emerged with a plurality of 43 seats. After a month of negotiations, a government was formed (June 1977) that aligned the Likud bloc with two religious parties (and later with the DMC, which reserved the right to disagree on questions including religion and occupied territories). Menachem Begin, the leader of Likud, became the new prime minister. The new government was conservative in domestic issues and aggressive in foreign policy: It advocated a selective dismantling of socialist policies in favor of private enterprise and the settlement of Israelis on land occupied since the 1967 war. Prime Minister Begin referred to the occupied area as being "liberated." As the new government became established, it remained unclear whether the basic shift away from Labor bloc positions would continue. Analysis of the 1977 election indicated that Israelis voted against the Labor alignment rather than for the Likud coalition.

The Likud coalition fell apart in early 1981. The results of the June 30, 1981, election gave Labor and Likud 49 seats each. The smaller parties generally lost seats but gained in bargaining power because Labor and Likud eagerly sought their favor in hope of forming the needed 61-seat majority. Likud finally patched together a fragile coalition, and Begin continued as prime minister. The coalition fell apart in two and a half years, and another election was held in July 1984. Israel was in the midst of a particularly difficult set of circumstances. Especially important were the heavy psychological, financial, and human costs exacted by continued Israeli presence in Lebanon, which they had invaded in 1982. Contributing factors included domestic and international antagonisms generated by the accelerated pace of settlement in the West Bank and an unusually harsh economic climate.

Prime Minister Begin dropped out of political life well before the election—he did not even campaign for or publicly endorse Likud candidates. Election results again yielded a stalemate (44 seats for Labor, 41 for Likud).

After prolonged negotiations, Likud and Labor joined forces to form a "National Unity Government." The Labor leader (Shimon Peres) was prime minister for the first two years, and the new Likud leader (Yitzhak Shamir) first filled the post of foreign minister and then switched with Peres. If nothing else, this unique arrangement of power sharing indicated the impossibility of either party forming a coalition government by bringing the increasingly contentious smaller parties into its fold. Analyses of the election indicated that there was a hardening of attitudes among the voters, and that voting by ethnic blocs increased (Ashkenazi to Labor; Oriental to Likud).

The 1988 elections yielded the same sort of stalemate. However, Labor (39) and Likud (40) won fewer seats than in the previous election. The religious parties gained seats, but Labor and Likud were unwilling to adopt certain religious party issues to form a coalition. Labor and Likud again formed a unity government. During the campaign both blocs had agreed that this cumbersome power sharing was to be avoided. Israel needed decisive action on several pressing issues, and a unity government essentially meant that any such action would be blocked by one of the blocs. The post-election realities dictated another round of power sharing, however. The debilitating results of an electoral system based on proportional representation were not ignored, and electoral reform became a serious issue again.

The coalition fell apart in March 1990, and a new government was formed in June. Labor failed to form a new government; Likud gathered the needed majority by hammering out an agreement with the religious and right-wing parties. In the interim, there was a rally of 100,000 in Tel Aviv calling for electoral reform. The call went unheeded, however.

The government fell apart again in January 1992, when two religious parties bolted from Likud. Israel had suffered through a tough year during 1991. It was forced to sit on the sidelines during the Gulf War, failed to settle

Soviet immigrants in a coherent fashion, was rebuffed by the United States when it requested a $10 billion loan guarantee to aid in the process, initiated a socially disruptive furious pace of settlement on the West Bank, and was pressured into the beginnings of a peace conference. If nothing else, the Israeli political process points to the dangers of having an electoral system that rewards fringe parties in a setting of social heterogeneity when core values are at stake.

Likud suffered a stunning defeat in the June 1992 election, winning only 32 seats. Labor won 44 seats, and, more important, the liberal lists gained enough seats to allow Labor to form a coalition with them without yielding to the demands of the ultranationalist and religious parties. Labor prime minister Rabin acted quickly to reinvigorate the peace process that had stalled under the Likud government.

Social Setting

The coming to power of a non-Labor government in 1977 was in many ways the political expression of the social change that had been occurring since 1948. The composition of the Israeli population in 1950 was markedly different from what it was two years earlier. Estimates (open to some question) made by the United Nations team that drew up the 1947 partition plan showed a total population of 1.8 million, two-thirds being Arabs. By the end of 1949, the Arab population had decreased to about 160,000 and represented one-eighth of the total; the Jewish population had roughly doubled to 1.2 million. The Arabs became a minority. Jewish immigration continued to be heavy through 1952. Thereafter, natural rates of increase and immigration contributed equally to the population growth. By 1990 the population of Israel was five million, 85 percent being Jewish. Also, by 1990, Israel was receiving large numbers of Jews emigrating from the Soviet Union (owing to the general Soviet relaxation of restrictions). Israeli authorities were quick to embrace these people, but they faced the daunting prospect of financing the absorption of one million new citizens within a couple of years.

Israeli society is a complex amalgam that nevertheless invites categorization and oversimplification. Perhaps it is easiest to begin with a three-way ethnic breakdown: European Jews, Oriental Jews, and Arabs. The European (**Ashkenazi**) group also includes Jews who immigrated to Israel from North and South America and South Africa, but the major distinguishing factor is the common parental or cultural lineage with European Jewry. Most Jews who came to Palestine during the five preindependence waves of immigration were from Europe; the first four were primarily from Russia and Eastern Europe; the fifth wave included a considerable number of Jews fleeing the Holocaust. The leaders who emerged from the first four waves set the ideological tone for the young state, a blend of socialism and Zionism that emphasized the virtues of working the soil. The fifth wave came to Palestine largely out of desperation. These people faced death in Nazi Germany and had been denied adequate refuge in the Allied countries. Their motivation was survival, not the socialist-Zionist pioneering spirit that had guided former immigrants. Although their impact on Israeli society should not be overemphasized, many of these immigrants were urban, middle class, skilled, and more closely in touch with Western European culture than previous immigrants from Eastern Europe and Russia. Their numbers were large, and their votes had to be counted. Nevertheless, immigrants of the first four waves headed every government save one—that of Rabin, a Sabra (native-born Israeli). The postindependence wave of Eastern European immigration was largely over by 1952.

In the first few years after independence, many Jews from Asia and Africa immigrated as Arab governments acted in increasingly unfriendly ways and as local populations sometimes vented their anger at Israel toward these people, who by and large had nothing to do with Israel. During the first 25 years of independence, Israel absorbed three-quarters of a million of these immigrants, the largest group, 255,000, coming from Morocco. The effect on the social structure of Israel has been profound. Jews of African-Asian origin, called imprecisely either **Sephardic** or Oriental Jews, came to Israel to escape hostility and did not share the Western values and orientations of the Ashkenazi Jews. Their shared Jewishness was all that bonded them with their fellow Israelis. Although there are notable exceptions, the Oriental Jews of Israel generally have a substantially lower than average per capita income, have had less education, hold less significant government posts, have less desirable housing, and are viewed in a disparaging light by many of their fellow citizens. They are the soft underbelly of the Jewish population of Israel. The most notable exceptions to these generalizations are the Sephardic Jews who were longtime residents of Palestine. The Sephardic Jews of Palestine were totally conversant with local Arab culture and had an articulated social structure in place well before the Zionist movement started. This small Sephardic elite tended to view all Jewish immigrants with some disdain.

Although many Sephardic Jews found government posts under the British mandate, neither they nor the Oriental Jews of more recent arrival shared fully in Israeli political life after independence. Their numbers swelled during the first decade of statehood until they became the Jewish majority by the 1970s, and the Ashkenazi-controlled major political parties had to woo their votes. The scene was complicated by the increase in numbers of another identifiable Jewish group, one that cut across Ashkenazi and Oriental distinctions: Sabras, or native-born Israelis. Although generally associated with their parents' group and marrying within that group, Sabras started to form another social force and constituted more than half the Jews in Israel by 1977, most of them of

European parentage. The immigration of Soviet Jews complicated the mix further.

If the Oriental Jews are the underside of Israeli Jewish society, many Arabs are in the position of belonging to a different culture while being citizens of Israel. The flight of Arabs out of Palestine from 1947 to 1949 was motivated largely by a concern for personal safety, the same concern that brought many Jews to Palestine. Because the fighting in Palestine in 1947–1948 was largely between Jewish and local Arab forces, it is not surprising that various Jewish groups actively sought to rid the fragile state of the hostile Arab population. The most famous—or infamous—terrorist act of this early period was the massacre in the village of Deir Yasin, where 250 Arab men, women, and children were killed. Although the political leaders of Israel officially opposed the act, they did not proceed in a forceful manner to end terrorism by the armed bands that cooperated with the military.

Arab migration from (and within) Israel destroyed any semblance of order and coherence in the remaining Arab population. The two sources of leadership, the urban professional elite and the traditional village leaders, generally had fled. Of the major cities of Israel, only Nazareth maintained a large Arab population; only a few thousand remained in the other urban centers. A wide-open and often bitter competition for power occurred in many rural areas. There was no center around which the Palestinian Arabs could rally. They were divided further along religious lines: 70 percent were Muslim; 21 percent, Christian; and 9 percent, Druze and other religions. In the immediate postwar years, Palestinian Arabs had no political leadership and suffered extreme economic deprivation.

Neither Zionist theory nor past political policy gave the leaders of the new state a clear formula on how to deal with an Arab minority in a Zionist state. Some Israelis hoped for a time that the problem would resolve itself— that the flight of the Arabs would continue until

none were left. In any case, the fledgling state had other pressing problems to deal with to survive. The economy was in chaos, the machinery of government was incomplete, and thousands of indigent, relatively unskilled immigrants were flowing in. The ad hoc policy toward Palestinian Arabs was mainly concerned with the maintenance of state security.

The geographic concentration of the Arab population made administration simple. A few months after Israel was formed, the army units that had occupied Arab-populated areas were formally charged with administering them. Because most of the Palestinian Arabs lived in areas that were Arab under the United Nations partition plan, a military administration was logical in that Israel was an occupying force. The military administration continued until 1966, however, well after annexation of these areas. Regardless of its other policy measures, the emplacement of what essentially was an army of occupation defined the basic attitude of the state toward these "part-citizens." Even within the military administration, however, the principles of administrative action were not clearly spelled out; security remained the only articulated goal. Security would be enhanced if the Arab population was fragmented geographically and politically, if their economic power was limited but not desperately low, and if their emerging leadership was placed in a dependent situation and co-opted. Many of the Israeli government's policies can be connected to one or more of these aims. Land use and land rights policies consistently had the effect of stripping land away from the Arab population, especially in areas the government deemed necessary to place under full Jewish control. Travel restrictions made it difficult for Arabs to reestablish political unity, and other policies established tight control over the Arab labor force. Occasionally, the policies of the military administration resulted in spectacular displays of violence. In October 1956, 49 residents of the Arab village of Kfar Kassim were killed for disobeying a curfew order of which they were unaware. The growing tensions surrounding the 1956 war and the need for absolute control led to the tragedy. That the responsible officers were given relatively light sentences confirmed the Arab view of the Israeli government's attitude toward them.

By the mid-1970s, the Arabs of Israel began to express a sense of nationalism, but it was not until the 1988 uprising in the occupied territories that they moved to build a unified political base with strictly Arab concerns at the forefront. Their formidable task was complicated, however, by the increasingly severe restrictions the government placed on their political activity.

Israel and the Border States

Following the May 14, 1948, declaration of statehood, Israel immediately was engaged in war by Egypt, Iraq, Lebanon, Syria, and Transjordan. The initial round of fighting lasted for a month and was followed by a month-long truce administered by the United Nations. Ten more days of fighting was followed by a second truce. Sporadic fighting and truce arrangements occurred throughout 1948. Finally, the British government declared that it would act on the 1936 treaty with Egypt that allowed British troops to enter Egypt to protect vital British interests. This announcement and pressures from the U.S. government on Israel helped bring about a series of bilateral armistice agreements between Israel and its neighbors.

The war and the armistice agreements increased Israeli territory by more than 30 percent beyond what was allowed for in the partition plan. The Israeli army, although outnumbered substantially, mounted a series of crisp and well-coordinated attacks on the various Arab armies. However, the Israeli success was due at least as much to the ineptitude of the Arab armies and the lack of coordination between them. Although various Arab leaders charged that Israel won because of Western support, several Arab nationalist

spokesmen expressed their dissatisfaction with the kind of leadership that resulted in such humiliation. Terrorist activities ripped through Egypt in the latter part of 1948 and throughout 1949; the Egyptian prime minister was assassinated. The winds of discontent in Egypt continued to blow until the Free Officers' revolution in 1952. Three coups occurred in Syria during 1949–1950; none of the leaders, however, engaged the public's imagination. King Abdullah of Jordan was assassinated in July 1951. The shame of the 1948 defeat resulted in more Arab reprisals against their own governments than against Israel. Their anger was well placed, but it would take another quarter century before Arab armies could begin to match Israeli forces.

The task of creating and maintaining stability in newly created states generally has proved to be a formidable task. Israeli leaders had their job complicated by continued hostile relations with Arab states and by Israel's special population and economic problems. The flood of Jews coming from Europe after the close of World War II and from Arab countries during the late 1940s and early 1950s put the new state under tremendous strain. Israel, after all, was to be the homeland for all Jews. The Israeli declaration of independence implied and subsequent legislation (the Law of Return) granted this right. All immigrants had to be accepted. The economic and social system was put under an enormous burden, so enormous that many feared Israel would collapse. In 1952 the Jewish Agency, the organizers and financiers of most of this immigration, in an attempt to ease the crisis, introduced certain financial criteria for immigration. The new criteria for immigration did not solve other pressing problems, however, including the fact that many immigrants did not adhere to the Zionist-socialist ideology on which the early settlers had founded Israeli society, and that the flight of Arab farmers and the cessation of agricultural trade with Arab states caused a food shortage that assumed crisis proportions.

Many immigrants had to be settled on the land, but most were not ideologically suited to life on a kibbutz (a form of collective farm developed by earlier settlers) or in the cooperative agricultural villages, the moshav. The government placed many immigrants in farming villages under the supervision of instructors who gave technical information, executive direction, and ideological guidance. Ideally the villages were to be located behind the border settlements and evolve into autonomous cooperatives. This process was carried out by fits and starts, with successes and failures.

The first several years of statehood were difficult. However, the population, food, shelter, and state security problems were adequately solved by the mid-1950s. A considerable amount of ingenuity and hard work had been required, but the job was eased a great deal by a large amount of foreign aid flowing into the country that made it possible for Israel to cope with the situation. Immediately after independence, the ratio of the value of exports to imports was about 15 percent—that is, for every dollar spent on imports, only 15 cents was earned from exports. The ratio increased to 60 percent in the 1970s, but the absolute value of the gap increased. The gap between international spending and earning was covered by international remittances—gifts and loans from governments and individuals. About $15 billion was received during the new nation's first 25 years. Twenty-five percent came from Jewish Fund collections; 25 percent from German reparation and restitution payments; 9 percent from bond sales; 13 percent from direct, unilateral transfers (generally from individual to individual); 13 percent from U.S. government loans and gifts; 7 percent from direct private investment; and 8 percent from various short-term and medium-term loans. Much of Israel's economic growth was due to these sources.

The economic successes of the first couple of decades of statehood were not to be sustained. Israel's international debt position deteriorated considerably. Per capita external debt ranked among the highest in the world by 1980, and debt service payments became increasingly onerous, averaging around 20 percent of the value of export earnings in the 1980s. Growth slowed, inflation sometimes topped 100 percent,[1] and the extensive social welfare state constructed in the first two decades did not allow for a flexible response by the government. Solutions to these problems required a strong government; as it was, Israel went through most of the 1980s and early 1990s with coalition governments unable to reach agreement on crucial policy issues.

The 1956 Arab-Israeli War

As Israel steadied its economy and settled its immigrants, the Arab nations limited their anti-Israeli activity. They generally did not have firm control over their own internal political situations and shied away from full-scale conflict. However, Nasser's success in nationalizing the Suez Canal aroused Israeli fears of Arab unity. A few years earlier, Israel had initiated its policy of severe military reprisals against any government from whose territory attacks on Israel were launched. The policy was designed to discourage further attacks by making the punishment exceed the transgression. Although Israel was censured by the United Nations on several occasions, it held firm to the policy. Israel and the West were deeply concerned with the pan-Arab sentiment that was growing under Nasser's leadership and Egypt's drift toward the Soviet bloc. Israel also was concerned with the increasing number of raids from Egyptian territory and Egypt's refusal to allow Israeli ships through the Suez Canal and especially the Straits of Tiran.

Israel invaded Egypt on October 30, 1956. Within four days, Israel was in control of

---

[1] The disruptive effects of the enormous rate of inflation are ameliorated considerably because the economy is indexed. That is, wages rise automatically with inflation, lessening the usual kinds of redistribution of income generally associated with inflation.

the Sinai and the Gaza Strip. One day after the start of the Israeli invasion, the British and French announced a joint expedition to seize the Suez Canal, an action that the United States vigorously and decisively opposed. When the fighting ended a few days later, the British and French held Port Said at the northern terminus of the canal. An eventual settlement called for the removal of the invading forces from Egyptian soil and the stationing of United Nations troops along the Egyptian-Israeli borders (primarily the Gaza Strip and the important Straits of Tiran, through which Israeli shipping could reach the port of Aqaba and avoid the Suez Canal).

The Arabs henceforth considered Nasser a hero. He had turned back Israel, France, and Britain and had earlier rebuffed U.S. attempts to limit Egyptian military strength. Israel had scored an impressive military victory but found itself in a more delicate position than before as Nasser's influence and the pan-Arab movement gathered momentum. During the decade after the 1956 war, Nasser remained the undisputed leader of the Arab world, although he had to share some of his prestige with Ahmed ben Bella after the success of the Algerian revolution. Nasser also was concerned with the situation in Yemen and sent 70,000 troops to support the republicans against the Saudi-backed royalists.

The 1967 Arab-Israeli War

From 1956 to 1966, Israeli-Arab tensions remained just below the boiling point as a host of large and small issues—including important disputes over water rights in the Jordan River, changing relative military strength, and shifting Arab alliances—threatened to fan the conflict again. For two years the Syrian government had permitted Al-Fatah, a military arm of the fledgling PLO, to use Syria as a base for raids into Israel. In May 1967, various Arab leaders became convinced that Israel was about to launch a massive reprisal attack against Syria. As a visible display

of Egypt's willingness to go to war, Nasser had Egyptian troops march through Cairo on their way to the Suez Canal. This action sounded like a battle cry in the Arab world, which then called on Nasser to crush Israel. Nasser's popularity had begun to wane; he needed to be firm and decisive if he was to remain the leader of the Arab world. Confrontation politics are always dangerous, but especially so when each side has developed a worst-case scenario. On May 19, 1967, Egypt requested that United Nations troops be withdrawn from Egyptian territory. The United Nations complied promptly—too promptly to suit many observers. On May 24, Nasser announced that the Straits of Tiran were closed to Israeli ships.

The die was cast. The Six-Day War started in the morning of June 5; the Israeli air force destroyed most of the Egyptian air force while it was still on the ground. Quickly and efficiently Israel pressed the advantage it secured by air; within a week it had taken the Sinai and Gaza from Egypt, Jordanian territory west of the Jordan River, and the Golan area from Syria. In contrast to the postwar agreements of 1956, Israeli troops continued to occupy territory where more than one million Arabs lived. The war was another crushing humiliation for the Arabs, and Nasser offered his resignation.

Israel gained a clear military victory and established three buffer areas it considered vital to its security. It also had to control more than one million additional Arabs at a time when the Palestinian movement was gathering steam. Israel's occupation of Arab territories put it in a difficult position in the United Nations. The Security Council of the United Nations responded by adopting Resolution 242, which required Israel to withdraw its forces from occupied territory and Arab states to recognize Israel's right to exist, among other things.

The 1973 Arab-Israeli War

The end of the 1967 Arab-Israeli war did not bring peace. Israel continued to hold the occupied territories and even built settlements on them. It faced a line of hostile Arab states, especially Egypt, and was burdened with an enormous defense budget.

By 1973 Egypt's president Anwar Sadat had had three years of experience in office. He had ceased to be viewed as a weak, sometimes comical, figure and had begun to assert his own brand of leadership. The 1967 war had been devastating to the Egyptian military and economy. Because the economy already had been extremely weak, partially as a result of the abrupt and untimely way in which Nasser nationalized many industries in the early 1960s and the high population growth rate, the capacity of the average Egyptian to endure hardship was being severely strained. The Soviet Union was reluctant to give President Sadat the military aid he needed, probably because of the possibility of upsetting the movement toward détente with the United States. In July 1972, President Sadat ordered the immediate departure of 40,000 Soviet military personnel and their dependents from Egypt. The oil-rich Arab states already were supplying Egypt with considerable aid but could not be expected to deliver military hardware. If Egypt had allowed the status quo to continue, the minimal demands of the military would have worsened the already dangerous economic situation. The government of Israel, seeing Egypt's plight, set down more stringent conditions for peace, hoping that President Sadat would accede. However, acceptance of the Israeli position would have endangered Egypt's aid from the oil-rich states and possibly triggered a coup. President Sadat embarked on a fruitless international diplomatic offensive as a last step short of war.

Because he saw no other way out of the stalemate, Sadat and President Assad of Syria planned a joint attack on Israel for October 6, 1973. The war, called the Ramadan or Yom Kippur War, was launched on time. Carefully trained Egyptian forces managed to penetrate Israel's defenses for the objective of seizing a strip of the Sinai east of the canal. Israeli forces crossed the canal at another point, however, and isolated the Egyptian army. A major reason for the turnaround in Israeli fortunes was the large and swift replacement of military equipment by the United States. A cease-fire, sponsored by the United Nations with the encouragement of the great powers, took effect on October 24. It took until the following May for terms to be worked out on the Syrian-Israeli front.

The Israeli army had again proved capable of meeting the Arab threat. It had recovered from the initial forays of the Egyptian army and mounted its own offensive; it also beat back Syrian attempts to regain the Golan Heights. The results of this conflict were different, however, from the earlier wars on at least a couple of counts. First, the cost of the effort in terms of money and men was staggering. It was obvious that neither side could afford many more such ventures. Second, the Egyptian army performed as a tough, skilled unit. Although it did not in any sense win the military battle, a limited Egyptian victory was well within the realm of possibility.

President Sadat's gamble in initiating the war seemed to have paid off. The Egyptians had mounted a successful limited strike and invited the great powers to help Egypt find a way to break the stalemate with Israel. It was a high-risk strategy, one that came dangerously close to forcing direct military involvement by the United States and the Soviet Union. The stalemate was broken, however, as the U.S. secretary of state, Henry Kissinger, took the lead in promoting a new settlement. In the months after the war, Kissinger and numerous other interested parties flew repeatedly from one capital to another in what was called "shuttle diplomacy." After a time, terms of peace were established between Egypt and Israel. President Sadat had put much stock in efforts of the United States to bring the needed settlement. The Syrians, still engaged in combat against the Israelis and unable to win back any territory, were understandably upset by Egypt's separate agreement with Israel. Sadat's actions were considered to be a form of appeasement, and Egypt became isolated in the Arab world. Syria's president Assad assumed the leadership of the front-line states.

Nevertheless, President Sadat continued his efforts to bring a lasting peace to Egypt. His most spectacular move was to go before the Israeli Knesset in November 1977. Although the major issues between Egypt and Israel were not resolved by this dramatic initiative, it did set the stage for further negotiations, the most important being the Camp David talks between Prime Minister Begin, President Sadat, and President Carter. These resulted in a formal peace treaty and diplomatic relations. Egypt and Israel continued their sometimes fractious negotiations through the remainder of the 1970s, resulting in a gradual Israeli withdrawal from the Sinai and a partial normalization of relations between Egypt and Israel. Israeli withdrawal was completed in April 1982.

Egypt's partial accommodation with Israel continued to alienate it from Syria and its supporters and the Palestinians. It was charged that Egypt forgot the Palestinians in a selfish and short-sighted attempt to gain temporary security. Sadat's dismantling of Nasser's social-ist economy was seen as further evidence of his Western bias. Syria, the new claimant to Arab leadership in the struggle against Israel, was caught in an ironic swirl of events. As noted earlier, Syria had found it necessary to place troops in Lebanon to control Palestinian activi-ties and avoid Israeli reprisal attacks. By 1982 Christian separatist forces controlled a sizable strip of southern Lebanon, with the help of Israeli supplies and military aid. Syria effectively controlled the rest of Lebanon (not including parts of Beirut and some mountainous areas), including the Palestinians.

The 1982 Invasion of Lebanon

The 1982 Israeli invasion of Lebanon pro-foundly changed the character of several key

political relationships in the Middle East. It has been argued that the 1967 war resulted in an Arab moral crisis. It became clear that visions of Arab unity were pure illusion; Nasser's dream was dead. In the same light, the invasion of Lebanon marks a profound moral cleavage in the Israeli polity. Israeli opponents of the invasion tended to view it as brutal aggression that undermined Israel's moral foundations. Israeli peace groups gained new life; a protest demonstration in Tel Aviv drew several hun-dred thousand participants. Supporters of the government saw the action as necessary, arguing that the last PLO foothold had to be destroyed. Political divisions hardened.

The 1982 invasion of Lebanon did not occur without reference to Israeli security on other borders. Israel's separate peace with Egypt culminated with the April 1982 with-drawal of Israeli forces from Sinai. The process of withdrawal was aided by the presence of a multinational peacekeeping force. Included in the agreement were scheduled, and continually postponed, talks that were to lead to eventual autonomy in the Gaza Strip.

Withdrawal from the Sinai necessitated that Israelis be removed forcibly from their illegal settlements. This threatened the fragile domestic coalition that depended on the support of the members of the Knesset favoring virtually unlimited settlement in occupied terri-tories. Prime Minister Begin weathered the storm, partially as a result of prior decisions on the rapid settlement of the West Bank and the extension of Israeli civilian law (December 1981) in the Golan Heights, an action that translated into de facto annexation.

In early May 1982, the Knesset formally supported Prime Minister Begin's statement that Israeli settlements would not be dismantled as part of any peace negotiations, and that Israeli sovereignty over the West Bank would be estab-lished after the interim arrangements called for in the Camp David Accords had run their course. During the first several months of 1982, there was considerable unrest in Gaza and the West Bank.

Israel apparently thought that if the PLO were crushed in Lebanon, and if Syrian forces were neutralized, it could establish more secure borders to the north and east; the agreement with Egypt had provided breathing space to the south. The invasion and occupation of Lebanon (1982–1985) accomplished some objectives— the PLO in Lebanon was severely weakened, and time was afforded for the continued rapid settlement of the West Bank. But it carried substantial liabilities, including the weakening of Christian power in Lebanon; an ultimately more powerful Syrian presence; a rapprochement between the PLO, Egypt, and Jordan; and considerable domestic unrest.

These adverse conditions were but surface manifestations of deeper seismic rumblings caused by the war. Of prime importance was the subsequent regrouping of the PLO and its 1985 acceptance of the "Jordanian option." Although it is dangerous to draw specific long-range implications, it is quite clear that there are straightforward connections between the 1982 invasion and the Palestinian uprising.

THE PALESTINIANS AND THE 1988 UPRISING

The Palestinian diaspora that resulted from the Israeli victory of 1948 was largely to Arab countries. In 1950 about 900,000 Palestinian refugees were in camps operated by the United Nations in Lebanon, Jordan (and the West Bank), Syria, and the Gaza Strip. The plight of these people was deplorable. The United Nations relief effort was minimal; the food ration was limited to 1,600 calories a day, and housing often consisted of scraps of material loosely thrown together to form primitive shelters. No national Palestinian leadership had arisen before the establishment of Israel, and refugees grouped together on a traditional village basis. Throughout the 1950s, the outside world heard little about the refugee camps except for occasional news shorts showing their humiliating and stultifying living conditions. The rest of the

world seemed to wish the Palestinians away; the Palestinians were unable to generate any coherent response to their plight. On the few occasions when the Palestinians protested their conditions, they were suppressed by the host Arab governments, the most notable early example being Egypt's actions in the Gaza Strip in the 1950s.

Organized resistance eventually did develop, beginning with the formation of Al-Fatah in the late 1950s and the creation of the PLO in 1964 through an initiative of the Arab League. It was apparent to the various national leaders that the festering discontent in the refugee camps was being used to form effective paramilitary units dedicated to the overthrow of Israel. These groups took heart in the success of the Algerians in thwarting the best efforts of France through a combination of tight organization, urban guerrilla terrorist activity, and tenacity. Palestinians began to think that they too could bring a Western power to its knees. There were significant differences between the two situations, however, one being that the bulk of the Palestinians and the heart of the resistance movement were outside Israel. Israel's reprisals against any nation from which anti-Israeli actions originated, coupled with its military superiority, deterred the Arab League. The League decided to control the Palestinian activists. It thought that the PLO could serve as a Palestinian umbrella organization and at the same time be subject to the League's control. Al-Fatah, under the leadership of Yasir Arafat, remained active, however.

With the end of the 1967 war, Palestinian fortunes began to rise. For most of the 1960s, Palestinian leaders had disagreed with Nasser's dictum "Unity Is the Road to Palestine," preferring instead "Palestine Is the Road to Unity." The outcome of the 1967 war made it clear to them that their hopes for nationhood would be dashed if they followed Nasser's proposition. The Palestinians believed that only they could and would act to defeat Israel. They ignored Arab pleas for unity. The various "front-line" nations bordering Israel faced the prospect of having independent armies in their territories, armies bent on destroying an enemy that the nations themselves were not prepared to attack. The PLO no longer could be expected to control the different Palestinian groups or obey the wishes of the Arab League. Each country gave tacit support to a particular Palestinian organization, supported its growth, and tried to control its activity. More than a dozen sizable groups and a bewildering array of splinter groups formed between 1967 and 1969. In 1969, Yasir Arafat of Al-Fatah became the head of the PLO. Apparently, the thinking in Arab capitals was that Arafat's successful organization would be controlled more easily if he were given a new mantle of authority.

King Hussein of Jordan tended to view the Palestinians as potential citizens of Jordan, rather than aspirants to a separate nation. Because the PLO had between 30,000 and 50,000 troops in Jordan by 1970—forces better described as a conventional army than as guerrilla fighters—and because the fractious liberation movement was demanding more and more autonomy in Jordan, the king could either sit back and watch his country being dismantled or take decisive action. "Black September" is the name the Palestinian movement gave his response; in September 1970, Hussein ordered regular Jordanian troops against the PLO. Thousands of Palestinians were killed, and Palestinian power in Jordan was broken. The only remaining sanctuary close to the Palestinian homeland, Lebanon, absorbed large numbers of refugees and found itself traveling down a dangerous road. The Palestinians were in decline, but they remained a force to reckon with.

The PLO was not significantly involved in the 1973 Arab-Israeli war except for promoting strikes in the occupied West Bank. In November 1973, the Arab heads of state declared the PLO the sole legitimate representative of the Palestinian people. To Arab leaders, the move made sense for several reasons. Jordan's King Hussein had been

discredited as a representative of Palestinian interests because of the events of Black September, it was necessary to include the PLO in any peace negotiations, and the PLO now seemed to be more flexible than before on many issues. In November 1974, Yasir Arafat addressed the United Nations and saw that body pass resolutions declaring the right of Palestinians to seek independence and granting the PLO permanent observer status in the United Nations. The PLO had attained international legitimacy, but it was not recognized by Israel and could not enter into direct negotiations. The PLO was not accorded more independence of movement by the Arab nations.

The fortunes of the Palestinian Liberation Organization took a turn for the worse during 1975 when Lebanon fell into civil disorder. The PLO had been hinting that it could accept the continued existence of Israel if Palestinians were granted an independent status on West Bank territory. Israel indicated that it could accept a Palestinian "entity" on the West Bank only as long as that entity was formally part of Jordan and as long as Israel was allowed to maintain defense forces in the area. Although these positions were far apart, they at least allowed the participants room to negotiate and continue the slow process of finding a mutually acceptable solution. The moderating forces in the PLO lost ground to the "rejectionists," however—those who saw the elimination of Israel as the only possible foundation for a Palestinian state. Because the PLO could not control rejectionist activities during the collapse of Lebanon, its claim to preeminence was compromised.

Events following the evacuation of PLO forces from Lebanon in the aftermath of the Israeli invasion of 1982 point to a couple of facts. First, the PLO is a multinational organization. It did not collapse because of the evacuation; the organization simply changed the primary locus of activity away from that country. In addition, people evicted from

Lebanon were afforded considerable prestige in parts of the Arab world because of the tenacity of their forces in the face of the clearly superior firepower of the Israelis, and they gained a more cordial relationship with several important Arab governments, especially Egypt and Jordan. The well-established organizational structure of the PLO and the financing offered by several Arab governments (along with a Palestinian income tax) indicated that the PLO would be a force to reckon with for some time.

Second, Al-Fatah continued to be the most powerful group within the PLO, and Yasir Arafat maintained his position as head of Al-Fatah and the PLO. Rejectionist forces and breakaway Al-Fatah groups failed in their attempts to wrest power away from this now clearly dominant group. The most prominent of these rejections of Arafat's leadership occurred after the first PLO evacuation from Beirut. Al-Fatah forces located close to Syrian positions in Lebanon took up arms against their brethren when the PLO was seen as entertaining notions of compromise that would have yielded considerable territory to Israel. The same group, with Syrian support, wrested control of large camps around Beirut from Al-Fatah.

Third, the PLO strategy for the struggle for Palestine allowed more accommodation. In the 1970s, the PLO abandoned the notion that Israel needed to be destroyed if Palestine were to exist; that is, it moved from a military to a political strategy. By the 1980s, it was giving strong indications that the establishment of a Palestinian "entity," which need not include all of the territory occupied by Israel, would be acceptable if assurances could be given for eventual independence. King Hussein of Jordan and Arafat held discussions on these matters a little more than a decade after Black September. Irreconcilable differences have a transient quality.

The First Intifadah

The widespread Western, and especially American, view of Israel as a beleaguered David struggling against an Arab Goliath was shattered in 1988. Television screens around the world showed confrontations between stone-throwing Palestinian youth of Gaza and the West Bank and the Israeli Defense Forces. Palestinian teenagers took on the persona of the stone-throwing David, and the Israeli crack troops with sophisticated weapons appeared as Goliath. Television cameras revealed instances of the inevitable excessive use of force by the Israeli Defense Forces. As the 1982 invasion of Lebanon had thrown Israel into moral crisis, so the uprising intensified it and laid to rest notions of a beneficent military occupation.

An auto accident in Gaza in December 1987 provided the spark that ignited the uprising, popularly called **intifadah** by the Palestinians. Apparently all of the principals were surprised by the strength, depth, and spread of the initial stages of the rebellion. The PLO was among those surprised and quickly scrambled to coordinate the civil disorder. Although the auto accident provided the catalyst for the intifadah, the discontent had been growing for some time.

The 1967 war resulted in Israeli occupation of Gaza, the Sinai, the Golan, and the West Bank (including East Jerusalem). Each of the areas presented Israel with different opportunities and problems. The Sinai provided a massive buffer against Egypt. A decade later this land was traded for peace as part of the Camp David Accords. The Golan district was earmarked for permanent control almost immediately after the war's conclusion. Because Israel feared Syria more than any other belligerent neighboring Arab state, this strategic border area would not be relinquished. The task of maintaining control was eased because almost 90 percent of the prewar population had fled.

Gaza had been militarily administered by Egypt since 1949. Although it lost 15 to 20 percent of its population owing to the 1967 war, it still contained about a third of a million residents in a very small area. A large percentage of these families were refugees from the 1948 war, still openly hostile to Israel. Consequently, Israeli policy in Gaza was dominated by police action rather than settlement.

East Jerusalem was claimed as Israeli territory shortly after the war. It was a piece of property that Israeli politicians could not contemplate giving back. The West Bank was more problematic. Immediately after the cessation of hostilities in 1949, King Abdullah of Jordan hastily convened a conference of West Bank Palestinian notables who gave their blessings to the formal annexation of the West Bank by Jordan. The international community never accepted the result, but it did allow the de facto administration of the territory by Jordan. Most of the Palestinian population never accepted Hashemite rule, however. The disputed status of the West Bank allowed each interested party to frame arguments and policies consistent with its most convenient premise. Israel held that it could negotiate only with the government of Jordan, whereas the PLO claimed that it alone represented the occupants of the occupied territories. After six months of the intifadah, and some 40 years after the annexation announcement, Jordan formally renounced any claim to the West Bank.

The West Bank lost about a quarter of its population in 1967. Especially important was the fact that more than 90 percent of the population of the West Jordan Valley, located between the Jordan River and the western mountains of the rift, fled to the East Bank or other nearby places of rural refuge. Only 10,000 Palestinians remained.

Israeli's Allon Plan, although never formally accepted as official policy, provided the basic blueprint for Israeli action in the first decade of occupation. The plan called for settlement of (1) the Jordan Valley rift from the northern Israeli border to just north of the Dead Sea and (2) an area from Jerusalem south past Hebron to the border and from Jerusalem to the Dead Sea in the east. This meant that the

Palestinian area of the West Bank was divided into two parts, which the Israelis called Judea and Samaria. The northern enclave (Samaria) had a corridor that joined Jordan at the northern end of the Dead Sea. The areas marked for Israeli settlement (including a strip west of Samaria and one running along the Sinai border) were designed primarily with defense in mind.

Although the Allon Plan served defense interests, it did not satisfy the increasingly popular goal of settling throughout the West Bank—including the religiously important and heavily Palestinian-populated central areas ignored by the Allon Plan. The Likud bloc victory of 1977 extended the settlement policy to include Judea and Samaria. In 1977 Prime Minister Begin declared that the "Green Line" (the 1967 borders) had "vanished." To the Labor government's security rationale for settlement, the Likud government added a theological imperative: The land had been promised to them by God. Although believing in the same God, the Palestinians did not receive the same message. Nevertheless, colonization proceeded apace.

By 1990 about 100,000 Israelis had settled in the occupied territories, mostly on the West Bank, mostly in bedroom suburbs of Jerusalem and Tel Aviv. The bulk of these settlers were not religious zealots but middle-class Israelis trading a crowded urban environment with scarce and expensive housing for newly constructed subsidized units 15 minutes from the city center. These units also served a military purpose. Called "fortress settlements," they generally are multistory apartment complexes built on high ground, close to each other (or interlocking) to prevent enemy penetration, and with other defense-type features, such as narrow windows with metal shutters. Jerusalem is virtually surrounded by these fortress settlements. The 1991 acceleration of settlements guided by the Minister of Housing, Ariel Sharon, largely followed this policy by "thickening" the urban clusters.

Numerous settlers in the earlier years went to newly constructed towns throughout the West Bank. To build these settlements, land rights had to be secured, transport and power grids constructed, and water systems put in place. By 1988 half of the West Bank's land had been ceded to Israelis through the application of a wide range of measures. A road network was in place, connecting the cities, bypassing Arab towns, and preventing the development of ribbon settlement of Palestinians next to the roads. Access to water, especially for agricultural use, became increasingly difficult for Palestinians. Although the placement of some settlements was dictated by the desire to control a particularly important religious site, the overall pattern was designed to isolate the Palestinian towns.

Israelis opposed to the settlements complained about the expense of the program in times of economic hardship. They argued that annexation would undermine Israel's stature as a Jewish state if the Palestinians were given full citizenship rights or destroy the democratic character of the state if they were denied citizenship. But colonization continued; de facto annexation took place.

Many of the refugee camps were 40 years old at the time of the uprising. The tents of four decades ago had been replaced by concrete block structures that had rooms added to them as the camps took on more the character of permanent settlements than places of temporary refuge. Some camp residents owned autos, many homes sprouted television antennas, and an articulated economic order brought increases in material well-being. Some material conditions remained appalling, however, such as open sewers draining into disease-ridden, fetid pools of filth. Residents were reminded daily of their occupied status. Men of Gaza gathered every morning to get transport to Tel Aviv for regular jobs or day labor. Israel demanded that they return to the camps every night or have identity cards that permitted their stay in Israel.

The usual colonial pattern of discrimination in wages and types of jobs available prevailed. More than 100,000 Palestinians of the occupied territories worked in Israel. Economic dependence was not limited to the labor market or the camps. Agricultural produce and industrial output of the occupied territories were denied ready access to Israel when they would compete with Israeli-produced goods; licenses to produce goods in potential competition with Israel were denied; water rights were curtailed. The military plan for maintaining civil order was called the "Iron Fist": long-term detentions without charge or trial, collective punishment, deportations, and strict control of basic political expression. When this plan is placed in the context of a systematic loss of land rights and increased economic dependence, it is not surprising that the Palestinian population became more embittered and desperate.

The widespread nature of the rebellion meant that a decisive response by the Israeli Defense Forces would result in unacceptable levels of carnage. As it was, the limited response still resulted in an average of a Palestinian death per day. As Israel groped for solutions, the revolt continued. In addition to some widely reported excesses of the military, several largely symbolic statements and actions by Israeli officials fanned the flames. Prime Minister Shamir at one point said that the troublemakers were mere "grasshoppers" and would be dealt with as such. Ariel Sharon, early architect of the settlement policy on the West Bank and of the 1982 invasion of Lebanon, moved his residence to the Muslim quarter of the old city of Jerusalem. Some members of the Knesset called for the forcible removal of all Palestinians from the West Bank. Substantive actions supported these symbolic acts. In April 1988, Abu Jihad, the supposed PLO coordinator of the uprising, was assassinated in Tunis by a team widely assumed to be associated with official Israel. Deportations, detentions, and other restrictive measures increased, but the rebellion continued. Israel was a few months away from elections, and the Palestinian National Congress was preparing a declaration of independence.

It was no surprise that the 1988 election campaign in Israel was vicious. Israel's position in the occupied territories was increasingly precarious, and international opinion was increasingly sympathetic to the Palestinian position. The crisis of conscience brought to center stage by the 1982 invasion of Lebanon intensified. The Labor bloc advocated (with many provisos) the convening of an international conference that would trade land for peace. Likud was not so disposed. The religious parties, always important, hardened their positions.

The religious parties gained seats in the November 1988 election. Likud (40 seats) and Labor (39 seats) garnered about an equal number of seats. A coalition was put together after six weeks of negotiations. Likud, which was called on to form a government, initially negotiated with the religious parties but finally found the positions of the religious bloc to be unacceptable. Particularly controversial was the policy proposed by religious conservatives of redefining the Law of Return so that the only converts to Judaism eligible for "return status" would be those converted by Orthodox rabbis. Many Jews outside Israel, especially in the United States, expressed deep shock and hinted that acceptance of this policy would change their attitude toward Israel. Also, after the election and before the formation of the new government, the Palestinian National Congress declared an independent Palestinian state (November 15, 1988), a move that received warm worldwide support. A month later Yasir Arafat addressed the United Nations. In the address, and in subsequent clarifying remarks in the next several days, the PLO stated its recognition of the state of Israel and renounced terrorism. A few days later, and after much diplomatic dancing, the United States opened official discussions with the PLO, something it had not done for 13 years.

The new coalition in Israel again joined Likud and Labor in a marriage of inconvenience.

Before the election, all parties agreed that the policy paralysis of the last such government should not be repeated. There were differences in the composition of the new government, the most important being that Likud would hold the posts of prime minister and foreign minister throughout the coalition (instead of the Labor–Likud split and midterm switching), but many of the debilitating aspects of power sharing remained. The major actors of the new government declared agreement on their unwillingness to talk to the PLO and the need to end the intifadah. They disagreed on most other important matters. As stated earlier, the coalition fell apart by 1990. The subsequent Likud–Religious Party government met a similar fate in 1992.

CONCLUSION

The nations of the industrialized world had many decades to develop their forms of government, economic structures, and cultural perspectives. Most countries of the Middle East have not had time to sift and winnow such weighty ideas. These countries have been thrown headlong into the race for "modernity" and are still in the process of defining their identity. We can expect to see many changes in the Middle East, although we can identify only the broad contours.

Many important issues in the Middle East are connected to the drive for self-determination. Although most of the countries had gained formal political independence by 1950, they still faced the tasks of establishing an effective government, charting an independent economic course, and settling on a coherent cultural identity. Their job was complicated by the acceleration of worldwide technological and organizational revolutions, which acted to make the world more interdependent. Greater world interdependence meant that one nation's policy changes could conflict easily with the interests of other nations, and that they would have to make a greater number of decisions between mutually beneficial and harmful interdependencies. Statements of many third-world leaders still reflect the dilemma; they generally have been quick to point to the difficulties, but have not been able to arrive at affirmative policies. However, some guides to the future are identifiable from the decisions of the past.

None of the powerful countries of the world can feel sure of having this or that bloc of Middle Eastern nations in its camp. The nations of the Middle East are now able to act more independently. It also seems likely that the various regional relationships will continue to be fluid. Libya sought political union at times with Egypt and the Sudan, but has had hostile relations with these nations at other times. It also strongly backed the "progressive" government of Iraq during some periods and strongly opposed it at other times. The rise of independent and majority Muslim republics in the southern reaches of the former Soviet Union in the early 1990s led Iran and Turkey to scramble into new regional alliances. The changing alliances and relationships reflect that the actors are still in the process of searching for fundamental common interests that will transcend transitory conflicts.

The Middle East's dominance of world petroleum markets will continue to have a major effect on regional and global politics. Gulf tensions regularly bring statements of neutrality from Western governments along with warnings that the West will not tolerate actions that might close the petroleum spigot. Such pressures on the Middle East are certain to continue. The financial strength of the petroleum-rich countries will continue to alter regional relationships between have and have-not nations. Conflicting interests also will continue to surface between the have nations (e.g., Iran, which has low petroleum reserves, can be expected to have an attitude toward petroleum pricing different from Saudi Arabia, which has large reserves).

Perhaps of greatest ultimate importance, Middle Eastern societies will continue to change at a rapid pace. Rapid change has stimulated a search for a new sense of identity that is bound to take different directions across countries and through time. The most arresting manifestation of this search has been the resurgence of Islam as a regional, national, and personal symbol of identity. It is difficult to predict whether this resurgence will act as a vehicle through which social tensions will be played out, will serve as a causal agent itself, or will create its own dynamic. In any case, the Islamic resurgence promises to continue to be a significant political force.

Key Terms

Baath *80*	Ashkenazi *100*	intifadah *109*
Hizbollah *86*	Sephardic *100*	

7 | TURNING POINTS

This chapter is designed to explain and link together selected significant events of three time periods. During the late 1980s and early 1990s three events dominated the structure of much of Middle East politics: a Palestinian rebellion, the meltdown of the U.S.S.R., and the 1990–1991 Gulf War. The years around 2000 saw the attacks of September 11, another Palestinian rebellion, and the second Gulf War. In the latter years of the decade, the Palestinians essentially broke into two governments (Hamas in Gaza and Fatah in the West Bank); Israel had significant engagements with Hibzbollah and Hamas; the United States started to untangle itself from Iraq; and Iran convulsed over a disputed election.

Although the events and threads of causation are given some detail in this and following chapters, the major emphasis is on the broad contours that help explain some root issues involved in patterns of conflict and attempts for resolution.

CIRCA 1990

First, Palestinians in the territories occupied by Israel since 1967 rebelled in December 1987. The intifadah brought increasing domestic and international pressure on the Israeli government finally to resolve the "Palestinian issue." Israeli Defense Forces (IDF) acted to suppress the rebellion but to little avail, even though more than one Palestinian per day was killed for several years. By early 1996 Palestinians held elections that signaled the opening steps of the establishment of a Palestinian state. By early 2000, after a three-year hiatus, negotiations between Palestinians and Israelis addressed core issues. By 2003 many Palestinians came to see the promising turning point of the early 1990s come full circle. Occupation had been reasserted, the Palestinian Authority was woefully ineffectual, and the chances for true independence and peace were almost nil.

Second, the collapse of the U.S.S.R. as a superpower ushered in a series of dramatic changes in official ideology, demography, and international political alignments. The states that received aid from the U.S.S.R.—notably Syria, Iraq, and South Yemen—were cut adrift financially and militarily. During this period, the Soviets announced that they would allow the emigration of a large number of Jews—up to one million people. Israel faced the prospect of having its Jewish population increase by 20 percent in a couple of years, enhancing its position as a Jewish state but also presenting it with an immense financial and social burden. Also, the rise of nations with a majority Muslim population (the central Asian republics) from the ashes of the Soviet empire meant that westward-leaning Turkey, more religiously oriented Iran, conservative Saudi Arabia, and others scrambled to forge new alliances. The collapse of the U.S.S.R. also presented the United States, the sole remaining superpower, with unique challenges. One of the most prominent of these was the extent to which the United States was to posture itself as the leader of wide-ranging multinational coalitions, or essentially to define and execute policy in a more unilateral fashion. The Clinton Administration leaned toward the multilateral approach. The second Bush Administration favored unilateral action.

Third, the 1990 invasion of Kuwait by Iraq and the subsequent war shook the foundations of the area. The combination of the collapse of the Soviet Union, the intifadah, and the Iraqi invasion signaled changes so deep-seated that they rivaled in importance the mandate system that gave the basic geopolitical boundaries to the region.

In the early morning of August 2, 1990, Iraqi forces invaded Kuwait and within a couple of days were dug in at the Saudi border (with Kuwait) after having an easy time with the totally outmatched Kuwaiti defense forces. Six months later, an allied force, led by more than one-half million U.S. troops and supplied with a stunning display of high-tech weapons, liberated Kuwait and crippled the Iraqi military and economic infrastructure. The military victory came with surprising ease. The campaign was over in about a month with very low allied losses. The effects of the invasion and war, however, will take decades to play out.

In the immediate aftermath, Saddam Hussein was still in power, had crushed a Shia revolt in the south, and bargained an uneasy and unstable compromise with the Kurdish resistance in the north. Jordan, a nervous

supporter of Iraq after the invasion, partially owing to the domestic popularity of Saddam Hussein's postinvasion call for the liberation of Palestine as part of Iraq's comprehensive bid for a settlement, suffered a loss of Western and Gulf financial aid and had to deal with the burden of several hundred thousand Palestinians who had been expelled from Kuwait because of their "support" of Iraq. On the other side of the war front, about one million Egyptians returned home after Iraq expelled them because of Egyptian support of Iraq's enemies. Several hundred thousand Yemeni workers were evicted from Saudi Arabia because the Yemeni government "supported" Iraq. Syria, a crucial ally of the United States in the coalition against Iraq, gained the ability to reinforce their control over Lebanon. Israel suffered missile attacks from Iraq during the war and faced increased pressure to settle with the Palestinians after the conflict.

Also, terrorist networks associated with Middle Eastern causes became global and were likely to remain global. U.S. forces remained in Afghanistan and Iraq. Terrorist bombings of Westerners in those countries and in Western countries continued.

CIRCA 2000

September 11, 2001, has been described (with some hyperbole) as "the day the world changed." For the purposes of this text, there is little need to retell the full story of the suicide bombings of the World Trade Center and the Pentagon in the United States. It also is unnecessary to detail the U.S.-led coalition that intervened militarily in Afghanistan, pursuing Al-Qaeda and toppling the Taliban government. It is important to point out, however, some of the Middle Eastern seeds of these events and the subsequent repercussions.

Fifteen of the nineteen individuals who hijacked the planes were Saudi nationals, reasonably well educated and obviously highly motivated. What were their rationales? One rationale was that the United States was seen as the primary force supporting what they saw as corrupt regimes in the area, especially (but not exclusively) Saudi Arabia. They viewed the Saudi government as corrupt, profoundly undemocratic, and traitors to Islam for (among other things) allowing U.S. forces to use Saudi soil for military actions. This rationale as well as others was cloaked with religious certainty—a profound belief that these actions were in defense of core values.

The events of September 11 impacted, directly and indirectly, the contours of U.S. antiterrorist policy in the Middle East. President Bush declared that the United States was determined to end the regime of Saddam Hussein in Iraq, declaring it (along with Iran and North Korea) to be an "axis of evil." The U.S. government drew up plans for an invasion of Iraq. European and Arab governments generally strongly advised against any such action, at least in public pronouncements. The United States submitted a resolution to the United Nations demanding a return of UN-mandated weapons inspectors to Iraq; they left Iraq in 1998 after being frustrated by Iraq's refusal to comply fully. The U.S. resolution also called for military action if Iraq did not accept the inspectors.

In the summer of 2002 important opinion makers in Washington painted the government of Saudi Arabia as one not to be trusted and Saudi Arabia as a nation that needed to engage in serious reform if it was to remain a U.S. ally. The people attacking Saudi Arabia apparently were convinced that the Saudi government's well-known acquiescence to the religious authorities was at the root of much of the spread of "Islamic terrorism" in the world. The contention was that the government's financial largesse nurtured the proliferation of religious schools, especially in Pakistan, that led to the profoundly anti-American sentiments of the Taliban and Al-Qaeda, among others. Other observers noted the irony that the United States encouraged these developments in the 1980s as a countermeasure to the Soviet occupation of Afghanistan. Some people found it to be more than coincidence that the attacks on Saudi Arabia heated up several weeks after Crown Prince Abdullah of Saudi Arabia presented a peace plan that, among other things, would have brought diplomatic recognition of Israel by all Arab states in return for a comprehensive settlement between the Israelis and the Palestinians.

Finally, the second Palestinian intifadah, which began in September 2000, took a horrific turn. During the first half of 2002 Palestinian suicide bombers targeted Israeli civilians, resulting in many hundreds of deaths. Israel responded with massive military force, occupying almost all key Palestinian Authority–controlled areas in the West Bank. The Israeli military crushed the infrastructure of the Palestinian Authority, including surrounding the compound of Yasir Arafat, virtually holding him under house arrest. Many hundreds of casualties ensued, many thousands of Palestinians were arrested, and finally a lull in the suicide bombings took place. After the Israelis withdrew their forces, the bombings resumed. The Israelis returned, now for a longer stay. The political crisis forced the Palestinians to call for elections in early 2003. Shortly thereafter, the Israeli government collapsed, and they also called for elections in early 2003.

These turning points affected the region and the world. But the outlook in the early years of the new millennium was far bleaker than that of the "turning points" of a decade earlier. First, the earlier era witnessed the beginnings of a peace process between Israel and its neighbors. By 2002 the peace process was in shambles, and violence increased spectacularly. By 2005 there again were faint signs of hope. By early 2006 hope faded. At midyear 2006 Israeli forces retaliated against Hizbollah after the latter kidnapped two Israeli soldiers. Israeli airpower did extensive damage to Lebanese infrastructure throughout the country. They also attempted to root out Hizbollah forces from their bases in southern Lebanon. Hizbollah, however, was deeply dug in and heavily armed. They were not defeated. After surviving the initial attacks, they fired hundreds of rockets from their positions into Israeli cities. When Israel finally quit Lebanon, Hizbollah gained enormous prestige, and Israeli went though an existential crisis.

Second, Iraq was put on center stage again. By November 2002 the United Nations passed a resolution demanding that Iraq accept U.N. inspectors looking for weapons of mass destruction (after a four-year hiatus) or face invasion. The inspectors returned, but the crisis remained. After a couple of months, the United States complained that Iraq was not fully complying with the United Nations resolution. After failing to convince the United Nations that military action was needed, the United States (and Britain and a group of minor participants) geared up for war. Military action started mid-March. Within a month the war was finished, and the Iraqi regime was vanquished. The physical and political reconstruction of Iraq was fraught with danger, but the United States stated that its forces would remain until the tasks were completed. As pointed out later in this chapter, securing the peace proved to be very difficult.

Third, Iran was put back in the limelight. The United Nations imposed (mild) sanctions on Iran due to their noncompliance with international inspectors of the nuclear enrichment program.

CIRCA 2010

The election of Barack Obama signaled a change of U.S. military policy on a couple of fronts. President Obama indicated that after a military "surge" in Iraq the United States would withdraw its combat forces from urban areas in 2010 with a goal of (almost) complete withdrawal thereafter. The new administration also pledged to vigorously seek a solution to the Israeli/Palestinian issue. Obama also gave an important speech in

Cairo in an attempt to assure Muslims that the United States held no bias against them.

The promised departure of most U.S. forces meant that Iraq had to scramble to clear up significant issues of provincial revenue sharing, provincial borders (especially around Kirkuk), and political lines of authority. There were national elections in early 2010. As pointed out later, the results called for a coalition government that was difficult to cobble together.

Iran held elections in 2009. When it was announced that Mr. Amadinejad won, massive protests occurred. The protesters claimed that Amadinejad won only because of fraud. It was estimated that about a million people took to the streets of Tehran. Given modern communications, the world saw the protests and some of the brutal actions of the government in their attempt to suppress the protesters. The country had not convulsed like that since the revolution. The protesters failed in their ultimate goal, but discontent remained widespread, including some prominent clergy. Iran also faced increasing international pressure to open their nuclear program to inspection. Iran failed to satisfy U.N. demands and subsequently faced a new round of sanctions imposed by the U.N. The plight of the Palestinians continued. Israel launched a major military attack on Gaza in response to rocket launches into Israel. Much of the Gazan infrastructure was destroyed. Israel then imposed a blockade of most goods destined for Gaza. At the time, an Israeli official commented that they did not want to starve the population but merely put it on "a diet." This led to a major humanitarian crisis in Gaza. The territory had to depend on goods smuggled in through tunnels crossing the border with Egypt. In mid-2010 a flotilla of ships attempted to bring humanitarian aid into Gaza. The Israeli military responded by firing on and boarding the ships. They killed 9 of those attempting to break the blockade. An international furor was brought against Israel. By mid-year, the Israeli government announced that it would allow foodstuffs and basic medicines to enter Gaza.

However, they remained firm on continuing the blockade of most materials needed to repair the infrastructure destroyed during the invasion, claiming that these materials could be used to enhance military capability.

GLOBALIZATION

The rise of globalization and the demise of the bipolar world have complicated area studies in general and the study of the Middle East in particular. This section begins with a discussion of globalization. It then addresses the related notion of why it may be wise to rethink ideas about what we mean by an "area." This notion can become complicated quickly, but the complications are necessary. Because notions of "academic scribblers" lay behind many policy decisions, and because in this case radically different views of the coming shape of the world result from the adoption of different assumptions, it becomes vital that we examine some core issues.

Globalization usually refers to increasing economic, political, and cultural interdependence. There are significant arguments over the identification of the most important motive forces of globalization. Economic globalization often is said to have been caused by the (putative) triumph of free markets in combination with the information revolution. Although there is some merit to the argument that free markets enhance globalization, it seems overly restrictive to mark it as the most important cause of the phenomenon. In a similar vein, the rise of free markets generally is associated with democratic gains. This also has merit, but the lines of causation are not always clear or complete: Aspects of ideological cheerleading color many analyses.

Although the root causes of "globalization" are not known with certainty, there is no doubt that the demise of the U.S.S.R. further muddied the analytical waters. The absence of a bipolar world has led numerous analysts to venture hypotheses of the future nature of the international order. One highly contentious theme centers on what is meant by "an area," or if the concept holds much meaning. Financial capital markets are so highly integrated that it makes little difference if you are trading in Hong Kong or Chicago. From this lens, analysis of financial markets in terms of geographic areas is of little use. Others argue that the notion of areas of the world will continue to hold central importance, albeit in a different fashion than that of the bipolar world. In one such version, the core commonalities of areas no longer will be based on political and economic ideologies (e.g., free enterprise versus state control of the economy) but on core cultural, especially religious, values. This notion was first famously put forth by Samuel Huntington in his provocatively titled article, "The Clash of Civilizations?" Specifically, Huntington argued that the emerging Islamic civilization posed the greatest danger to the (Christian) West. Although he added nuances to the basic argument since the writing of the original article, the basic point remains: Islam and the West are and will continue to be at odds.

The emerging alternate views of what ought to be contained in the analysis of "areas" are not neatly defined, but they offer valuable insights. There seem to be at least three key jumping-off points: (1) considering borders as "thick" rather than thin, (2) thinking of areas in ways that transcend a land-based geography, and (3) looking at processes rather than traits as being more useful for analysis.

Area studies originated as a distinct subject of academic inquiry in the United States because of national security needs after the close of World War II. Lines were drawn on maps to block out areas of the world that presumably had enough in common so that coherent foreign policies could be established. The "Great Game" of the four decades after World War II largely involved the material and ideological battles of the U.S.S.R. and the United States. Although all serious analysts clearly recognized that the pencil point–thin borders delineating areas, such as the Middle East and South Asia, involved some fiction, it nevertheless was thought to be useful. For example, Iran generally is considered to be part of the Middle East, whereas Afghanistan and Pakistan are not. Yet even the most casual analyst knows that there is much commonality.

Geographical demarcation necessitates a degree of arbitrariness: A line has to be drawn somewhere. Perhaps an initial caution is that "areas" defined solely in terms of a sharply delineated geography do not carry as much intellectual heft as is usually thought. The meltdown of the U.S.S.R. further complicated the picture. Areas initially were defined with respect to national security needs. Now the rules had changed, so it seemed sensible to reexamine the notion of what was meant by an area. Globalization provided another motivation to engage in a fundamental rethinking. Although Huntington provided one such new view, his concept did not go unchallenged.

The notion of using "thick" borders as an analytical device is not controversial when standing alone; it is widely recognized that geographic fault lines neatly separating areas are not universally present and may shift with time. Examples are easy to cite. Turkey generally is considered to be part of the Middle East. On one hand, this makes sense; after all, the Ottoman Empire ruled most of the area for centuries. On the other hand, the Turkey of today aspires to be a part of the new Europe; this also is credible, as witnessed by a 1999 European Union (EU) decision to make Turkey a candidate for membership. A line that puts Turkey firmly in the Middle East, with all of the important traits used to define the area (e.g., Islamic), does not do justice to the rich diversity of beliefs and behavior. Perhaps it is better to think about shadings based on civilization or physical areas rather than razor-thin lines.

A related argument deals with the efficacy of thinking of areas solely in terms of geographic space. The (usually implicit) defenders of "areas as geography" argue that the effect of the (undisputed) proliferation of international interdependencies on basic political, economic, and cultural groupings is minimal. This group largely calls to mind the last third of the nineteenth century, when significant revolutions in communications and transportation allowed for massive increases in the international movement of goods and people. A polar view prognosticates basic changes in human organizations and relations. The more radical interpretations see the weakening (some would say demise) of the nation in the offing. The argument is that important aspects of the current wave of globalization encourage individuals to develop vectors of primary identity that would be stronger than loyalties to the nation. Immigration to the United States at the beginning of the twentieth century generally meant that individuals were cut off from their place of birth. Transport and communication were relatively time consuming and expensive. Over time, the immigrants adopted the lifestyle of their new home; they developed new sets of loyalties and attachments, the nation being of prime importance. By the end of the twentieth century, the remarkable decrease in travel and communication time and expense meant that many millions of immigrants could stay connected through frequent air travel, telephones, and most recently the Internet. Will these groups to some significant degree retain old loyalties? Will they develop "hybrid" loyalties? Will nonimmigrants also change because of this?

The growth in the number, size, and influence of nongovernmental organizations (NGOs) often is offered as partial evidence of this trend. To what extent will the use of the Internet help environmentalists band together in a fashion that significantly strengthens loyalties to the worldwide environmental community? Will the women's movement further transcend national borders? The foregoing considerations have led some analysts to believe that the notion of geographically defined areas, with each area having a set of distinguishable traits, is less valuable than commonly perceived. A geographic and trait-based definition views the Middle East as an Arab/Muslim world with undemocratic or unstable governments. The West has Christian and democratic traits. The detractors of this sort of classification argue that it runs the risk of overstating the differences in geographic locations in an age of increasing interdependence. Professor Arjun Appadurai prefers to think of "scapes" rather than areas. By this he wants to convey that the replication and mutation of civilizational affinities is not limited to geographic space. He further argues that the static notion of traits detracts attention from another, possibly more important concept. He prefers to think of "processes." This refers to the dynamics of world culture, politics, and economics. It places weight on the (dynamic) fashion in which people interact, solve problems, and change in a world of globalization.

Why is this border discussion a matter of serious contention? Remember that Huntington contends that geographically based civilizational areas are likely to produce the next source of international conflict, and that Islam poses the greatest threat to the West. Detractors claim that Huntington has constructed a false dichotomy, that the assigned traits are overdrawn and placed in a static framework. They contend that Huntington's conclusion of "Islam versus the West" does violence to reality, and that the ongoing globalization process will tend to show Huntington's argument increasingly less useful. They further argue that an acceptance of the "clash of civilizations" argument will lead to wrongheaded and possibly tragic policies.

The rise to prominence of Al-Qaeda provided a straightforward example of the difficulty of sorting through these complications. It represented par excellence the dark side of the NGO phenomenon. Its members and operations were multinational, cloaked with nationalist and Islamic motivations and rhetoric.

Transcending the expected limits of national borders, Al-Qaeda supposedly operated in more than 60 countries, a truly global terrorist organization.

ARAB NATIONALISM

Almost every border in the Middle East initially was defined by European powers—by way of the Balfour Declaration, the mandate system, and various territorial realignments thereafter. Middle Eastern governments, almost without exception, railed orally, if not through policy, against the artificial nature of the imposed borders. This notion held special force for the Arab nations. Arab unity, they said, would be denied as long as the borders remained. However, these same governments actively sought to build and strengthen loyalties to the nation-states described by the hated European-imposed boundaries. They succeeded in these efforts to various degrees, but the ideologically convenient dream of Arab unity, albeit moribund after 1967, continued to be part of the required rhetoric of some leaders until the invasion of Kuwait by Iraq.

The invasion was universally condemned as an illegitimate exercise of state power. Several regional participants (Algeria, Libya, Jordan, the PLO, Sudan, and Yemen) contended that an "Arab solution" would be the only acceptable solution. The countries of the Gulf (except Yemen) disagreed; they called for Western military intervention. Egypt and Syria were persuaded to accept this view and, importantly, to contribute troops to defend Saudi soil (but not to invade Iraq). It is difficult to overstate the enormity of these actions. The invasion of Kuwait marked the first time that a modern Arab state engaged in a full-scale invasion of another. The Arab world was quick to point to the sanctity of the borders. Then the United States, a longtime staunch supporter of Israel, along with ex-colonists France and the United Kingdom (and others), were invited to Saudi soil to do battle.

The Arab allies in the war against Iraq consisted of the petroleum-rich and population-poor countries of Arabia (except Yemen), Egypt, Syria, and distant Morocco. Egypt essentially had laid to rest notions of pan-Arab unity a decade earlier in the Camp David Accords, when it reached a separate peace agreement with Israel, ignoring the Israeli-occupied territories except to the extent that reference was made to vague and unworkable linkages concerning negotiations for the formation of Palestinian "autonomy." By 1990, Egypt was in a difficult economic situation—a situation eased, after its participation in the allied cause, by U.S. and Gulf economic aid and significant debt forgiveness. Syria also faced a long-standing malaise: a burdensome defense outlay in Lebanon, continued Israeli occupation (and settlement) of the Golan (Quneitra) territory, and cutbacks in aid from the Soviet bloc. It needed to repair relations with the United States; the crisis in Kuwait provided a convenient entrée.

Although the allied forces crippled Iraq quickly and easily, Saddam Hussein remained in power after the conflict. There are a couple of reasons why the allies did not press their advantage until Hussein fell. Although Iran generally watched the spectacle from the sidelines and had shown signs of considerable political moderation, neither the United States nor the Gulf States wanted to see the postwar Gulf dominated by Iran, an event that would be more likely if Iraq fell into prolonged chaos. The removal of Saddam Hussein likely would have assured such a case because his brutally repressive regime had decimated opponents and rid the country of an identifiable alternative leadership. The communal nature of Iraq—the Shia of the south and the Kurds of the north—meant that it was likely that the country would crumble without a strong central authority. Without a center holding the country together, the allies, especially the United States, would have had to settle in for a long-term military occupation. This idea was rejected out of hand. As it was, the Shia and

Kurds revolted against Baghdad. The Shia were repressed quickly and savagely by Saddam Hussein as the allied forces sat less than 50 miles away. Thousands of Shia continued the revolt despite increasingly energetic campaigns by the Iraqi military. By 2002 the Shia remained in a precarious position; they continued to be under the thumb of official Baghdad, experienced internal conflict, and suffered economically.

The Kurdish revolt in the north took longer to sort out, partially because of the long-standing organized Kurdish resistance forces and the flight of millions of Kurds into Turkey and Iran. As has been the case since the 1920s, Kurdish resistance briefly gained the sympathy of the wider world. As before, the world soon grew bored with news clips of the Kurdish plight. As always, the countries with substantial Kurdish populations, most notably Iran and Turkey, were not particularly anxious to see the Kurdish independence movement succeed. The Kurds of Iraq were given some protection through the application of measures designed by the United Nations to keep Iraq's military from unleashing its full force on the Kurds. Official Iraq viewed the U.N. actions as violations of its national sovereignty. While Iraq pressed for greater access to the Kurdish areas, the Kurdish opposition supplied the world with documentation to support their claim that even before the war there was an Iraqi policy of the systematic extermination of the Kurds.

Finally, there were the Kuwaiti oil fields. Before the war, the world had never seen more than five wells burning at the same time. The Iraqis torched 640 at the time of their retreat. The extent of the ecological damage probably will never be known. As with many such events, the worldwide media provided immediate footage of the spectacular fires. Then the coverage all but stopped; it became old news. To the surprise of all observers, the last burning well was doused in nine months (December 1991) instead of the originally estimated two to five years.

United Nations sanctions against Iraq as well as the Iraqi reluctance to meet the terms of the United Nations kept tensions high. Iraqi citizens were suffering terrible consequences from the sanctions, but the government of Iraq did not change its position. A particularly bothersome sanction was the issue of U.N. inspection teams charged with finding and disarming Iraq's stockpile and production facilities for weapons of mass destruction. The teams were denied access several times. As the years passed, Iraq engaged in a piecemeal compliance—yielding on one site to be inspected, calling for the end to sanctions, having these calls rejected by the United Nations, and then relenting a bit more. The common citizens continued to suffer. The sanctions worked in this sense, but it was unclear how much they weakened the power of Saddam Hussein.

During 1995–1996, there were several indications that Iraq was increasingly ready to relent on some of the U.N. demands. The regime suffered a setback when two of Saddam's inner circle, his sons-in-law, defected. They gave information on growing dissatisfaction in Iraq and evidence that Iraq had not told the truth to U.N. authorities on compliance with U.N. resolutions. Some European nations that had been urging a softer line, most notably France, were forced to distance themselves from that approach. Jordan, a vital lifeline for supplies, had largely patched up its relations with the Gulf States, and Iraq had to wonder if Jordan's transport routes would continue to remain open. The hope of a possible "opening" of Iraq faded on two counts. First, and most important, the United Nations was dissatisfied with conditions the Iraqis wanted to impose on the investigations. The second reason for pause was a bit bizarre. The defected sons-in-law were asked to return to Iraq. They were given assurances from official Baghdad that all was forgiven. They returned and were murdered two days later by members of their own extended family. The U.N. inspectors were withdrawn from Iraq in 1998.

The civilian population of Iraq suffered the horror of war from 1980 to 1988, and then again in 1991. Thereafter, their suffering continued; some would say it increased. Iraq had increasing rates of infant mortality, disease, and malnutrition. The country with arguably the best balance of resources in the Middle East, Iraq had a precipitous and continual decline in real per capita income. A United Nations study reported that child (younger than 5 years old) mortality rates increased dramatically: from 56 per 1,000 live births from 1984 to 1989, to 131 per 1,000 live births from 1994 to 1999. The report concluded that Iraq ought to be given an expanded "food-for-oil" allotment.

The (northern) Kurdish regions of Iraq continued to be under the control of the United Nations, albeit with (different) local administrative authorities and associated militias in charge of day-to-day decisions. In the north, the child mortality rate decreased from 80 to 52 in the same time frame as the dramatic increase in the country as a whole. A major goal of the sanctions was to pressure the Iraqi government to comply with the U.N. inspection teams charged with ferreting out weapons of mass destruction. Because the teams destroyed many (but not all) weapons, and because they were excluded from working in Iraq through all of 1999, after the United States and Britain mounted a substantial air campaign, there was much argument that the sanctions should be scrapped or at least eased. People in favor of continuing the sanctions replied that the increased child mortality rate and other horrors suffered by the common Iraqi had more to do with decisions of the government than the sanctions; they argued that an easing of sanctions would only help the inner circle of the regime. The suffering continued. By the end of 1999, the United Nations was trying to shape a program that would end the sanctions if Iraq agreed to more inspections. These efforts failed. All along, the United States continued its "quiet" air war against the Iraqi military.

As stated earlier, Iraq had national elections in 2005. The government that was cobbled together after bitter negotiations was thought to be weak. To the surprise of many observers, it held together. The next round of national elections was hotly contested, but the amount of violence was diminished from the previous elections. It is likely that this was because of the combination of the putative success of the U.S. troop surge, the subsequent increased responsibility of Iraqi forces, and the political accommodations that were forged since 2005. The firm intention of the United States to withdraw certainly played a role in persuading Iraqi politicians that they had to proceed in an orderly fashion or face chaos.

While the Kurds of Iraq experienced increased security, if not full prosperity, under the protective U.N. umbrella, and despite violent squabbles among the major political blocs contending for Kurdish loyalties, the Kurds of Turkey had a different experience. The Turkish military destroyed more than 3,000 Kurdish villages during the 1990s in an attempt to quash the Kurdish independence movement. The government regularly had about 50,000 troops in eastern Turkey and spent perhaps $8 million (U.S.) annually in these actions. In February 1999 Abdullal Ocalan—the long-time leader of the PKK, the Kurdistan Workers Party, and a sought-after terrorist—was captured, put on trial, and convicted of murder. Kurds throughout Europe expressed their outrage; the Turkish government breathed a sigh of relief. The Kurdish revolt quieted until 2004 when it heated up again. The Kurdish issue remained fundamentally the same as at the time of the mandates. The Kurds are divided among countries and among themselves.

Turkey's actions toward the Kurds were complicated by the desire to become full members of the European Union. The EU stated that a full consideration of Turkish membership would not be put on the table until (among other things) the Turkish government considerably improved its human rights record

with respect to the Kurds. This situation was brought to a head in summer 2002 in the midst of a political and economic crisis. The aging, infirm, and politically besieged prime minister apparently saw an advantage in supporting civil rights reforms for the Kurds in hopes of gaining the considerable popular support of joining the EU. The picture was muddled further when the U.S. government sought to weld together the various Iraqi forces opposed to the government of Saddam Hussein. This complicated matters for the Turks because of their fear that Kurdish success in Iraq would spill over into Turkey.

The long and severely deep economic recession in Turkey, coupled with political paralysis, led to national elections in November 2002. The results were stunning. An Islamic party rode to victory, and the party claiming roots to Ataturk was crushed. It was difficult, however, to interpret this as a rejection of secularism in Turkey. The victors in the election publicly endorsed the secular political traditions of Turkey. It also seemed that the voters were sick of economic decline and massive corruption of the old order; they sought a fresh approach. The leadership of the Islamist party voiced the same opinion—"Islam Lite," it seemed. But tensions between the secularists and Islamists persisted. In 2007, the Turkish military leadership issued a stern warning to the (Islamist) government that their proposed action of supporting an Islamist for the presidency was unacceptable.

International Organizations

It is sometimes useful to distinguish between international organizations under control of the constituent member states (e.g., the United Nations and the International Monetary Fund) and international NGOs (e.g., Amnesty International). Both groups face enormous challenges, and they often are in conflict with each other and with single governments. The role of the United Nations in Iraq signaled something more than a straightforward consequence of the dissolution of the bipolar world. The role of many NGOs would become more important in the affairs of countries. It remained unclear, however, how they would function. It is unclear if they would be effective in conflict resolution or if they would simply add more complications. The importance of the emerging role of NGOs goes far beyond the roles of watchdog and enforcer of international opinion that the United Nations took on in Iraq. Scores of NGOs pledged aid to the emerging state of Palestine. During the 1999 relief efforts in Kosovo, several Arab Gulf countries, led by local NGOs, provided significant (and, significantly, highly visible) aid to refugees.

It also seemed that regional alliances were assuming more importance. At the end of the 1991 war, a series of pronouncements called for a "new order" in the Middle East. The Gulf Cooperation Council countries along with Egypt and Syria were to provide for regional military security on a cooperative basis, providing a vehicle for dissuading further invasions. The Gulf States apparently feared the brawn and long-term intentions of Egypt and Syria, however. Consequently, they immediately started to back away from the agreement. For their part, Egypt and Syria were not ready to engage in significant military expenditures and risk loss of life without receiving substantial compensation—a compensation not being offered by the Gulf States. The members of the Gulf Cooperation Council significantly increased their defense spending, and they attempted, with limited success, to coordinate their defense forces.

After the war, it was recognized that the extreme disparity in income and wealth between the haves and have-nots posed considerable danger to stability. Various participants dreamed up schemes that allowed petroleum-inspired Gulf charity to flow into the income-poor and population-rich countries. But the petroleum-rich countries would have difficulty in the best of times satisfying the appetites of Syria and especially Egypt, and these were not the best of times; the oil-rich states felt a considerable financial pinch as oil prices wobbled downward and as defense expenditures increased. Also, some Gulf countries felt betrayed by the lack of support in quelling the Iraqi threat by Jordan, Yemen, and the PLO during the war. It would be quite extraordinary if large-scale income distribution occurred. The rich states probably will continue to write checks to pay for defense and otherwise defang the nettlesome desires of some neighbor. The basic schisms are likely to remain. These schisms are likely to continue to excite resentments on the part of the poorer nations. After all, the extremely high income of, say, Kuwait resulted from being lucky; if vast amounts of petroleum had not been found under its patch of territory, Kuwait would be yet another small and poor country.

Although a study of the complicated international actions in the former Yugoslavia is beyond the scope of this book, there are some overarching points of interest. First, significant military actions were taken by the North Atlantic Treaty Organization (NATO), the U.S.-European defense organization, not the United Nations. If nothing else, this indicates the complicated interactions of organizations controlled by member governments. Second, NATO actions in Kosovo were designed to protect ethnic Albanians against the politically dominant Serbs. Using a different set of descriptors, differences in "traits," the actions could be described as Western Christians defending a group of Muslims against Orthodox Christians. Although this should not be seen as the centerpiece of the conflict, it does point to the complications encountered when the more simplistic formulations of the "Clash of Civilizations" argument are accepted. Richer explanations are called for. In the midst of the drama in Kosovo, scores of NGOs (among them, the Red Cross and the Red Crescent) scrambled to provide relief to the Muslim Albanians.

These calls for international cooperation, wealth sharing, and a greater role for NGOs may not be as important as the ability of individual governments in the region to engage their citizens as the process of nation building develops. As every student of politics knows, there is no simple and straightforward model or plan of action that guarantees success. It involves a host of issues, including the construction of a set of meaningful symbols that convey attributes of the nation that are believable and behavior of the government that reinforces the believability of the symbols. When significant economic and political reforms are called for to meet the goal, the process becomes more complicated.

ECONOMIC LIBERALIZATION

During the 1980s, it became increasingly clear that many government policies were detrimental to the process of economic growth. The presumed need to intervene in the economy through the establishment of state-owned enterprises and various rules and regulations constraining private economic behavior has deep and complicated roots that often are tied to the structure of the colonial economy. The statist economic programs of several Middle East countries tended to lose favor during the 1980s. Privatization programs became a worldwide phenomenon, including such diverse countries as the United States, Ghana, India, Mexico, and Malaysia, along with many others. Among the promoters of a scaling back of government involvement in the economy were major international institutions, such as the International Monetary Fund and the World Bank.

The nub of the argument was, and is, that many government programs were grossly inefficient, stifled individual initiative in the bargain, and as a result guaranteed low economic growth and bureaucratic arrogance. Although this view of the consequences of an "overly activist" government has considerable merits,

the emphasis on economic efficiency does not speak (at least explicitly) to notions of distributive justice. Although many Middle Easterners could agree with the diagnosis of the sickness of their government, they had difficulty accepting the prescription; after all, unshackling businesses could be viewed as a policy of widening the income gap in a country.

It is not only the fear of the "rich getting richer and the poor poorer" that accounts for resistance to the opening of markets. The time-tested notion of comparative advantage states that the opening of trade between countries would enhance the economic well-being of each, owing to each specializing in the production and sale of a good of which it is the relative low-cost producer. The theory is applicable to most real-world situations that can be imagined. Some potentially significant complications must be considered, however. First, although each country would benefit, there would be winners and losers in each country. Owners of the resources specialized in the good or service that faces competition from imports would lose. Owners facing an expanded market through exports would gain. Social and political conflict should be expected.

Second, other questions buried in the comparative advantage argument are those of price trends, export earning volatility, and the potential for a country to lose its comparative advantage quickly. The price trend question is as follows: Are there forces that would drive the price of primary products (e.g., cotton and petroleum) lower relative to imports (i.e., manufactured goods)? If so, the country exporting primary products would have to export a greater volume each year simply to pay for the same volume of imports. Even if this is the case (and the results are mixed), there is the question of price volatility. Wildly gyrating prices make planning more difficult.

Finally, there is the question of the length of time that a country will hold a comparative advantage in a product. Petroleum is a good example. The high petroleum prices of the

1970s prompted research for new sources of petroleum and for different energy sources. The world seeks a low-cost energy source to meet its needs, not simply more petroleum. So, as solar and other energy sources are developed, the cost advantage in the production of petroleum by Saudi Arabia loses some significance: Why would people pay more to buy the cheapest petroleum if they could get energy from other sources (e.g., solar) at a lower price? The more a country is dependent on a single product to provide export earnings, the more pressing these questions become.

It has been appreciated only more recently that the process of reform can be exceedingly difficult. Although some issues are technical, a primary basic reason is straightforward: Significant groups prosper from the status quo, groups that would be harmed by reform. Likewise, the prospects for successful reform differ depending on what is going to be reformed and in what country; power relationships depend on complex political and economic relationships. It also is sometimes the case that a country in the midst of a liberalization program experiences economic downturns before the fruits of liberalization are realized. Some countries fix food prices below their free market level, but this tends to reduce the supply of food coming to market. Abolishing maximum prices for food would increase food production. But this takes time; in the interim, the average consumer may see food prices increase without an increased supply. Even right-minded reform can carry a high political cost. Economic liberalization has great appeal to most economists. The process of moving to more open markets may be disruptive and expensive in political and economic terms.

By the late 1990s, some important international organizations largely controlled by the rich countries of the world, notably the International Monetary Fund and the World Bank, started to pay more attention to the "poorest of the poor." They argued that if the poor were not beneficiaries of economic development policies, there would be a greater probability of lower national growth and increased social instability. The onset of terror against the rich symbolized by the events of September 11, 2001, strengthened this view. It remains, however, an abstract aim.

It often is said that there is a link between economic liberalization and political liberalization. The rationale is that businesses need to know the intentions of governments and will press for greater transparency. The Saudi Majlis Al-Shura is a case in point. Its importance as a player (albeit consultative) in policy decisions has increased steadily. This argument, however, is rather easily contested.

Political Islam

Because complete economic reform often involves the acceptance of a different role for the state in economic affairs, this can translate into questions regarding the nature of the "good" society. These issues tend to become explicit during periods of considerable flux; the argument of this chapter is that this is such a time in the Middle East as a result of the aftermath of the dramas of the past quarter century. These events did not occur in a vacuum; they occurred in a context of rapid economic and social change in some countries, of stultifying stagnation in others, of some ideological frameworks becoming stale, of others gaining in appeal, and sometimes of a profound distrust of the people in charge of the mechanics of government.

Religious movements often provide the context in which these concerns are played out. This is not surprising because concern about "the good life" is central to religion. In Algeria, an Arab country generally not covered in this book, civil order essentially broke down, with many thousands of lives lost, when the secularly oriented authorities repressed an Islamic political movement when it seemed assured of winning elections and fulfilling its promise to install an Islamic government.

Islamists gained power in Sudan, and that desperately poor and war-racked country started to be viewed by the international community as a prime safe haven and training ground for terrorists, replacing an ideologically evolving Iran as the premier rogue nation in the area. Relations between Sudan and Egypt, never free of some contention, soured as official Egypt blamed Sudan for the increasingly popular, powerful, and disruptive groups of religiously based movements in Egypt.

There are indications that the leadership of some of the more prominent "extremist" organizations (e.g., Turabi of Sudan) changed their tactics during the 1990s. Running the risk of oversimplification, during the 1980s the attitude of these groups was characterized by a total rejection of existing governments and a heavy reliance on displays of violence. Although this view and behavior did not disappear during the 1990s, there was a greater tendency for compromise and for use of the political arena to secure victories. Hizbollah participated in Lebanese elections (with surprising results), Hamas was persuaded not to boycott (1996) Palestinian elections, and an Islamic party gained more votes (December 1995) than any other party in supposedly secular Turkey. It is difficult to sort out the meaning of these events. Some commentators believe that the softening of rhetoric and action was primarily due to the fact that the Islamists suffered significant failures through the decade, that the change of tactics grew out of failure, and that the age of "Political Islam" is over. This may be the case, but another view must be considered. It may be that the Islamists are becoming woven into the political fabric and will gain strength in coming decades.

Finally, it may simply be that the 1990s represented a lull. Wealthy disaffected Saudi citizen Osama bin Laden gained prominence during the late 1990s by providing the financing and training of terrorists. The United States sent its warplanes to bomb his training site in Afghanistan and a chemical factory in Sudan that U.S. officials (on slim reeds of evidence, it seems) thought was producing biological weapons. This occurred after U.S. embassies in Kenya and Tanzania were bombed with considerable loss of life. The U.S. government reported that its attack on bin Laden was designed to prevent another round of attacks on U.S. facilities in scattered parts of the world. The terrorists intensified the attacks after the invasion of Iraq. Globalization has many faces.

These conflicting currents were readily seen in Egypt during the 1990s. During the early years of the decade, various groups engaged in acts of violence against the Egyptian government, Egyptian secularists thought to be their enemies, and foreign tourists. They also acted within the law to harass their enemies, bringing legal suits charging apostasy. The government acted by changing various laws to protect people being harassed mainly with a complete repression of the "religious extremists." During the mid-1990s, more than 50 individuals convicted of terrorist activities were sentenced to death, and thousands lingered in prison. Although it is understandable that the Egyptian government viewed the extremists solely as security threats, it also meant that this stance precluded an examination of the root causes of the desperation and despair.

The various radical groups—groups often with wildly different rationales—reacted in a variety of ways. In March 1993, a huge bomb ripped away part of New York City's World Trade Center. In short order, a group of individuals were arrested and subsequently convicted not only of that act but also of planning to blow up many important New York buildings and bridges and planning for the assassinations of numerous prominent people. The leader of the group was an aged Egyptian cleric. He and his followers apparently believed that a series of strikes at the United States would further their aim of returning Egypt to Islamic traditionalism. In 1995, a suicide bomber crippled the Egyptian embassy in Pakistan. Islamic Jihad claimed responsibility for this attack, and they promised more. On the other side of the ledger, members of the Muslim Brotherhood, an organization barred from formal political action, and the group that probably suffered most from the government crackdown, announced in 1996 the formation of a new party (the Center Party); the leadership of the Muslim Brotherhood gave public assurances that they would not act outside the law. By 2002 there were indications that many in Egypt who had called for or tacitly supported violence had changed their thinking. Personal piety started to be favored over political action, or so some people argued.

The conviction of a prominent Egyptian (secular) civil rights activist led the U.S. government to criticize Egypt openly in mid-2002. The United States also indicated that they would withhold supplemental economic aid to Egypt because of the conviction. Before this time, U.S. criticism of the Egyptian civil rights record was muted and not placed on center stage.

Generally, people struggle for significant changes in the ordering of government and society when they see no way to meet their goals through the present system. Often they seek power to root out what they see as a growing cancer in the body politic. It is interesting to speculate on a potential conflict between this call, or cacophony of calls, and the acceptance of many governments of a "liberalized" economic order. In the second half of the first decade of the new century groups of Middle Eastern intellectuals, both secular and religious, began to voice the opinion that violence justified by Islam was misplaced.

It is difficult to predict any definite outcome to these various swirls of activity. Middle East nations seem to have developed distinct, if sometimes fractious, identities. The nations are striving to strengthen these identities. However, economic liberalization within countries and the growing interdependence between countries tend to constrain the actions of governments and weaken notions of national identity.

Occupation of Iraq

The invasion of Iraq caused considerable controversy in the United States and internationally. The prime reason given by the U.S. government and its supporters for going to war was that Iraq had weapons of mass destruction and was primed to use them. The reasoning went as follows: The United States had an obligation to mount a presumptive attack to stave off a future catastrophe. The U.N. inspection teams disagreed, but their arguments were rejected out of hand. No weapons of mass destruction were found. The United States was unable to garner support of numerous significant allies to help in the effort. Another stated reason for going to war was that postwar Iraq would become a democratic state and, like dominos, other nations in the area would follow. The region would be better off. The need for stable petroleum supplies from the region was a largely unstated reason for the resort to war.

After the military victory, things started to go downhill. During the preparation for the war, the U.S. military chief of staff told a congressional committee that several hundred thousand troops would be needed for the effort, and that they would have to stay in Iraq for several years because of the difficult task of restoring order in the reconstruction effort. His reasoning was straightforward; if progress was to be made, security had to be assured. Security demanded that a large force needed to be maintained, especially in urban areas. The Department of Defense civilian leadership rejected the argument out of hand. Shortly thereafter, and unusually, they announced well before the chairman's term was to expire his replacement, effectively neutering him and sending a clear signal to naysayers. Apparently, the civilian core in the Department of Defense and the White House thought that their Iraqi champion of the time, Chalabi, was right in that the United States would be greeted with "rice and rose petals," and that the transition would be smooth and rapid. They apparently also ignored State Department and Central Intelligence Agency documents (among others) detailing the complicated path of occupation and transition.

After the war there was little security; looting and killing were plentiful. Significantly, immediately after the war the Iraqi army was disbanded, and Baathists were disqualified from employment in the public sector. This left the U.S.-dominated coalition forces without indigenous help. Baath Party membership many times was gained solely to secure employment, not because of ideological fervor. This was especially important for the professional classes. The decision to ban all Baathists from employment carried a high price tag; the Iraqi specialists were on the sidelines, and there was no national army (but there were some significant regional militia). Although it would have been difficult to sort through the ranks to root out undesirable individuals, the decision to forgo this task guaranteed that the job of the coalition would be even more difficult.

Iraq was on the brink of civil war as sectarian forces lined up in an attempt to strengthen their respective positions. The situation was complicated further by an inflow of a substantial number of foreign jihadis bent on punishing coalition forces and Iraqis that supported them. The capture of Saddam Hussein by coalition forces did little to change the situation.

The Shia of the southern portions of Iraq wanted to have their substantial militias control Shia-dominated areas. The coalition disagreed. Fierce fighting erupted between the militia and coalition forces until, after much negotiation, the leading Shia cleric in the country called for an end to the uprising.

The Kurds to the north had gained substantial autonomy from the central government since the end of the first Gulf war. They were calling for even greater power in Kurdistan. They also wanted to widen their area of control

to include areas around and including Kirkuk, an important petroleum-producing area. They claimed, with substantial evidence at hand, that Kirkuk was essentially a Kurdish-majority city before Baghdad systematically deported them to the north. Kurds started to return to Kirkuk after the military victory.

The Sunni population in the middle of the country provided the core of the insurgency. There were several reasons for this. The Sunni population was relatively privileged under the Hussein regime, and now many of their leaders had tough questions to answer; they had much to lose with a reconfiguration of power. They also realized that their minority status likely would lead to them being frozen out of petroleum revenues. They used their considerable financial resources to fund the insurrection.

Coalition forces and a far greater number of Iraqis were killed. The worldwide jihadi movement started to punish countries of the coalition with attacks on civilians; spectacular bombings in Madrid and London were the most prominent. Attacks also were mounted in Egypt, Kuwait, Qatar, Saudi Arabia, and Jordan.

The Sunnis were deeply troubled by the manner in which the march to Iraqi self-government was outlined. There was to be an election of a Provisional Assembly; this was to be followed by the creation of a draft constitution, elections ratifying the constitution, and finally elections for a new government. If elections were to be conducted on a nationwide basis, they would be consigned to have highly limited representation because they were only about 20 percent of the population. Representation based on districtwide elections would have put them in a more favorable position, but that would have required a national census, something impossible given the rapid timetable of the transition and the lack of security. Most Sunnis walked away from the elections to the provisional assembly.

The Provisional Assembly was dominated by the Shia and Kurds. After considerable haggling, especially with the reluctant Sunnis, a draft constitution was created. In October 2005 a referendum was held. This time the Sunnis participated; they wanted to defeat the referendum. This desire was due in part to the considerable autonomy granted to each province; because petroleum was concentrated in the Shia and Kurdish areas, the resource-poor Sunni provinces could lose much. Their efforts led to an overwhelming defeat of the referendum in all three Sunni provinces. The election rules stated that if three provinces had two-thirds of the voters reject the referendum, it would fail. Only two of the provinces met this high bar. The referendum passed. The killings continued.

An election was held in late 2005. The religious Shia did very well, but they did not have a majority. The difficult process of forming a government started. The killing continued. By mid-2007 the Iraqi political scene remained fragile and acrimonious. American troops continued to be killed at a very high rate. This led to the U.S. Congress (then controlled by Democrats) to draft an amendment that included a timetable for withdrawal in the Iraq war-funding legislation. Eventually, the timetable was dropped and the funding was approved, but passions continued to run high in both the United States and Iraq.

As stated earlier, the United States started to leave Iraq in 2010 and the Iraqis held their second nationwide election. International observers thought that it was a fair election. A secular Sunni/Shia coalition gained 91 of the 163 seats needed for a majority. The party of Prime Minister Malliki won 89 seats. The party associated with Moktada Al-Sadr won 70 seats, and the main Kurdish party had 43. Because of the sharply different political orientations of the parties it was difficult to put together a stable government. For example, the party that gained a plurality could not court the Kurdish parties due to bitter boundary disputes, especially around oil-rich Kirkuk. Much uncertainty remains with respect to the future of Iraq and the fate of its beleaguered population.

Political Legitimacy in the Gulf

The monarchies of the Gulf faced another set of difficulties regarding the proper extent of political participation. Officials could argue that their majlis-based tradition of consultation and consensus gave the average citizen a more meaningful voice in national policy than countries that professed democratic forms, but it did not actually allow opposition. They still had to deal with the issue of formal political participation and power sharing.

It was obvious to all serious observers that the massive response against Iraq's invasion of Kuwait in 1990 had more to do with protecting supplies of petroleum than preserving the Kuwaiti government. Iraq and Kuwait each supplied about 10 percent of the world's petroleum. Saudi Arabia supplied another 25 percent (and most of the Saudi supply came from the area bordering Kuwait). Because industrialized economies must have adequate supplies of petroleum to function, having Iraq control a large percentage of world output was unacceptable to the industrialized countries.

The war was enormously expensive for Saudi Arabia (possibly $60 billion directly and the same total indirectly), but the Saudi leadership knew that the expenditure had to be made, given the alternative. Victory did not mean that the kingdom was free of trouble, however. Mobilization gave focus to some of the more problematic aspects of the state. The royal family came under attack from numerous sources. Some people in the worldwide Muslim community wondered if the Saudis abrogated their function of guardian of the holy sites of Mecca and Medina by inviting more than one-half million infidels into the country. Some saw the sprawling royal family as engaging in wasteful and sometimes corrupt policies. Saudis from the left and right wondered if the role of women in the society was properly defined. Some people made calls for Western-style democratic reform.

Traditionally the royal family used the power of the purse to quiet dissent. Postwar Saudi Arabia faced a harsh budgetary reality, however; they had been spending beyond their means for more than a decade, drawing down their international financial reserves in the process. In 1994 the government announced a 20 percent cut in expenditures. They cut expenditures again the following year. The government also started to cut back on its lavish system of subsidies—education, gasoline, water, telephone services, and electricity—to become financially sound. Unless the price of petroleum increased dramatically, the Saudis would have to continue to tighten their fiscal belt.

In 1993 the government created a 61-member consultative council (Majlis Al-Shura), all appointed, in response to calls for more political voice. The government also arrested some dissidents and made significant policy changes favored by senior members of the religious establishment. In November 1995, a car bomb exploded in a Riyadh military building where U.S. personnel were training Saudi military forces (five Americans died, and scores of individuals were injured). Official Saudi Arabia blamed the attack, generally received with skepticism, on foreigners. In January 1996 King Fahd, weakened by illness (probably a stroke), handed over responsibility for running the government to Prince Abdullah, Fahd's half-brother. By the middle of the next decade, Abdullah assumed formal designation as head of state after Fahd died. Abdullah wanted to quicken the pace of Saudi economic and political liberalization. He did this but in a partial fashion due to considerable opposition, especially from the clergy. His task was eased by the bonanza brought about by the trebling of petroleum prices. It is not surprising that the amount of Saudi public discontent with the government increased markedly during the 1990s and in the early years of this century. After all, the war against Iraq was a major trauma, one that called many basic precepts of the society into question. It was unclear, however,

how these pressures would be played out. The legitimacy of the state rested on the dual pillars of the royal family and the religious establishment. In the last quarter century, a third pillar grew, that of the professional middle-class: businessmen, bureaucrats, and academics. Many of these people either were trained in Western universities or assimilated a range of Western values and lifestyles. The government of Saudi Arabia responded with conciliation and repression, depending on the presumed offense and the source. Although this is an understandable set of responses, the net result may not lead to a stable reordered system.

As stated earlier, it was not lost on many observers that most of the September 11 bombers were Saudi Arabian citizens. The U.S. government began a process of distancing itself from Saudi Arabia, quietly and not so quietly calling for substantial reform, especially actions that would mute the public policy role of the clergy. The government of Saudi Arabia then faced terrorist attacks within the kingdom. The pace of rooting out the domestic terrorists increased substantially. This, in turn, led to a strengthening of U.S.-Saudi relations. The other monarchies of the Gulf also had to deal with significant changes after the first Gulf war. Kuwait was torched and pillaged by Iraq. Not long after the invasion, Iraq announced that Kuwait was properly (historically speaking) part of Iraq. Because the Iraqis planned to stay in Kuwait, structural damage to buildings initially was limited, but anything movable was potential booty. The University of Kuwait lost its 700,000-book library and all of its computing facilities. Office buildings and hotels were systematically cleared of furniture, autos were stripped, the national museum was looted, and medical supplies were taken.

After the war, the physical reconstruction of Kuwait City happened quickly. The Kuwaitis had accumulated a fortune in international reserves to pay for whatever was needed. But there were tougher "reconstruction" projects with uncertain futures. First, more than a third of a million Palestinians living in preinvasion

Kuwait had to leave; their perceived pro-Iraqi stance during the occupation deeply embittered the Kuwaitis. Second, along the same lines, Kuwait announced that it would reduce its prewar population (2.2 million) by one-half by placing limits on the number of foreign nationals allowed in the country; only then could Kuwaitis become a majority in their own country. They found this goal impossible to carry out. Third, calls for increased political participation resumed. In 2004 Kuwaiti women were given the right to vote, a sure sign that reform was being taken seriously.

The other monarchies of the Gulf experienced serious political rumblings during the 1990s, albeit with short-term outcomes that favored a continuation of the status quo. A coup in Qatar resulted in a change of power within the ruling family; inner circle intrigue in Oman failed; the (Sunni) Bahraini leadership continued to worry about their Shia majority, including serious rioting; and the U.A.E. was forced to clamp down on expressions of opposition. A basic question remains: Are the monarchies of the Gulf becoming increasingly anachronistic, or will they develop creative solutions so as to remain in power?

There was a change of leadership during 1999 in Bahrain (March) and in Morocco (July) with the death of long-standing King Hassan. In addition, the small Gulf country of Qatar continued to undergo significant change. In 1995, a son toppled his father in a bloodless palace coup. There was a failed countercoup in 1996 and one of the putative designers of that coup was arrested in 1999. The new Qatari leadership significantly increased media freedom (especially if the host government was not the subject of media scrutiny), promised a democratically elected parliament sometime in the future, and generally attempted to "open" the country to significant political and social change, including a political role for women. The Qatari TV station Al-Jazeerah caused a significant stir, first in the Arab world and then worldwide. The proliferation of satellite TV reception meant that the wider Arab world was receiving news relatively free from government control. Several Arab governments complained when unfavorable news of their country was broadcast, but the Qataris held firm. Within a year, the station had established itself as an Arab version of CNN. Then it gained wider notice because it, virtually alone, reported and interviewed prominent leaders of the Taliban and Al-Qaeda.

Oman, Kuwait, and the United Arab Emirates (UAE) also experienced rapid change in social relations, including open discussions of a role for women in political life. Although it is too early to be definitive, it may be that 2000 signaled the "beginning of the end" of the old monarchical ways of organizing political and social life in the Gulf kingdoms.

Although the international situation of Iran remained markedly different from that of Saudi Arabia, there were some broad commonalities on the domestic scene. Sanctions imposed by the United States (since 1979) constrained the ability of Iran to rebuild its infrastructure, military, and petroleum facilities, although Western European reluctance to follow the U.S. lead meant that Iran was not close to the dire situation faced by Iraq. In an apparent attempt at partial rapprochement, in 1995 the Iranian government awarded Conoco, a U.S.-based firm, a chance to invest in Iranian oil and gas production. The U.S. government forced Conoco to reject the offer. Whatever the reasons given by the United States, the offer and the rejection point to a salient set of facts: It seems that the Iranian "pragmatists" were reaching out to the wider international community, and the United States was not ready to accede. The government of Iran faced domestic discontent from a variety of sources. Although President Rafsanjani managed to stay in power, his range of domestic policy options remained limited because of his reluctance to alienate any of the major political blocs. The continued poor performance of the economy initially was blamed on international sanctions, but it became apparent over time that domestic policy shared the blame. Because the Iranian revolution promised a full renaissance of the country under the banner of a reinvigorated Islam, the discontent over economic failure was intimately tied to larger issues of faith—that is, of self-definition. The revolution defined this religious renaissance as applying to the entire Muslim world, and many of the clerics close to the seat of government power saw Iran as the locus of the movement. There is evidence to suggest, however, that the revolution also engendered a renewed pride in the Iranian nation, that religion did not provide the sole source of continued inspiration.

Khatami followed Rafsanjani to the post of president. The election was spirited, and the landslide victory seemed to signal the desire for political reform, especially in the softening of religious dicta on everyday life. The transition, if indeed it was a transition, was not smooth. Many clerics opposed to reform used their considerable levers of power. An especially important battlefield concerns the proper extent of freedom of the press. During 1999 a conservative clerical court banned two progressive newspapers and arrested the editors. University students took to the streets, and some died. Then a reformist ministry of the government brought a lawsuit against three conservative newspapers. The conservatives returned the salvo by calling for the imprisonment (some called for the death) of two students who wrote a satirical play that the conservatives thought blasphemed Islam. We could view this series of events as a sideshow, but it can be profitably seen as the core of the struggle for reform. If the conservative clerics-cum-politicians lose their struggle on being the sole definers of proper political expression, we would expect a different set of debates (and policies) than if they won. The struggle over fundamental political issues continues in Iran. In 2002, President Khatami directly called into question the authority of the clerical establishment to overturn legislative initiatives. He called for changes in the constitution that would weaken their right to change summarily the course of Iranian history to fit their vision of a just society. However, the conservatives rallied. They effectively muted all attempts at reform. In 2005, a fiery populist, Muhammad Amadinejad, took over the reigns of government. In the space of a few months, he made a series of statements that seemed to signal an attempt to rekindle revolutionary fervor and rebalance their relations with the West. First, the United States and then the United Nations stepped up pressure on Iran to stop its nuclear enrichment program and to allow international inspectors to come into the country. Iran refused. The United Nations imposed (mild) sanctions in March, 2007. Iran had argued that the program was for peaceful means. Despite a very inefficient economy, the torrent of petroleum revenue meant that the demand for electricity (at subsidized rates) was increasing dramatically. By 2007 Iran consumed about 40 percent of its production for internal uses, and they had to import refined petroleum. Adding peaceful nuclear capacity could ease the strain. On the other hand, they refused to let the U.N. inspectors do their job. In 2010 this refusal culminated in sanctions imposed by the United Nations.

As stated earlier, the results of the 2009 elections in Iran were hotly contested. Millions of protesters took to the streets in many cities. These largely peaceful protests were quashed by the government through brute force. The protesters were quieted, but the legitimacy of the government remained tattered.

The United States, among others, was also deeply concerned about the extent of Iranian involvement in Iraq and Lebanon.

FROM OSLO TO JERUSALEM TO GAZA

The 1999 election of Barak as prime minister of Israel was hailed by many as a turning point in the long process of creating a sustainable peace between Israel and the Palestinians. It was a turning point; with bitter irony, it marked the beginning of a downward spiral.

A 1993 accord signed by Yasir Arafat and Yitzhak Rabin seemed promising. Although negotiations were slow and fractious, there was some movement toward a resolution. Then an assassin seemed to halt the process. On November 5, 1995, Israeli prime minister Rabin was assassinated by a lone Israeli Jew who objected to the hotly contested peace negotiations between Israel and the Palestinians. Shimon Peres inherited Labor bloc leadership and the office of prime minister. It was first feared that the peace negotiations would be derailed by the assassination. The road to peace started after the conclusion of the Gulf War. Many bumps and roadblocks had to be negotiated between that time and January 1996, when Palestinians held elections in Gaza and the West Bank, presumably entering the final stage of their long battle for independence.

The implications of the first Gulf War for Israel were secondary in the physical sense, but emotionally and politically profound. The intifadah was droning on at the time of the invasion, enervating all parties. After facing a universal diplomatic firestorm during the first week of the occupation of Kuwait, Saddam Hussein announced that Iraq would withdraw if Israel quit the occupied territories and if Syria withdrew from Lebanon. Despite Saddam Hussein's past indifference to the Palestinian cause, the PLO embraced him, and the Palestinian people took heart. When faced with such threats in the past, Israel often responded with a preemptive strike. It was constrained this time; the allies needed Arab participation in the war effort, and it would not happen if Israel were to strike Iraq. Israel was pressured to sit back—they even maintained this stance during the war when Iraq lobbed psychologically devastating and physically ineffective Scud missiles into Israel. Israelis went through the war donning their gas masks at every air raid warning: There was a fear (unrealized) that the Scuds would be armed with biological or chemical warheads. Palestinians "danced on the rooftops" as the Scuds sped toward their targets. Israeli attitudes toward the Palestinians hardened, and the already dispirited Israeli peace movement collapsed. Ironically, however, the June 1992 elections resulted in a government that was closer to meeting the goals of the peace movement than any government since the territories were occupied in 1967.

Israel also was affected by U.S. agreements with other members of the coalition. First, Syria was given a green light to root out Christian General Aoun from his fortified Beirut position. He had denied the implementation of a new power-sharing agreement because he saw it as bringing grief to the Christian population of Lebanon. Syria quickly routed Aoun, saw the new government installed, had the new government request Syrian help in disarming the various militia, and signed a treaty ensuring a strong Syrian voice in Lebanon. A united and Syrian-dominated Lebanon placed Israel in an awkward position. For more than a decade, Israel controlled much of southern Lebanon directly or through a Christian militia proxy. Withdrawal would remove a buffer for the northern Israel border and weaken the Israeli position in the Golan. To remain meant that Israel would face increasing international pressure. Israel remained. The Syrians agreed to withdraw their forces from all of Lebanon except the Bekka valley. The Syrians ensured their prominent position in Lebanon, however, through the engineering of a 1992 election in Lebanon that yielded a government friendly to Syrian interests. Israel finally quit Lebanon. Syria dominated Lebanon until their withdrawal some 13 years later. The withdrawal was prompted by a U.N. resolution calling for Syria to quit Lebanon after the Syrians manipulated Lebanese election laws and the constitution in an attempt to keep their Lebanese puppet president in power.

After the conclusion of the conflict, the United States placed considerable pressure on Israel to come to a peace conference. As the only remaining superpower, and with newly forged ties to important Arab governments, the United States was in a unique position. After a considerable amount of posturing, initial meetings between Israel, various Arab governments, and Palestinians (but not the PLO directly) were held (the "Madrid" meetings) in late 1991 and 1992. Over the next couple of years, the process continued slowly. Some observers thought that there would not be any further significant movement. This perspective was confounded by an announcement that the Israeli government and the PLO had been talking secretly in Oslo and had entered into an agreement (the Oslo Accords) that would bring the two parties into open direct negotiation for the first time. The accords were brokered without the active engagement of the United States.

By 1993, Prime Minister Rabin and Yasir Arafat shook hands on the White House lawn, a startling scene symbolizing their agreement to work toward peace. In 1994, Jordan signed a peace treaty with Israel. Syria and Lebanon remained out of the fold, although intense negotiations brokered through the United States brought the parties ever closer.

It will take some years to unravel connections between the details of the various negotiations. Several points, however, are obvious. First, the details of the peace arrangements between Israel and the Palestinians angered significant elements in each camp. Hamas initially rejected the idea of peace with Israel; they viewed it as a capitulation, and they promised resistance. But they were persuaded to change their views, probably because peace seemed inevitable, but that view was not firmly rooted, as subsequent events showed. Hizbollah, a champion of the Shia of southern Lebanon (occupied by Israel), seemed to moderate their stance when it became clear that attacks on Israel by them would call forth massive Israeli retaliation—but now Hizbollah could not count on the support of the Palestinians. This is not to say that violence on the part of these groups and their comrades ceased—far from it.

The Palestinians did not have a monopoly on peace plan–inspired violence. Various groups, often settlers in the territories, took arms against Palestinians, the most spectacular display being a massacre in Hebron, when a settler killed more than 20 Palestinians praying in a mosque located in the Tomb of the Patriarchs. It was profoundly shocking to many Israelis that many of his fellow settlers considered him to be a hero and martyr. In January 1996, a Palestinian terrorist dubbed "the Engineer" because of his sophisticated use of bombs was assassinated in Gaza by unknown individuals widely believed to be associated with Israeli intelligence. Because "the Engineer" had been responsible for scores of deaths, the Israeli population would have liked to breathe a sigh of relief, but "the Engineer" had become a hero in Gaza, and more than 100,000 marched in Gaza City the next day, calling for revenge. By this time, Israel had withdrawn its military forces from Gaza in favor of Palestinian Authority police. Palestinian critics of the peace plan pointed to the Israeli action as yet another reminder of the extremely limited extent of Palestinian freedom of action—another indication to them that the peace plan was a sham.

The November 5, 1995, assassination of Prime Minister Rabin—by a Jewish religious student who thought that God had directed his actions as a way of stopping the peace process—sent profound shock through Israel. There were deeply disturbing aspects of Rabin's death beyond that of clouding the prospects for peace. This was the first time in Israel that a politician had been assassinated. Israeli political debates have always been raucous, often punctuated by references to violence. During all of 1995, the level of bitterness and hate expressed by the enemies of the peace process increased, some of the most vicious attacks calling for the death of leaders who entered into such a peace. Some more radical individuals combed religious texts for a justification of such violent acts. Some commentators asked whether Israeli society had crossed a Rubicon, whether more political violence could now be expected. A related matter, and one that required less speculation, was the fact that a small but significant portion of the Israeli population were dangers to the functioning of the state. They had to be controlled in some fashion, but at what price? One problem relates to the continuing need for coalition building to form a political majority in the Knesset; religious parties of one stripe or another often have provided the votes necessary for the party with a plurality to form a majority. The obvious implication is that control had to be accomplished without alienation.

The agreement touched the definition of Israel itself. Israel has always had two potentially conflicting notions of self-identity. It operates as a democratic and largely secular state by definition of basic political rights such as voting. Many other rights and relations to the government are defined through the dual notions of ethnic Jewishness and religious Judaism. Israeli Arabs generally are not allowed to serve in the Israeli Defense Forces, and IDF service is a prerequisite for eligibility for a wide range of government subsidies and services. On a more fundamental level, the raison d'être of Israel is tied to religion in a more immediate sense than it is for most nations. Loyalty to the nation and loyalty to religious precepts can come into conflict.

Israeli settlements on the West Bank and in Gaza provided an important example of the kinds of difficulties the peace negotiators faced. It was impossible for the Israeli government to consider the dismantling of the settlements; it was thought, with considerable evidence, that no government could survive such a policy. The settlers had to be protected after control of the areas passed to Palestinian hands. Adequate protection demanded that safe transport to Israel proper had to be assured and water rights needed to be guaranteed. Many Palestinians objected to the notion that the settlements would remain, and that Israel would have an effective veto power in other realms of activity. They contended that Palestinian independence in this context would be meaningless, that a subservient dependence would remain. On the other side of the ledger, some Israelis said that the plan in essence was an abandonment of the settlements and the settlers.

The status of Jerusalem was left to future negotiations. Both sides knew that this was the single issue on which neither side could compromise, at least for the moment. Israel continued to regard Jerusalem as its capital; the Palestinians regarded it as their future capital. In this fashion, Israeli and Palestinian negotiators could tell their respective constituencies that they held firm to the all-important issue of the status of Jerusalem. The January 20, 1996, Palestinian elections included voters in Jerusalem. But Israel stated that those votes were to be treated as absentee votes from another area. Each side ignored the call of the other. The Palestinians could elect representatives from Jerusalem, whereas the Israelis could say that those votes were for representatives of other areas (because Israel claimed all of Jerusalem). As it happened, the voter turnout in Jerusalem (and Hebron) was far lower than in the rest of the West Bank and Gaza.

The Palestinian elections of January 20, 1996, were for an interim 88-member legislative council. Although the Palestinians were in control of only patches of West Bank territory, the victorious Arafat was correct in stating, "This is the foundation stone for our Palestinian State." About 70 percent of the registered voters turned out—a strong indication that calls for a boycott from "rejectionist" elements were not heeded. Although the formation of the legislative council could be considered to be a foundation stone, plenty of work was needed before an independent state could be constructed on it. Israel needed to leave the rural areas of the West Bank and urban Hebron, and the PLO had to reject its charter calling for the destruction of Israel, before the permanent-status talks scheduled for May 1996 could even begin. In addition, there would be much hard bargaining in the talks.

Syrian-Israeli negotiations centered on the familiar problems of Israeli settlers, water rights questions, and border control. Syria needed to have the Quneitra District (the Golan), first captured by Israel in 1967, free of Israeli settlers. Over time, the Israelis moved to accept this position—but they would accept it only if water rights would be guaranteed and Israeli towns bordering Syria would be safe from attack. In January 1996, the United States offered to station peacekeeping forces at the border, attempting to meet Israeli security needs and Syrian demands that they have full control of the use of their soil. An agreement with Syria was important to Israel beyond constructing peace with that particular neighbor; it was thought that formal relations with the Gulf States would follow if an agreement with Syria could be brokered. This would leave Lebanon as the only border state without a formal peace agreement with Israel—a Lebanon with Israelis in control of the southern part of the country, Iranian-supported groups in the south-central areas, and considerable Syrian influence throughout.

The proposed timetable for an Israeli-Syrian agreement became clouded in February 1996 when Prime Minister Peres called for elections in May 1996 instead of waiting the full term and having the elections take place in October. Apparently, Peres calculated that an election victory was more likely the closer the election was to the drama of Rabin's assassination. He began to interpret the election as a vote for peace with Syria and continuing "normalization" with the Palestinians. There also was the risk, however, that the election might disrupt the fragile peace talks.

In February and March 1996, spectacular terrorist bomb attacks for which Hamas claimed responsibility threatened the Israeli-Palestinian peace talks. In the first large-scale terrorist action, one that broke a period of relative calm, bomb blasts killed 25 (22 Israelis, the bomber,

and 2 U.S. citizens). The nation was horrified and stunned. Peace talks were put on hold, the borders between Israel and the territories were sealed, and the proponents of continued negotiations scrambled to avoid having the incident lead to a series of deadly reprisals. Hamas said that the attacks were reprisals for the death of "the Engineer" several months earlier. During the following week, the Israeli leadership of those opposed to the peace negotiations (as constituted) gained voice and public support for the first time since the death of Rabin. A week later (March 3), another bomb exploded in central Jerusalem, killing 19. Hamas claimed responsibility. Peres and Arafat vowed to root out the terrorists. Vital security issues dominated the scene; negotiating for peace would be impossible without a set of acceptable assurances that terrorist actions had permanently ceased. Israeli public opinion markedly turned against peace with the Palestinians.

In the elections of May 1996, Benjamin Netanyahu was elected prime minister. Due to electoral reform, this was the first time that the post was filled through general elections. After some time, he cobbled together enough allies in the Knesset to form a government. The elections marked an overall slowing of the peace movement, although a dramatic peace initiative occurred in August 1998 (the Wye Accords) when President Clinton presided over a meeting between Netanyahu and Arafat. The meeting ended with a timetable for Israeli withdrawal from portions of the territories it occupied (and after cancer-ridden King Hussein made an appearance calling for peace). The optimism of the day quickly faded, however. The language was familiar: Israel wanted the Palestinian Authority to do a better job controlling the Palestinians opposed to the peace process. The Palestinian Authority claimed to be doing all that was possible, and that the situation would be eased only after Israel fully complied with the withdrawals and other parts of the agreement. Negotiations with Syria ended. The peace process had ground to a halt.

Israel held another election in 1999. A relative political novice, Ehud Barak, defeated Netanyahu on the promise to speed the peace process. He also promised to bring any peace settlement to the vote of the electorate. As usual, it took time to cobble together a coalition government. Significantly, the Shas, an ultra-Orthodox (religious) party, gained enough seats in the election to become the third largest party in the Knesset. Prime Minister Barak gained his majority by including the Shas in the government (along with three ministerial posts). The Shas leadership agreed not to block peace negotiations.

By the end of 1999, a series of steps had been taken that revived the moribund peace initiative. For the first time in three years, Israel and Syria negotiated, and confidence-building measures were taken by the Israelis and the Palestinians. As always, the leadership of each side had to account for their constituents who were hostile to the process. Building permits on Israeli settlements continued apace, and the Shas gained budgetary approval for their financially strapped school system. The leadership of all parties (Israel-Syria, Israel-Palestine) agreed that they would construct the framework for a final agreement by February 2000.

The Palestinian leadership viewed the Israeli-Syrian negotiations with some trepidation; they worried that an early Israeli-Syrian accord would isolate the Palestinians. It seemed likely that this agreement could occur quickly, especially after Prime Minister Barak indicated that Israel was ready to relinquish most of the Golan, an area to which Israel does not have strong ideological claims (as opposed to Gaza and the West Bank). The struggle between the Israelis and the Syrians was strategic, overwhelmed by issues of security. When an agreement was reached, it was very likely that Lebanon would follow. That would leave the Palestinians alone. In addition, Barak indicated that the several million Palestinians living in U.N. camps or in the wider diaspora would not

be allowed to return. As always, the issue of Jerusalem was off the table.

All of these movements toward a peaceful settlement were dashed in short order. As seems to be habitual in the Middle East, events confound prediction. Yasir Arafat struggled to exact ever-greater gains out of the peace process while attempting to convince the Palestinians that the deal he was seeking was the best possible. On the other side, Prime Minister Barak's proposed concessions to the Palestinians severely eroded his support in the Knesset. Opposition groups on both sides acted to subvert the peace process. A visit by Ariel Sharon to the Muslim holy sites on the Temple Mount was the catalyst that sparked the unraveling of the peace process. The scenario was familiar enough: Palestinians rioted, Israel responded, deaths resulted, the voices of moderation were subdued, and the position of the "hard liners" in each camp strengthened. Finally, Barak was forced to call elections. Ariel Sharon became prime minister, and the Israeli position hardened. It was significant that Sharon was forced to accept Labor bloc members into his cabinet to form a majority in the Knesset.

The second Palestinian intifadah started in September 2000. Until the early months of 2002, militant Palestinian action focused primarily on the assets of official Israel, mostly in the occupied territories. But tactics changed: A spate of suicide bombers entered the fray; their targets were Israeli civilians. After some time, the Israeli military responded by invading most Palestinian cities, severely disrupting the infrastructures for water, transportation, and electricity and crippling Palestinian Authority centers of control and command. Thousands of Palestinians were arrested. Many on each side died. The IDF withdrew, only to return one month later as suicide bombing resumed. In July 2002, the Israeli air force (using an F-16) dropped a 1,000-pound "smart bomb" into a crowded apartment complex in Gaza City. The attack was successful in that it killed the leader of the military wing of Hamas, an individual the Israelis claimed planned many of the suicide attacks. The bomb also killed 14 others and wounded more than 100 people. A firestorm of international criticism followed. Over the years, many in the international community had criticized other Israeli policies and actions deemed contrary to international law, such as collective punishment. This case was different. The Israelis had to know that a bomb of such size would kill innocent civilians. They had to know that U.S. law prohibiting the use of U.S. weapons from knowingly targeting civilians was violated by such an action. They weathered the international criticism. The bombing occurred one day after the spiritual leader of Hamas had issued a statement that the suicide bombings could cease if the Israelis withdrew from Palestinian territory. The Israelis did not offer an explanation for the bombing in light of this apparent opening to the end of suicide attacks.

The Palestinian government and the population suffered in ways other than the loss of life and assorted indignities of occupation. The Palestinian Authority depended on Israel to hand over tax revenues collected by the Israelis. These transfers ended with the onset of the intifadah. The funds that the Palestinian Authority did have seemed to have been grossly mismanaged, with numerous agencies controlling funds, refusing to be accountable to the Palestinian Authority. By mid-2002, the Palestinian Authority started to assert its authority over its finances—a first step in assuring accountability.

Palestinian citizens also suffered physically. A 2002 study commissioned by the U.S. Agency for International Development indicated that 30 percent of Palestinian children younger than age 6 had chronic malnutrition, an increase from 7 percent two years earlier. About 50 percent of women of childbearing age were anemic. Fifty percent of the population depended on outside assistance for food, largely because the unemployment rates were more than 50 percent. The Israelis also stepped up their policy of collective

punishment. For many years, they destroyed homes of families who had members thought to have been engaged in terrorist activities. During 2002, the Israelis extended this punishment to include deportation.

Both leaders—Arafat and Sharon—scrambled to maintain internal support while weathering substantial international criticism. In late 2002, the Labor members of the coalition quit Sharon's government, eventually forcing him to call for early elections. Labor quit the coalition because they thought that the continual endorsement of settlements was self-defeating. Members of the Knesset in support of the settlements refused to join Sharon's government because they perceived him as being too "soft" on the Palestinians. Sharon had to patch up his shaky coalition to remain in power. As the intifadah became bloodier, Israel laid siege to the Palestinian Authority headquarters, convinced that Arafat gave a "green light" to individuals responsible for the suicide bombings.

After Arafat died in 2004, many Palestinians called for a change in the manner in which the Palestinian Authority acted. Corruption was deep and widespread, with various agencies squabbling over their areas of authority and power and money. The calls for greater accountability and transparency were agreed to by the new leadership, but action was slow and shallow.

Israel built a security wall separating it from the occupied territories of the West Bank. The announcement of the plans drew widespread international condemnation, but the wall was built. Sharon also announced that Israel was going to withdraw from Gaza, including the removal of Israeli settlers (about 8,000). Prime Minister Sharon weathered a political storm. Israel pulled out of Gaza in mid-2005. The "thickening" of settlements on the West Bank continued. It is difficult to sort through these Israeli initiatives. Some analysts suggest that the moves would lead the parties back to the "roadmap," a plan devised in 2003 outlining a sequence of steps that would lead to a final status solution. Others saw the actions as the death of the roadmap, an Israeli strategy designed to rid the state of some settlements, while strengthening its hold on the West Bank.

In November 2005, Sharon announced that he was quitting Likud, the party he helped to found, to form a new party. Apparently, he thought that members of Likud who opposed the retreat from Gaza would continue to block his efforts to govern. Elections were to be held in early 2006. Although the odds were high that the election would result in another coalition government, nobody knew its composition and its policies. A couple of weeks after the Sharon announcement, Peres, who had lost his post as head of the Labor bloc to an individual to his political left, announced that he was quitting Labor to join Sharon in the new "centrist" party. There was a guarded optimism regarding the peace process because of this move. In early January 2006 Sharon had a massive stroke, removing him from the political scene. The Israeli political scene was one of extreme uncertainty. By extension, the Palestinians entered a dangerous phase. The Palestinian elections of 2006 brought Hamas to power in the Palestinian parliament (Fatah still controlled the executive). This was a stunning result. Hamas was dedicated to the destruction of Israel. This meant that Israel could not contemplate any negotiations with them. Israeli elections resulted in the new centrist party, Kadima, winning a plurality. This necessitated the cobbling together of another coalition government.

Again, the past was but prologue. By 2006 Hizbollah was well entrenched and heavily armed in southern Lebanon. They crossed into Israeli territory and kidnapped two Israeli soldiers. Israel responded with massive force. The targets were not limited to Hizbollah forces; they included attacks on Lebanese infrastructure throughout that country. Two prominent reasons for the widespread response were an attempt to cut off military supply routes and to

punish the Lebanese government (members of Hizbollah, after all, are citizens of Lebanon). The Hizbollah response to the attacks was effective and furious. Their bunkers were constructed to withstand Israeli air attacks, and they also were able to thwart Israeli ground assaults. They also launched hundreds of rockets aimed at Israeli cities, reaching as far south as Haifa. After a few months, Israel withdrew without defeating the enemy. This proved to be an existential moment for Israel: An enemy sworn to the destruction of Israel had beaten back the considerable power of the IDF. For its part, Hizbollah emerged as a hero to many Shia Lebanese. They used this popularity to intensify their demand for greater voice in the government.

For the next year, the Lebanese government, relatively friendly to the West and opposed to a reassertion of Syrian influence, struggled to stay in power. In May 2007, a new threat emerged. Rockets rained down on northern Lebanese cities from one of the Palestinian refugee camps. By a decades-old agreement, the Lebanese military were not to enter the camps. The attackers were from a recently founded and relatively small jihadist group. They vowed to fight to the death. Lebanon responded with its own shelling. Thousands of Palestinians in the camp fled. Negotiations followed. Official Lebanon pointed fingers at Syria. In June 2007, a bomb killed a prominent Lebanese politician; he was the sixth politician assassinated in two years. All were vocally against Syrian involvement in Lebanon. The future of Lebanon is uncertain.

Israel also faced a number of vexing problems. Mr. Sharon had worked to forge a policy to dismantle the settlements. He had ordered the unilateral disengagement from Gaza in 2005. The election of Ehud Olmert (March 2006), Sharon's successor as head of the Kadima, indirectly indicated an acceptance of the policy. Olmert had then turned to the settlements on the West Bank. The policy was to have Israelis out of 90 percent of the area.

He wanted to have an agreement with the Palestinians on this point, but the election of Hamas dashed that issue. Olmert then decided to go forward with the plan unilaterally. But the engagement with Hizbollah dashed those plans; Israeli public opinion turned sharply against withdrawing from the West Bank without there being an effective government in the area.

The war effort was sharply criticized by the public and through an official commission of inquiry. Then the Olmert government was hit by a series of corruption scandals. The government could not be expected to chart a forward-looking course when it was concentrating its efforts on holding the government together.

The Palestinians had their own problems. Fatah controlled the executive branch. It was widely perceived as being profoundly corrupt and ineffectual. Hamas was viewed as being relatively clean and more staunchly ideological; especially bothersome was its continued call for the destruction of Israel. At one point, there were hints that it could be willing to accept a "suspension" for some years of the call for the destruction of Israel in return for a strengthening of their position. In other words, "kick the can down the road." This notion was doomed by the reality of events.

The military forces of Hamas and Fatah engaged in intermittent armed battles in Gaza throughout the period. There were no serious signs of progress to form an effective and stable Palestinian government. In June 2007 Hamas and Fatah fought for control of Gaza. After several days, Hamas controlled Gaza after overrunning Fatah forces. Fatah controlled the West Bank. The Palestinian president dissolved the cabinet and installed an "emergency cabinet" devoid of members of Hamas and declared that the government still represented all Palestinians, though nobody knew how they could effectively help those in Gaza. This allowed the Israelis to call for negotiations between it and the new government since Hamas was not

represented. They also announced that they would release the tax revenues they collected for the Palestinian government but refused to hand over after Hamas won the legislative elections. The United States announced that it would end restrictions on financial institutions doing business with Palestine and also would earmark substantial aid designed to help build credible institutions. The 1.4 million residents of Gaza were facing a humanitarian crisis. Several governments, including the United States, promised money to the United Nations for humanitarian aid in Gaza. Israel faced a dilemma since they controlled most of the routes into Gaza. Should (and could) they allow the trans-shipment of goods into Gaza?

To complicate matters further, it was evident that Iran and Syria were at play in the funding and training various groups promoting instability. It was widely believed that Hizbollah was the main beneficiary of this policy (other smaller groups also benefited). Sunni Arab governments of the area were deeply disturbed by the prospect of a Shia "arc of influence." The scenario was that post–civil war Iraq would be Shia. And Lebanon would be the same once Hizboallah took power there. It would be surprising if the Sunni governments did not put pressure on the United States to defuse the situation. However, given the lack of diplomatic relations between the United States and Iran, coupled with the enormous strains on the United States due to Afghanistan and Iraq, it was not clear what the United States could do. In the early months of 2007, the United States did (very softly) indicate that direct talks with Iran could be fruitful. It also banged the war drum a bit louder.

President Obama promised to bring a renewed effort to reach a two-state solution. He appointed a respected diplomat to work with the parties to affect such a change. In 2009 the Israelis promised to suspend all settlement expansion. This was a "non-negotiable" demand of the Palestinian Authority. as it was apparent

that ever-more territory was used for settlements over the past couple of decades.
Although the suspension was useful in moving
forward, there were significant loopholes.
First, the Israelis continued to assert the right
to "thicken" existing settlements. Second, they
stated that this did not apply to East
(Palestinian) Jerusalem since they had previously declared all of Jerusalem to be their
capital. Apparently it made no difference that
this was clearly against international law.

In March 2010 Vice President Biden was
sent to Israel in order to ratchet up the process.
While he was there, Israel announced that it
planned on building settlements in East
Jerusalem beyond those previously announced.
Prime Minister Netanyahu apologized for the timing of the announcement, but he did not indicate
that the policy would be dropped. Since the
Palestinians were firmly opposed to any expansion, this amounted to a de facto rejection of the
peace process. The United States sharply
criticized Israel. Relations between the two countries became decidedly cool. The Israeli attack on
the flotilla of ships attempting to deliver humanitarian aid to Gaza by ignoring the Israeli blockade led to more tension.

CONCLUSION

Interpreting the past, to say nothing of predicting the future, is a dicey business. It is a necessarily subjective process, one of sorting through
various "facts," picking the important ones, and
fitting them into a conceptual pattern, a pattern
that the analyst has chosen as most appropriate. Saying that, history ought to be more than
"the latest fairytale": History ought to inform
and guide.

There is a strong temptation for the
analyst to choose a single motive force underlying human action. For example, the Christian
crusades in the Middle East originally were
presented as an ideological cause—to regain
control of the Holy Land. The crusades subsequently were given various materialistic explanations—the onset of Western imperialism in
the search for greater power, the need to solve
basic property rights issues in Europe, and so
on. Then explanations again tended to include
religious idealism. Although we could appro-
priately argue that each variety of explanation
yields insights into the past, the acceptance of
any one view also helps to define the present
and guide predictions of the future. Simple
explanations usually are simplistic.

The failure of analysts to predict the tu-
mult of the past couple of decades, the turning
points, attests more to the enormous complexity of the world rather than to some fundamental
analytical flaw in the ruminations of the experts.
Will the Palestinians gain meaningful independence? Will peace between Israel and its Arab
neighbors be stable? Will Iraq emerge from its
long nightmare, and if so, in what form? Will the
monarchies of the Gulf (and Jordan) survive in
their present form? Will Egyptian reformers
have their dreams realized? How will Turkey's
Islamic leaders chart their country's political and
economic course? Will Islam be employed as an
increasingly powerful motivation for political
change, or will it retreat from political life? The
list could go on, but the point should be clear:
More fundamental changes will occur in the
character and behavior of the nations of the
Middle East. The remaining chapters discuss in
detail economic, cultural, and political contexts
of these changes.

8 THE POLITICS OF RELIGION, CULTURE, AND SOCIAL LIFE

In recent years, the role of religion and culture in Middle Eastern politics has attracted increased attention. Few aspects of Middle Eastern politics are so difficult to understand, however, without introducing our own cultural biases and distortions. Try as we may to transcend ethnocentric prejudices and pursue a deeper insight, the goal remains elusive. In this book's Introduction, the authors cautioned against certain popular but misleading assumptions. These assumptions include the conception of non-Western cultures as inherently stagnant and of non-Western individuals as unreflective and unimaginative with regard to the choices facing them. This is the sort of view reflected in some Western writers' condescending depiction of "the Arab" as "a child of tradition." Western journalists frequently portray a renewed commitment to Islam as an unthinking "return" to some irrelevant and regressive past, whereas Christian or Jewish renewal in the West tends to receive a more nuanced and tactful treatment and to be placed in a richer explanatory context.

We also have mentioned the limitations of the "modernization" theories popular from the 1950s to the 1980s, which attempted to explain social change in developing countries as the result of the adoption of a more rational cultural outlook. According to this theoretical paradigm, people achieve modernity when they trade in their unthinking obedience to tradition for a set of attitudes more appropriate to life in a changing, cosmopolitan world. Although each theorist had a slightly different list, these imputed traits tended to draw a distinction between "modern" and "traditional" people that was as self-congratulatory to the former as it was unflattering to the latter. So-called modern people are purportedly empathic, mentally flexible, ambitious, rational, democratic, egalitarian, open to change, punctual, and hard working. Implicit in much writing about modernization was an unstated premise that "modern" equals "Western."

Although some modernization theorists were more cautious and sensitive than others, this general approach had some inherent faults apart from its frequent descent into outright ethnocentrism. First, it tended to understate the diversity, dynamism, and critical awareness that can exist in so-called traditional cultures. Second, by treating such a broad range of social transformations simply as the product of an attitude adjustment, this type of analysis ignored (among other things) the relations of political and economic inequality central to the colonial and postcolonial order, implicitly recasting colonialism as an educational outreach program. This politically self-serving interpretation, vestiges of which still survive in some social science literature, can cloud understanding of the complex historical processes that have led to current political realities. This brings us to a third flaw in modernization theory, to which we shall return momentarily: its failure to shed much light on the resurgence of Middle Eastern religious and cultural values that have become so central to the contemporary scene.

The modernization theories were based on an element of truth: Certain ways of living and thinking have become more widespread, especially among people in urban-industrial settings and people whose social circles are the most cosmopolitan. In the Introduction, the authors characterized many of the emerging traits of contemporary life in terms of Marshall Hodgson's relatively value-neutral concept of "technicalization," a social trend in which the demands of specialized technical efficiency come to play a more central role than they did in preindustrial and precapitalist societies. Throughout this book, the terms *modern* and *modernizing* refer to the complex set of changes that accompany the technicalizing trend. This is not meant to suggest that these developments are necessarily desirable or that they define the inevitable direction of social change; in fact, they have sometimes raised moral questions and provoked negative reactions in the West as in other parts of the world.

Any discussion of the politics of cross-cultural understanding, especially with regard to the Middle East, should include some reference to the work of the prominent literary and cultural critic Edward Said. In *Orientalism* and other works, Said discusses the intricate web of assumptions by which Westerners characterize Muslims and Middle Easterners in terms of timeless, exotic essences.[1] Such depictions,

Said argues, have more to do with the West's need to define itself by contrast with an imaginary "other" than with any genuine traits, interests, or motives of so-called Oriental people. Said maintains that the "Orientalist" (whether the classic colonial sort or the modern "expert") shows surprisingly little interest in how actual "Orientals" view themselves or what they have to say on their own behalf. In Said's view, loose generalizations about such things as "the Arab mind" provide convenient substitutes for a deeper look at the common human motives, historical developments, and specific concerns that motivate flesh-and-blood people.

Although critiques of this sort may be taken to ethnocentric extremes, the problem Said describes is very real. Some of these pitfalls may be unavoidable whenever different peoples try to understand one another—especially when doing so from a distance. But if we want to demystify the motives of Muslims and other Middle Easterners and to understand them in plausible human terms, it is in our interest to move beyond wholesale characterizations and to examine the maze of challenges, strategies, and interests that characterize the interactions of individuals and collectivities in the region. This is especially difficult when we turn to such emotionally charged issues as cultural identity, religion, and social values.

THE POLITICS OF CULTURE

It is often suggested in the Western press that Middle Easterners either must side with the forces of growth and progress (rashly equated with Westernization) or remain in the clutches of the dead hand of tradition. This view is based on a notion of non-Western cultures as static and unreflective, stifled by authoritarian doctrines and unchanging consensus on social, moral, and intellectual issues. The hand of tradition, however, turns out to be more animated (and more manipulated) than one might suppose. Even in the most stable societies, cultural consensus is partially offset

---

[1] Edward Said, *Orientalism* (New York: Pantheon Books, 1978).

by ambiguities within the traditions and by diverse strategies of interpretation.

Social theorists increasingly have come to view cultural tradition not so much as an inert body of rules and beliefs as a battleground of shifting, contested meanings. Tradition is a perpetually unfinished project; how people comprehend their traditions and apply them to practical situations is subject to constant negotiation. In complex situations such as that of the contemporary Middle East, the process of interpretation is complicated by conflicting—and often disguised—power interests at various levels ranging from the individual, communal, class, and ethnic to the international and intersocietal arenas. The range of acceptable cultural interpretations within any given community is defined as much by their relation to social forces as by any logical justification or compatibility. In keeping with the broad definition of *politics* as the conflict and accommodation of competing demands for control of limited resources, the struggle over authoritative definitions of cultural meaning can be called a "politics of culture." In the arena of cultural politics, power interests assert competing claims to the labels, ideals, and symbols that a community holds in high esteem.

Politics of Culture in Islamic History

Islamic civilization was characterized from the start by a complex cultural and political dialogue. The ideal of a religiously inspired social order has always embroiled Islam in the politics of cultural belief and everyday social practice. To begin with, there was the question of how impeccable the religious credentials of the Umma's leadership must be, with the Shia insisting on leadership in the Prophet's genealogical line and the Sunnis more inclined to accept any overtly Islamic leadership able to govern effectively. Beneath this rift lies a deeper concern shared by Sunni and Shia alike—the danger of apostasy, of falling away from true Islamic guidance.

The time before the Prophet is viewed by Muslims as an age of great wickedness and barbarity (**jahiliyya**), but the original Muslim community under the Prophet's leadership (and in a different way, the great age of the caliphate) was a golden age, an exemplary time that later societies will never excel but can only hope to emulate. Because Muhammad was the Seal of the Prophets and his revelations completed God's message to humankind, there will be no future prophecies and no improvements on the rightly guided life of the Prophet's community. To turn away from that model is to renounce God and to slip backward into the darkness of jahiliyya. Innovation (**bida**), in the sense of forsaking the essential elements revealed by Muhammad and practiced in the Islamic golden age, is the slippery slope to apostasy. The early Islamic period was an era of unequaled cohesion and expansion, a fact that reinforces the association of political success with piety and political decline with apostasy.

Because Islam has been grafted onto a variety of local cultural traditions and has spanned long periods of social change, the question has often arisen as to how far everyday practices may depart from those of the Prophet's community without subverting Islam. To compound the problem further, there is plenty of room for disagreement as to just what is authentically Islamic and what is innovative. Ordinary people in past-oriented societies have tended to project their own practices back in time, so that any custom may seem to be validated by tradition and, in the case of Muslim societies, to merge with Islam itself. The high ulema have despaired of this tendency and sporadically denounced folk practices as innovations, even though they may not always agree on what deserves this sort of condemnation. For example, is the seclusion of women a tenet of Islam or is it really a folk custom that departs from the practices of the Prophet and the original Muslim community? Is the veneration of the Black Stone in Mecca a central part of Muslim worship as most Muslims believe, or is it, as some purists have claimed, an example of idolatry? Islamic civilization displays an inbuilt tension over such issues of social and cultural correctness, a tension that has energized and shaped much of its political dialogue. Over the whole of Muslim history, we can see cyclical periods of sociocultural "decline" followed by zealous revitalizing movements, often led by charismatic warriors under the banner of a purified Islam. Although these movements were deeply intertwined with the play of secular power factions, their capacity to mobilize support often depended on their claim to cultural, and ultimately religious, authenticity.

Colonialism and Cultural Politics

The confrontation with the West has added a profound dimension to cultural politics in the Muslim Middle East. Prior to the colonial career of the West, Christian Europe represented an external military threat and a challenge to Islam's universality. It also reinforced the Muslim perception of the unbeliever as uncivilized and insignificant. All this was to change radically with the rapid rise of European influence, a cultural and political explosion unequaled since the expansion of early Islam. It was not until the seventeenth and eighteenth centuries that Europe, which had previously lagged behind the Middle East, decisively surpassed it technologically. By the end of the nineteenth century, Europe had established its power throughout the Muslim Middle East. This came as a bitter blow to a civilization that, despite occasional setbacks, had remained the most powerful and cohesive force in world politics for more than a millennium.

The relation of colonialism to economic and formal political hegemony has been discussed in previous chapters, but it also is important to consider the profound cultural meanings that colonialism had for both the colonizers and the colonized. Whatever their material motives, the colonial powers generally thought of their efforts as part of an inexorable pattern of universal progress, in which culturally advanced peoples acted as benevolent protectors and teachers of the "backward" elements of humankind. From the colonial point of view, acquiescence seemed a small price to pay for the generous tutelage of a higher culture, and those people who resisted seemed obtuse and ungrateful. In recent decades, Western influence has shifted from overt political rule to various modes of cultural and economic hegemony, supported less by a conscious ideology of domination than by a set of cultural assumptions that make Western preeminence seem a natural consequence of living rationally in the modern world. The latent ethnocentrism of this neocolonialist outlook, cloaked in the seemingly neutral language of reason and modernity, can be more seductive and threatening than was the older, cruder ideology of colonial subjugation.

In addition to the effects of domination, colonialism has brought about a special set of problems with regard to sociopolitical identity. The Middle East, particularly under the Ottoman Empire, was an intricate mosaic of linguistic, regional, and religious groupings, the balance among which was disturbed by colonial intervention and the ensuing political changes. The impulse to assert local identity raised such questions as Who are we first and foremost? Are we citizens of the Ottoman Empire, or Arabs (Turks, Persians, etc.), or Egyptians (Iraqis, etc.), or Muslims (Christians, Jews, etc), or Shia (Sunni)? The problem of local identities was compounded by the drawing of modern national boundaries, most of which reflected the concerns of colonial powers rather than those of the peoples contained within—or divided by—those boundaries.

The confrontation with Europe has posed some philosophical problems for Muslims. As mentioned previously, Islam generally has looked to the past—the Islam of the Prophet and the splendor of the caliphs—to define its ideals. The post-Enlightenment Western secular worldview, by contrast, embraced the idea of unlimited human progress through reason.

Although the presence of a progress-oriented ideology is neither a necessary nor a sufficient condition for actual improvement of the human condition, it lent Western ascendancy a philosophic dimension that challenged orthodox Muslim thought and invited some kind of response. Muslims had to find a way of linking profound social changes with their own cultural conceptions of a golden age.

THE CONTEMPORARY POLITICS OF ISLAM

One of the most dramatic shortfalls of classic "modernization" theory was, as has been suggested, its failure to anticipate the phenomenal resurgence from the 1970s onward of Islam as a political force. To understand the Islamic revival, it is not enough to place it within a simplistic dichotomy of reason versus tradition; we must relate it to the specific problems of Middle Eastern societies and the diverse tactics that have been employed to address them. We already have noted the internal dynamic of Islamic civilization as it struggled to maintain political and social viability over the centuries and the important role that religious renewal has played in this internal process. In the modern global context, Muslim civilization must contend not only with these perennial problems of internal cohesion and growth, but also with the threat of being overwhelmed by economic, political, and cultural forces from the outside. The response to these challenges since the beginning of the twentieth century has embraced a wide range of possibilities. Some movements or leaders have tried to align the Middle East culturally with the modern world by the wholesale adoption of Western practices and values in many areas of social life. Others have used Western ideas more selectively, aggressively asserting national identities and goals at odds with some Western interests, while embracing modernizing technical and social reforms that seem to further those objectives. Still others have supported a

reassertion of Middle Eastern social and religious ideals, in some cases rejecting modern social values as inimical to Islam, or at other times claiming Islam to be compatible with (or even uniquely supportive of) such modern ideas. The past two centuries have seen these diverse strategies combined in various ways to form a rich internal dialogue in the Muslim Middle East, a dialogue in which cultural values and historical symbols—both local and imported—are interpreted in conflicting ways. The Islamic revival is a part of this discourse, and it must be understood in relation to the other parts.

The phenomenon referred to has been variously labeled *Islamic resurgence, Islamic revival, Islamic renaissance, the Islamic revolution, Islamic fundamentalism, and radical Islam,* among other terms. The authors will use *Islamism, Islamic revival,* or *resurgent Islam* to refer to the whole spectrum of movements whose aim is to strengthen Islamic influences in political, economic, and social life. The Islamic revival is real and pervasive and raises challenges to most forms of constituted authority, whether modern bureaucratic, charismatic, democratic, or authoritarian.

Not all Islamic revivalists share the same vision. The conservative revivalist wants to see the prevailing version of Islam taken more seriously, but does not envision any radically new interpretations or any purging of accepted religious practices. The Islamic fundamentalist, on the other hand, advocates a return to what is perceived as a lost purity in religious practice. This may entail not only the reimposition of the Sharia law and Koranic education but also a rejection of many locally accepted traditions of belief and ritual that do not strictly agree with the vision of a pure and uncorrupted Islam. Fundamentalists often take a dim view of cultural values and social practices originating in the West, although they may be quite accepting of technical innovation. The term *Islamic extremists* refers to people who would use violent or coercive means to implement a fundamentalist Islamic political agenda.

Although the Western press has given considerable attention to the fundamentalists, who seem to exemplify Muslim fanaticism, it has less to say about another kind of Islamic revival. Islamic **modernism** is predicated on the belief that Islam can be adapted to the circumstances of modern life without losing sight of the fundamental truths of Muhammad's revelations. In opposition to the fundamentalists, who see the Koran as a strict, literal, and unvarying prescription for righteous behavior, modernists wish to preserve the spirit and intent of Islam in a modern social context. Modernists begin with some of the same premises as the fundamentalists, including the need to cleanse Islam of accumulated human innovations that depart from the original purity and intent of God's revelations. In contrast to the fundamentalists, however, the modernists locate the core of Islamic truth in its liberal ideals of justice and reason, arguing that Islam is entirely compatible with modern life—or at least with a version of modern life that steers away from the godlessness, hedonism, social injustice, and abuse of power that they see in many developed nations. Although modernism and fundamentalism at times can lead to radically different positions, at other times they may be difficult to distinguish. Some of the differences and convergences of these two positions are illustrated in the discussion of sexual politics later in this chapter.

An irony concerning the modernist wing of the Islamic revival is that it achieved considerable visibility long before the recent wave of fundamentalism rose to prominence. Modernist arguments were articulated in the well-known writings of Jamal al-din al-Afghani (1838–1897), who traveled widely in the Muslim world, and his pupil Muhammad Abdu (1849–1905), whose ideas contributed to social reforms in Egypt, Turkey, and elsewhere. Islamic modernism has had a considerable following among educated and liberal-minded Muslims and still has influential advocates. Although this kind of moderation may prevail in the end, the mildness of the modernist position does not seem to make for good political drama and news headlines or, more important, to address forcefully enough the concerns of the average Muslim in times of social upheaval. This does not suggest that the Islamic revival is entirely dominated by fundamentalists. It would be rash to say that most Muslims today are fundamentalists, much less Islamic political extremists. For various reasons, however, it is the most extreme variants of Islamic resurgence that achieve a disproportionate amount of local and international visibility.

The contemporary Islamic revival springs from numerous political and historical sources. First and foremost, the movement attempts to address the current predicament of the Umma: the subjection of Islam to foreign control; the apparent falling away from simple pious faith, particularly among the urban intelligentsia and ruling elites; the Western technological challenge to time-honored social conventions; and the fall of Arab and Islamic influence to an all-time low. All this can be explained as the consequence of turning away from the true and uncorrupted revelation of Islam. Implicit in the movement is the expectation that a return to Islamic purity would restore the Umma to its rightful place on earth and bring Allah's beneficence again to his people.

Before the Iranian revolution, none of the successful Middle Eastern political movements of the twentieth century was driven primarily by the sort of religious concerns that had remained important to the average person. The leaders of the Egyptian revolution first seized power and only later turned their attention to the articulation of their (largely secular) principles. Baathism, despite its origin among Levantine intellectuals, was at best ambivalent in its recognition of Islam as a guiding moral force. Similar observations could be made of the Shah's White Revolution in Iran or the Turkish revolution under Ataturk. They all subordinated Islam to a broader secular framework, excluding it from the specifics of their ideology and policy. They denied the connection of Islam with political practice, thereby failing to address some basic concerns of the pious masses and neglecting a powerful source of political legitimation.

Modernization in the Middle East in the 1960s and 1970s became increasingly a program of Westernization and technological development lacking any consistent social or moral vision responsive to public sentiments. In the educational systems, secular government-controlled institutions replaced religious schools. From the perspective of its fundamentalist critics, Westernization brought increasingly immodest dress; permissive attitudes toward sex; the consumption of alcohol; and "corrupt" entertainment, including movies, television, pornography, and rock music. The growing wealth of the cities enhanced this image; as the political and social elites consumed Western products more extravagantly, the pious folk became more and more estranged from the elites of their societies.

The growth of urban wealth, concentrated in the elites, has given rise to perceptions of a widening economic gulf between the rich and the poor. Such a gulf is particularly obnoxious to pious Muslims who take seriously the Koranic injunctions regarding charity. The failure of elites to support a more equitable distribution of national resources has become a rallying point of revivalist Muslim opposition demanding social justice. In this setting, the Islamic resurgence draws on the radical egalitarian and democratic impulse associated with Islam in its earliest forms. Thus, a particular interpretation of values rooted in the Islamic tradition has been used to express dissatisfaction with existing patterns of social relations and with existing political authority.

The notion of the West as a source of moral degeneracy is in some respects a reaction to the humiliating colonial doctrines of Western cultural superiority, but it is also moved by specific opposition to certain Western-inspired social trends. The Islamic revival often calls for the rejection and expelling of Western influences depicted as "Satanic" in origin. During the cold war, many proponents of Islamic revival professed to see little difference between the social systems of capitalism and communism, a view adopted by some secular Middle Eastern leaders as well.

The existing tension between the worldviews of Muslim fundamentalists and Western modernists found a focus in the controversy that followed the 1988 publication in England of Salman Rushdie's *The Satanic Verses*, a novel that includes in its narrative a thinly disguised interpretation of Muhammad's revelation. The novel, although strongly critical of the moral decay and racism of colonialism and the modern Western societies, also contains material relating to Islam that many religious authorities, particularly in the Shia clergy, found overtly blasphemous. On this basis, Iran's Ayatollah Khomeini pronounced a death sentence on Rushdie and announced a bounty of $5 million for whoever carried it out.

Western governments were initially incredulous at this death sentence and ultimately were outraged. Muted criticism of the decision also was heard from the less fundamentalist Sunni ulema, suggesting that the Islamic world did not universally share this judgment. Nonetheless, most other countries with substantial Muslim populations banned the book, if only to head off communal conflict (a major consideration in India's decision). Rushdie condemned the censorship, expressing surprise over the reaction and protesting that he only wanted to present a "secular humanist view of the creation of a religion."

That such a view would be unacceptable to anyone believing in divine revelation seems obvious. Whatever Rushdie's intent or readers' judgments, the controversy expressed forcefully the divergent assumptions on which we predicate our views of the world. Even within the Muslim world, there has been evidence of differing views, and some Muslims have defended Rushdie's freedom of expression despite the book's offensiveness to them. Many years after the publication of his controversial book, Rushdie cautiously reentered public life.

Groups espousing an Islamic revival gained political power in Iran, Sudan, Libya, Afghanistan, Pakistan, and, arguably, Turkey. They contended for power in Lebanon, Morocco, and Algeria, and they figure in the politics of every Middle Eastern nation. They are actively, if irregularly, advocating the inclusion of Islam in government or even promoting an Islamic Republic in which the Sharia would be established as the law of the land. Their progress has been uneven to date, and the obstacles to their programs are serious. These experiences notwithstanding, such movements have gained in strength since the 1970s. At the same time, there are signs that the coming years may see a gradual revitalization of modernist Islam.

The phenomenon of Islamic revivalism cannot be treated in isolation from the larger dialogue of which it is part. This dialogue includes not only religious issues but also the problems of cultural identity; the challenge of serious moral, social, and economic problems; and the quest for collective self-esteem and self-direction. The resulting discourse brings up diverse and often conflicting perspectives from which to address the challenges of a changing world. The examples of Turkey, Egypt, Saudi Arabia, and Iran illustrate some of the complex forms this dialogue has taken.

TURKEY: RADICAL WESTERNIZATION AND THE DURABILITY OF ISLAM

Turkey's unique historical circumstances have placed it in an ambiguous position with regard to Western Europe. At the height of the Ottoman Empire, Turkey functioned as a frontier state that directly confronted, and at times threatened, the Christian West. Europe itself was regarded as a less accomplished civilization, and Christian Europeans were among the

subject peoples within the Empire. At the same time, Turkey's proximity and long commercial association with the West, its cultural distinctiveness from other Muslim groups, and its political strength compared with other Middle Eastern nations in the colonial period allowed for an exceptional policy toward the West. No other Muslim nation has so explicitly committed itself to the project of cultural Westernization, and Turkey's experience reveals the limits of a westernizing strategy.

The Tanzimat reforms from 1839 to 1876 (see Chapter 4) were aimed not at fundamentally changing Turkish culture or society, but at strengthening its military and government structures. Nevertheless, these reforms helped shape the attitudes of a generation of middle-level government officials with strong sympathies toward Western humanitarian and libertarian ideals. The liberalizing trend found strong expression in the Young Ottoman movement of the 1860s. Far from leading to an acceptance of colonialism, liberal ideals were linked with the project of casting off foreign control and pursuing the sort of self-determination achieved by the European nation-states. The liberals viewed with extreme distrust the sort of Westernizing elites who collaborated in European domination. The liberal movement emphasized the potential contributions of Turkish national culture to modern life; for example, the florescent Turkish literature of the time emphasized a more colloquial language and democratic idiom than the classical forms and expressed the ideals of the liberal intelligentsia. In this setting, a modernist interpretation of Islam flourished that located the core of Islamic tradition in its liberal values. According to this interpretation, Islam's pure monotheism, its commitment to freedom and social justice, and its opposition to superstition make it the most rational of world religions and therefore the most compatible with modern life. Such an interpretation not only validated Islam but it also suggested that the reversal of fortunes lately suffered by the Muslim world might be only temporary. It gave a traditionalist mandate for rooting out, in the name of a purified (i.e., rationalist) Islam, the "superstitions" and customary practices associated with Islam by the common folk and the conservative ulema.

During the period from 1876 to 1909, modernizing changes continued, not under the auspices of liberalism but under the authoritarian rule of Sultan Abdulhamit, who suspended the recently adopted constitution and ruled by means of a despotic police state. Abdulhamit's use of religious legitimation was different from that of the Young Ottomans. Initially appealing to the conservative ulema against the liberal modernists, he soon turned to a new brand of pan-Islamism, pressing his claim (contrary to existing Islamic interpretation) as "caliph," not in the restricted capacity of overseer of the Sharia and the Muslim community but as political ruler of an Islamic empire. Abdulhamit's project of building a Hijaz railway to carry pilgrims to Mecca, symbolic of his attempt to unify the Umma, drew material support from Muslims throughout the world. Despite his restrictions on freedom of expression, he continued to develop modern schools, build literacy, and promote Western science and technicalization.

The Young Turks rebellion of 1908, which restored the constitution and eventually forced Abdulhamit from power, had to face anew the confusing question of Turkey's identity. Should Turks align themselves with the Muslim world or with Europe? Should they form a Turkish nation based on a common language and culture, or unite with other Muslims under the banner of pan-Islamism, or try to maintain control over a religiously diverse Ottoman realm, even as Christian and other fragments of that Empire seemed intent on going their own way? Military conflicts over territory gave the Young Turks little respite, and events connected with World War I soon put an end to the Ottoman Empire and nearly to Turkey itself. Turkey struggled for its very life, and Mustafa Kemal, who emerged in the

1920s as the hero of that struggle and "father" of the Turks ("Ataturk"), was in a uniquely powerful position to make sweeping changes in Turkish society.

Ataturk's vision of the Turkish nation was influenced by European nationalist romanticism by way of the Turkish social theorist Ziya Gok-Alp. Arguing against the pan-Islamic and pan-Ottoman ideologies popular at the beginning of the twentieth century, Gok-Alp had promulgated a vision of a strictly Turkish, Westernized nation-state. Humankind, he argued, is naturally divided into "nations," each marked by a distinctive language, culture, and folk "spirit." Turkey could adopt whatever outward forms of government and elite culture were most progressive at the time without compromising its immutable national character; the ascendant Western cultural forms could serve Turkish development as a world power in the twentieth century, just as the Persian-Arabic civilization had served the purpose centuries earlier. Gok-Alp adopted a liberal modernist view of Islam, arguing for its place in Turkish national culture but not in a capacity that would damage Turkey's aspirations as a modern westernized state.

Ataturk resolutely implemented this vision of Turkey as a modern state in the Western mold. In a series of measures from the mid to the late 1920s, Islam was disestablished as a state religion. Sufi orders were officially abolished and their property was seized by the government; the madrasah schools were closed, and the state-sponsored training of the ulema came to an end; and Sharia law was replaced in its official capacity by a slightly modified version of the Swiss personal law. The interplay of symbolic and pragmatic elements is dramatically evident in certain of Ataturk's policies. In 1928 he abolished the use of Arabic script, decreeing that Turkish must be written with occidental letters; this was not only a symbolic alignment with Western culture, but in practical terms it cut succeeding generations off from the literary heritage of

Ottoman civilization. Similarly, the purging of Persian and Arabic elements from the Turkish language celebrated the language of the ordinary Turkish people at the expense of the classical Persian-Arabic high culture. (When non-Turkish roots were necessary, preference often was given to Latin and French.) The Muslim call to prayer, heard the world over in Arabic, was changed to Turkish.

Perhaps Ataturk's most deeply symbolic political gesture—and the one that prompted the most riots—was the 1925 ruling that adopted the Western brimmed hat and outlawed the fez and all other brimless headgear. The various hats, caps, and turbans had distinguished the many traditional ethnic groups, religious orders, and statuses within the Islamic community while serving the common practical function of allowing believers to touch forehead to ground during the performance of Muslim prayer. As Hodgson observes, Ataturk's policy served

> several functions at once. It symbolized the rejection of the Perso-Arabic and the adoption of the Western heritage (in itself the brimmed hat was not particularly modern—for instance, it was not particularly efficient—but it was very explicitly Occidental). More substantively, it [abolished] for the whole population the old distinctions of status which headdress had marked and which were incompatible with the interchangeable homogeneity which a modern nation-state presupposes; and it particularly reduced the visibility of those religious classes whose prestige and influence Kemal had to eliminate if the secular Republic were to survive. Finally, it served as a psychological coup. Even in language, "the hatted man" had meant a European, and "to put on a hat" had, as a phrase, meant "to Europeanize"—that is, "to desert

Islam, or the state" (which came to the same). Kemal was demanding, in effect, that every Turkish man own himself a traitor to all that the Ottoman state had stood for. It was one of those blows which forces people to come to an inner decision: either they must resist now, or acknowledge defeat and henceforth hold their peace. Those most so minded did resist and were crushed; the rest now had overtly to admit Kemal's authority, if not his wisdom, and found themselves implicitly committed to whatever more might be implied in Westernization.[2]

Ataturk's policies helped strengthen Turkey's educational system and its industrial economy and promote economic and social reforms associated with modernizing societies. Turkey has moved toward a closer association with the West, but the movement has not been as all-encompassing as Ataturk might have envisioned. His policies themselves departed so radically from popular sentiments that he could ill afford to promote the kind of political freedoms that might have brought Turkey closer to the political ethos of the West. Despite his veneration of the common people, Ataturk's policies went against the current of popular religious commitments.

The Kemalists never intended to abolish Islam but rather to guide it toward a more personal, rationalized, Westernized form similar to Protestantism. To some degree, however, the closing of the madrasahs had the contrary effect of reducing the influence of educated (and modernist) ulema and promoting more folk-oriented versions of Islam. Despite the Kemalist ideas taught in the school systems, local imams continued to compete for the

---

[2] Marshall G. S. Hodgon, *The Venture of Islam,* Vol. 3 (Chicago: University of Chicago Press, 1974), pp. 264–265.

loyalty of most villagers. Sufism, far from being crippled by the dismantling of the tariqahs, was purified by it and flourished at the grass-roots level. The growth of religious freedom after World War II saw the return of formal religious training and of the tariqahs, and in this atmosphere some factions became openly dedicated to undoing Ataturk's policies.

Turkey today, although still officially adhering to the fundamentals of Kemalism, is characterized by a wide array of positions on Islam and Westernization, from secularism and Islamic modernism to fundamentalism aimed at reestablishing Sharia law. In the 1995 national elections, the Islamist Refah ("welfare") party made significant gains, suggesting that, in some broad sense, the Islamists were in a position to move forward toward their goal of enhancing the influence of Islam in Turkish state politics and law. Subsequent elections confirmed this trend. The reemergence of Islam in Turkish national politics stands as a testimony to the durability of Islam.

EGYPT: THE LABYRINTH OF POSSIBILITIES

Egypt's brush with French colonization at the beginning of the nineteenth century dramatized its need for an effective strategy of self-definition and self-determination. Its unique position in the Middle East suggested many particular qualities, needs, and possibilities. Egypt possessed an ancient pre-Islamic urban and agrarian heritage, and its long history of urban culture had helped it to become one of the premier centers of learning and culture in the Islamic world; al-Azhar in Cairo was the recognized center of Sharia scholarship. Located at the fringes of Ottoman control, Egypt was semi-independent and a ripe target for European colonization. During the nineteenth century, the European powers, particularly Britain, established a strong social, political, and economic hegemony in Egypt that fell just short of outright colonial rule and that was to

last until the middle of the twentieth century. At the same time, Egypt could and sometimes did define itself as a legitimately Western nation, pointing to its active role in the classical Greek and Roman world at a time when Western Europe was still at or beyond the periphery of Western civilization.

In the first half of the nineteenth century, Muhammad Ali tried to bring Egypt into the modern world on a basis of cultural and material strength. His program of selective assimilation stressed military technicalization, economic development, and modern forms of education and government. Even at this early date, rural Islamic-oriented resistance to these modernizing changes posed a significant challenge, leading Muhammad Ali to attempt control of the Sufi orders by manipulating and co-opting their leadership.

Islam was not simply a conservative force, however. The Persian scholar Jamal al-din al-Afghani (1838–1897) traveled throughout the Muslim world, including Egypt, promoting ideas foundational to much of twentieth-century pan-Islamic, Islamic nationalist, and Islamic modernist thought. Similar to other restorers of the faith, he held that Muslims should return to the example set by the first caliphs and the early Muslim community. At the core of al-Afghani's teaching was the natural affinity of Islam with science and reason, the unity of the Umma against local and ethnic loyalties, and the need for a unifying political leadership modeled on the pious early caliphs.

His student Muhammad Abdu (1849–1905) became the chief religious authority of Egypt and a seminal spokesman for Islamic modernism as a model for Egyptian sociocultural development. Like al-Afghani, he rejected the wholesale adoption of Western ideas in principle, preferring instead to use the disciplined methods of reasoning developed by certain prestigious early Islamic scholars, and employing established ideas from Sharia interpretation, such as the principle of *maslahah* (preservation of the public welfare). He saw reason as given by God to protect humankind from either excess or adulteration in religion. Abdu placed more emphasis than did the Persian al-Afghani on the glories of classical Arab civilization and on Egypt as an exemplar of Arab culture. But like al-Afghani, he saw Islam as providing a superior basis for social justice, moral cohesion, and intellectual progress—a vehicle for outdoing Europe even in the areas of its greatest strength, while retaining the moral-religious virtues of Islamic civilization and the full benefit of local cultural integrity.

Some of Abdu's scholarly disciples interpreted his ideas of *salafiyya*, or the true wisdom of the pious ancestors, in a manner sympathetic to the conservative Muwahhidun (Wahhabi) movement of Saudi Arabia. But for most of the urban middle and upper classes, a loose interpretation of Islamic modernism became a license to adopt secular and Western ideas at their convenience without the stigma of religious apostasy. This is not to say that Islamic modernism eliminated the role of Islam either as a personally meaningful element or as a symbol of Egyptian identity. It did not make conflicts over cultural identity any less troublesome. While foreign-sponsored schools taught European ideas in European languages, a native flowering of Arabic literature struggled to reconcile the vastly different worlds of classical Arabic language and literary forms, the local Arabic vernacular and popular literary culture of the Egyptians, and the foreign literary genres that expressed "modern" individualistic conceptions of the self. Meanwhile, the discovery of the tomb of King Tutankhamen in 1922 renewed a popular interest in the glories of pre-Islamic Egypt that coexisted uneasily with the sentiments of either Arabism or Islamic renewal. In short, Egyptians faced a bewildering smorgasbord of different, and partly incompatible, cultural symbols and identities.

The first half of the twentieth century saw a growth of specific social problems besides those of economic and political self-determination

referred to in previous chapters. Social changes were creating new sources of discontent, including uncontrolled population growth; urban migration that greatly outstripped economic development and resulted in endemic unemployment; and a highly unequal distribution of land, capital, and other social resources. The effect of growing inequality was worsened by the breakup of communal village holdings and a weakening of familial and other networks of support for the destitute. These structural problems were accompanied by the growing prominence of films, popular songs, and sundry entertainments that, according to their critics, extolled individualism, romantic love, and other harbingers of hedonist immorality.

Although Gamal Adbel Nasser rose to power in 1952 by seizing a political opportunity, he became the first Egyptian leader in many decades to develop doctrines addressing a broad spectrum of his country's social problems. Eschewing the "borrowed ideologies" of the capitalist West and the communist bloc, he employed Islamic slogans and vocabulary in support of policies whose ultimate objectives were essentially secular. Nasser's ambition to bring the Arab world together under Egyptian leadership was based on a doctrine of Arab nationalism, which promoted the idea of a single Arab nation united by language, culture, and historical achievements. (Arab nationalism gained by its representation of Israel as a Western colonial settler state and of the Palestinian cause as a symbolic rallying point for Arab resistance to foreign domination.) The pursuit of social equality in the form of "Arab socialism," oriented toward state control of the means of production and redistribution of income and land holdings, was linked with Islamic concepts of equity, the care of the needy through zakat (alms), and the ideal of the unity and common good of the Umma. Nasser reformed the great mosque school of al-Azhar to resemble more closely a modern university, and he persuaded the high ulema to issue religious decrees, or fatwas, in support of such government policies as birth control. Islamic organizations and publications were organized and sponsored by the Nasser government to legitimize official policies at home and abroad. Although Nasser did much to reintroduce Islam into Egypt's political rhetoric, its use was selective and was essentially a means to other ends. By this time, however, a far more serious movement for the Islamic redemption of Egyptian society had been gathering strength at the grass roots.

The Muslim Brotherhood was founded in 1928 as a Muslim young men's association promoting personal piety, but by the 1940s it had become a radical, sometimes violent, political faction highly critical of Egyptian government, society, and culture. Drawing its membership largely from the ranks of educated and professional people—traders, teachers, and engineers—it advocated the restoration of Islamic law and government as an antidote to the decadence it saw everywhere in Egyptian life. Sayyid Qutb, a modernist literary critic whose two years in America had helped to turn him against Western lifestyles and modes of thought, led the Brotherhood through some of its most radical years until his execution in 1966. At first sympathetic to Nasser and the Young Officers, the Brotherhood soon parted ways with the government on a variety of issues.

Similar to the modernists, the Muslim Brotherhood sought a return to the roots of Islam to create a more just and decent society, hoping to reopen the process of *ijtihad* (Sharia interpretation) and reapply the values of the past to the problems of the present. The Brotherhood's vision of Islamic values drew on different traditions of Sharia interpretation, however, resulting in a fundamentalist ideology that contrasted starkly with the liberal-rationalist Islam of the modernists. They opposed Western-style democracy and Marxism alike as incompatible with Sharia rule, questioned the teaching of Western philosophy and modernist Islam in the schools, and opposed the formal separation of religion from government. They

had less tolerance than the modernists for religious minorities, Sufism, or folk religious practices. They targeted for criticism a broad array of "anti-Islamic" values and decadent practices that they associated with modern life—from exploitation, domination, materialism, and bank interest to "entertainment," consumerism, romantic song lyrics, popular women singers, mixing of the sexes, and birth control. Although they opposed Nasser's Arabism as an anti-Islamic attempt to draw distinctions within the Umma, they nevertheless criticized the lack of attention to classical Arabic—the language of the Koran and of high Islamic culture—in the schools and media. Where Abdu and the modernists had chided the ulema's hidebound conservatism, Qutb's Muslim Brotherhood attacked them for their timidity in defending Islamic traditions.

So vehement was the Muslim Brothers' opposition to the Nasser government that they considered resistance to it a higher cause than the struggle against Israel. In the political rhetoric of the Brotherhood, Nasser was equated with every enemy of Islam from Crusaders, Jews, and Mongols to Turkey's Kemal Ataturk. Almost from the beginning, the Brotherhood was divided between individuals (including Qutb) who shunned violence and individuals who were willing to use assassination and other forms of terror. The latter gave the government an excuse for suppressing the Brotherhood by force.

The Brotherhood and the establishment used symbols and concepts from Islamic history to revile one another. Qutb drew on the writings of a prestigious medieval Islamic thinker, Ibn Taymiyya, to press the argument that any Islamic leader who fails to apply a significant part of the Sharia has abandoned Islam. The Brotherhood equated the state of Egyptian society with jahiliyya, the period of utter wickedness before the coming of Islam. The pro-Nasser faction, speaking through sympathetic ulema, countered that the concept of jahiliyya properly applies only to a specific historical time and reversed the charges of apostasy by labeling the militants as *Kharijites* (the fanatical sect, which, claiming "sinners" to be outside the Umma, assassinated the Prophet's son-in-law Ali), contending that it was actually they who had left the Umma.

After Nasser's death, the fundamentalists at first were encouraged by Anwar Sadat's apparent interest in Islam. Sadat began and ended his speeches with Muslim benedictions, he declared the Sharia as the basis of all legislation (a matter more of labeling than of substantive reform), and during the 1973 "Ramadan" war against Israel (code-named "Badr" after one of the Prophet's famous victories) he employed the Muslim battle cry "Allahu Akbar" ("God is great"). He encouraged Muslim student associations in order to combat residual Nasserite Arab socialism. But Sadat wanted it both ways, declaring the separation of religion and government and instituting in 1979 family laws that liberalized women's rights in divorce, alimony, and child custody. His assassination by Jihad, a militant army cell including some former members of the Muslim Brotherhood, was a sobering lesson for Sadat's successor Hosni Mubarak.

The Muslim Brothers were as much a factor in the 1990s as in Nasser's time. The 1980s saw the growth of widespread popular interest in various forms and degrees of Islamic revival. Most Egyptians in all walks of life continue to be devout Muslims, and the visible expressions of that faith became more evident during the decade after the Iranian revolution. Muslim student associations earnestly promoted Islamic morality, politicians debated whether Egyptian laws are in keeping with the Sharia, and television shifted away from such fare as *Dallas* toward a greater emphasis on religious programs. Attendance at mosques increased. Merchants and bureaucrats were more likely to interrupt official business for daily prayers. The government, responding to both international and domestic Muslim pressures, prohibited the sale or consumption of alcohol except to

non-Muslim foreigners. A movement toward quasi-traditional forms of Islamic dress, especially for women, not only symbolized an interest in Muslim norms of sexual modesty but also asserted local resistance to Western fashions and subdued the display of differences in wealth and social status. Bearded men and veiled women were seen more often in the streets of Cairo. The label "imported ideas" became a common expression of disapproval, and rationalist interpretations of Islam were often stigmatized as irreligious innovations (*bida*). Despite more recent signs of a liberal reaction, the symbols of Islamic resurgence are no longer the exclusive province of radical fundamentalism but are often associated with popular, middle-of-the-road conservatism.

Although the Muslim Brothers are still censured by the government, their influence and affiliation reach into the officially tolerated Islamist Center Party on one end of the spectrum. At the other end of the political spectrum, they may have connections with the radical fringe of extremist groups inclined toward violence against the Christian Copts, foreign tourists, and others seen as enemies of the faith. The Egyptian government has, in turn, singled these groups out for harshly repressive countermeasures that have drawn criticism from international human rights observers. It is not easy to predict with any confidence what path Egyptian society may find through this labyrinth of conflicting factions, visions, and possibilities. In the 2005 legislative elections, about 20 percent of the seats were won by individuals associated with the Muslim Brothers.

Many social forces have conspired to encourage cultural nativism and religious conservatism in modern Egypt: a succession of modernizing leaders who underestimated the importance of popular religious sentiments; the failure of modernizing secular policies to deal with internal social and economic problems; the humiliating defeat by Israel in the 1967 war, interpreted by some Muslims as a divine punishment; the example of the 1979 Iranian

Revolution; the long-standing presence of a minority Christian community; cultural strains caused by tourism; pressure from Saudi Arabia to adopt stricter laws as a condition for aid; the example of Sadat's assassination; the increasingly dangerous cauldron of Islamic political extremism in the Sudan; the critique by third-world intellectuals of Western cultural domination; and perhaps even the West's own disaffection with some aspects of modern life.

Egypt illustrates many of the diverse cultural issues and possibilities facing modern Muslim nations. Although the interpretation of cultural tradition lends itself to manifold possibilities, it is no longer prudent for political leaders to ignore popular religious and cultural values on the assumption that they will soon fall before the juggernaut of secular Western ideas. Not surprisingly, President Mubarak's public policies and personal lifestyle show an appreciation of the importance of religious and cultural symbolism in contemporary Egypt.

SAUDI ARABIA

It is hard to imagine a nation commanding more of the symbols of Islamic legitimacy than does Saudi Arabia. Its roots lie in an Islamic purification movement begun by Muhammad ibn Abd al-Wahhab in the mid-eighteenth century and carried forward by the Saudi family, which unified the present nation in 1932 under the leadership of Abdulaziz ibn Saud (1879–1953). Inspired by the strict Hanbali school of Sharia law, ibn Wahhab's teachings (whose adherents prefer the designation *Muwahhidun* [unitarian] over the popular term *Wahhabi*) embraced a puritanical version of Islam that today forms the core of Saudi Arabia's religion, politics, society, and culture. Saudi Arabia is formally dedicated to the ideal of jihad, or struggle on behalf of the faith. Its flag displays the shahada (declaration of faith) and a sword.

Saudi Arabia had from the beginning what many Muslim fundamentalists elsewhere still struggle for: the Sharia as virtually the sole

law of the land. When King Khalid ascended to the throne in 1975, he reaffirmed that "Islamic law is and will remain our standard, our source of inspiration, and our goal." (His homage to the Sharia was astute because the consent of the ulema is needed for all transfers of power and was instrumental in the deposition of the dissolute King Saud in 1964.) Lawyers are scarce in Saudi Arabia, for Sharia religious courts decide all legal cases except for certain commercial actions and suits against the state (the latter are adjudicated by appointees of the royal family). This stern interpretation of the Hanbali legal code, with its provisions for beheadings and amputations, has become for most Westerners (and for many non-Saudi fundamentalists) a vivid symbol of zealous Islamic justice.

U.S. troops stationed in Saudi Arabia during the 1991 Persian Gulf War were surprised at the strictness of Saudi social norms. Saudi women wear full facial veils in public; non-Saudi and even non-Muslim foreign women may be publicly upbraided for failing to cover their hair. Men too must dress modestly and could never appear in public wearing tank tops or shorts. The ubiquitous semiofficial "religious police" patrol the streets ready to rap the exposed ankles of immodestly dressed women, to ensure that shops are closed promptly at prayer times, to enforce the fast of Ramadan, and generally to scold or even detain individuals behaving in a manner that strikes them as un-Islamic. Mingling of the sexes in public is considered inappropriate, schools and universities are segregated, and even foreign men caught in the company of women who are not their spouses may find themselves in trouble. Possession of alcohol is a serious criminal offense. U.S. forces in Saudi Arabia during the Persian Gulf War were obliged to rename chaplains "spiritual advisors," avoid wearing their religious insignia, and go through the motions of concealing the nature of Christian and Jewish religious services (ironically, the "enemy" regime in Iraq not only tolerated but even subsidized Christian worship).

Saudi Arabia is unique among Muslim nations in being the birthplace of the Prophet and the site of Islam's holiest places. The Saudi royal family makes much of this; King Fahd has the official title "Guardian of the Two Holy Mosques" (Mecca and Medina). The government has gone to great lengths to provide facilities and services for pilgrims during the hajj, and the royal family may be seen participating in the yearly ritual cleansing of Mecca's holiest shrine, the Kaaba.

In many respects, then, Saudi Arabia might appear to be an Islamic fundamentalist's Camelot, confidently enforcing strict Islamic norms while occupying a place of privilege in Muslim ritual and history and wielding the power of a premier oil-producing state. Beneath this apparent self-assurance, one detects a certain precariousness and insecurity in the position of the Saudi elites. So far, the regime has been reasonably successful at pursuing three potentially incompatible goals: (1) the maintenance of a credibly devout Islamicism safe from fundamentalist challenges, although the success of Al-Qaeda in recruiting Saudi nationals is disconcerting; (2) the pursuit of a permanent place in the modern global economy; and (3) the preservation of the Saudi monarchy. The third element, Saudi rule, is important not only from the viewpoint of elite self-interest but also because it has so far tried to head off a direct collision between the first two aims. The strategies used so far to reconcile these diverse ideals eventually could shatter, however, along the fault lines of inherent contradictions and double-edged political tactics.

The Prophet Muhammad is reported to have said, "The princes will corrupt the earth, so one of my people will be sent to bring back justice." In November 1979, on the first day of the Muslim year 1400, several hundred followers of a man who claimed to be the Muslim deliverer, or Mahdi, produced weapons from under their cloaks and seized the Grand Mosque at Mecca. Securing the permission of the ulema, Saudi forces retook the mosque after many days of combat during which more than 200 soldiers, hostages, and rebels, along with their family members, lost their lives. Most of the rebels were Saudis, some of whom were driven by old political grievances with the government. But their stated complaints had to do with the erosion of religion and the breakdown of morals in the kingdom, as evidenced by working women, Western entertainments, and the surreptitious consumption of alcohol. At the root of their protest were issues of religious purity, Western influence, and the alleged moral corruption of the Saudi rulers. Although the Saudi populace and the Muslim world were appalled at the audacity of these rebels, their claims resulted in numerous symbolic gestures toward increased moral strictness. The incident dramatized before a world audience the vulnerability of Saudi prestige.

The Saudi public takes pride in its royal family because it symbolizes the lofty, independent spirit of a people who have never submitted to foreign rule and the immense progress that the nation has made from the isolation and poverty of only a couple of generations ago. At the same time, however, the notion of monarchy is not in strict accordance with Koranic ideals of equality before God, and it is not in keeping with the contemporary fundamentalist preference for rule by popularly chosen religious experts. The monarchy is at pains to show that its rule is dedicated not to its own aggrandizement but to the welfare of the Umma. However, the huge influx of oil wealth in the past few decades has enabled the royal family (which has thousands of recognized members) to lead lives of privilege and self-indulgence, provoking criticism throughout the Muslim world, especially among the poor and the devout. The display of privilege and materialism is not only unseemly but it is also unjust and un-Islamic. The Saudi rulers make an important ritual gesture toward traditional modes of public access by holding royal audiences where the humblest citizens can bring their troubles to be adjudicated.

Not all the problems facing the House of Saud involve questions of lifestyle; some have to do with conflicting requirements of the society. The Saudi government has declared that the Saudi educational system is, above all, Islamic in its intent. Another important goal of the Saudi state is to establish an economy that can continue to develop and be self-sufficient without dependence on the single, exhaustible resource of petroleum exports. In doing so, it must emphasize high-tech industry, communications, and international commerce, for which a religiously oriented educational system is not particularly well suited. The Saudi universities must place religious goals in the background if they are to compete with the best Western institutions (where many Saudi royalty are still educated), but to turn away from traditional educational goals is to incur the wrath of religious critics.

Saudis sometimes are led to inconvenient or inconsistent practices by the contradictions of a society that is highly technicalized in some ways but that hopes not to compromise moral norms developed in a different social context. Because women are not allowed to drive, a male professional might have to leave work to take his wife or child to the doctor (or entrust them to a chauffeur, who is usually a foreigner and sometimes an infidel). Although alcohol is legally forbidden, it is a mark of prestige and hospitality among certain affluent, cosmopolitan Saudis to offer a guest fine Scotch whiskey worth hundreds of dollars a bottle on the black market. This nation of great affluence and sophisticated information technology submits every imported videotape to rigid censorship; *Muppets* videos are censored because one of the characters is a pig. Trivial enough in themselves, these examples point to the coexistence of extremely different social values within a single system. All societies involve significant contradictions; it is unknown whether the

contradictions in Saudi society will continue in their present form or resolve themselves in some particular direction.

Saudi relations with the United States pose something of a dilemma for the Saudi leadership. Islamists of the past few decades have been adamant in their opposition to communism, but the United States is equally disliked in some circles, not only because of its power and its secular materialism but also for its role as Israel's closest ally. Saudi Arabia's educational, commercial, and military security needs—to say nothing of its prestige in the West—are well served by friendship with the United States. Yet, the social policies required to promote one's image in the United States are sometimes the opposite of those needed for a nation aspiring to Islamic legitimacy, and any concessions to foreign influence are certain to arouse fundamentalist antagonism. Even as U.S. troops went into battle in the Gulf War defending Saudi interests, religious fundamentalists abused Saudi women's rights advocates by calling them "American sympathizers." The latent cultural tensions that surfaced during the Gulf War may continue to complicate the Saudi government's difficult task of reconciling its American connections with Islamic legitimacy, a problem dramatized by a November 1995 attack by Saudi extremists on a U.S. military training mission in Riyadh.

The issue of Saudi Arabia's image in the West was highlighted by its official opposition to the 1980 British-produced television documentary *The Death of a Princess*. Broadcast in the United States and Britain, the program dealt—somewhat loosely, its critics say—with the execution of an adulterous Saudi princess and her commoner lover. The program, which the Saudis tried to prevent from airing, outraged Saudi honor by making public the shame of the royal family and by suggesting that Saudi princesses cruised the desert in limousines looking for sex. Whatever its factual basis, the "documentary" reveled in Western stereotypes of Islamic justice and Saudi extremism. In the end, some stations chose not to air the show, and others followed it with a panel discussion including Arab (but not Saudi) speakers. Although the program reached only a small audience, the incident suggests the degree to which even conservative Muslim nations are sensitive to the way they are perceived elsewhere in the modern global village.

Saudi prestige in the West took a substantial drop in the aftermath of the attacks on the Pentagon and the World Trade Center in New York on September 11, 2001. Saudi Arabia was criticized for the large number of its citizens involved in the attack (15 of the 19 involved) and for tolerating Islamic extremism among its ulema and religious institutions. The government responded with an ambitious public relations campaign designed to rehabilitate Saudi Arabia's public image in the West in general and the United States in particular.

There seems to be a growing worldwide consensus on human rights and essential freedoms (although many nations prefer to make exceptions in their own cases), and international prestige and internal order seem to be increasingly linked to these criteria. However, the rights and freedoms widely accepted in the modern world may not always be compatible with the demands of the Muslim conservatives and fundamentalists whose opposition the Saudi government wishes to avoid. The country's Shia minority is economically and politically underprivileged and ripe for agitation from Saudi's archrival, the revolutionary Islamic government of Iran. Several disturbances occurred, including one indirectly related to the Grand Mosque incident of 1979. For the Saudi government to assuage Shia demands for improved rights and economic conditions would be to inflame Sunni fundamentalist sentiments of the sort that provoked the Mosque takeover. Any move toward equal rights for women and religious minorities, freedom of worship, or certain other rights recognized in the West and elsewhere is likely to incite radical Islamic opposition that conceivably could unseat the government.

Having taken the road of Islamic legitimation, Saudi Arabia has not only tapped a powerful force in its favor but it also has limited some of its political options.

Saudi Arabia's self-cultivated role of world Islamic leadership also poses serious challenges and problems that partially offset the rewards of prestige. Although the guardianship of the holy places gives the Saudi regime a high religious standing, it also puts it under the burden of maintaining the ritual purity of Saudi soil; the presence of U.S. troops during the Gulf War was seen by some purists as a desecration. Although the exposure of pilgrims to Saudi Islam sometimes may help promote it as the normative model for world Islam, interregional contact during the hajj also keeps alive the dialogue of diverse possibilities for Islamic culture. Saudi Arabia's sponsorship of countless international Islamic conferences has had a similar effect, bringing forth both liberal and ultrafundamentalist perspectives potentially critical of Saudi practices.

The Saudi Arabian ulema, like the royal family, are in a delicate position. Although they enjoy exceptional power in government and the courts, their co-optation by the monarchy has led them to relinquish much of the oppositional function historically exercised by the ulema in Muslim society. Should they become too closely allied with the ruling elite, they could lose their credibility among the more stringent Muslim factions and with it their usefulness to the monarchy. On the other hand, if they express too much opposition to government policies, they could find their influence in government diminished. Saudi monarchs already have shown a willingness to circumvent conservative ulema with rulings designed to win international credibility, as when King Faisal mollified President Kennedy by abolishing slavery and permitting television in private Saudi homes.

The Gulf War drew international attention to Saudi Arabia, its social and political order, its political restrictions, and its dissenters. In

March 1992, after years of lobbying from a coalition of Saudi liberals and religious conservatives, King Fahd announced the formation of a long-promised *Majlis Asshura*, or consultative council. Accompanying the announcement was a carefully worded decree spelling out the regime's doctrines of political legitimacy and answering numerous implicit questions about Saudi rule. It asserts that the announced changes are not innovations, but simply the continuation in a new form of religiously mandated practices that have always existed in the kingdom. The principle of "mutual consultation," which is mentioned in the Koran, is said to have been present all along in various arrangements for consultation with the ulema. The decree also pledges to "ensure the rights of individuals and their freedom and refrain from any action that will affect these rights and freedoms except within the limits stipulated in the laws and regulations." Protection of property and freedom from illegal search, arrest, or imprisonment are affirmed. Concerning the monarchy, the decree states that the Sharia "identifies the nature of the state, its goals and responsibilities, as well as the relationship between the ruler and the subjects." The king notes that this relationship is based on "fraternity, justice, mutual respect, and loyalty," and that "there is no difference between a ruler and a subject. All are equal before the divine laws of Allah." Above all, the decree declares unequivocally that the Sharia is the law of the Saudi state, and that "the Kingdom's constitution is the Holy Qur'an and the Sunnah (sayings) of the Prophet."

King Fahd's astute attempts to clarify the basis of Saudi political legitimacy showed a keen understanding of political forces, but not everyone was satisfied. Because the council is appointed by the ruling family rather than elected and would place no real limitations on royal authority, it falls short of the hopes of either the liberals or the conservatives. Each of these groups favors popular election and freedom of speech, but this apparent agreement of goals may conceal deeper divisions that could surface if the base of participation broadens. The experience of Algeria shows that religious extremists may envision democracy and freedom of speech as a means rather than an end, employing them to establish a strict reign of religious and cultural authoritarianism. An opening up of Saudi political processes may reveal a deep rift between the long-term objectives of the fundamentalist and the liberal wings of the opposition. The liberals might see reform as leading to greater rights for women and the Shia minorities, whereas religious conservatives might envision democracy as a process of installing pious ulema who would protect the community from just such changes.

IRAN AND THE ISLAMIC REPUBLIC

Iran's Twelver Shiism is based on the premise that, until the reappearance of the Hidden Imam, no earthly government is truly legitimate. This philosophy is well suited to an oppositional role, but the rise of the Shia-based Safavid Empire in the fifteenth century prompted a modification of this theory: Although the Hidden Imam is the only true ruler, the Shia ulema can and should lead the people in his absence, and their guidance can legitimatize secular rule.

At the beginning of the twentieth century, two factions were vying for control of the government: one advocating active guidance from the ulema according to the rationale stated above, and one pressing for a modern constitutional government. In 1906 these factions reached a compromise that provided for constitutional government, but with guarantees as to the Islamic nature of the government and a stipulation that all laws would conform to the Sharia. This compromise was set aside, however, with the ascendance of the Pahlevi dynasty in 1925. As he moved away from the representative government provided by the constitution, Reza Shah paid little attention to Islamic values and did much to suppress the visible manifestations of

Islam. A split between secularizing and Islamic factions began to grow. With the forced abdication of Reza Shah and the partial return to democracy in the 1940s, a renaissance of Islam led to the reappearance of veiling, religious garb, and public ritual.

The young Mohammad Reza Shah at first was allied with the moderate religious establishment. During the 1950s, however, the United States colluded with him to eliminate the popular nationalist prime minister, Dr. Mohammed Mossadegh, and the shah moved steadily toward autocracy. Aided by U.S. assistance and growing oil revenues, he launched a program of modernization that he dubbed the "White Revolution." His programs included much that was potentially beneficial, including land reform, industrialization, and the advancement of public health and education. He had little appreciation for the social and cultural context of these developments, however, forcing a pace of change that was self-defeating and that brought severe social upheavals.

Land reform stripped power from the clergy, and it moved faster than the ability of the people—including its peasant beneficiaries—to adapt to it. Ships loaded with goods arrived to find no docking facilities; thousands of cars and trucks sat idle without adequate roads or trained drivers; millions of dollars of oil revenues went for imported goods rather than the development of home manufacture, while urban migrants from the countryside looked for employment. The shah refused to listen to competent advisors, Muslim clergy, or popular sentiment, ruthlessly suppressing all dissent with brutal police state tactics. Despite important contributions to the material standard of living, the shah's policies resulted in a political condition that was more repressive and less promising than in 1906 when the first Iranian constitution had been adopted.

Perhaps looking for a source of legitimation that would not bind him to the authority of the Shia clergy, the shah turned to the political

symbolism of the pre-Islamic Persian Empire. He was not the first to think of this; during the nineteenth century, certain critics had attributed the decline of Iran to the dilution of Persian culture by Arab and Turkish influences, and some even blamed Islam itself. They advocated turning away from these influences to a renaissance of Persian culture. The shah's regime chose this strain of nationalism: He dubbed himself the "Sun of the Aryans" and had his wife Farah crowned empress—the first since 632 C.E. Although the shah's "Peacock Throne" ideology did not renounce Islam, it dismantled a long-standing balance between nationalist and Islamic definitions of political authority and turned Islam from a potentially powerful source of legitimation into a lethal weapon for the opposition.

Although the opposition to the shah included a broad spectrum of religious, secular modernist, Marxist, and other viewpoints, the shah's brutal tyranny tended to unite them and to make their differences seem less significant. The opposition ideology derived much of its character from the negation of the shah's excesses—his denial of human rights and free speech, insensitivity to popular opinion, and submissiveness to U.S. interests. Whatever their diverse social ideals, the dissenters were brothers in oppression, and a bravely resisting figure such as the Ayatollah Ruhollah Khomeini seemed in some sense to speak for the common cause of the disaffected. In the case of the Iranian revolution—as in so many others—it proved easier to unite in opposition to evil than to join in a vision of the good. The Iranian Revolution of 1979 was followed by a reign of terror in which thousands were executed, beginning with the minions of the old regime and proceeding gradually to the leftists and other out-of-favor elements among the dissidents and to social misfits and ethnic or religious minorities.

At the core of the revolutionary ideology was the total institutionalization of Islam in government. The revolutionary "Council of

Experts" articulated a theory of government by "the jurist" (*faqib*), a religious figure chosen to represent Islam; Khomeini was, of course, the jurist. Ironically, the traditional Shia opposition to worldly rule has elements that can be used to legitimize forms of political-religious leadership that make Sunni political authority seem humble by comparison. The chiliastic concept of a Hidden Imam who will eventually appear to redeem the world and punish the wicked (and who may send a deputy to rule in his name until his arrival) led many to see Khomeini as a divinely appointed spokesman for the Imam, or even as the Imam himself. (Most of Iran's Shia clergy have opposed such extremes, and many reject involvement in worldly politics both on theological and practical grounds.)

Postrevolutionary Iran was steeped in Islamic values and symbols. The educational system was aimed at purging Western influences and making people better Muslims, and college entrance examinations stressed religious education and attitudes. "Islamic dress" became the norm. The language of politics and the mass media was rich in religious symbolism. Chiliastic imagery and the Shia idealization of martyrdom figured prominently in patriotic rhetoric, and major political announcements were timed in accordance with auspicious dates in the Muslim calender. As a reaction against the shah's choice of cultural and historical symbols, "nationalist tendencies" were eschewed as contrary to Islam: Persian literature and poetry fell into disfavor, and it was even suggested that the Persian Gulf be renamed the "Islamic Gulf," at once symbolizing the unity of the Umma and rejecting the celebration of a pre-Islamic cultural identity. Although some of these expressions of revolutionary Islamic zeal have mellowed, especially in the cosmopolitan circles of Tehran and other urban centers, the revolution has profoundly altered the nation's culture, society, and politics in a way that will be felt for generations to come.

The identification of the United States as "Number One Satan" expresses many themes in the revolution. To begin with, there is a secular political grievance: The United States supported the shah and helped to depose Mossadegh, a charismatic popular leader who might have changed Iranian history for the better. SAVAK, the shah's notoriously cruel secret police force, was organized and trained with the help of the FBI and CIA to search out "internal enemies." The United States also functions in radical Iranian Shia thinking as a potent symbol of the powerful, antireligious, worldly oppressor—as opposed to the oppressed, righteous, martyred victim who will triumph with God's help in the end. The United States is associated in political rhetoric with the satanic figure of "Caliph Yazid," the historical caliph who martyred Ali's son Husayn. Symbols of American or Western influence, such as clothing and entertainments, are excoriated as anti-Islamic. Any victory in the conflict with the Great Satan is claimed as evidence of God's favor, whereas a defeat may be seen in light of the perennial martyrdom of the righteous. Of course, it is not only Iran that uses common enemies to promote internal unity, and it is not only the United States that is demonized in Iranian political rhetoric—Iraq, for example, also symbolizes the irreligious oppressor. Furthermore, it should be kept in mind that not all factions in Iran are comfortable either with the extremism or the international isolation that this militant rhetoric entails.

Khomeini's political philosophy placed great emphasis on the conflict between the oppressor and the oppressed. The oppressors included both the West and the former communist bloc as well as assorted local and internal villains. The regime has expressed its commitment to Iran's poor, favoring them for rationed goods and offering them government employment. It also endeavored to raise their condition through rural development and nationalization of private commercial assets.

The Islamic Republic

One way in which the revolutionary government of Iran has attempted to address "oppression" is by exporting its style of Islamic revolution to other Muslim countries. The direct appeal of Iran's strategy is greatest where there are substantial Shia populations, as in Iraq, Lebanon, and the Gulf States. Even non-Shia Muslim militants may be inspired by the success of the Iranian Revolution, and the decade following 1979 was one in which the whole Muslim world reverberated with the concept of "the Islamic Republic." Although many in the Muslim world reacted with distaste to some of the excesses of the Iranian formula, Iran continues to enjoy a certain kind of prestige as the first modern Islamic Republic and the harbinger of a hoped-for age of Islamic ascendance.

The concept of an Islamic state has an understandable appeal for Muslim activists accustomed to being on the defensive. The Islamic Republic raises a new set of troublesome issues, however. Although the Koran regulates social life in a variety of ways, it makes no provision for government as such. Nothing is said about leadership, succession, or the structures and institutions that compose a system of government. Some Islamic modernists have argued that it was not the intent of God's revelations to establish any particular system of government, and that whatever their moral and religious responsibilities, governments are entirely human creations.

If one does accept the notion that the Koran requires an Islamic government, the exact form of that government must rest on elaborate, and potentially debatable, interpretations of the Koran and Sunna. The body of preexisting interpretation in the Sharia is concerned mostly with personal conduct in ritual, family, and business matters—and of course, it does not refer to uniquely modern situations and problems. Although the Sharia cannot in principle be modified, its application to contemporary legal and political affairs would require considerable extrapolation. It could be argued that the extension of Islam and the Sharia into highly contested social and political applications might weaken it by tying its fortunes to the vagaries of politics. The same kind of issue arises with regard to the role of the ulema. Historically, participation of the ulema in government has tended to weaken their oppositional role (as in the Ottoman and Saudi cases) and potentially to diminish their status as an independent moral force. Strong links with governing factions or structures can quickly become liabilities when the tide of politics turns against them. For these reasons, many ulema are wary of excessive direct involvement in politics.

The supporting ideology of the Islamic Republic parallels in many respects the doctrines of third-world liberation. For example, there is the emphasis on social justice, dignity and empowerment of the common people, rejection of foreign domination, and celebration of indigenous spiritual and cultural values. At the same time, the Islamic Republic is theoretically incompatible with one of the classic elements of most third-world movements—nationalism. There is only one Umma, and it includes all believers in Islam. Any less inclusive Islamic republic that pursues its own national interests in opposition to the rest of the Umma can expect its status as an Islamic republic to be contested. The pursuit of a single, universal Islamic Republic offers little hope of success in the contemporary world, but the existence of competing Islamic Republics is a contradiction in terms.

Democracy also poses a problem for the Islamic Republic. As long as the will of the people is suppressed by a non-Islamic establishment, it is easy enough to use the demand for popular participation as a blanket concept for a variety of different and incompatible goals. Islam has a long history of populist thought that defines popular participation largely as participation by the ulema, insofar as they embody accepted religious ideas and apply the Sharia in a manner consistent with social justice and equality before God. This is quite different from the Western conception of democracy, and it raises urgent practical issues, including the right of dissent, political rights of religious minorities, limits on suffrage and representational government, and constraints on legislation. The Islamic concept of unity, or **tawhid**, refers not only to the oneness of God but also to "unity" in a variety of other meanings, including the political. Although tawhid is part of the ideal Islamic state, it is difficult to reconcile tawhid with the actual plurality of ethnicity, political views, culture, and religion encompassed within any modern state. Although Islamic-based governments such as Saudi Arabia and Iran have tried to equate the will of God with the will of all the People, it is inevitable that one or the other would be compromised to the detriment—in someone's eyes—of the regimes' legitimacy.

SEXUAL POLITICS

Throughout this book, politics has been treated as a dynamic process of conflict and accommodation, a process that connects in complex ways with cultural, societal, religious, and economic factors. The authors have referred to arenas and levels of conflict and resolution that dip and swirl irregularly so that issues on one level may have ramifications for others. More specifically, the authors have identified *cultural politics* as the arena of conflict that centers on conflicting definitions of cultural norms, categories, and symbols. Few problems better illustrate these kinds of conflict than male–female relations in the Middle East. These relations deserve to be termed *sexual politics*—not only because of their potential for conflict and resolution but also because of their relevance to the struggle for power and authority in domestic, community, national, and international contexts and their multifaceted relations with other political problems discussed in this book.

Sexual Equality in Islam: The Modernist Interpretation

Despite Western stereotypes to the contrary, there is a case to be made for Islam as a liberating and egalitarian influence in opposition to rigidly sexist traditions. This case has been made by a variety of Middle Eastern Muslims and outside apologists since the middle of the twentieth century, in an attempt to free Islam of the taint of "backward" folk traditions and reconcile it with modernizing trends. The view that many of the standard, prevailing interpretations of Islam are actually un-Islamic, and that the true, original Islam is more compatible with "modernization" than the pseudo-Islamic social traditions, is characteristic of "Muslim modernism." There is much in the historical record to support a modernist interpretation of Islam with regard to sex roles. Few would deny that the Koran ended many abuses against women, or that it established inheritance and property rights that were extremely liberal by the standards of the time; Muslim feminists sometimes refer to these provisions of the Koran as a "feminist bill of rights." Beginning with Muhammad's wife Khadija, the women of the early Muslim community were active in public life, even to the occasional extreme of serving as warriors or instructing men in religion. After a delegation of women converts questioned the Prophet about the male-oriented language of his earlier revelations, certain key Koranic verses used a "he or she" locution similar to that of modern "nonsexist" writing. As noted in Chapter 2, the Koran seems relatively free of the intimations of spiritual and moral inequality that one may find in parts of the Christian Bible.

The modernists have rightly pointed out that many of the "Muslim" customs that outsiders criticize as sexist are not necessarily Islamic in origin. It has already been noted that the veiling of women existed in pre-Muslim times as a symbol of social status. Koranic references to the veil are ambiguous at best and can be read merely as prescribing modest dress in public. Similarly, many modernists deny that the Koran provides any general support for the custom of secluding women in the home. The exclusion of women (until more recently) from public worship in the mosques is said to be a reflection of folk tradition directly at variance with the practice of the Prophet and his early followers. The Prophet's admonition against a man taking a second wife if he doubts that he can treat both wives equally, together with his statement elsewhere as to the impossibility of equal treatment, is offered as evidence that Islam really meant to rule out polygamy. Others have pointed out that polygamy is mentioned in the Koran only in connection with certain special and unusual circumstances and is nowhere endorsed as a general practice. The Koranic basis for the rule of evidence in Islamic courts, that a woman's testimony is worth only half that of a man's, is also noted as applying to certain (perhaps obsolete) social circumstances and not, the argument goes, intended to be universal. Modernist writers have also pointed out that some antifeminist sentiments commonly attributed to the Prophet are based not on the Koran but on the less reliable hadiths.

The apologists state that even unequal institutions sometimes may be better than they appear. Seclusion in the harem, for example, accustomed women to a considerable degree of freedom and achievement in a predominantly female world. Women physicians were (and are) surprisingly common in the Middle East, as are all-female workgroups in the contemporary mass communications industry and elsewhere. Similarly, polygamy is sometimes said to have relieved the burden on the traditional wife, while providing sororal companionship. The fact that the Koran allocates to women only one-half the man's share of inheritance must be balanced against the recognition that men are required to provide for women but not vice versa, and that the dowry paid by the husband at marriage becomes the wife's personal property.

Perhaps the strongest point on behalf of the egalitarian interpretation is that the main thrust of the Koran is the elimination of injustice and the protection of the weak from abuses by the strong. If one accepts this as the overriding message of Islam, even customs once considered as Muslim might be superseded in the name of this ultimate Islamic principle.

Sexual Inequality in Islamic Tradition

The previous arguments notwithstanding, there are certain historical realities that even the most devoted modernist is obliged to recognize. To begin with, the social regulations of the Koran do portray a world in which public affairs were handled mainly by men, a world in which women usually moved in a domestic sphere circumscribed by male authority. The inequality recognized in the Koran is social rather than spiritual in nature, entailing numerous sexually asymmetrical regulations, such as the difference in inheritance shares, the fact that only men can take more than one spouse, and the exclusively male ability to obtain a divorce without publicly showing cause. Although the outlook of the Koran is probably no more male-oriented than that of Jewish and Christian scriptures, the Koran is explicit in its regulation of domestic life, and its detailed implementation in Sharia law leaves little latitude for interpretation.

There is no mistaking the trend in sex roles after the Prophet's death. Conservative views arising from folk tradition and from the practice of the Persian and Byzantine upper classes led to consistently antifeminist interpretations of the Koran and the accumulation of antifeminist hadiths attributed to the Prophet. By the time Sharia law had taken its definitive form in the ninth century, these conservative interpretations had taken on the authority of divine command. The Sharia gives legal force to the husband's right of unilateral divorce, but it leaves up to the man's judgment the fulfillment of the Koranic requirements that the man has good cause and will seek reconciliation. Similarly, it gives legal status to the Prophet's permission to marry four wives, but it leaves up to the husband the fulfillment of the Koran's clearly stated precondition of equal treatment. The Sharia occasionally even sanctifies customs that cannot be documented in the Koran and seem at odds with the Prophet's attempts to strengthen the family. This particularly includes the custom of "triple divorce," in which a husband can divorce his wife simply by saying, "I repudiate thee" three times in one sitting. In most schools of Muslim jurisprudence, this divorce is binding and cannot be rescinded even at the husband's will. Most ulema, although disapproving of the practice, must recognize its legality as an established part of the Sharia. The Sharia, technically at least, is not subject to modification; its explicitly conservative interpretations of sex role issues pose an inconvenience to the modernists.

Equally problematic is the tendency of rank-and-file Muslims and even the ulema to imbue traditional practices and attitudes with the sanctity of Islam. Whether or not the Koran actually insists on traditional female subordination, ordinary people may believe that they are defending Islam whenever they resist innovative, especially Westernizing, influences in favor of their own traditions. There is even a basis for this in Islamic theology because the Prophet is reported to have said that God will not let His people agree in an error. Hence, Muslim jurisprudence recognizes consensus (i.e., the consensus of the ulema) as one criterion of religious truth. Traditional attitudes about women and sexuality achieve a quasi-religious status despite their lack of any direct basis in scripture or theology.

Important among these attitudes is the notion that female unchastity is the most potent threat to family honor, and that women's sexuality threatens the social order. It is taken for granted that men will be possessive and protective of the women in their own families and opportunistic toward others. Women are thought of not as self-controlling but as being controlled by others; a good woman submits to

the control of her father, brothers, and later her husband, whereas a bad woman submits to the predatory stranger. Women are not to be trusted but rather contained—confined within the circle of male overseers, within the veil, and whenever possible, secluded and protected in the women's quarters of the household. Many Muslim men may see this private patriarchal domain as their last bastion of authority in a world otherwise dominated by exogenous forces. A sense of helplessness in the face of other changes might even lead to a retrenchment of this miniature polity within the home.

Struggle for Reform

Much of the modernization of sex roles in the Middle East has stemmed indirectly from international politics. Turkey and Egypt, as the two main centers of Middle Eastern Muslim power in the early nineteenth century, were the first to feel the threat of the Western incursion. Their response in each case was a judicious attempt to modernize the military and other sectors of society that might help stave off foreign rule. These programs of modernization, implemented by Western-educated cadres, led to a general fascination with, and grudging respect for, Western culture. Colonialism was, of course, as much a cultural as a military onslaught, and Middle Easterners were faced with a significant challenge in the West's claims of cultural superiority. It was in this context that the first Muslim modernists began their attempt to rediscover Islam, purified of its misguided "folk" interpretations, as the progressive religion par excellence. By the turn of the twentieth century, the Egyptian modernist scholar Qasim Amin had produced such works as *The Emancipation of Women* and *The Modern Women*. Decades ahead of their time, these works set out such modernist arguments as those discussed earlier, for which they were publicly condemned as un-Islamic. Amin argued that full equality of the sexes was required by Islam, and that it was necessary for Egypt's national development.

Although such ideas were unpopular, they provided a basis for a more active wave of feminism. In 1923 educated Egyptian women formed the Feminist Union, publicly cast off their veils, and began to campaign for legal reform. The same year saw the establishment of the Republic of Turkey under the leadership of Kemal Ataturk, the ardent modernist reformer. Building not only on his role as founder of the modern Turkish state but also on nearly a century of reform in women's status and other social issues, Ataturk instituted sweeping reforms that eliminated legal distinctions between the sexes, abolished polygamy, and allowed women to vote and stand for office. Although he did not outlaw the veil and could take no direct action against the deeper attitudes that gave rise to it, he never missed an opportunity to dramatize publicly his support of sexual equality. Although he replaced the Sharia with the Swiss Civil Code, Ataturk claimed to be purifying Islam of its latter-day misinterpretations.

In 1956 Habib Bourgiba, after leading Tunisia to independence, initiated a process of reform that placed his country alongside Turkey and Egypt in the vanguard of sexual egalitarianism. In contrast to Ataturk, who disestablished the Sharia as the law of the land, Bourgiba based his program on his own radically modernist reading of the Sharia. His reforms, generally similar to Turkey's, banned polygamy, required informed consent of a bride as a precondition of marriage, set a minimum age for marriage, gave the sexes equal rights in divorce and child custody, and provided equal educational opportunity. Justifying these changes in the name of purifying Islam and catching up with the West, Bourgiba even provided free abortions to married or single women without the need of a husband's or guardian's permission. Similar to Ataturk, however, Bourgiba has left an unintended legacy of backlash against what is increasingly seen by Islamists in the post-Bourgiba era as a campaign against Islam.

If Ataturk's and Bourgiba's initial successes were due largely to their favorable political positions, reforms in some other countries have failed for equally political reasons. In Algeria and Morocco, for example, schooling for girls and other egalitarian reforms were sponsored by the hated French colonial regime and became associated with the taint of cultural imperialism. Despite the important role played by women in the war of independence, postcolonial Algeria and Morocco deliberately adopted a conservative interpretation of Muslim women's roles as part of the repudiation of Western culture. These sentiments, along with a fear that working women would add to the severe male unemployment, have led to policies aimed at keeping women in the home. In Saudi Arabia, where political legitimacy rests on Muwahhidun conservatism, the veiling and segregation of women are actively enforced and have encountered only weak opposition. An organized demonstration during the 1990 Gulf War, in which Saudi women defied the rule against driving automobiles, resulted in widespread denunciation not only of the women involved, but also of the U.S. influence on which the protest was blamed.

Most Middle Eastern countries lie between these extremes and are characterized by a dialogue between the forces of conservatism and change. Modernizing economies, urbanization, a greater variety of role models, and women's education provide the foundation for fundamental, although often very slow, changes; in the meantime, legal reforms gradually accumulate.

Women in the Islamic Revival

Since the mid-1970s, the plodding pace of social and legal reforms in women's roles has been overshadowed by a more dramatic turn of events: a widespread popular movement devoted to a restoration of Islamic behavior and dress. If this movement were simple conservatism among the traditionally oriented rural population, it would hardly be surprising. It is understandable that even 75 years after Ataturk's reforms, rural Turkish villagers still continue in the patterns of marriage, dress, and sex roles that prevailed in the old days. Paradoxically, however, the most self-conscious reassertion of Islamic roles for women is found in places where Westernization, social reform, and education have proceeded the furthest. Again ironically, the protest is often most evident among educated middle-class women, the daughters and granddaughters of the women who boldly emerged from their harems, cast away their veils, and campaigned for legal reforms. In Egypt, female university students have taken increasingly to wearing various forms of modest "Shari" dress, some go veiled in public, and a few have even elected to seclude themselves in their homes. In Tunisia, where reforms of family and divorce laws had gone particularly far, educated women clad in veils publicly confronted President Bourgiba to protest his liberalizing policies and reaffirm the value of traditional feminine roles. Today, Muslim women take part in lively discussions on the Internet, testifying to the liberating value of Islamic dress and Islamic concepts of womanhood. These events reflect more than mere inertia against change; they constitute a political phenomenon in their own right.

A comparison between the Middle East and China with regard to sex role changes might be instructive. In postrevolutionary China, the ideal for sex role change was clearly and unequivocally portrayed: The old patriarchal order was to be abolished and replaced by sexual equality. Of course, changes in behavior have not entirely lived up to the ideal, and they have not been painless. Nevertheless, the degree of change within only a generation or two has been remarkable, especially compared with the Middle East, when one considers the strength of patriarchal attitudes and institutions in Chinese tradition. The Middle East as a whole has not experienced anything like the upheaval of the Chinese Revolution, but there are other differences as well. The role of Islam in establishing the cultural and social forms of the

Middle East, in placing it so centrally in world history, and in structuring a centuries-old competition with the Christian West contributes to the importance of Islam as a vehicle for the political response to Western domination. The Middle Easterners' struggle for self-determination is expressed in the need to be Muslim. But Islam, as we have seen, is uniquely concerned with marriage and family life, and thus the domestic arena becomes, in a sense, a setting in which the drama of international domination and resistance is symbolized and is acted out.

Seen in this context, the West's vocal concern over the plight of Middle Eastern women is itself an example of cultural politics—another blow in the age-old rivalry over "who is more civilized than whom." Western feminists may add to this sense of rivalry by unconsciously equating Westernization with progress—a habit of thought that tends to muddle the issues and to divide those who could be united by deeper common interests. In this setting of cultural and political rivalry, departure from traditional family and sex-role patterns in favor of those prevailing in the West—even when sponsored by popular nationalist leaders or justified in the name of purified Islam—is widely seen as a capitulation to foreign domination.

The case of Iran aptly illustrates the interplay of sexual politics with the national and international arenas. Interest in greater opportunities for women began during the nineteenth century among the Western-oriented middle class, and by the early decades of the twentieth century, women were involved in forceful public demonstrations in support of nationalist and democratic causes. In the 1920s some educated women braved persecution to operate private schools for girls. The cause of sexual equality was, however, unwittingly sabotaged by the policies of the Pahlevi rulers. Reza Shah, who came to the throne in 1925, pursued a program of Westernization that included public schooling for girls, forced abolition of the veil, and other changes in family life. Reza Shah's high-handed methods fostered an ulema-led opposition that, after his abdication in 1941, led to a dramatic backlash against his policies. Legal reforms were reversed, and the ulema publicly called for a return to the veil.

During the 1960s and 1970s Mohammad Reza Shah attempted another program of legal changes, including women's suffrage and the Family Protection Laws of 1967 and 1973, which modified in women's favor the prevailing practices regarding polygamy, divorce, child custody, and related matters. It seems, however, that the shah valued these changes more as symbols of "modernization" than as actual advances toward equality. In a much-publicized interview with an Italian journalist, he scorned "women's lib," pronounced women inferior to men in ability, and remarked that "women count only if they are beautiful and graceful."

Authoritarian in his methods and reliant on the United States for support, the shah came increasingly to be seen not only as an agent of cruel outside oppression, but more specifically as a harbinger of Western-style profligacy whose "feminism" was really nothing more than an attempt to turn women into painted playthings. Through an ironic twist of politics, a strong ulema-led opposition to the shah's policy of women's suffrage became (for some, at least) an important rallying symbol of popular empowerment. The movement against the shah appealed to people's sense of social justice, personal freedom, national pride, and religious piety. The appeal was equally to women and to men, and both participated actively in the revolution. As often happens, the success of the revolution brought rude surprises for some. Although perhaps many women had never aspired to a growing personal freedom or equality with men, others felt betrayed by the repeal of the Family Protection Laws and the attempt to return women to their traditional roles. Some women who had worn veils as symbols of protest against the shah felt differently when the new government began to require "Islamic" dress.

Beneath the apparent unity of Khomeini's Iran lies a great diversity of assumptions and opinions about the direction of progress. Iran's religious leaders claim that it is they who truly respect women's equality with men, whereas the chief threat to women comes from people who would plunge them into Western-style "immorality." Although many women seem to accept this claim, others see it as a rationalization for reactionary, sexist policies that amount to a betrayal of their trust.

The changes in Iran, although dramatic, are not entirely unique. In Egypt, modest Islamic dress has been voluntarily adopted by a growing number of young women, often from the educated middle class. Liberal family and marriage laws championed by Mrs. Sadat were later repealed following repeated protests by veiled Egyptian women, and a leading Egyptian feminist and film director was pressured into self-exile by opponents who labeled her a "foreign agent" for her feminist views.

The authors have argued that these reversals against women's rights are in part a spinoff from the Islamic resistance to Western domination. This is aided by the inevitable tendency of any culture to form inaccurate and ethnocentric stereotypes about another—in this case, an exaggerated notion of promiscuity, materialism, and breakdown of family life in the West. It may be more difficult for the Westerner to see, however, that some elements of the "revival" also may stem from informed reflection, women's self-interest, and intelligent cultural criticism. Middle Eastern women directly familiar with Western culture have pointed out its flaws as a model for women's fulfillment. Accustomed to moving in a segregated women's world, they see Western women as obsessed with dating, pairing, and heterosexual attraction. While criticizing the traditional Middle Eastern domination of women within the domestic setting, they are shocked and repulsed by what they see as the tasteless public exploitation of women and femininity for hedonistic and commercial purposes. In this light, veiling and other forms of neo-Islamic dress take on still another meaning: Islamic dress is for many women an assertion of personal choice, a way of preserving their privacy and dignity in a public or work setting, and an affirmation of their cultural pride in the face of a smug and domineering West.

It is not always easy to distinguish reactionary elements from modernizing ones. Although one might expect fundamentalist and modernist Islam to be irreconcilable opposites, the two at times may be almost indistinguishable. The writings of Ali Shariati (1933–1977) provide a case in point. Educated in sociology at the Sorbonne, Shariati endured two decades of imprisonment, surveillance, and exile from his native Iran because of his opinions. As an articulate defender of Islam and critic of Western society, Shariati became a spokesman for the anti-shah movement and a veritable saint of the Iranian revolution after his death, and his writings continue to provide guidance for Muslim revivalism in postrevolutionary Iran and elsewhere. Shariati, however, was an Islamic modernist in the tradition of Muhammad Abdu, Qasim Amin, and al-Afghani; although he defended Islam in the face of Western secular thought, he was equally eloquent in his attack on the traditionalists who "confuse being old-fashioned with being religious." He blamed tradition for depriving women of their rightful place in Muslim society, for excluding them from religious life, and for ranking them in social standing "at the level of a washing machine." To the discomfort of many Shiite ulema, Shariati flatly proclaimed the equality of the sexes and advocated their equal participation in social life. His ideal, however, was not the "superficial" modernity of the Western woman. Instead, he offered as his ideal woman the Prophet's daughter Fatima, the perfect wife and mother, exemplar of courage and social

responsibility, and leader in the protest against the materialistic trends in the religion of her time. Was Shariati a modernist or a traditionalist? The very fact that this question is so difficult to answer may suggest that, in the end, the meaning of modernity must be defined within the terms of each society's historical experience.

CONCLUSION

The authors have defined *politics* as the process of conflict and resolution involved in the pursuit of limited good, and have suggested that this good may include the privilege of defining the symbols and values by which people live. Political behavior everywhere shows patterns that, if not always strictly rational, display a more or less intelligible logic when the underlying premises are understood. Those premises are invariably rooted, however, in cultural values and symbolic relationships that cannot be reduced to pure rationality. This is not a situation that people and nations are likely to outgrow in the forseeable future—perhaps not ever. Religious and cultural symbols are a defining source of social goals and a reflection of historical striving toward those goals. In our discussion of the Islamic revival, we have steered away from explanations that would reduce religion and its associated values to the status of mere political devices or, at the other extreme, make politics simply the tool of religious dogmas. History shows a dynamic, evolving relationship between social life and changing interpretations of religious and cultural heritage. To see one as a mere puppet of the other, or to reduce either to nonhistorical essences, is to pursue a comforting simplicity at the expense of genuine understanding.

Key Terms

jahiliyya *145*
bida *145*

modernism *148*
tawhid *165*

9 | POLITICAL ELITES

The study of political and social elites has been extraordinarily rewarding to social scientists. Most complex societies have well-defined elites. These elites are prominent; they are easily identified and studied. Elites are intimately involved in the processes that produce and resolve group conflict over the allocation of resources; they exist in all arenas of conflict—local, regional, national, or international. Elites prompt, resist, or reflect changes in the social, economic, and political processes.

In all but the simplest societies, certain people perform political functions; they make the binding decisions of the society. These people are the elite and can be distinguished from people who do not exercise substantial power—the public or the masses. At one level or another, and with varying degrees of effectiveness, the elite is comprised of people who decide who gets what, when, and how. Because those decisions are going to satisfy and disappoint members of that society, especially as allocations take place in an environment of relative scarcity, the activities of the elite resolve and generate conflicts. A decision to transfer land from traditional landowners to the previous tenant farmers satisfies the demands of the tenant farmers but motivates the landlords to seek some form of compensation for their losses. The elite in its action creates new demands on the system as it attempts to reconcile existing conflicts.

Members of the elite tend to represent the interests of the group of society from which they spring. A member of the elite whose ancestors were small farmers can be expected to represent the interests of people with similar backgrounds, *to a predictable degree*. A member of the elite whose ancestors were landless peasants would be expected to represent a substantially different point of view, especially on problems that directly involve the conflicting interests of landholders and tenant farmers.

If members of the elite represent their own groups of origin with some predictability, the composition of the elite can reveal much about the state of politics in a society. The overrepresentation of one segment of society in the elite would imply that disproportionate shares of that society's produce were going to that group. The absence of a potentially important elite group, such as the educated professional class, would imply that the group was being disproportionately penalized by the actions of government. The composition of the elite is important to a society attempting to modernize because a modern society attempts to involve most or all of its citizenry in the pursuit of a new social and political consensus. Consensus is not built by excluding large or important groups from the political process or the elite. The general representativeness of the elite is an important indicator for anyone attempting to understand the political process in a country or region.

The analysis of the elite in a transitional society—and most of the systems under study here are in a transitional state between traditional and modern—generally reveals an elite of changing composition. In particular, we should be alert to changes in the elite that indicate an expansion of the elements of society participating in political decisions and to evidence that indicates traditional opposition to that change. It is axiomatic that established elites oppose such changes because the changes involve a dilution of the elites' past influence. Conflict is implicit between the elements of the elite proposing and supporting technical modernization and the elements of the elite opposing such changes. In most of the countries of the Middle East, this process expresses itself in terms of religious elite opposition to the modernizing efforts of the bureaucracy, professional classes, and military. Since World War II and the nominal political independence of the nations of the area, this conflict has occurred between the traditional religious elite of the Middle East—the ulema—and the government, usually dominated by the military bureaucracy.

Although we have discussed the peculiarities of the ulema in earlier chapters, it is important to recall some of its primary characteristics, particularly because it complicates our analysis. First, the ulema is unusually diffuse; it has no clear hierarchy or rules of membership or formal organization. Existing independent of the political order, it has nonetheless historically penetrated and influenced that order, reflecting the pervasiveness of Islam in general. The ulema is consequently difficult to pin down in sociographic terms. There is no denying its existence, however, and no denying its desire to maintain its authority deriving from sacred or religious sources. The ulema's maintenance of sacred sources of authority and knowledge brings it into conflict with the focus of modernization because modernization, as it developed in the West, recognized the authority of man, not God.

The ulema, as the front-line bastion against secular authority, is often in fundamental opposition to the secular values of Western-style modernizers. As we shall see, this opposition takes various forms in the political systems of the Middle East. Historically, the ulema sought to influence and advise government rather than serve formally as officers of the state. It preferred to exercise moral vetoes over unacceptable policy. There are indications that this policy has changed in Iran, Saudi Arabia, Libya, the Sudan, Egypt, and the Gulf States, but historically, the political power of the ulema has been negative—oppositional power rather than the power of positive influence or accommodation.

A prominent exception to this situation involves the Shia community in Iran. Here the clergy, more formally organized than in Sunni-dominated areas, has taken direct control of the government for the purposes of implementing an Islamic republic. Although this experience is important, it is also important to remember that the Shia account for only approximately 10 percent of the world's Muslims. In most states, the ulema still keeps its distance from government, seeking to exert moral or oppositional influence in contrast to the direct exercise of political power. There are growing numbers of ulema in many states, however, anxious to take a direct role in the affairs of state.

The relatively recent spread of "political" Islam (the term is controversial) has involved the ulema in overt political activity in many Middle Eastern countries. Although in most situations the proportion of the ulema taking direct roles in political organizations and formal oppositions is relatively small, the consequences can be momentous. This is the case in Algeria, where a determined and well-organized Islamic party confronts the government politically and militarily; in the Sudan, where the ulema effectively direct the affairs of state; in Egypt, where ongoing Muslim opposition to the Mubarak government is apparent; in Turkey, where an Islamic party successfully challenged the dominance of both major secular parties, only to be removed from office by the military; in Saudi Arabia, where conservative ulema have increased their criticism of the royal family and its policies; and in Israel and Palestine, where Hamas is supported by numerous politically committed ulema, many uncomfortable with the secular posture of the Palestinian Authority and Israel. It is difficult to identify patterns of behavior here that transcend local or particular political systems. Nonetheless, ulemic activism is one of the emerging realities in the Middle Eastern constellation of elites.

The inability of the ulema to respond effectively to the rising challenges of extremism and jihadist groups has been widely noted in the Western press. A brief review of the websites commonly available paint a different picture. In fact, there are multiple examples of prominent ulema and groups of ulema incorporating these concerns into their analysis and advice. The ulema now speaks with a strong voice on these controversial topics, rejecting the claims of extremist and jihadist organizations such as Al-Qaeda and related organizations. These analyses are generally presented in the context of fatwas, scholarly opinions binding on the faithful. They receive widespread public attention in the ummah, but unfortunately not in Western mass media where the few extremist alims dominate the attention of the press. Hopefully, a more balanced appraisal of the modern ulema will come forward in the next few years.

By contrast, the modernizing forces in the Middle East can be described as adopting the opposite of the political style of the ulema.

The forces generally supporting technical modernization in the Middle East are the governmental entities that gained political power in the aftermath of independence. Although nominal power at that time was held by hereditary monarchs (e.g., Farouk in Egypt and the Hashemite monarchs of Jordan and Iraq), more actual political power was held by the bureaucrats and military officer corps of those governments. As the political pressures of independence grew, the actual formal political power of these elites grew, ultimately displacing the hereditary traditional authorities in countries such as Egypt, Iraq, and Libya. In other countries, such as Saudi Arabia, Iran, Oman, and the U.A.E., a system of shared powers between the traditional and the bureaucratic/military elites developed.

It is not surprising that the technically modernizing elements in the political elites of the Middle East should come so often from the bureaucratic/military cadres, for the preceding colonial regimes tried to create a capable, modernized bureaucracy without an attendant modernized, independent political structure. At independence, the elements that had been most exposed to the logic and philosophy of secular modernity were the bureaucrats and the military.

Consequently, we expect to find the elite structures of these Middle Eastern political systems in a state of flux, reflecting the low level of consensus in the society as a whole. The historical traditional order preceding the transitional stage to modernization was characterized by relatively high levels of consensus and elite congruence, and presumably the emergent modern order will be as well. Just as predictably, the intermediate transitional state will reflect the growing conflict over the objectives and basis of sociopolitical organization.

One of the most interesting and pervasive changes in the elite environment has revolved around more recent changes in communications technology. Satellite-based broadcasting has resulted in the exposure of new sources of information and worldviews for individuals and groups that could be characterized as "information poor" less than a decade ago. Computer-based communications systems, primarily the Internet and the World Wide Web, have allowed instantaneous communication among individuals and groups widely separated by space and culture. The result of this is that elites and counterelites are in much wider and more intimate contact than was true a decade ago. We no longer can think of elites as bound by state or nation. Quite the opposite is true.

The consequences of these new information flows are important for government. It is more difficult for governments to "manage" news or information flows. The system is nearly anarchic in the sense that it resists management from the top. The result is a public with greater sources of information and with greater possibilities for coordination. Individuals and groups formerly isolated in diasporic living situations now can communicate and participate in conversations and exchanges literally half a world away. There will be consequences to these new realities, although they are unclear at this time. Higher levels of elite consensus could be possible than under previous conditions of information scarcity. Counterelites may find it easier to maintain relations with like-minded dissidents within and outside any particular country.

During periods in a country's history when elite consensus and integration predominate, the leadership of the country can be indifferent or undistinguished without great cost because the widespread agreement on processes, institutions, and goals provides adequate direction to even the most unimaginative regimes. When elite conflict and competition are evident, and consensus is absent, the resources, imagination, and capability of the individual head of state become of great consequence. Because the Middle East is in just such a transitional situation, we analyze the emergent styles of political leadership in the region in Chapter 10. We attempt to show

the political and social consequences of varying political leadership styles, including styles that we shall call traditional, modern bureaucratic, and charismatic.

TRADITIONAL, TRANSITIONAL, AND TECHNICALLY MODERNIZING ELITES

Figures 9.1, 9.2, and 9.3 present models of the elite structures of traditional, transitional, and modern Middle Eastern societies. Before discussing each of these elite categories, a few remarks on the diagrams themselves are in order.

In these models, we distinguish between three levels, or strata, of society: *the elite,* represented by the smallest group of circles in the center of each diagram; *the ruling class,* the groups from whom the elite is regularly recruited; and *the mass public,* the members of society with considerably fewer resources and influence, who constitute most of the society. The broken lines surrounding the ruling class vary in the three diagrams; they are intended to indicate the ease with which movement from the mass public to the ruling class can occur. If there is real opportunity for individuals of demonstrated merit or capability to move from the mass public to the ruling class, we describe the society as having open, or permeable, boundaries. If there is little possibility of an individual moving from one class to another, we label the society closed, or impermeable. The quality of permeability is of great importance to a society's ability to adjust to the changing demands of modernization.

Another feature of the models reflects the degree of cohesion, or consensus, in the elite. In each model, the closer the elite elements are, the higher the degree of consensus among them. Two of the identified elite models have relatively high degrees of association, whereas the transitional model indicates a high degree of bifurcation and internal conflict. Finally, although these models describe national elites, they also can apply to regional and local elites. All countries in this area are, in effect, mosaics of elite structures.

Traditional Elites

In many respects, we already have discussed the traditional elite structure in the preceding chapters dealing with classic Islamic social organization and the early stages of modernization. We need to put that knowledge into the context of elite competition in the contemporary world. A short review of the main components of each elite is appropriate here, and we shall begin with the center of the traditional elite, the monarch (caliph, sultan, bey, or sheikh) and his immediate subordinates (traditionally, the *diwan*).

In most classic Islamic states, the ruler perpetuated his control largely on the basis of the elite's acceptance of his traditional right to rule. Particularly in Sunni political systems, a high priority was placed on the maintenance of

the established rule, with many theorists claiming that even tyrants should be obeyed until the very structure of the Islamic community itself was threatened. Shia communities were less disposed to accept established authority, but even in these communities, established authority had high credibility. In most traditional Islamic states, the head of state ruled on the basis of a widespread belief that such rule was correct and divinely determined.

The bureaucratic apparatus that supported the monarch was subject to greater vagaries. The diwan, drawn primarily from privileged families in the nobility and ruling class, were much more subject to being removed from office, commonly at the caprice of the hereditary monarch. In some traditional systems, notably the Turkish Janissary corps and the Egyptian Mameluks, rulers and high ministers might come from slave origins, devoid of family connections. Such arrangements were designed to minimize family-related or clan-related court intrigues, but often succeeded only in substituting one form of intrigue for another.

The diwan and their aides and staffs administered the kingdom; they collected the taxes and maintained the appropriate records. The record keepers, the **katib**, provided the source from which many of the ministers of the diwan were recruited and exerted much influence on the matters of court. The caliph, diwan, and katib, combined with the caliph's favorites, constituted the bulk of the court in a traditional Islamic state.

Also of the elite, but not so regularly or intimately a part of courtly life, were the wealthy merchants of the capital city, large landowners, military officers, and the higher ulema. All of these elements had a restraining role on government—practically, in the merchants' and landowners' reaction to taxation, and morally, in the higher ulema's criticisms of policy. The ulema, in particular, limited the role of government by deciding which questions should be resolved by the caliphate, and which questions were in the exclusive domain of the Islamic

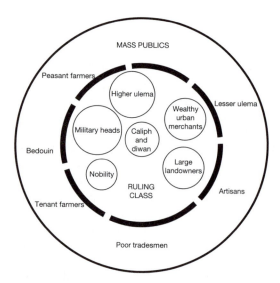

Elite Characteristics:
—Low permeability
—High elite consensus
—Small ruling class

Nation in Traditional Classification:
  Kuwait

FIGURE 9.1 The Traditional Elite

community—essentially the greater and lesser ulema. The relationship between caliphate and ulema was periodically rocky, and many traditional authorities defied the moral sanction of the ulema, formally and informally, successfully and unsuccessfully.

Many of the conflicts between caliph and higher ulema in Sunni states centered on religious opposition to efforts at modernization or changes in the social and political structure of the state. One major exception to this pattern has been the continually strained relationship between the monarchy and the Shia higher ulema in Iran. In this case, the Shia mistrust of political authority (see Chapter 3) has resulted in the higher ulema's espousing a strong form of constitutionalism as a basis for government. In this restrictive sense, the Iranian ulema has been among the forces striving for a more modern political system, fomenting conflict with the authoritarian aspirations of the Iranian shahs. This conflict has persisted to the present day in Iran. In other areas of life, however, such as the liberalization of women's roles or secular education, the Iranian ulema's position is nearly indistinguishable from that of the Sunni ulema.

The military hierarchy also has been a persistent element in the ruling class and the elite of the Islamic state and of traditional political authority. There is no Islamic tradition separating military authority from political, social, or religious authority. Military life traditionally has been a means of social access and upward mobility. Particularly in linking outlying Bedouin military forces with the urban caliphate and elite, the military played an important role in the integration of the traditional elite. And as we shall see, the military is an important force in the transitional and modernizing elites.

Generally, the traditional elite has a low permeability—that is, the ruling class is very stable, and outsiders move into it only with great difficulty. With the exception of the ulema (particularly the lesser ulema) and the military

to some degree, social mobility was largely unknown in the traditional elite. Elite circulation historically was confined to the established ruling class and resulted in considerable unresolved tension. Many of the theorists of Islamic society, including the well-known Ibn Khaldun, attributed the decline and fall of the caliphates to the increasing restiveness of the mass publics (peasants and Bedouins), and the inability of the ruling class and elite to respond to them. The very cohesiveness of the traditional elite—its homogeneity and small size—contributed to its ultimate demise.

The weakness of the traditional state becomes most obvious when conflicts arise. In the traditional Middle East, political control, as a rule, declined proportionately to the distance from the political center. With the ruling class and elite centered primarily in the capital city, it was a matter of time until the periphery suffered from neglect or exploitation. Common causes of provincial unrest came from factors such as deteriorating irrigation systems, increasingly exploitive taxes, and failure of the government to protect farmers and merchants from banditry and other forms of predation. As opportunists perceived the possibilities deriving from these growing demands, the power of the central authority dwindled to a point of crisis. If the traditional authority was lucky or aggressive, the threats might be laid to rest. If not, new elites and political structures, often drawn from restive elements within the ruling class and not from the mass publics, would be constituted and the whole process continued.

In the late nineteenth and early twentieth centuries, these traditional Middle Eastern political systems—notably the Ottomans and their client states—came under heavy pressure from the national systems of Europe. The traditional political elites found themselves hard pressed to respond adequately to superior European political, military, and economic power. At this time the only surviving traditional political system in the Middle East is in Kuwait, where the rulers have retreated from most of the initiatives at political reform that occurred before or in the immediate aftermath of the Gulf War. Other countries previously classified as having traditional elites—Oman, the U.A.E., and Qatar—can now be classified as transitional. In each of these countries, we can recognize changes in the political system that have resulted in broader, more representative elites and changes in governments allowing limited movement toward democratic institutions.

Transitional Elites

Elite disagreement over the basic forms and derivations of authority produces a type of structure called *transitional*. The term is used most often to denote the stage between the disruption of traditional authority and the triumph of technical modernization; however, it might just as easily occur before an aggressive reassertion of traditional leadership, although this is unusual. It does seem to apply to the turmoil affecting contemporary Iran and the rise of conservative Islamic political parties.

The transitional elite (see Figure 9.2) has a dotted line separating the elite and ruling class into two polarized and contending groups. Although the specific composition of the elite can vary from country to country, certain groups or elements are likely to have a prominent role. Wealthy landowners who owe their prosperity to the support of the traditional leadership still participate in political decisions. The military, often the first group to be systematically exposed to the influence of secular modernity by reason of their education, usually can be counted on to support modernizing programs. The bureaucracy, trained in the science of public administration by a prior colonial administration, also tends to support modernizing change. The elements of the

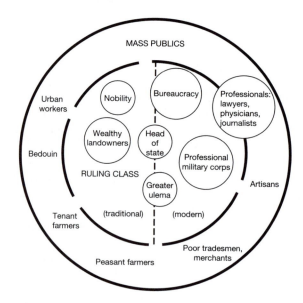

Elite Characteristics:
—Regular permeability
—Low elite consensus, internal elite conflict
—Growing ruling class, presence of
    "new" groups in ruling class

Nations in Transitional Classification:
Bahrain   Libya
Iran   Saudi Arabia
Jordan   Yemen
Oman   U.A.E.
Qatar

FIGURE 9.2   The Transitional Elite

traditional elite with hereditary power can be counted on to cling to that power. Most of the greater and lesser ulema also can be counted on to take sides in the issues at hand, although their decisions can frustrate traditional and modernizing elements in the elite.

The transitional elite generally is composed of and represents more social groups than the traditional elite, despite the transitional elite's disagreement over the means and ends of political, social, and economic life. Internal conflict in the elite can produce irregular policy, wavering between the demands and desires of a fragmented society. This often may lead to frustrating inconsistencies that produce growing dissatisfaction from traditional and modernizing elements. Transitional societies are subject to growing internal pressures that demand resolution. Commonly, these pressures build up to political violence, including demonstrations and assassinations. On a more positive note, such behavior, short of violence, bespeaks a broader level of political participation and is one of the early signs that the pressures of change are building. The transitional society and its elite—as disorganized and chaotic as they sometimes seem—carry the seeds of a new social order based on greater participation and wider social consensus.

Oil has been a major factor affecting the prominence of transitional elites in the Middle East. Two relatively large and influential oil producers—Iran and Saudi Arabia—are transitional in character, as are the smaller Gulf States of Bahrain, Oman, Qatar, and the U.A.E. In combination, they account for the bulk of oil production and reserves in the Middle East and the world. As a group, these countries also exhibit radically different political styles: modernizing monarchies and two variants of the Islamic republic.

The transitional elites in the Middle East have provided the arenas for some of the most important political changes in the entire region. The fall of the shah of Iran in 1979 is the most dramatic of these changes and in some respects the most important. The styles of politics and elite organization in Libya and Saudi Arabia have been equally as important, however, and warrant mention here.

IRAN. The fall of the shah of Iran can be directly related to the strains placed on his political authority by a failure to accommodate new groups in the political elite and by a parallel failure to maintain the support of the more traditional groups in Iran. The newly emergent professional middle class was largely uninfluential in the shah's autocracy. Because this group holds a near monopoly of modern technology and skill, it can be ignored only at the ruler's peril. Ironically, the ambitious technical modernization program of the shah simultaneously enhanced the size and potential power of the middle class at the same time as it alienated them. Disaffected professionals found it advantageous to join with the forces of the traditional Muslim leadership against the shah. The opposition of the Shia ulema, again ironically, was based on the disruptive and secularizing influence of the shah's modernization program. The combination of traditional and modern opposition was too much for the shah's primarily military base of support, and he was forced to leave the country. The results of the change—particularly the attempt to establish an Islamic republic—are now clear. The theocratic regime in Iran seems to be fully in control of the country. Considerable institutionalization has occurred, and there are indications that the relevant elite has expanded, reincorporating professional and middle-class elements that had previously been excluded in the early days of the revolution.

The initial political coalition that governed Iran during the transition from the shah's rule to the new republic can be characterized as a "temporary pluralism" dominated by the Shia clergy under Ayatollah Khomeini. The new government organized by Mehdi Bazargan was heavily populated with ministers representing the urban professional and secular political groups that combined with the Shia opposition against the shah. As the design of the new republic became apparent, Bazargan's secular/professional government was replaced by a government under Bani-Sadr, a government dominated by nonclergy Shia leaders committed to the implementation of the Islamic Republic. Under Bani-Sadr's stewardship, and partially responsive to the strains of the U.S. hostage crisis, the Shia clergy began to play a growing political role in the government. By the early 1980s, after the fall of Bani-Sadr, the clergy had consolidated their power, assuming most of the important positions in the Islamic Republic.

The last months of the Iran–Iraq war placed the Iranian government and elite under terrific strain. As a consequence, Iran's governing elite was divided between the poles of the Iranian moderates, led by Rafsanjani, the Speaker at the time, and more conservative groups committed to even greater levels of Islamization and further prosecution of the war. The stakes in the controversy included the right to nominate the successor to Ayatollah Khomeini as the "religious expert," the faqih of the Islamic Republic. Reports from Iran in late 1988 indicated the execution of many members of the leadership of the most moderate factions of the ruling Islamic coalition, particularly among the followers of Ayatollah Montazeri. Commentators equated this action with the consolidation of power within the elite by the Rafsanjani faction, empowered by Khomeini's public stand in favor of ending the war. Ultimately this version proved to be true, with Rafsanjani and his followers consolidating their control over the Republic's institutions.

The complexity of Iranian politics was exemplified in the political ramifications of Khomeini's reaction to the novel *The Satanic Verses*, written by Salman Rushdie, an Indian citizen living in London. This novel, found blasphemous by many Shia mullahs, prompted Khomeini to sentence Rushdie to death and place a price on his head. Ayatollah Montazeri

opposed this action, and in the process questioned the direction of government generally. Khomeini responded by demanding and receiving Montazeri's resignation as the faqih designate. In a related move, Khomeini attempted to kick Speaker Rafsanjani upstairs to a more ceremonial post as president of the republic. Other commentators have assumed that these actions indicated the increasing influence of the uncompromising conservative faction within the governing coalition.

Two other equally plausible explanations deserve consideration, however. First, this may be just one more example of a charismatic leader finding it difficult to relinquish power, a common phenomenon in the later stages of charismatic rule. Second, Khomeini may have been concerned that the revolution was losing ideological momentum and, like Mao Tse-Tung in the Great Cultural Revolution in China, sought to institutionalize the ideological/revolutionary fervor of his movement. In truth, all of these observations may be appropriate.

After the war with Iraq and Khomeini's death, the Rafsanjani faction consolidated its power. The elevation of Ayatollah Khomeini to the position of the faqih increased the moderates' influence because Khomeini lacked the prestige of his predecessor. Under the leadership of President Rafsanjani, the government of Iran adopted relatively moderate foreign policies. Iran's neutral posture during the Iraqi invasion of Kuwait improved its prestige and positioned it as one of the influential states of the Gulf region. But the conservative factions were not totally excluded from power; and leftist revolutionary groups began modest terrorist operations against the government in the early 1990s. The government was unable to secure agreement to lifting the sentence imposed on Salman Rushdie, although considerable economic benefits were likely to follow from such a decision.

The politically active Shia clergy now dominates the Iranian elite, but there is new evidence that the urban professional classes and important ethnic and religious minorities are regaining some influence in the political process. The election of Muhammad Khatami as president of Iran in 1997 and his subsequent reelection revealed the political muscle of moderate opposition to conservative clerical rule. President Khatami pursued a gentle relaxation of the most conservative domestic policies and pushed for better relations with the West and the United States.

Most surprising to many analysts have been apparent changes within the Iranian ulema, with moderate and even liberal leaders coming into public prominence, challenging the authority of the traditional mujtahids. One popular cleric of moderate disposition, Hojatoislami Nouri, has been a focus of conservative attempts to deny him public voice, convicting him of various offenses against the revolution and the religion. His experience set the tone for future conflicts within the Iranian ulema.

The presidential election of summer 2005 returned the Iranian presidency to conservative control, with the election of Mohammad Ahmadinejad, defeating long-standing moderate politician Hashemi Rafsanjani. The new president was not enthusiastically welcomed in the European West and confirmed many expectations by quickly excoriating Israel and the United States. To many pundits, the election of the new president was a harbinger of reversal of the moderating policies of the Khatami administration. To others, this was a clear affirmation of the democratic nature of Iranian political institutions, institutions that ratified changes in government made by a broadly enfranchised electorate. In the area of foreign policy, the new president intensified Iran's development of nuclear capabilities and rejected the efforts of the United Nations and the International Atomic Energy Agency (IAEA) to resume inspection and supervision of the nuclear fuel cycle. There is little doubt that the democratic process has produced concrete change in government and policy in Iran—changes not always consistent with the preferences and policies of Iran's international opponents.

The hotly contested presidential elections of 2009 caused considerable turmoil in Iran. Critics of the election claimed that the government interfered in the election, producing a false victory for President Ahmadinejad over his primary opponent, Mir-Hossein Mousavi, a veteran Iranian politician running as a reformist. Analysts claim that the election results were apparently tampered with, producing a major victory for Ahmadinejad, receiving 63 percent of the vote over Mousavi's 33 percent. Although it is possible that Ahmadinejad actually won the election, it would be most likely by a dramatically smaller margin.

In any event, the resulting protests to the election revealed real lines of conflict and cleavage, within both the Iranian electorate and Iran's political elites. Considerable violence was apparent in the weeks immediately following the election, with large demonstrations repressed by equally determined government security forces. Dozens of protestors were killed, thousands jailed, and the international reputation of Iran suffered.

In terms of elite conflict, the reactions to this flawed election revealed fault lines within the government and even within the clerical establishment, with important Ayatollahs and other clerics publically criticizing Grand Ayatollah Khamenei and other members of his ruling council. These fracture lines demonstrate key vulnerabilities to Iran's governing elites. Although in the short term the government was able to repress the protests over the elections, it is less clear that the government will be able to turn back or repress the demands for change and reform that expressed themselves volubly and visibly during the protests. Change is afoot in Iran, fortified by generational conflicts and now increasingly focused on the democratic institutions of that country. We also note the important role played by Internet platforms such as Facebook and Twitter in coordinating the protest movement, a technology that the Iranian government has not been able to fully control. The political genie is out of the bottle, so to speak, and it is unlikely that the senior clerical establishment can reverse the trend.

SAUDI ARABIA. The elite changes occurring in Saudi Arabia have been occurring more *within* the ruling family and its coalitions. King Fahd announced a broad reorganization of his cabinet in 1995, changing some key assignments. Early in 1996, failing physically, Fahd relinquished daily responsibility for the government to his brother, Prince Abdullah. Both changes came in the context of increasing criticism of the royal family and its policies by a coalition of conservative ulema and critics of the economic excesses and domination of the royal family. The flow of delegated power to the king's heirs accelerated in the last days of the twentieth century, constituting a de facto political transition. In the early twenty-first century, the crown prince and other senior princes took increasingly visible roles as administrators and spokesmen for the kingdom.

Given these adjustments and preparations, the death of Kind Fahd in 2005 brought a political succession to Saudi Arabia with little disruptions and no disturbance in the organization of government. The new king, Abdullah, reaffirmed most of the existing power arrangements within the royal family and personally conveyed the prospects of moderate political change in the kingdom. Among the promulgations and observations of the new ruler were the observations that restrictions on women driving cars would be lifted, and the ritual kissing of the monarch's hand would be abolished.

As princes and retainers of the monarchy have received educations in the elite institutions of the West (e.g., Oxford, Cambridge, M.I.T., Harvard, and the Sorbonne), they have become increasingly aware of the need to adapt to the pressures and advantages of modern social organization. The Organization

of the Petroleum Exporting Countries (OPEC) has often been attributed directly to such influences. The Saudi elite seem to be attempting to modernize the economic and technical facets of Saudi society without making corresponding changes in the political and social facets. This is a difficult maneuver because as the experience in Iran suggests, the educated and professional classes begin to desire power and influence. Ordinarily, analysts would be inclined to predict failure in this effort and disagree only on the timing of the ouster of the monarch and his ruling family. But the extraordinary wealth of Saudi Arabia, combined with its relatively small indigenous population, may allow for unusual and unanticipated developments. It is clear at this point that the Saudi system has gone from traditional to transitional elite politics in a fairly short time, largely within the framework of the hugely extended royal family. The abdication of King Saud in favor of his more progressive brother, Faisal, and the publicly emerging differences of opinion between the royal princes under King Khalid provided evidence of the changes and the relatively short time frame within which they occurred.

Rivalry within the royal family has come down more recently to competition between three branches: the Sudairi, which includes many of the technically trained and sophisticated bureaucrats; the Jilwa, the branch traditionally concerned with the cultivation of the tribal loyalties that have supported Saudi rule; and the religious branch of the family, the Al-Baz, descendents from the Wahhabi reformers of the nineteenth century and the dominant force in the ulema. The death of King Khalid in 1982 and the resulting transfer of power to King Fahd consolidated the power of the Saudi modernist factions in the elite, but not completely at the expense of the opposition.

Members and associates of the religious faction became progressively dissatisfied with the social and religious policies under King Fahd. Several prominent members of the Saudi ulema were placed under arrest in 1995 for advocating and petitioning for government reforms. The activities of Osama bin Laden, a Saudi exile from a prominent family, accused of masterminding several terrorist plots against U.S. interests, allegedly received financial and moral support from dissatisfied Saudi citizens. The attack on the World Trade Center and the Pentagon on September 11, 2001, organized by bin Laden's terrorist organization, Al-Qaeda, strongly embarrassed the Saudi elite. Under enormous pressure from the United States, the government has been forced to take a closer look at the radical ulema preaching in the kingdom and make attempts to identify and detain members of Al-Qaeda and other radical groups. By 2006, many of the most radical leaders of the Saudi ulema had been removed from their pulpits or severely censored. Members of Al-Qaeda and other radical political and Islamist groups have been arrested or hunted down and killed. Jihadist organizations in Saudi Arabia, although not eliminated from the society, have been severely repressed. This fact suggests a higher level of internal elite dissatisfaction and conflict than conventional analyses would identify.

The Saudi elite has conceded extensive social power to the religious branch of the family, with the result that Saudi Arabia maintains one of the most conservative social atmospheres in the Middle East. The quasi-official religious police, the **mutawwa**, are responsive to leadership from the religious branch of the royal family. They are responsible for maintaining the codes of propriety in dress and worship. In the aftermath of Desert Storm, this branch of the royal family complained publicly about declining standards of personal conduct, demanding even more restrictive rules and punishments. At the same time, other elements in Saudi society encouraged the creation of a consultative assembly, and King Fahd did so, appointing a national assembly and other local assemblies (in Arabic, **as shura**). The importance of these assemblies has grown slowly, and in the long run these assemblies may

provide a small opening to more democratic participation in the kingdom. Many observers connect the demands for political liberalization and opposing demands for greater conservatism with the catalytic presence of foreign troops during the confrontation with Iraq. The political elite of Saudi Arabia found itself under considerable political strain.

The role of women in Saudi Arabia is also changing, albeit slowly. Some women ran for local government offices, although unsuccessfully. Female representation in the professions has increased, particularly in the health and business sectors of the economy. Many local pundits were surprised and pleased at the election in 2005 of two women candidates to the board of the Jiddah Chamber of Commerce, an important and influential economic entity. Such an election would have been unheard of decades earlier. Progress, incremental and slow, is nonetheless visible. A small number of women appointed to important political positions in the Kingdom in 2008 and 2009 also indicate a slow, if inexorable and deliberate, relaxation of traditional gender roles in the country.

Responding to increasing criticism of his government, King Fahd announced a broad reorganization of his cabinet in 1995, changing some key assignments, including the top management of the Saudi oil company. As discussed before, early in 1996, failing physically, Fahd relinquished daily responsibility for the government to his brother, Prince Abdullah. Both changes came in the context of increasing criticism of the royal family and its policies by a coalition of conservative ulema and critics of the economic excesses and domination of the royal family. As a consequence of these arrangements, the death of King Fahd in 2005 and the accession of King Abdullah were accompanied by little tension and disorganization. King Abdullah has intensified the government's suppression of the Islamist and radical ulema in the kingdom and allowed a modicum of social liberalization. Intrafamily adjustment to political realities continues to characterize

Saudi rule. Saudi pragmatism, combined with its great wealth, should allow it more latitude for maneuver than most monarchical regimes under similar pressure.

It is clear in hindsight that the bombing of the Khobar Towers barracks, the bombing of a U.S. advisory mission in Riyadh late in 1995 (with considerable loss of life), and the 1998 attack on the U.S. embassies in Kenya and Tanzania signaled an important change in the strategy and tactics of the opposition to the monarchy. The Al-Qaeda attack on the New York World Trade Center and the Pentagon involved a large percentage of Saudi citizens. The emergence of the exiled Saudi citizen Osama bin Laden as the chief architect of international terrorism against the United States and the West has damaged the international reputation of the Saudi elites. Bin Laden's continuing ability to garner financial resources from Saudi nationals suggests that visible public dissatisfaction with the regime is but the tip of the iceberg. Similar to the other states of the Gulf, Saudi Arabia finds itself increasingly under pressure to change, internally and internationally.

It is not surprising, then, that both the opponents to the regime and the regime itself have stepped up their efforts. In 2006 and 2007, the Saudi government successfully thwarted several attempts to attack the petroleum infrastructure of the kingdom. Sensing the importance of this shift in terrorist tactics, the Saudi government embarked on a more aggressive effort to isolate and control dissident elements, particularly of the jihadist movements. These efforts to date appear to have been successful. In particular, reports from Saudi Arabia claim considerable progress in reprogramming and then reintegrating former jihadists back into the Saudi system. If these programs continue successfully, it will constitute one of the few programs capable of reversing commitments to jihadist ideology.

KUWAIT. Developments in Kuwait in the early 1990s were traumatic and violent. The brutal, and largely unanticipated, invasion of Kuwait by Iraq in August 1990 threatened to terminate Kuwait's long-standing monarchy. The diplomatic and military responses to the occupation are discussed in detail in subsequent chapters. From an elite perspective, the results of the events were significant.

Returned to power by an international coalition led by the United States, the Kuwaiti royal family was widely expected to institute long-awaited democratic reforms. They did not materialize. Instead, the government of Kuwait embarked on a program of reestablishing the traditional government and increased "nativization," an attempt to ensure security by drastically reducing the guest population in Kuwait. Hundreds of thousands of foreign nationals—particularly, but not exclusively, Palestinians, Jordanians, and Iraqis—streamed out of Kuwait. Many of these individuals held important positions in the government and in the professions. A series of public trials of individuals accused of collaboration with the Iraqi occupiers contributed to an already negative environment for foreign workers. Collaborators and noncollaborators were expelled or fled. As a result, the political elite of Kuwait has narrowed in the years since Desert Storm. Democratic reforms have been considered but not implemented, and in late 1999, the Kuwaiti assembly vetoed a proposal to extend political rights to women.

Whether or not this reassertion of more traditional elite domination will work remains to be seen. It is unclear whether there are enough native Kuwaitis willing or able to staff the offices of a complex modern bureaucracy. But like Saudi Arabia and the other Gulf monarchies, the vast oil wealth of Kuwait gives it more possibilities than less affluent regimes. There are no signs that the ruling family of Kuwait is interested in sharing power or expanding the scope of the Kuwaiti political elite. For these reasons, we have left Kuwait in the traditional elite category.

BAHRAIN. Changes are afoot in Bahrain, at least partially a product of a change in leadership. The death of Amir Issa in 1999 brought his son Hamad to power. Amir Hamad has taken his new position as an opportunity to engage in modest political reform, expanding the role of the consultative assembly and in 2002 conducting elections for a Bahraini parliament.

High unemployment has exacerbated Bahraini Shia anger at what is perceived as policies preferential toward the extended royal family, its retainers, and the Sunni minority. Street demonstrations, critical pamphlets, and campus seminars have placed the issue squarely in public view. The government of Bahrain has conceded some of the points and promises to ameliorate the causes of discontent. A slow process of extending elite boundaries to include more of Bahrain's Shia in the government is underway.

LIBYA. The prevailing situation in Libya is in great contrast to that in Iran and Saudi Arabia. In Libya, the change from traditional to transitional status came with the elimination of the monarchy in 1969. In its place, a unique blend of Muslim puritanism and radical Arab nationalism has developed, personified by Qadaffi, a charismatic leader. The Libyan regime is run largely by its military bureaucracy, within which are recognized competing factions. There are some contributions from a small professional elite and equally small traditional ulema. Libya, one of the major oil exporters of the region, is particularly uneven in its development. Changes within the transitional elite structure of the country can be anticipated, although constrained by the erratic influence of Colonel Qadaffi. Qadaffi's attempts to replace regular bureaucratic organization with democratic delegations have confused the situation in Libya substantially, and he plays this confusion to his own benefit. Elite consequences are sure to follow from these innovations and strains, but their character and direction are uncertain.

In the past, Libya's substantive support of radical and terrorist groups, including the

Palestinians, brought substantial benefit to these movements. The U.S. raid on Libya in April 1986 seemed to have reduced Libyan predilections for international intrigue or the support of terrorist movements, however. Nonetheless, Libya continued to pay for its past sins. Early in 1992, Britain and the United States accused two Libyan diplomats of directing the bombing of Pan Am Flight 103 over Lockerbie, Scotland. Both countries demanded the extradition of the two diplomats, and, uncharacteristically, the Libyan government finally conditionally agreed to such surrender and allowed their trial to proceed. One of the alleged terrorists was convicted, and the other was acquitted.

In 2005, Libya surprised many analysts by admitting to a nuclear weapons program and turning its nuclear materials over to the United States. Analysts were surprised by the action and by the quality of the technology that Libya had acquired. The decision to abandon its quest for nuclear capability dramatically improved Libya's standing in the European West and allowed for the "rehabilitation" of its leader, Muammar Qadaffi.

All of this has resulted in growing legitimacy for Libya in Western Europe. For whatever reasons, internal or external, the Libyan elite now seem more focused on its internal problems and less interested in staking out an international role.

JORDAN. The Jordanian political system has few tangible economic resources. It also has had the unenviable role of being a front-line state in the conflict with Israel and of being a neighbor of Iraq and Syria, both countries with a historical interest in regional dominance. During the Iraq–Kuwait war, it managed to alienate both sides in the conflict. Despite these negatives, Jordan has survived to transform itself into a relatively stable country with reasonable short-term prospects and a growing tradition of democratic government. At least part of the responsibility for this state of affairs could be attributed to the leadership of King

Hussein and his ability to maneuver adroitly between contending powers. His death in 1999 brought his son Abdullah to power, displacing the crown prince in the line of succession. With this change in leadership came another political opening.

Jordan's political system has many internal political fractures. Chief among them is the division between the Jordanian Bedouin populations and the large native and refugee Palestinian population. This fact led to the bloody confrontation between Palestinian guerrillas and the Royal Jordanian Army in 1970–1971. This confrontation, important for the Palestinian and Jordanian elites, was caused by a growing recognition by both parties that political power was slipping increasingly into the hands of the Palestinian-dominated bureaucracy. Relying primarily on the Bedouin-dominated Arab Legion, King Hussein managed to expel the most militant of the Palestinians at that time to southern Lebanon and elsewhere.

It has long been recognized that one possible solution to the Palestinian problem—the integration of the West Bank and Gaza Strip into Jordan, or some other form of federation—held great risks for the existing Jordanian elite, as great numbers of well-educated Palestinians unsympathetic to the Jordanian regime became politically active and legitimate. The relationship between King Hussein and the Palestinian Liberation Organization (PLO) has been a turbulent one, oscillating between periods of cooperation and outright conflict. Nonetheless, King Hussein's announcement in July 1988, abdicating political and administrative responsibility for Gaza and the West Bank, surprised many observers, particularly in Israel and the United States, where fanciful hopes for a "Jordanian solution" had been kept alive. Hussein's action, although distressing to people seeking a "moderate" solution to the Palestinian problem, was probably of positive consequence to the Jordanian political elite, removing the major threat to its continued existence and eliminating many Jordanian-Palestinian officials from its ruling class.

In the twenty-first century, Jordan found itself in the unprecedented situation of having been a beneficiary of the Israeli-Arab relationship, with dramatic increases in trade, tourism, and investment, only to have these gains put at risk by the collapse of the Oslo Accords and the peace negotiations and the presumptive, preemptive U.S. war against Iraq.

King Abdullah has attempted to maneuver between these hazards and to maintain Jordan's standing in both the region and with the United States. Balancing the Jordanian elite's comfort with the United States and the West in general with the sentiments of the Jordanian "street," with its strong sympathies for the Palestinians and resistance to a punitive war with Iraq, has prompted King Abdullah to retrench on some of the political liberalizations pursued by his father.

From 1988 to 1990, political liberalization appeared in Jordan. Elections to the legislature provided a substantial broadening of the political elite. Men and women from a variety of parties and professions gained office. The king and his counselors seemed willing to accept the practical limitations on monarchical power implicit in such changes. The future for democracy appeared much brighter. But events since 1990 prompted both King Hussein and King Abdullah to rein in the legislature, limiting its role and purging some of its membership.

Earlier gains were put at risk during the events of Desert Storm. Jordan, highly dependent on its trade with Iraq, attempted to maintain a neutral posture. Neither side would tolerate such diplomatic niceties, and as a result Jordan paid a high political price for its attempted independence. Aid from the United States and Gulf States virtually disappeared, and Jordan found itself diplomatically isolated and the subject of great suspicion. Street demonstrations in support of Saddam Hussein and Iraq did little to dignify King Hussein's argument that he was attempting to broker a negotiated settlement between the parties. During Desert Storm and its aftermath, Jordan became the terminus of a massive migration of its nationals from Iraq, Kuwait, and the Gulf States. A near doubling of the refugee population in Jordan further strained the already inadequate resources of the state, while at the same time remittances from workers abroad declined.

Jordan's emerging democratic institutions and its changing elite were severely tested after King Hussein's rule. In the aftermath of the signing of the Israeli–Palestinian peace accords, King Hussein boldly placed Jordan as a proponent of regional peace. Israeli–Jordanian tourism became a major factor in Jordan's economy, and many joint ventures between Israeli capitalists and Jordanian businessmen were launched. Ironically, legislative dissatisfaction with the king's intimate relations with Israel kept the pressure on, and the promising democratic reforms begun in 1988 slowed. Membership in the Jordanian elite depended to no small degree on an individual's stance vis-à-vis the Palestinian or Israeli question.

The Muslim Brotherhood opposed the Jordanian rapprochement with Israel, and the government responded with limitations on press and political freedoms, particularly for the representatives of the Islamic conservatives and the ulema. Jordan had as much (or more) to gain as any state in the region from the solution of this long-standing problem, and it is ironic that closer economic and political ties with Israel and its Palestinian entity should result in increasing tension within the Jordanian political system.

The political transition from King Hussein to King Abdullah has alleviated some of these strains. The new king reinstated many key advisors to his father, isolated the extremist elements from the legislative system, and brought responsible elements of the Muslim Brotherhood into the government. Press freedoms were partially restored. Jordan's commitment to the peace process

was reconfirmed. All of these positive trends were put at risk, however, by the collapse of the Palestinian–Israeli negotiations, the terrorist attack on the World Trade Center and the Pentagon, and the U.S. efforts to accomplish "regime change" in Iraq. Al-Qaeda sponsored attacks in Jordan in late 2005 further increased fear and political tension in Jordan, and the government instituted security measures aimed at minimizing such attacks and, unfortunately, retrenching on the liberalization initiatives that began with King Abdullah's ascension. In the short run, at least, unintended consequences of the Iraq war have retarded democratization in Jordan.

GULF EMIRATES. Positive change can also be recorded among the Gulf Emirates: Bahrain, Oman, Qatar, and the U.A.E. In each of these countries, progress has been made toward the nativization of the national bureaucracies. Consultative assemblies were put in place in these countries and given wider responsibility in advising on government policies. In Oman and Qatar, the political leaders have publicly speculated on the desirability of eventual democratization. Qatar has allowed the establishment of an important Arab-language satellite channel, Al-Jazeerah, which has become noted for its independence and somewhat fearless coverage of global political issues. Qatar also is in the process of creating a set of basic laws that would provide the basis of an eventual Qatari constitution.

The oil and gas wealth of Qatar and the U.A.E. have allowed considerable investment in the education and development of the indigenous populations. As a result, the "emirization" of government positions has proceeded with great dispatch. The U.A.E. experimented in 2006 with limited elections to the national assembly, although half of the assembly continues to be appointed by the government. Even in the Gulf countries with greater economic constraints—Bahrain and Oman—progress in elite modernization is apparent.

Some mention should be made here of the stresses on Dubai, consequences of the global recession beginning in 2008. Dubai was caught in the end-game of an extremely ambitious set of projects, including the construction of the symbolically important Burj Tower. As government revenues declined, construction slowed, many guest workers exited the country, and the previously unbridled prosperity of the emirate declined. It is hoped that the downturn in prospects for Dubai is short-lived. But there is little doubt that Dubai's reputation as the richest of the rich and the most ambitious of the transformative microstates was tarnished.

All of the transitional regimes of the Middle East are important to the region and to the larger world community. As indicated earlier in this chapter, these regimes are all in an incipient state of change. This incipient change is magnified further by elements in the new global system, facilitating communication through satellite links and the Internet, economic change contingent on the higher levels of international trade, and the unprecedented physical mobility of average people. It is unrealistic to think of traditional or transitional elites as naive or place-bound. Increasingly, the major differences between them lie in their preference or ambivalence toward democratic institutions. All of that understood, they constitute much of the kindling for the Middle Eastern tinderbox, and the general direction of their change will have profound implications all over the world.

The global economic crisis (2008–2011) has had a disproportional impact on the UAE, particularly in Dubai where many ambitious building projects have either been downsized or terminated. This is a serious reversal in a community that has prided itself on its excessive and/or dramatic architecture and global modernism. Two results have been a major exodus of guest workers and the dismissal of highly paid expatriate experts. Both are indicators of the magnitude of the economic crisis afflicting the Dubai elites.

Modern Elites

In contrast to the traditional elites, the modern elite is one whose day has come. The traditional elite has been either excluded from rule completely or had its influence substantially reduced. Emergent groups who represent larger sections of the population now hold sway. These new groups find themselves in the heady but unaccustomed position of being able to exercise real political power. The political experimentation following the power consolidations of the modern elite may cause instability in policy at first, but eventually equilibrium should be reached in which the decisions of the new elite will begin to have discernible effects on the society.

Figure 9.3 illustrates the composition of the modern elite. The central figures in the elite will generally be the head of state and his government ministers. It is likely, but not certain, that the head of state will have reached that position through a career in the bureaucracy or the military. A more unusual approach may be through the emergent party system, or even through the professional modern elites, such as medicine, law, or related fields. Even less probable but still possible is advancement from the mass public because the modern elite is characterized by greater permeability. The established officer corps and nonpolitical middle-level and upper-level civil servants complete this rough outline of the modern elite. The ulema and the wealthy landowners still may be present, however. They continue to occupy positions of privilege in a modern society, but they have lost much or all of their political influence.

Several things distinguish modern elites from traditional and transitional elites. One of the greatest differences lies in the modern elites' worldview or philosophy. In contrast to the traditional and transitional elites, modern elites are much more likely to see the world as a place that can be radically changed by political, social, and economic policies. In other

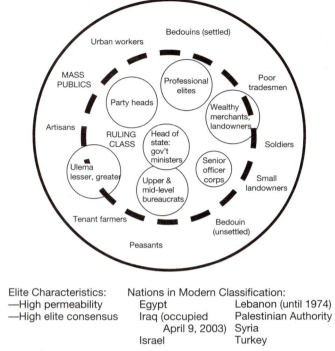

FIGURE 9.3 The Modern Elite

Elite Characteristics: Nations in Modern Classification:
—High permeability   Egypt   Lebanon (until 1974)
—High elite consensus   Iraq (occupied   Palestinian Authority
                          April 9, 2003) Syria
                        Israel   Turkey

words, they see the social and political order as a consequence of human activity and policy, rather than as the result of divine order or some asserted tradition. This point of view often, but not always, associates itself with a secular belief system—that is, a belief system centered on human rather than divine values. For this reason, the modern elite often finds itself in fundamental conflict with religious or sacred values. Some modernizing leaders—such as the former shah of Iran or the late Prime Minister Bhutto of Pakistan—have found religious opposition to their rule to be fierce and ultimately successful. Other modern Arab leaders—Qadaffi of Libya—claim that a modern viewpoint can be supported by traditional Muslim authority and law. The ulema itself is split over this problem, some inveighing against any semblance of human-centered values or policy and others adopting a more flexible viewpoint. Many political leaders now show increasing

interest in Muslim sensibilities, balancing the demands of technical innovation with new concerns for the agenda of Muslim fundamentalists.

One of the most prominent features of contemporary Muslim politics is the growing interest in the possibility of establishing modern Islamic republics, states capable of modern control over environment and policy without relinquishing the claims of Islam over social life generally. Islamic republics have been officially established in Pakistan, Libya, Sudan, and Iran; many other countries are currently wrestling with the problematic relationship between Islam and political authority. Of the countries in the process of establishing an Islamic republic, Iran has made the most progress, but even here progress has been uneven and fraught with controversy. The specific design of the republic is likely to inject substantial conflict into elite dynamics in most Middle Eastern countries. These experiments hold the seeds of substantial transformation of the policies in question and thus are of substantial contemporary and future significance.

The triumph of a modern elite does not in any way eliminate group conflict or for that matter even minimize it. To the contrary, the composition of the modern elite includes more groups in the political process than do the traditional or transitional political systems. The intensity of conflict may increase as well, particularly as more elements in society make stronger and stronger claims on social services and goods. For example, traditional and transitional societies generally have low levels of public literacy. As modern societies increase literacy, they also increase the social and political awareness of groups of their particular situations vis-à-vis other groups in the society. The social good—literacy—carries with it the premise of higher political consciousness and more and greater political participation. The result is an increase in the scope of conflict and subsequent greater attention to conflict resolution. Issues and publics that are simply not relevant to the traditional regime are suddenly and irreversibly part and parcel of a geometrically expanding political process. Both mischief and progress attend this change.

International conflict also can affect these elite systems. The secular-modern regimes of Egypt, Syria, and Iraq have often found themselves individually in conflict with the transitional regimes of the Sudan and Iran or the traditional regimes of Saudi Arabia (under Saud and Faisal) and Kuwait. Their respective beliefs are often seen as mutually exclusive and irreconcilable.

Our contemporary focus on the Arab–Israeli conflict in the Middle East often blinds us to the equally valid differences existing within the Arab and Muslim world. These differences are likely to play larger roles in the immediate future, particularly as different elites make claims on the political loyalties and sensibilities of citizens in other countries. This level of conflict is difficult to resolve without resorting to widespread violence—violence that is all too capable of spilling over into other arenas of international conflict. The long and stubborn war between Iran and Iraq is a good example. The story of the events surrounding Iraq's occupation of Kuwait in 1990 is an even more forceful example.

Modern elite systems—Turkey, Egypt, Syria, Iraq, Lebanon, and Israel, and, very problematically, Palestine—although sharing the characteristics of a more open and competitive structure, are clearly a heterogeneous group of nations that have substantially different histories and cultures. The specific compositions of their elites are also different, although they tend to share similar outlooks on modernization.

TURKEY.   Under the Ottoman sultans, Turkey was the model of a traditional elite. But it was the first Middle Eastern nation to throw off the mantle of the traditional past and embrace European modernization, perhaps because it alone straddles Europe and Asia. Although many political and economic changes occurred in Turkey under the sultanate, Turkey emerged as a modern political system with the remarkable innovations of Mustafa Kemal Ataturk, who proclaimed a new, secular republic in 1923. Ataturk, supported by his political party, the Republican People's Party, mounted a strong and sustained attack on the traditional order. Reforms ranged from the general to the specific, but the major thrust was the secularization of political power, a corresponding reduction of the power of the Muslim hierarchy, and the virtual elimination of the institutions of traditional rule. Ataturk aimed at no less than the total transformation of Turkey from a weak, illiterate, agricultural nation to an industrial nation with all the attendant skills and attitudes that this implies. The very idea of a political party, even a single-party system, implied levels of public political participation undreamed of in the preceding regime.

From these revolutionary beginnings, Turkey has moved toward a complex, industrial, participatory system. Truly competitive political parties now exist in Turkey, although periods of military rule occurred in 1960, 1971, and 1980–1981. Military-approved reforms in the early 1980s and later in the 1990s seem to have eliminated some of the fragmentary tendencies of the Turkish party system, and the system continues a slow move toward independent democratic institutions and greater representation of Muslim organizations and groups.

The Turkish political elite has made significant progress toward its goals. The vision of Ataturk has yet to jell in the economic sector, and some traditional elements—particularly Muslim conservative groups and separatist Kurdish groups—have put considerable strain on the country's political institutions. Yet, progress has been made. Turkey's politics are remarkably participatory compared with politics in the transitional countries and freer than most other modern countries in the Middle East—no mean achievement for any country developing democratic institutions.

In 1995–1996, conservative Muslim parties emerged as a potent element within the Turkish electoral system. The Welfare Party (Islamic) received the largest percentage of votes in the December 1995 parliamentary elections, prompting the resignation of Prime Minister Ciller and subsequent negotiations between the two minority parties (True Path and Motherland) to organize the government. Clearly, Islamic democrats had become a force to be reckoned with in Turkey, with concomitant changes in the Turkish elite. It was encouraging that the Welfare Party leadership was willing to negotiate within the arena that included secular as well as religious parties.

In a related vein, emergent demands for policy reform from Turkey's small Shia populations were reported; and many Kurds, fleeing repression in Iran and Iraq, entered the country, amplifying the demands addressed to the government. In a major setback for the Kurdish People's Party, the Turkish government apprehended the leader of the party, Abdullah Ocalan. His trial, conviction, and death sentence ratified the Turkish military's continued campaign against Kurdish separatism in western Anatolia.

Ultimately, the political successes of the Welfare Party drew attention from militant secularists in the military. In 1996, the military intervened, forcing the resignation of the Welfare government and reestablishing secular party rule. A decision of the Constitutional Court in 1998 forbade the participation of the Welfare Party in electoral politics and prohibited its key leaders from political participation for five years. Suspicion of Islamist parties prompted the Turkish government to reject earthquake relief aid from international Islamic organizations and governments. Given the severity of the earthquakes and their damage to Turkish infrastructure, this decision was not taken lightly. This setback for Islamist groups in Turkey has not apparently dampened their mass appeal and the desire of some Turkish groups for a higher level of Islamization in Turkey.

Consequently, in the Turkish elections held in fall 2002, another Muslim party dominated the election. This party, the Justice and Development Party, went out of its way in the aftermath of the elections to emphasize its commitment to the secular constitution of Turkey. This electoral victory suggested a maturing of the Muslim elements in the Turkish political process and notably improved Turkey's chances for membership in the European Union, a highly significant objective for the new Turkish government. Turkey's newly won status as a candidate for membership in the European Union was dashed when the EU declined to admit Turkey to membership. The immediate political result was a major reorientation in Turkey away from Europe and toward the Middle East, Asia, and the non-Western world. The Israeli attack on a Turkish relief convoy headed for Gaza in 2010 provided a rationale for acceleration of this trend. Contemporary Turkey enjoys substantial international prestige, and the Turkish political elite has broadened to include a larger representation of Muslim participants.

As noted earlier, the achievement of a modern elite structure does *not* signify an end to internal political conflict, but rather signals a change of arena and scope of conflict. In this regard, Turkey has shown itself capable of adjusting to serious political conflicts in recent history; and the future promises more and tougher challenges. As Turkey again approached national elections in 2007, the Turkish military felt it necessary to warn the Muslim affiliated parties again that it would not tolerate a breach in the wall separating religion and the state in Turkey. The permeability and representativeness of the Turkish elite should be a considerable asset in meeting these tests.

EGYPT.   In contrast to Turkey, Egypt had long been a victim of direct imperialist control and continued to be until more recent times. The Egyptian revolution occurred in 1952 with the revolt of the Free Officers. This revolt, which expelled the corrupt and ineffective monarchy of King Farouk, brought to power in Egypt a junta of young army officers, most of them trained abroad. This group of officers subsequently showed extraordinary cohesiveness, bringing a revolution of considerable scope to a faltering Egypt. Initially led by General M. Naguib, the group was ultimately headed by Colonel Gamal Abdel Nasser, one of the most remarkable leaders to grace the political landscape of the Middle East.

Under Nasser, attempts were made to create a party of national revolution. Several formulas were tried, and in 1962, the efforts jelled in the formation of the Arab Socialist Union. The union was conceived of as a party of national integration and ideology, bringing the masses into political contact and cooperation with the central regime. Under Nasser, the party took on some distinct characteristics that were to have profound effects in Egypt in particular and in the Middle East in general.

Nasser, a charismatic leader of the first order, tapped or created a reservoir of sentiment that is now called *Arab nationalism*. Essentially arguing that the Arab people were split unnecessarily and unwisely into many competing camps and nations, Nasser made an emotional appeal for a new Arab unity, one that would reclaim a prominent world role. Nasser's vision inspired many movements across the Middle East that were often viewed with suspicion outside of Egypt. Cynical observers were to see in Nasser's calls for Arab unity the distinct possibility of Egyptian political dominance. Others were disturbed by the coincidence of Nasser's Arab unity with his concept of Arab socialism and mass political participation. Nasser's forthright opposition to the traditional elites of Egypt did not endear him to the beleaguered traditional and transitional elites of other Middle Eastern countries.

Nasser had a particular vision of Arab socialism. This combination of politics and economics should not be viewed as socialism in any European or Marxist sense; rather, it was more a socialism of secular Islam. Its practical expression came in terms of the nationalization of basic industries; the elimination of foreign ownership; and the construction of hospitals, mosques, and schools in as many Egyptian villages as possible. There was no sophisticated understanding of socialist economics in Nasser's formula. There was instead an interest in the common man, expressed in terms of daily needs and concerns—concerns such as food, a place of worship, employment, and national ethnic pride.

The implementation of Nasser's socialism had benign political effects: mass public participation in the Arab Socialist Union, a real improvement in Egypt's international prestige, and the integration of the professional and political classes with the military bureaucracy. But it nearly created an economic disaster: high inflation, low industrial productivity, and high unemployment. As critical as we may justifiably be of Nasser's economic policies, however, we cannot deny his beneficial influence on Egyptian and Arab politics. His symbolic value to the emergence of an appropriate twentieth-century Arab identity is enormous.

Nasser's death and the consolidation of control under Anwar Sadat brought many substantial changes to Egypt and its elite. Under Sadat, the scope of the elite broadened as government policy became more tolerant of people and institutions in the private sector. In the mid-1970s, Sadat launched an ambitious program to create a parallel private economic structure; he attempted to create competition between left, right, and center parties in the Arab Socialist Union. These efforts broadened the representativeness of the elite.

Sadat's bold changes to Nasser's political vision did not come cheaply or without opposition. Attempts in 1978 to increase the artificially low price of bread met with widespread and angry public demonstrations, forcing the government to back down. Nasser is still a potent symbol in the hearts and minds of the Egyptian peasantry and bureaucracy, and one is more likely to encounter his picture in a peasant home than that of Anwar Sadat. Much of the thrust of the Egyptian revolution under Nasser survives. Sadat made a mark on that revolution himself, as demonstrated by the Egyptian treaty with Israel (1978), the dramatic break with the Soviet Union, and the wooing of Western industry to the Nile.

Sadat's government, however, came under increasing domestic pressure from groups dissatisfied with these changes. Palestinian organizations placed a price on his head, as did Libya's volatile Colonel Qadaffi. The Muslim Brotherhood, violently repressed by Nasser in the early days of the revolution, showed signs of resurgence, encouraged by the Islamic revolutions in Libya, Iran, and Pakistan.

Arab nationalists, unhappy with Sadat's unilateral peace with Israel, began to oppose Sadat's rule. These factors ultimately coalesced in the fall of 1981 in the assassination of Anwar Sadat by members of a Muslim fundamentalist cell in the Egyptian army.

Sadat's successor, Hosni Mubarak, was more careful to avoid direct conflict with these alienated groups, and ample evidence documents a broadening of the ruling class under his rule. Mubarak allowed limited representation of conservative Muslim groups in the Egyptian political elite and has avoided the personal displays of consumption and irreverence that brought Sadat into disrepute with Egyptian fundamentalists. At the same time, Mubarak moved forcefully to reduce fundamentalist influence in the Egyptian military and government bureaucracy. Some incremental and modest Islamization has occurred, particularly in the areas of family law. Muslim political groups have been allowed to contest for seats in the legislature. The government seems to be at great pains to avoid antagonizing the fundamentalist ulema. The prospects seemed to suggest continued conflict between groups in the Egyptian elite, successfully moderated through existing Egyptian political institutions and modest electoral freedom. The Egyptian role in international affairs—particularly Desert Storm and the Oslo-era Mideast peace negotiations—increased the prestige of the government domestically, an asset it needed as domestic pressures on government capacity increased.

Contemporary Egypt is under enormous pressure from competing ideologies, population growth, economic stagnation, and religious extremism, at home and abroad. The elite structure of Egypt has apparently broadened and expanded in recent years. The emergence of political terror in Egypt, particularly the occasional targeting of foreign tourists, Egyptian Copts, and governmental officials for assassination, including the attempt on President Mubarak's life in Ethiopia in late 1995, and successive terrorist attacks on

Egyptian targets on the Sinai (2005), has led the government to retrench on its emphasis on democratization. The government has reacted firmly to attempts by politically extremist and even moderate Muslim organizations to take over important Egyptian unions and professional associations, and the government continues to manipulate election rules effectively to disenfranchise smaller or fringe Islamic parties. Serious complaints were raised by the Muslim Brotherhood about the conduct of presidential and legislative elections in 2005. As a result, there are growing political strains on the Egyptian political system and decreasing permeability to the Egyptian elite. Future domestic conflict is highly likely. The prestige of moderate Islamist groups in Egypt grows as the legitimacy of the Egyptian government declines. These factors hold the seeds of future political conflict as new generations of restive citizens attain political maturity.

In an effort to contain the growing Islamist groups, the Egyptian government promulgated a number of constitutional reforms in a referendum in 2007. The thrust of the reforms is to effectively disenfranchise the Muslim Brotherhood and affiliated organizations. The effort constitutionalizes and legalizes widespread government practices of the past decade. The long-term effectiveness of these efforts will play out in the next few years. In spite of these restrictions and policies, legislators nominally sympathetic to the Muslim Brotherhood have managed election to the Egyptian legislature, where they have played a cautious and restrained role; and the number of businessmen elected to the legislature has increased dramatically, leading to a potential shift in the overall politics of the legislature.

These changes are important as Egypt faces an imminent political transition. President Mubarak, now in his early eighties, can be expected to retire from politics in the next couple of years. His retirement and succession will create both new strains and opportunities politically in Egypt, perhaps allowing dissident groups in government a louder and more influential voice in national politics.

SYRIA. Syria shares many characteristics with Lebanon and the people of Palestine. One of the most economically viable of the Middle Eastern countries, Syria has considerable arable land, reasonable water resources, and a well-educated population. The country has exported its professional and commercial expertise for many years, an indicator of its well-developed and sophisticated elites. Syria's borders were the result of arbitrary decisions by the victorious European allies; it is also one of the front-line states in the Arab–Israeli conflict. Similar to Egypt and Lebanon, Syria carried much of the financial and personal burden of the confrontation.

Syrian politics have been dominated since the early 1950s by a combination of party ideology (the Baath Party) and military opportunism. Currently, Syria is run by a military-bureaucratic elite whose power is periodically confirmed by national elections. Most influential positions, including that of the president, are currently held by Alawite Muslims, a small and obscure sect. There is substantial resentment in the Sunni and Shia communities over this inequity, a resentment leading at least in part to broad-scale uprisings in Aleppo (1980) and Hama (1982), forcefully put down by the government. Sunni and Shia participation in Syrian government since that time has been cautious and deliberate.

Although the Baath Party in Syria (and in Iraq before its occupation) has a substantial ideology of nationalism and moderate socialism, pragmatism is a strong influence in contemporary Syrian policy. The collapse of the Soviet Union left Syria exposed diplomatically and militarily. As a consequence, since the late 1980s, Syria has moved slowly toward the West and the United States. In the 1990s, Syria abandoned many of the hallmarks of association with the Soviet alliance, pursuing modified market economics and improved diplomatic and trade relations with the West. The education of Syrian students in the West has increased dramatically, and English has eclipsed Russian and French as the second language of commerce and culture.

Syria gained a measure of political stability under Baathist military rule, a stability that stands in marked contrast to the highly unstable early days of its independence, when the coups d'état were literally too numerous to count reliably. A modicum of economic growth has been achieved, and internationally Syria has achieved a far greater influence in the Arab bloc than her size and power would indicate. The aftermath of the Israeli invasion of Lebanon led to a dramatic increase in Syrian prestige in the region, an opportunity carefully exploited in President Assad's diplomacy. Syria's key role in the U.S.-led coalition against Iraq in 1990–1991 contributed greatly to its regional prestige. Syrian foreign policy in the 1990s centered on the recovery of the Golan, a related peace with Israel, and consolidation of its influence in Lebanon.

Syria's diplomatic gains and its influence in Lebanon were largely eroded in the first decade of the twenty-first century. Identified by the Bush administration as a center of terrorism, Syria found itself at odds with the Western alliance after the September 11 attacks. As a result, Syrian international prestige, globally and regionally, plummeted. Syria's 30-year occupation of Lebanon ended in fall 2005 as many of the elements of the Lebanese political system called for Syrian withdrawal, demands to which Syria acceded. Syrian negotiations with Israel over the return of the Golan also stalled, and Syria found itself increasingly isolated—an isolation encouraged and supported by the United States.

All of these reversals of fortune aside, the Syrian political elite has become progressively more representative in the past decade, as national elections and the promulgation of a

more or less democratic constitution demonstrate. Syria is one of the most socially progressive Middle Eastern nations—the status of women is traditionally higher in Syria than in the rest of the Middle East. Syria, with adequate water and growing petroleum reserves, is potentially one of the economic bright spots outside the Gulf area. Bashaar Assad has managed simultaneously to accommodate loyal followers of his father, while expanding the elite to include broader representation of his own political supporters and moderate Muslim groups and organizations. Analysts note the increasing representation of businessmen in Syria's national elite, a product of President Assad's private-sector economic initiatives. Relations with the United States and the West have improved in the last few years, opening the door for new elite members with growing connections outside Syria.

IRAQ. Politics in Iraq were changed dramatically when the U.S.-led coalition invaded the country in March 2003, displacing the Baathist regime and driving Saddam Hussein from power. During three years of occupation, the coalition authorities and their Iraqi allies pursued an aggressive policy of "de-Baathification," purging the army, the government, and civil organizations of Baathist sympathizers. As a result, the elite structure of Iraq entered a period of intense reorganization, the results of which will not be apparent for some time.

In March 2003, an exasperated United States launched Operation Iraqi Freedom, a unilateral invasion of Iraq to accomplish regime change. By April 9, the Baathist government under Saddam Hussein had been destroyed and the beginnings of an occupation administration initiated. Apparent conflicts among Sunni, Shia, Kurdish, and Turkoman communities were aggravated as the occupying power looked for a formula that would restore order, reestablish basic services, and facilitate a transition to an Iraqi regime democratic in nature.

The political situation in Iraq since the beginning of the occupation can only be described as chaotic. It would have been misleading and disingenuous at that juncture to discuss a national political elite there. There were definable and observable elites in the Shia south of Iraq and in Kurdistan in the north. They eventually became the national elites of a reconstructing Iraq. To some degree, the current composition of the Iraqi political elite, broadly defined, are the unintended consequences of shortsighted policies. Or they may constitute the rudimentary beginnings of a truly national Iraqi elite. Only the future will reveal the contours of the Iraqi elite over the next few years.

A disconcerting trend regarding the Iraqi elite is the dramatic expatriation of the Iraqi professional classes. It is estimated that up to two million well-educated members of the Iraqi society have fled Iraq, including teachers, doctors, social workers, and college professors. As these highly valued professionals found occupational relief in neighboring countries and around the world, it became less likely that they would return to their homeland, continuing the pattern of social disorganization occasioned by the occupation.

There were some Iraqi bright spots, however. After three years of occupation, the coalition had organized an Iraqi government sufficiently strong to conduct three national elections in 2005, ultimately adopting a constitution and electing the first members of an Iraqi parliament. Although these developments were encouraging, they did not yet represent a sovereign government capable of standing alone. In late 2006 and into 2007, the government itself became increasingly vulnerable to violent attacks. Snipers, suicide bombers, and mortar attacks succeeded in breaching the sanctity of the Green Zone, the heavily fortified and protected center of Iraqi government. A small number of Iraqi officials were assassinated, and a larger number resigned their positions, adding to the stress on the government.

The surprising military successes of the U.S. "surge" in 2007–2008 created a political opportunity for the nascent Iraqi political institutions. From a perspective on Iraq's political elite, the results have been disappointing. Sunni Iraqi's have more or less been denied access to the government jobs and positions (electoral and appointed) that would confer elite status. Instead, the government of Iraq has become dominated almost exclusively by Iraqi Shi'a and (in Kurdistan) by ethnic Kurds. This near-exclusion of Sunni citizens from the political elite of Iraq promises to be politically problematic in the next few years. As U.S. troops are gradually withdrawn from Iraq, Iraq's security forces will be placed under greater pressure as the discontented Sunnis protest their lack of power and influence. The breathing space bought by the success of the military surge is unlikely to be followed by a similar political breathing space. The consequences will be evident when they occur: more terrorist attacks, growing political instability, and ultimately a possible civil conflict. This unpleasant scenario could be aggravated and accelerated if the Kurdish majority in the north seeks greater autonomy or independence from Baghdad. Again, the long-term prospects in Iraq appear problematic from a number of perspectives.

There is serious political work to be done in Iraq in the next decade. The construction of a responsible political elite representative of the complex social divisions in the country is a high priority for the nascent Iraqi regime. The Iraqi parliamentary elections of March 2010 illustrated these problems. In an election that produced a virtual tie between secular-Sunni lists and the two major Shi'a lists, the organization of a new government continued for months without resolution. It seems apparent now that the social and political divides between secular and religious elites make national coalitions difficult, at best. Iraq is in serious need of a coherent national elite capable of negotiating these divides.

LEBANON. Until the spillover of the Arab–Israeli conflict literally tore it asunder, Lebanon was the most cosmopolitan country in the Middle East. Beirut, a city of charm and energy, was a center of commerce and finance; it had attracted a highly skilled and mobile international population. Blessed with considerable national resources, including a well-educated and ambitious population, Lebanon seemed to have a bright future.

The Israeli invasion of Lebanon in 1978, primarily to eliminate Palestinian terrorist bases, put an effective end to the dream of the Lebanese. The dream was fragile long before, however. Lebanon, another of those countries based on a series of unwise and shallow judgments made in Europe, was composed of at least three highly differentiated ethnic groups: Christians, Muslims, and Druze. Never integrated into a national political or economic unit, these groups lived in proximity but not intimacy. The National Pact or charter of Lebanon, promulgated at a time when the Muslim and Christian populations were nearly equal, parceled out political offices to particular ethnic groups. The president was required to be a Maronite Christian, whereas the prime minister had to be a Sunni Muslim and the speaker of the Assembly a Shia Muslim. These and other offices were apportioned on the basis of the supposed relative balance of religious-ethnic groups at the time of the National Pact. National censuses were forbidden for fear of upsetting the delicate balance between the groups.

The fiction of stable, counterbalancing religious groups served Lebanon well until it was forced, seemingly against its will, into the mainstream of the Arab–Israeli confrontation. After the invasion of Lebanon by Israeli units in 1978, Lebanon was plagued by a civil war that was aided and abetted by foreign intrigue. Links between Israel and right-wing Christian groups, formalized in the aftermath of the 1982 invasion, deteriorated in subsequent years. Syrian troops occupied much of Beirut and

Lebanon, with little pretense of peacekeeping and with the open intention of exercising political control. What remained of Lebanese independence was completely destroyed in the aftermath of the Israeli invasion of Lebanon in the summer of 1982, an invasion and occupation disastrous for nearly every participant concerned. The expulsion of the Arafat wing of the PLO created a vacuum of power in the elite, leading to the rise of the Shia militias (particularly the Amal and Hizbollah), Syrian-backed factions of the Palestinians, and the Syrians themselves. Lebanon was in a state of civil war.

There have been many efforts to "fix" the situation in Lebanon, and most have failed. The Taif Accords, however, midwifed in 1989 by Saudi Arabia and Lebanese legislators, produced substantial progress. In effect, Syria became an active participant in stabilizing Lebanon, forcing substantial disarmament among the independent militias and establishing a governmental military presence. As a result, Lebanon by the early 1990s enjoyed a modicum of stability. Many of the Lebanese social, economic, and political elite that had fled to Jordan, the Gulf States, and Europe announced plans to return. For the first time in 20 years, there was real cause for optimism that Lebanon might resolve its civil war. The Lebanese elite seemed to be broadening, with greater representation of the previously disenfranchised Shia. This boded well for the establishment of effective government in the 1990s. Certainly, the diplomatic aftereffects of Desert Storm reduced some of the international pressure on Lebanon, making it less attractive as an international battlefield. The release of all American hostages in Lebanon in late 1991 was apparently a joint venture of Lebanon, Syria, and Iran, and the United Nations. The release reduced the rhetorical conflict in the Middle East, to Lebanon's advantage.

As was noted in the preceding discussion, progress on the Israeli–Syrian peace negotiations seemed to strengthen the Syrian hand in

Lebanese politics. The unexpected withdrawal of Israel's occupying forces from southern Lebanon reduced much of the pressure on the Lebanese government, with salutary effects. This seemed to contribute to the progress made in Lebanon in the last few years, continuing the trend toward development of an independent stable and effective government.

Syria's military and administrative position in Lebanon came to a fast and surprising end in fall 2005. After nearly 30 years of occupation, many in Lebanon had lost their patience with the Syrian presence. The assassination by car bomb of a prominent Lebanese businessman and politician, Rafik Hariri, was widely blamed on the Syrians, further exacerbating the problem. After parliamentary resolutions and public demonstrations put Syrian withdrawal squarely on the world stage, Syria quickly withdrew.

Elections in Lebanon after the Syrian withdrawal were inconclusive. Although anti-Syrian parties gained some representation in the parliament, pro-Syrian groups also were successful in defending their interests. Hizbollah, a resistance organization backed by Iran and Syria, gained a number of seats and seemed prepared to take a responsible role in the governance of Lebanon.

Events in August 2006 put Lebanon's fragile coalitions back in danger. Hizbollah, attempting to goad Israel into an exchange of prisoners, attacked an Israeli patrol, killing several Israeli soldiers and taking two captive. Under the conditions of previous negotiations, this could have led to an exchange of prisoners. In this particular instance, it provoked a massive military reaction, placing most of Lebanon under intense Israeli attack. Billions of dollars of damage to the Lebanese infrastructure occurred, hundreds of Lebanese civilians were killed, and tens of thousands were displaced or made homeless. After weeks of intensive bombardment, supported by periodic U.S. resupply of munitions for the Israeli Defense Forces, international forces entered

southern Lebanon and separated the two combatants.

The results of the month-long war were surprising. Hizbollah was able to weather the barrage in its bunkers in South Lebanon and emerged to offer relief and support to the Lebanese public. Hizbollah emerged from the conflict substantially strengthened politically and assumed a more prominent and influential role in the Lebanese elite and government.

The aftermath of the Syrian withdrawal has seen an expansion of the Lebanese political elite, incorporating a wider range of political organizations and interest groups into the Lebanese state. All in all, Lebanon has moved toward a mature democracy, and its elite structure represents and supports that fact. National elections in Lebanon were held in June 2009. The results of the election were encouraging, with the incumbent party and government winning the election in a relatively close contest with Hizbollah. Although Hizbollah's representation in the legislature increased, it did not displace the coalition government. The short-term result is that both parties have behaved responsibly in the new alignment. Many analysts note the transformation of Hizbollah from a primarily terrorist/resistance organization into a conventional political party. If this transformation is genuine and complete, Lebanon and the larger Middle East will be the beneficiaries. At this point, cautious optimism seems appropriate. The Lebanese elite has expanded marginally in the aftermath of the 2009 elections, and Hizbollah shows signs of transformation into a genuine political party giving voice to the disenfranchised Shi'a of Lebanon. The summer 2010 death of Ayatollah Fadlallah, the titular head of Hizbollah for decades, will necessitate further changes and probable expansion in the Lebanese elite. Hopefully Fadlallah's successor will be able to continue Hizbollah's political maturation. Fadlallah was very influential in the extended Shi'a community, commanding great respect in Iraq, Iran, and, of course, Lebanon.

ISRAEL. In some respects, the Israeli elite is the most modern of the Middle Eastern elites; in other respects, it is among the most traditional. It is modern in that its members are highly educated and technically competent. There has been an important infusion of Russian émigrés into the elite in the past decade, permitting some elite expansion in size and experience. The Israeli elite has mastered the technological skills and values necessary for a modern society. For those who qualify for elite status—primarily on the basis of religious preference, technical competence, and social origin—the established political process is participatory and representative.

Recent political trends in Israel have enhanced (perhaps exaggerated) the presence of the religious Orthodox and Ultraorthodox elements in the Israeli elite. Their influence as the swing factions in the coalitions in the Knesset has given them influence out of proportion to their numbers. They now compete effectively with the previously dominant secular factions, and their presence in any government's ruling coalition is crucial to its survival there. The withdrawal of support by two very small parties in January 1992 forced general elections, and similar defections led to the demise of the Netanyahu government in 1999 and the Sharon government in 2002. Ultraorthodox parties continue to enjoy disproportional influence in government and the Israeli elite.

Large groups of citizens are effectively disenfranchised in the Israeli system. First and most obvious are the Arabs, who number in the hundreds of thousands and who live in Israel. From the government point of view, the Arabs constitute a serious security problem, and as a consequence they are subject to a wide range of political, economic, and social controls. These controls greatly increased during the Palestinian intifadahs, indicating a growing

government resolve to stamp out any vestige of sympathy for independence. The Palestinian intifadah eventually motivated civil disobedience and demonstrations among Israeli–Arab citizens as well, leading to more problems for this poorly represented constituency. Ironically, the growing legitimacy of the Palestinian Authority in the West Bank and Gaza has resulted in higher levels of estrangement for Arabs living within Israel proper, citizens or not.

The withdrawal of Israel from Gaza in 2005 mitigated the problem of Arab disenfranchisement considerably. If proposed withdrawals from the West Bank are eventually accomplished, the problem will be reduced yet again. This will open up the prospects for developing a Palestinian elite in its own territory, a transformation of the political situation facing the Palestinians since the establishment of the Israeli state in 1948. Construction of a modern Palestinian elite would be a function of the success or failure of the Palestinian state currently under negotiation and development.

Disenfranchisement was not the fate only of the Arabs, however. Intra-Jewish conflict has been well documented in recent decades, showing that certain Jewish groups have little access to the ruling class. Tensions continue between the politically dominant European Jews (Ashkenazi) and the more recently arrived and less modern Oriental Jews (Sephardim) from Asia and Africa. There are growing separations between recent immigrants from the Ashkenazi and Sephardic communities and the native-born descendants of the founders, the Sabras. Hundreds of thousands of Jews from the former Soviet Union have immigrated to Israel. They are not well integrated into the Israeli political system and have not yet found their economic or social niche. Many African Jewish immigrants are living lives of unemployed marginality in hotels originally built for the tourist trade. Their isolation is palpable and begs for solution. The revelation in 1996 that thousands of units of blood donated by Ethiopian Jews (Falasha) had been destroyed for fear of "contamination" led to public demonstrations by this disadvantaged group. Israel has been swallowing considerably more immigrants than it can effectively integrate into its system, resulting in large numbers of European and African Jews living in political and economic limbo. Growing levels of inflation have exacerbated these problems.

The implementation of the Israeli–Palestinian peace continues to strain the Israeli and Palestinian political elites. This has been true during the entire history of the conflict. The return of Gaza and Jericho to Palestinian control brought vehement opposition from fundamentalist Jewish groups, particularly the settler movements in the West Bank. Increasing tensions between the nonobservant Israeli leadership and the observant leadership became public and vitriolic. Further grants of responsibility to the new Palestinian Authority increased friction even more. This situation led directly to the assassination of Prime Minister Yitzhak Rabin by a fundamentalist Jewish extremist in October 1995.

Public and media reactions to the assassination, to the unseemly celebrations of the event among settler and American Jewish communities, and to the evidence that ultraconservative rabbis had at least indirectly approved of the murder led to a swing in public opinion toward continuation of the peace process and a decline of support for extremist groups in Israel. But a spate of terrorist bombings from a militant wing of Hamas in winter 1996 placed this momentum in jeopardy and allowed a reemergence of antipeace sentiment in political discourse. As Prime Minister Barak proceeded in the implementation of the peace accords in 1999, increasing tension between the settler groups and the government became apparent. Polarization between the Israeli left and right occurred.

To many analysts, the ascension of Ariel Sharon to the prime minister's office signaled a "get tough" phase in this relationship. Many were surprised when, in the spring of 2005, the prime minister announced the government's intention of pursuing a unilateral withdrawal from Gaza and an eventual withdrawal from most of the West Bank. Domestic opposition to the withdrawal was furious, but the government prevailed, and in fall 2005, Israel withdrew all Israelis—troops as well as settlers—from Gaza, turning the administration of the region over to the fledgling Palestine state. Events subsequent to the withdrawal saw the resignation of the prime minister from the Likud Party, through which he had previously governed, to create a new centrist party composed of moderate elements of the Likud and Labor coalitions. These events set the stage for a dramatic conflict in twenty-first-century Israeli politics, played out in the elections of 2006.

In December 2005, Prime Minister Sharon suffered a debilitating stroke, plunging Israel into a political crisis. Prior to his illness, Sharon had abandoned the Likud Party in favor of a new, centrist political party, the Kadima. The Kadima Party was dedicated to the unilateral withdrawal of Israel from Gaza and the West Bank and widely expected to win in the March Knesset elections. The prime minister's precarious health put those assumptions to the test, particularly as the Palestinian Authority conducted earlier elections in February.

The results of both elections, Palestinian and Israeli, surprised many analysts. The Palestinian surprise came in the form of a Hamas electoral victory over the Fatah Party of Mahmoud Abbas. The Israeli surprise, in late March, came with a decisive victory by Kadima over the Likud and Labor Party, staking out a broad center in Israeli politics. Acting Prime Minister Ehud Olmert was formally inducted as Prime Minister and immediately found himself in a confrontation with the new Hamas-led "government" in Palestine, led by Prime Minister Ismail Haneya. Early relations were clearly strained.

Both elections—Israeli and Palestinian— changed the contours of their respective political elites. The Hamas victory brought new players into the Palestinian elite, displacing many leaders with Fatah/PLO backgrounds. In Israel, the Kadima victory clearly reduced the influence and prestige of the Ultraorthodox parties in the Knesset and reduced their influence in the Israeli elite. Both Israel and the emerging Palestinian state were now faced with the difficult task of finding a working relationship between two adversaries.

Israeli–Palestinian conflict in 2006 and 2007 brought new and stronger strains on this fragile relationship. Rocket and military-type attacks from Gaza brought swift and deadly Israeli responses, both on the ground and from the air. As the Fatah faction of the Palestinian Authority sought to restrain its Hamas partners, a near civil war erupted within Palestine. This was immeasurably complicated by the military conflict between Israel and Lebanon/Hizbollah in late summer of 2006. The result of these conflicts was simultaneous conflict between Israel and Lebanon, conflict between Israel and the Palestinian Authority, and intra-Palestinian conflict between Hamas and Fatah. Many of the Hamas leaders were targeted for assassination, and a large number of Palestinian parliamentary delegates were imprisoned in Israeli jails. Things on the ground in Israel and Palestine have not looked any dimmer than in the darkest minutes of the conflict decades earlier.

Israel itself has not escaped the consequences of this multiple conflict. Widespread dissatisfaction in Israel over the management of the Lebanese conflict, substantive charges of corruption against the government and the military, and a sense of futility regarding Palestinian relations led to widespread public demonstrations against the Olmert government. Israel appears to be swinging further to the

right politically, with all of the implications and consequences that shift entails. The Israeli elite is in danger again of splintering over the questions of the occupation and settlements in the West Bank. What progress seemed evident two years before seemed lost by 2007.

The result of the intermittent and uneven progress toward Israeli–Palestinian peace has resulted in the emergence of two competing political elites, Israeli and Palestinian, with a common stake in the success of the peace effort. The genie of Palestinian autonomy, even Palestinian independence, was out of the bottle. A two-state solution was now on the horizon. It cannot be contained again without wreaking havoc and destruction on both parties.

This cautiously optimistic scenario for Israeli–Palestinian resolution was sharply dashed by the Israel elections of February 2009. In a tightly contested election between two party coalitions, Kadima and Likud, the Likud coalition won, bringing Benjamin Netanyahu, a previous holder of the office of prime minister, back into power. Netanyahu, an unapologetic conservative, came to power with a slim parliamentary majority and the desire to halt the two-state solution that has been the dominant paradigm for peace. Netanyahu's history and policies put Israel on an immediate collision course with the new Obama administration in the United States. In terms of the Israeli political elite, the immediate results of the election were clear, bringing representatives of the settler communities and other conservative religious groups prominently back into elite status. Netanyahu's military suppression of the Hamas government in Gaza in the months following his election was wildly popular among the conservative and extremist elements in the Israeli electorate, creating greater strains with the Palestinians, the larger Arab world, the United States, and the West in general. Ironically, as the Arab states moved toward a two-state solution to the conflict, Israel moved toward a radical one-state solution. "The more things change . . . ."

CONCLUSION

Political, social, and economic pressures in the Middle East ultimately affect the elite structure of politics. The Middle East is unusual in having a wide variety of elites—traditional, transitional, and modern. Changes in the composition of an elite ultimately can cause profound changes in the policies and worldview of a political system. These effects are not specifically predictable.

We can safely predict that these changes will produce new strains and demands on the political system, and that these strains and demands will create new and often unexpected domestic and international conflicts. We can predict with some confidence a continuation of the unsettled nature of contemporary Middle Eastern politics. Without doubt, we can predict that Islam, in its various forms, will be intimately involved in that process. These factors, combined with the commonplace but accurate observation that the world is growing smaller, suggest that the political implications of these changes in elite structure will influence all our hopes and lives.

Key Terms

katib   *177*
mutawwa   *183*
as shura   *184*

10 POLITICAL LEADERSHIP IN THE CONTEMPORARY MIDDLE EAST

Having discussed the ruling elites in the Middle East, we shall now focus on those individuals in the highest political offices: monarchs, generals, and presidents. Although effective leadership is important to the world's affluent and powerful societies, it is even more important to the disadvantaged and recently independent countries that are confronting serious internal and external challenges. Countries in which the institutions of governments are new, fragile, or discredited have a far greater need for effective leadership than countries with long histories of political order and stability.

There are three basic styles of political leadership: traditional, modern technical bureaucratic, and charismatic.[1] We shall examine a leader representative of each style and show how his career exemplifies that style's essential nature. We will then discuss other contemporary Middle Eastern leaders and see how their styles of rule fit the pattern. Finally, we shall briefly look at how these leadership styles affect domestic and international politics.

The three basic leadership styles are broad and general and do not account for fine differences, and they do not accurately predict the political consequences of any one kind of leadership; they are only rough guides. To illustrate the three types, we will focus on four prominent figures in twentieth-century Egyptian politics: King Farouk (traditional), Gamal Abdel Nasser (charismatic), and Anwar Sadat and Hosni Mubarak (modern bureaucratic).

TRADITIONAL LEADERSHIP

Traditional leaders base their claim to leadership on the assertion that they are the clear and logical successors to a line of leaders that stretches back in time and that is legitimized by practice. They are leaders because of historical forces, and they claim the right and obligation to continue. They often imply that their leadership is necessary to maintain the social order on the right course. Traditional political

---

[1] This leadership typology originated with Max Weber, the great German sociologist. Our use of it, however, differs substantially from his. See Hans Gerth and C. Wright Mills, eds. *From Max Weber* (New York: Oxford University Press, 1964).

orders, although conservative, are not rigid or unyielding to change, but they may be slow to implement a schedule of changes or react to changing conditions. They expect change to occur over relatively extended periods of time. As Almond and Powell observe, a definite promise of performance is implied in the assertion of the right to rule:

> Most traditional societies have some long-range performance expectations built into their norms of legitimacy; if crops fail, enemies invade, or floods destroy, then the emperor may lose the "mandate of heaven," as in Imperial China; or the chiefs their authority; or the feudal lords, their claim to the loyalty of their serfs.[2]

The traditional leader depends on the force of tradition, or his interpretation of it, to establish his legitimacy as a ruler. *Legitimacy* refers to the public perception of the ruler's right to his position of leadership and is not restricted to traditional leaders alone. The willingness of the populace to accept a particular leadership structure as right and defensible legitimizes the political process as it exists. Tradition is no substitute for effective policy, however, and it cannot protect an ineffective ruler forever.

Some examples of traditional legitimization may clarify the problem. There is logic to the use of tradition as a legitimizing symbol. The shah of Iran often publicly argued that the Persian cultural tradition demanded monarchical leadership, that the Iranian political practice for thousands of years found its most effective and satisfying expression in a monarch. As monarch, Mohammed Reza Pahlevi was performing an important service for the Iranian people. The rulers of Egypt made similar arguments.

Shah Muhammad Reza Pahlevi (Modernizing Traditional Leader).

That tradition may legitimize but not stifle change is also well demonstrated in Saudi Arabia. There is no gainsaying the importance of tradition in legitimizing the Saudi leadership. Tradition has not been a logical reason for continuing a weak leader in office, however. The transition from King Saud to King Faisal, based on decisions within the royal family itself, suggests that this traditional elite was responsive to contemporary difficulties. Tradition was mobilized to legitimize the change and the new leadership.

The right or legitimacy of traditional leaders is often bound up in the intersection of political and religious tradition: The king or sultan also may be the defender of the faith, or the sheikh may be patron of the ulema, as in the relationship of the Egyptian monarchy with the mosque university of Al-Azhar. These roles and symbols, given great weight by their persistence over time, are the most important factors in legitimizing the traditional regimes.

In the absence of competing claims, traditional leaders may find the invocation of ancient roles and symbols adequate to protect their base of power. Given the twentieth-century

---

[2]Gabriel Almond and Bingham Powell, *Comparative Politics* (Boston: Little, Brown, 1978), pp. 31–32.

phenomenon of competing claims from charismatic or modern bureaucratic aspirants to office, traditional leaders have often been forced to attempt limited reforms within the recognized tradition. Traditional leaders have attempted to modernize their political, social, and economic systems without sacrificing their right to rule. The Tanzimat reforms in Ottoman Turkey can be interpreted in this light, as can the White Revolution of the shah of Iran. In both cases, the traditional leader attempted to come to terms with modern technology and administrative procedures without relinquishing his monopoly of political power. It is instructive that both efforts ultimately failed.

King Farouk of Egypt

Many characteristics of traditional political leaders are exhibited in the experience of King Farouk of Egypt, the last Egyptian monarch. Farouk's rule (1936–1952) embraced a period that saw a fundamental redrawing of the international political order, including the rise of Soviet and American power, the concomitant decline of European—especially British—influence in the Middle East, the emergence of mass political parties, and the political reassertion of Islam and Islamic groups. Farouk's response to these changes demonstrates the essence of traditional leadership and its fundamental defects.

Born in 1920 into the royal lineage founded by the great Egyptian leader Muhammad Ali, Farouk was raised in a strong tradition of royal absolutism. The line of Muhammad Ali treated the whole of Egypt as its personal possession. King Farouk proved himself to be no stranger to this tradition.

The royal family, similar to most of the ruling houses of Egypt for the past 3,000 years, was not of Egyptian extraction. In the case of Farouk's family, the line was founded by an Albanian adventurer, Muhammad Ali, with tenuous ties of loyalty to the Ottoman Empire. Enormously successful at realizing the political, social, and economic potential of

King Farouk (Traditional Leader).

nineteenth-century Egypt, Muhammad Ali was frustrated by European, especially English, intervention. A large extended family buttressed by extensive retainers and officials saw Egypt as a private fief run for its own benefit. With few ties to the Egyptian masses, the royal family routinely assumed its right to absolute rule and consistently opposed the extension of political rights or influence to native Egyptians.

Farouk himself was educated and socialized in a conservative atmosphere; he was exposed to periodically rabid Anglophobia and persistently pro-Italian sympathies. Farouk's tutors included the most notable ulema of Al-Azhar University, who instilled in him a serious appreciation of his role as protector of the faith. King Fuad's death placed Farouk on the throne at age 16, still in his minority. A regency council was formed to advise and educate him in his responsibilities as ruler of Egypt.

Farouk's father, King Fuad, saw the emergence of the first legitimate mass political party in Egypt, the Wafd. Much of Fuad's political labors in later life were devoted to frustrating Wafd aspirations to power, a policy continued by the young king. The combination of mass political activity and growing nationalism had a disquieting effect on the royal house. By complex political maneuvers, Fuad and Farouk attempted to exclude the Wafd from power. They both demonstrated one of the chief characteristics of traditional political leadership: a great reluctance to *share* political power with anyone, particularly with mass or nationalist groups. This is not to imply that Farouk was bereft of policy or ambition; there is evidence to the contrary. The point is that these ambitions never included a broadening of the base of political power.

Farouk showed his traditional orientation to political power in other ways. His fascination with ceremony, pomp, and circumstance reflected the concern of the traditional leader for rituals and rite that confirm the assertion and maintenance of traditional authority. Arrayed in rich uniforms for every occasion, Farouk's movements around his kingdom were spectacles in themselves: elegant livery, scores of retainers and entertainers, international celebrities, and sumptuous banquets in luxurious palaces or country estates. Grandeur was not only a perquisite of office, it was an obligation, and Farouk became increasingly enthusiastic about it.

In a similar vein, the royal house under Farouk became internationally noted for its hedonism. Drunkenness, particularly offensive to the emerging Muslim Brotherhood, sexual abandon (often reported graphically in the international press), and disturbingly regular accusations of official corruption involving minor members of the royal family were commonplace. Farouk's appreciation for attractive women became an international symbol of Egyptian royal decadence, set in the most luxurious spas of Mediterranean Europe.

There was a curious tension between Farouk's hedonism and his public attitude toward Islam. One could not call him personally pious, particularly in view of his devotion to Koranically prohibited pleasures—wine, women, and pornography. However, Farouk took his role as "defender of the faith" seriously; he made substantial contributions to the maintenance of Al-Azhar and welcomed numerous political exiles to Cairo. He also subsidized programs designed to maintain Egyptian prestige in the larger community of Muslim nations, which lacked any focus of authority since the abolition of the caliphate. These practices solidified his relationship to the higher ulema at the same time that his hedonism was coming under growing criticism by fundamentalist Muslim groups.

Despite these irritants to the prestige of the royal house, Farouk's rule and government enjoyed a legitimacy that shows the strength of traditional leadership. Most analysts of the period assert that Farouk's government far outlasted its effectiveness. Aside from noting the population's predisposition to accept the traditional, little in the last ten years of Farouk's rule suggests that his political, social, or economic *performance* commanded popular support for the government.

The demise of Farouk's rule in Egypt resulted from a combination of domestic and international forces. Farouk's pro-Italian sympathies quickly ran afoul of international events in World War II, resolving in favor of his British enemies. In addition, the public became dissatisfied with his opposition to the Wafd party, and the increasingly militant fundamentalist Muslim Brotherhood was disillusioned by his personal licentiousness. Riots in Cairo involving the Wafd, extremist groups, the Muslim Brotherhood, and students became commonplace. The final blow came with the miserable performance of the Egyptian military in the war against Israel in 1948, although the full implications of the war were not to become clear to the public until the revolution of July 23, 1952. Charges of corruption and ineptitude gained widespread circulation and validity. The war became a focus of resentment against the low level to which Arab and Egyptian prestige had sunk. Farouk became increasingly unable to manipulate the forces of Egyptian politics, and instability and drift became the governmental norms.

Farouk's fall and abdication were a result of actions by the military, not the political forces that opposed him for so long. His final attempts to abrogate the Anglo-Egyptian treaty in 1951 produced a series of ugly confrontations between Egyptian and British forces, which set off a series of antigovernment and antiforeign riots in the urban centers of Egypt. The army's inability to handle these incidents further inflamed the king's opponents, and British efforts to reinforce their garrisons made the situation worse. Finally, on July 23, 1952, a group of military officers known as the Committee of Free Officers overthrew the government and established the Revolutionary Command Council under the titular leadership of General Naguib. On July 26, the council requested the formal abdication of King Farouk. Farouk complied, abdicating in favor of his son, and promptly departed for Italy. Farouk never recovered his influence in Egypt. His abdication itself demonstrated his inability to come to terms with the emerging political order.

> Towards the middle of the afternoon, it was announced in a broadcast from Cairo that "some very important news would be given at six o'clock." Everybody understood and prepared to listen.
>
> All round the Ras El Tin palace and along the coast road to Alexandria an enormous crowd had gathered, tense with expectation and with mixed feelings of anguish and joy. Then came the prodigious sight: the royal exit in the rays of the setting sun, on to the sea which a hundred and fifty years earlier had brought, to the Egyptian shore, the Albanian soldier of fortune, Muhammad Ali, the great-great-grandfather of the sovereign who was now taking his leave.

> At ten minutes to six . . . Farouk, in his splendid white uniform of *Admiral of the Fleet*, came slowly down the palace steps towards the sea. He was followed by Queen Narriman, carrying the new king, six months old. . . . While the royal flag was being fetched from the palace, a cruiser in the bay fired a twenty-one-gun salute.
>
> General Naguib went aboard. . . . Farouk appeared to be touched, behind the screen of his dark glasses. "Take care of my army," he said. "It is now in good hands, sire," Naguib replied. The answer did not please Farouk, who said in a hard voice, "What you have done to me, I was getting ready to have done to you." Then, turning on his heel, he took leave of the conquerors.[3]

Farouk's final years became a mishmash of sybaritic excess in the most expensive and exclusive resorts of Europe. Throwing himself with abandon onto the gambling tables, onto the dining tables, and into the arms of many an attractive companion, Farouk ended his life as a corpulent playboy dedicated to pleasures of the flesh and the moment—a sad ending in many respects, far removed from the promise of leadership in the 16-year-old youth who ascended the throne in 1936.

King Farouk is hardly the best example to use of a traditional ruler. He was weak and was unable to rise effectively to the challenges of his times. Indeed, he helps to maintain the myth of decadent Middle Eastern rulers. Compared with the historical importance of the shah of Iran or Ibn Saud of Saudi Arabia, Farouk's importance is a footnote to contemporary history.

---

[3]Jeanne and Simone Lacouture, *Egypt in Transition* (New York: Criterion Books, 1958), pp. 156–159.

However, King Farouk's example is important for several reasons. First, the crises of leadership that have afflicted the decolonializing world have often involved the reluctant departure of ineffective traditional leaders. To focus on strong leaders would distort our analysis. Second, the myth of decadence is not a myth. Absolute rulers, traditional and otherwise, have not shown themselves to be disinterested in pleasure or pomp or luxury. Much of the basis for their legitimacy comes from just such a claim to the perquisites of royalty. Finally, the influence of weak and ineffective leaders on world history is arguably as important as the impact of the few "great men" of our times.

We will return to the subject of traditional leadership at the end of this chapter. The crisis of confidence in traditional leadership, which undermined King Farouk just as it undermined many other Middle Eastern leaders in the twentieth century, leads to three possible alternatives:

1. Traditional political governance from a different political ruler, an apparently unlikely and short-term phenomenon
2. Leadership based on the claims of the modern bureaucratic managers in the society, such as the military or a nascent political party
3. Charismatic leaders who offer their transcendent leadership as a substitute for the claims of tradition or bureaucratic efficiency

In the period after the fall of the Egyptian monarch, the third alternative materialized in the form of Gamal Abdel Nasser, a young officer in the movement that called for Farouk's abdication. Definitely a charismatic leader, Nasser was to have an important effect on Egypt and the Middle East.

CHARISMATIC LEADERSHIP

As defined by Max Weber, a charismatic leader possesses particular characteristics that set him apart from normal leaders. A charismatic leader is, in a word, unique. He possesses personal characteristics that are suited to a peculiarly intense leadership style, and he is capable of creating or participating in an intense, reciprocal psychological exchange with his followers. His actions and proposals are legitimized by reference to some transcendent source—religious, historical, natural, or mystical. Recent world leaders recognized as charismatic include Adolph Hitler, Charles de Gaulle, Tito, Sukarno, and Gamal Abdel Nasser.[4]

Our definition and description of charismatic leadership is complicated by two factors. First, charismatic leadership is often erroneously equated with other leadership characteristics, such as personal beauty, rhetorical skill, or popularity. The use of the term in general circulation may distract us from the necessary distinguishing characteristics of the charismatic leader. Second, charismatic leadership seems to be idiosyncratic to the culture in which it occurs; the characteristics of a charismatic leader in Egypt would differ from those of a charismatic leader in, say, France or England. The chemistry of the relationship between leader and followers changes according to the particulars of the culture and historical circumstance. Despite these difficulties, the phenomenon of charismatic leadership is real and is important in any analysis of Middle Eastern politics. Charismatic leaders have had, and continue to have, enormous impact on the politics of the region. The Sudanese Mahdi, Gamal Abdel Nasser, Ayatollah Ruhollah Khomeini, and Colonel Muammar Qadaffi—all have had, or have, the potential to alter dramatically the course of political events.

Despite the idiosyncratic qualities of charisma, we can make some general observations about the phenomenon. Charismatic leadership almost always appears during a social or

---

[4]For a broad treatment of charismatic leadership, see Ann Ruth Willner, *The Spellbinders: Charismatic Political Leadership* (New Haven, CT: Yale University Press, 1984).

political crisis—particularly a crisis in which the prevailing institutions of government have been discredited or destroyed. Examples include the ruinous inflation in Germany that preceded the rise of Hitler or the legislative-executive deadlocks that preceded de Gaulle's second entrance into French politics. Theoretically, the public in these situations is predisposed to seek a heroic leader to provide a substitute for discredited authority.

Another expectation is that the charismatic leader will promulgate substantial and convincing images of a new order, perhaps ordained in heaven, that will raise the community to new levels of activity and accomplishment, or, in another variant, restore the community to its rightful place in the world. In giving substance to the visionary demands of a disillusioned populace, the charismatic leader provides them with psychological sustenance and heightened self-esteem.

Another characteristic of charismatic leaders is their resonant rhetorical gift—resonant in the sense that they can raise sympathetic responses from their followers. This rhetorical gift may vary dramatically in style. Compare the dramatic histrionics of Adolph Hitler with the icy, Olympian quality of de Gaulle's pronouncements. Whatever the style, the successful charismatic leader has the ability to move a nation by the power of his rhetoric. In many cases the rhetoric may be more politically important than the substance of the policies articulated.

Finally, the charismatic leader leads by example. This quality seems idiosyncratic to culture. The simple, introspective life of Gandhi can be contrasted with the cheerful hedonism of Sukarno in Indonesia or Marcos in the Philippines. The leader in his personal life sets a standard of personal behavior that strikes the populace as desirable and ennobling.

These characteristics provide the public with personal knowledge of the leader. He has a place in the collective psychology of the nation. The leader gains a larger-than-life perspective on himself, thriving and growing on the demands and support of the followers. A powerful, reciprocal psychological exchange is established, which ultimately allows a single personality to substitute for a complex of institutions.

As powerful as this reciprocal dynamic can be, there is a crucial defect in charismatic leadership—the mortality of the leader, on whom the whole social transaction is based. Charismatic leaders, like ordinary mortals, die, and the transition from a charismatic leader to his successor is fraught with hazard. Charismatic leaders do not appear on demand. One cannot count on replacing one charismatic leader with another. Usually, charismatic leadership must give way to traditional rule or modern bureaucratic leadership—so nature and the human condition dictate. Let us now turn to the charismatic leadership of Gamal Abdel Nasser.

Gamal Abdel Nasser

Nasser presents an interesting counterpoint to King Farouk. Born in Alexandria in 1918 into the family of a low-level civil servant, Nasser was ethnically Egyptian, as opposed to the Albanian origins of Farouk. Educated in the new modern schools of the time, Nasser entered the Egyptian military academy in 1936. Farouk's first military job was as chief of state at age 16. Where Farouk was elegant and pampered, Nasser was simple and ascetic.

Nasser's physical and personal qualities have inspired many writers to attempt to capture the factors that contributed to his commanding presence. The following passages by Jeanne and Simone Lacouture are representative:

> What first impresses you is his massive, thickset build, the dazzlingly white smile in his dark face. He is tall, tough, African. As he comes toward you on the steps of his small villa on the outskirts of the city, or strides across his huge office at the Presidency, he has the emphatic gait

Gamal Abdel Nasser (Charismatic Leader).
Agence France Presse/Getty Images.

of some Covent Garden porter or some heavy, feline creature, while he stretches his brawny hand out with the wide gesture of a reaper, completely sure of himself. His eyes have an Asiatic slant and almost close as he laughs. His voice is metallic, brassy, full, the kind of voice that would be useful on maneuvers in the open country. . . .

The impression of strength remains when he relaxes. He has an air of youthfulness, together with a certain timidity. He is gray at the temples but his hard face, that reminds you of a ploughshare, sometimes takes on an adolescent look.[5]

Nasser, in short, was heady tonic to a people accustomed to foreign rule and previously convinced that government was not an Egyptian aptitude. His personal presence, reflecting real and potential power, combined

_____
[5]Jeanne and Simone Lacouture, *Egypt in Transition*, p. 453.

with an electrifying rhetorical style, spoke directly to the powerlessness of the masses. Nasser, it seems, became the personal embodiment of the aspirations of the people. He in turn grew in response to their fervent commitment.

Nasser entered politics indirectly. His biographies indicate an early dissatisfaction with foreign rule and political corruption, but he originally intended to reform the Egyptian military. Nasser and his associates did not come to power in the revolution of July 23, 1952, with any plan for political rule. Instead, it seems that political power and responsibility were thrust on the officers as they began to recognize the inability of Farouk and the Wafd to work cooperatively for reform.

Ideologically, Nasser's early political views can be summarized by the formula "Fight Against Imperialism, Monarchy, and Feudalism." Only later, as he matured in the office of president, did Nasser's political views develop. These views reflected the cosmological quality of Nasser's leadership. Particularly in his promotion of Arab socialism and pan-Arabism, Nasser demonstrated the charismatic leader's claim to some cosmological source of authority. In making regular symbolic reference in his speeches and writings to the greatness of the Arab past, the Egyptian past, and to Islam and the Umma, Nasser not only provided a cultural and historical identity to the Egyptian people, but he also legitimized contemporary policy in non-Western terms. In many respects, this can be labeled a triumph of form over substance, for Nasser never specified the policy implications of his ideology consistently. Nevertheless, for the fragmented and uncertain Egyptian community of the 1950s and 1960s, the Nasser prescription was just what was needed.

Nasser's relationship to Islam reveals his lack of ideological precision. Although he recognized a direct relationship between Islam and Egypt's past and present, and although he seemed to be personally pious and upright,

Nasser was nevertheless a secular political leader. Early on in the revolution, the Free Officers came into conflict with traditional Islamic forces: the ulema, which was in league with the monarchy and was opposed to the revolution, and the Muslim Brotherhood, which did not recognize any distinction between politics and religion. In steering a course between these forces, Nasser and the Free Officers opted for a view that derived inspiration from Islam and its writings but simultaneously honored the principle of separation of church and state. This separation was anathema to the leadership of the Brotherhood, and a nasty confrontation was inevitable.

Nasser's socialism was ambiguous and imprecise. Essentially a philosophy of equitable distribution, Nasser's socialism has been rightly criticized for economic naiveté and a devotion to publicly managed projects of dubious value. Although these projects were politically palatable, their contribution to a coherent economic policy was negligible. The steel complex at Helwan is a case in point. The claims of this grandiose project could not be justified by even the most optimistic economic projections. The project was to supply most of Egypt's need for steel, employ large numbers of Egyptian workers, and ultimately contribute to the balance of payments through export. Of these goals, only the employment of more and more Egyptians was accomplished.

Similarly, the revolution's effort to guarantee jobs to every college graduate created a swollen bureaucracy that operated on the principle of disguised unemployment. This policy often resulted in several people sharing a job that could be handled more effectively by one employee. Intolerable inefficiencies were thus built into state enterprises and made administration very difficult. Once again, the political gain outstripped the economic realities.

The differences between Nasser and Farouk are quite sharp. There is one point, however, in which their leadership styles converge. The personal presence and lifestyle of each leader supported his claim to political authority. Of course, their lifestyles differed dramatically; Farouk's love of pomp and ceremony contrasted sharply with Nasser's modest private life. Each to a great degree personally demonstrated in his private life the basis of his claim to power.

Finally, both leaders' careers came to abrupt ends. Farouk abdicated to a life of leisure one jump ahead of the executioner; Nasser died unexpectedly of a heart attack in 1970. Neither of them left office under "normal" circumstances—that is, as the result of regular or normal political processes. Of the two leaders, Nasser clearly left the greater impression on Egyptian politics. As Bruce Borthwick pointed out, despite the difficulties besetting the regime,

> Nasser had . . . received the "gift of grace" that endows charismatic leaders. He and the Egyptian people were one; his actions and his voice were theirs. They would not let him resign in June, 1967, and when he died suddenly on September 28, 1970, the masses poured out their emotions for him in a frenzy of grief."[6]

To this day, portraits of Nasser occupy the place of honor in the simple homes of the Egyptian peasantry. The imprint of Farouk is a historical curiosity, and no more.

The ultimate consequences of Nasser's charismatic leadership are manifold. First, through his charismatic claim on political power, Nasser gave Egypt a focus of legitimate power. In a time when the existing institutions of power were discredited (the monarchy, nobility, and political parties), his exercise of charismatic power filled what would have been a dangerous vacuum. The cosmological qualities of Nasser's

---

[6]Bruce Borthwick, *Comparative Politics of the Middle East: An Introduction* (Englewood Cliffs, NJ: Prentice Hall, 1985), p. 182.

leadership, such as his commitment to the Islamic Umma, Arab culture, and the Egyptian nation, provided a potent national identity for the Egyptian masses. His powerful rhetoric and commanding presence provided real evidence that his claims and goals were viable and realizable, if difficult to achieve.

Nasser's rule had its negative aspects. His economic policies were at best naive. His international adventures, as in the case of his military intervention in Yemen, often strained Egyptian capabilities beyond their limit. His persistent confrontations with Israel committed vast proportions of the Egyptian economy to wartime production. Finally, his flirtation with international communism (domestic communists were suppressed and jailed) could have generated yet another wave of foreign intervention in the Middle East.

All in all, Nasser's leadership was of great benefit to Egypt. Ultimately, the force of his leadership spilled over to the new institutions that implemented the revolution and prepared the way for modern bureaucratic politics. Egypt moved from a political process dependent on a single, fragile personality to a political system characterized more by institutional stability and strength.

MODERN BUREAUCRATIC LEADERSHIP

Modern bureaucratic leadership is predicated on the promise of adequate short-term performance in government. Claiming technical and organizational superiority over the older, traditional means of governance, modern bureaucratic leaders promise to transform society through the application of management skills. These leaders believe that contemporary problems can be solved; that humans can purposively change their physical and social environment if only given the chance and the right organization; and that these changes can lead to several possible social, economic, and political outcomes.

Muhammad Ahmadinejad (Modern Bureaucratic Leader).

Although all modern bureaucratic leaders base their right to rule on their ability to perform and solve problems, some rule within publicly accountable systems (democratic) and others within authoritarian systems. Publicly accountable modern bureaucratic leaders recognize the right of the public to evaluate periodically their performance and decide whether to retain them in office. Authoritarian, or Kemalist, modern bureaucratic leaders reject the regular review of their right to rule, arguing instead that no one has the ability to judge their leadership or its performance.[7] Authoritarian leaders often conceive of their political rule as a period of political trust and tutelage during which society learns and practices the skills and procedures that will lead to genuine publicly accountable politics. In most cases, authoritarian modern bureaucratic regimes are military in nature; publicly accountable regimes usually emerge from a political party

---

[7]*Kemalist* refers to the modernizing authoritarian rule of Kemal Ataturk in Turkey that was aimed ultimately at the creation of a democratic process.

background. In the emerging countries, where modernization was first achieved among the military, it is not surprising that Kemalist regimes predominate.

Anwar Sadat and Hosni Mubarak

The immediate successor to Nasser in Egypt was another member of the original Free Officers, Anwar Sadat. Original predictions suggested a relatively short tenure in office for Sadat, seeing him presiding over a period of transition during which more capable leaders would contest for the mantle of power. (Similar predictions had been made for the institutions of governance that had developed during Nasser's rule, particularly the Arab Socialist Union and the People's Assembly.) Both Sadat and those institutions proved much more durable than anticipated. By 1981, the Sadat regime had been in office for more than 10 years and had made many substantial changes in political emphasis and direction. Far from being a caretaker or transitional leader, Sadat proved himself to be a legitimate and strong leader in his own right.

Sadat's personal history was similar to that of Nasser. Sadat was born into a peasant family and benefited from a liberalization in education policy. He entered the Egyptian military academy during the time when the regime was trying to develop an Egyptian officer corps. And like Nasser, Sadat participated in the Free Officer movement that led to the coup of 1952. It is surprising, then, that there should be so few similarities in the leadership styles and political views of these two men.

Anwar Sadat was not a charismatic leader. His claims to the loyalty of the government and the public were based on his performance. He hoped for a low-keyed, coherent managed solution to Egypt's problems of the 1970s. To compare Sadat's political thought with Nasser's is to compare the thought of a technician with that of a dreamer. Sadat's rhetorical style bore little or no similarity to Nasser's impassioned, moving speeches.

Sadat's personal style contrasted sharply with those of Nasser and Farouk. Comfortable in Western dress, Sadat often appeared in a conventional Western suit and tie, as opposed to Nasser's simple tunics and Farouk's elaborate uniforms. Sadat lived in an impressive villa, although it hardly compared with Farouk's palaces. Mrs. Sadat wore the latest Paris fashions and moved in the highest international social circles. Sadat was comfortable with modern political leaders around the world. He cultivated an image of international sophistication in dress, language, and personal manner.

Nothing underscores the difference between Sadat and Nasser more than their respective treatment in the U.S. press. Where Nasser was often presented in uncomplimentary terms with thinly veiled suggestions that he was a communist or radical, Sadat was presented as a leader of quiet authority and dignity. As regular guests on U.S. talk and interview shows in the 1970s, Mr. and Mrs. Sadat personally raised Egypt's national image by their humane, warm, and comfortable styles. Such democratic sophistication would not have occurred to Farouk or have been tolerated by the mercurial Nasser. Sadat was definitely a different kind of political animal.

Sadat reversed Nasser's economic policies, particularly those toward private industry. He openly sought foreign private investment in Egypt, strengthened ties with the United States and Western Europe, and pursued a political solution to the Israeli question and Palestinian demands. Domestically, he permitted new political parties to develop, although they were carefully controlled. He subtly tried, and failed, to demythologize Nasser.

Sadat believed that his reforms had relieved much of Egypt's economic and military burdens, and to some degree he has been proved correct. The Sinai had been recovered, and commercially exploitable oil resources expanded. The West gave military and technological support, but foreign investors were reluctant to enter the mixed Egyptian economy.

Ultimately, the failure of the Egyptian-Israeli peace talks over the question of Palestinian autonomy gave ammunition to his enemies in and out of Egypt. As a result, Sadat retrenched on many of his political reforms, the secret police became more active, and numerous political opponents were placed under house arrest.

Some of Sadat's reforms met with widespread resistance. In 1977, he attempted to raise the price of bread, which had been subsidized at artificially low prices since the revolution; there were riots in Cairo in which mobs burned luxury hotels and nightclubs catering to foreigners and chanted "Sadat-Bey, Sadat-Bey," equating Sadat with the hated Ottoman rulers of an earlier age. Foreign corporations attempting to enter the Egyptian economy reported that despite sympathy at high government levels, mid-level and low-level bureaucrats did not share this enthusiasm and made life miserable for Western business managers.

In governing Egypt, Sadat had certain advantages that were not available to Nasser or Farouk. He had a tested set of bureaucratic and technocratic institutions on which he relied for counsel and for implementation of policy. These institutions were less efficient than many of their counterparts outside Egypt, but they were a distinct improvement over the administrative vacuum that attended Egyptian political crises earlier in the twentieth century.

Anwar Sadat's rule ended on October 6, 1981, with his assassination while viewing a military parade. The assassins were members of a fundamentalist Muslim group within the Egyptian military and reportedly had strong ties to other fundamentalist groups active in Egypt. The transition of rule was remarkably smooth, and Sadat's vice president, Hosni Mubarak, was elevated to the presidency. The orderly transfer of power and the quiescent acceptance of the events by the Egyptian masses evidence the remarkable progress toward institutionalization of government since Nasser.

Under Mubarak's rule, Egypt recovered much of the prestige lost in the Arab world as a

Hosni Mubarak (Modern Bureaucratic Leader).

consequence of Sadat's peacemaking with Israel. Mubarak has been able to capitalize on Sadat's close relationship with the United States, the economic gains stemming from the military disengagement with Israel, and the aftermath of the disastrous Israeli invasion and occupation of south Lebanon. Mubarak's key role in the U.S.-led coalition that confronted Iraq in 1991 also contributed greatly to his domestic and international prestige. His leadership style has proved to be relatively low key and accommodative, with the result that many of the Egyptian groups dissatisfied with Sadat's policies or personal style now find themselves cooperating with the government. Political conflict or tension has not been eliminated from Egyptian politics, and it is clear that the government has strenuously suppressed extremist Islamist opposition groups, but there has been substantial improvement since Sadat's death, and the scope of political participation in Egypt has modestly widened. Because the political equation in Egypt is crucial to the larger political equations of the Middle East, stability and progress there generally benefit the larger system. Mubarak must continue to deal with the problems of economic growth, population explosion, Muslim fundamentalism, and international conflict that bedeviled his predecessors. But he can do so with a significantly stronger set of political institutions than any of his twentieth-century predecessors.

The aftermath of September 11, 2001, placed Mubarak in a difficult position with his American allies. Uncritical U.S. support of Israel was not politically popular in Egypt, and great popular enthusiasm for the U.S. efforts to marginalize Saddam Hussein in Iraq was lacking. Internal and external complaints about the lack of democracy in Egypt occurred simultaneously with an increase in the militancy of jihadist Islamist organizations, including increasing numbers of assassinations and bombings. The presidential and parliamentary elections of 2005 did little to allay critics' concerns. The future will likely produce continued tests of Mubarak's leadership, with important consequences for Egypt and the Middle East.

CONSEQUENCES OF LEADERSHIP STYLES

The contemporary Middle East presents a melange of leadership styles. Traditional and modern technicalist bureaucratic leaders predominate numerically (see Table 10.1), but charismatic leaders such as Ayatollah Khomeini

and Colonel Qadaffi have had disproportionate influence. Many of the international strains and tensions in the Middle East are partially a result of divergences among leadership styles.

Traditional leaders compose the largest group in the Middle East. Historically, these leaders tended to oppose modernization or modernize in only strictly technological ways; they all resisted any substantial sharing of powers. In recent times, some traditional leaders have looked toward political reform, advocating changes that would result ultimately in a diminution of traditional authority in favor of more democratically constituted future rule. All traditional leaders, however, including those with modernization on their minds, depend greatly on formal assertions of their traditional right to rule, undergirding these claims with the performance of traditional rituals and the maintenance of complex interpersonal relationships with other leaders.

TRADITIONAL STATES

The enormous oil revenues of Saudi Arabia, Oman, the U.A.E., Qatar, and Kuwait permit them to manage their economies and give them some political breathing time. For traditional leaders in poorer countries—King Abdullah of Jordan or Emir Hamad of Bahrain—the maneuvering time is considerably reduced. In the case

Table 10.1 Contemporary Leadership Styles in the Middle East

Traditional	Modern Bureaucratic	Charismatic
Bahrain	Egypt (K)*	Egypt under Nasser
Egypt under Farouk	Iran	Iran under Khomeini
Iran (Pahlevis)	Iraq (K) under U.S. occupation, April 9, 2003–	Libya under Qadaffi
Jordan	Israel (for Jewish citizens)	
Kuwait	Lebanon	
Oman	Syria (K)	
Qatar	Turkey	
Saudi Arabia	Yemen (K)	
U.A.E.	Palestinian Authority	

*K = Kemalist Modern Bureaucratic.

of Jordan, Bahrain, and Yemen, foreign subsidies have been crucial in maintaining the existing political authority, a compromise with independence distasteful to all leaders. The discoveries and development of exploitable petroleum reserves in Yemen are producing major changes there, however.

Serious challenges to existing authority have emerged in all of the countries under traditional leadership. The fall of the shah of Iran was a harbinger of things to come. In Kuwait, a traditional ruling class traumatized by the Iraqi occupation in 1990–1991 searched for security by expelling most of the Palestinian and Jordanian guest workers who manned their institutions, substituting guest workers from more distant and less politically risky origins. Promises of greater democratization have not materialized, and the al-Sabah family seems content with maintaining its traditional political authority even as small groups of Kuwaiti citizens petition for greater democratization.

Kuwait suffered a leadership crisis in early 2006 with the death of its emir, Sheikh Jaber al Ahmad al-Sabah. Arrangements for the transfer of power to the Crown Prince Sheikh Saad al-Sabah were complicated by his ill health. Critics of the proposed succession complained that the health of the candidate was so poor as to impair his function as emir. At the last minute, the Kuwaiti Parliament and the council of ministers declared the Sheikh unfit by reasons of health to serve as emir. He was replaced by his half-brother, Sheikh Sabah al-Ahmad al-Sabah. Because the new emir is also a septuagenarian, this situation may repeat itself in the near future.

In Jordan, King Abdullah must continue to deal with the domestic and international tensions that nearly toppled his father, King Hussein, numerous times. Early indicators suggest that King Abdullah will confront political issues in Jordan aggressively, and he has succeeded in working out practical compromises with Islamist factions in the Jordanian legislature. He also has continued his father's participation in the Israeli–Arab negotiations,

forcefully insisting that both sides negotiate fairly and implement agreements in a timely fashion. He has been willing to support and criticize both sides in the conflict. On the other hand, the king has scaled back the commitment to developing democratic institutions; disbanding the legislature and postponing scheduled elections. King Abdullah also seems willing and able to take a publicly visible role in the political life of Jordan. This has become equally true for his wife, the Queen, who appears quite regularly in Western media. U.S. and Israeli pressures on Jordan to take stronger, pro-Western positions on the Israeli occupation and the suppression of Iraq have put the king in a difficult position, particularly given strong public opinion in favor of the Palestinian resistance and public sentiment against the U.S. occupation of Iraq. Jordan was hard-pressed by the United States to take an active role in the 2003 war with Iraq, a pressure largely resisted by the king. King Abdullah has largely lamented the plight of the Palestinians (rhetorical support) and refused to allow Jordan to be the base for U.S. troops attacking Iraq. Despite the king's maneuvers, Jordan was attacked late in 2005 by Iraqi Al-Qaeda suicide bombers targeting Western-owned hotels in Amman. For King Abdullah and most other Middle Eastern leaders, there is no safe distance from the extreme jihadist organizations of the region.

Oman, increasingly important in the international politics of the Persian Gulf, is bordered by Yemen to the west, conservative Arab states to the northwest, and an unpredictable Iran across the straits. Sultan Qabus has established close military relations with the United States, a relationship exercised during Desert Storm. Similar to most of the current rulers in the Gulf, however, he has refused to allow Omani bases to be used in the U.S. war against Iraq.

The eventual and inevitable end of Qabus's rule (he has no heirs) apparently precipitated an in-government coup attempt in 1995, one that resulted in the removal and arrest of many important Omani officials and influentials. The situation in Oman is unclear at best, however, and even the sultan himself has publicly speculated on the form of governmental transition and the eventual emergence of democratic institutions. Omani economic conditions have improved, and educational programs have produced a capable, growing native elite capable of handling a transition to a new government or system in the coming future. Planning for a future transition continues.

The collective leadership in the U.A.E. have made similar arrangements, as have the leaders of Bahrain and Qatar, all pursuing policies of "nativization" and modest political reforms, including consultative assemblies. They all seem aware of the necessity of future changes in the form and structure of governance. The new leadership in Bahrain under Sheikh Hamad al-Khalifa has allowed the development of new institutions of representation, and elections have been scheduled. The restive Shia population of Bahrain has been the focus of economic and social reforms and apparently is responding positively to them. Bahrain, similar to its other Gulf neighbors, has responded negatively to U.S. attempts to use Bahraini bases in the war against Iraq.

The U.A.E. changed its leadership in 2004 with the death of Sheik Zayed, a true visionary largely responsible for the creation of the Emirati state. In keeping with the political design implemented by Sheikh Zayed, political power in the state is shared between two principal families, the al-Nahyan of Abu Dhabi and the Maktoums of Dubai. The new president of the U.A.E. is Sheikh Khalifa bin Zayed al-Nahyan; the prime minister was Sheik Maktoum bin Khalifa al-Maktoum, until his unexpected and untimely death in January 2006. He was succeeded by Muhammad bin Rashid al-Maktoum, continuing the power-sharing arrangement between the emirates and Abu Dhabi and Dubai in particular. As in neighboring Saudi Arabia, this change came without turmoil or political strife.

Perhaps the most dramatic changes in the Gulf States have occurred in the small state of Qatar under the leadership of Sheikh Hamad al-Thani. Qatar's experiment with modern communication, the independent Arab news service Al-Jazeerah, has injected a new element of mass communication into the Middle East generally. Its broadcasts of communiqués from Osama bin Laden and his lieutenants have incited furious negative reactions from other Middle Eastern and Western states. Qatar has allowed the United States to develop a large military facility as an alternative to similar facilities in Saudi Arabia and other Gulf States. Qatar was the only Gulf State to support publicly the proposed U.S. assault against Iraq. Modest democratic reforms at the municipal level also are under way.

All the Gulf States have serious security problems occasioned by their small size and the attractiveness of their oil reserves. As many observers remark, these small states live in a "bad neighborhood" with strong and aggressive neighbors. They all rely increasingly on the coordination of their foreign policies through the Gulf Cooperation Council, seeking a measure of security in collective defense relationships. Calls for Gulf Cooperation Council–organized trade and customs union have been positively received, suggesting a growing role for this important regional participant.

Saudi Arabia is the dominant political actor among the traditional states of the region and plays a key role in the larger Middle Eastern system. The Saudi decision to invite U.S. troops onto Saudi soil to defend against Iraq clearly had a high risk-to-reward ratio. The aftermath of Desert Storm placed the Saudi royal family under new pressures from the left and the right. Both groups have been energized by what they observed during the coalition presence in Saudi Arabia. Groups interested in increasing democratization and social liberalization petitioned the leadership for a consultative assembly and a liberalization of the strict Saudi social rules. The religious right called for increased emphasis on conservative social values, opposing the liberalization espoused by the left. The royal family cannot satisfy both camps, and an increasing level of domestic political conflict results.

In the spring of 1992, King Fahd announced the creation of a national consultative assembly and numerous local consultative bodies. These assemblies are constituted with no power other than the persuasive quality of their advice. Nonetheless, they are widely interpreted as a first, although cautious, move by the royal family in the direction of democratization.

Increasing internal pressures associated with economic strains and increasing polarization between conservative and liberalizing factions, punctuated by the terrorist bombing of a U.S. military facility in Riyadh in 1995, led to many political and administrative changes in the Saudi leadership in 1995 and 1996. King Fahd rearranged the cabinet and replaced many senior bureaucrats. In early 1996, he delegated day-to-day political responsibilities to Crown Prince Abdullah. King Fahd's personal health seemed to play a decisive role in these actions, but it is probable that demands for reform within and outside the royal family also helped to precipitate these changes.

The death of King Fahd in 2005 brought the Crown Prince Abdullah to the throne. The transition was smooth and without disruption, as befits an intergenerational transition. The new king shares many fundamental assumptions with his predecessor. Nonetheless, King Abdullah has permitted a small measure of liberalization in the kingdom and moved quickly to curtail the political influence of the most conservative Saudi ulema. He is determined to reduce the influence of radical jihadists in the country. His rule also has benefited substantially from the dramatic increase in oil prices, giving the new government more room for expansion of social programs.

The events of September 11, 2001, have had important effects for the Saudi government. More than any other state in the region, the Saudi relationship with the United States, its

King Abdullah, Saudi Arabia (Modernizing Traditional Leader).
AP Wide World Photos.

principal ally and guarantor, was strained by the attack on the World Trade Center. What seems to have been an intentional Al-Qaeda strategy of using mostly Saudi nationals in the attack has created great stress for the Saudi government, as an orchestrated public relations attack on the Saudi government followed in the wake of the disaster.

What may be a low point in the U.S.–Saudi relationship occurred in late 2002 as an advisory board to the U.S. Department of Defense heard a research report labeling the Saudis as unworthy allies and basic enemies of the United States. Saudi prestige plummeted dramatically in the United States under a withering public relations campaign against it. Although the official organs of the U.S. government (president, state department, defense department) denied holding such opinions and asserted the strength of the relationship, it was also clear that Saudi opposition to a unilateral U.S. attack on Iraq strained the alliance. The relationship also was strained by U.S. insistence that the Saudi leadership dismantle much of the Islamist/fundamentalist infrastructure in the kingdom, citing the strident anti-Western rhetoric of many Saudi ulema, and the "money trail" between the kingdom and many of the jihadist organizations supporting terrorism.

The rule of King Abdullah was welcomed by the Bush Administration. A public appearance between the King and President George W. Bush ratified their relationship in a widely distributed image of the two of them walking hand in hand on the grounds of the president's ranch in Crawford, Texas. Cynicism over the photo opportunity aside, it is clear that the Saudi leadership made considerable progress in repairing its relationship with the Bush Administration. Saudi increases in petroleum production in the weeks following Hurricane Katrina in the early fall of 2005 were critical in blunting the worst effects of a bull market in petroleum. The old formula of Saudi petroleum in exchange for U.S. assurances of regional security appears to have survived the transition from Fahd to Abdullah.

In short, the traditional states of the Middle East, rich and poor alike, appear to be subject to increasing domestic and international pressure for change. Some of these traditional polities are fighting a rearguard action (Kuwait, Saudi Arabia). Others have been embracing moderate democratic change (Bahrain, Oman, Qatar, the U.A.E.). The inevitable transition to constitutional/democratic monarchies, modern bureaucratic leadership, or charismatic rule will be quite stressful to these traditional leaders and to those nations dependent on their petroleum and natural gas exports.

MODERN BUREAUCRATIC STATES

The second largest group of political systems in the Middle East is governed by some kind of modern bureaucratic leadership. Three of these states—Egypt, Yemen, and Syria—are ruled by Kemalist regimes. Iraq, under U.S. occupation, is no longer ruled by the Baath Party, while the Syrian Baath Party remains in power. In Egypt, President Mubarak apparently believes in the principal of public accountability of leaders, but he has not yet entrusted substantial political authority to the parties or legislature. The Arab Socialist Union and the National Assembly, although influential, are still subject to his veto. These special executive powers were recently raised to a constitutional level by a series of referenda in early 2007 with the effect of reducing the influence of Islamist organizations in Egyptian government. Critics of the Mubarak government see in the reforms an attempt to secure political power for Mubarak's son. Others see the reforms as the logical response to the increasingly dangerous Islamist movements in Egypt and the region.

Egypt, Syria, and Yemen seem unlikely to face serious internal challenges in the immediate future. In Syria, the transition of power from Hafez el-Asad to his son Bashar appears to have proceeded with little opposition or difficulty. In Yemen, the government is challenged by an increasingly vigorous Islamist minority, but there does not appear to be a serious challenge to the legitimacy of that government.

The government of Iraq, however, was under serious political pressure internally and externally. Although it was plagued for some time by feuding within the ruling Baathist military group, by the late 1980s Iraq appeared to be emerging as a stable and competent political regime. Encouraged by its growing petroleum revenues, in the mid-1970s Iraq had embarked on an ambitious program of economic and social investment. Simultaneously, the leadership's anti-Western posture softened, and growing numbers of Iraqi students had enrolled in European and American universities, particularly in management and technology programs. A growing disenchantment with communist influence in the Iraqi army led to a number of executions and imprisonments and explorations with non-Soviet European governments regarding trade and technology.

The long war with Iran accelerated these tendencies, as Iraq became increasingly dependent on the Europeasn West and the moderate Arab states for financial and military support. American aid to Iraq was channeled mainly through other governments. The war was extraordinarily expensive to both Iran and Iraq, in terms of money, military and civilian casualties, and deferred public projects. Both countries, however, managed to avoid widespread domestic discontent, an indication of effective leadership and progress in political institutionalization. Saddam Hussein, during the darkest periods of the Iran–Iraq war, appeared to initiate a "cult of personality" to offset public dissatisfaction with the conduct of the war. In fact, his personal presence rose dramatically, through use of techniques often associated with charismatic leadership. The lack of a charismatic public response, however, was equally obvious, leaving us with the impression of Saddam Hussein as an aspiring charismatic leader in search of a constituency. That said, the reins of power seemed firmly in his hands.

All apparent progress in Iraq was put at risk by Saddam Hussein's decision to invade Kuwait in l990. This invasion, and the subsequent ejection of Iraq from Kuwait by a U.S.-led coalition of Western, Arab, and other third-world states, changed the trajectory of development for Iraq. Saddam Hussein's inept military leadership resulted in the deaths of tens of thousands of his countrymen and the rekindling of two serious revolts by the Kurds in the north and the Shia in the south. Iraq was placed under onerous economic embargo and political isolation by the U.N. Security Council. United Nations inspection teams roamed Iraq in search of Iraq's programs to produce "weapons of mass destruction." All in all, Iraq and its government received heavy punishment for its transgressions in Kuwait.

Saddam Hussein's survival of this humiliation amazed commentators everywhere. Although his removal was not an official objective of the Desert Storm coalition, the rhetoric of the conflict left little doubt that this was an unarticulated goal. It was believed that the military humiliation of Iraq and attendant economic and social disruptions would lead the Iraqi elite to remove him from office. This did not occur and Saddam Hussein remained in power years after the war. The survival of his key military establishment—the Republican Guards—gave him the breathing space necessary to suppress the Kurdish and Shia revolts. And given the highly integrated nature of Iraq's political elite, he was able to forestall political opposition among his influential rivals in government. External opponents of the Saddam government were cheered in 1995, when several key members of Saddam's ruling clique defected and sought refuge in Jordan. The cheering was short-lived, however, when the dissidents returned to Iraq months later to face death at the hands of their own families for "treason." The whole affair did little to change the internal political equation in Iraq. It appeared to many observers that Saddam Hussein was grooming his son, Uday, as a probable successor to his rule.

The United States and Western opposition to Saddam Hussein was implacable. Efforts by the Clinton Administration to oust Hussein ranged from large-scale air campaigns, to an ongoing "airwar of attrition" launched during the Kosovo crisis, to renewed emphasis on support for opposition groups and espionage. All failed to push Saddam Hussein from his perch or generate substantial opposition to his rule. The biggest losers in the conflict appeared to be the children of Iraq, damaged in nearly unprecedented ways by a combination of repeated attacks on crucial infrastructure and the embargo of critical medical supplies and foodstuffs.

In the aftermath of 9/11, the Bush Administration pushed the removal of Saddam Hussein toward the top of the U.S. international agenda, superseding even the war against terrorism and Al-Qaeda. In a speech that stupefied many scholars of the region, President Bush pronounced the existence of an "axis of evil" constituted of Iraq, Iran, and North Korea, the logic of which is not immediately evident. This notion quickly evolved into the idea of "regime change" and "preemptive war." World and regional opinions notwithstanding, the United States proceeded on a course designed to remove Saddam Hussein from power and replace the regime with a more acceptable leadership and democratic institutions. The regime of Saddam Hussein officially collapsed on April 9, 2003, the victim of U.S. unilateral military invasion and occupation of Iraq. Saddam himself was captured many months after the invasion, and his public trial began in the fall of 2005.

The final chapter in the life of Saddam Hussein came on December 30, 2006, when he was hung at a U.S. military base in Baghdad. Initial media reports indicated that his execution was a low-key, dignified event. Unfortunately, at least for the news managers in the Iraqi government, a different story ultimately emerged. A member of the execution party recorded the actual execution on his cell phone camera, showing a much different sequence of events.

The subsequent publication of that film showed Saddam Hussein escorted to the gallows by a gang of Shia "toughs" wearing ski masks and tormenting Saddam with insults and praise for his enemies. The execution itself was flawed, not only breaking his neck in the fall but nearly decapitating him in the process. A final complication was the timing of the hanging, corresponding with the celebration of Eid al-Adha, an important day in the Islamic calendar, emphasizing the importance of forgiveness. Leaders around the world, and particularly those in Sunni states, expressed horror at the details of the execution. Saddam Hussein continued to be controversial, even in his own death.

The construction of a new Iraqi political regime continued. Some three years after the invasion of Iraq, a series of elections and a constitutional referendum signaled the establishment of a new Iraqi regime. The emergent Iraqi "federation" appears to be based on religious regional affiliations. The Shia majority in the south garnered the largest bloc of support in the new parliament, followed by the Kurdish parties in the north. Sunni and secular Shia lists did poorly in the parliamentary elections and had little influence on the choice of leadership for the new republic.

The first president and prime minister of the new government reflected these on the ground realities. Fully five months after the conduct of the elections, in April 2006 and with great pressure from the United States, the newly elected parliament formed a "national unity" government. President Talabani was reappointed. A new prime minister, Nuri al Maliki, replaced the previous interim prime minister and a slate of Shia, Sunni, and Kurdish ministers was chosen. The Sunni representation in the government appeared nominal and cosmetic. Al Maliki's background and qualification appeared similar to Ibrahim al-Jafaari, the interim prime minister he replaced. Most analysts saw in the new government the continued dominance of the Shia and Kurdish movements that had controlled the interim government.

Parliamentary elections scheduled for March 2010 were carried off with little evidence of fraud or manipulation. Unfortunately, the election produced the moral equivalent of a tie between a secular-Sunni coalition led by Ayad Alawi, an interim prime minister during the formal U.S. occupation, and two Shia coalitions, one led by current Prime Minister Nuri al-Maliki and the other by Shia cleric Moktada al-Sadr, an anti-American leader with significant communal power.. Months after the election, the Sunni-secular group had been mostly disenfranchised by the selective disqualification of several of its leaders for previous Baathist connections; the government continued through the summer of 2010 in the hands of a caretaker regime from the al-Maliki government. Nine months after the election, Maliki was asked to form a new government. The situation is complicated by the imminent withdrawal of U.S. forces in 2011, an event that could precipitate a greater political crisis, the consequences of which are largely unknown and/or unpredictable. Stay tuned.

Of the two non-Kemalist modern bureaucratic regimes, one country, Turkey, has a recent history of relatively free and open review of its leadership. Only occasionally has the military intervened and suspended the political processes, and then back off after a period of adjustment. The military rule established in 1980 was progressively withdrawn in favor of a civilian government. To date, the Turkish military has taken steps to minimize the number of parties allowed to contest elections, in the hopes of avoiding the legislative stalemates characteristic of the prior multiparty government, and has allowed an extensive experiment in free-market economics begun by President Turgut Ozal. The apparent success of the reforms and the ability of the existing leadership to deal effectively with restive political minorities have resulted in a continued reduction of the military role in Turkish politics. Turkey's aggressive pursuit of full membership in the European Community seems to support a continued trend in this democratic direction.

The viability of Turkey's democratic system was tested in 1992 when the party coalition supporting President Turgut Ozal lost its majority in the parliament. The election of Suleiman Demirel to the prime minister's position brought an old political enemy to an important position in the government. Ozal and Demirel subsequently demonstrated their ability to work together, an important improvement in institutional legitimacy and pragmatic political leadership. The Turkish government also was able to effect an orderly transition in its leadership after the death of President Ozal to a new leader, Prime Minister Tansu Ciller.

The success of an Islamist political party in 1995 brought committed Muslim leaders to power in a coalition government. Uneasy with the religious implications of this change, the military intervened again in the Turkish

political process, dislodging the Welfare Party and its Prime Minister Erbakan in favor of secular leadership. The Welfare Party was dissolved, and its leadership was banned from political elections for a period of years. Turkey was ruled now by a coalition government of secular parties, led by Prime Minister Bulent Ecevit.

In late fall 2002 another moderate Islamist party won the national elections. The Justice and Development Party celebrated its electoral victory with great modesty, as its leadership asked its followers to omit cries of "Allahu Akhbar" after the election and went out of its way to endorse the secular assumptions of Turkish government.

This form of very moderate Muslim political activity did not trigger a Turkish military intervention. The success of the venture—an electorally and governmentally successful moderate Muslim political initiative—provides a useful example to other states in the region. Turkey's success in this arena led to its acceptance as a candidate for membership in the European Union, long a high priority of Turkish governments. Turkey is widely recognized as one of a few Middle Eastern states successful in its efforts at democratization.

National elections scheduled for 2007 again tested the delicate balance between secular government and Muslim political organizations. The Turkish military in mid-2007 issued another reminder that a radical or extremist victory would not be tolerated and would result in yet another intervention. The warning seemed to be taken seriously by the contending Turkish parties.

Turkey is currently led by Prime Minister Erdogan, a Muslim politician of moderate disposition. Under his stewardship several critical events occurred. First and foremost, the European Union demurred acceptance of Turkey into the union. Turkey has since turned increasingly toward the East, and the Middle East in particular, in its pursuit of political and economic partners. The important alliance between Turkey, Israel, and India was severely strained by an Israeli commando assault on a Turkish relief convoy headed for Gaza. In the assault in international waters, nine Turkish nationals were killed. Turkey has demanded an official apology and the Netanyahu government in Israel has bluntly refused. The future of Turkish–Israeli relations at this juncture does not look promising. Turkey itself enjoys growing prestige in the Muslim world and is increasingly recognized for its economic and political power.

Lebanon, in a state of civil war for decades and occupied intermittently by Syrian, United Nations, and Israeli forces, all of whom shared power with private Christian, Muslim, Palestinian, and independent armies, was proof of just how bad things can get when domestic and international forces combine to challenge or undermine existing political authority. The pre-1976 government of Lebanon, predicated on the fiction of relatively equal and stable Muslim, Christian, and Druze populations, functioned in an effective and publicly accountable way. It was, in many respects, something of a showplace for democracy in difficult circumstances. The enormous contrast between then and now suggests that when all pretense of political civility disappears, the potential for political and social disorganization is great.

The disastrous invasion and occupation of Lebanon by Israel (1982–1985) succeeded in removing the Arafat elements of the Palestinian Liberation Organization in and south of Beirut, but it did not succeed in removing other Palestinian groups or their military bases. The occupation also failed to tip the equation of forces in Lebanon in favor of the Christian militias and apparently stimulated the political and military growth of the Shia organizations, particularly the AMAL and Hizbollah. The result was the government of Lebanon ruling less and less of East Beirut while political and military groups with ties to major international participants (Syria, Iran, Iraq, Israel, Libya, the PLO, and the United States) jockeyed for position.

Frustration with this situation led eventually to a regional conference in Taif, Saudi Arabia, in 1989. In the adopted accords, Syria assumed a major role in disarming the competing militias and supporting a nonsectarian parliamentary government. Key events included the disarmament of General Aoun's army in 1990 and the systematic reestablishment of the regular Lebanese army under governmental direction. By 1992, it was clear that this initiative had changed the political equation in Lebanon dramatically, allowing the potential emergence of genuine national political leadership and the establishment of a second republic. Some progress has been made in this regard, although Syria still played a major role in domestic Lebanese politics.

Israel's withdrawal from southern Lebanon in 1999 surprised nearly everyone. Dispirited by the incremental loss of military personnel to Hizbollah attacks in the zone of occupation, Prime Minister Barak decided to cut Israel's losses in Lebanon and concentrate on its dealings with the Palestinians. This event allowed a considerable reprieve for Lebanon, and the short-term effects have been lugubrious. By late 2002, the government of Lebanon had made substantial strides toward institutionalization of its government and legitimization of government in general.

Syria maintained its presence in Lebanon until fall 2005, when, submitting to domestic Lebanese and international pressure, it withdrew its military and intelligence forces. Syria still wields considerable influence in domestic Lebanese politics, but for the first time since the 1982 invasion, internal developments in Lebanon have been positive. Elections in fall 2005 changed the internal composition of the legislature without completely dismissing the pro-Syrian bloc. Significantly, the political party affiliated with Hizbollah won numerous seats, allowing a measure of representation for this controversial political organization.

Lebanon's fragile democracy was severely tested by the events of 2006 and 2007. The month-long "war" between Hizbollah and Israel in August of 2006 resulted in extensive physical damage to the Lebanese infrastructure. The aftermath of the war saw the emergence of Hizbollah as a serious partner in the Siniora government. Sheikh Nasrallah, the official leader of Hizbollah, became both a Lebanese power broker and a target of Israeli attempts at assassination.

A serious test of the Lebanese leadership occurred in mid-2007 when the Lebanese army attempted the suppression of an Al-Qaeda related group based in a Palestinian refugee camp near Tripoli, in the north. Hizbollah apparently supported the effort, providing some evidence of its maturing role in the Lebanese government. And in yet another surprising dimension to Lebanese politics, the United States provided arms and ammunition to the Lebanese government in its effort to suppress the Al-Qaeda affiliates, putting Hizbollah and the United States on the same page, to some degree. Politics are definitely evolving in Lebanon.

The Lebanese elections of 2009 produced an interesting cascade of events. In a hotly contested but fair election, the Sinora government maintained its majority status and continued to rule. The Hizbollah lists returned a substantial number of its candidates to a minority status in the parliament, a platform from which it has demonstrated its willingness and ability to participate in government as a minority party. Many observers see in this outcome a maturation of Hizbollah into a more conventional political organization. The long-term implication of this transformation augurs well for democratic process in Lebanon.

The leadership situation in Israel deserves discussion. Our categorization of the regime as certainly modern bureaucratic but uncertainly democratic or Kemalist depended on whether one was focused on Israeli citizens within the normal confines of Israel (pre-1967 boundaries) or the administered Arab populations of the West Bank, Gaza Strip, and Golan Heights. The problem would not be so great were the populations involved not so large. We must distinguish between the democratically responsible leadership of conventional Israel and its authoritarian rule over what remains as the occupied territories, minus Gaza.

The apparent progress of the Israeli–Palestinian peace negotiations changed with the initiation of Intifadah 2, the Palestinian reaction to a visit by Israeli extremist Ariel Sharon to the Haram al Sharif/Temple Mount in August 2000. Sharon's electoral victory over Barak in the ensuing elections changed everything, as the Israeli government changed the assumptions of the peace process from "land for peace" to "peace for security," a formula that called for Palestinian destruction of internal Palestinian resistance to the occupation. The result was to set the Israeli–Palestinian relationship on a track of reciprocal violence to a point unprecedented since the return of the PLO to Israel more than a decade earlier.

Sharon's conduct of repression in the West Bank and Gaza initiated unprecedented levels of "asymmetric war," the application of full military coercion against a nongovernmental foe. For its part, the Palestinian Authority replied with a series of escalating violence against the Israeli military and more significantly against Israel's civilian population. The increase of suicide bombings from desperate Palestinians precipitated increasingly deadly reprisals from the Israeli military in a spiral of violence that brought a series of brutal military "incursions" into the occupied territories. Neither side seemed willing to back down, which resulted in an increasingly horrific war with large numbers of civilian casualties. This presented a nightmare conclusion to the Oslo Peace Accords, initiated so hopefully a decade earlier and abrogated in 2002 by the Sharon government.

The brutality of the confrontation plunged Israel into its deepest political divisions since the 1973 Yom Kippur/Ramadan war. Public opinion became highly polarized, and Sharon's government was weakened by defections from the moderate parties that initially supported him. The parties of the left, mostly Labor or Labor affiliated, continued their opposition to the policies advocated by the Likud government. To the Israeli right, Sharon was embraced as a genuine hero of Israel's expansion, its settlements and continued control of the occupied territories, and its hard-line response to Palestinian resistance. His periodic attempts to embarrass, dismiss, or injure Yasir Arafat played to rave reviews in the Israeli right. To the left, he became the apotheosis of violence and repression, an embarrassment to historical Israeli values. Internal divisions grew deeper and more vituperative.

The legitimacy of Arafat's leadership increased substantially among the Palestinian public. It was difficult to envision a scenario in which the Israeli government could remove him from the political system, despite Sharon and Bush's dismissal of him as "irrelevant." As Israel systematically demolished the physical and social infrastructure of the Palestinian Authority in the summer and fall of 2002 and periodically laid siege to Arafat's government headquarters in Ramallah, Palestinian resistance stiffened, and the prospects for a moderate Palestinian leadership also dimmed. Things at the end of 2002 looked as black as in any period in the preceding 50 years of Palestinian–Israeli conflict, personified in the head-to-head conflict of two irreconcilable enemies: Ariel Sharon and Yasir Arafat.

Ariel Sharon and Yasir Arafat presented disconcertingly similar leadership history and styles to their constituencies. Both leaders played important roles in their countries' political travails over the last 50 years. Both were admired within their own constituencies and just as equally vilified and demonized in the opposing constituencies. Both had significant blood on their hands contingent on their roles and responsibilities over the past decades. Both were widely considered to be war criminals and terrorists, within and outside their respective political systems. Finally, each despised the other. The result was a sort of mirror image of the Israeli and Palestinian leaders. This personal symmetry complicated the negotiations between the two entities dramatically.

Things do change, however. In spring 2003, yielding to wide-ranging and insistent pressure from the international community and Israel, Arafat appointed Mahmoud Abbas (also known as Abu Mazen) as the prime minister of the Palestinian Authority, ceding substantial administrative authority to the new minister. An immediate consequence of this appointment was the acceptance in principle (with reservations) of the road map to Middle Eastern peace proposed by the Quartet (United Nations, European Union, Russia, and the United States), promising an independent Palestinian state by 2005.

Yasir Arafat's death in 2004 changed the Palestinian political equation considerably. The Palestinian Authority moved incrementally toward a set of democratic institutions, although under difficult and frustrating circumstances. President Mahmoud Abbas, supported largely by the Fatah faction of the old PLO, must contend with the political activity and ambitions

Mahmoud Abbas (Modern Bureaucratic Transitional).
AP Wide World Photos.

of competing factions, notably Hamas, and with resistance movements reluctant to give up on the strategy of violence they have been committed to for so long. Political change, the death of its longtime leader, and the changing policies of Israel toward Palestine made for a frustrating and difficult set of problems for this government in the making.

These problems were compounded in January 2006. In the parliamentary elections, Hamas defeated Fatah decisively, leading to the immediate resignation of the Quereia-led government. Hamas, widely condemned in Israel, Western Europe, and the United States as a terrorist organization, capitalized on Palestinian frustrations with the aftermath of the Gaza turnover, the continued construction of the wall separating the West Bank from Israel proper, and the alleged corruption and administrative ineffectiveness of the Fatah-dominated government. Polls did not indicate support for Hamas based on religious concerns. In the short run, the success of Hamas seriously jeopardized the negotiations between Israel and the Palestinian Authority, already traumatized by the medical impairment of former Prime Minister Ariel Sharon. Tensions between the victorious Hamas supporters and the ousted Fatah partisans led to chaotic confrontations in Gaza and the West Bank. Sharp divisions between Palestinian Authority Mahmoud Abbas and the new Hamas-affiliated Prime Minister Ismail Haniyeh were evident.

During the chaos and confusion of the Israeli war with Hizbollah, elements in the Hamas coalition mounted attacks on Israel, mostly from the Gaza frontier. Israel responded to these attacks with increased air and ground incursions into the area, and with increasingly repressive interventions on the West Bank. Eventually, by the summer of 2007, a miniature civil war between Hamas and Fatah emerged, all but destroying the weak civil administration of the Palestinian Authority. Palestine is close to becoming a failed state before it actually becomes a state.

Israel has proved many times over its ability to change leadership within the structure of public accountability. The multiparty electoral system in Israel has made for complicated elections and sometimes-opaque negotiations between parties, lists, and leaders. Nonetheless, for the most part political leadership changes in Israel have occurred in a clearly democratic context. The one major exception to this observation was the assassination of Prime Minister Rabin in 1995 by an Ultraorthodox religious extremist.

Israeli elections often have resulted in substantial changes in the composition of the Israeli political elite, its formal leadership, and its domestic and international policies. The election of the Likud slate and the elevation of Menachem Begin to prime minister in 1977 signaled considerable changes in political direction for Israel. Similarly, the election of 1992 ended 15 years of Likud dominance, bringing the Labor Party and Yitzhak Rabin into power. Succeeding elections have had similar dramatic effects.

In 2000, the Israeli electorate brought former general Ariel Sharon to power. Long an advocate of tough sanctions against the Palestinians, Sharon enacted a wide range of repressive policies focused on the West Bank and Gaza. Elections in January 2003 reconfirmed Sharon and his strategy for dealing with the Palestinians.

Prime Minister Sharon surprised many of his critics and supporters alike when in early 2005 he announced his intention to withdraw unilaterally from Gaza. Israeli settler groups were particularly outraged and resisted the effort. Palestinians were disconcerted at being left completely out of the decision and its subsequent administration, and international participants, particularly the United States, were angered over the unilateral nature of the decision.

In late summer 2005, Israel withdrew from Gaza, turning the area over to the administration of the Palestinian Authority, which candidly was ill prepared for the responsibility.

Israel's withdrawal was accompanied by the eviction of Israeli settlers from the area and from a near-total closure of transit points to Israel and the West Bank.

The unilateral withdrawal from Gaza and the construction of a physical barrier (a wall) between Israel and the West Bank and Gaza show clearly the ability of Ariel Sharon to change policy directions. This was demonstrated politically in late 2005, when Sharon abruptly resigned from the Likud and announced the creation of a new centrist party, the Kadima Party. Elections were scheduled for spring 2006, and early polls showed the new centrist coalition with good prospects in the upcoming election. Sharon was credited with a successful and daring set of political maneuvers and praised for his political acumen in managing the reactions to them.

Celebrations turned out to be premature. In December 2005, Sharon suffered a stroke and was hospitalized for treatment. Given Sharon's overall health and personality profile (septuagenarian, overweight with complications, workaholic), his viability as a candidate was thrown into question. Sharon recovered

Ariel Sharon (Modern Bureaucratic Leader). Getty Images, Inc.

quickly from the effects of the stroke, but questions about his overall health remained.

Early in January 2006, the prime minister suffered a massive stroke that effectively ended his political career. Sharon's deputy, Ehud Olmert, a former mayor of Jerusalem and member of the Knesset and one of Sharon's partners in the organization of the Kadima, took over the duties of the prime minister on an interim basis. National elections were held in March 2006. The Kadima Party was successful in the election and Olmert formally became the prime minister. Prime Minister Olmert brought a very different style and background to the office. Whether or not the new prime minister would continue the policies set by his predecessor was an open question.

Olmert's initial reactions to the new Hamas-controlled Palestinian government suggest that his responses would be measured and careful. The August 2006 war with Lebanon eliminated the measured and careful dimension from the Olmert government. The government found itself in conflict with the Israeli right wing critical of the conduct of the war, and in the middle of an increasingly violent confrontation between Hamas (which Israel opposes) and Fatah (which Israel reluctantly supports). The governments of both Israel and Palestine are under internal and external pressure. Leadership changes were likely on both sides.

All of this suggests that Israeli leadership is conventional in its base of authority. Begin, Peres, Rabin, Shamir, Netanyahu, Barak, Sharon, and Olmert all can be described as modern bureaucratic leaders. Their survival in power was or is directly dependent on the consequences of their policy choices, not their charismatic or traditional appeal.

The Israeli elections early in 2009 brought the return of Binyamin Netanyahu to the office of Prime Minister. In order to create a successful governing coalition, Netanyahu moved far to the right of Israeli politics, bringing many ultra-religious parties into the government and embarking on a campaign of suppression in Gaza and expanded settlement in the West Bank. Importantly, the support from government for a "two-state solution" to the Israeli–Palestinian conflict declined and negotiations with the Fatah faction of the Palestinian "government" also declined. This has placed the vaunted U.S.–Israeli relationship in a difficult situation, as the Obama Administration continues its push for an independent Palestinian state.

That said, the political leadership of Israel is aging. Many Israeli leaders, including Shimon Peres, are septuagenarians and facing the end of their long careers as party and government leaders. A new generation of Israeli leaders is appearing. As Israel faces a range of difficult problems—economic, political, racial, international, ethical—the quality of her leadership will be of great importance.

Ayatollah Khomeini (Charismatic Leader).

CHARISMATIC RULE

Two Middle Eastern countries, Iran and Libya, were under charismatic rule throughout the 1980s. Both rulers can be described as irregular, unpredictable, and dramatic, but their governments and ideologies were inherently different.

Ayatollah Ruhollah Khomeini

Ascetic and gaunt, Ayatollah Ruhollah Khomeini appeared to confirm the trite Western stereotypes of Muslim fanaticism. This predisposition to judge harshly was exacerbated by the outrage generated by the Iranian militants' seizure of U.S. diplomats and embassy employees in November 1979. It is hard to find a publicly sanctioned, dispassionate description and analysis of Khomeini and his beliefs.

Khomeini was clearly a charismatic leader. He believed that his ultimate authority was derived from Allah, an indisputably cosmological referent. His speech was laced with hyperbole and jeremiads against the West, the shah, the devil, and all corruption and debasement. His followers responded with

strong outpourings of emotion. His branch of Islam, Iranian Shiism, is mystical and chiliastic. He used the Shia tenets of Islam as the basis of a new, revolutionary economic, social, and political organization.

Khomeini's opposition to the shah's regime and to Western influence in Iran was based partly on his personal history. His father was allegedly murdered by a landlord closely allied with Shah Reza Pahlevi. Raised as an orphan, Khomeini was passed from relative to relative largely out of charitable obligation. His training, exclusively in traditional religious schools and subjects, was exactly opposite to the modern education promoted by the Pahlevis. As an adult, Khomeini was often in trouble with the regime, which restricted his movements and preaching and finally exiled him. His promotion to the rank of Ayatollah was prompted, it is claimed, by other Muslim clergymen's attempts to protect him from the shah's courts and certain imprisonment or execution. Long periods of exile awaited the Ayatollah, during which his son was murdered, allegedly by SAVAK. Ayatollah Khomeini had a long history of personal and religious opposition to the Pahlevi regime.

Khomeini's political behavior bewildered most Western correspondents. Two Shia traditions may explain some of it. First, the Shia community in Iran has long practiced the right of **taqiyyah**, or dissimulation. If the defense of the faith requires it, the faithful may say or do anything that would allow them to pursue the true way, including the denial of adherence or membership. In the darkest days of SAVAK's repression, many Iranians protected themselves by exercising this right. Public political statements were often contradictory or misleading. It is indicative of Khomeini's moral status with the Shia faithful that he was able to dictate the abandonment of taqiyyah during the last stages of the fight against the shah, and from a position of exile at that.

The second tradition is the low status of political officialdom in Shia Islam. Ayatollah Khomeini instinctively avoided the regular, continual exercise of political power characteristic of the "normal politician." Khomeini apparently wished instead to correct or direct politicians by exercising a moral veto when they deviated from the divine will. Khomeini's exercise of power was irregular and intermittent, a fact of life that confounded and confused the Western observer accustomed to administrative regularity and continuity. His role as faqih in the Islamic Republic also confused Western observers, particularly those who simply did not comprehend institutions of mixed sovereignty—in this case, of God and man.

One also needs to understand something of the political and religious history of Iran. The doctrine of taqiyyah developed in response to the persecution of the Shia faithful by established Iranian political authority. Dissimulation, when necessary, advanced the interests of the good community. It was not a simple or universal justification for lying. The Ayatollah's symbolically rich speech similarly derived from the long Persian tradition of complex, poetic language. Much of it is impossible to translate accurately into English. An example of the difficulty is the *heech* controversy of 1979.

Heech is an Iranian word of some subtlety. It can mean "nothing" in a literal and an ironic sense. On returning to Iran from exile in Iraq and France, Khomeini was asked by Western newsmen how it felt to return to Iran after all those years in exile. Khomeini expressed his contempt for such a superficial question with the observation, "Heech." The newsmen interpreted his response to mean that he had no feelings, emotional or otherwise, about his return and concluded that he was coldly self-controlled. Khomeini intended to convey his disgust at being asked such an obvious and superficial question. Khomeini's efforts were rewarded with misunderstanding. Khomeini's behavior and justifications remain valid for Iran and largely misunderstood in the world arenas.

Khomeini's charismatic power was not restricted to Iran; it also operated among Shia minorities along the Persian Gulf and in Jordan, Syria, Iraq, and Lebanon. In addition, many fundamentalist Sunni Muslim groups recognized Khomeini's impact and wished to emulate his success without adopting the Shia disciplines. Finally, Khomeini's rabid anti-Western attitude taps a venerable tradition of opposition that dates back to the maturation of European imperial power in the area. As a successful leader, attempting the radical de-Westernization of Iran based on the tenets of Islam, Khomeini was a living example of the political potential of Islamic revival.

In the late 1980s, as Khomeini aged and his health deteriorated, he was frequently absent from the seat of government. Nonetheless, as the Iran–Iraq war degenerated into a human sacrifice of epic proportion, Khomeini was able to provide moral support to the faction in government seeking a settlement. Without his influence, it is likely that a greater protraction of the controversy would have occurred. Khomeini backed the settlement at great risk to his own political reputation, potentially sullied by "backing down" to Iraq and Saddam Hussein.

Khomeini's political maneuvering in the aftermath of the war gives good insight into some of the difficulties of exercising charismatic power and ensuring an appropriate succession to the charismatic leader. The publication and reaction in the Muslim world to the book *The Satanic Verses* provided Khomeini with an opportunity to exercise the moral dimensions of his leadership to disadvantage his political opponents. His pronouncement of a death sentence and bounty for the author of the book prompted criticism by Ayatollah Montazeri, Khomeini's designated successor as faqih of the republic. This reaction and earlier statements by Montazeri critical of the policy directions of the regime gave Khomeini the opening he desired. He demanded Montazeri's resignation, arguing that in opposing his actions Montazeri had demonstrated his unfitness to interpret God's will. Montazeri resigned, and no prominent successor of his public status was nominated to succeed Khomeini. Speaker Rafsanjani, who might have benefited from Montazeri's fall, was unable to capitalize on the situation until much later. The most conservative factions of the ruling coalitions were empowered in the short-term by this sequence of events. Ali Khamenei ultimately succeeded Khomeini as faqih, but his less prestigious reputation signaled a de facto decrease in the institution's role.

This question almost asks itself: Why did Khomeini impeach his personally designated successor? The answer may reside in the character of charismatic leadership qualities in the leader that militate against the sharing of power. It just as well may offer evidence of the implicit conflict between charismatic leadership and the institutional/bureaucratic leadership it eventually spawns. Whatever the reason, these actions seemed to make the inevitable transition of power from Khomeini to a successor more problematic and difficult than ever, a prospect that did not augur well for stability within the regime or the revolution. That the transition from Khomeini's charismatic rule to the more pragmatic bureaucratic rule of Rafsanjani and

Khamenei occurred without great public disorder is a monument to the progress in political institutionalization that developed in the later years of the Iranian revolution.

Under the divided leadership of Ayatollah Khamenei and President Khatami, Iran clearly moved in a moderating direction in the domestic and international arenas. Broad public support for the loosening of Islamic dress and behavior resulted in the reemergence of a middle class less interested in a revolutionary religious life and more interested in life in the larger, global sense. This progress was evident in public life, where Iranian nationals felt freer to express their political opinions, and in the public behavior of women, many of whom put off the chador in favor of conventional, nontraditional dress.

Iran's moderating social and political life was put on hold or reversed with the 2005 election of Muhammad Ahmadinejad as president. A committed Iranian "conservative," Ahmadinejad moved quickly and vigorously to reassert policies more acceptable to the Iranian clerical class. Many of the social changes evident during the thawing of revolutionary fervor were prohibited. A ban against "Western music" was promulgated, dramatically changing the mix of music allowable on Iranian radio and television. Many women readopted the Islamic dress of the revolutionary period.

Of greater political significance, Ahmadinejad announced Iran's intentions to continue full speed in the development of its nuclear program and called for the destruction of Israel, in the process questioning the reality of the Holocaust and of the Western motives for the establishment of Israel in the first place. None of this was well received in the European West or in Israel, but there was clearly some resonance with the Arab "street" throughout the Middle East.

As bizarre and radical as President Ahmadinejad's pronouncements are perceived by his domestic opposition and his international critics, his base of authority was initially based in democratic process and modern bureaucratic leadership conventions. Iranian leadership is not based on assertions of tradition or charisma. It remains to be seen whether or not these same institutions and political processes can moderate or offset this tendency toward belligerent and aggressive policies.

Colonel Muammar Qadaffi

No less an enigma is Colonel Muammar Qadaffi, the unofficial head of state of Libya, a country with few people and considerable oil wealth, located next to Egypt on the Mediterranean coast of Africa. Qadaffi has held power since the Revolutionary Command Council removed King Idris from power in 1969. Since that time, Qadaffi has consolidated and expanded his political power. His position is currently secure as head of the military group ruling Libya.

Qadaffi's power is also indisputably charismatic, although it differs substantially from that of Khomeini. Qadaffi is a radical, modernizing charismatic leader who has based his policy on unique, innovative interpretations of the Koran. Personally pious and reputedly ascetic, Qadaffi rejected the authority of the hadith and sunnah, preferring instead his own reading of the Koran as the sole authority. His personal philosophy is detailed in the Green Book, the handbook of the Libyan revolution. Qadaffi finds himself in opposition to the conservative ulema, whereas Khomeini's power derived from it. Although both men were anti-Western and anti-imperialist, Qadaffi is enthralled by Western technology and science.

Qadaffi and Khomeini also differed markedly in physical appearance. Khomeini appeared dour, dark, and sober, with downcast eyes, and dressed in the traditional garb of the mullah. Qadaffi is quick to flash a bright, toothy smile and dresses in flattering quasi-military tunics. Where Khomeini's rhetoric was apocalyptic, Qadaffi's is more persuasive and personal.

Similar to Khomeini and Nasser, Qadaffi aspires to leadership in the larger Muslim community. Qadaffi has openly espoused the causes of numerous revolutionary and terrorist groups around the world and offered hospitality to their leaders. Qadaffi's influence has spread to the Philippines, where Libya has supported the Moro National Liberation Front. It also has spread to Uganda and to Egypt and the Sudan, where Libya had been openly hostile toward the modern bureaucratic regimes of Sadat and Numeiri. In 1981, Libya intervened in the civil war in Chad, ostensibly to aid the Muslim groups in their consolidation of power. The government in Chad backed away from a proposed formal union, however, and the extent of Libyan control or influence there is problematic.

One of the staunchest of anti-Israeli Muslim leaders, Qadaffi has in the past provided aid, comfort, and a base for operations to diverse groups in the Palestinian nationalist coali-tion. These causes and his personal claim to a universally valid view of Muslim revolutionary government have not been well received in the conservative or secular governments of the Middle East. The disappearance of Imam Musa'Sadr in Libya in 1977 increased Qadaffi's distance from the Shia community. Increasingly visible Libyan assassination squads targeted against Qadaffi's political opposition in exile in England and Italy further blackened Libya's international image. Libya tilted decidedly toward the U.S.S.R. in its foreign policy, although the relationship was not sufficiently strong to prevent the 1986 U.S. air raid against its capital.

The sudden transformation of the international system resulted in the growing isolation of Libya and Qadaffi. The collapse of the Soviet Union deprived Libya of its major international protector. The stabilization of petroleum prices reduced Libya's discretionary income. The emergence of a moderate to conservative Arab alliance in the region has effectively eliminated Libya as a major player in international events.

The international support received by Britain and the United States in 1991–1992 as they demanded the surrender of two Libyan diplomats allegedly involved in the bombing of Pan Am Flight 103 is a strong indicator of Qadaffi's rapidly declining international prestige. Qadaffi's surrender of the two Lockerbie suspects to a U.N. court in Amsterdam was a dramatic departure for Qadaffi from his previous policies. The conviction of one of the bombers and the acquittal of the other has allowed Libya to seek new economic and political relationships, particularly with Mediterranean Europe.

In 2005, Qadaffi confounded his international critics by unexpectedly admitting to a Libyan program for the production of nuclear weapons. Qadaffi not only admitted the program but he also identified his sources of technology and materials and turned them over to the custody of the United States. The Bush Administration, viewing these events as vindications of their overall preemptive policies toward nuclear proliferation, welcomed Qadaffi and Libya back into the Western alliance, removing most of the sanctions that had been in place for the past two decades.

Nonetheless, Qadaffi keeps Libya on a revolutionary course. Based on his philosophy as expressed in the Green Book, Qadaffi has continued on a course of radical democratization in the context of the original Islamic revelation. Detractors are quick to point out that Qadaffi may be confusing his own role with that of the Prophet. Nevertheless, Qadaffi seems intent on working through a system of "people's power" committees, unions, and boards. Ultimately, these peoples' committees are intended to replace the Revolutionary Command Council, although the Revolutionary Command Council and Qadaffi still seem to be in control of the Libyan political process. The increasing roles of Muslim fundamentalist movements in the Maghreb have occurred without any direct Libyan involvement. This fact alone suggests that the international consequences of Qadaffi's charismatic leadership

have declined. Qadaffi's charismatic leadership is increasingly a domestic fact and not an international one.

CONCLUSION

The contemporary Middle East presents a mosaic of leadership styles with definite implications for conflict and conflict accommodation. The traditional Muslim leaders of the Middle East are conservative. Fighting a rearguard action against increasing demands for a larger share of political power, traditional leaders are coming under increasing domestic and international political pressure. Although traditional leaders of rich or potentially rich states may be able to buy time politically, in the long run, their right to power will be undermined by the social effects of such wealth.

Most traditional regimes will be replaced eventually by modernizing bureaucratic regimes, either democratic or authoritarian in nature. We see confirmation of this point of view and these trends in the reforms enacted in the countries of the Gulf. These regimes will try to mobilize mass political sentiment but keep it under strict control. Technological and economic progress is likely under these regimes, but they are not guaranteed. These regimes will come increasingly under the pressure of fundamentalist Islamic groups seeking to establish Islamic republics that derive their form and mandate from the Koran and Islamic tradition. They will remain vulnerable to mischief from other groups and countries.

This assault on the secular aspects of the modern bureaucratic regime may lead to instability and internal conflict, with predictable negative consequences for the systems. Modern bureaucratic leaders such as Mubarak of Egypt and Assad of Syria, basing their claim to power on demonstrated policy results, will find themselves increasingly challenged by credible alternative concepts of the public good and public order. These concepts, arising from a mixture of religious, political, and foreign influences, will produce potent claims for future performance, finding root in increasingly sophisticated political publics.

It is impossible to predict when charismatic leaders will appear or what the consequences of their regimes will be. They are capable of creating emotional political storms that float over the fragile boundaries of nation-states. Nasser, Khomeini, and Qadaffi, all of whom enjoyed at one time substantial support outside their own countries, challenged the authority of traditional monarchs and modern bureaucratic leaders. Their potential for destabilization and mischief or political good was great. Currently, Ayatollah Khomeini's sermons reportedly enjoy a wide circulation in the Fertile Crescent and now in the independent republics of central Asia, inspiring many active organizations. Colonel Qadaffi attempted to oust Sadat from Egypt and succeeded in ousting Numeiri from the Sudan in an attempt to extend his leadership into new areas. The more recent decline of his influence does not negate the possibility of other charismatic leaders emerging. It does not take a political soothsayer to predict the probable consequences of charismatic rule in Saudi Arabia with its petroleum wealth or in Egypt with its large population and crucial geopolitical position. On a much more abstract level, we must recognize the potential for charismatic leadership in the Muslim Umma

generally, a leadership capable of transcending familiar national entities. Such leadership would have worldwide impact. Islamic tradition is predisposed in this direction.

Finally, the U.S. "war on terror" has placed all Middle Eastern leaders in a difficult position, particularly as the United States identified organizations as terrorists that other leaders understand as "freedom fighters" or part of a legitimate resistance to oppressive rule. Hamas and Hizbollah present those leaders with just such a problem. The U.S. enthusiasm for war with Iraq was not shared by most political leaders or their followers throughout the region. The U.S. assertion that states are either "with us or against us" in both areas placed all of these leaders in a difficult political situation, torn between cooperating with Washington and staying true to the beliefs of their respective publics. How this resolves remains to be seen. Common sense in and out of the Middle East crucible maintains and expects serious political consequences for Middle Eastern leaders, from both policy questions.

The emerging international strategy of the Obama Administration puts less strain on Middle Eastern leaders. Committed to more multilateral policy initiatives, Middle Eastern heads of state are less individually seen as bending to U.S. will and more independent in their management of international conflicts.

Key Terms

taqiyyah *229*

11

THE ECONOMIC SETTING

The Middle East presents a remarkably wide spectrum of economic circumstances. It includes some of the richest and poorest nations in the world and some of the most fertile and most barren land. Some of these nations have been cosmopolitan for a millennium or more, whereas others only more recently peeked beyond their boundaries. Some mix religion and politics in puritanical systems, and others have advocated secular socialism. The Middle East's unusual diversity of conditions generally is unappreciated.

Some cautions should be mentioned at the outset. Nations are complex, and most short statements about them tend to be incomplete. This is understandable: The interplay of cultural, economic, and political forces is difficult to understand in the most straightforward of circumstances. When the forces are rapidly changing in a context of a quest for meaningful political independence, growing economic interdependence, and sometimes spectacular instances of instability, the task becomes daunting. Many works—from Baedekers to sophisticated technical analyses—deal with the economic conditions of the individual countries under study. Our approach is to deal with central themes of conflict and resolution rather than geographic or national entities. Students also should realize that the precision implied by statistics is often illusory. Some of the available statistics purporting to describe the Middle East are in gross error due to faulty measurement or to bias. Numbers have political uses. Petroleum production figures must be viewed with caution because of the frequent and frequently acknowledged tendency of members of Organization of Petroleum Exporting Countries (OPEC) to cheat on their production quotas. Migrant labor statistics are suspect for a variety of reasons. Sometimes all parties agree to ignore a changing reality. For example, the government of Lebanon consistently lacked data on the measurable economic and social characteristics of its Muslim and Christian populations. The always precarious balance between the groups could have been thrown into disarray through political action premised on such information.

The economy of Israel has many problems common to the various Arab states, but it differs considerably in other respects. In contrast to its Arab neighbors, its labor force is more highly educated and from a different cultural setting, its agriculture is more capital intensive, its industry contributes relatively more to national income, and it has received greater amounts of international aid. Common problems include significant migration, serious water management problems, and the need for a large and expensive military sector.

The traditional way of comparing the economic ranking of a country was simply to compute per capita income. Generally, by 2010 the oil-rich Gulf countries had gross domestic products per capita in the $20,000 to $45,000 range. The poorest country, Yemen, was close to $1,000. Most others were between $5,000 and $10,000. However, it has been persuasively argued, especially by those associated with the United Nations Development Program, that this simple notion often gives an inaccurate picture of well-being. They developed something called the Human Development Index, a measure that includes measures of per capita income, health, and literacy. After all, a country can be income rich while having low life expectancy and high rates of illiteracy. This was the position of the petroleum-exporting countries in 1974, the time of very high petroleum prices. Their per capita income ranking was much higher than their Human Development ranking. Since that time, the Human Development rank has increased due to the fact that a substantial portion of the petroleum earning was invested in education and health. Even so, this view of the human condition can be criticized for being too simple. For instance, it says nothing about the distribution of income, the role of females, the amount spent on the military, and a host of other factors. Scholars are grappling with the construction of more sophisticated versions to measure "the good life" in a more meaningful fashion. Table 11.1 shows the differences in per capita income along with health and military expenditures.

Per capita income figures do not show what each citizen has available to spend; rather, the figures indicate how much of national income each individual would have if the income were evenly distributed. The enormous gulf between the rich and the poor found in some of the states is ignored, as are military expenditures. The fact that Egypt has devoted about one-fifth of its gross national product to military needs, whereas the U.A.E. has spent a much smaller percentage, means that the gap between the two countries is much larger than indicated.

Per capita income figures for the small-population, petroleum-rich countries can vary substantially from year to year. Income earned in these economies closely follows petroleum export earnings. The measured per capita income in Saudi Arabia in 2005 was about $13,650. By 2008 it stood at over $19,000, reflecting the substantial increase in petroleum prices. This does not mean that the average Saudi citizen experienced a $5,000 gain in income. The government increased its international reserves for a time (by 2010 it went on a spending spree). The opposite happened in the 1980s. Then to cushion the decrease in income earned, the government spent reserves accumulated in earlier years. But even the fabled Saudi wealth has finite limits. By the 1990s, the government was forced to adopt a more modest budget; continued weak petroleum prices along with enormous expenditures related to the 1991 war against Iraq meant that relative budget austerity continued through the 1990s. Kuwait was more insulated from petroleum price shocks. Interest earnings from international investments exceeded revenue from petroleum sales during the 1985 to 1990 period. These earnings also financed the massive reconstruction project after Iraq was pushed out of Kuwait in 1991. Countries (e.g., Jordan, Egypt, and Yemen) that export labor to the petroleum-exporting countries also must worry about petroleum prices; remittances of migrant workers to the home country constitute a substantial percentage of foreign exchange earnings.

Sometimes massive changes in population affect the per capita income figures substantially. With the success of OPEC, the small-population petroleum exporters allowed large numbers of foreigners to enter the country (mostly in low-paying jobs).

	Table 11.1 Selected Economic Indicators				
Country	Real Per Capita Income U.S. $ 2008 (PPP)	Avg. Annual Growth		Health Exp Per Capita 2007 U.S. $	.Mil. Exp %GDP 2008
		2005	2008		
BAHRAIN	33,430	7.8	6.3	902	14
EGYPT	5,470	4.5	7.2	101	7.6
IRAN	10,850	4.6	7.8	253	12.6
ISRAEL	27,450	5.1	4	1,893	19.7
JORDAN	5,720	8.1	7.9	248	16.1
KUWAIT	53,480	10.6	4.4	901	13.2
LEBANON	11,750	1	8.5	525	14.6
OMAN	22,170	4.9	7.7	375	NA
SAUDI ARABIA	24,500	5.6	4.4	531	NA
SUDAN	1,920	6.3	8.3	40	NA
SYRIA	4,490	4.5	5.2	68	NA
TURKEY	13,420	8.4	0.9	465	9.5
U.A.E	NA	8.2		1,253	NA
YEMEN	2,220	5.6	3.9	43	NA

Source: World Bank. WORLD BANK DATA WORLD DEVELOPMENT INDICATORS.

The growth record, whether viewed from the simplicity of per capita income or from a more sophisticated framework, was reasonably satisfactory during the 1960s if one ignores Egypt and impoverished Yemen. Petroleum price increases in the 1970s assured some countries of phenomenal growth and put the countries without petroleum under ever greater strain, especially the countries that had established an industrial base and needed oil.

The decade of the 1980s was not good for most Middle Eastern economies. Wars (e.g., Iran–Iraq), virtual anarchy (Lebanon), insurrection (Palestine–Israel), wildly fluctuating petroleum prices, continued high rates of population growth (adding more than one million per year to Egypt alone), significant droughts, and clumsy government intervention in economic life all contributed to the record. By the end of the decade, many countries (e.g., Egypt, Israel,

Iraq) had significant debt-servicing problems, and others (e.g., Syria) saw their sources of economic and military aid dry up because of the sudden collapse of the Soviet Union. The 1990s and first half of the decade of the new century were characterized by continued modest growth in some countries, negative growth in others, and a move toward more private enterprise in several countries. Substantial increases in petroleum prices in the last half of the decade led to substantial growth.

In 2002 the United Nations Development Program issued the first Arab Human Development Report, a study (by Arab analysts) of the roots of economic and social stagnation in the Arab world. The conclusion was that three basic causes explain why the growth of real per capita income was a dismal 0.5 percent per year in the two decades preceding 2000. The first was autocratic governments that supported incompetent and sometimes venal civil administrations, despite the outward trappings of elections and seemingly open civil codes. This situation lessens the chances for growth-inducing economic action. The second identified shortcoming was the low quality of education. The third was the inferior status of women, even though female literacy rates increased more than threefold in the last three decades.

ECONOMIC RECORD

Three overriding phenomena have shaped the economic record of the Middle East in the past half-century—the previously mentioned failures of government, war or the threat of war, and the changing nature of the petroleum industry. On a more general level, the major long-term economic issue is that of resource imbalances. High rates of population increase when placed in the context of a limited supply of water and arable land is the most obvious set of problems. Likewise, petroleum is a non-renewable resource; supplies are exhaustible. Economic growth in these circumstances may not be sustainable. Additionally, growing resource imbalances increase the probability of conflict within and between nations.

The Persian (Arabian) Gulf and Israel have been the focus of most major military conflicts. Israel and the countries bordering it have consumed a substantial amount of their resources for military strength in the past half-century—resources that could have been directed toward economic growth. Wars have deleterious economic effects beyond the pure waste of committing resources to nonproductive uses; the occasional outbreaks of war and the constant possibility of war disrupt plans and projects, discourage investment, and divert attention from nonmilitary objectives. The disruptive effects are greater in the less-developed countries than in their richer counterparts because the less-developed economies are far more fragile than the developed ones. A poor country is poor, in part, because it does not

have the physical infrastructure (networks of communication, transportation, education, and electrical power); the right variety and amounts of economic resources; and the social and political complements necessary for sustained growth. These countries experience significant setbacks when they have to absorb shocks to their economies. This is exactly what happens when the local military machine is obliged to garner resources that otherwise could be used to build a stronger national economic foundation. Local circumstances, however, dictate that this statement needs to be tempered. Although the long (1980 to 1988) war between Iran and Iraq was enormously expensive in terms of material and human life, the effect on Iraq was ameliorated substantially by the receipt of tens of billions of dollars of grants and loans, especially from the petroleum-rich Gulf States. By the time of the cease-fire, Iraq had in their workforce two million foreigners, almost all Arab, most being Egyptian. Their externally financed presence meant that the Iraqi economy was able to grow throughout the conflict.

By 1990, however, Iraq was facing a set of stringent economic conditions that represented an important cluster of motivations for their invasion of Kuwait. Gulf grants had ended and debt servicing was burdensome; OPEC production exceeded agreed limits, lowering the price and depriving Iraq of foreign exchange earnings (Iraq lost about $1 billion per year for every dollar drop in the price of petroleum); and the port city of Basra would be closed indefinitely because the Shatt Al-Arab was clogged with mines, sunken ships, and silt.

If war generally is very expensive, so is the establishment of peace. The Camp David Accords between Egypt and Israel provide a useful case history to keep in mind as more comprehensive peace processes involving Israel are contemplated. An essential element of the Camp David Accords was Israeli withdrawal from the Egyptian Siani territory captured in 1967. This meant that Israel was asked to relinquish a formidable natural buffer between it and Egypt. Neither Israel nor Egypt had the financial resources necessary to construct and maintain an "electronic fence" to serve as a substitute for the buffer of the desert. Neither side could afford peace. It was necessary for the United States to foot the bill.

Negotiations of "land for peace" in the 1990s involved the same sort of financial bind. All parties face severe water problems, and Israel receives a substantial percentage of its supply from the territories it occupies. It must be assured of secure water supplies. One way to accomplish this is through the construction of (very expensive) desalination plants. The only other way is through detailed negotiations that allow for an equitable system of water sharing and ironclad guarantees that water supplies will not be interrupted.

Egypt engaged in four wars with Israel, had a consequential involvement in a civil war in Yemen, had several confrontations with Libya, and participated (with compensation) in the 1991 effort against Iraq. In the best of circumstances, the task of creating an economy capable of sustained growth is difficult; the need to be in an almost constant state of military readiness has greatly compounded the problem. Jordan has had to contend with a tremendous influx of Palestinians on several occasions, Syria has been engaged with Israel, the delicate balance in Lebanon unraveled, and so on. Israel has felt particularly beleaguered, being constantly under threat, although massive international aid for many years buffered the problem. Given these conditions, the countries under study have experienced more rapid growth than one would expect. But the prospects for sustained rapid growth were dim until 1974.

One of the most remarkable transfers of wealth the world has ever seen occurred as a result of changes in the petroleum industry. The members of OPEC roughly quadrupled (to $12) the price of petroleum between October 1973 and January 1974, not so much as acting as a cartel, but by taking advantage of worldwide changes in supply/demand conditions. The

price doubled (from $15 to $30) in 1979–1980, largely in response to the disruption of petroleum supplies caused by the outbreak of the war between Iraq and Iran. Saudi Arabia, the largest producer of OPEC, had accumulated more financial reserves than most other countries of the world by 1980. The other petroleum producers in the area, most notably Iraq and Iran, along with some of the small Gulf States, also had spectacular increases in revenue. The results of this accumulation of financial power were felt, in greater or lesser degree, throughout the world. The Middle East became a more important trading partner for Japan (as measured by the value of trade) than the European Community. The petroleum-producing countries had the financial wherewithal to promote economic development; their allies benefited through various direct and indirect measures, and their enemies suffered. Much of the Middle East changed forever, and because of this, the world changed, but the situation did not last. High prices invited substantial exploration and a subsequent increase in worldwide supplies coming to the market. Weak petroleum prices through most of the 1990s severely restricted the ability of the petroleum-exporting countries to continue the spending spree they engaged in during the previous two decades. The real (inflation adjusted) price of petroleum wobbled around pre-1973 levels toward the end of the 1990s. At the end of the decade, as worldwide demand increased, petroleum prices increased substantially. The price was just shy of $150 in mid-2008 before settling down to the $70 range by early 2010.

ORGANIZATION OF ECONOMIC ACTIVITY

The three major economic goals of most countries are growth, stability, and an equitable distribution of income. There is much debate as to which of these is the most important and how the goals are best pursued when a reasonable consensus is reached on the "correct" mix.

Governments and universities resound with arguments that champion a range of solutions from private enterprise to socialism. The issues have importance beyond scholarly debate; the choices are real and the stakes are high.

Several countries have been proponents of "Arab Socialism." Other countries have monarchies that directly influence much of the "private" enterprise of any note. Others have taken a more eclectic stance, and a few are attempting to give coherence to the phrase *Islamic economics.*

There seems to be little consensus about the specific contours of Arab Socialism, a concept that receives increasingly less support as the years pass. The lack of a clearly defined and consistent ideology is due to several factors, including disagreements across national boundaries and espousals of an idea without any particular plan of action. What is clear is that most Middle Eastern "socialist" governments came to power with a definite desire to provide greater economic growth, stability, and a more equitable distribution of income and wealth. To meet these goals, the leaders initiated land reforms, froze prices, and nationalized major industries. These measures are better described as nationalistic than socialistic, however—especially when they are designed to lessen foreign influences in the economy.

During the 1980s, a pronounced shift occurred in the ideological stance of many of the proponents of Arab Socialism. There was a generalized worldwide shift away from government involvement in economic life in favor of private markets. During the preceding decades, most academics and policymakers favored large-scale government involvement. Their preference was rooted in various notions of the development process, from Marxist to neoclassical renditions of the failures of the marketplace in the specialized settings of low-income countries. National leaders often adopted one or another of these moorings, either from intellectual conviction or as a convenient excuse to pursue another goal. By the 1990s, the blame for the miserable economic performance in many of these countries was placed on government, the agent that was seen as the driving force of development only a few years earlier. It was claimed, with a considerable number of case studies at hand, that government action stunted growth. At the same time, the U.S.S.R. was falling apart.

It is probable that some countries professed socialism because it was a convenient way for their political leaders to eliminate business opposition or to strike an appropriate international posture; the professed ideals often faded as circumstances warranted. In 1973, three years after the death of Gamal Abdel Nasser, clearly the leading proponent of Arab Socialism in the region, Anwar Sadat declared an Egyptian "open door policy" to foreign investment. A little more than a decade earlier, Nasser had severely restricted not only foreign business operations but also private domestic investments. Nasser's relationship to the business class probably had something to do with his decisions. The abrupt change in Egyptian policy may have been based on Sadat's desire to curry favor with conservative King Faisal (d. 1975) of Saudi Arabia. Ideologies may shift dramatically with the political climate.

Iraq, considered a radical state in the 1970s, reacted strongly against the post-Nasser economic drift in Egypt. A few months after the open door policy was announced in Egypt, and after the 1973 Arab–Israeli war, Iraq proposed that the Western supporters of Israel should be punished through a boycott of petroleum sales. By adopting this policy, they proved their radical mettle to the world at large. The world at large may not have known that Iraq was selling its petroleum to the U.S.S.R., which sold petroleum to Western Europe. Without impugning Iraq's motives, it is fair to say that it was able to maintain its international reputation as a "hardline" state without having to suffer significant revenue losses from decreased petroleum sales.

Through the 1980s, Syria depended on the Soviet bloc for the bulk of their economic and military aid. Especially noteworthy is that much of the aid (especially educational) was given by the respective communist parties to the Syrian Baath Party. But then the Soviet bloc crumbled. The consequent almost total shutoff of the aid spigot coincided with a series of drought years in Syria—an agricultural system particularly sensitive to rainfall. It also became increasingly apparent that the extensive system of government ownership of industry and rigid price fixing was becoming increasingly burdensome. The Syrian government responded to their economic crisis by drawing closer to the remaining great power, the United States. They adopted a series of measures designed to "liberalize" the economy, along with an attempt to make some of their political policies more acceptable to the United States. The 1990 U.S. call for Arab participation in the coalition against Iraq presented Syria with a unique opportunity.

After the war, Syria continued to change its orientation in several ways. Among the changes was an official reinterpretation of Baathist notions of the "Arab Nation" and the role of the government in the economy. Although always in foggy and dreamlike terms, the keepers of Baathist ideology had spoken of some future time when there would be a pan-Arab nation free of boundaries imposed by Western powers. By 1991, they were speaking of the "Arab Nation" in the same tones as the members of the European Community were speaking of a united Europe—a closely cooperating group of nations, each with its sovereignty. Likewise, the past record of heavy government involvement in the economy was explained as a phase necessary to fit the objective conditions of the 1970s and 1980s; the "new objective conditions" dictated that it was time for the private sector to take a greater role. The widely reported weak health of President Assad fueled speculation as to the future direction of the Syrian economy. Although one of his sons (the first potential claimant, Basil, died in an accident) assumed power after Assad's death, it was uncertain that this potential economic liberalizer would have enough political power to bring about significant changes in the organization of

economic life. If not, would the mantle of leadership pass to long-established politicians who had a hidebound devotion to Baathist notions of the organization of the economy? Significant reforms started in 2004. By 2007, the economy was growing at a robust rate although they absorbed over a million Iraqi refugees (about 8 percent of the Syrian population). Reforms slowed significantly after that.

The same kinds of observations concerning ideologically flexible pronouncements and policies can be made about the growing list of countries that profess to follow private enterprise as an operating principle. In a few countries, most significant ventures initiated by the private sector are tied directly to the government through formal public participation or through the intervention of well-placed individuals in the government. The Iranian royal family gained ownership shares in many significant industrial ventures in that country. The royal family participated because it desired wealth and because it perceived a need to exert control over industrialists and the growing industrial sector. The same pattern of heavy, and sometimes hidden, government involvement persisted in the Islamic Republic. In many cases, this kind of intervention has had a profound effect on the functioning of the marketplace. Competitive private enterprise markets in the Western world tend to be impersonal, ideally excluding all considerations except for those of price and performance. The highly personalized industrial ventures in Iran under the shah or in Saudi Arabia should not be expected to yield the same results. It is difficult to know what to call such systems: perhaps *etatism* suffices. In any case, they are not private enterprise systems as generally thought of in the West.

Islamic Economics

The study of Islamic economics became a growth industry after the success of OPEC and the increased interest in the formation of an Islamic state. Before this, first-rate work was relatively rare or obscure. The term *Islamic economics* covers a wide variety of issues and problems, although Western attention has focused almost exclusively on the Koranic proscription on the taking of interest and the consequent need to redesign the financial system. Because the range of inquiry is so comprehensive and the analyses so recent, many questions remain, but there are many points of agreement.

The fundamental starting point of mainstream (Western, neoclassical) economic analysis is extreme: "Well-offness," utility, is maximized by an individual solely with reference to material goods (and services). The theory usually posits that "I make myself better off by ignoring the well-being of others." That is, it adopts an extreme individualistic and materialistic stance. Although Western economists generally agree that this narrow definition defies reality, they argue that it is a useful starting point, and that the analysis can be adjusted further down the line. However, a group of Muslim theorists believes that this abstraction from reality is not warranted: that the Koranic concern for the well-being of the Umma is so central that the "complications" need to be introduced at the outset. Consequently, some Muslim theorists have grappled with the complex issue of modeling individual utility functions that jettison extreme individualism and materialism. This meant that thorny issues of the "proper" distribution of income and wealth (including the assignment of property rights) were brought center stage at the outset.

There are many other issues that hold the attention of individuals concerned with Islamic economics. There are specific Koranic guidelines dealing with the scope of inheritance, the proper system of taxation (including zakat), the nature of government expenditures, and, more generally, the proper role of government in meeting the wider material and ethical concerns of the Umma. On some matters basic principles are clear, but the mechanisms for goal achievement are not. The principle of the obligation of zakat is straightforward; the manner in which it is to be levied, and by whom, is unclear. On a more general level, the Koran does not express explicit hostility toward private enterprise, but its egalitarian concerns for the Umma leave open some basic questions relating to the proper extent of property rights, limits on the accumulation of wealth, and other fundamental issues.

The Koranic proscription against the taking of interest has captured most Western attention concerning Islamic economics. Most Muslim theorists are convinced that the taking of interest is forbidden—after all, the Koran seems to be clear on the issue. We should realize, however, that although the Koran specifically declares that interest is forbidden (haram), straightforward acceptance of even this involves a theological position. Some theorists argue that the words of the Koran reflect a prohibition against usury—"exploitatively high" interest rates—rather than interest per se. A strict literalist position, one that takes the Word as immutable through time and not subject to interpretation, renders the modernist view as heretical. In any case, there now is widespread agreement on the need to develop an interest-free banking system.

As with any price, the price for the use of money, the interest rate, balances supply and demand forces. In general, individuals need to be compensated for deferring consumption (saving). That is, Western banks pay interest to encourage a flow of loanable funds. Borrowers create the demand. They are willing to pay interest because the rate of return they expect from investing the borrowed money (e.g., building a factory) is greater than the interest payment they are obligated to pay the bank. The bank serves the function of making this market, of bringing together people who gain from deferring consumption and people who gain from investing. The equilibrium interest rate, that which yields the same quantity demanded as the quantity supplied, also serves the economy as a whole by matching the community's desire to forgo present consumption with future rewards; that is, it helps determine the upper limit of growth.

How can an interest-free system operate efficiently? How does a financial institution encourage deposits and choose among potential borrowers? Islamic institutions provide an answer: a profit/loss share system. The banks compete for deposits by indicating that the depositor gains shares—claims on potential bank profits—and they advertise what they have paid out per share in past years. Depositors in an Islamic bank do not have the contractual guarantee of a return promised by a Western bank, but they do have some knowledge of the track record of the bank and could earn more if the bank has a particularly good year. This method of gathering loanable funds is in place in several countries, including Iran and Pakistan, and seems to work well—there is no fundamental difference from interest banking if competitive conditions prevail.

The lending decisions of the bank follow the same share principle. Instead of a firm borrowing money and having a fixed repayment schedule, the bank essentially buys shares in the activity of the borrowing company, with the provision that the firm has the ability to repurchase the shares (and an obligation to share profits). Because the banks are competing for the funds of potential savers, they must endeavor to deliver the highest share of profits. This forces them to lend to individuals who have the highest probable rate of return. As in the interest system, competition enforces efficiency on the market.

Although zero-interest banking can mirror an interest-paying system with respect to efficiency, there are several important differences that reflect Koranic concerns for equity. General Koranic ethical norms state that it is unacceptable to profit from an individual in dire straits. The share system satisfies this norm. The borrower is not obligated to make repayments to the financial institution if the investment goes sour. The farmer who faces a crop loss because of bad weather is not obligated to make a payment to the bank in the same period. The bank,

as partner, shares the burden. In the same fashion, the bank is not obligated to pay a return to depositors if the bank has a bad year. Gains and misfortunes are shared.

The Islamic system of zero-interest banking provides for the usual efficiency conditions of interest banking, and it fits Koranic ethical norms. Actually, the system is far more complex, and some of the details of operation and policy implications are not fully understood. It is clear, however, that the system can be economically rational and managerially feasible.

The need for more sophisticated financial instruments increased with economic growth. Much of the impetus for Islamic financial innovation has come from Malaysia, not the Middle East. For example, floating corporate bonds became ever-more important. This could be accomplished through a lend-lease arrangement. The borrower puts productive assets as collateral (in a special-purpose vehicle); the lender receives regular payments. The payments generally are benchmarked to the interest rate. Another innovation involves savings accounts. Although the saver shares in the profit fortunes of the bank, potentially high volatility of earnings discourages savings. The innovation is that the bank draws on a "profit reserve" to be paid to savers when bank profits are low. There are many more innovations in the pipeline. The basic issue faced by Sharia scholars is the determination of Islamic legitimacy. Does the innovation conform to Islamic norms, or is it merely a ruse throwing a thin veil over an interest-based system? These Malaysian innovations have prompted Gulf countries to view the financial system from another prism.

Economic Liberalization

The three large-population countries in the Middle East—Egypt, Iran, and Turkey—changed their economic orientation markedly during the last four decades. The 1973 pronouncement (legislated in 1974) by Sadat of a policy of *infitah* ("opening up") of the Egyptian economy to private foreign and domestic investment was a clear political statement rejecting Nasser's policies. The movement was to be toward building "market socialism" and away from the Soviet-type material balances approach. This meant that many prices were to be market determined rather than set by a planning agency. It also meant that the private sector would be strengthened. Although the Egyptian economy grew at a robust pace for the next decade, about 8 percent per annum, the proximate causes of the growth cannot be attributed to the new policy. Rather, a surge in foreign exchange earnings, emanating from forces largely out of the control of Egypt, seems to have been responsible. The four major items were petroleum exports, receipts from the (newly reopened) Suez Canal, remittances from Egyptians working in the petroleum-rich states, and substantial international aid programs. Beginning in the 1980s, President Mubarak slowly nudged Egypt toward more private enterprise and less government price fixing. By 2010, it seemed that the reform movement was secure.

A host of domestic forces consigned Egyptian policymakers to a narrow range of options in the 1970s and 1980s. It seems as though a policy stasis emerged. The fundamental problems of a high rate of population growth, an urban and industrial bias, and a troublesome income distribution were not matters given priority. Although the root causes of this policy stasis are not fully understood, it seems that one significant factor was the emergence of a new amalgam of social forces. The technocratic class gained members and prominence under Nasser. Many of this class were members of the bloated government, and Sadat's emphasis on the private sector was a clear threat to their power. As a result, the usually cumbersome bureaucratic apparatus seemed to cease to function altogether when private investors sought government approval for some aspect of their operations. The agricultural sector was another source of resistance to Sadat's policy shift. The peasants who had moved toward the top of the agricultural ladder through the Nasser-initiated land reform policies would lose if there was a significant change in the system. The best off of those in agriculture stood to lose because they received substantial subsidies (and important exemptions from regulations). In counterpoint to the technocrats and new agricultural elite, the old elite class came to the surface under Sadat after many years of quietness under Nasser. They pressed for favors for the private sector.

The debt crisis of the 1870s led to a reordering of Egypt. One hundred years later, Egypt again was in the middle of a nervous game in the international marketplace. The opening of the Egyptian economy removed some gross inefficiency. Its foreign exchange earnings were subject, however, to the volatile petroleum market (for petroleum sales and migrant worker remittances to Egypt) and the equally uncertain political environment (Suez Canal earnings and international aid). The basic issues of population and income distribution were largely ignored. The U.S. government forgave Egypt $7 billion in loans after Egyptian participation in the 1991 war against Iraq; the Egyptian economy was carrying a very heavy debt burden.

The process of economic liberalization in Egypt took root, and there were decent gains until the regional slowdown of the late 1980s resulting from the fall of petroleum prices in 1986. Egypt suffered again during the early 1990s and then showed a substantial recovery. A good deal of the recovery was attributed to the opening of international trade coupled with international investors' increased confidence that Egypt would stay the course. Reforms developed and picked up pace after 2000. On the other side of the ledger, the service sector and government bureaucracy remain very inefficient. It is difficult to dismantle quickly decades of inefficiency.

TURKEY. The Turkish solution to a faltering economy mirrored Egypt in that the economy was opened to foreign trade, but it differed in other basic aspects. Although the primary reason for the 1980 military takeover in Turkey was to curb the alarming amount of politically motivated violence (about 180 deaths per month by mid-1980), it was clear that a grossly inefficient economy also was of concern.

The military leaders of the 1980 coup thoroughly reformed the Turkish political system by (1) disbanding all political parties and confiscating their property, (2) barring political activity (10 years) for all individuals who at the time of the takeover were in leadership positions or in the Grand National Assembly (five years), and (3) initiating and guiding to passage a new constitution (November 1982). One important set of provisions in the new constitution dealt with electoral reform. In particular, proportional representation was ended, and national parties needed to receive at least 10 percent of the national vote to have a candidate seated. This blunted the efforts of many small parties and made it easier for the largest party to govern without being saddled by debilitating coalitions.

The election of 1982 brought a technocrat, Turgot Ozal, to power and gave his Motherland Party a majority in the Grand National Assembly, a majority that was increased substantially in the 1987 elections. This majority cleared the way for Ozal to act decisively to bring order in the streets and coherence in the economy to meet the constitutional provision that stated the economy was to be based on private enterprise. He initiated a set of "liberalizing" policies—policies designed to strengthen the free market, such as tariff reduction, foreign investment promotion, a wholesale dismantling of state-owned enterprises, a bid to join the European Economic Community, and (after the breakup of the U.S.S.R.) the formation of a Black Sea economic cooperation group of nations. Although the Motherland Party lost its legislative majority in 1991, the die had been cast; the majority in the legislature differed from Ozal in many ways, but they framed their differences within the basic market-liberalizing blueprint laid down in the 1980s. Similar to Egypt, involved Western

participants, from governments to private creditors, worried over the seeming inability of Turkey to service its debt, assisted in the effort. Also similar to Egypt, the Turkish economy seemed to be more vibrant during the last decade of the twentieth century as economic reforms, albeit highly incomplete, took root. However, the vibrancy was lost by 2000, and the Turkish economy went into a deep and serious depression. An election in 2002 toppled the old ruling alliances. A party that claimed to be Islamic took power in a stunning victory. They stated that their main goal was not to infuse religion into the center of Turkish political life; rather, they claimed that the goal was to end decades of corruption to restore economic growth. They acted on this premise without abandoning Turkey's secular status.

During the 1980s, the International Monetary Fund, the major international organization capable of providing financing to beleaguered governments, joined the academic world in their disillusionment with extensive government control of the economy. Countries seeking financial assistance always had to meet "conditionality" clauses if their requests were to be met. By the 1980s, these clauses more explicitly argued for economic "liberalization," the strengthening of the private sector. The financial weakness of the country often meant that they had little choice but to accept the conditions. Economic liberalization often meant, however, that policies had to be initiated that made things worse before they got better. This was an increasingly bitter pill to swallow for the countries already in deep trouble. It also seemed unfair to the countries that arrived at their poor status because of wild gyrations in the international marketplace rather than internally generated failings.

For example, in 1989 Jordan completed negotiations with the International Monetary Fund that allowed it to borrow from the International Monetary Fund on the condition that prices of key basic commodities in Jordan would be increased to reflect economic costs.

This is the usual procedure for the International Monetary Fund; they approve loans only if the country institutes a program that corrects fundamental imbalances. The case of Jordan illustrates why many countries object to this "conditionality." Substantial increases in food and fuel prices designed to limit imports were met by civil unrest among the elements of the population thought to be the most loyal to the government. In response to the unrest, Jordan's prime minister was forced to resign, and the king promised more political participation. The political costs of economic adjustment can be high. Through the 1990s, the International Monetary Fund (and major international lending countries) came under increasing pressure to temper their conditionality clauses through a recognition of political realities.

IRAN. Iran, the other large-population country of the Middle East, took a course different from that of Egypt and Turkey. Its revolutionary government rejected moves toward a more globally interdependent economy, whether under the market socialism of Egypt under Sadat or the free market goal of Turkey. Although there was considerable debate in Iran about the economic role of the state and private enterprise, there also was widespread agreement that there would be no infitah in Iran. If anything, the goal would be that of removing foreign influence from the internal economy. Thirty years after the revolution, Iran was still fitfully dealing its position on foreign investment. Iran also had to deal with Western, especially U.S., obstacles to foreign investment. Through most of the 1990s, liberalizing forces in Iran made modest gains, almost always hotly contested. Elections in 2005 brought a populist to the presidency. His first months in office indicated that he wanted Iran to redefine economic and political relations with the West, but events and a strong clerical backlash ended the reformers hopes.

In late 2006, a high-level delegation from Iran visited China with the express purpose of seeing what parts of the Chinese path to a (partial) market economy could be transferred to Iran. Although buoyed by record petroleum prices, the Iranian economy is grossly inefficient, partially due to the preponderance of the state in the economy. What the Iranians wanted to learn from the Chinese was this: How can Iran privatize the economy without ceding political power?

In 1976, under the shah, Iran was pumping petroleum at about 6 million barrels per day. Three decades later, it produced about 4 million barrels per day. The long (1980 to 1988) war with Iraq destroyed many production and refining facilities. Production fell to under 1.5 million barrels. There were difficulties in the reconstruction process, including U.S. sanctions, limited Iranian financial capability, and companies not under the sanctions umbrella unwilling to commit billions of dollars in an era of low petroleum prices and high probability of political instability. Internal political frictions added to the difficulties; Iranian conservatives often put contract provisions so strict that private investors rejected them.

Iran has a long history of heavily subsidizing energy use. In 2006, gasoline prices at the pump cost the equivalent of 45 (U.S.) cents. It has been estimated that energy subsidies account for about one-quarter of Iran's GDP. Due to high petroleum prices, the economy has been growing at 4 to 6 percent per year in the recent past. This meant that more autos, refrigerators, and air-conditioning units were being sold. Decreased supply and sharply increased demand have put Iran in a bind. In 2006, about 40 percent of Iran's petroleum output was for internal use. Indeed, they had to spend about $7 billion to import gasoline. If these trends continue, Iran's total output would go to internal use in a couple of decades. Petroleum accounts for the overwhelming percentage of foreign exchange earnings; the problem is obvious.

At times, it has been called "the curse of natural resource abundance." Heavy reliance on one product placed in a market characterized by extreme price volatility is problematic. There are three basic strategies, often complementary, to ease the problem. First, different energy sources can be developed; that is, supply could be diversified. Nuclear energy is one prominent option. However, as we have seen, Iran faces U.N. sanctions due to their refusal to allow U.N. inspectors ensure that its program is for peaceful means only. Sharply increased demand for energy has led Egypt and Saudi Arabia to consider the nuclear option.

Second, attempts could be made to constrain demand. While overall GDP growth in Iran has been good, most of the gains have not been seen by the common person. There is considerable unrest in the streets due to the perceived lackluster performance. The best way to constrain the demand for petroleum is to remove subsidies and allow prices to reflect their scarcity value. The government was reluctant to do this given the high probability of significant social unrest. By mid-2007, the government imposed a gasoline rationing scheme on government vehicles. A couple of years later they added most private vehicles to the rationing scheme.

The third way out is to diversify the economy. The best (and cheapest) way to do this is to embark on a program of (selective) privatization. But privatization brings with it the potential loss of political control, hence the visit to China.

China managed to maintain political control (to date) partially through selective and well-sequenced privatizations. But it is overwhelmingly due to the monopoly of power held by the Communist Party. In Iran, the president has to deal with fractious legislature as well as the Supreme Leader who has considerable autonomous authority to override the wishes of the president and legislature. The Iranian setting is further muddled by the existence of two other semi-autonomous institutions: the Revolutionary Guard and Waqf-like institutions, called *bonyads* in Iran.

The Revolutionary Guard was formed shortly after the revolution (1979). It is accountable to the Supreme Leader. The original aim was to stoke the revolutionary fires and to act as a counterweight to the military. As guardians of the revolution, they tried to enforce morality as they saw it. As a military counterweight, they were allowed to have their own military forces. At the end of the war with Iraq (1988), apparently it was thought that many of these zealots would be disaffected after having many thousands of its members killed in battle only to end up with a truce—the very thing that they were assured would never happen. Thousands of them were employed by the Guard to engage in government reconstruction projects. The goal was to give them work and thereby lessen the chances of significant social unrest. The scope of their activities gradually widened to include large construction and petroleum projects. Many of the projects were given to the Guard without the pretense of competitive bidding. It became an economic powerhouse.

Many mosques have affiliated bonyads. Most are modest in size. These institutions are best viewed as religious trusts. They pay virtually no taxes on their earnings, which, for the largest trusts, apparently are many millions of dollars per year. Nominally, they report to the Supreme Leader. The president and legislature have virtually no power or oversight. The largest bonyad, the Imam Raza foundation, may be the largest corporate enterprise in Iran. The profits of the enterprises it owns should be devoted to furthering Islamic causes, supposedly only in Iran. The organization also can be viewed as a major money spigot for the conservative clerical establishment. It wields considerable power.

While these thumbnail sketches of the Revolutionary Guard and the Imam Raza foundation may seem overly brief, they do point to additional complications faced by any potential reformer in Iran. It also makes it difficult for U.S. analysts to interpret Iranian actions. For example, it is reported that the millions of dollars that Hizbollah used in its reconstruction efforts in Lebanon after the Israeli invasion came from the Imam Raza bonyad. In a similar fashion, the Revolutionary Guard often is involved in actions generally directed by the executive branch of most governments. In mid-2007, in the middle of a dispute it was having about leasing oil rigs (U.S. pressure had led to the cancellation of a lease for these hard-to-get rigs), members of the Revolutionary Guard boarded a British patrol boat and detained several sailors. The bottom line is that it is very difficult to sort through the complexities of governmental decision making in Iran.

LIBERALIZATION AND GLOBALIZATION

The difficulties of the transition to a greater reliance on the free market generally were not well appreciated during the 1980s; painful experiences in the 1990s brought the lesson home. Free markets do not exist in a vacuum; to function properly, private enterprise must have a set of institutions that support it. There must be a legal system that can dispose of contract disputes in a fair and timely manner. There must be an administrative network that translates law into action. The financial system must be reasonably competitive and free of undue restrictions. The list could go on, but the point has been made. The putative triumph of free markets over statist systems makes sense from some perspectives, but free markets will not provide an answer to economic malaise without an institutional environment that supports the functioning of the market. In many cases, that environment was incomplete in the liberalizing countries of the Middle East. By the close of the twentieth century, the International Monetary Fund seemed to recognize that it was essential that governmental institutions needed to be reformed if economic liberalization was to succeed. They also paid much more attention to the plight of the poorest of the poor; the International Monetary Fund

argued that the poor needed to be directly involved and gain from economic development schemes. Their previous, albeit implicit, assumption that benefits would quickly "trickle down" to the poor was quietly shelved.

Liberalization was complicated further by globalization. The opening of economies can be painful to some segments of the society as markets are lost to global competitors, and income within the country is redistributed as a result. Free capital markets allow foreign investment to flow into the country, but as several Asian countries found out in the mid-1990s, that freedom also means that there can be quick and massive capital flight.

To complicate the picture further, the increasingly worldwide reach of the Internet, sometimes called "the death of distance," probably will have a profound effect on local companies everywhere. The local manufacturer used to having firms within its geographic space buy from it will increasingly find their customers surfing the Internet for the best worldwide buy. Because transportation costs have been decreasing, the advantage of buying locally is eroded further. The upshot is that global competition will seep into local geographic spaces—the death of distance.

Although the ideological stance of the various nations may be important, we must look beyond surface pronouncements and deeds. The remaining sections of this chapter analyze how different circumstances lead to different policy measures, and why the same policy measures may lead to different results.

LAND DISTRIBUTION POLICIES

Table 11.2 gives the geographic area of the various Middle Eastern countries. Saudi Arabia is the twelfth largest country in the world; Iran ranks fifteenth, being about one-half the size of India; Sudan and Algeria are the two largest countries in Africa. In comparison, Kuwait, Bahrain, Qatar, the U.A.E., Israel, and Lebanon are very small.

Table 11.2 Land and Urbanization 2008			
Country	Surface Area Sq. Km	Agr. Land % Total	Urban Pop. % Total
Bahrain	710	14.1	88.5
Egypt	995,450	3.6	42.7
Iran	1,628,550	29.5	68.5
Israel	21,640	23.2	91.7
Jordan	88,240	10.9	78.4
Kuwait	17,820	8.6	98.4
Lebanon	10,230	67.2	87
Oman	309,500	5.8	71.6
Saudi Arabia	2,000,000	N/A	82.4
Sudan	2,376,000	57.6	43.4
Syria	183,630	75.7	54.2
Turkey	769,630	51.3	68.7
U.A.E	83,600	7.1	77.9
Yemen	527,970	44.7	30.6
Iraq	437,370	21.6	66.6

Source: World Bank. World Development Indicators.

A great percentage of the land in the Middle East is either not arable or only marginally so. With a few minor exceptions, all of the arable land in Egypt runs along the Nile; that of Libya is contained in a narrow band of land along the Mediterranean. The Arabian Peninsula has significant arable land only in parts of Oman, Yemen, and the Hijaz region of Saudi Arabia. Much of the Iranian steppe and the mountainous terrain of Turkey are unsuitable for high-yield agriculture. The vast deserts of the Middle East often have been compared to a sea; although they have an unrelenting, harsh, and beautiful power, they are difficult to control. These formidable deserts are barriers and vast havens. However, their power to promote insularity has eroded considerably in the twentieth century. The finances necessary to overcome the power of the deserts—to cross them with roads, build airports, purchase transportation systems, dam rivers, and build radio transmitters—were generated in some countries by colonial administrations and in others by nationalist modernizing forces, by

means of taxes and oil revenues. Whatever the source, the deserts are slowly being changed. However, they will continue to present severe constraints on life in the Middle East.

Agricultural land distribution and ownership patterns generally are considered to affect productivity. They are also indices of economic justice and power. All of the countries in this survey have seen significant changes in the pattern of land ownership in the twentieth century. There have been formal agrarian reform programs in six of the countries—Egypt, Iran, Iraq, Syria, Libya, and (South) Yemen. There have been no reform programs in Jordan, Lebanon, the U.A.E., or Saudi Arabia. Land ownership and use patterns have changed considerably in Israel, but it is best to consider Israel apart because the circumstances of these changes have been unique.

Various land ownership patterns exist in the Middle East, but three types are most common. The first is **mulk**, or private ownership. The second is **miri sirf**, land owned by the state, generally with strong usufruct rights (right of use without ownership) granted to the tenant. In practice, this is often little different than mulk. The third is **waqf**, a uniquely Islamic institution. One type of waqf allows for title to the land to be given to some officially recognized religious or social institution, sometimes with the condition that the family and heirs of the donor are to receive some share of the proceeds from the land until the family line no longer exists or for some specified period. Another form is strictly private. A rough Western equivalent is a trust fund. As with trust funds, a waqf may be established and administered with the most honorable of intentions or simply to protect individual assets from the tax collector. In any case, modifications of waqf status can involve massive changes in the distribution of wealth and political power.

The following brief reports on some countries' experiences with land and agricultural policy illustrate several points beyond the gleaning of country-specific information. First, policies often have unintended results. Second, there is a wide range of ideological flexibility in the adoption of programs. Third, there can be serious international consequences to internal actions. Fourth, some policies can be very wasteful. Fifth, agricultural policies are intertwined with population and water issues. And finally, profound political tremors can be triggered by changes in policy.

Turkey

Turkey put itself on the path of modernization with the thoroughgoing westernizing revolution of Kemal Ataturk. Years of Ottoman neglect of agriculture except as a tax base were quickly reversed. At least four distinct periods stand out in Turkish agricultural history since the formation of the republic in 1923. First, during the years of Ataturk (1923–1938), the oppressive tax structure was reformed, and a host of infrastructure projects were developed. The second era began after the close of World War II. The government engaged in a considerable effort to improve storage and marketing facilities and to introduce mechanization. Up to 1960, agricultural output expanded tremendously. Wheat production nearly doubled between 1948 and 1953, allowing Turkey to become a net exporter of this grain for a short time.

A great deal of this expansion came about by extending the area under cultivation as opposed to increasing the yields per hectare. This resulted in two deleterious effects that slowed the agricultural growth rate after 1960, the third phase. First, because most of the new lands were marginal, they lost whatever productivity they had during each period of drought, as there was relatively little irrigation. Second, the methods used to expand the area under cultivation resulted in a loss of soil fertility and a greater runoff of water. The fourth phase has been characterized by an extensive series of irrigation projects made possible by the construction of dams, especially on the Euphrates. This has caused intense concern in Syria and Iraq, the other countries that depend heavily on the flow of Euphrates waters.

Egypt

The 1952 revolution in Egypt ushered in a substantial program of land reform and redistribution that proceeded by fits and starts for the next two decades. In 1952 about 1.2 percent of the largest holdings encompassed 45 percent of the agricultural land. By contrast, 72 percent of the smallest holdings accounted for 13 percent of the land, an average of about one feddan (1.038 acres) per holding. Because of population pressures and a lack of alternative employment, the rental rates charged by the mostly absentee owners of the large estates were high. The first lands to be expropriated were those of the royal family. These lands, plus the waqf lands in their possession, accounted for 5.5 percent of the total agricultural land. Land reforms also lowered the maximum feddans that an individual could hold, from 200 in 1952 to 100 in 1961 and finally to 50 in 1969.

At first, the larger landowning families simply split their holdings among various family members and avoided being severely affected. The law was gradually tightened, however, and by 1970 the government had redistributed 18.6 percent of all agricultural land. In 1981 the laws were modified to stimulate settlement on what otherwise was desert. Small holders were allowed to own up to 300 feddans, and agribusinesses could own up to 50,000 feddans. The record indicates that the large agribusinesses have been more successful than the small holders, partially because of their ability to move the creaky Egyptian civil service.

Syria

The process of land reform followed the same general pattern in Syria. Because of the extreme variability in land productivity, however, the redistribution was based on estimated incomes to be derived from the land; larger parcels were given to individuals on low-productivity land. As with many countries, the redistribution effort proved far more difficult than the promulgation of laws restricting maximum size. In Syria, as in Egypt, the class of large landholders was more tenacious than anticipated. The reforms quickened in pace only as the political power base of this group diminished. However, a new group of agriculturists-cum-capitalists took the place of the traditional landholding elite and complicated issues of government control.

Libya, Iraq, and Iran

In Libya and Iraq, large landholders were suddenly shut out of the political decision-making process, although the situation in each country was different. Libyan agricultural landholdings were of two polar types: a small number of large estates located on relatively good and well-irrigated land, mostly owned by Italian nationals, and vast stretches of marginal land, partially (about one-third in 1960) owned on a tribal basis. The 1969 overthrow of the monarchy led to the expropriation of the Italian farms in 1970. The Libyan agricultural reform methods fit the ideology of the "socialist" government and the agricultural situation. A mere redistribution of the poor lands would not accomplish much, if any gain in productivity. Likewise, the average yields of the large productive farms probably could not have been retained if the farms were split up. These large units were transformed into state farms. The redistribution of marginal lands was tied to an ambitious scheme to invest some of the country's considerable oil revenues to increase agricultural productivity; wells, roads, and marketing facilities were included in this effort. Attempts also have been made to discourage, if not eliminate, absentee ownership of arable land.

In Iraq, local sheikhs—generally better described as political dignitaries rather than religious leaders—were transformed into landholders in the twentieth century largely because the British attempted to transform the communal tribal ownership patterns into those of private ownership. The 1958 revolution left the sheiks without a political power base, and the carving up of their holdings was assured. State lands, the miri sirf, also provided a base for redistribution. But the state of Iraqi agriculture and the country's political instability led to highly uneven results for this potentially highly productive nation.

Most agricultural land in Iraq is dependent on irrigation to support even reasonable levels of productivity; declines in agricultural productivity occur when the central authority neglects its responsibilities in this area. The neglect lasted for more than 1,000 years. The relative political stability and petroleum-generated wealth of the 1970s and 1980s finally reversed the process. But the process stopped because of the ravages of war and the U.N.-imposed sanctions.

Large-scale land reform started in Iran in 1962 and without the impetus of a true revolution. The shah redistributed some royal lands in the 1950s, but the White Revolution, promulgated in January 1963, promised for the first time a set of sweeping changes throughout the economy, including substantial land reform (the "revolution" was called "white" because it was to be peaceful). Before the redistribution, absentee landlords controlled much of the fertile lands in Iran; the peasants generally had no tenancy rights. The landowners often owned huge tracts of land that encompassed many villages. To minimize evasion of the law, the legislation stated redistribution in terms of villages rather than area. Legislation in 1965 closed some loopholes in the law, transferred waqf land administration to the central government, and presented the landholders not affected by the 1962 legislation with five basic choices: (1) lease the land, (2) sell the land, (3) divide the land between themselves and the peasants on the basis of old sharecropping agreements, (4) form a cooperative with the peasants, or (5) purchase peasant rights to the land and continue farming. This wide range of choices reflected the triangle of tensions then present between landlords, peasants, and the shah. The shah needed to reduce the landowners' power, or at least give the appearance of doing so, but it was so great that an attempt at outright expropriation seemed inadvisable.

The results of this land reform can be analyzed fairly accurately by examining what happened in a particular village.[1] Before redistribution, about half the land in this village was in (public) waqf status, the other half being owned by a single individual. The peasants farming the waqf lands secured tenancy rights through the government. The landlord chose to split his property in half (the basis of the old sharecropping agreement), keeping, as might be expected, the most fertile land under his control. The peasants who worked this land were excluded from redistribution policies. Other similar results followed: The largest and most fertile parcels lying outside the new

domain of the landlord were worked by the family and friends of the village headman who until then had been the manager of the lands. On gaining property rights, almost half of these village elites rented their land to the headman and became absentee landlords themselves. Also, the custom of drawing lots every three to five years to ensure that particular peasants would not be permanently consigned to the least fertile land ended when title was assigned. This meant that some of the landed peasants were put in a permanently disadvantageous position.

It is difficult to assess the effects of these events on agricultural productivity. The peasants became increasingly stratified socially and economically, a new class of absentee landlords developed, and the de facto changes in power relationships with the central bureaucracy were different than stated. Especially important in this respect was the shearing away of clerical power in rural areas. Some of the goals of the program were achieved—many peasants gained ownership or secured tenancy rights to the land. But in a country plagued with low productivity in the best of times, the new sets of problems generated from the reforms did much to blunt the overall positive effect.

Issues of land reform also vexed the revolutionary government. There was widespread appeal for fundamental land reform, an appeal that had been given voice by prominent members of the new government and Aytollah Khomeini well before the revolution. But there was no clearly defined program. In the year after the fall of the shah, a confused picture emerged.

In some areas, villagers seized large estates and farmed them on a communal basis; in other seizures, estates were broken into private plots; and in some areas, disgruntled tribal leaders recaptured their feudal lord status, which had been stripped away by prerevolutionary reform. Because provincial courts and administrators gave contradictory rulings, the issue was brought to the Majlis for resolution. The attitude

[1]Craig, D. "The Impact of Land Reform on an Iranian Village," *Middle East Journal*, X(Spring, 1978):141–154.

of members of the Majlis toward private property varied considerably, and much haggling ensued. As more "progressive" members consolidated power, proposals were brought forth that severely restricted landowning. However, several prominent clergy gave opinions that indicated that the proposed legislation was at variance with Islamic principles. On another ideological level, arguments were made that raised questions about the power of Islamic jurists on this matter. Although legislation finally passed, numerous fundamental land-related issues remain unsettled.

AGRICULTURAL POLICIES

Most countries of the world prefer to be self-sufficient in agricultural production and most have made considerable efforts to achieve this goal. Most have failed. The countries of the Middle East are no exception. Although all of the Middle Eastern countries are unlikely to meet the goal of self-sufficiency in the foreseeable future, the region could make considerable strides in this direction.

Total agricultural output can be increased in two general ways: an increase in the yield per unit of existing agricultural land, and an increase in the number of units cultivated. The post–World War II record of the countries under consideration is mixed. Yields for the important foodstuffs grown in Egypt (wheat, rice, and barley) increased substantially and compare favorably on a worldwide basis. This was accomplished through labor-intensive cultivation and without much aid from the high technology of Western (and some Israeli) agriculture. The record of Iraq, although not as good as that of Egypt and suffering decades of war and sanctions, shows the same general trend. These are the two countries that have access to long stretches of major rivers. The record of the remaining countries, except for Israel, is mixed. Syria and Iran have shown increases in the yields of some crops and decreases in others. The yields of wheat have

decreased in Syria because marginal land has been brought under cultivation. Such poor yields, however, are not due to the chemical composition of the soil. Water is the scarce resource; its availability could change the situation markedly. Underground water deposits in Jordan, Libya, and Syria could call forth relatively high yields per unit if they could be brought into the production process at a reasonable cost. Another potential bright spot is that except for Israel, the gains so far have been made without heavy capital expenditures or a relatively heavy reliance on fertilizers or pesticides by individual farmers.

A Saudi experience illustrates that increased agricultural output can waste resources. In the early 1980s, the Saudi government decided that it could make the desert bloom—with wheat—through the application of a system of generous subsidies to farmers. Land, water, seeds, and fertilizers were provided well below cost. Within a few years Saudi Arabia had become an exporter of wheat. It also became painfully aware of the cost of this "success" when the exported wheat was sold at the world price of $3 a bushel. The cost of production was about $18 per bushel, meaning that the Saudis were using their resources to subsidize world wheat consumption. When the government announced that the system of subsidies had to stop, the wheat growers, who had invested on the assumption that the subsidies were to remain in place, voiced considerable opposition. Although the Saudi Arabian government was in the enviable position of being able to compensate the farmers to stop this wasteful use of resources, most countries are not so blessed.

It is difficult to project these production trends into the future because the ecological balance is particularly sensitive in the Middle East. The productivity gains have not resulted primarily from a wholesale transfer of Western technology, and they have not simply appeared as manna from heaven. The successful innovations have been those that have considered the particular needs of the area. Whether or not enough of these successful innovations will continue to occur is a highly problematic and important question. It is problematic because of our inability to identify the forces that lead to sustained innovation and growth. It is important because of the area's high rate of population growth and relative scarcity of water.

WATER

By 1990 it was apparent to most Middle East policymakers and analysts that water shortages were becoming more acute in most of the area. Some observers were predicting that the age of "oil wars" would be supplanted by "water wars." They may be correct; the looming water crisis is staggering.

Water is the scarcest resource in the Middle East. There are only a few significant rivers in the area. Egypt has the Nile. The Tigris and Euphrates start in mountainous Turkey and wind through Iraq; the Euphrates also cuts across Syria. The most fertile areas of the Middle East lie in the valleys of these great rivers and the Levant. Other agricultural areas generally must depend on rainfall.

The Nile is the lifeline of Egypt. At Aswan, the width of productive land is only a few hundred meters on each bank. The productive valley widens as one travels north, fanning out into the great Delta, north of Cairo. For thousands of years the annual flooding, occurring with great regularity, provided a natural replenishment of necessary soil nutrients and drainage. The Delta long was viewed as the breadbasket of the region and later as the source of cotton for English textile mills. Harnessing the great power of the Nile would give farmers a dependable source of water year round, increase the yields from a single planting, enhance the region's ability to double crop, and meet the nation's demand for electricity. The building of the massive Aswan Dam and the filling of Lake Nasser behind it were hailed as a project that would alter the face of Egypt. The financing was beyond the government's

ability, however. In the mid-1950s, the United States negotiated with Egypt to provide financing and technical assistance to the then young government headed by Gamal Abdel Nasser. The Egyptian government was groping for a positive course; it was trying to end the corrupt and inefficient rule of the royal family that was overthrown in 1952. As part of the move toward a nonaligned status, and because it needed to be ready for war with Israel, the Egyptian government shopped in the world arms market for military goods. Rebuffed by the United States, it signed an arms agreement with Czechoslovakia in 1955. This prompted the United States to withdraw its support for the Aswan Dam project and implicitly invited Soviet sponsorship and a consequent ascendancy of Soviet influence in Egypt. Consonant with its history, Egypt became a focal point for world politics. This time, however, Egyptian nationalism provided a check on the benefits to be gained by world powers.

The building of the Aswan Dam necessitated a massive movement of people from villages located where Lake Nasser would form. The Nubian villagers, well out of the mainstream of modernizing influences and culturally more akin to the citizens of Khartoum to the south than the citizens of Cairo, were uprooted in a wholesale fashion and relocated in parts of existing towns or in newly formed villages. Because the rhythm of the river was the heartbeat of the local culture and economy, the relocation amounted to radical surgery. These people were forced to rely on the central government much more than previously. They had to abide by new rules, as compensation was calculated, rents and land rights were established, and a new social order was set in place.

The dam had different consequences for the fellahin to the north because the river level was now constant. The water table began to rise, and as it did so, the soil became saturated with salt. By the mid-1970s, the centuries-old high productivity of certain parts of the Delta had decreased dramatically. The decrease was especially marked in cotton production; cotton is particularly sensitive to the level of salinity in the soil. Keeping the Delta region productive by lowering the water table required two basic strategies: control over water use and improved drainage. Each of these efforts required the government to impose regulations and spend considerable sums of money. The government had to control the operation tightly because individual economic incentives worked against actions that corrected the problem. Ironically, the increased availability of water led to tighter water controls.

Although the government controls the amount of water flowing into many irrigated areas, it cannot easily control how it is shared, a difficulty that has caused hostility between neighboring farmers. The allocation of water for individual farm use was complicated by the introduction of machine-driven pumps and by the land reforms that significantly reduced average farm acreage and increased the number of farm units to be controlled. The provision of adequate drainage presents similar difficulties. Substantial capital expenditures are needed for drainage, but an individual landholder would not significantly improve productivity acting alone. Likewise, if all of the farmer's neighbors spend their precious capital for adequate drainage, the lone party who resists would share in the benefits as the water table recedes. The government must finance and control drainage in a systematic fashion.

The boon to agricultural productivity, which was the *raison d'être* of the Aswan Dam, has been offset by important negative side effects that have strained the scarce financial and administrative resources of the government. Some estimates placed the cost of the delta-wide drainage expenditures as greater than the cost of the dam. Many of these side effects were anticipated before the building of the dam. However, the need to feed a quickly growing population and provide adequate electricity was thought to be more important.

The Tigris and Euphrates rivers originate in the Armenian highlands of Turkey, are fed by melting snow, and flow into the Persian Gulf. But the rivers are dissimilar in some important ways and present different kinds of opportunities and problems. The Euphrates cuts across Syria and Iraq on its journey. It has only a few major tributaries and is slow moving and has a regular flow. The Tigris passes directly from Turkey into Iraq and has many tributaries. It is liable to heavy flooding, has a swift current, and carries a large volume of water. Irrigation from the Tigris is complicated by the timing of the floods and the irregular level of the river. Flooding usually occurs in the spring, in about the middle of the growing season for most crops (except rice and barley). The land cannot simply be inundated as in Egypt. A system of catchment areas must be employed so that the water can be released at the appropriate times. Provision has to be made for adequate drainage to prevent excess soil salinity.

These problems were faced 1,000 years ago by the Abbasid caliphate. They exploited the fact that the Euphrates, a western neighbor of the Tigris around Baghdad, has a higher elevation than the Tigris. A canal system was built between the two rivers that allowed for catchment, irrigation, and drainage. Regular maintenance was required because the Euphrates carried a substantial amount of silt. If the Tigris flooded, a considerable additional effort was needed to clear the irrigation system. Relatively large and continuous infusions of capital were necessary to keep the system running. Because the irrigated lands were owned by many different parties, and the benefits of maintenance and repair were spread unevenly among them, the absence of a well-defined and enforced set of rules discouraged private investment in the canal system. An effective and stable government was needed to maintain agricultural productivity on the irrigated lands. When the Abbasids passed their zenith, the system fell into decay for a millennium.

This situation contrasts markedly with that of Egypt. Government actions maintaining adequate drainage have affected agricultural productivity in Egypt, but short-term neglect did not lead to a total failure of the system—at least not until the Aswan Dam was built.

The Euphrates cuts across Syria and Iraq before emptying into the Gulf. The construction of dams in Turkey, especially the massive Great Anatolia Project (GAP), caused considerable anxiety in Syria and Iraq. Although officials from the three countries have held regular meetings on the principles and details of water sharing, considerable tension remains. The problem is complicated further by the fact that a large percentage of the farmers of Syria and Iraq who are heavy Euphrates water users have been troublesome to the central government in the best of times. So when the Syrians cut back on downstream flows to fill the lake behind their huge dam, it was Shia farmers of southern Iraq who suffered.

Israeli water demands may serve as a significant roadblock to any proposed peace settlement. Israel garners a large percentage of its water from the territories occupied since the 1967 war. Especially relevant is Israeli control of the Golan, an area generally described by Israel as a military stronghold necessary to avert attacks from Syria. Although this argument does not hold much water, the Golan does. The Israelis are taking water from this source (largely via the Sea of Galilee) securing a sizable percentage of its national water needs (through the National Water Carrier). South of the lake, the Jordan River has been reduced to a small polluted stream; this causes obvious water shortage problems for Jordan. The Israeli presence in southern Lebanon had a water security dimension; the Litani River is located there and flows largely unimpeded to the sea. Israel also pumps water from the (largely rain fed) aquifers in the West Bank for use of settlers there and for general Israeli water use. By the early 1990s, they were pumping water out at an unsustainable rate; the water table was so low that substantial saltwater infiltration became a problem. Substantial Soviet Jewish immigration

heightened the problem. Rainfall helps ease the problem, but there is a significant drought in this region every four years or so. One cannot expect Israel to leave the West Bank without ironclad assurances of a secure water supply. Desalination plants are one potential answer, but these plants are very expensive.

Saudi Arabia faces its own water problems. First, there was great fear during the worst days of the 1991 war against Iraq that the desalination plants in the Gulf would become clogged with millions of barrels of petroleum that were floating down from Kuwait. That crisis was averted. The ecology of the Gulf is very fragile; the massive amount of petroleum transported through it poses a continual danger. Because the Gulf is an international waterway, this points to the need for international agreements on the protection of these waters. Second, several studies have indicated that the Saudis are rapidly depleting their (nonrenewable) aquifers in the central regions of the country.

Comprehensive water management programs should be employed, and research programs, such as the United Nations–affiliated International Center for Agricultural Research in the Semi-Arid Areas, should be funded adequately, especially because agriculture accounts for more than three-quarters of the annual water consumption in most areas. The research aim is to increase agricultural yields without an increase in water usage.

When water sources become overburdened in the face of increasingly densely packed populations, human disease flourishes (e.g., schistosomiases, malaria), property rights need to be redefined, the role of government water policies becomes critical, and, more generally, social conflicts increase in number and severity. As it is, rivers and (renewable) underground sources account for about half of the water in the entire region. This translates into severe water shortages in many areas of the Middle East. With the prospect of increased populations, annoying shortages will become crises in the near future.

POPULATION

Although the population of the Middle East has been increasing for at least a century, the post–World War II growth rate acceleration and subsequent decline is of particular interest. It is one of the ironies of history that local, national, and international efforts to prolong life have led, albeit indirectly, to more suffering. Increasing the population base without increasing the food supply results in less food per person. The average annual rates of population increase in the Middle East ranged from 2 to 3 percent in the last couple of decades of the last century; at these rates, the population doubles every quarter century. By 2010 the rate was less than 2 percent.

Rates of population increase are expected to decline more during the coming decade. This deserves some explanation. During the last quarter of the twentieth century, infant mortality decreased and the average age of death increased substantially, as indicated in Table 11.3. These changes will not be repeated during the next quarter century; there is not the same "room" to lower infant mortality or increase the average age of death. The major sources of population growth during the last three decades were absent; rates of population increase declined. Also, during the last decade of the twentieth century, fertility rates unexpectedly declined worldwide, including the Arab world. However, Arab countries still had higher fertility rates than most other areas of the world.

Despite the decrease in fertility rates, the mathematics of demography means that populations will continue to increase rapidly in the next couple of decades. An enormous number of young people will continue to put pressure on the beleaguered educational systems. Large numbers of young people will enter the workforce in economies that have not been creating jobs. This could be a potent force causing social discontent.

Migration

A significant portion of the population increases of a few countries have come about through

Table 11.3 Population and Fertility, 2008				
Country	Pop Growth Rate	Life Exp. at Birth	Pop Age 0–14 % Total	Fertility Rate per Woman
Bahrain	2.1	76	26.7	2.27
Egypt	1.8	70	32.5	2.86
Iran	1.3	71	24.4	1.81
Iraq	2.5	68	41.4	4.05
Israel	1.8	81	27.8	2.96
Jordan	3.2	73	35.1	3.49
Kuwait	2.4	78	23.4	2.17
Lebanon	0.7	72	25.8	1.85
Oman	2.1	76	32	3.05
Saudi Arabia	2	73	32.9	3.12
Sudan	2.2	58	39.5	4.17
Syria	2.5	74	35.3	3.25
Turkey	1.2	72	27.2	2.11
U.A.E	2.7	78	19.2	1.94
Yemen	2.9	63	44.2	5.22

Source: World Bank. World Development Indicators.

massive movements of people rather than natural increases in the indigenous population. The exodus of Palestinians in 1948 markedly altered conditions in Israel and Jordan. The event has dominated much of what has happened in Jordan since independence. At independence Jordan was an extremely poor country and had few natural resources. The flood of Palestinians into Jordan after the formation of Israel more than tripled the population. Already impoverished, Jordan faced seemingly insurmountable problems because most of the refugees were destitute. The addition of the West Bank to Jordanian "territory" added only 7 percent to the total land area but 30 percent to the total of arable land. However, these benefits did not come close to compensating for the massive influx of humanity.

During the 1950s, almost all expert opinion was pessimistic on the ability of the Jordanian economy to function in a reasonably coherent and growth-inducing fashion. Throughout that period, Jordan received a substantial amount of international aid. Although it remained a poor country, during the 1960s signs of positive movement started to appear. Many Palestinian refugees were highly skilled and experienced in commerce and industry. This "imported" skilled labor, along with considerable Jordanian efforts to improve education, especially at the postsecondary level, began to increase the country's productivity.

The 1967 Israeli occupation of the West Bank and the success of OPEC since 1973 complicated Jordan's problems. The occupation meant that a good portion of Jordan's arable land was lost, and that a new wave of refugees entered the country, putting an even greater strain on the system.

The mobilization of PLO forces in Jordan and the consequent pressure that these forces put on Israel, coupled with the Israeli policy of retaliation, led to King Hussein's decision to have Jordanian troops do battle against the armed Palestinians in September 1970. This decision brought home in stark and tragic relief the fact that many of the residents of Jordan held another national allegiance. The East Bank, an area showing progress amid the abject poverty of the refugee camps, was not fully under the control of the Jordanian government.

The success of OPEC signaled another wave of population movement as Jordanians rushed to fill positions in petroleum-rich countries. From 1975 forward, about 40 percent of the Jordanian workforce (a large percentage being Palestinian) were abroad. Remittances from these workers assumed staggering proportions by 1981, measured as a percentage of GNP (27.8%), imports (39%), or exports (168.2%). There are some difficulties associated with this influx of foreign exchange. One is the obvious heavy dependence of the Jordanian economy on the continued flow of remittances. Also, a major asset of Jordan, human capital, was depleted to the point that skilled positions within Jordan were understaffed. It is probable that several other labor-exporting countries faced selective labor shortages because of migration; the Egyptian construction industry seems to have suffered substantially. Jordan fell on hard times in the last years of the 1980s. Remittances (private and official) decreased, the current account deficit increased, and international financial reserves were depleted. In addition, in 1991, Jordan had to accommodate several hundred thousand Palestinians fleeing Kuwait (and generally without their hard-currency savings) and had Gulf aid dry up. In the five years after the invasion of Iraq, the population of Amman increased by about 40 percent as a result of an influx of Iraqis fleeing the war. Obviously, this created significant economic and social tensions. Syria received over a million Iraqi refugees, straining the Syrian budget and adding to inflationary pressures (especially in rental housing).

The small-population, petroleum-producing countries have been the major importers of skilled labor. They include Saudi Arabia, Bahrain, Kuwait, Libya, Qatar, and the U.A.E. Iraq also imported labor during the 1980s during their war with Iran. Egypt, Yemen, and Jordan were the major suppliers from the area. Indigenous entrants to the workforce in the rich countries often have been absorbed in government service as a matter of policy rather than need. Although this policy tends to keep measured unemployment lower than otherwise and serves to pacify potentially disgruntled members of the workforce, it also results in a considerable amount of disguised unemployment because the measured productivity of these workers is often nil. Apparently, notions of economic efficiency have taken a back seat to political and social issues.

The extent of labor migration has been dramatic. In 1975 about one-quarter of the population of these countries were migrants; by 1985 it was close to 40 percent. Twenty-five years later it remained at that level. Nationals are a minority in most Gulf countries. Because most of the migrants do not bring their families, the percentage of foreigners in the workforce is more dramatic. This situation significantly influences foreign and domestic policies. In Kuwait, about one-quarter of the expatriates (one in every five workers) were classified as coming from Jordan, a high percentage of them being Palestinians. The government of Kuwait found itself in a delicate position whenever Arab states had to stand up and be counted on Palestinian issues. The generally conservative government had to guard against a reaction from the Palestinian expatriates if it took the wrong stance.

The most dramatic change in the composition of the migrant labor force was the increase in the number of Asians—mainly Indians, Pakistanis, and Koreans—working in the Gulf States in the 1970s and 1980s. There are several complementary reasons why the increased demand for labor was not met exclusively by Arabs. First, the major suppliers already had substantial percentages of their workforce abroad. Second, skilled and semiskilled workers were in particularly short supply in the Arab

supplier nations. Third, the Asian labor market was well organized, Asian labor was relatively cheap, and the labor force was sometimes tied to construction projects awarded to Asian firms. Fourth, Asian workers tended to be less politically troublesome. By 1985, the percentage of total migrants to Middle Eastern labor-importing countries who came from India (8.6 percent), Pakistan (13.1 percent), and Southeast Asia (10.9 percent) was substantial. About 150,000 of the migrants were Korean. In total, about one-half of the migrants were not Arab.

The 1991 war against Iraq displaced millions of people. Several hundred thousand Kurds fled to Turkey, and more than a million went to Iran to escape Iraqi forces attempting to reestablish control after the war. Tens of thousands of Shia in the south fled either to Iraq or to the fabled Iraqi marshlands after their postwar resistance was crushed. Before the war, Iraq had more than one million Egyptian guest workers—all of these, and others, were expelled. Between 350,000 and 400,000 Palestinians were forced out of Kuwait, and several hundred thousand Yemeni guest workers had to leave Saudi Arabia after their government tilted toward Iraq.

The perceived consequences of having "too many" foreigners in a country was faced squarely by Saudi Arabia a decade before the 1991 war; they slowed the implementation of their development plans partially because of a fear that the cultural influences of the foreigners would erode important traditional Saudi values. The U.A.E. (especially Dubai and Abu Dhabi) provides a living illustration of Saudi concerns; the overwhelming majority of the population is foreign. It is clear to the most casual observer that much of traditional emirate culture is being swept away by a tidal wave of international commerce.

Kuwait decided to lower the foreign share of the population in a different fashion than Saudi Arabia. It had a preinvasion population of about 2.2 million; only 600,000 were Kuwaiti citizens. After the war with Iraq, they decided to stabilize the population at 1.1 million—the notion being that they needed to be a majority in their own country. Because the infrastructure of Kuwait needed more than 1.1 million people to function smoothly, the goal had to be modified. Almost all Palestinians were forced to leave, however, and many other "guest" workers, mainly from Asia, were restricted in number. The government also changed the terms of (nonprofessional) guest worker employment. No longer were they allowed to bring their families with them, and the work permits were to expire after three years, more or less assuring that the foreign population would not develop roots in the country, as in the U.A.E. However, by 2002 the population of Kuwait had climbed back to 2.3 million, with foreigners accounting for about the same percentage of the population as before the war and about 80 percent of the workforce. Expatriates accounted for more than one-half of the workforce in every Gulf State, ranging from about 55 percent in Saudi Arabia to 90 percent in Qatar.

Israel had a different sort of population influx during the last decades of the twentieth century: Jews emigrating from the former Soviet Union. Israel absorbed about 350,000 people from the beginning of the influx in the late 1980s through 1991, and more than that number waited—although limits of Israeli absorptive capacity and the breakup of the U.S.S.R. stemmed the flow. This potential massive influx, a 20 percent addition to the population, was greeted with much fanfare in Israel; after all, the *raison d'être* of the state was the ingathering of world Jewry. The timing also seemed propitious: The Israeli psyche was in a moral quandary—large numbers of its citizens believed that the continued occupation of the territories was tragically misguided. The influx also eased the fears of some Israelis who thought that the higher Arab birthrate was leading to some future point where the Jews would be a minority in the Jewish state. The Israeli government worked hard to assure that Jews could leave the Soviet Union and that Israel was the only haven.

The influx also carried significant problems. The immigrants had to be housed, fed, and otherwise assimilated into the society. The government budget was not up to the task, so they asked the U.S. government to guarantee $10 billion in loans they had to raise. The United States balked—mainly because Israel was at the same time quickening the settlement of Jews in the occupied territories, a policy against international law. Many of the Soviet Jews took over jobs otherwise given to Palestinians, worsening the economic condition of these people. Over time, they became a significant force in Israeli political life. During the last half of the 1990s, Israel thought it proper to limit the number of work permits issued to Palestinians in the West Bank and Gaza. The shortfall in the (largely) unskilled labor force was made up by allowing Asian migrants to come to Israel for relatively short-term stays. The second Intifadah brought a new group of immigrants to Israel—mostly from Eastern Europe, Romania, Philippines, and Thailand—as the restrictions on Palestinian labor tightened. By 2002, migrants constituted almost 10 percent of the workforce.

Urbanization

There are different sources and consequences of population problems—the overarching problem being one of resource imbalances. Population increases and rapid urbanization are related in an integral fashion to many of the cultural, economic, political, and social problems many Middle Eastern nations are struggling with. It is politically dangerous to attack the population issue squarely, however; it is the rare politician who opts to champion a policy of population control. After all, the issue strikes at the core of family life. More often, governments simply do not enter public discussion of the issue. Some governments, notably Iraq, provided explicit economic incentives and public applause to people with large families. By the late 1990s, Iran had established a formidable family planning program.

Egypt provides a classic and sad case of an "overpopulated" country. Its population doubled in less than 30 years, standing at about 80 million in 2010. Virtually all of the increase is attributable to natural increases. Because almost all of the arable land in Egypt is along the Nile River and Delta, this narrow strip is one of the most densely populated areas in the world. Because the amount of arable land, although increasing through irrigation, is close to being constant, there has been ever-increasing pressure on the land to produce more. The additional labor could do little to add to production, however, because the methods employed already were highly labor intensive. This combination of population increases and a constant amount of land to be worked is close to fitting the Malthusian dilemma of population increases resulting in permanent subsistence living. Egypt has avoided taking the dreary course predicted by Malthus through the application of modest technological advances, a reorganization of landholding patterns, greater availability of water from the Aswan Dam, and the shifting of crops from cotton to food. The race between productivity and population has been close. A sanguine outcome is not assured partially because the continuing high rate of population increase has led to urban sprawl that is covering prime agricultural land. Land reclamation has proved to be difficult, and water shortages have been felt.

Cairo holds about 20 percent of the population of Egypt. Although some of the increase in the past half-century can be attributed to flight from the war-torn cities of the Suez Canal area, most of it has been due to people leaving the farms. In the cities, the rural people have not been assimilated easily or quickly. They often form pockets of essentially rural culture and lifestyles that are resistant to change. The Middle Eastern urban populations in 2000 included four cities exceeding 10 million: Cairo (13 million), Tehran (11 million), Istanbul (11 million), and Baghdad (11 million).

By 2010, the population of Riyadh was close to 6 million, about half of them being foreigners. There are obvious social concerns attendant to having such a large percentage of the population of the city being foreigners. But there are other problems associated with rapid urban growth; the provision of adequate sanitation, roads, power, and other infrastructure concerns are important. The relatively large numbers of young Saudis who are mobile within the country present another set of problems. For example, in 2006, Riyadh could house the elderly who did not have family to care for them with the provision of less than 50 beds; traditionally, Saudi children took in their elders. The mobility within the country means that the number of elderly who will need government assistance will balloon in the near future.

The movement of people from rural to urban settings upsets traditional patterns, but it is unclear whether these changes should be considered beneficial or dysfunctional. Generally rural migrants do not have skills useful in the urban environment. There is considerable worldwide evidence that at least for the first several years in an urban setting, individuals are apt to be alienated from the urban society and have considerable difficulties adapting to the regimen of factory life if they are lucky enough to land a job in the first place. Tardiness, absenteeism, and quit rates generally are high. The factory seems to be a particularly difficult place to adjust to. At the same time, evidence (from areas other than the Middle East) indicates that the factory is the most effective source from which to accumulate that set of attitudes that are considered "modern." A rapid increase in the population of major cities also can lead to the breakdown of city services. Transportation becomes a nightmare as thousands of vehicles are jammed into what is essentially a pre–twentieth century road network; electrical supply capacity is strained; and telephone systems become virtually unworkable. However, it is easy to generate arguments to indicate that if the migrants stayed in a rural setting per capita income and possibly agricultural production would decrease. Besides having one less mouth to feed, the farmer often receives remittances from the family member in the city; this can finance technical change. Because government actions, fiscal and otherwise, have pronounced effects on the flow of labor to urban areas, one also must consider how those flows would change when particular measures are being considered. Would an attempt to improve urban conditions merely lead to an increased flow into the cities and thwart the original effort and disrupt agricultural planning? A related urban bias problem is that usually one city is favored. Damascus garners many more resources than Aleppo, but the resource base of the country is closer to Aleppo than Damascus.

Employment

Most countries profess full employment as a primary goal. A brief account of a government's problems in attempting to meet this goal may give the reader a sense of the complexity of designing a coherent employment scheme. The first job is to figure out what percentage of the population is to be counted as part of the labor force. Dependency ratios are good shorthand indicators of the issue. A dependency ratio is the ratio of people defined as being out of the labor force (younger than age 15 and older than age 65), people dependent on others to produce goods and services (the numerator), to people of working force age (ages 15 to 65, the denominator). The dependency ratio for most high-income Western countries is about 0.5. This means roughly that two workers are available to help "support" one person not in the labor force. In the Middle East, the ratio approached 1. The very high ratios of the earlier period are due to the rapid increase in population as a result of the decrease in infant mortality rates and increase in the average age of death. These are not expected to change as much in the coming decades, but as noted

earlier, female fertility rates have decreased, decreasing the dependency ratio (relatively fewer children to support).

Defining potential members of the labor force involves questions concerning the role of women and the minimum acceptable age of entry into the labor force—issues that are not easily resolved. The task of the planner and analyst of the labor force is complicated further by the fact that individuals are not interchangeable parts—the illiterate construction worker cannot be placed in a job for a materials engineer. An economy may have labor shortages in some areas and surpluses in others. Correcting the perceived imbalances is not an easy task, especially considering that many of the high-skill positions demand relatively advanced formal education. It is unclear to what extent the goal should be that of universal primary education, the strengthening of the secondary school environment, or expanded opportunities for higher education. Several governments adopted policies that virtually guaranteed employment to indigenous workers of a certain level of educational attainment. These policies are not limited to petroleum-rich states. For many years Egypt guaranteed government employment to all college graduates. The combination of limited employment opportunities and heavy government subsidization of university education resulted in a bloated bureaucracy. Studies, including one commissioned by the government, indicated that in Cairo alone about one-quarter of a million government employees had no function except to receive their salary. Although this policy lowers the measured level of unemployment, there are gross inefficiencies. Throughout the region, public-sector employment is high relative to world averages.

When education is provided and employment opportunities are lacking, bitterness and social unrest can result. Palestinian earnings and unemployment in the West Bank and Gaza changed markedly after the 1980s. Before 1972, there were no institutions in the area that granted postsecondary school degrees. By 1986, there were 20 (funded largely by outside sources). The flood of Palestinians with higher education resulted in a large decrease in the wage difference between skilled and unskilled labor; that is, the rate of return to education decreased dramatically. Also, unemployment among the more highly educated increased significantly. One reason for this is the remarkable increase in supply. Another reason was due to living in conditions of occupation. Israeli policies often acted to limit employment potential.

Youth unemployment is high in all of the countries, including Israel. Continued long stretches of unemployment lead to frustration and bitterness. It forms a fertile ground for recruitment into organizations opposed to the current order. As a whole, youth unemployment is about 25 percent with more than two million new entrants expected each year.

The workforce participation rate of women in the Middle East is much lower than that of men. It is much lower than most other areas of the world. In short, Middle Eastern growth is lower than it otherwise would be because of the low female participation rate. One could argue that placing the productive power of women in the labor force runs against long-standing cultural norms. However, it cannot be denied that the disparity has enormous consequences. The rates of increase in female literacy and average number of years of schooling relative to men were substantial during the last several decades (see Table 11.4). This is likely to have a positive impact on health and productivity even if women continue to be consigned to household chores. An overwhelming amount of evidence collected worldwide indicates that when women are literate, infant mortality, low birth weights, wasting, and child stunting all decrease. More generally, the breathless pace of social and economic change in the Middle East in the past several decades has led to substantial change in the role of women and substantial confusion with respect to what could and ought to follow.

It seems that many Saudi women now use the Internet not only to shop but also to run businesses. Without this technological change, Saudi restrictions on the activity of women in public places all but ruled out significant business ventures of women. It should be noted that Saudi females are gaining more civil space. For example, prominent members of the Jiddah Chamber of Commerce are females.

Most observers would agree that there are significant labor problems in the agricultural sector of most less-developed countries. Typically, however, one does not find much open unemployment in agriculture; rather, the problem is one of underemployment. *Underemployment* is described as a situation in which at least some of the labor force is not working to full capacity. The usual implication is that these "surplus" workers could be freed from agricultural work with little or no decrease in output. But this conclusion is not the correct one and is, in any case, too simplistic. There is a tremendous seasonal fluctuation in the demand for agricultural labor in most of the Middle East. Labor must be available on a standby basis to perform essential tasks. Another qualification is that the labor force in agriculture is not homogeneous; custom dictates that some tasks are to be performed by men and others by women and children. Because the household (extended or nuclear) is the basis of most small farms in the Middle East, it becomes difficult to sort out the work patterns of the various types of labor. Generally, it seems that the cycle of seasonal work for men, although substantial, is less pronounced than that for women and children.

Equity considerations and efficiency also may clash when rural land use and labor deployment policies are being considered. It seems that large plots require less seasonal labor than small plots. Although the reasons for this tend to be specific to the area under study, generally we can assume that the cultivator of the larger plot has greater access to capital inputs (e.g., chemical fertilizers, pesticides, tractors). A

Table 11.4 Literacy and Gender

Country	Total % Age 15 or More	Female % Ages 15–24	Male % Ages 15–24	Progression to Secondary School	
				Females	**Males**
				Percent	
BAHRAIN	90.8	99.7	99.8	97.9	94.7
EGYPT	66.4	81.8	87.9	NA	NA
IRAN	82.3	96.1	97.1	73.7	83.9
IRAQ	77.6	80.2	84.5	NA	NA
ISRAEL	NA	NA	NA	NA	NA
JORDAN	92.2	98.9	99	97.5	97.9
KUWAIT	94.5	98.5	98.4	99.5	100
LEBANON	89.6	99.1	98.4	89	83.2
OMAN	86.7	97.6	97.6	97	97
SAUDI ARABIA	85.5	96.2	98.4	96.5	91.9
SUDAN	69.3	81.7	88.6	98	90.3
SYRIA	83.6	92.5	95.6	96.2	94.9
TURKEY	88.7	94.3	98.6	NA	NA
U.A.E	90	97	93.6	98.5	98.3
YEMEN	60.9	70	95.1	NA	NA

Progression to secondary school refers to the percentage of students in the first year of secondary school who were enrolled in the last year of primary school.

Source: World Bank. World Development Indicators.

policy of creating larger plots would free underemployed labor and make it available for other productive uses. There are several conflicts involved in this approach, however; a move toward larger plots is not accomplished easily. Considerations of equity have led many countries to legislate land reform programs designed to result in smaller-sized holdings. If seasonal laborers could be released from the land, one must determine where they would be employed. Industrial growth on a substantial scale is needed to absorb this labor, and that growth has not been forthcoming in most of the countries under consideration. Also, because women and children are most apt to be seasonal workers, it presumably would be they who would be freed for alternative employment. There would be considerable resistance to any such move.

Another problem in evaluating the workforce is that urban unemployment is open and obvious as contrasted to that in the agricultural sector. The planner may begin with a bias and develop plans that commit more resources to urban areas than are warranted by strict economic criteria. This tendency is buttressed because of the politically volatile nature of the urban population and because most notions of modernity, both naive and sophisticated, are linked to industrialization, and industry is linked to urbanization.

INDUSTRY

Because of OPEC's success, industry in the Middle East has grown dramatically. There are several prerequisites for large-scale, sustained industrial growth. Systems of communication, power, transportation, and education are needed if a modern industrial structure is to emerge and prosper. The history of all of the industrialized countries of the world indicates that this process takes a long time, that it generally proceeds by fits and starts, and that "economic miracles" have their roots in earlier centuries, not decades. Because of OPEC, several oil-rich economies are being transformed at an unprecedented rate.

Until the spectacular increase in the price of petroleum, Egypt, Turkey, and Iran were the focus of most speculation about the course of industrialization in the Middle East. They have large populations, providing the potential for domestic markets, and a longer history of significant industrial activity than the other countries of the region. Industrialization in Egypt received its first substantial impetus under Muhammad Ali in the 1820s. This ambitious attempt ground to a halt after a couple of decades and was largely moribund until the 1920s, when Egypt received a measure of independence. Industrialization in Egypt moved slowly for the next 30 years; it finally began to receive close attention in the 1950s under Nasser. The 1960s in Egypt saw the large-scale nationalization (and weak industrial performance) of major industries; during the post-Nasser period, there was a selective encouragement of private enterprise. A series of reforms during the 1980s and 1990s encouraged foreigners to invest in Egyptian manufacturing. Direct foreign investment in Egypt increased from $400 million in 1995 to more than $1.2 billion in 1997; about one-half was in manufacturing and 30 percent in banking. Foreign investors in manufacturing were not solely responding to liberalizing economic policies; they also began to sense that the reforms had "staying power," and that there was a commitment to strengthen the institutional framework that supports private enterprise.

Iran began to industrialize more than a century later than Egypt. The years between World War II and 1960 were spent laying a foundation on which industrialization could occur. Fueled by petroleum revenues, the growth process accelerated. By the mid-1970s, per capita income in Iran was about five times that of Egypt, up from less than double in 1960. In any discussion of the future of industrialization in the two countries, most observers favored Iran. Petroleum sales provided the money to purchase capital goods and to train a "modern" labor force quickly. (In 1978 one out of every nine international students studying in the United States was Iranian.) The Iranian revolution and the war with Iraq (1980 to 1989) seriously disrupted economic activity in Iran, however, and made the predictions of sustained industrial growth questionable. The decade of the 1990s provided some breathing space for the leaders of the government to sort through economic policies, including significant overtures to rejoin the international economic community fully. But there was serious opposition, and with the revolution more than two decades old, Iran remained tentative, and the United States continued to press, albeit less forcefully than earlier, for continued restrictions on trade and investment in Iran. By 2006, the new Iranian leadership fully rejected Western overtures, especially with the stated intention to resume the nuclear program.

Lebanon and Kuwait provide another set of contrasts. Lebanon has a long history of commercial and industrial development. Its relatively mature economy, its geographic position, and its tradition as the financial hub of the Middle East allowed some impressive industrial growth during the 1960s and the first half of the 1970s. Because most of the industrial establishments were centered in and around Beirut, however, the devastation of that city beginning in 1976 halted Lebanon's industrial and financial activity. It was not until the mid-1990s that sustained significant investment in Beirut resumed. Instability during the period from 2000 to 2010 led to substantial decreases in investment. Kuwait, long an earner of substantial amounts of foreign exchange through petroleum sales, attempted to diversify its industry and not rely exclusively on petroleum-related production. The Iraqi invasion of 1991 put that process on hold. Most of the oil-producing Gulf States sought economic diversification, especially after petroleum prices took a long downward slide during most of the 1990s. The search to diversify continued with high petroleum prices; petroleum, after all, is a nonrenewable resource.

Bahrain has a different set of problems. The Shia of Bahrain constitute most of the population but are in a disadvantageous economic and social position. Because many of the Bahraini Shia have close cultural and ethnic ties to Iran, the Sunni leadership has evinced considerable concern. But Bahrain does not produce enough petroleum to finance large-scale, employment-generating industry. Bahrain has been in the forefront of Gulf Cooperation Council members calling for closer economic cooperation in ways that would ameliorate unemployment.

When petroleum prices rose dramatically during the first decade of the new century, Saudi Arabia announced plans to build six large cities from scratch. In each case, the primary economic function was designed to diversify the economy.

PETROLEUM

Oil has been called black gold—and for good reason. Petroleum has been the focus of many a country's national and international affairs during the twentieth century. Petroleum has been so important to everyday life that this has been dubbed the Age of Hydrocarbon Man.

The vital need to secure adequate supplies of petroleum has been complicated by the fact that it has been exceedingly difficult to predict when supplies will run dry or be multiplied by the development of a new field. It is only with mild hyperbole that European control of Middle Eastern petroleum at the onset of World War I prompted Britain's Lord Curzon to remark that "the Allies floated to victory on a wave of oil." About a half a century later, some were predicting that the rise in petroleum prices would create a new Arab Golden Age. The clearest recent example of the worldwide importance of steady petroleum supplies is shown by the Western response to Iraq's 1991 invasion of Kuwait. Petroleum is the dominant economic influence in the Middle East, and Middle Eastern petroleum is vital to the economies of the world. Finally, petroleum has been responsible for one of the most rapid transfers of wealth in world history—a true revolution.

Early Years

The half-century preceding World War I was a time of rapid change in the Middle East. The Ottoman Empire was in disarray and decaying despite sporadic bursts of energy and direction. Turkey and Egypt accumulated heavy public debts; one-third of Turkey's government expenditures and one-half of Egypt's were applied to debt servicing. Turkey was declared bankrupt in 1875, and Egypt was declared bankrupt in 1876. European interests in the area were becoming more pervasive and were setting the stage for twentieth-century events.

By the turn of the twentieth century, most major investments in the Middle East were European in origin and ownership. European domination did not begin with these investments. Western influence was substantial well before Napoleon occupied Egypt in 1798, as commerce between the two areas grew. European investments in dams, canals, railroads, and electrical systems built up gradually as the Middle East became more secure. However, the surge of nationalism in the Middle East around the beginning of the twentieth century forced Europeans to relinquish direct control of some of their investments.

In the two centuries preceding the opening of the Suez Canal, Britain gained control of the Persian Gulf through a series of military maneuvers and treaties with local sheikhs. The route from India through the Persian Gulf, up through Basra and Baghdad, and then to Mediterranean ports provided a vital communications link for the empire until the opening of the Suez Canal. The area was again central to British interests in the 1890s because Britain wished to thwart German influences and because of the discovery of substantial amounts of petroleum in Iran.

After securing control of the Suez Canal, the British had been content to control commerce on the Persian Gulf and not travel inland, but the discovery of a large petroleum field in Iran in 1907 changed their intentions. The industrial revolution, although first fueled by coal, was becoming increasingly dependent on oil and other petroleum products. Petroleum products also were becoming increasingly valuable for military uses. Large consumers sought a steady and dependable supply. By 1900 the United States and Russia produced 90 percent of the world's petroleum. When the Iranian field east of Abadan was discovered, the British moved to ensure their control over the area. Although the British had concessions for Iranian petroleum in 1872 (and then in 1889 and 1901), the rights were not considered particularly valuable. In 1908 the Anglo/Persian Oil Company (later changed to Anglo/Iranian) was founded. As tensions in Europe heightened, British needs for a dependable source of petroleum increased, partially because the British navy was converting its fleet from coal to oil. In May 1914, about one week before European hostilities broke into widespread conflict, the British government acquired a 50 percent interest in the venture.

The finds in Iran stimulated exploration for petroleum in southern Iraq. The results of negotiations completed in 1912 allowed for the formation of the Turkish Petroleum Company. The Turkish Petroleum Company was reorganized in 1914 and again in 1920, when German interests were removed, and France and the United States moved in. The participation of U.S. firms was accomplished through vigorous diplomatic activity. In 1920 there was widespread fear of an impending oil shortage in the United States. The U.S. government even considered direct government participation instead of relying on private enterprise, but decided against it.

The agreement that formed the Turkish Petroleum Company, later renamed the Iraqi Petroleum Company (IPC), contained a proviso that limited the seeking of concessions to the area within the Ottoman Empire that was shown by a red line drawn on a map. The Red Line Agreement stated that the individual companies in the IPC would not act in a fashion that would upset the balance of company power within the red line. They were not to operate any other fields in the area and gain relative power.

Although British interests had the only concessions in Arabia, there was no production until 1934. In 1930, Standard Oil of California (SoCal) had gained an option from a British syndicate for Bahrain. Petroleum was found in 1932, and exports started to flow two years later. In 1933 SoCal gained the concession for the Al-Hasa province of Saudi Arabia. Petroleum was found a few years later. In 1934 Gulf Oil and British Petroleum entered Kuwait. The entry of U.S. firms into Saudi Arabia, and the subsequent development of the huge oil fields found there, threatened the dominance of the IPC, especially after SoCal joined with Texaco in 1936 to form the Arabian-American Oil Company (ARAMCO) to take advantage of the Far Eastern marketing network of Texaco.

The fear of a petroleum shortage immediately after World War I sparked a flurry of exploration during the next two decades. World supply had increased markedly by 1930 through various major fields coming into production, most notably in the Far East, Middle East, Venezuela, and the United States. With the increased world supply and more oil firms in the market, the "majors" maneuvered futilely to retain control of the world petroleum market.

Petroleum was in abundant supply during the worldwide Great Depression of the 1930s. As machines were turned off because of the depression, so also was the demand for petroleum products; the fears of an oil shortage turned into fears of a large and continuing glut. The sustained depression, especially in the United States, caused changes in the structure of the petroleum industry. Weak firms, especially the firms that were not vertically integrated, generally failed.

World War II to 1970

By the beginning of World War II, it was apparent that Middle Eastern petroleum would be vital to the world oil market. The United States, although supplying much of the petroleum products needed by the Allies during World War II, feared that its postwar position would be weak. Again there was talk of the need for direct government participation and for protecting the U.S. position in the Middle East. Saudi Arabia provided the United States with a major foothold in the Middle East. In efforts to keep the support of the Saudis, lend-lease agreements were put into force whereby the British actually extended the aid because Saudi Arabia was not eligible. Saudi Arabia was still a very poor country and received only modest revenues from the petroleum industry. The Saudis needed aid. Largely because the United States feared that the British would use their influence as intermediaries to curry Saudi favor, Saudi Arabia was made eligible for direct lend-lease aid in 1944. But there was another problem; the Saudi government wanted to increase production to increase its revenue. The U.S. government wanted to ensure an adequate supply, but ARAMCO did not have the financial resources necessary to expand Saudi production substantially. The U.S. government first planned to buy directly into ARAMCO and then to build a pipeline to the Mediterranean in return for preferential prices and guaranteed strategic reserves. Both plans failed to come to

fruition, and the U.S. government finally (1948) arranged with the financially stronger Standard Oil of New Jersey (later named Exxon) and Mobil, both IPC members, to buy into ARAMCO (30 percent and 10 percent). The entry of these IPC members signaled the end of the Red Line Agreement. By 1948 seven Western companies controlled Middle Eastern oil: Four were based in the United States (Standard Oil of New Jersey, Mobil, SoCal, and Texaco); one was British (British Petroleum); and one was a joint British-Dutch venture (Royal Dutch/Shell).

The selling price of any product is determined by the interaction of supply and demand. Although the record of the petroleum industry after World War II is too complex to be forced into a couple of equations, it is nevertheless instructive to highlight these two basic forces. The tremendous worldwide economic expansion that occurred in the decades after World War II increased the demand for petroleum products considerably. In addition, the Western nations and Japan were building energy-intensive societies and shifting increasingly greater percentages of their energy sources from coal to oil. The combination of these forces meant that the demand for petroleum was doubling every six and a half years.

The steady price of petroleum throughout the 1950s and most of the 1960s indicates that the supply of petroleum was increasing at about the same pace as the demand. The character of the industry, however, was changing in substantial ways. New independent firms were entering the petroleum industry, and the producing countries themselves began to feel new strength. The entry of more firms into the industry meant that the seven firms that controlled Middle Eastern petroleum production were slowly losing their influence in the market. Governments demanding greater revenues from petroleum exploitation were in a better position to bargain. Because of its heavy reliance on Libyan production, Occidental Oil was more likely to respect Libyan demands for increased monies than if it had widely diversified holdings. By contrast, the Iranian attempts at nationalization of the petroleum producers in 1951 failed in large part because of the relatively plentiful and more diversified world supply. During the 1950s and 1960s, the Middle East also was becoming relatively more important with respect to production and proven reserves. During the 1960s, it became clear to close observers of the scene that there had been a fundamental change in the market: A greater percentage of world supply originated in the Middle East, petroleum supplies started to lag behind demand in the latter part of the decade, and an upward pressure on prices began to be felt.

OPEC Revolution

The OPEC did not have any significant power in the first decade of its existence (1960 to 1970). The organization of the industry and the plentiful and diversified supply of oil blunted any thoughts about manipulating the market. However, the situation had changed markedly by 1970. During that year, the postrevolution government of Libya started negotiations for substantially increased payments from the petroleum companies. Algeria and Iran had gained better concessions in 1969. Although these actions represented a breakthrough for the producing countries, they were also viewed as special cases. Revolutionary Libya, strongly backed by "radical" Algeria and Iraq, called for much greater revenue increases than previously sought and threatened outright expropriation if its demands were not met. Libya succeeded for various reasons. World supply and demand conditions, aggravated by the 1967 closure of the Suez Canal, caused prices to rise; the Occidental Oil Company was vulnerable because almost all of the petroleum for its European operations came from Libya; the companies operating in the Middle East were unable to form a common front; the home governments of the oil companies could not bring any unified pressure to bear on the

producing countries; and OPEC was presenting a relatively united front. Prices were increased further after President Nixon's August 1971 announcement of a proposed devaluation of the U.S. dollar (which meant that the dollar earnings of the petroleum exporting countries would lose purchasing power). They also rose because of a continuing decline in U.S. petroleum production, worldwide inflation, and unabated increases in petroleum demand. Upward pressure on prices and calls for increased participation, partial ownership, and outright expropriation continued through 1973.

Intense negotiations between OPEC and the oil companies through the first ten months of 1973 resulted in substantially higher posted prices. These increases came without direct reference to the Arab-Israeli situation. Members of OPEC, Arab and non-Arab, were simply exploiting worldwide market conditions; they were seeking to get as much revenue as possible before their precious natural resource was depleted. The decline in the value of the U.S. dollar was eroding the purchasing power of petrodollar earnings, giving more reason to increase prices.

The 1973 Arab–Israeli war provided the catalyst that permitted the Arab members of OPEC an opportunity to flex some economic muscle and to see petroleum prices (roughly) quadruple in less than a year. Any such dramatic OPEC action needed the support of the largest producing nation, Saudi Arabia. King Faisal needed to be convinced that this bold and dangerous move was the proper policy: Saudi conservatism and substantial Saudi ties to the United States dictated against a precipitous break with past policy. However, Western, and particularly United States, support for Israel during and immediately after the 1973 war convinced the Saudi leadership that a dramatic increase in the price of petroleum and a selective boycott by the Arab members of OPEC were necessary to change Western policy.

The boycott was lifted in March 1974. The higher prices remained. The industrial world struggled through the next couple of years attempting to adjust to the change. Of particular importance were the massive balance-of-payments problems that resulted from the price increase and the related—but not causally determined—inflation that continued to plague them. A simple example clarifies what was happening. Assume that the United States was producing the same amount of goods each year. Now suppose that the price of imported oil increased, and the United States continued to import the same number of barrels. More dollars were flowing out of the United States, and less were being spent by U.S. consumers on U.S. goods. Now suppose that the exporting country spent all of those earned dollars on U.S. goods. With the same total amount of money being spent on the same total amount of goods, the straightforward result is that the oil producer had more goods and the United States had less. The only way out of this situation was to eliminate spending on imports by conserving energy and developing internal sources.

The U.S. government failed to respond with a clearly defined program. Attempts to develop comprehensive energy programs floundered throughout the decade. Instead, individual participants, aided by a pliant government, attempted to recoup their losses by spending more. In terms of our simple scenario, they pumped more money into the system. More money chasing the same amount of goods results in inflation. Inflation meant that members of OPEC could purchase less with each "petrodollar" earned. OPEC raised prices to recoup its position. The 1970s inflation in the United States was not caused primarily by OPEC actions; rather, continued U.S. inflation virtually guaranteed further rounds of OPEC price increases. Because the United States remained the most powerful economy in the industrialized world, it transmitted these problems to other countries.

Although the situation was far more complicated than the foregoing description suggests—especially important were the

complications that arose from the exporting countries not spending all of the petrodollars they earned—it represents the nub of the issue. The members of OPEC had control of a large enough percentage of world petroleum supplies to call the tune. They had become a full-fledged cartel that controlled the supply in the supply-demand equations. Most petroleum companies clearly understood these shifting power relationships by the late 1960s. At least one went so far as to launch an advertising campaign calling for a more sympathetic view of the Arab cause with respect to Israel. Others sent similar messages to official Washington. They knew that they were engaged in a rearguard action and were attempting to forestall the inevitable. The U.S. public had another point of view. Most people saw the situation as resulting from a U.S. government blunder or from oil company actions. Conspiracy theories abounded. It was as if the public could not believe that a group of third-world countries could have the power to foment such disorder and then "get away with it." It was the first time that a group of third-world countries had secured such a position.

The third-world countries that had begun to industrialize but had no oil could not fully share in the jubilation. Instead, they suffered. They were not economically strong enough to adopt the Western attitude of considering the price increases to be an unfortunate irritant that caused problems but nevertheless could be lived with. The major Arab members of OPEC responded to the plight of the poorer countries by increasing their aid programs. The Western nations had surrendered their grip on the political systems of the third world during the preceding years of the century. Was the success of OPEC the first major victory of a future economic trend?

None of the foregoing should suggest that the OPEC members all agree on the extent of the price increases. The position of any individual country depends on its particular economic needs. The countries aiming for very high prices generally had economies that could absorb all of the goods that petrodollars could buy; they had reasonably solid industrial bases or large populations or both. Iran and Iraq were the Middle Eastern members of OPEC that most readily fit this pattern. The price moderates, led by Saudi Arabia, generally were countries with large petroleum reserves, small populations, and less developed economies. At least in the early years of OPEC success, they did not have the ability (or the desire) to spend all of the petroleum earnings to strengthen their economies.

Another round of significant petroleum price increases was initiated by OPEC in 1979–1980, and aided by the onset of the Iran–Iraq war—this time the price was roughly doubled (from $15 to $30 a barrel). Worldwide inflation since the first (1973) round of increases eroded the purchasing power of their earnings considerably. Several objective conditions affecting the petroleum market had changed markedly, however, since the first round of price increases. First, there were more significant non-OPEC sources of petroleum that came on-line in the intervening period, the Mexican and North Sea fields being two prominent examples. Second, many heavy petroleum-using countries had adopted some conservation measures. Third, the industrialized world experienced a deep recession from 1980 to 1982. These increases in supplies and decreases in demand put downward pressure on prices. Reductions in individual supplier output are the mechanism through which price increases can be made effective. But several members of OPEC believed that they could not reduce supplies and their foreign exchange earnings without causing harm to their economies. There were significant defections from the posted price and output goals, Nigeria being the most important.

During the first half of the 1980s, OPEC managed to hold together through a series of complex technical maneuvers and price rollbacks. The organization was aided in its efforts

through a reduction of Iranian and Iraqi output caused by the war and a strong U.S. dollar. Most petroleum sales are denominated in U.S. dollars. When the U.S. economy began (1982) growing at a robust rate with lower inflation and high real interest rates, the value of the dollar increased relative to the currencies of most of its trading partners. This meant, for example, that the petrodollars could buy more Deutsch marks than before and more German goods. A constant dollar petroleum price translated into increased purchasing power.

Petroleum prices started a remarkable downward slide in late 1985. By the end of the first quarter of 1986, petroleum prices were close to the 1974 level (about $12 per barrel). There were several reasons for the decline, including larger worldwide supplies from new fields and a decision by Saudi Arabia to increase its output. The Saudi decision deserves some comment.

Saudi Arabia is the largest producer in OPEC. It acted as the "swing" producer—it was Saudi Arabia more than any other that changed its supplies so as to have the supply–demand equations yield the agreed price. As more non-OPEC petroleum entered the world market, the Saudis decreased production. Because of a complex of unfavorable worldwide economic conditions, many OPEC producers found themselves financially strapped by the early 1980s. They responded by increasing production beyond the limit they agreed to as members of OPEC. Saudi Arabia was in an increasingly tenuous situation. Finally, by late 1985, it thought that it had to increase production. It doubled production in the following months—and at that was producing only one-half of its capacity.

The slide of petroleum prices would have occurred without Saudi action. Their decision, however, made the decline steep and rapid. Petroleum exporters with massive debt problems (e.g., Mexico, Nigeria, Indonesia) were dealt a harsh blow. So was Iran. Petroleum accounted for most of the foreign exchange earnings of Iran. It is not by chance that Iran initiated a vigorous offensive against Iraq in early 1986 and threatened to widen the war to the Gulf States if the Saudis insisted on driving the price of petroleum down by producing more and by continuing to provide Iraq with financial aid for the war effort.

OPEC reached another agreement in 1988: The price of petroleum was to increase several dollars (to $18) through a complicated rearrangement of production quotas. It was impossible to increase the price to previous peaks because of increased world supplies. However, some action was needed to ease national budgetary burdens. Despite massive war-related aid from Saudi Arabia and Kuwait, Iraq had accumulated a staggering debt burden. Even the Saudis felt the pinch; their petroleum revenues decreased to about $20 billion in 1988 from a peak exceeding $100 billion in the early 1980s. Although the price of petroleum increased to $40 after the invasion of Kuwait, increased Saudi supplies quickly brought it back to about $18. The real (purchasing power) price of petroleum in 1996 was lower than the mid-1960s.

Many analysts interpreted the weakened position of OPEC as the long-predicted demise of the cartel. Although the spectacular successes of OPEC during the 1970s and early 1980s are not likely to be repeated, the Middle Eastern members of OPEC still hold the lion's share of world petroleum reserves, and they have the ability to influence the market substantially again, albeit only on a short-run basis. Petroleum prices decreased and then increased dramatically during the late 1990s. Some of the decrease is attributable to a unique set of circumstances. There was El Niño causing an unusually warm winter in much of the Northern Hemisphere. The Asian economic meltdown and consequent fall in demand were another force. As the economies of OPEC countries felt the pinch, there was more cheating on agreed-on quotas, increasing the supply of petroleum. It seems likely that the incentive structures imbedded in the price system will continue to depress petroleum prices over the longer run. First, relatively high prices call forth

alternate sources of petroleum supply. Second, substitution takes place; people demand energy, not petroleum per se. Research geared to develop nonpetroleum sources of energy at competitive prices (e.g., solar energy) intensify. Third, and probably not as important, high prices call forth conservation efforts, reducing demand. This has been recognized by the leading petroleum producers of the Middle East; several times during the late 1990s real (inflation adjusted) petroleum prices dipped to pre-1973 levels. This is one reason that several Gulf producers scrambled to establish themselves as the regional finance centers; they know that economic diversification is essential for long-term growth. But the widely agreed-on demise of OPEC as a major player in the petroleum market could be premature. As world demand for petroleum increased in 1998 and 1999, OPEC, led again by Saudi Arabia, cut supplies and sent prices from $10 to levels not seen since the 1980s (about $25 per barrel).

By September 2005, petroleum prices had shot up close to $70. What happened? As opposed to previous price spikes, this did not occur primarily because of supply disruptions. The cause was a surge in demand, led by rapidly growing China and India, countries accounting for about 40 percent of the world's population. The less important factors include limited refining capacity. It seems that companies were not willing to increase capacity substantially by spending billions of dollars in an industry that experienced wild price gyrations (hence the possibility of huge losses). By mid-2008 prices approached $150. Then, with the worldwide financial meltdown and resulting depression prices, oil prices slid back to the $70 range.

This meant that the rentier states of the Middle East, those heavily dependent on petroleum exports, had an enormous financial windfall. This allowed them to open their pocketbooks to pass out substantial subsidies and wage increases.

There also was a surge in domestic demand for petroleum in the major exporting countries. Increased demand for autos, air conditioning, and other goods sought by middle-income families grew quickly. The percentage of petroleum that was exported declined. The countries importing petroleum suffered. It is estimated that by 2020 domestic consumption will account for one-third of Saudi oil production. The implications for the petroleum importing countries are obvious.

Petroleum production is highly capital intensive; it does not produce many jobs. The same can be said of most subsidies and cash handouts. As stated earlier, there will be an enormous number of young people joining the labor force in the next couple of decades. The question is if the increased flow of petrodollars will be used to fuel reform in the job-creating sector, or will those profiting from the current system block reform? The answer is important.

The future of OPEC is uncertain. Its history is remarkable. The powerful industrialized countries of the world depend on OPEC supplies. Being dependent, these countries have had to reorder their policies toward the Middle East.Petroleum became a political tool of the first order after 1973; alliances had to be altered and new approaches to conflict resolution developed.

CONCLUSION

Economic growth depends on a complex array of factors beyond the technical blending of labor, natural resources, and physical capital. There must be a coherent set of institutions and policies properly related to economic resources if there is to be sustained growth.

Increasing resource imbalances led by rapid population growth have a distinct tendency to accelerate a degradation of the quality of life without triggering self-corrective mechanisms. The growing resource disparities in the Middle East are straining the capabilities of the political system. Conflicts are bound to multiply as the system spins out of control. A major challenge exists. One nettlesome dimension is

that a forward-looking policy often demands the imposition of painful short-run measures (e.g., placing a price on water use) that would yield noticeable benefits only in the long run, and that most political leaders have a short time to satisfy the demands of their populations. There are powerful political incentives to ignore fundamental problems until they cannot be avoided; that is, until there is a crisis. Lives hang in the balance.

Not all instances of a degraded quality of life result from the long accretion of pressures and ignored long-term remedies; war quickly can undo decades or even centuries of change. The 1991 deliberate torching of 640 of Kuwait's petroleum wells by Iraqi forces is the most spectacular case in point. The last of the fires was snuffed out much quicker than anticipated (by December 1991 instead of a few years later). The Kuwaiti desert, the air, and the Gulf water experienced immediate trauma. But more subtle effects were at work. Bahrain, some 200 miles to the south, experienced its coldest summer in a millennium; oil-soaked rain fell thousands of miles away; and it is anybody's guess to what happened to the geological structure of the fields.

The coalition's destruction of the Iraqi infrastructure brought another set of shocks. Iraqi infant mortality quadrupled in the year after the end of the war. The U.N.-imposed sanctions on imports to Iraq had another set of consequences—many more thousands died for want of medicine and hundreds of thousands suffered malnutrition, a condition that has profound lifelong implications for the young. Massive epidemics became highly probable. The sanctions imposed by the United Nations, along with a quietly sustained U.S.-led bombing campaign through the 1990s meant that the misery of the average Iraqi continued, and continued to suffer after the 2003 U.S. invasion.

The sudden and spectacular loss of life caused by war sometimes blinds observers to the relatively gradual and potentially more pernicious effects of high rates of population growth in a setting where complementary resources are growing more slowly. The following simple linear causal chain illustrates one aspect of the problem: Population growth increases the demand for food, which calls for more irrigated land, which strains water resources and leads to contaminated water supplies, which spreads disease, which decreases human productivity, which leads to lower real income. The issues are far more complicated: Property rights conflicts surface, the health care system becomes overburdened, the educational system falls into crisis, and social conflicts generally increase.

A prudent analyst shuns the opportunity to predict the specific path and shape of future Middle Eastern economic realities and ideologies. One of the central lessons of chaos theory is that the course of complex systems is impossible to predict. A related maxim from that body of theory is that there are complex causal links and feedback mechanisms between variables usually thought to be unrelated—folk culture, economics, the physical environment, the arts, and notions of the "good life" are part of the same cloth. At the same time, humans organize themselves for purposive ends; the behavior of purposive participants counts. Because of the obvious resource imbalances in the Middle East, thoughtful policies must be devised and tinkered with as conditions change.

Key Terms

mulk *248*
miri sirf *248*
waqf *249*

12 INTERNATIONAL RELATIONS IN THE MIDDLE EAST, 1945–1990

A predictable characteristic of all international orders is the concentration of power in a small number of states. At any moment, one can identify a short list of international actors with power and influence well beyond the capacities of most other states. It is inevitable that these states, at some point, come into conflict with one another. It is equally plausible that they externalize those conflicts into their relations with other states. Earlier chapters in this book have described the role played by the great powers of Europe in the establishment of the contemporary state system in the Middle East. In Chapters 13 and 14, we place great emphasis on the architectonic effect of the bipolar conflict between the United States and the Soviet Union. Until the late 1980s, the way in which most people looked at the world was determined by this contest for global hegemony.

Although one can define international relations strictly in terms of the contests between great powers for relative advantages over the others (the "Great Game," as it has been called), to restrict the analysis to these actors would eliminate much that is important. The effect of this competition on weaker states is important as well, particularly to the weaker states themselves. It also would be inappropriate to assume that because the so-called great powers were economically and militarily powerful, their diplomacy and decision making were more rational or insightful than the diplomacy of other states. Finally, we caution against the assumption that great-power status is immune to the laws of nature or physics. The inevitability of the decline of great powers is a well-known fact.[1] The dissolution of the Soviet Union in 1991 and U.S. attempts to orchestrate world events from a position of relative decline are the latest demonstrations of this process.

The international system has many features not found in national political orders. The most important of these features is the lack of a legitimate sovereign power, or even of some entity with a viable claim to the exercise of sovereign power. Compared with the average national system, the international system is nearly anarchic—political power is broadly diffused among its actors

---

[1] See Paul Kennedy, *The Rise and Fall of the Great Powers: Economic Change and Military Conflict from 1500–2000* (New York: Random House, 1987).

and yet enormously concentrated among a few. International power is transitory and difficult to assess comparatively.

The actors that constitute the international order have a power base that can be broken down into three areas: *economic power*, the power to produce or acquire material goods; *political power*, the power to coerce or influence their own populations or the populations of other states; and *military power*, the ability to gain goals through the direct application of organized coercive force. These capabilities are not distributed evenly among the actors in the international system. Saudi Arabia possesses enormous economic power based on its extensive oil reserves, but it has a population insufficient in size and technical sophistication to maintain a truly international military capability. Egypt, by contrast, has a large population sufficiently skilled to maintain a large military machine, but lacks the economic base to develop it without foreign aid. The relative international power of Saudi Arabia and Egypt must be calculated on different bases— quantitative and qualitative. This enormously complicates the calculations involved in international politics, particularly because one actor's analysis of the capability of another is a core determinant of its foreign policy.

The relationships between international actors embrace a wide field of human activity. International relations occur at many levels and in many functional arenas. No state can isolate itself from international trade because to do so it would have to reduce its economic activity greatly. Any nation finds it necessary and desirable to allow the movements of goods and services into its territory as varying amounts of goods and services flow out. Most states are involved in some level of international economic exchange that requires cooperation with friendly and potentially unfriendly powers. At the nadir of Iranian–U.S. relations, Iranian oil was still being imported by the United States at the rate of some 80,000 barrels per day—a fact as politically unpalatable to President Carter as to Ayatollah

Khomeini. International relations possess a logic that is to some degree independent of the best wishes or intentions of their actors; to put it another way, international politics and economics make strange bedfellows.

Actors in the international system pursue a combination of specific and general goals that can be lumped together under the term *national interest*. The national interest presumably directs the foreign policy of a nation, at least at the strategic level. The national interest of the Soviet Union (now the Commonwealth of Independent States [C.I.S.]) has long required a safe, warm-water port, whereas the contemporary U.S. national interest requires regular delivery of petroleum from its Middle Eastern sources. Needless to say, these two national interest goals have a potential for conflict in the area of the Persian Gulf.

The problem in analyzing international relations strictly from the national interest viewpoint can be summarized briefly. First, nations may not perceive their true national interests clearly. U.S. involvement in Vietnam in the 1960s is a case in point. Second, power—the base of implementation of national interest—is an enormously complex entity. Miscalculations of one's own power or of the reputed power of another actor inject a quality of uncertainty into international relations. An example is Nasser's miscalculation of Israeli responses to his mobilization in 1967. Finally, international relations are only rarely dyadic—that is, involving only two nations. Although for analytic purposes we often discuss foreign policy in dyadic terms, most international exchanges involve the interests of secondary and tertiary actors. These complex intersections of national interests—primary and secondary, immediate and long-term—create the Gordian knots of the international process. Often the solution to these problems is war, with its attendant human miseries and material losses.

In viewing the international system from the perspective of decades and centuries, we perceive dramatic changes taking place.

Nations, even entire civilizations, change their positions in the relative power hierarchies of the international system, rising and falling for reasons that are often idiosyncratic or obscure. It is even possible, as was the case with the nineteenth-century Ottoman Empire, for a country to improve its absolute power—to have more financial, military, and human resources—and still decline relative to its competitors (in this case, the emerging national powers of Western Europe and Russia). As intellectually disconcerting as this may be to students of the international system, we live in a time in which just such changes are occurring. The demise transformation of the U.S.S.R., the newfound political independence of Eastern Europe, the political integration of Western Europe, the dispersal of economic power to new centers, the dramatic change in policy directions in China, the quantum increases in the sophistication and use of conventional and chemical weapons, and the dramatic and unlikely diplomatic initiatives (e.g., the Palestinian declaration of statehood in December 1988) force a reevaluation of basic premises on which foreign policy is predicated.

None of the preceding should be interpreted as denying order or process in international relations. The Middle East, in particular, has seen the rise and fall of many separate international systems. The region witnessed the development of an international theocratic movement during the early days of Islamic expansion, in which the world was seen as a contrast between the *Dar al Islam* (world of peace) and the *Dar al Harb* (world of war); centralized bureaucratic empires based successively in Damascus, Baghdad, and Cairo; loose relationships between competing centers of power, as peripheral kingdoms arose in the Maghreb, Spain, Europe, Central Asia, Persia, and India; the consolidation of power in the decentralized millet system of the Ottoman Empire; the intrusion of European imperial power, predicated on a classic balance of

power in Europe; and, after World War II, the bipolar conflict between the United States and the Soviet Union. As we settle into the new millennium, yet another international order presents itself, with concomitant challenges and changes in the international environment.

The origins of the contemporary international order can be found in the deterioration of the system that emerged just after World War II and prevailed until the early 1970s. This first order, the bipolar international system, was produced by an unusual concentration of military and economic power in two rival political systems, the United States and the Soviet Union, which saw each other as threats to their own national interest and to the larger political order. In this situation, the alliances surrounding these two superpowers grew rigid and confrontational. The term *cold war*, which applied to the early period after World War II, suggests a confrontation between the two blocs just short of overt military hostilities. During this time, the two superpowers enjoyed a nuclear monopoly and rapidly growing economies. Stymied in their confrontation in Europe, the United States and the U.S.S.R. turned to the nations of the third world—Africa, Asia, Latin America, and the Middle East—for potential alliance partners in their crusade against international communism and international capitalism, respectively.

From the point of view of international actors in the Middle East, this transition was frustrating. Neither the United States nor the Soviet Union had well-established bases in the area. European power, although waning and definitely inferior to that of either superpower, was nonetheless still something to contend with. Finally, the ideological claims of capitalism and communism did not find fertile intellectual soil in the Middle East.

Regional factors also injected themselves into the emerging international order. Primary among them was the creation of Israel in 1948 and its subsequent protection by the United States. This issue, transcending such questions as Arab unity, water resources, economic growth and development, or Islamic resurgence, provided the mechanism for the entrance of bipolar politics in the area. The unevenness of U.S. policy toward the Arab states, combined with U.S. unwillingness to hedge on the question of Israeli security, provided the Soviet Union with an entree, particularly to Egypt, Syria, and Iraq, the major powers confronting the Israeli state. Despite great Egyptian, Syrian, and Iraqi dependence on Eastern-bloc sources for weapons and expertise, the U.S.S.R. was unable to capitalize on its advantages domestically in these countries. The United States, for its part, confused the desire for independence in these countries with a drift toward communism and reacted hostilely to Soviet gains there. The bipolar alliance system did not extend completely into the Middle East, and Soviet and U.S. policy goals were frustrated.

The 1960s saw the gradual erosion of the "eyeball-to-eyeball" confrontation between Soviet and American global power. The age of détente ushered in a period in which Soviet and American ability to control their alliances and dictate policy declined. The emergence of competing centers of economic and political power—Japan, Western Europe, and China—ultimately produced an international system in which the great powers of the United States and the Soviet Union were reduced by the growing economic powers of their allies and by the loss of their nuclear monopoly. The resulting international system, maturing in the late 1980s and ultimately transformed by the dissolution of the U.S.S.R. can best be described as an emerging set of relatively independent power centers orbiting loosely and often erratically around the United States as the last surviving superpower. Additional sources of international power seemed to be maturing, based on the growing economic and political systems of Asia, Africa, the Middle East, and Latin America. These centers of power were increasingly inclined to define national interest in their own terms. All of this contributed to the complexity and potential instability of the international order. Many saw in all of this the emergence of a new international order, a topic we shall address specifically in Chapter 14.

Let us now examine the implications of these changes for the international system that is the Middle East. Our method will be to move from macroanalysis in Chapter 12; to regional analysis in Chapter 13; and finally to consideration of dyadic relations involving the foreign policies of Egypt, Saudi Arabia, Iran, Iraq, Syria, and Israel. In each of these chapters, we shall discuss the phases of international relations in the Middle East. Phase I, 1945–1948, embraces the immediate postwar period; phase II, 1948–1974, includes the period of transition from tight bipolar confrontation to loose bipolar competition; phase III covers the period from the 1973 Arab–Israeli war and the Arab oil embargo to 1990; and finally in Chapters 14 and 15, from 1991 to the present, and including the dramatic changes occasioned by the collapse of Soviet power, covers the causes and consequences of Desert Storm and the prospects for negotiated peace between Israel and the Arabs.

THE GREAT-POWER SYSTEM AND THE MIDDLE EAST

In the relatively short span of 40 years, actors in the Middle East have gone from a system in which their policies were largely reactive to the policy goals of the United States and the Soviet Union, through a period in which international power seemed to disperse toward other industrial states of the temperate zones, to an international system in which many Middle Eastern nations realistically can view themselves as capable of originating international exchange, politically, economically, and militarily. Some Middle Eastern actors—most notably Saudi Arabia, Egypt, Iraq, Syria, and Iran—see themselves as major actors in the international arena. Decisions reached in Riyadh, Cairo, and Tehran now have repercussions in Moscow, Washington, and Tokyo.

The current system contains numerous international power centers that have altered substantially the relative influence of the United States and the U.S.S.R. This is not to say that the power and national interests of these two megapowers are unimportant. On the contrary, their pursuit of their national interests is in many ways more important and more dangerous today given the greater number of probable actors. The primary effects of policy shifts may be predictable, but the secondary and tertiary effects, involving other actors indirectly, are rarely predictable or controllable. As the United States reduced its dependence on Iranian oil imports in the late 1970s (a primary policy decision), Japan and other U.S. allies simultaneously increased their imports of Iranian crude (a secondary effect), which increased their vulnerability to pressure from Soviet intervention in the Persian Gulf. Of the two great superpowers, the United States held the more enviable position of power in the Middle East. European (specifically British and French) power in the area generally was replaced by American power. The United States was historically removed from the abuses of colonial policy in the area, and many Arab leaders looked with affection toward the United States. The period after World War II saw an extension and expansion of U.S. power in the Middle East, oriented toward an alliance system aimed at frustrating Soviet moves, particularly in Turkey and Iran.

Table 12.1 summarizes the foreign policy objectives of the great powers in the Middle East from the end of World War II to the present. The table suggests some sharp changes in policy over that relatively brief period of time.

U.S. FOREIGN POLICY

Phase I

U.S. policy toward the Middle East was not coherent or logical during phase I. After World War II, the U.S. concern for the Middle East grew directly as it recognized that its allies (Britain and France) were unable to play their traditional roles. The United States also feared that the Soviet Union, the other principal winner in World War II, would attempt to exploit the political uncertainties in Greece, Turkey, and Iran. This concern led to the Truman Doctrine, a statement of real opposition to Soviet imperialism in the area, which committed the United States to direct military and economic support for the threatened areas.

As in other areas of the world, the United States found itself moving into unfamiliar political seas to fill what was generally recognized as an incipient power vacuum. The exploitation and importation of crude petroleum was clearly of a secondary nature in its foreign policy priorities. Critically, the United States, in honoring its commitments to the governments and policies of its allies, set itself squarely in the camp of Middle Eastern conservatism. This early commitment, as we shall see, ultimately played havoc with U.S. credibility and prestige in the area.

Phase II

During phase II, U.S. policy and presence in the Middle East were inextricably linked with Israel. President Truman's hurried recognition of Israel, combined with U.S. influence in the United Nations, placed the United States squarely in the role of protector of the Israeli state. This role, coupled with intractable Arab opposition to Israel, provided the Soviet Union with its first major successes in Middle Eastern policy. From 1958 to 1975, the U.S.S.R. was able to exploit the situation resulting from U.S. support for Israel by supplying arms and advisors to Egypt, Syria, and Iraq. The United States attempted to maintain a preeminent power position, while the Soviet Union attempted to exploit potential weaknesses in the U.S. posture. It may be a tribute to the diplomacy of Middle Eastern nations that neither power managed to envelop the area within its alliance systems or to dictate policy in the area systematically.

Table 12.1 Foreign Policy Priorities in the Middle East, 1945–Present

Phase	United States	Soviet Union (C.I.S. after 1990)	Europe (England, France, Germany, European Community)
I (1945–1948)	1. Extension of influence	1. Extension of influence into Mediterranean, Turkey, and Iran	1. Reestablishment of prewar influence
	2. Exploitation and protection of promising petroleum production in Saudi Arabia and Iran	2. Frustration of U.S. power and prestige in Middle East	2. Exploitation and protection of petroleum production and trade relations in Middle East
		3. Support of Jewish community in Palestine	3. Limited support of Jewish migration to Palestine
II (1948–1974)	1. Support and protection of Israel	1. Extension of military influence into Middle East via anti-Israeli governments in Syria, Egypt, and Iraq	1. Maintenance and expansion of petroleum production and trade relations
	2. Maintenance of influence and prestige against Soviet invasion; Baghdad Pact	2. Frustration of U.S. power and prestige in Middle East	2. Maintenance of prestige and influence in Middle East
	3. Exploitation and protection of petroleum production in Saudi Arabia and U.A.E.		3. Support of Israel
III (1974–1990)	1. Support and protection of Israel	1. Maintenance of influence in Syria and Iraq	1. Maintenance and expansion of petroleum production and trade relations
	2. Maintenance of influence and prestige	2. Frustration of U.S. power and prestige in Middle East; support of national liberation movements in Yemen and Oman, PLO	2. Compete with U.S.–U.S.S.R. efforts in Middle East
	3. Exploitation and protection of petroleum production in Saudi Arabia and U.A.E.	3. Access to Middle East petroleum and warm-water ports	
IV (1990–present)	1. Ensure stability of region; maintenance of Desert Storm Coalition	1. Russia seeks new diplomatic relations, trade relations	1. Protect petroleum production, establish European Community trade relations
	2. Protect petroleum production in Persian Gulf		2. Solution of Arab–Israeli conflict
	3. Solution of Arab–Israel conflict		3. Support of Israel
	4. Support for Israel		

This period in international relations saw a determined U.S. effort to extend the tight bipolar alliance system into the Middle East and to link North Atlantic Treaty Organization (NATO) in Europe with the Southeast Asia Treaty Organization (SEATO) alliance in Asia. The Baghdad Pact (1955) represented the greatest success of the United States in this regard. It was seen in the United States as a logical response to Soviet aggression; many Middle Eastern leaders, however, saw themselves in danger of being pulled headlong into the ideological confrontation between the United States and the U.S.S.R. Nasser succeeded in popularizing the concept of nonalignment in the area; the pact, lacking full support by the signatories after Iraq's withdrawal in 1958, was replaced by direct aid to Iran. Full support of the shah by the United States was implemented by means of a bilateral mutual assistance treaty in 1959.

During this period, Middle Eastern petroleum production was a relatively low order of priority: The U.S. oil fields until the early 1960s were more than capable of supplying most domestic petroleum needs. The maintenance of its influence, the protection of Israel, and the frustration of Soviet ambitions provided the motivation for U.S. policy. Until the late 1960s, the United States was able to accomplish all of its objectives simultaneously. The emergence of the Palestine independence organizations, however, coupled with growing international recognition of their rights and legitimacy, made the support of Israel costly to U.S. influence and prestige. The Soviet Union capitalized on this situation by breaking relations with Israel and providing arms and aid to Egypt, Syria, and Iraq. Decision makers in the United States assumed the worst—that Soviet aid meant Soviet control. A period of very tense, even hostile, relations between the United States and these nations ensued.

In short, during phase II, the United States was able to consolidate its alliance positions with the "northern tier" states—Turkey, Iran,

and Pakistan—while its relations with the core states of Syria, Egypt, and Iraq deteriorated. Strains even appeared between the United States and its client states Jordan and Saudi Arabia, simultaneously pro-American and increasingly anti-Israeli. The maintenance of any alliance in which conflicting goals are present is extraordinarily difficult. Consequently, the United States was called on many times to put out "brush fires" in the area. The attempted nationalization of Iranian oil in 1953, the Suez Crisis of 1956, and the crisis in Lebanon in 1958 are examples. Ultimately, these foreign policy objectives were to become more clearly and forcefully contradictory. Particularly clear by 1974 was the incompatibility of maintaining and expanding the Middle East's petroleum flow to the West and the unyielding support of Israel.

INTERVENTIONS IN IRAN. During the early phase II diplomacy, the United States was forced to intervene directly in the Middle East. The first of these interventions was prompted by developments in Iran from 1951 to 1953, a period in which Iranian politics were dominated by the leadership of Premier Mohammed Mossadegh. Mossadegh effectively challenged the Anglo-Iranian oil agreements and moved to nationalize the company's holdings. Simultaneously, Mossadegh virtually isolated the young shah from political power, taking control of the army and moving to abolish the representative assembly, all with strong support from the Iranian public. American and British interests responded with a carefully orchestrated policy of intrigue that ultimately brought Mossadegh's downfall and the return of the shah.

The shah's power, based on his increasingly effective control of the military, waxed from that period on. The petroleum production of Iran was finally organized on a consortium basis in which American and European corporations shared the profits on a 50–50 basis with the Iranian National Oil Company. From this time onward, and particularly during the White Revolution, the shah had generous support from the United States, which perceived Iran as playing a "policeman's role" in the important Persian Gulf. Resentment over U.S. support for the shah became an important factor in Iranian politics after the successful revolution of 1979. The United States labored unsuccessfully to escape the consequences of its support for that repressive regime.

SUEZ WAR. The second major U.S. involvement in the Middle East also had long-term consequences for U.S. interests in the area. From 1948 onward, Egypt and Israel were periodically at some level of armed hostility, ranging from small guerrilla raids to larger punitive expeditions. Egypt sought U.S. arms, the better to engage the superior capabilities of the Israeli armed forces. The successful Israeli raid on the Gaza Strip in February 1955 led Colonel Nasser to request arms sales from the United States and Great Britain. These requests were emphatically denied.

Rebuffed by the Americans and the British, Nasser turned to the Eastern bloc for relief, concluding a barter deal (cotton for arms) with Czechoslovakia. Reactions in the United States were abrupt, resulting in the July 1956 cancellation of U.S. support for the construction of the high dam at Aswan. The connection between this refusal and Nasser's independent pursuit of Soviet arms through Czechoslovakia was made clear by the United States. In backing out of its commitment to the dam, the United States threatened the heart of Nasser's development plan for Egypt. Relations between Egypt and the United States deteriorated rapidly from this point.

Nasser reacted to this great-power action by nationalizing the Suez Canal Company in July 1956. The canal, of great importance to Europe as a trade route and defense link, heretofore had been operated by a corporation dominated by Britain and France. Their immediate response was to oppose the nationalization, freeze Egyptian funds in their respective banks, and seek a solution to the problem

from the United Nations. U.S. interest in the proceedings was indirect until Nasser made it clear that Israeli shipping would continue to be denied access to the canal. Britain and France became increasingly restive about the failure of the United States to condemn Egypt. This frustration led ultimately to the Suez War of 1956.

The events of the Suez War suggest collusion between Israel, France, and Great Britain. The war began with Israeli occupation of Gaza and penetration and control of the Sinai up to the canal. France and Britain demanded that the belligerents (Egypt and Israel) withdraw to positions ten miles on either side of the canal. Egypt's rejection of this ultimatum prompted the invasion of the canal zone by British and French paratroops and the occupation of Port Said.

After a period of intense collective and unilateral diplomacy by the United States, U.N. troops (UNEF) were placed between the belligerents, and they were exhorted to withdraw from the territory. The United States placed heavy pressure on its allies, particularly Israel, to withdraw. French and British troops quit the area by December 1956. Finally, in March 1957, an agreement was reached for Israeli withdrawal from the Sinai.

The resolution of the Suez War found the United States opposing the actions of its strongest allies—Israel, France, and Great Britain. This pro-Arab action led to considerable strains in the Western alliance but did little to persuade Nasser that U.S. policy was ultimately benevolent.

LEBANON CRISIS OF 1958. The third U.S. intervention in Middle Eastern affairs was generated by the Lebanon crisis of 1958, an intervention that saw the movement of U.S. marines into Beirut on July 15. The details of the Lebanese situation that produced the U.S. intervention were complex, involuted, and confusing. The Lebanese political situation was becoming increasingly unstable, and the delicate balance between Muslim, Christian, and Druze interests was deteriorating. This deterioration had attracted the attention of Egypt, which directly intervened in the struggle on behalf of the Sunni Muslims. The successful revolution in Iraq, on July 14, heightened the feeling of tension. At the request for aid by President Chamoun, the U.S. Sixth Fleet moved 3,600 marines into Beirut to stabilize the situation. This tactic, combined with intense behind-the-scenes negotiations, brought some order to the Lebanese conflict and helped to forestall a civil war. The action was successful, and the Lebanese regime survived until the civil war in 1975 and the Israeli-Syrian interventions from 1976 onward. Nonetheless, this event revealed the willingness of the United States to intervene directly in Middle Eastern affairs if it believed its national interest was at stake—a right it steadfastly denied to its allies and adversaries alike.

Phase III

The United States as well as all of the recognized powers and superpowers had entered a period in which international political power was shared, a dramatic change from the era of unilateral intervention that preceded it. U.S. foreign policy in the phase III era was conceived and executed by "postmodern" presidents, beginning with President Carter. As Richard Rose succinctly puts it:

> A postmodern President no longer enjoys isolation from other nations. The White House retains the attributes of the modern presidency, but in a changing world these resources are no longer adequate. A postmodern President cannot secure success simply by influencing Congress and public opinion; the President must also influence leaders of other nations and events in the international system.[2]

---

[2] Richard Rose, *The Post-Modern Presidency*, 2nd ed. (Chatham, NJ: Chatham House, 1991), 25.

During phase III of its Middle East policy, U.S. commitments to Israel were strained by its need for regular supplies of Middle East petroleum. The seven-month Arab oil embargo of 1973–1974 was initiated in direct retaliation for U.S. support for Israel in the war of October 1973. This war, initiated by a surprise attack by Egyptian forces, was ultimately concluded by means of intervention via the United Nations. As a result, the United States, by shipping arms to Israel, first prevented the collapse of the Israeli military, and then, through its diplomatic activity in the United Nations, rescued Egypt from probable defeat.

From the October war of 1973 until the 1991 Gulf War, U.S. attempts to play both sides of the Arab–Israeli conflict were unsuccessful in rescuing its prestige in the area. U.S. policy seems to have alienated both sides in the conflict. Israeli complaints about U.S. waffling on aid became more frequent in the 1980s, characterized by the public complaints of Prime Minister Menachem Begin and his successor Yitzhak Shamir. The Arab "rejectionist" states were not satisfied or mollified by U.S. economic support for Egypt or increasing U.S. arms sales to Egypt and Saudi Arabia. Increasingly, the United States was pressured to consider the Arab view in the Arab–Israeli conflict. The diplomacy of the Carter administration, in particular the Camp David Accords, which led to bilateral negotiations between Egypt and Israel, was most probably the only realistic option for the United States.

The Camp David agreements resulted in the cessation of diplomatic hostilities, the return of most Sinai territory to Egypt, and the opening of genuine diplomatic and trade relations between the two countries. The negotiations, however, did not engage the most basic questions regarding Palestinian autonomy in the West Bank and Gaza. The problem of Jerusalem, claimed by Israel as its historic capital and an important religious site for Christianity and Islam as well, also proves to be difficult. Because Egypt bore the brunt of past military confrontations with Israel, an outbreak of war became unlikely.

The early foreign policy of the Reagan administration did not hold the promise of substantial change in U.S. Middle Eastern policy. Early administration decisions to accede to Saudi requests for longer range and more sophisticated fighter-bombers were balanced by promises to increase military aid to Israel. As in the preceding administration's foreign policy, neither side was ecstatic about the U.S. effort to play both sides.

Reagan administration's efforts to organize an anti-Soviet alliance in the Middle East were gently but firmly rebuffed in the early months of 1981. Administration concern for Saudi security prompted its approval of the sale of sophisticated radar planes (AWAC) to Saudi Arabia, a decision that produced considerable pro-Israeli objections in the U.S. Congress. The June 1981 Israeli air raid on the Iraqi nuclear facility near Baghdad prompted the administration to suspend shipment of four F-16s to Israel, which also strained relations. The U.N. resolution condemning the Israeli raid and calling for compensation was a joint product of American and Iraqi diplomats at the United Nations. Such a collaboration would have been unthinkable a decade earlier and became unthinkable a decade later. All of these examples underscore the difficulty of maintaining traditional U.S. policy priorities in the 1980s. No less an authority on U.S.–Israeli relations than former president Jimmy Carter has observed that on many fundamental issues, the interests of Israel and the United States diverge.

The issue of Palestinian rights led the Reagan administration to offer "the Reagan Plan." The plan, which was based on the creation of a "Palestinian entity" nominally attached to Jordan, was rejected by Israel and alternately rejected and accepted by other Middle Eastern actors, never simultaneously and never with enough consensus to get the proposals a serious hearing. Israeli objections centered on Prime Minister Begin's flat refusal to consider in any way the return of areas considered part of historical Israel, particularly Judea and Samaria. This, in effect, announced a de facto annexation of the West Bank, a point of policy firmly opposed by the United States. Prime Minister Shamir continued this emphasis under his administration, with just as much rigidity and energy.

These growing disagreements were minor compared with the difficulties engendered for the United States by the massive Israeli invasion of Lebanon in June 1982. What was announced initially as a limited-objective foray against Palestinian bases in south Lebanon quickly became a drive to Beirut. Israeli Defense Forces stopped only just short of a complete occupation of Beirut and all of southern Lebanon. The United States was apparently caught unprepared by the scope of this military action and hastily created a U.S. military presence in Beirut, ostensibly to police the withdrawal of Palestinian troops from the area.

Shortly thereafter, U.S. marines were reintroduced into the Beirut area in the role of guarantor of the Bashir Gemayel government and tutor for the government's new army, composed primarily of Maronite Christian militia. The United States took a position opposing Israeli attempts to elevate other Christian groups, primarily the Army of South Lebanon, led by Major Saad Haddad. The United States and Israel failed to achieve their objectives. The formal U.S. presence in Beirut was demoralized by a terrorist bombing of the U.S. marine barracks with great loss of life and ultimately by a similar attack on the U.S. embassy annex. The U.S. hope for an effective national government based on the Gemayel administration deteriorated as other groups and countries controlled more Lebanese territory. What hopes Israel had countenanced for the creation of a neutral or pro-Israel government dissipated in the anarchy created by the sudden removal of the Palestinians from the military-political equation in Lebanon. The primary gains from the invasion of Lebanon seemed to accrue to the

Syrians, now the arbiter of political relations in Lebanon and consequently enjoying a substantial rise in diplomatic prestige, and the Shia groups, particularly AMAL and Hizbollah, who rose to oppose first the government, then the Palestinians, and finally the Israelis.

U.S. policy at this time seemed to be more reactive than active. The events in Lebanon proved a major setback to U.S. efforts to promote a negotiated settlement between the Israelis and their Arab neighbors and resulted in a dramatic decline in U.S. prestige in the area—a decline underscored by the Lebanese hostage crisis of June 1985. U.S. losses in Lebanon were slightly offset by the maintenance of close, even intimate, relations with Egypt and by a substantive but informal supportive relationship with Iraq. Neither policy vector was well received in Israel, and U.S. policy in the Middle East, yoked as it was to unqualified support for Israel, retained the internal inconsistencies apparent since World War II.

Two dramatic sets of events transformed Reagan administration policy from reactive to active. The first was direct U.S. involvement in the Iran–Iraq war, initially in an effort to secure the release of U.S. hostages, and later as an attempt to maintain open sea lanes in the Persian Gulf. The second involved the remarkable events of the Palestinian intifadah and the subsequent efforts of the Palestinian Liberation Organization (PLO) to gain multilateral support for direct negotiations toward the creation of a Palestinian state under United Nations Resolutions 242 and 338. Each of these events warrants separate discussion.

Direct U.S. intervention in the Iran–Iraq conflict occurred first during 1985–1986 as a covert effort to gain Iran's cooperation and intervention in the release of U.S. hostages held by various groups in Lebanon. The effort was directed in secrecy by an office in the National Security Council and eventually involved the U.S. government in a bizarre arrangement linking arms sales to Iran to support for covert Contra (anticommunist) operations in

Nicaragua. The details of the initiative are still unclear, but the effects of the policy are known: The sale of key weapon systems and badly needed spare parts to Iran (particularly antiaircraft and antitank missiles) neutralized much of Iraq's qualitative advantage in military equipment and put the Iraqi military in a dangerous corner. With its back against the wall, Iraq responded with missile attacks on key Iranian cities and the use of chemical weapons, chiefly gases, against Iranian troops and its domestic Kurdish opposition, who were sympathetic toward Iran. Simultaneously, Iraq and Iran extended their attacks on domestic shipping in the Persian Gulf, each attempting to damage the other's ability to earn foreign currency to continue prosecution of the war. These attacks, particularly against noncombatant Persian Gulf states, brought a U.S. naval presence into the Gulf.

The United States, prompted by Kuwait's threats to invite a Soviet naval force into the area, eventually moved a large naval task force into the Gulf, ostensibly to protect all shipping, regardless of source. Kuwaiti tankers were reflagged as American tankers. (In practical effect, this meant action against Iran.) The task force included most of the paraphernalia of modern superpower technology, including AWACs radar surveillance, AEGIS guided-missile cruisers, destroyers, minesweepers, helicopters, and smaller vessels. The Iranians deployed more mines and used small, high-speed boats for grenade and small-caliber attacks on slow-moving tankers. The Iraqis relied most heavily on air-launched missiles. The result of all this military activity was an increase in the complexity of traffic in the Gulf region, an area already congested in its sea and air lanes. This compression of traffic and activity increased the levels of uncertainty in the area, a fact that led to the May 1987 attack on the *U.S.S. Stark* by an Iraqi Exocet missile, with substantial loss of American lives. This incident was resolved by an Iraqi apology and payment of damages.

The U.S. response to this attack was to beef up its presence in the Gulf. Higher states of alert were required, and more ships were deployed. Petroleum continued to flow from the Gulf, protected by the U.S. Navy. U.S. encounters with Iranian attacks and mines led to limited action against Iranian bases, particularly converted oil platforms. The Iran–Iraq war ground on with appalling levels of military and civilian casualties culminating in the accidental shooting down of an Iranian jetliner in July 1988 by the *U.S.S. Vincennes*, a sophisticated AEGIS class cruiser. This attack, and the almost universal diplomatic indifference to it, contributed to the Iranian acceptance of a negotiated end to the conflict, through the auspices of the United Nations. A distraught Ayatollah Khomeini supported the decision to end the war, against his personal sentiments. A war that began badly, with some U.S. covert involvement at its inception, ended similarly, with U.S. covert and overt actions affecting the course and conduct of the war.

There are lessons to be learned from this protracted conflict and the U.S. role in it. The U.S. role in the world, although important, was no longer definitive. At the same time, it was clear that policy decisions in Washington did have effects, sometimes intended, as is the case in the Persian Gulf intervention, and sometimes unintended, as the hostage–arms sales relationship with Iran demonstrated, for it was clearly not in the interest of the United States to tip the balance of power in that conflict toward Iran. Yet in the short run, that was the clear impact of the policy. Some critics of U.S. policy in the Gulf conflict suggested a lack of clarity in U.S. objectives; others have pointed out the essentially reactive U.S. role there. Still other critics have suggested that a greater multilateral presence in the Gulf would have proved useful to U.S. purposes, sharing costs and blame more equally among those benefiting from the petroleum flow. These criticisms and suggestions reinforce our previous observations about the changing nature of the international system and the U.S.

role in it. (These commonplace criticisms of U.S. decision making in the Iran–Iraq war have an almost eerie resonance in the criticisms of U.S. shortsightedness in the Gulf War with Iraq in 1991.) In any case, the United States was now just one of many important actors in the arena. This reality became extremely clear through the remarkable events in Israel's occupied territories.

In December 1987, Palestinians on the West Bank and in Gaza began a civil insurrection against Israeli occupation. Most participating in this intifadah were Arab youths not directly affiliated with the PLO or other mainstream organizations professing Palestinian rights. Many analysts have concluded that this insurrection was sparked by the sense of alienation that many young Palestinians, bereft of a meaningful future, had come to experience. Israeli protestations to the contrary, there is little evidence to suggest that the early stages of the protests were conceived, organized, or executed by formal groups outside of Israel, including the PLO. This insurrection was indigenous to the occupied territories and sparked by a generalized sense of despair and frustration, particularly among third-generation and fourth-generation Palestinians in the refugee camps of Gaza and the West Bank.

The Shamir administration responded to these demonstrations and riots with ever-increasing firmness. The policy of the "Iron Fist," predicated on group responsibility for individual acts of resistance or rebellion, produced daily incidents of beatings, arrests, expulsions, jailing without charge, broken bones, and many deaths, mainly among Palestinian teenagers. That these protests could continue on a protracted basis suggests the depth of the feelings motivating both sides in the conflict. The Palestinian intifadah quickly became an element in the international equation in the Middle East, as the PLO attempted to control the rebellion for its own ends, Israel tried to contain it as a domestic dispute, and growing numbers of the international community perceived the events as a major human rights problem.

The attempt by the PLO to benefit from this uprising led to many strains within its ruling coalition. In November 1988, the Palestinian National Council, in a move that surprised many of its friends and foes alike, declared an independent Palestinian state and asked for diplomatic recognition. The specific resolution implied recognition of Israel, but stopped short of the unambiguous statement required by the supporters of Israel. The Israeli government reaction was strongly negative, although growing minority sentiment in Israel favored a "land-for-peace" trade. The U.S. official position at this time echoed formal Israeli policy.

Later in 1988, Yasir Arafat announced plans to speak before the United Nations General Assembly in New York for the purpose of presenting new proposals on the Arab–Israeli conflict. In a surprising move, Secretary of State Shultz refused Arafat a visa, on the grounds that he represented a terrorist organization. Earlier congressionally mandated efforts to close the information offices of the PLO set the stage for this development, but even so, Shultz's refusal shocked many in the international arena, and charges were made that the action violated the U.S. contract with the United Nations. After repeated efforts to change the State Department's decision failed, the meetings were moved at great expense to Geneva, Switzerland, where, in December 1988, Arafat addressed the General Assembly.

The content of Arafat's speech was astounding to all participants in the long-standing conflict. Arafat acceded to U.S. demands for unequivocal PLO positions on three points: (1) the right of Israel to exist in peace within secure boundaries, (2) acceptance of United Nations Resolutions 242 and 338, and (3) a specific renunciation of terrorism generally and of the use of terrorism as a political tool. Arafat ultimately accepted the explicit language required by the United States, as defined in multilateral discussions in Sweden, and the United States immediately moved to begin direct diplomatic discussions with the PLO in Tunisia. Supporters of Israel in the United States were hard put to explain the sudden change in U.S. policy, and the Israeli government formally expressed its "disappointment" with the American decision. The most likely explanation for this substantive change in direction is to be found in Secretary Shultz's earlier attempts late in the Reagan administration to revive the peace process. U.S. attempts were rebuffed by a recalcitrant Israeli government, a fact that angered the administration and began the erosion of administration support.

This sudden shift in U.S. policy energized the peace process in many ways—primarily in eliminating the last practical barrier to an international consensus (minus Israel) favoring multilateral discussions of the Pales-tinian question. The PLO proposals for the convening of a multilateral conference in Geneva ultimately provoked an Israeli response preferring U.S./U.S.S.R.–mediated discussions of the problem. Although there was no obvious solution to the problems immediately at hand, international diplomacy seemed at this juncture to be taking a more active role in bringing the conflict to some conclusion. Just what kind of "autonomy" or "independence" awaited the Palestinian people had yet to be determined. However, there was little doubt that the dramatic change in U.S. policy toward the PLO created more possibilities and probabilities for change than previously existed. The tacit approval of the Bush administration, during the presidential transition in the United States, further suggested continuity in U.S. policy for the next few years. Such prospects were realized in the U.S.-led peace negotiations that began in fall 1991, bringing multilateral diplomacy to bear on this difficult problem. The specifics of this process are discussed in greater detail in Chapter 13.

Despite the special relationship between the United States and Israel, and despite the presence of a highly visible and effective Israeli lobby in the United States, the realities of different interests ultimately expressed themselves. Optimistically, we can hope for a more mature relationship between Israel and the United States in the near future, one that facilitates growth and development for all states in this long-lasting conflict.

SOVIET FOREIGN POLICY

Initially, Soviet foreign policy toward the Middle East was opportunistic and reactive. It was opportunistic in that the Soviet Union attempted to exploit the postwar difficulties of Greece, Turkey, and Iran in its historic attempt to secure a year-round, warm-water port. It was reactive in that it attempted to exploit the consequences of U.S. policy in the Arab–Israeli conflict.

In phase I of its Middle Eastern policy, the Soviet Union attempted a combination of subversion and guerrilla intervention in the northern tier nations. Soviet diplomatic pressure on Turkey was intense, particularly with regard to its navigation rights in the Bosporus Straits and the redefinition of the Thracian border in favor of Bulgaria. This, combined with more direct military adventures in Iran, prompted President Truman to declare the Truman Doctrine and unilaterally commit the United States to the defense of these states. Soviet ambitions in these areas were frustrated, and Soviet policy in the Middle East became more reactive to U.S. policy.

In phase II, the Soviet Union seemed primarily interested in exploiting the difficulties raised by the U.S. commitment to Israel. To find a way to move its growing military capability into the Mediterranean, the Soviet Union began courting the most rabidly anti-Israel states. The first major opportunity came in Egypt, hard on the heels of the Israeli raid on Gaza, the French-British-Israeli attack on the Suez Canal, and the U.S. cancellation of support for the Aswan Dam. The Soviet Union abandoned its initial support for Israel, moved into the arms race in a major way, and ultimately committed

itself to the construction of the high dam in Egypt. Soviet arms aid was supplemented by a vigorous economic aid and trade policy that succeeded after 1958 in orienting the trade relations of Egypt, Syria, Yemen, and Iraq toward the Eastern bloc. Extensive cultural programs also were implemented, many involving educational opportunities for Arabs in Eastern Europe and the U.S.S.R. These programs, combined with its support of nonalignment movements worldwide, succeeded in raising Soviet prestige and influence at the expense of the United States. Until the events of the 1990s reversed the trend, Soviet-trained academics dominated the university systems of Syria, Iraq, and Yemen and remained influential in Egypt.

The Soviet Union was able to turn some of these gains into tangible results. It was given the use of military facilities in Egypt, most notably an extensive naval base at Alexandria, and communication and airfield facilities at Luxor. At one point, Soviet technical and military experts in Egypt numbered close to 20,000. Similar gains were scored in Syria and Iraq, although not on such a grand scale. Its support for the front-line states against Israel and later for the Palestinian guerrilla movements, some of which received technical aid and support from Soviet allies, also contributed to the heightening of Soviet prestige in the area.

Most of the Soviet Union's overt political gains during phase II were nonetheless intangible. Soviet attempts to influence directly the governments of Nasser and Sadat in Egypt were frustrated. The Egyptians seemed adept at taking gifts from the Russian bear while simultaneously avoiding its hug. To a lesser degree, similar events transpired in Syria and Iraq, where allegedly communist-inspired coups were detected and crushed, accompanied by army and university purges. When Sadat ordered the Soviets out of Egypt in 1972, American influence and prestige enjoyed some recovery. Syria and Iraq, in recent years, slowly reoriented themselves toward a more positive, but wary, relationship with the United States.

Phase III of Soviet foreign policy initially paralleled U.S. policy shifts. The Soviet Union aggressively supported wars of national liberation in the area. Frustrated in its attempts to consolidate its advantages in the Fertile Crescent, the Soviet Union turned to overt military aid and surrogate (Cuban) intervention, most notably in Yemen and Ethiopia, where it became involved in the Eritrean dispute. Its invasion of Afghanistan raised warning signs all over the Middle East, particularly among the states formally committed to Islamic rule. Its occupation of Afghanistan lowered its prestige and influence in the region and heightened Middle Eastern awareness of its poor treatment of Soviet Muslim groups. Afghani resistance to Soviet control continued to plague the Soviet and Afghan government troops, leading many commentators to regard this venture as "the Soviet Union's Vietnam." This probably overstates the case, but the fact is that the Afghani fighters (mujahedin) refused to go away and attracted greater external support. As the U.S.S.R. escalated its presence, Muslim governments throughout the area became more suspicious. A case in point is Iraq, where after considerable waffling, the Soviet Union offered substantial support for the war against Iran. Despite this, Iraq continued its pro-Western tilt. Soviet support for Syria, particularly during the Israeli invasion of Lebanon, increased Syrian prestige and indirectly improved Soviet prestige. But Syria is determinedly independent, and it is hard to imagine a less tractable or more unpredictable alliance partner in the Middle East. The 1988 decision to withdraw from the Afghan imbroglio eliminated one of the Soviet Union's negatives in dealing with the states of the Middle East, but this did not in and of itself increase Soviet prestige in the area.

From a geopolitical perspective, the turmoil in the Persian Gulf presented the Soviet Union with some opportunities and risks. Intervention in Iran conceivably could have produced a warm-water port and increased access to foreign petroleum. A successful venture in Oman could have placed the Soviet Union in a position of influence at the opening to the Persian Gulf. Success in the northern tier, bordering as it does on the Soviet Union itself, could have been exploited militarily and politically. The U.S. response to such success was hard to envision. The movement of Iran into the Soviet orbit could upset the international balance to such a degree that the United States would resort to military action. The Soviet Union had avoided such a direct confrontation with its nuclear adversary since the Cuban Missile Crisis of 1962. Soviet diplomacy during the worst days of the Iran–Iraq conflict was cautious and appropriate. Its attempts to improve relations with Israel reflected its growing interest in a greater diplomatic role in the region. Finally, its apparent withdrawal of overt support for wars of national liberation improved its standing in the international community.

The Soviet Union made other international moves that were astounding in view of past policies. Under Gorbachev, great efforts at internal reform were attempted, and it became clear that the Soviet regime equated declining international tension with an opportunity to put its own social and economic house in order. The 1988 nuclear disarmament treaty with the United States evidenced new assumptions in Soviet foreign policy, and the decision to implement a phased withdrawal from Afghanistan suggested a new realism in Moscow. Of great interest and importance to regional actors in the Middle East were new expressions of political activity occurring in Soviet Central Asia, particularly in Azerbaijan, where a regional dispute with the Armenian Republic flared into substantial communal violence. Reliable reports circulated of Soviet Muslim demonstrators carrying placards of Ayatollah Khomeini. Soviet policy toward these marginal elements was an important indicator of the true intent and character of Soviet reforms. With the benefit of hindsight, it now seems clear that the attraction of the republics of Azerbaijan, Kazakhstan, Uzbekistan, and Turkmenistan toward Turkey and Iran in the early 1990s suggests that Islam was an important social and religious fact of life of those former Soviet republics.

The consensus after 1988 conceding the U.S.S.R. a role in mediating the Israeli–Palestinian conflict was further evidence of the maturation of the Soviet role in the politics of the Middle East. A joint U.S.–U.S.S.R. initiative was understood to have considerable weight on both sides of the political divide and enhanced prospects for eventual solutions to existing problems. The events of the 1990s showed the viability of this model, as the United States and Russia jointly sponsored negotiations between Israel and the Arab states.

There is a substantial irony to this state of affairs. Many Middle Eastern intellectuals have long believed that the United States and the U.S.S.R. were basically identical—that they were both interested only in maintaining and extending their political and military power. For these two adversaries, accustomed to seeing each other in absolute, polarized terms, such a conclusion must have seemed outrageously inaccurate. The collapse of Soviet international power in 1990 and the dissolution of the Soviet Union in 1991 put an end to the bipolar structure of international relations and made the whole argument moot. Both states now recognize a fundamental convergence of their basic interests in international stability and relative peace.

BRITAIN AND FRANCE

As indicated in this chapter, the postwar international scene saw a substantial reduction of British and French power. Both nations emerged from World War II victorious but exhausted. Even with the direct help of the United States, these two countries were hard-pressed to reassert their authority over their former colonies. Both reluctantly began a series of retrenchments.

Of the two, Britain's withdrawal from strategic power was the more graceful, the less disruptive. While the French confronted two divisive and difficult wars of national liberation in Vietnam and in Algeria, the British planted supposedly independent, pro-British regimes in their former colonies. When things got out of hand, as they did in Iran in 1952–1953, Britain participated in intrigues designed to bring a friendly face to the throne—in this case the return of the shah from exile.

Both countries attempted to use World War I and World War II diplomacy to extend and develop their influence in the Middle East. Pursuing a course of naked self-interest, the British and the French promised, at one time or another, everything to everybody. In the end, the Middle Eastern state system, a pastiche of kings, emirs, presidents, and sheikhs presiding over geographic entities drawn by committees in Europe, emerged. In this emergence, the power of the British and the French paled in comparison with that of the United States and the U.S.S.R. In the phase I period, they contented themselves with attempting to perpetuate their cultural and economic influence in the area under U.S. military protection. Israel received enormous support in return for taking in the great numbers of displaced European Jews. Extensive oil resources were being developed in Iraq, Iran, Kuwait, and Saudi Arabia.

In phase II, the British and French turned their attention primarily to trade relations. The abortive Suez War in 1956 effectively ended what predisposition they had for an overt military role in the area. After that time, the orientation of the European powers became essentially commercial and focused on the exploitation of the increasingly important petroleum reserves. During this time, it also became evident that support of Israel had become secondary to other objectives. French and British arms were sold indiscriminately in the Middle East, to the anguish of the United States and Israel. These sales demonstrated the growing inability of the United States to control its alliances.

In phase III of their Middle Eastern policy, the U.S. allies grew even less dependent on American initiatives and policy direction. Since 1974, Britain, France, and West Germany have sold increasingly sophisticated weapons and technology to assorted Middle Eastern governments. Even nuclear technology, over specific, energetic U.S. opposition, has been made available to Iraq, Egypt, Libya, Algeria, and Iran. All of these countries have the combination of financial, physical, and intellectual resources necessary for the construction of nuclear devices. At some point, it seems likely that one or more of this aspirant group will succeed in building nuclear weapons. This possibility, combined with the nuclear arsenal in Israel, raises the specter of nuclear confrontation in some unspecified future. This recognition prompted the 1981 Israeli air raid on the Osirak reactor near Baghdad, a raid launched without regard to anticipated diplomatic fallout. Iraq's president Saddam Hussein subsequently called for aid from "peace-loving" nations to help in the development of Arab-controlled nuclear weapons, for the specific purpose of countering Israeli nuclear devices.

After the 1988 cease-fire, many European businesses reentered Iran, Iraq, and the threatened Gulf nations. A more unified, vital, and active Europe expanded its economic and political presence in the Middle East, yet another proof of the changes occurring in the international system. European states and businesses also continued to sell sophisticated technical equipment in the area. By 1990, Iraq had made substantial progress toward its goal of nuclear weapons, its success only incidentally put at risk by its ill-advised invasion of Kuwait and the subsequent coalition response.

Significantly, many European leaders have expressed dismay at U.S. hostility toward Libya, opinions representative of emerging differences in basic policy between Europe and the United States. During this period, the governments of Europe became even more dependent on Middle Eastern petroleum. France, Germany, Italy, Belgium, and The Netherlands must import much of their petroleum from the Middle East. They hastily separated themselves from the United States during the Arab oil embargo. By 1980, all of the major governments of Western Europe enjoyed privileged status in trade relations in the area, exchanging trade and technology for petroleum.

European relations with Israel generally have paralleled world opinion. Israel has found most European countries hostile toward its policies on Palestine and Jerusalem. In the United Nations, they have joined the majority in opposing Israeli aggression and imperialism and have been vocal in their insistence that Israel accept Resolution 242 (1967), which calls for a return to the prewar boundaries. The states of Europe were supportive and encouraging of the PLO initiative toward multilateral consideration of the Palestinian question. Israel found itself increasingly isolated in the court of European public opinion and under mounting pressure to enter into a dialogue with the PLO.

Western Europe, during phase III, began to act as though it were just one of many centers of world power. In 1980 and 1981, the European Common Market called for new peace talks in the Middle East that would exclude the Soviet Union and the United States. As the contemporary international system matures, we can expect to see more independent European and Japanese policy initiatives. As we have emphasized previously, the economic interdependence of Europe and the Middle East continued to grow throughout the 1980s. The fate of Turkey's application for full membership in the European Community should provide an indication of the future of the relationship. Should Turkey finally manage to gain entry, the levels of exchange between the two regions should grow even faster.

CHINA AND JAPAN

The foreign policies of China and Japan toward the Middle East have become important since the 1990s. During phase I, China and Japan deferred completely to the policy dictates of the U.S.S.R. and the United States. In the 1960s, during phase II, both countries turned their attention toward the Middle East, but not in the intense or manipulative way of the superpowers or the European powers. China historically has supported Arab movements toward nonalignment and occasionally offered minimal support to wars of national liberation in southern Arabia. Its interest in frustrating the growth of Soviet power has led China to supply military replacement parts to Egypt after the Soviet Union cut them off. Japan during this period became a progressively larger consumer of Middle Eastern oil, on which it is almost totally reliant to fuel its industry. Japan has placed a high premium on innocuous, positive diplomatic relations in the area.

In phase III, China became more directly active in its attempts to frustrate Soviet gains in the area. Overt Chinese support for anti-Soviet elements in Afghanistan was instrumental in frustrating the U.S.S.R. there. The Chinese also opposed Soviet interests in the horn of Africa. China seemed to be interested in a worldwide alliance designed to frustrate Soviet "hegemonism." The coordination of U.S.–Chinese policy in this regard has been minimal and of little importance to the contemporary Middle East except for Afghanistan and Pakistan. As indicated earlier, Japan has seen its dependence on Middle Eastern (particularly Iranian) oil increase to critical proportions. Japan has had its latitude of action severely restricted and has resorted to a low profile in its international policy in the area. This dependence characterized Japan's diplomatic posture during the entire Iran–Iraq conflict, a period in which Japanese imports of Iranian oil grew unabated. For the Japanese,

with few natural energy resources of their own, the need for regular and predictable supplies of Middle Eastern petroleum continued to militate against taking any position of risk or exposure in the area—a point underscored by the domestic controversy over its financial support of the coalition in Desert Storm. Japanese economic activity and trade in the area continues to grow, keeping Japan ahead of Europe in its total trade activity in the region.

Chinese domestic politics turned in an authoritarian direction after the horrifying suppression of dissidents in Tiananmen Square. Many of the progressive gains made in the decade preceding were dismantled. These changes were reflected in China's foreign policy. China has become something of an indiscriminate supplier of arms, including middling quality nuclear technology and Chinese-built Scud missiles. Middle Eastern states, including Iran and Syria, have been heavy buyers of these replacements for Soviet armaments. China is not the only non-European source of missile technology, but its participation in this type of international trade was and is potentially destabilizing. For its part, China seems more inclined to independence in its foreign policy than in the decade of the 1980s, less inclined to accept the strictures placed on it by the industrial West. It would seem inevitable that fundamental interests of China and Japan eventually would come into salient conflict.

CONCLUSION

All great and near-great power actors more recently have found the Middle East a difficult area in which to implement policy. Changes in the structure of the international system have frustrated Soviet and American policy initiatives in the area. The growth of economic power centers outside the bipolar axis increased the number of players in the game; the collapse of Soviet power further accelerated the trend. Middle Eastern leaders have shown themselves to be adept practitioners of classic diplomacy in this emergent balance-of-power system.

Many of these factors and actors came into play in the immediate aftermath of the Likud electoral victory in May 1996. Prime Minister Netanyahu's efforts to renegotiate details of the Oslo agreements led to a truly international effort to keep the process on course. Near-nonstop mediation by the United States, using special envoys and its diplomatic representation in Israel, was crucial in keeping the Israeli government and the Palestinian Authority negotiating. Periodic public exhortations by Egypt's President Mubarak and King Hussein of Jordan also proved important, and King Hussein's personal intervention in Israel in early 1997 was crucial at a moment when both sides were ready to break off negotiations. Other important players in this scenario included the Commission of the European Union, Prime Minister Chirac of France, Chancellor Schroeder of Germany, and the Islamic Conference, all of which contributed to the chorus calling for continued negotiation and implementation of the Oslo agreements. Events in this area of the world are considered of great importance in other regions and a legitimate arena within which to exercise the prerogatives and responsibilities of power.

13 | INTERNATIONAL RELATIONS IN THE MIDDLE EAST, 1945–1990: THE REGIONAL ACTORS

The international politics of the Middle East have been, in the current period, highly conditioned by the realities of great-power competition. The classic balance-of-power system that prevailed in Europe from the late eighteenth century through the early twentieth century put the region at the center of wars, intrigues, and maneuvers pitting variously England, France, Germany, and Russia against one another for influence and control. Regional actors found it necessary to define their policies largely in reaction to initiatives from the outside. Calculated reaction was complicated by the realities of spying, intrigue, subtle maneuver, double-dealing, and the sheer ignorance of many of the great-power decision makers.[1] Informed rationality was only occasionally important in the exercise of international relations in the region. Decision makers on all sides harbored appallingly inaccurate and inappropriate images of the "others."

Similar realities appeared in the heyday of the bipolar system, as the United States and the Soviet Union, ill-prepared for the role of international arbiters, blundered their way into and through the politics of the region. The U.S. belief that Nasser's Egypt had become a Soviet satellite poisoned relations with Egypt for many years. The Soviet Union's casual disregard for Muslim sensibilities led it into a political morass in Afghanistan, a policy that carried Soviet prestige to new lows regionally.

For newly independent states of the Middle East, foreign policy was a continuing challenge, combining their highest aspirations for independence with the overwhelming reality of their relative weakness. Contemporary regional international relations can be partially understood as the attempt by regional actors to acquire the capabilities (political, economic, social) that support their independence in the international system.

The Middle East is an area seemingly designed for intensive regional activity. As noted elsewhere in this text, the region's nations have many physical similarities: aridity, uneven population distributions, oil reserves, sophisticated communications

---

[1] The notion that the great powers conducted their international diplomacy with high-minded rationality was certainly destroyed by David Fromkin, *A Peace to End All Peace: The Fall of the Ottoman Empire and the Creation of the Modern Middle East* (New York: Avon Books, 1989).

systems, and trade centers. They share many ethnic and cultural similarities: large contiguous blocs of Arabs, Turks, and Persians; the predominance of the Arabic language; and the pervasive influence of Islam. There are many physical, ethnic, and cultural bridges across the national boundaries of the state system. There have been many attempts—public and private—to exploit these similarities.

The oldest of the regional associations in the Middle East is the Arab League. Founded in Cairo in 1945, the League initially was composed of Egypt, Iraq, Saudi Arabia, Syria, Transjordan, Lebanon, and Yemen. Although there were serious internal divisions within the League from the outset, it accomplished some positive action. Critical histories of the Arab League invariably stress its early difficulties in coordinating the war against Israel in 1948. In this war, the mutual suspicions between the Hashemites, Saudis, and Egyptians severely split the Arab forces. In the phase II period, the League was successful primarily in nonpolitical areas—for example, in social and economic cooperation. The Arab League has never been able to resolve the fractious politics of its Arab constituency and has survived by avoiding those difficult problems for the most part. More effective efforts at Arab unity have been pursued from the base of national power, as in Nasser's pan-Arab movement, the Baath Party, and OAPEC (Organization of Arab Petroleum Exporting Countries). In phase III, the League has been an important sounding board for diverse Arab interests.

During phase II (see Table 12.1 on page 279), there were two notable attempts to achieve Arab political unity. The first was the pan-Arab movement launched by Nasser in 1958; the second was the formation of the Baath Party, which was based on the philosophy of Michel Aflaq and found its most receptive constituency in Syria and Iraq. These two movements (pan-Arabism and Baathism) have often been at odds, supporters of each accusing the other of simply advancing the national interests of its leaders.

Nasser's pan-Arab objectives were couched largely in terms of national union. Based on a loosely articulated ideal of Arab unity and cooperation, Nasser's movement was considerably more pragmatic than the ideological basis of the Baath movement. Where the Baath Party depended on loyal cadres to spread its ideology and raise it to power, Nasser pursued the constitutional union of Egypt with a variety of potential partners. At one time or another, Egypt has proposed unification with Syria, Iraq, Yemen, Libya, and the Sudan.

Nasser's pan-Arab strategy produced some tangible results. The 1958 union of Egypt and Syria, the United Arab Republic, survived until 1961, when the federation succumbed to a Syrian army coup. Some critics argue that a failure of the union was prompted by Nasser's efforts in 1959 to effect a true economic, political, and military union—one that to some degree would extinguish remaining Syrian political identity. Others argue that Syrian nationalism simply proved too potent an obstacle for union. Nasser's attempts at federation with Yemen (1958) were much looser and much less ambitious. A proposed union with Iraq in the 1960s was frustrated by a military coup and the subsequent entrenchment of Baathist regimes in Syria and Iraq. Despite these frustrations and failures, Nasser maintained his commitment to Arab unity via political union. Most countries of the Middle East counted among their populations groups strongly supportive of Nasser's dream. These groups were in the main not strong enough to implement his vision of unity, although they were strong enough to worry their governments continually. These governments continued throughout Nasser's presidency to suspect his motives, question his actions, and frustrate his international ventures.

Baathism is a political party and a political philosophy. It is one of the few indigenous political party movements in the Middle East. Based on the work and writings of Michel Aflaq and Salal al-Din al-Bitar, it was founded in 1943 and is committed to the ultimate goal of Arab unity through nationalism, socialism, and pan-Arabism.

The Baath (Resurrection) Party specifically aims to recover past Arab greatness. Baathism found its normal constituency among the intellectuals and military of Syria, Lebanon, Jordan, and Iraq. Since 1963, it has successfully maintained itself in power in Syria and until more recently in Iraq. It should be noted that in Syria, Baathist support came largely from the civilian sector; in Iraq, Baathist power resided mainly in the military, many of whom had earlier supported union with Nasser's Egypt.

The Baathist regimes in Syria and Iraq have been in the forefront of the assault on Israel. Between 1965 and 1975, Iraq openly supported Palestinian separatist and terrorist organizations. Iraqi troops were moved into position during the 1967 and 1973 wars with Israel, although they were for the most part noncombatant.

Syrian policy during phase II moved closer and closer to the Soviet Union, particularly after dissolution of the union with Egypt. Syria was frigid in its relations with Israel and the United States, cool with the traditional Middle Eastern states (Saudi Arabia, Iran), and increasingly friendly with Libya and Algeria. Substantial economic and cultural ties with the Soviet Union and the Eastern bloc were maintained.

The dramatic expansion of Syrian influence after the Israeli invasion of Lebanon (1982) moved Syria into the forefront of diplomatic activity in the area. It seemed possible that this elevated role would lead Syria into the role of a strategic "broker" in regional conflicts. Syrian influence in the region has waxed steadily since that time.

Nonetheless, the Baathist regimes of Syria and Iraq were often at loggerheads despite their ostensible commitment to Arab unity. Both countries have relatively long and potent histories of nationalist feeling, and it is possible that these factors have been a determinant in their foreign policy. They have only given lip service to regional unity movements. Iraq and Syria split forcefully during the Iran–Iraq conflict, with Syria taking a publicly pro-Iranian position despite considerable pressure from

other regional actors backing Iraq. This position put the Syrians and the Israelis in common cause because Israel viewed the Iraqi regime as much more dangerous than any probable Iranian government.

The end of the Iran–Iraq conflict did not ameliorate relations between Damascus and Baghdad, and as Iraq sought ever-closer ties with the United States, Western Europe, and the moderate bloc of Arab states (Egypt, Saudi Arabia, Jordan), Syria burnished its already well-established ties with the Soviet Union and cautiously pursued improved relations with the United States. The events of 1991 occasioned by the Iraqi invasion of Kuwait stood this relationship on its head. Syria aligned itself with the U.S.-led coalition against Iraq and after the war moved aggressively to improve relations with the United States. Syria and Iraq still remained at loggerheads, however, despite the dramatic changes in alliance politics.

A digression on the role of Islam in the regional politics of the area is necessary here. During phase II, Nasser's pan-Arabism, Baathist ideology, and the traditional systems of the day all stressed the importance of Islam as a common source of tradition and identity. In nearly all of the participating states, however, Islam was conceived of in politically secular terms. It was fashionable to recognize the existence of Muslim society (a society composed primarily of Muslims) as a desirable reality, while rejecting the idea of an Islamic state (a state based on the Koran and Islamic tradition). Although there were exceptions to this professed secularism— mainly the Muslim Brotherhood and many Sufi orders—there were no effective challenges to the political orthodoxy of the day. Arab socialism in particular depended on Islamic sources for inspiration, but few economists were willing to suggest that modern economies could be based on the principles contained in the Koran, the hadith, or their subsequent commentaries and codifications. This complacency regarding the role of Islam in politics, economics, and social life was strongly challenged from the

1970s onward (see the discussion of Islamic economics in Chapter 11), and it would be foolish to dismiss the emergent role of Islam in the international relations of the region. Important political, intellectual, economic, and cultural links complement the established religious connections.

Islam was, is, and is likely to remain one of the major facts of international life in the Middle East. Reports of fundamentalist sympathies among Sunni groups in Egypt, Turkey, Jordan, Algeria, Morocco, the Gulf States, Saudi Arabia, and the occupied territories of the West Bank and (especially) Gaza indicate that Islamic fundamentalism has emerged as a potent force in previously secular political systems. Although these groups do not seem as radical in their views as their Shia counterparts in Iran and Lebanon, it does seem that Islam will be a growing element in the regional politics of the Middle East.

Growing fundamentalist influence in Algeria early in 1992 resulted in massive electoral victories. Unwilling to accept the prospects of a potential Islamic republic, the incumbent government and the military abrogated the elections and instituted emergency rule. The conflict in Algeria between fundamentalist Muslims and secular bureaucrats is representative of the tensions emerging in many Middle Eastern states. The international implications of these movements emerge as other governments support or oppose restrictions imposed on fundamentalist parties, and as these groups communicate and support each other across increasingly permeable state boundaries. For Middle Eastern states and their Western counterparts, the distinction between domestic and international politics becomes increasingly difficult to ascertain.

One of the most promising and important regional developments was the organization of the Gulf Cooperation Council (GCC). Founded in 1980, the GCC was based on the realization that only cooperative economic policies and collective security arrangements could ensure the continued independence of the small states

and sheikhdoms ranged along the south side of the Persian Gulf. These states—the U.A.E., Qatar, Oman, Bahrain, and Kuwait—joined with Saudi Arabia, their larger but still vulnerable neighbor, to form an organization that would coordinate the defense policies of the region. Among the early successes of the GCC was the standardization of key defense systems. The GCC members all committed themselves to the purchase of compatible French and British fighters and bombers. Compatible and integrated communication, command, and control systems were installed. Saudi AWAC planes provided a platform for coordinated early warning and air traffic control. A Rapid Deployment Force was organized to meet unexpected threats. A high level of military cooperation and coordination was established. Politically, the GCC was seen as a necessary response to the attempts of Iraq and Iran to establish dominance in the Gulf. The long-running war between those two states provided continual incentive to keep the development of the GCC as a high priority among member states. The rising tide of Muslim, and especially Shia, fundamentalism also kept pressure on the Gulf States.

Saudi Arabia, by geographic size and population, was destined to play a dominant role in the GCC. The GCC became the primary instrument of Saudi policy in the Gulf. In keeping with the established principles of Saudi diplomacy, the GCC attempted to keep at arm's length from entangling relationships with the superpowers or other regional powers. On this basis, Saudi Arabia criticized Oman for its participation with the United States in military maneuvers in 1981.

The diplomacy of the GCC states adopted much of the content and style of traditional Saudi diplomacy. For instance, although the GCC states formally aligned with Iraq in the Iran–Iraq war, the constituent states still kept formal diplomatic relations with Iran. "Burn no bridges, make no enemies" could easily be the diplomatic slogan of the GCC.

Political and economic cooperation slowly followed the military/diplomatic success of the GCC. Left to its own devices, the GCC likely would have moved slowly toward regional integration. With the added goad of the Iraqi invasion of Kuwait and the ensuing war, the immediate future of the GCC seems brighter. The small, and mostly rich, states of the Gulf still live in a "bad neighborhood" with untrustworthy and unfriendly neighbors. Further integration seems to be the most likely avenue of political survival.

The Gulf Cooperation Council's relations with the United States have paralleled Saudi relations with the United States. That means that the GCC has often expressed reservations about the desirability of accepting the U.S. security umbrella. Historical U.S. preferences for Israel and U.S. attempts to trade hostages for arms with Iran during the Iran–Iraq war (the Iran-Contra affair) make the GCC states wary of publicly visible linkages with the United States. The Iraqi invasion of Kuwait changed most of those reservations, and the GCC currently allows a high level of integration with the U.S. military. Linkages tested in Desert Storm remained in place afterward, and the U.S.-GCC strategic alliance is one of the new facts of Middle Eastern international relations.

PALESTINIAN INTERNATIONAL ACTION

It is unfortunate, but in much of the world, terrorism is equated with the Palestinians. It is unfortunate in the sense that the Palestinian people are for the most part no more engaged in the activities of international terror than are the members of any other nation. Nonetheless, the peculiar status of the Palestinians as a large, concentrated but stateless people struggling for some form of independence makes them particularly vulnerable to the kind of stereotyping that victimizes and dehumanizes them. That they struggle for independence against a government with a "special relationship" with the

United States also makes objective analysis difficult. For the reality is that although most Palestinians are normal people who simply want to work and live their lives, terrorism has been a necessary strategy for those Palestinians organizing their drive for independence. To a people without a state, a police force, an army, or a capital, terror is the only available instrument of revolt against established state power.

Any discussion of political terrorism, regardless of how dispassionate or neutral, inevitably raises emotional objections from those who initiate it or suffer from it. In these objections, the motives of either side in the equation of terror are reduced to the most simple and limited perspective. "Terrorists are simply bloodthirsty animals," say the objects of terrorist attacks. "No, we are freedom fighters attempting to overthrow a pitiless, merciless, repressive regime," respond the attackers, "and we must fight these monsters to the death with whatever means are at our disposal." In the final analysis, one person's terrorist is another person's freedom fighter. This fact, coupled with the widespread use of terror and political violence in the modern world, makes analysis difficult.

However, there are dispassionate and insightful observations that one may make about terrorists and their objectives and counterterrorists and theirs. Above all, terrorists seek the creation of a psychological mood. Terror works best in the glare of intense publicity and coverage by the mass media. This coverage can cause a small-scale and apparently random act to translate into a gnawing sense of anxiety in the target population. We know of no government overthrown simply by the cumulation of terrorist acts. Terror tactics, although morally reprehensible, can best be perceived as a sort of harassment or irritant, an activity that can claim the attention of government but rarely topple that government. Reprisals against terrorists ironically can result in losses to the afflicted government, especially if the reprisal is not cleanly and clearly focused against the terrorists themselves. Government attempts in Northern Ireland to suppress terrorism generally have created a fund of ill will among the nonterrorists who are nonetheless disadvantaged or hurt by the governmental policies. Policies of restraint are generally the most profitable in the long run, whereas policies of overreaction may have negative consequences in the climate of world public opinion.

All of these observations have direct applicability to the situation in the Middle East, particularly as regards the Arab–Israeli conflict. Only the most studiously isolated individual is unaware of the wide-scale use of terror by the Palestinian groups confronting Israel. Israel, particularly under the guidance of Prime Ministers Begin and Shamir, has made no secret of its intention to repay terrorist activity in kind, following the biblical injunction of "an eye for an eye, a tooth for a tooth." In keeping with the contemporary cry of "Never again," the government of Israel has invoked powerful symbols in its decision to use a counterterror strategy in its dealings with the Palestinian Arabs.

In the next few pages, we attempt to place this pattern of violence and reprisal into the flow of contemporary international relations. It is not an attempt to draw moral lessons from either side's use of terror or violence, but simply to identify the consequences of those actions. Our effort here is not to catalogue those activities, but rather to emphasize the events that had the most symbolic importance in defining and redefining adversary roles in the conflict.

Totally frustrated in their efforts to obtain relief before 1967, Palestinians began to express their frustrations by violent means. Lacking a national base or homeland, the Palestinians were a genuinely regional group, moving from country to country as the patience and tempers of their hosts wore thin. Of the many organizations they formed, the two major ones were the umbrella Palestinian Liberation Organization (PLO) and its most powerful constituent organization, the Harakat al-Tahrir al-Falastini (Al-Fatah). Both of these

organizations, between 1965 and 1975, accomplished a most dramatic change of status. From the image of bumbling PLO bureaucrats or of ragtag, terrorist revolutionaries (Al-Fatah) furtively slinking across the Middle East landscape, they became accepted internationally as the government in exile of the Palestinian nation and are welcomed in many of the capitals of the world and in the United Nations.

This transformation was not accomplished without difficulty and pain. Dispersed across the Middle East, substantial groups of Palestinians inhabited dehumanizing refugee camps in Lebanon, Syria, Jordan, Gaza, and the West Bank. Others who were more fortunate occupied expatriate positions in the economies of nearly all the nations of the Middle East; they have become a valued resource, given their high level of education. Leaders of this fractured community could with good reason suggest that the Arab states had little interest in solving the Palestinian question because to do so would reduce the pressure on Israel. It was not until the 1967 Arab–Israeli war that the Palestinian organizations found the tide of events moving, although sluggishly, in their direction.

Ironically, the Arab losses and the Israeli victory in 1967 gave the PLO and Al-Fatah the needed impetus. The movement of Israel into the West Bank created a new flood of dispossessed Palestinians, many of whom found the claims of the PLO and Al-Fatah attractive. Simultaneously, the defeat of the Arab armies undermined the prestige of the Arab states and their leaders, creating a power vacuum, at least where the confrontation with Israel was concerned. The two Palestinian organizations suddenly found themselves in positions of preeminence in the Palestinian diaspora.

Al-Fatah, under the leadership of Yasir Arafat, became the most successful group in terms of violent operations against Israel and in providing organized social services to its constituents. Operating initially out of bases in Jordan, Al-Fatah launched numerous attacks against Israel, which ultimately prompted an Israeli retaliatory raid on a Jordanian staging area. The Israeli raid, although successful, encountered stiff Palestinian resistance, which was perceived by many young Arabs as an effective action, bringing increased attention and more volunteers to the organization.

Between 1968 and 1970, Al-Fatah and other, smaller Palestinian groups engaged in increasingly violent guerrilla and terrorist activities, culminating in the hijacking of four jets—a Swissair DC-8, a TWA 707, a Pan American 747, and a BOAC VC-10. These audacious actions captured the attention of the international mass media, inevitably bringing the Palestinian organizations into public prominence. With this public prominence came discussion of Palestinian grievances. Ultimately, the PLO was granted observer status in the General Assembly by the United Nations.

The year 1970 marks a watershed for the Palestinian movements. The event known as Black September, the expulsion of the Palestinian guerrillas from Jordan, proved to be a serious setback to the movement. Moving to Lebanon, from 1970 to 1972, groups of Palestinians accelerated their military and terrorist activities, leading the Lebanese government to repressive measures. Palestinian units began to operate openly in southern Lebanon, in defiance of the government.

The growing role of the Palestinians in Lebanon was formalized in 1969 in a document midwifed by the Arab League and signed by the government and the PLO. Specific rights and areas of governmental competence were given to the PLO, supporting the war of attrition from southern Lebanon. Palestinian influence and position in Lebanon steadily improved until the PLO was generally recognized as one of the most potent political and military groups in the country. The Israeli invasion of Lebanon in 1982 radically altered this situation. The Israeli sweep placed the PLO between at least four dangerous enemies: the nascent Shia militias, the Syrian army, Syrian-backed factions of Palestinians

opposed to Fatah, and the assortment of Christian family armies centered in Beirut and the adjacent mountains. The withdrawal of Arafat and his fighters, under U.S. protection, transformed the loyal PLO groups from military to diplomatic actors, with the PLO headquartered in Tunisia. Other Palestinian groups quickly emerged to continue the military and terrorist pressure on Israel.

Conflict between the various factions of Palestinians often turned violent, producing what has been called the "war of the camps." The PLO itself became the focus of terror during the Israeli invasion and occupation. The horrifying massacres in the Palestinian refugee camps in 1982—carried out by Christian Lebanese militia while the Israeli army sealed off exit from the camps and provided logistical support—created substantial international sympathy for the beleaguered PLO. Yasir Arafat has shown himself more than able to exploit this drift of sympathy, and now realigned with his former foes in Jordan and Egypt, enjoys wide recognition as the only credible national leader of the Palestinian people.

The departure of the Arafat factions of the PLO did not result in a net reduction of terrorist activity in Lebanon. If anything, the scope of terrorism expanded, including not only Israel but other targets as well. Many of the terrorist actions were attributed to a shadowy organization called Islamic Jihad. This may in fact be a convenient clearinghouse for a variety of organizations. What is clear is that terrorism is widely considered an appropriate vehicle for political action. It is a fact of life, and not just in the contemporary Middle East.

Two events of 1985 and 1986—the hijacking of the cruise ship *Achille Lauro* and the coordinated attacks on the passenger lounges at the Vienna and Rome airports—demonstrate the complexity of dealing with terrorist action. In each case, initial assumptions about the origin and affiliations of the terrorists proved to be either wrong or oversimplifications. The centrality of the Libyan role in these actions initially was assumed to be clear and incontrovertible, but in the long run was shown to be problematic, with facts, motives, and organizational structure proving to be murky and diffuse. The identity of the terrorist organizations also proved to be difficult and accountability hard to establish.

A final resolution of who was responsible for the bombing of Pan American Flight 103 over Lockerbie, Scotland, may never be accomplished. The string of credible accusations showed the difficulty of affixing responsibility. U.S. and British authorities initially charged the Abu Nidal faction of the Palestinian movement with responsibility. Syrian involvement was eventually added, and at other times it was claimed that Iran had contracted for the bombing, in an act of revenge for its passenger liner shot down over the Gulf by a U.S. warship. Ultimately, the responsibility was pinned on Libya, and U.S. and British spokesmen demanded the extradition of the Libyan diplomats charged in the bombing. By 1991, Syria, Iran, and the Palestinians, all had been exonerated in the bombing. But political pressures and realities may yet reverse even that finding. Accountability for terrorist activity is as difficult to determine today as it was when it began in earnest in the 1970s.

Phase III Palestinian activity benefited from a growing world recognition of the fact that Jewish relief had resulted in Palestinian injustice. It also benefited from growing financial support from OAPEC members, including Kuwait, Saudi Arabia, the U.A.E., and Khomeini's Iran; from the growing inability of the United States to ignore Arab wishes in regard to the Palestinian question; and finally, significantly, from what was perceived as Israeli tendencies to overreact to terrorist raids on its territory. The West Bank settlement policies of Israel, in particular, convinced many governments of Israeli intransigence toward negotiated Palestinian autonomy on the West Bank.

The Palestinian intifadah beginning in late 1987 prompted Israeli reprisals and draconian attempts to suppress this insurrection. The televised images of public beatings, tear-gassings, shootings, deportations, destruction of housing, and the like by the Israeli army did much to change international public opinion, particularly in the United States, where many Jewish political action organizations professed public distaste for the violence in Israel. American television networks and newswires began carrying information revealing Israeli repression, further contributing to a change in public opinion in the United States. Most important, protest emerged within Israel itself, further polarizing the Israeli polity and influencing the elections in fall 1988.

For this and other reasons, the PLO decided that the fall of 1988 was the right time for a "peace offensive" of major proportions, including a public disavowal of terrorism. Arafat's difficulties in enforcing such a line among the complex set of organizations that make up the Palestinian diaspora was dramatized in the December bombing of Pan American flight 103, en route from Frankfurt to New York, with large loss of life and attendant publicity. Although the PLO ultimately was found innocent in the bombing, it was nonetheless embarrassing to Arafat and was greeted by a chorus of "I told you so's" from Israeli leaders. Nonetheless, the transformation of the PLO into a legitimate governmental organization that speaks for Palestinian interests was under way.

OPEC AND ISLAM

Regional Arab relations in phase III were dominated by two emergent trends: first, the effect of OPEC petroleum pricing on the incomes of Saudi Arabia, Iran, Libya, Kuwait, Iraq, the U.A.E., and others; second, the emergence of Islamic fundamentalism as a potent force in Arab politics. These two trends were intertwined.

With the exception of Iraq, the major petroleum-producing countries in this region were also religiously conservative: Saudi Arabia is dominated by the severe Wahhabi school of Islam; Iran is governed by fundamentalist Shia revolutionaries led by the ulema; Kuwait and the U.A.E. are ruled by traditional leaders who rely on the support of the ulema; and Libya is currently dominated by a unique Islamic fundamentalism developed by Muammar Qadaffi. These countries have used their substantial oil revenues to support religious goals. Kuwait and Saudi Arabia have tied loans and investments to specific Islamic reforms in Egypt and the Sudan. Iran and Libya have supported a variety of anti-Israel, anti-Western movements across the Middle East, both Sunni and Shia. Fundamentalist movements have gained ground in Syria, Lebanon, Iraq, Jordan, Egypt, Turkey, and Algeria, all working toward the establishment of an Islamic state—a government based specifically and exclusively on the precepts of Islam. The Muslim Brotherhood, long proscribed in Egypt since its conflict with Nasser early in the revolution, found new bases of support in Egypt and the Fertile Crescent. These movements, fragmented across many lines, nonetheless posed a singular threat to the prevailing secularism of the earlier international order.

Coordination of policy and collective action have tended to increase in the area in recent years. The early success of OPEC, and of its Arab subgroup OAPEC, led to numerous international development projects funded out of the growing revenues of the petroleum-rich states. Some of these projects had at the minimum a semblance of collective control. Joint economic ventures between OAPEC members, such as the huge dry-dock facility in Bahrain, were also examples of collective action. The successful pursuit of Palestinian rights in the United Nations has been mentioned earlier, and Arab members occasionally have coordinated the freezing of deposits for World Bank projects seen as hostile to the Palestinian cause.

Islam itself has spawned numerous international conferences and organizations, as a growing Islamic international community searches for ways to implement Islamic principles in banking, commerce, and social and political organizations. A group of 42 Islamic nations met in 1980 to consider and protest the Soviet action in Afghanistan, and a few of them broke off relations with the U.S.S.R. as a result. A similar meeting was held in Taif, Saudi Arabia, early in 1981. This meeting affirmed the earlier position taken on Afghanistan and took a dim view of the Iran–Iraq war, which was perceived as damaging to the Umma. The conference was persistent, although unsuccessful, in its efforts to mediate the Iran–Iraq conflict.

Nuclear Arms and Regional Politics

Nuclear politics seem to have taken on a regional flavor. The Israeli nuclear arsenal has long been recognized as a major factor in any major Middle Eastern confrontation, although the specifics of the nuclear weapons are carefully guarded secrets. Arab responses to the Israeli nuclear capability have included regional support for the development of nuclear weapons, often described as the "Islamic bomb." Documented reports of cooperation between Iran, Pakistan, and Libya have circulated. The Israeli preemptive strike against Iraq's nuclear reactor was set against a backdrop of a changing nuclear world. Complicating matters was the fact that nuclear technology was no longer the dark secret that it once was: The technology was now available for purchase, and many Middle Eastern states had sufficient financial resources to do so. The aftermath of the collapse of the Soviet Union put many sophisticated Soviet nuclear scientists on the world market.

In the aftermath of Desert Storm, it was clear that Iraq had made substantial progress in its drive for nuclear capability, using a combination of domestic and international human and technical resources. All of this suggests an enormously complicated international system, one capable of taking the world to the edge of nuclear catastrophe from a regional level of conflict. If these trends play out as it appears they may, we will have to abandon the metaphor of the "tinderbox" Middle East and replace it with more apocalyptic imagery.

Nuclear weapons were not the only area of armament concern. In the last stages of the Iran–Iraq war, Iraq and Iran fought with chemical weapons and with independently modified ballistic missiles. The lack of effective international condemnation of these uses apparently spurred production in Iraq and in many other countries. In 1988, U.S. accusations that Libya was building a chemical weapons facility in the guise of a pharmaceutical plant led to a confrontation between U.S. and Libyan aircraft, resulting in the shooting down of two Libyan Mig-23s over international water. President Reagan, in the waning days of his administration, publicly speculated on the desirability of a "surgical strike" to eliminate the Libyan facility. Intentions and facts are difficult to pin down because facilities that can produce fertilizers, soaps, or pharmaceuticals can be transformed easily to produce gases, explosives, and other chemical weapons. The evidence from Iraq confirmed the hypothesis that chemical and biological weapons of mass destruction were technically and economically feasible in third-world countries. This feasibility, combined with the fact that a consortium of third-world nations now produces missile delivery systems independent of great-power technology, suggests that the world is becoming a more dangerous place. The Middle East is a case in point.

FOREIGN POLICIES OF EGYPT, SAUDI ARABIA, IRAN, AND ISRAEL

In this section, we discuss the respective foreign policies of Egypt, Saudi Arabia, Iran, and Israel. Collectively or independently, these nations have been responsible for most of the international initiatives and exchanges in the region.

Egyptian Foreign Policy

In the post-1948 Middle East, Egyptian foreign policy concerned itself with the following major issues: opposition to colonialism-imperialism, opposition to Israel, opposition to Arab unity, and, after the revolution, opposition to conservative Arab regimes. For some 2,000 years, Egypt had been the prime example of a colonized state. In that long span of time, rarely had the Egyptians been ruled by anything faintly resembling an Egyptian ruling class. The rejection received by Napoleon when he proposed self-rule to the Egyptian ulema was characteristic of the relationship between Egypt and her rulers: Egyptians were intrinsically suspicious of outside powers. All of this was to end after World War II, when Egypt struggled to free itself of European domination. Farouk's foreign policy consisted of attempts to play one set of European powers (England and France) off against another (Germany and Italy). With the Egyptian revolution and the rise of Nasser, however, the concept of anti-imperialism took on greater depth and meaning, until it meant to many the complete removal of foreign influence from Egypt. This rejection of foreign influence was an issue with domestic origins and consequences—an issue to which the Egyptian masses would respond wholeheartedly. Opposition to colonialism-imperialism became as important to domestic policy as it did to foreign policy.

Nationalism and anti-imperialism are often delicately intertwined, producing a complex fabric of action and reaction. The question is in some final sense unresolvable: Does an anti-imperialistic movement create nationalism, or is anti-imperialism itself created by emergent nationalistic feeling? The resolution of this question must await further study. At this point, and especially in the case of Egypt, we must note the existence of a symbiotic relationship between the two forces—a relationship that has enormously complicated Egypt's pursuit of a consistent foreign policy.

Although Egypt was nominally independent of direct foreign control before Nasser's rise to power, many postcolonial problems needed resolution. These problems dominated Egyptian foreign policy in early phase II. Among them were the relationship between Egypt and the Sudan, both former British dependencies (political union was one of the early ideological goals of the revolutionary movement); British rights to control and defend the Suez Canal; and a pattern of mutual defense agreements negotiated before and during World War II. The range of possible solutions was limited because these issues evoked powerful emotions in the Egyptian public, particularly in Cairo, where any agreement with a foreign power would be seen as suspect. The great powers insisted that these problems were only a subset of the larger bipolar confrontation of East and West.

The question of the Sudan's relationship to Egypt was resolved peacefully, but not in a way that was consistent with Egypt's initial objectives. A series of elections led the Sudan ultimately to opt for independence rather than union. The other problems were more complicated and led to international tensions. The sensitive problem of Egypt's relations with the West and the problem of its security goals, conflicting as they did with Egypt's difficulties with Israel, resulted in the Suez crisis and the frustrations over the Aswan High Dam detailed earlier in this book.

The Suez crisis and the Aswan High Dam controversy confirmed Nasser's belief that relations with the Western alliance were going to be uneven. The U.S. and European response to Egypt's negotiations for Eastern-bloc arms was hostile and proved that promised economic and technical aid had clearly visible political strings. Accordingly, Nasser moved increasingly to a posture of nonalignment and began to play an important role in that world movement.

Egypt took a leadership role at the first major nonalignment conference in Bandung, Indonesia (April 1955). Spurred on by his distaste for the Baghdad Pact and the extension of

the bipolar conflict into the Middle East, Nasser subsequently hosted many of the major meetings of the nonaligned powers and forcefully argued for nonaligned foreign policy in the region. Nasser attempted to coordinate his nonaligned foreign policy with such neutralist leaders as Nehru of India, Tito of Yugoslavia, and Sukarno of Indonesia. He attacked the Eisenhower Doctrine of 1957 and continued his unrelenting opposition to European imperialism.

In the 1960s, Egypt's opposition to Western imperialism and to Israel necessitated closer military relations with the Soviet Union, on which it was now solely dependent for arms. This relationship, combined with the growing number of Soviet technicians assigned to the Aswan High Dam project, confirmed many Western judgments that Egypt, along with Syria and Iraq, had slipped irretrievably into the orbit of the Eastern bloc. These reactions were premature and underestimated Nasser's ability to take aid and maintain his own independence of action. The Soviet Union, for its part, was never able to consolidate its gains in Egypt, and in 1972 it departed on Sadat's orders.

Egypt's relationship with Israel has been paradoxical; Egypt has lost every military encounter with Israel but has won much more in the peace settlements. Israel's obviously superior military forces defeated Egyptian armies in 1948, 1956, 1967, and 1973; Israel also intervened with small tactical units in neighboring Arab nations at will during the same period. Each victory became more expensive to Israel and Egypt alike, requiring extensive and speedy military rearmament. Egyptian losses in these encounters far outstripped the losses of its allies, leading to the widespread observation that other Arab states were willing to fight the Israelis "to the last Egyptian."

Despite these consistent military losses, Egyptian prestige in the Arab world was enhanced by these defeats. World public opinion turned gradually in a pro-Egyptian direction, and Israeli interests in the United Nations began to wane. In Egypt and the wider world, the struggle against imperialism and colonialism came increasingly to be seen as continuous with the struggle against Israel.

The political results of the 1967 Arab-Israeli war illustrate Nasser's gift at turning liabilities into assets. The war itself began as a result of Nasser's miscalculation. Increasingly irritated by the presence of United Nations Emergency Force (UNEF) on Egypt's territory but not on Israel's, Nasser ordered the removal of the UN barrier troops. Shortly thereafter, he announced his intention to blockade Israeli shipping at the Straits of Tiran. Nasser at the time was involved in a costly and frustrating venture in Yemen, and it is doubtful that he expected the Israeli attack that occurred on June 5, 1967. At the end of the brief war, the Israeli army occupied all of the Sinai, had taken the Golan Heights from Syria, had destroyed most of the Iraqi air force on the ground, and had occupied Jerusalem and the West Bank of the Jordan River. These losses were traumatic to Nasser and the Arab states. Intervention by the United Nations brought a cease-fire and an end to the fighting. On June 9, Nasser submitted his resignation as president, citing his failure in the war. The Cairo masses refused the resignation with an outpouring of support, prompting Nasser to rescind his resignation and resume his leadership role. What in military terms could be described as a rout became a reaffirmation of Nasser's leadership.

Involvement by the United Nations did not stop with the cease-fire. Most important was the passage of United Nations Resolution 242 on November 22, 1967. This resolution called for the removal of Israeli armed forces from territories gained in the 1967 war and called on all the nations of the region to recognize each other's rights to "live in peace within secure and recognized boundaries free from threats or acts of force." This resolution was greeted with mixed emotions by Egypt and its allies. Although they approved of the return of the conquered territory, they were not pleased with the second point of the resolution, which

would permanently recognize Israel's right to exist in peace. Events in the 1970s found the Arab states anxious to accept the resolution and Israel reluctant to surrender the territory. In the final analysis, Arab support of Resolution 242 became a key item in the Arab propaganda conflict with Israel. The support for the resolution was an important factor in the shift of world opinion toward the Arab and Palestinian cause.

Egypt's venture in Yemen also was frustrating. The Egyptian army was largely removed from Yemen on an emergency basis to shore up defenses after the 1967 war. From 1962 to 1967, the Egyptians had intervened substantially in the Yemeni civil war on the side of the republican forces. During this period, Egyptian troop strength increased to around 80,000 in Yemen. They were opposed by Saudi Arabia, which provided logistical and communication support to the ousted imam, and by tribesmen in the Yemeni hill country. As with the 1967 war, there was no clear solution to this conflict in sight. The expenditure of many lives and dollars resulted in a coalition government, with the royalists and the republicans sharing power. The Egyptian goal, the establishment of a pan-Arab revolutionary regime, was frustrated. The Saudi goal of rescuing a traditional system from revolutionary pressure also was frustrated. The conflict between the modernizing pan-Arabs led by Nasser and the conservative traditional leaders led by Saudi Arabia was not resolved: Saudi and Egyptian relations reached a low point.

From the 1967 war until his death in 1970, Nasser pursued a political solution to the Arab–Israeli conflict. This political strategy necessitated regional cooperation, both formal and informal. Egypt's encouragement of the PLO and Al-Fatah during this period is an example of its informal diplomacy. At the time of his death, Nasser was presiding over a pan-Arab conference in Cairo designed to resolve the Black September conflict between the Palestinian fedayeen and the Jordanian army; this exemplified his formal diplomacy in the post-1967 period.

Egyptian relations with Libya, its western neighbor, were relatively uneventful before the emergence in 1969 of Colonel Muammar Qadaffi as the Libyan ruler. A charismatic leader, Qadaffi possessed a sense of mission and saw himself as Nasser's heir apparent as head of the pan-Arab movement. The tension between the leadership styles of Sadat and Qadaffi soon became quite apparent, although Sadat acquiesced in a proposed Egyptian–Libyan union in 1972–1973. Sadat's reluctance was probably based equally on his misgivings about the great differences between the two countries demographically and economically and his appraisal of Qadaffi's erratic and radicalizing leadership. The union never got off the ground, and it brought the two leaders into open confrontation. In 1974, the Egyptians claimed they had discovered a Libyan plot against Sadat's government.

Since that time, relations between the two states have been cold, occasionally erupting into overt conflict. Libya's support of terrorist movements and its leadership role in the anti-Israeli rejectionist bloc have set it at formal diplomatic odds with Egypt. Libya took the severest stand against Sadat for his bilateral negotiations with the Israelis and reputedly placed a price on his head. As the promise of the Camp David Accords dimmed, Libya's pressure on the Egyptian leader took on more international weight. Egypt thus found itself, in phase III, increasingly estranged from the Arab states that it once sought to lead. Egyptian diplomatic efforts during the Iran–Iraq war were largely ignored in the Arab states, confirming Egyptian isolation. For its part, Iraq accepted limited Egyptian military aid during its conflict with Iran.

EGYPTIAN FOREIGN POLICY UNDER SADAT AND MUBARAK. The foreign policy of Anwar Sadat constituted a dramatic shift in emphasis from that of Nasser. Under Nasser, Egypt had pursued a policy of Arab unity through revolutionary action and development. Sadat sought friendly relations with all Arab states, regardless of their revolutionary status. The hostility that previously marked Egyptian relations with Saudi Arabia and Jordan declined markedly. Sadat put great emphasis on the political resolution of the Israeli question, building on Nasser's belated conversion to this policy. Sadat's personal gifts allowed a public-relations offensive to be launched in the West, particularly in the United States, where he showed himself to be adept at talk shows and news interviews.

Soviet influence also declined under Sadat's leadership. Soviet involvement in the attempted coup against Sadat in 1971, and its hesitance to supply sophisticated new weaponry to the Egyptian army, eventually resulted in its abrupt expulsion from the country in July 1972. Since that time, U.S. influence and arms have gradually replaced the Soviet presence.

Sadat's commitment to a political solution to the Arab–Israeli conflict did not prevent him from initiating the war of October 6, 1973—the Ramadan, or Yom Kippur, War. Sadat's attack on the Israeli Bar-Lev line met with short-term success but incurred heavy armaments losses on both sides; Egypt and Israel called for immediate arms deliveries. The United States responded with airlifts to Israel, which the Israeli army was quick to exploit. The Israeli army was able shortly thereafter to reverse the Egyptian gains and reestablish its positions along part of the Suez Canal. The Egyptian Third Army was effectively surrounded when the Israelis crossed the canal. The threat of the annihilation of the Egyptian force brought a threat of intervention from the Soviet Union.

At this point, the Arab states proclaimed an oil embargo against the United States and its Western allies. This embargo caused the United States to exercise its influence more evenly; as a result of U.S. pressure, the Israeli army did not follow up on its advantages in the Sinai, and the Egyptian Third Army was extricated from the cul-de-sac into which it had been thrown. Subsequent "shuttle diplomacy" conducted largely by U.S. Secretary of State Henry Kissinger and his assistant Joseph Sisco resulted in a cease-fire and the initiation of many rounds of diplomacy between the United States, Israel, and Egypt. Once again, having lost the war, Egypt may be said to have won the peace.

These diplomatic exchanges, referred to collectively as Sinai I and Sinai II, resulted in the following: the withdrawal of Israeli forces back to the Mitla and Gidi Passes, the monitoring of the neutral zone between the passes and the canal by U.S. electronic surveillance, recovery by Egypt of the oil fields in the western Sinai, and the reopening of the Suez Canal with its attendant revenues. Most importantly, the United States had been drawn into the Arab-Israeli confrontation in a more balanced manner. From this time on, Sadat sought closer relations with the United States and attempted to use these relations to bring increased diplomatic pressure to bear on Israel. The stage was set for Egyptian foreign policy in phase III.

Sadat's postwar diplomatic offensive reached its zenith in his dramatic November 1977 address to the Israeli Knesset. The visit of an Arab head of state to Israel was an enormous symbolic and substantive act. His speech effectively broke the diplomatic deadlock. From that point on, Egypt engaged in bilateral negotiations with Israel, a policy bitterly opposed by the Arab rejectionists—Syria, Iraq, Libya, South Yemen, Algeria, and the PLO. These negotiations produced little or no tangible results. They did prepare the way, however, for the remarkable events associated with the Camp David Accords, reached in September 1978.

The Camp David Accords have been described as a triumph of personal diplomacy for President Carter. During 11 days of face-to-face negotiation at Camp David, Maryland, Carter convinced Sadat and Begin to agree to a set of accords that would create a "framework for peace" in the Arab-Israeli conflict. The accords can be divided into two sections. The first accord dealt with the bilateral relations between Egypt

and Israel. It involved the return, by stages, of Egyptian territory in the Sinai and the normalization of relations, including the eventual exchange of ambassadors. By 1980 large numbers of Israelis were touring in Egypt, at least one Jewish temple was reopened in Cairo, and reports of the opening of kosher restaurants circulated in the Western press. To protect Egypt from the potential criticism of the rejectionist states, however, the first accord was linked in principle to a second accord dealing with the West Bank and the Gaza Strip. The second accord directly addressed the problem of the occupied territories and the future of the Palestinian people. The Palestinians, in the loosely worded agreement, were to be granted "autonomy" on the West Bank, although the implications of this term were not spelled out.

The negotiations that followed between Egypt and Israel proceeded fairly smoothly where the disengagement of their forces and the return of Sinai territory were concerned. Simultaneous negotiations on the second accord immediately began to stall, however, on the question of the West Bank. Ultimately, whereas the first part of the accords was fully implemented, resulting in a near normalization of relations between Israel and Egypt, no discernible progress was made on the subject of Palestinian autonomy. Shortly after the Camp David Accords were announced, the Begin government began to increase the number of Jewish settlements on the West Bank; and late in 1980, it announced that henceforth Jerusalem would become the indivisible capital of Israel by action of the Knesset. Apparently, Israel's leaders did not share Egypt's concepts of autonomy.

Predictably, Egypt came under intense Arab criticism for backsliding on the confrontation with Israel. Even the more conservative states of Saudi Arabia and Kuwait joined in the condemnation of Egypt. Radical groups announced the formation of assassination teams aimed at Sadat. Egypt, for its part, gained economically and socially in the bilateral agreement with Israel, but at the cost of its leadership position in the Arab world. Israel gained a secure border that was guaranteed by its most dependable international ally, the United States. The Palestinians, as usual, lost another chance for self-determination and independence.

As Egypt came more into confrontation with its Arab neighbors, it became more dependent on U.S. aid and support. Cooperation between the two nations occurred in the economic, political, and military areas. Nasser's cherished nonalignment policy became a casualty of Sadat's pragmatism.

Ultimately, Sadat himself became a casualty of his domestic and international policies. Egyptian foreign policy under Sadat's successor, Hosni Mubarak, recaptured much of the prestige and status that had eroded in the Arab world since Camp David. Mubarak successfully sought the restoration of relations with the Arab states and cooled his relations with Israel to a diplomatically "correct" temperature, particularly after the invasion of Lebanon. Mubarak's relationship with Washington also remained strong, and growing U.S. economic and military aid to Egypt indicates that Washington perceived Cairo as a trustworthy ally. The two countries in recent years have conducted joint military exercises (Operation Bright Star) predicated on joint operations. All in all, Mubarak has been able to improve his relations with his Arab neighbors (including Arafat's PLO) substantially without threatening the close Egyptian–U.S. relationship. Egypt provided much of the venue for U.S. support of Iraq during the war with Iran, a posture palatable to all of the major Middle Eastern actors except Libya, Syria, and Iran. Mubarak engaged in "personal diplomacy" in his ongoing attempts to facilitate political "conversations" between the PLO, Jordan, the United States, and, ultimately, Israel. In this sense, he continued the broad reconciliation policy initiated by Sadat.

Egyptian–Israeli relations were greatly strained by the Israeli effort to control the intifadah in the occupied territories. One result of the cooling in relations was strong pressure by Egypt on Arafat and the PLO for an initiative that would bring some movement on the Palestinian question. As Arafat acquiesced to pressure from Egypt and other moderate Arab states, and from the United States and the Soviet Union alike, the prestige of Egypt increased. This growing prestige was given a great boost from Egypt's early participation in the coalition formed against Iraq after its invasion of Kuwait. Egyptian prestige grew again as the United States pressed forward with an attempt to solve the Palestinian question through Arab-Israeli negotiations. At one point, facing destructive public rhetoric from Yitzhak Shamir and Hafez al-Assad, Mubarak threatened to make public their earlier "private" meetings and conversations. Egypt is clearly one of the premier international actors in the region. The election of an Egyptian, Boutros Boutros-Ghali, in 1992 as secretary-general of the United Nations further increased Egypt's international visibility and prestige. On the negative side, Mubarak's growing international prestige as a regional "moderate" may result in growing friction with the fundamentalists gaining political strength in Egypt.

The special relationship between Egypt and the United States has remained intact since the Camp David Accords and strengthened during and after the Iraq–Kuwait crisis, assuring Egypt a generous flow of U.S. aid and the forgiveness of $6 billion in debt. One should not overestimate the influence that this aid garners the United States in Cairo, but there is clearly a relationship of mutual respect between the two countries that translates into specific policy gains for both parties.

Saudi Arabian Foreign Policy

Saudi Arabia is the one Arab country that immediately after World War II could point to a long-standing relationship with the United States. This relationship began in the 1930s as American oil companies began to appreciate and exploit the enormous petroleum reserves of this recently consolidated kingdom. The earliest relationships between Saudi Arabia and the West were exclusively the product of the oil companies' initiatives. King Ibn Saud, in desperate financial straits in 1933, required a loan of £30,000 in gold sovereigns as part of the original oil concession agreements. This loan, put up not by the U.S. government but rather by the participating oil companies, came at a critical time for the king, allowing him to maintain the loyalties of key elements in his new tribal coalition. The U.S. government was at this time relatively uninvolved in the affairs of this remote region. The loan apparently produced enormous goodwill toward the oil companies in particular and toward the United States in general. From that point on, despite cordial relations with Britain and concerted efforts by the Germans and Japanese just before World War II, Ibn Saud expressed his preference for the United States. He was to pursue this preference during World War II, despite his experts' counsel to the contrary and despite lost potential oil revenues from sales to the Axis powers. His loyalty proved to be an enormous asset to the United States during the war and immediately thereafter.

The emerging relationship between the United States and Saudi Arabia just after World War II can be fairly characterized as "special," a term connoting an unusual mutuality of interests and policy between the two states. U.S. interest in Saudi oil was complemented by its interest in maintaining and expanding its air base at Dharan, a base that linked Western interests in India with the Mediterranean, as part of the larger Western attempt to contain possible Soviet expansion. U.S. payments to Saudi Arabia, both governmental and corporate, began to increase annually. The newfound wealth prompted the initiation of many ambitious development projects from 1947 on, which in turn necessitated the movement of numerous American technicians and advisors to the kingdom. The development projects,

which ran the gamut from communications, transportation, and electrification to public health and public education, significantly increased Saudi prestige in the Middle East. Ibn Saud's ministers fully entered into the international relations of the region. From this time, Saudi Arabia was to be one of the major actors in the Middle Eastern international order.

One of King Ibn Saud's first international ventures in the postwar period concerned the future of the Palestinians. Relying on the special relationship he had had with President Roosevelt, King Ibn Saud sought and received assurances that no decisions affecting the future of the Palestinians and Jerusalem would be made without consideration of Arab wishes. Ibn Saud's public espousal of the Palestinian cause heightened his prestige among the Arab states. It also made for his first major disappointment in U.S. policy, as President Truman virtually ignored Roosevelt's promise of consultation in his hasty recognition of Israel in 1948.

Saudi Arabian prestige and power were clearly on the rise at the time of King Ibn Saud's death in 1953. He was succeeded in power by his son Saud ibn Abdulaziz. Simultaneously, the new king's younger brother Faisal was named crown prince. The new King Saud was a far less effective monarch than his father.

King Saud, from 1953 onward, changed the basic thrust of Saudi foreign policy. Where his father had pursued a policy of close alignment with the United States, Saud moved into a closer alliance with revolutionary Egypt, accepting the principles of nonalignment put forward by Nasser. Simultaneously, Saudi Arabia opposed the Hashemite kingdoms of Jordan and Iraq. The Hashemite family, long influential in the tribal politics of the Arabian Peninsula, had been among the final obstacles to Ibn Saud's consolidation of his kingdom. Fear of possible Hashemite reprisals from bases in Jordan and Iraq motivated much of Saudi international policy.

Ibn Saud had protected himself against potential Hashemite intrigue by allying himself with England, the major international guarantor of the Hashemite house. King Saud approached this problem by formally adopting in 1955 the Egyptian revolutionary policy toward Jordan and Iraq. This policy essentially involved a continuing attempt to isolate the two countries diplomatically and to support actively anti-monarchical movements there. However, although Egypt and Saudi Arabia had common interests, including opposition to Israel, it was becoming increasingly clear to the Saudi elite that Saudi Arabian interests ultimately would conflict with Egypt's.

Growing dissatisfaction over King Saud's conduct of domestic and foreign policy led to efforts within the royal family to limit his power and to enhance the power of Crown Prince Faisal, acting as prime minister. These efforts bore fruit in 1958. The emergence of Faisal as the primary decision maker signaled what was to become an important shift in the foreign policy posture of Saudi Arabia. Under Faisal's influence, King Saud became increasingly cool toward Cairo and increasingly cordial toward Iraq and Jordan. Encouraged by the United States, which feared growing Soviet influence in the area, Saudi Arabia ceased its attempted destabilization of Jordan and Iraq. This is the same period in which the Eisenhower Doctrine was pronounced, offering and guaranteeing necessary aid to any Middle Eastern state suffering foreign aggression. King Saud endorsed this declaration after a state visit to the United States.

Crown Prince Faisal proved to be an effective leader. His domestic reforms quickly restored fiscal stability to the kingdom. His foreign policy was more finely balanced and moderate, a foreign policy informed more by Saudi self-interest than by international alliance politics. Substantial domestic policy gains were scored, all of which contributed to a recovery of Saudi prestige in the Middle East. Relations with Cairo became formal and correct, but not warm. Soon, the two countries would enter into protracted hostilities in Yemen.

Faisal's initial period of rule was challenged by dissident elements in the ruling family. These elements persuaded King Saud to place certain policy demands on Faisal that he was unwilling to accept. Faisal resigned and was replaced by a candidate from the dissident ranks. The new prime minister, Prince Talal, fell victim to jealous intrigues himself, some eight months after his rise to power. From 1962 to 1964, Crown Prince Faisal gradually reacquired his lost power and gained more, until he became the virtual ruler and Saud became a figurehead. This situation was finally resolved in November 1964 when Saud was deposed by royal family consensus and Faisal was made king. Saud died in 1969.

King Faisal continued the close relationship between the United States and Saudi Arabia, but the relationship changed substantially between 1964 and 1975. Faisal became increasingly bewildered and irritated by U.S. unconditional support of Israel. This developing tension between the two countries did not suffice to reorient Saudi policy toward the revolutionary Arab states or the Soviet Union, but it was undoubtedly instrumental in Faisal's decision to participate in the Arab oil embargo immediately after the 1973 Arab–Israeli war. That embargo, which shook the U.S. economy, was indicative of a new Saudi attitude toward the United States and the U.S.S.R.—an attitude that emphasized the growing independence of Saudi Arabia in foreign policy. Saudi Arabia moved into phase III of its foreign policy. In this phase, relations were based increasingly on the grounds of pragmatism and national interest, a new posture at least partially facilitated by the increasing income generated by its petroleum sales. Although Saudi Arabia participated fully in the 1973 oil embargo against the United States, it continued to maintain close economic and military relations with the United States. Saudi Arabia, under Faisal and his successor, Khalid, attempted to improve substantially its independent military strength through the purchase of sophisticated armaments and training from the United States and elsewhere.

In 1980–1981, the Saudis sought to upgrade their tactical air capabilities significantly and to purchase sophisticated U.S. radar planes (AWACs). Israeli opposition to such transfers was vehement.

The assassination of Faisal in March 1975 by a minor and mentally unstable member of the royal family ended the administration of this remarkable leader. He was succeeded in office by King Khalid. The transition was smooth and involved minimal administrative disruption. Of some importance from an elite perspective was the continued influence of Prince Fahd, whose influence on Saudi government continued unabated from the reign of King Faisal through the reign of King Khalid. Under Khalid, Fahd would assume even more direct control over the conduct of foreign policy.

From 1978 to 1980, Saudi Arabia became even more disillusioned with U.S. policy in the Middle East. Saudi spokesmen such as Prince Fahd and Sheikh Yamani (minister of petroleum) were openly critical of U.S. policy. In their view, a quid pro quo between the United States and Saudi Arabia developed shortly after the 1973 oil embargo. This agreement required Saudi Arabia to increase its oil production and oppose extreme price increases by the militant members of OPEC and OAPEC. In return, the United States committed itself to an evenhanded Middle Eastern policy; it agreed to sell sophisticated military technology to Saudi Arabia and Egypt and to pressure Israel to return the occupied territories and settle the Palestinian question. In the Saudi view, they were faithful to their part of the bargain, whereas the United States dragged its heels on armament sales and failed to force the Begin government to implement the Camp David Accords regarding Palestinian autonomy. In the immediate aftermath of Desert Storm, in 1992, the Saudis reluctantly joined in the multi-lateral peace conference organized by the Bush administration, demonstrating their continuing reservations about U.S. policy.

King Khalid's death in 1982 brought Prince Fahd to the throne. Fahd's stewardship of Saudi foreign policy continued a modest activism, culminating in the presentation of a comprehensive peace plan for the Middle East. Similar to other Saudi efforts, it was predicated on the United States taking a more active role in constraining and influencing Israeli policy. Also similar to other efforts, the initiatives failed to bear fruit. The Saudis continued to place much of the responsibility on the United States for its reluctance to "play tough" with Israel. Another constraint on Saudi foreign policy was declining petroleum revenues, forcing harder domestic and international choices. Both of these factors were important influences in the Saudi decision to commit its leadership and resources strongly to the GCC, an organization that Saudi Arabia dominates and that demonstrated its importance as a diplomatic and military coordinating body during the Iraqi invasion of Kuwait.

The Saudi complaints about the U.S. policy inconsistencies have substance, but in fairness the Saudi elite probably overestimates the independence of the American president in the conduct of foreign policy. Israeli influence in Congress and in presidential elections has been strong enough historically to make a pro-Arab stance a severe political liability. The United States and Saudi Arabia continue to maintain a strong military and economic relationship. Saudi and U.S. interests, at base, are predicated on numerous similar assumptions: primarily, that the political status quo is preferable to revolutionary change.

It is also clear that in the past 20 years Saudi Arabia changed from being an uncritical ally of the United States to a country pursuing its self-interest based on its growing financial and economic power. The elites of Saudi Arabia increasingly have turned away from dependent international alliances and toward independent national pragmatism. The Islamic revolution and attendant events in Iran did much to undermine Saudi confidence in the ability of the United States to protect the Saudi monarchy and Saudi territory unilaterally; the danger to

Saudi Arabia during the Iraqi invasion of Kuwait made this realization even more tangible and manifest. Saudi Arabia can be expected to pursue an even more independent foreign policy in the coming years—years that will see growing internal pressure on the Saudi elite. These internal pressures, combined with the potent forces of revolutionary Islam in the contemporary Middle East, could thrust Saudi Arabia into new domestic and international conflicts.

Saudi Arabia's increasingly paternalistic posture toward its Gulf neighbors, the U.A.E., Qatar, Bahrain, Kuwait, and Oman, is also an indication of its growing international independence and regional influence. Its commitment to the coordination of regional defense and economic policy was implemented in the organization of the GCC. Saudi Arabia saw these states as part of its defense perimeter and sought closer relationships. For the most part, these efforts proved successful. All of the Gulf States exist in the shadow of two much larger neighbors, Iran and Iraq, both of which have been determined to achieve military and political dominance in the area. Both have actively courted the Shia populations of the GCC states and constantly raise the suspicions of those governments.

Oman became a primary focus of U.S. attempts to improve its position on the Gulf and the Strait of Hormuz after the Iranian revolution; this focus also indirectly improved the scope and quality of U.S. relations with Saudi Arabia, allowing the coordination of defense planning through the GCC without unwelcome visibility. Yemen is another sensitive area of concern. Saudi Arabia has intervened in Yemen whenever necessary since 1962, and there are no signs that this concern for Yemeni stability will abate, especially given the unification of Yemen. Yemen is now a potentially stronger neighbor than before, with a dramatically different worldview. Saudi Arabia expelled many Yemeni guest workers during and after Desert Storm, perceiving Yemeni sympathies for Iraq as potentially dangerous. Tensions remain high along their mutual border.

Saudi Arabia has taken the initiative in all of these relationships. As Saudi Arabia seeks a greater degree of partnership with the United States, as opposed to a more dependent relationship, it stands to reason that it will become even more aggressive diplomatically. These issues will be discussed in greater detail in Chapter 14.

The precipitous decline in petroleum prices in the mid-1980s reduced Saudi Arabia's ability to accomplish its diplomatic agenda strictly with grants-in-aid or other payments. Relatively speaking, the moderation in petroleum prices and the declining rate of increase in demand during the period strained Saudi Arabia's ability to complete its ambitious development programs on schedule. Although the country still enjoyed considerable revenue from petroleum exports, less and less of the revenue could be considered "excess" and available for diplomatic purposes. One consequence of this situation has been greater Saudi involvement in the efforts to reinvigorate OPEC and reestablish a sounder relationship between petroleum supply and demand. Iran and Iraq, desperate to improve their economic conditions, were loath to accept production restrictions, as were other non-Middle Eastern producers, Nigeria especially. Dramatically increased Saudi production, put in place as a retaliatory measure to punish those states unwilling to join in production limits, was implemented, with the effect of falling prices for petroleum worldwide. Given Saudi Arabia's growing levels of proven petroleum reserves, a factor that differentiates this country from many other producers, this policy promises to remain a centerpiece of Saudi foreign policy.

During the events of the Iraq–Kuwait conflict in 1991 and 1992, Saudi Arabia dramatically increased its petroleum production to offset losses in Iraq and Kuwait. In the recovery following, Saudi Arabia was positioned as even more of a dominant influence in the pricing and marketing of petroleum internationally. Saudi Arabia has continued to support moderate prices that stimulate continued demand for the product without instigating a search for viable alternatives.

Events in Afghanistan in 1979–1980 brought a heightened awareness of Soviet power in western Asia. This new awareness produced some cooperation between old adversaries. Iran and Saudi Arabia tried to frustrate the Soviet-sponsored war of national liberation that was launched against Oman from South Yemen, and Iraq and Saudi Arabia agreed finally during the Iran–Iraq war to divide the "neutral zone" between them, a long-standing source of conflict. Healthy fear of Soviet penetration in the area had produced "discussions" between the conservative states of the Middle East and all but the most radical revolutionary states. Saudi Arabia was deeply involved in these developments. The dramatic events that first occasioned the collapse of Soviet international power and then precipitated the dissolution of the union itself in 1991 changed the equation completely. The Soviet Union (now the Commonwealth of Independent States) was completely out of Afghanistan; even more important, it was no longer an influential international actor in a bipolar world. This fact changed the face of international relations in the Middle East. Saudi Arabia reacted to those changes by seeking diplomatic relationships with countries it had shunned earlier, particularly Syria and Iran.

Because of its security concerns in the emerging international order in the Middle East, and because of its unique role in Islam as the custodian of Mecca and Medina, Saudi Arabia has become a center of pan-Islamic activity. Many conferences have been held in the past decade in Saudi Arabia that embrace a variety of questions confronting the Islamic world. Conferences on Islamic banking and finance, Islamic law, and economic development have been held in Riyadh, Mecca, Taif, and Dharan. In these conferences, the weight and prestige of the Saudi government have been prominent. The emergence of revivalist Islam as a potent force in the Middle East may have presented the Saudi elite with a counter-strategy against the revolutionary secular governments of the region. Prestige politics of this kind are not without some hazards. Iranian attempts to exploit the hajj for propaganda purposes have disrupted the pilgrimage on more than one occasion and prompted Saudi police action against the demonstrators. Although Saudi Arabia obviously benefits as custodian of the holiest shrines of Islam, its stewardship also raises envy and provides opportunities for embarrassment. To some degree, the fundamentalist movements in Islam exacerbate this problem, a topic discussed in more detail in other chapters in this book.

Iranian Foreign Policy

Iran's geopolitical position in the Middle East has always assured it of a central role in the international relations of the region and the world. This role has not always worked to its advantage. It frequently has been involved in the ambitious plans of stronger nations. In the nineteenth and twentieth centuries, Russia attempted to extend its influence in Iran to gain control over Iranian territory. Britain, the Ottoman Empire, and Germany tried to frustrate Russian gains. These international pressures were compounded by the complicated domestic makeup of Iran, composed of many diverse cultures and nations. The Persian-Shia core of Iran is surrounded by large concentrations of Kurds, Azeris, Baluchis, Turks, and Arabs, all of whom nurtured dreams of relative autonomy or independence at one time or another. Although Iran is predominantly Shia, there are substantial populations of Sunnis and Bahais. This makes for a political system of great complexity and potential conflict, inviting foreign intervention.

The rise to power of Shah Mohammed Reza Pahlevi in 1941 indicates the degree to which Iranian domestic politics have been influenced by international relations. The shah came to power after his father, Reza Shah, was forced to abdicate by a combination of Soviet and British pressure. In deference to the pro-German sympathies of Iran's ruling class, Reza Shah had tried to keep Iran neutral in World War II. Soviet and British leaders would have none of this and demanded his abdication. The reorientation of Iran from neutrality to alliance with the West was accomplished during the war. A definite policy of pro-Western and anti-Soviet international relations was pursued deliberately by the shah from that time on, often causing domestic opposition to the policy. The period of stress and disorder from 1951 to 1953, engendered by Premier Mossadegh's attempts to nationalize British oil holdings, is an example of the domestic opposition to the shah's foreign policy.

From the immediate postwar period through the 1970s, the shah of Iran pursued a foreign policy predicated on close, even intimate, relations with the United States, rabid anticommunism, and the systematic expansion of Iranian military power. The shah envisioned Iran as the dominant political and military force in the Middle East policing an area of growing economic and strategic importance. Associated with these goals were the recovery of Persian greatness and the transformation of Iran into a modern industrial complex ruled by a benevolent monarchy. The petroleum reserves of Iran made such grandiose ambitions distinctly possible. Iran's sharing of a boundary with an increasingly powerful Soviet Union added the necessary note of urgency.

Iranian relations with the United States were not a one-way street. The United States played an important role in the shah's return to Iran in 1953. Subsequent U.S. aid under the Eisenhower administration—aid denied to Premier Mossadegh during his brief stay in power—helped stabilize the shah's power. Shortly after this consolidation, American oil companies successfully negotiated entry to the Iranian oil concessions. The "love affair" between the shah and the United States was definitely reciprocal. A charter member of the Baghdad Pact, Iran was a major success in U.S.

strategy among the northern tier nations. Substantial aid and trade followed. Relations with the Soviet Union, already cool, cooled further.

The 1958 revolution in Iraq signaled the onset of strained relations between Iraq and Iran. The border became the scene of tension and frequent armed hostilities. The Kurdish minorities were exploited by each side in their attempts to embarrass or occupy the attention of the other. As the revolution in Iraq moved into its Baathist phase in 1963, relations became even more strained. Conflicting claims over territory at the Shatt al-Arab of the Persian Gulf aggravated an already unfriendly relationship, as did concern over the safety of Iranian pilgrims in southern Iraq. Both sides viewed each other's military growth with alarm. With the Soviet Union supplying arms and material to Iraq, and the United States fulfilling a similar role for Iran, the bipolar confrontation manifested itself in the regional politics of the Middle East.

Iranian relations with the United States were not unduly complicated by the Arab–Israeli conflict, at least not to the degree seen in the foreign policies of Egypt and Saudi Arabia. As a Persian rather than Arab nation, Iran did not share the rabid anti-Israel sentiments of its neighbors, particularly Syria and Iraq. During most of the shah's reign, Iranian relations with Israel were cordial and constructive, with Iranian oil fueling the Israeli economy. Cooperation also existed in other spheres, with both countries exchanging intelligence, espionage, and police technology. Iran, alone among Middle Eastern oil producers, declined to participate in the Arab oil embargo of 1973–1974 and continued to sell oil to the United States and Israel.

During phase II, the shah committed Iran to a series of major reforms that he called the White Revolution (1963). These reforms were prompted in part by the international course charted earlier. Growing Iranian military and economic power necessitated a skilled population capable of managing the complicated machines of war and production. Predictably, the changes attendant on the White Revolution produced strains and tensions in Iran. These tensions, which included the growing alienation of the landed gentry from the shah, the outrage of the Shia ulema over the secular thrust of the reforms, and the political frustrations of groups wanting social and economic modernization, prompted increased political repression. The instrument of this political repression was SAVAK, the Iranian secret police.

SAVAK became a nightmarish fact of life in Iran, presiding over a pervasive network of spies and informants, using the latest in surveillance and interrogation techniques. Widely recognized in Iran as a client of the U.S. Central Intelligence Agency and the Israeli Mossad, SAVAK killed tens of thousands of Iranians and tortured and mutilated many more. SAVAK became increasingly linked in the public mind with the shah and the United States. These factors combined with other political forces to bring on the revolution of 1978. Before the final act was played out, however, the shah managed to acquire one of the largest military machines in the world.

It would be simplistic and incorrect to portray the shah of Iran as a mere puppet of U.S. interests. Toward the end of his rule, particularly after the success of OPEC greatly increased Iran's oil revenues, the shah pursued policies sometimes at odds with the United States. This situation is particularly evident where oil pricing was concerned. In this policy area, the shah pursued a course best described as militant, arguing for massive increases in the royalties paid the producing countries. The shah was aware of the limited nature of Iran's petroleum reserves and wished to use the remaining production to build a postpetroleum economy. Needless to say, the dramatic increases in petroleum prices he advocated were not perceived as in U.S. interests, or in the interests of its European and Japanese allies. The shah pursued the price increases vigorously, in spite of American discomfort and pressure. In point of fact, the shah was one of

the earliest supporters of OPEC and played a key role in ushering in the third phase of post–World War II international relations in the Middle East. The shah, even given the most conservative assumptions about his rule, contributed greatly to the changing face of Middle Eastern politics.

In phase III diplomacy, the foreign policy of Iran was increasingly influenced by domestic politics. After 1975, rising domestic opposition to the shah's regime and to SAVAK repression prompted the shah to pursue even more drastic measures to control his opposition. Many of the opposition were exiled or fled to Iraq, whose government lent support and a podium for verbal attacks. The success of these attacks contributed materially to the ultimate decline of the shah's national prestige.

In this phase of its foreign policy, Iran became even more involved in the politics of the states neighboring the Persian Gulf. Iran sought close and amicable relationships with the smaller states of the Gulf and with Saudi Arabia. Despite this policy, Iranian troops occupied three small islands near the Straits of Hormuz in 1971, achieving potential control over traffic in and out of the Gulf. When a Marxist-backed rebellion threatened the security of Sultan Qabus of Oman, Iranian troops were dispatched to Oman to help suppress it. All in all, from 1972 to 1978, Iran enjoyed something approaching military hegemony in the Persian Gulf. This was the high point of Iran's international power and influence under the shah.

The year 1978 saw the effective consolidation of the shah's opposition, leading to a virtual state of anarchy in Iran's cities. On January 16, 1979, the shah left Iran with his family. He would not return. Iran, under its revolutionary Islamic leaders, would enter a new age of Iranian diplomacy and foreign policy.

FOREIGN POLICY OF THE IRANIAN REVOLUTION. Iranian foreign policy under Ayatollah Khomeini was nearly diametrically opposed to that of the shah. The United States, instead of being seen as a steady and respected ally, became the personification of imperialism and decadence, rivaled only by the Soviet Union. The foreign policy of Iran was to be based on the principles of Shia Islam, not on the interests of Persian nationalism. Iranian ideology reflected an imperfect combination of Islamic social and political thought with the drives for political independence and nonalignment characteristic of phase III developments in the region. Compounded by the irregular and intermittent leadership of Ayatollah Khomeini, Iranian foreign policy appeared to its detractors as a mishmash of contradictory impulses and goals.

A low point in U.S.–Iranian relations occurred with the seizure of the U.S. embassy and the taking of its employees as hostages on November 4, 1979. The degree of complicity between the government and the students who seized the embassy was unknown, but the seizure was triggered when the United States admitted the shah for medical treatment. Many in Iran believed that the United States, so instrumental in returning him to power once before, would attempt to do so again. The seizure of the embassy was seen by these groups as one way to forestall such an effort.

The seizure and continued holding of the hostages was contrary to international law in its symbolic and pragmatic dimensions. Negotiation proved fruitless, especially because the Iranian regime connected the future of the hostages with the return of the shah by the United States for trial. Traditional U.S. contacts with the Iranian elite had been obliterated by the revolution. In April 1980, the United States attempted a military rescue of the hostages, but it failed. Increasingly, the situation began to resemble a classic no-win situation for both sides. The international prestige and patience of the United States were severely tested by the seizure. Iran suffered from the U.S.-imposed and -inspired economic sanctions initiated in early 1980.

The resolution of the conflict came in January 1981, on the day of the inauguration of President Reagan, and some 15 months after the hostages had been seized. Although both sides attempted to portray the outcome as a great victory, more sober judgments prevailed. As ABC correspondent Pierre Salinger concluded after his exhaustive analysis of the negotiations, it may have been a victory for the human spirit of the hostages themselves, but it was not a victory for the United States or for Iran. Both sides lost considerable prestige and influence in the exchange.

Subsequent events later in the 1980s provided more opportunities for pain and embarrassment. The Iran-Contra initiative was revealed as a bungled U.S. attempt to free hostages in Lebanon by selling badly needed arms to Iran at the moment that the United States was attempting to organize an international boycott of weapons sales to Iran. The accidental shooting down of an Iranian domestic airliner over the Persian Gulf showed Iranian weakness in the face of U.S. power, while it simultaneously embarrassed the United States in revealing the operational weaknesses of its high-technology warfare.

Iranian relations with the United States continued to be cold and antagonistic. Although the hostage situation held the spotlight for most of 1980, other shifts in Iranian foreign policy could be observed. First, Iran became one of the rejectionist states in the Arab–Israeli conflict. Yasir Arafat met with Khomeini shortly after the latter's return to Iran in 1979, and the two pledged to work together for the liberation of the occupied territories and for Palestinian independence. The Israeli mission was turned over to the PLO. Iranian proxy groups in Lebanon carried on much of the terrorist initiative against Israel—particularly Hizbollah, a Shia fundamentalist group in southern and central Lebanon. Iranian opposition to Israel became a major premise of Iranian foreign policy.

The Soviet Union, although enjoying the U.S. predicament in Iran, was unable to capitalize on the Iranian revolution. Virulently anticommunist, the Iranian revolutionary elite was in domestic conflict with pro-Soviet elements, particularly in the cities and the oil fields near Abadan. As a consequence, Iran did little to reverse the shah's anti-Soviet foreign policy. The Soviet Union, with large populations of Muslims bordering on Iran, contemplated the disorder in Iran with apprehension. The Soviet invasion of Afghanistan in 1980 brought Soviet-Iranian relations to their lowest point. Soviet withdrawal from Afghanistan did not in itself notably improve Soviet-Iranian relations. Soviet willingness to reflag Kuwaiti tankers to protect them from Iranian attacks during the last stages of the Iran–Iraq war removed any vestige of the idea that the U.S.S.R. might be neutral in that conflict. Soviet diplomacy in the area reassured no one and renewed suspicions about the underlying motives of great-power diplomacy in the region. Iranian foreign policy continued to identify the United States and the Soviet Union through 1991 as unwelcome interlopers.

Iranian relations with Iraq, always troublesome, turned violent after Iraq's seizure of disputed territory in the Shatt-al-Arab on the Persian Gulf. For eight years, Iran and Iraq engaged in a war of varying intensity: periods of relative quiescence followed by short bursts of vicious fighting. The conflict quickly spilled over into the Gulf region, with both sides attacking tankers headed to enemy ports. Both Iraq and Iran suffered substantial declines in petroleum revenues and horrifying casualties.

With its larger population base and substantial economic infrastructure, Iran was probably best situated for a protracted conflict. Iraq, given this reality, was the recipient of substantial foreign military aid. Conservative and moderate Arab states—notably Egypt and Saudi Arabia—provided money and arms to keep Iraq from defeat. Egypt channeled European and American arms to Iraq. Syria, Libya, and Israel independently aided Iran, obviously for different reasons.

The end of hostilities in the Iran–Iraq conflict was a bitter pill for the government of Iran. The prosecution of the war exacted high costs financially and in human terms. Reportedly, Ayatollah Khomeini concluded reluctantly that further prosecution of the war would be disastrous, and with great pain he endorsed Speaker Rafsanjani's plan to accept U.N. mediation to end the conflict. The result prompted a hiatus in Iran's role as fomenter of radical change in the area—a turning inward toward domestic conflicts and problems. The diplomatic isolation of Iran, apparent in the muted world reaction to the shooting down of its airliner over the Gulf, continued.

Iran's regional influence and international prestige received a great boost in the early 1990s, benefiting from the confluence of events in Europe and the Middle East. Specifically, the collapse of Soviet power and the reorganization of the now-independent republics (Commonwealth of Independent States) created an area of fluid potential in the region. The miscalculations in Iraq that led to Desert Storm pitted two of Iran's most bitter enemies against each other. By taking a relatively neutral position, Iran became one of the most immediate beneficiaries of Desert Storm.

Iran was able to gain politically and economically in this scenario. It has used revenue from its increasing petroleum sales to shop for arms, reportedly spending nearly $20 billion in 1992 to reequip its armed forces. One of the possible applications of this new power just might be in Central Asia, where Iran supports movements of fundamentalist Muslims intent on establishing an Islamic republic. Much of the military materiel, ironically, came from the former Soviet Union.

Simultaneously, the Rafsanjani government embarked on efforts to improve Iran's relationship with the Western powers. Relations improved slightly, going from cold to chilly, and the United States allowed the release of some of the funds seized during the hostage crisis of more than a decade earlier. Iran reportedly paid millions of dollars to the Lebanese groups holding American hostages, with resulting releases in late 1991 of all American hostages held there. Similar advances were made in Europe, although some problems continued to beset Iran's efforts. The death sentence imposed on novelist Salman Rushdie for the publication of *The Satanic Verses*, a novel widely regarded as blasphemous by fundamentalist Muslims, still rankled Great Britain; and Iranian terrorist reprisals in other European states prevented the development of "normal" diplomatic relations.

Iranian influence in the foreign relations of the Middle East is still best thought of in moral and symbolic terms, although circumstances could change quickly. The Islamic revolution in Iran, with its Islamic constitution and its stress on Islamic sources of social, economic, and political policies, is still a dramatic demonstration of the revolutionary potential of Islam in the contemporary world. Coming, as it did, during widespread disenchantment with the politics of bipolar confrontation, the Iranian revolution spoke to the ability of peoples in the Middle East to organize domestic and international politics on their own terms, in their own way. And now, with the bipolar system a memory of history, peoples and movements in the region are even less constrained by external influences on their political life. Iranian influence is indirectly evident in the fundamentalist political movements in Jordan, Egypt, the Sudan, Algeria, and Morocco. These movements ultimately may have momentous consequences for the international system.

Israeli Foreign Policy

More than any other Middle Eastern state, Israel was formed in the crucible of international relations. The difficulties that beset the Jewish community in Europe in the late nineteenth and early twentieth centuries produced the international Zionist movement. This diverse group of Europeans was able, against heavy odds, to establish a Jewish state in the Middle East. In the Zionists' view, this state symbolized a return to the historical site of

their religion and civilization. In the view of the Palestinians living there at the time, the state symbolized an aggressive invasion of their homeland by European colonists. Neither side perceived a middle ground between these two positions. Consequently, Israel's foreign policy is also its domestic policy. Domestic security in Israel has always been a function of its international situation.

During phase I of Middle Eastern diplomacy, the leaders of Israel were concerned with the physical establishment of the state. To accomplish this, they resorted to a variety of legal and illegal international efforts. Above all they sought international approval for their efforts, both unilaterally and bilaterally. In this they were successful, much more so than their Arab opponents. Unanimous great-power recognition of the state of Israel came virtually on the announcement of sovereignty. The fledgling United Nations provided the necessary diplomatic midwifery. All of this occurred in the immediate context of Arab diplomatic and military opposition.

Support in the United States for the young Israeli state was widespread. In addition to formal U.S. aid, Israel received great infusions of financial and political aid from the American Jewish community. This private aid proved to be crucial for Israel. Support for Israel assumed a mantle of inviolability in the United States, particularly in election years. Opposition to support for Israel was characterized as anti-Semitic or baldly fascistic. To say the least, Arab prestige was not high.

During phase II, Israeli foreign policy was linked tightly to its domestic policy. Domestic development depended on safe and secure boundaries; domestic development would help provide those same boundaries. In this stage of Israeli policy, successive governments of Israel sought to capitalize on their diplomatic advantages over their Arab neighbors. Israel moved enthusiastically and fully into the bipolar alliance structure of the postwar period. American arms and aid flowed freely into Israel from its founding until phase III diplomacy necessitated an American reappraisal of the relationship.

In its relations with its Arab neighbors, Israel pursued a carrot-and-stick policy. The carrot in the relationship was the supposed benefit of bilateral negotiations with Israel—the carrot ultimately nibbled by Sadat at Camp David. The stick was Israel's undisputed military superiority. The statement that the best defense is a good offense was put into practice by Israel in the Suez War of 1956 and the 1967 war. In both instances, Israeli first strikes initiated armed conflict.

Although the Israeli military actions were impressive for their speed and their effectiveness, the price was high. During this period, military superiority and preparedness began to take a higher and higher toll on the Israeli economy. This toll was reflected in increasing levels of inflation and in the economic losses connected with the full mobilization of the Israeli military. Israel, with a small population, found it increasingly difficult to sustain full military mobilization and a thriving economy simultaneously.

Repeated confrontations with superior Israeli military forces made the Arab states reluctant to do battle with Israel. Instead, the Arab states chose a strategy of diplomatic confrontation and isolation, a strategy that began to pay off first in the United Nations. The 1967 conflict, in which Israel occupied the West Bank, Gaza, and the Golan Heights, prompted United Nations Resolution 242, calling for the full restoration of those areas. Israel found itself increasingly isolated in the United Nations and relied more and more on friendly vetoes from the United States. World public opinion began to turn, resulting in a repolarization of attitudes toward Israel.

This period of Middle Eastern history also saw the beginning of Palestinian diplomatic and military activity against Israel. This activity was not confined to Israeli territory; it included many harassment actions such as the hijacking of commercial airliners and horrifying acts such as the seizure and murder of Israeli athletes at the Munich Olympics in 1972. Israeli reprisals included assassination squads sent into Beirut, the imposition of punitive curfews and penalties for political agitation, the shooting down of a Libyan commercial airliner that strayed over Israeli air space, an air strike in 1985 on PLO headquarters in Tunisia, and multiple routine air strikes on PLO staging areas throughout Lebanon.

By the mid-1970s, world opinion had shifted markedly in a pro-Palestinian, anti-Israeli direction. In 1975 the United Nations General Assembly adopted a resolution condemning Zionism as a form of racism. Semiofficial "observer" status was extended to the PLO at the United Nations. Israel's treatment of imprisoned Palestinian Arabs was condemned by Amnesty International, and a similarly critical U.S. State Department report surfaced in the mass media. Israeli prestige, initially created and supported by the larger world community and the United Nations, was now on the defensive in the same forums.

The same set of circumstances that ushered in phase III diplomacy and resulted in a heightening of Arab prestige also signaled the growing diplomatic isolation of Israel. During this period, Israel became increasingly protective of its special relationship with the United States. At the same time, the Nixon, Ford, and Carter administrations became more evenhanded toward the Middle East. The result was an inevitable and growing political strain between Washington and Tel Aviv. The United States, more and more dependent on Middle Eastern petroleum production, found unyielding support for Israel increasingly expensive.

The Camp David agreements of 1978 demonstrate one dramatic attempt to reconcile the security needs of Israel with the economic problems confronting the United States. The first section of the agreements, implementing a bilateral disengagement between Egypt and Israel, proceeded smoothly; section 2, which would have established Palestinian "autonomy" on the West Bank and Gaza, made little progress. Prime Minister Begin, after the implementation of section 1 of the accords, began a policy of new Jewish settlement in the "occupied territories." Israel was determined to maintain an effective presence in the West Bank, regardless of what Palestinian autonomy entailed.

The inability of Egypt and Israel to make progress on section 2 of the accords was aggravated symbolically by the Knesset's decision in 1980 to make Jerusalem the undivided capital of Israel. Arab reaction to this was predictably strong. As we have seen, King Khalid of Saudi Arabia called for jihad to bring East Jerusalem back under Arab control. Coming as it did from a leader who had cultivated an image of restraint and control, such a call was indeed a sign of the growing Arab irritation over the expansionist policies of the Begin government. The PLO fueled these flames of discontent by increasing its raids against Israel. Israel responded with air strikes, commando raids, and a tightening of security precautions, all of which served to heighten the sense of urgency among the Arab states.

The Israeli elections of June 1981 injected another note of uncertainty into Middle Eastern politics. The elections were called after the Begin government found it increasingly difficult to control its parliamentary coalition. At the onset of the campaign, the Labor bloc enjoyed a healthy lead, at least as reported in national polls, but by the end of the campaign the Labor and Likud blocs were in a virtual dead heat. This turn of events was at least partially attributable to the prevailing atmosphere of international confrontation.

Two major conflicts dominated the period before the elections. The first involved Israeli expansion of its role and activity in Lebanon, including stepped-up counter-Palestinian raids in southern Lebanon, air surveillance of virtually all of Lebanon, and strong financial and military support for right-wing

Christian paramilitary groups. Syrian action involved increased pressure on the Christian units, particularly to the east of Beirut, and the introduction of numerous Soviet-supplied SAM antiaircraft missiles into eastern Lebanon and especially in the Bekaa Valley. Prime Minister Begin vowed to remove the missiles by force if Syria failed to withdraw them. A nasty diplomatic confrontation between Syria and Israel emerged. It is difficult and perhaps meaningless to try to determine the sequence of events that led to this confrontation. What is important is to recognize the seriousness of both sides in the conflict and its potential for widening the Arab-Israeli conflict. U.S. shuttle diplomacy, utilizing the talents of retired State Department official Philip Habib, focused on keeping the confrontation contained, using international diplomatic pressure. In this, Habib was at least partially successful.

The second, and much more dramatic, international action involved the Israeli raid on Iraq's nuclear reactor complex (Osirak) near Baghdad. The raid, using American-built F-15 and F-16 fighters, succeeded in knocking out the reactor in what must be described as a flawlessly executed exercise. World opinion nearly unanimously condemned the raid, and the United Nations formally condemned Israel for the raid and asked for compensation to Iraq. Significantly, the U.N. resolution condemning Israel was a joint product of the U.S. and Iraqi delegations to the United Nations—a collaboration unthinkable a decade earlier. Many saw in this reaction an increasing international isolation of Israel and growing resolve of Prime Minister Begin to go it alone, regardless of the consequences. For his part, Prime Minister Begin characterized the attack as defensive in nature, given the reactor's ability to produce weapons-grade plutonium, and argued that the raid was a moral imperative to avoid another Holocaust.

Controversy over these two actions—the confrontation with Syria and the raid on Iraq—polarized Israeli politics more than any previous time in its political history. Many backed Begin for his firm handling of the Arab danger, and just as many criticized him for unnecessary reliance on military action where diplomacy might have been successful. The virtual dead heat between Labor and Likud doubtless found much of its cause in this internal division.

Instead of caution, the confused internal politics of Israel resulted in a more aggressive foreign policy. Moves toward the annexation of the West Bank and the Golan Heights were initiated. In spring 1982, the Israeli army began an invasion of Lebanon, ostensibly to remove Palestinian terrorists from bases adjacent to the Israeli border.

What was initially presented as a limited action was instead, it was soon apparent, a full-scale invasion. Israeli troops quickly seized the southern cities of Sidon and Tyre and began a fast-paced move up to and into Beirut itself. The professed goal of the invasion changed to the elimination of the PLO presence in Lebanon, not simply the removal of bases near the Litani River. It seems that the architects of the invasion hoped not only for the removal of the Palestinians, but also to tip the political equation in Lebanon in favor of conservative Christian groups with whom they could negotiate a favorable peace treaty. None of these goals were achieved. It is difficult to identify any positive short-term results attendant on the invasion.

From the perspective of international and regional relations, the invasion introduced serious strains between Israel and the United States, strains increased by revelations of systematic Israeli spying on U.S. intelligence agencies; led to a substantial enhancement of Syria's power and prestige; failed to eliminate Palestinian terrorist groups in Lebanon, although the Arafat factions of the PLO were forced to leave; further reinforced images of Israel as intransigent and militaristic; created circumstances that led to the politicization of hitherto quiescent Shia groups, particularly AMAL and Hizbollah; and ultimately failed to create a sympathetic government in Beirut.

Domestically, the invasion produced substantial internal political division over the wisdom of the invasion and its moral consequences. The Kahan Commission investigating the massacres at the Palestinian refugee camps was very critical of the Israeli Defense Forces officer corps, and a public discussion of Shin Bet executions of Palestinian terrorists damaged governmental secrecy, while simultaneously polarizing public opinion. The growing number of Israeli casualties during the three-year occupation disheartened many families. The Israeli economy went into a tailspin, at least in part a function of the costs of invasion and occupation. Politically, the invasion was a major factor in the resignation and withdrawal from politics of Prime Minister Begin and the progenitor of the odd sequential coalition between the Likud and Labor blocs in the face of a divisive and yet indeterminate election.

The aftermath of the Israeli withdrawal from Lebanon in summer 1985 saw the Arab-Israeli conflict taking on new coloration. The U.S. role in the area was visibly reduced, and Israel's self-confidence in its moral rectitude was challenged. The Palestinians had more faces than ever, and the prospects for a negotiated settlement seemed dim. Courageous leadership, of the type exhibited by Sadat during his trip to Jerusalem, seemed a scarcer commodity than ever. Arabs and Jews have paid a high price for the privilege of settling disputes through violence.

The assassination of President Sadat on October 6, 1981, served to emphasize the degree to which the United States and Israel had predicated their policies on the particulars of Egyptian policy. They, most of all, found themselves in the process of agonizing reappraisal of their foreign policies. In the main, these reappraisals centered on the question of whether or not the policies of Sadat would survive his administration or would fall victim to the new political realities likely to follow.

The continuity in Egyptian foreign policy under Mubarak placed Egypt in a position of high prestige with nearly all of the international actors in the region. Mubarak complied with the letter of the Camp David Accords, reclaiming the Sinai territory lost in previous conflicts. Egypt did not repudiate the treaty even after the Israeli invasion of Lebanon, an act repugnant to most Egyptians. Egypt provided a warm welcome to the exiled Arafat and recovered a measure of its revolutionary bona fides in the process.

The relative calm of U.S.–Israeli relations was jarred when the Palestinian revolt prompted renewed U.S. efforts to promote a settlement. Secretary of State George Shultz personally engaged in an extensive round of regional diplomacy, alternately needling and wheedling the respective players for substantive action. Israeli leaders were successful in ignoring these pressures until fall 1988, when the actions of the PLO reenergized the U.S. effort. Other powers entered the discussions; even England, long stalwart in its refusal to talk with PLO representatives, relented and opened lines of communication. This effectively left Israel isolated and with a diminishing set of possibilities. Israeli diplomatic maneuvers centered on discrediting the PLO for continuing terrorist activity and attempting to define a different set of Palestinian leaders with whom to negotiate. International pressure in favor of some form of "autonomy" for the occupied territories was building, and the Israeli government, fragile coalition that it was, was hard pressed to find palatable and practical policies. Short-run solutions to the problem seemed unlikely, but it also seemed that a process had begun that *could* in time lead to an amelioration of the plight facing the Palestinians under Israeli control.

Public opinion in the United States, reacting to the brutal suppression of the intifadah and Israeli unwillingness to enter into substantive dialogue with a changing PLO, reflected declining support for Israel—particularly among the American Jewish community, long noted for its unwavering support but now disconcerted by the repressive

policies of the Israeli government in the West Bank and Gaza. These changes presented a serious challenge for Israeli leadership, particularly given the importance of U.S. aid in maintaining the security and economic vitality of the country. As is so often the case, clear linkages between domestic and international policy existed, complicating already complex calculations.

The collapse of the coalition government in 1988 brought the Likud back to power and ushered in another Shamir administration. The foreign policy of the Shamir government was predicated on a hard line toward Palestinian independence, increased Jewish settlement in the occupied territories, and a willingness to accept deteriorating relations with the Bush administration as the price for this set of policies. This initially resulted in growing tensions between Washington and Tel Aviv and increasing rhetorical conflict between Israel and its Arab neighbors. The continuing Israeli response to the Palestinian intifadah added to this declining prestige.

Israel also found its foreign policies affected by the emergence of a new world order. The decline of the bipolar system devalued Israel's purely military value to the United States. The changes in the Soviet Union allowed dramatic increases in Soviet emigration to Israel, straining the economy with dramatically growing resettlement and housing expenses.

Iraq's invasion of Kuwait proved both a blessing and a problem for Israel. Excluded from the formal coalition, Israel was not a front-line state in Desert Storm, and its losses were confined to a few Scud attacks with little loss of life or property. Palestinian sympathy for Iraq increased the latitude of the government in its attempts to control the Palestinians. Onerous curfews, the closing of schools and other institutions, deportations, and increased settlement activity placed even greater pressure on the Palestinian community. Israel's officially low-profile role in the conflict gave it the opportunity to increase the pressure on its Palestinian population.

On the debit side of the ledger, the aftermath of Desert Storm found the Bush administration pushing hard for multilateral talks aimed at settling the Palestinian question. Implicit in the effort was a "land for peace" formula that the right wing of Israeli politics found absolutely unpalatable. Kicking and screaming, the Shamir government was forced to the conference table in late 1991 and 1992 by a combination of "carrots and sticks." Israel's detention of Palestinian staff traveling to the peace conference and its military operations in southern Lebanon in the winter of 1992 contributed further to the existing strains. The domestic political consequences of entering into these discussions prompted two religious parties to drop out of the Likud coalition in the Knesset, necessitating new elections in summer 1992.

The international events of the early 1990s damaged the prestige and reputation of Israel and brought it into increased confrontation with the United States. Major changes in the structure and dynamics of the new emerging international order present serious challenges to the Israeli government today. As high-technology weaponry suffuses the area, bringing even relatively small states substantial increases in military capability, simple and direct military action becomes ever more destabilizing and less likely to produce the desired effects. Perhaps the events of the turn of the millennium herald the beginning of more pragmatic initiatives from all parties to the conflict. In this political mare's nest, we dare not hope for less.

CONCLUSION

In the years since the end of World War II, the Middle East has been the scene of intense international exchange. The forces of great-power interests, emerging national self-interest, international economic interdependence, and secular and Islamic revolutions have changed the international relations of the Middle East. No longer reacting primarily to the bipolar strategies of the United States and the Soviet Union, the Middle Eastern states now initiate international moves to which other powers must respond. Pragmatic self-interest pervaded the policy atmosphere of phase III diplomacy. This attitudinal change, together with the real financial power of the petroleum-rich Arab states, signaled the emergence of the Middle East as one of the several independent power centers that make up the multipolar world.

Thinking about the world as a bipolar system yielded powerful insights from 1948 through the 1980s. In the midst of 1980s, however, the explanatory power of the model declined, and the behavior of states seemed to be less and less conditioned and constrained by bipolar considerations. We now see the end of that system and the emergence of a new, multipolar world. This change is sufficiently significant that we have added another chapter to this book, examining the possible consequences of this new world order for the domestic and international politics of the Middle East. In particular, Chapter 14 examines the dimensions of the newly emergent international system; the effect of Desert Storm on that system; and the prospects for real peace between the Arabs and Israelis.

14 | THE MIDDLE EAST AND THE CHANGING INTERNATIONAL ORDER: 1991–2001

By the end of the 1980s, it was clear to most observers that the prevailing international system was in the process of change. However, few foresaw the rapidity and implications of that change. Processes that were assumed to be stable deteriorated in a matter of years, even months. The result was the disruption of the old order before the dimensions of the new order were clear. Many statesmen spoke glibly of the "new international order," but few were clear about the contours and details of the new system. As is so often the case in this new age, changes occurred faster than the ability of governments to perceive or understand them.

Reviewing the signal events occurring from 1988 to 1991 gives us some idea of the early direction of change. Events began with uncharacteristic agreement on nuclear weapons treaties between the United States and the Union of Soviet Socialist Republics (U.S.S.R.). With hindsight, it seems that both protagonists in the great cold war were economically exhausted by the competition. These agreements were followed closely by Soviet retrenchment throughout the world, including its withdrawal from Afghanistan and drastic reductions in its support for its allies elsewhere.

These emerging trends assumed the proportions of an avalanche by early 1990, and in short order the Soviet Union abandoned its political and military role in Eastern Europe. "Velvet revolutions" occurred in Poland, Czechoslovakia, and Hungary. The Berlin Wall fell, and German reunification was permitted and quickly implemented. The Warsaw Pact was dissolved, and many of its members, including the Soviet Union, unsuccessfully petitioned for membership in NATO. The "eye-ball to eye-ball nuclear confrontation" of some 40 years' duration took less than 40 months to evaporate. The bipolar world order was defunct.

Emboldened, perhaps, by the events in Eastern Europe, the Baltic states of the Soviet Union increased their demands for independence. Events again outpaced the expectations of statesmen and scholars. In fairly short order, Lithuania, Latvia, and Estonia gained a measure of independence from the Soviet center. These changes precipitated others until the chain of events eventually challenged the Soviet government itself. Decades of pent-up regional and nationalist sentiments were released. As republic after republic in the Soviet Union declared its independence, the authority of the Communist Party and the central government progressively declined. The reform movement headed by Mikhail Gorbachev lost momentum to the forces of revolutionary change, increasingly symbolized in the leadership of Boris Yeltsin and the political and economic centrality of the Russian Republic.

The forces of radical change were energized again in August 1991 when threatened members of the old Soviet elite attempted a coup against Gorbachev and his government. The failure of the coup resulted in the formal dissolution of the Communist Party and the progressive transfer of power from the Gorbachev government to the governments of the republics. In December 1991, a majority of the republics of the old Soviet Union ratified a new Commonwealth of Independent States (C.I.S.). This entity of confederation—a system of relative autonomy and cooperation between ethnically and historically defined regions—formally replaced the Soviet Union and finally and practically signified the last gasp of the old communist order.

Even the names of the players changed, and most probably not for the last time. Although the Soviet Union has been reconstituted as the C.I.S., events occurring after January 1992 reduced the vitality of the new C.I.S. and demonstrated the emergence of a newer and more intense Russian nationalism. The mixed success of the Yeltsin government in 1995, 1996, and 1999–2000 to suppress the attempted secession of Chechnaya is a case in point. Attempts to negotiate a settlement failed, and periodic violence from each side seemed to strengthen the resolve of the other. Similar observations regarding resurgent nationalism, separatism, Christian and Islamic religious extremism, and basic political uncertainty characterize many Russian provinces (e.g., Chechen Republic, Dagestan, Ingushetsia), and many of the new states of central Asia. These include notably Azerbaijan, Georgia, Turkmenistan, Kyrgyzistan, and Armenia and the fragmenting components of the former Yugoslavia, particularly in Bosnia and Kosovo—all within or bordering on the nominal cultural and political region we understand as the Middle East.

The immediacy of the changing world order finds its most dramatic evidence in the emerging relationship between Israel and the Palestinians. After decades of intransigence, two old and battle-scarred combatants—Itzhak Rabin and Yasir Arafat—warily exchanged handshakes in Washington in September 1993, under the beaming countenance of President Clinton. This handshake and the subsequent encounters between Israeli and Palestinian officials began the process of negotiation that would lead eventually to real transfers of power to the Palestinian National Authority, under the elected leadership of Yasir Arafat. This image—Yasir Arafat and the Palestinian Liberation Organization (PLO) exercising real administrative power in Gaza and the West Bank, armed Palestinian police officers patrolling in cities and villages—is one that would have been inconceivable a decade earlier.

Also inconceivable would have been the cast of characters active in the process that led to such change. Secret diplomacy exercised by the government of Norway, not the United States or any of the so-called "great powers," broke the deadlocks between Arafat and Rabin in 1993 and 1995. King Hussein of Jordan, by his presence and his remarks, contributed to the healing of Israel after the assassination of Prime Minister Rabin and literally left his hospital bed to restart stalled Palestinian-Israeli negotiations at Wye Plantation in Maryland in 1998. Regional and world actors acting in good faith for idealistic reasons have been of great importance in bringing the Palestinian–Israeli relationship to its current state and condition.

There is no doubt that the old international bipolar system is gone. But the system replacing it is an act in progress, not a finished product. Change, and its handmaiden of uncertainty, is in the air and on the land. Consider the collaborators in the decision to intervene in Bosnia in 1995 and Kosovo in 1999. Who would have predicted only a year or two earlier that NATO, under the nominal direction of the United Nations, would put troops on the ground in an area far removed from its normal theater of operations? Who would have predicted broad support for the reintroduction of German troops into the Balkans? Who would have predicted the combination of U.S. and Russian troops working together to establish a peaceful climate in which a government born of negotiations in Dayton, Ohio, could come to fruition? We truly live in a dramatically changing world. However, there are trends and developments that suggest the outlines of a new international order.

DIMENSIONS OF THE EMERGING INTERNATIONAL ORDER

Although it is early to specify the full dimensions of the emerging world system, some trends are apparent. In order of importance we note the following:

1. The new world order is *not* unipolar. The collapse of the Soviet Union did not automatically elevate the United States to the level of a hegemonic power. The same pressures that caused the collapse of Soviet power seem to constrain U.S. power as well. Both are counting on reductions in military appropriations to reinvigorate their lagging economies, and so are the other principal world powers. Finally, the former Soviet Union is a nuclear power of great importance even in the chaotic situations attending its reorganization and partial democratization.

2. The emerging world order is apparently *multipolar*, a world system in which military, economic, and political power is more widely dispersed than in the previous bipolar system. It also is likely that few countries in this system will have across-the-board capability. The new order will be characterized by the economic and military power of one actor combining with the military and political power of others, in a relatively free-floating set of international combinations.

3. The movement toward *regional integration* will continue. Economic regional integration will proceed in Western Europe, North America, Eastern Europe, Southeast Asia, East Asia, North Africa, and the Persian Gulf. There are potentials for increased integration in Latin America and sub-Saharan Africa as well. These new institutions eventually will constitute power centers with consequences for the conduct of international affairs. At the minimum, their existence implies a system of shared powers and responsibilities, a system quite different from the one it replaces.

4. In this environment, *international organizations* will become increasingly important. Multinational organizations such as the United Nations and NATO will perform important coordinating roles in the international order. Nongovernmental international actors also will take on an increasingly important role in international affairs, organizations like Médecins Sans Frontières or the International Red Cross/Red Crescent.

5. Global political, social, and economic *interdependence* (globalization, as this process is often called) will continue to accelerate, considerably reducing the independence of governments and their actions. Resource scarcity (water, fuels) and global pollution (ozone depletion, ground water contamination) and population control will require international cooperation for solutions. Nearly instantaneous international communication will keep us all aware of the human costs of disease, famine, war, and natural disaster; national politics will be ever more visible to attentive publics on the outside. Technology will continue to diffuse independently of the attempts of governments to restrict it.

6. *Regional conflicts* will become more active and numerous as the restraining effect of the bipolar competition fades. War and conflict will not disappear because of the changing international system, but the size and consequences of conflict will change. The arenas of conflict are being redefined by the changes at the system level. The great powers of the world will face increasing levels of regional and local risk as the dangers of global nuclear threat recede. Smaller conflicts and more of them are likely occurrences in the brave new world we all now face. The civil war in Yugoslavia is a good example of this, and the plight of the Kurds, spanning the boundaries of Turkey, Iran, Iraq, and Syria, is another.

7. The *north–south conflict* is likely to intensify. As the previous system of ideological competition fades, conflict between economically and socially defined groups is likely. Demand for more equitable sharing of the world's resources is a likely nuance of the emerging world order. Global conflict between rich and poor is likely to become a political and moral, if not military, fact.

8. Finally, and in many ways most important, a blurring of the distinction between domestic and international policies confronts all major nations. The domestication of the international and the internationalization of the domestic make coherent policy making difficult. As Robert Pranger has observed, "Because the demands placed on national interests by international and domestic environments differ in ends and means, foreign policy . . . is more complicated than domestic policy . . . and requires areas of expertise not normally available in any abundance to leaders whose legitimacy usually depends on domestic political authority."[1]

THE MIDDLE EAST IN THE EMERGING INTERNATIONAL ORDER

These profound changes in the international system have resonant effects in the international relations of the Middle East. Many corollaries

[1] Robert Pranger, "Foreign Policy Capacity in the Middle East," in Judith Kipper and Harold Saunders, eds., *The Middle East in Global Perspective* (Boulder, CO: American Enterprise Institute, Westview Press, 1991), pp. 20–21.

and consequences of the change had begun to emerge in the late 1980s, maturing in the mid-1990s. Chief among these were a new caution in Soviet relations with the area and visible changes in the U.S. posture toward the area as the Soviet threat retreated. The Soviet retrenchment in Afghanistan was only the most visible of what became a general withdrawal of the U.S.S.R. from the region's conflicts. Allied states such as Syria, Iraq, and South Yemen received smaller amounts of foreign and military aid and less encouragement in the support of wars of national liberation. The PLO sensed these changes and sought dialogue with the West, attempting awkwardly to adjust to the new realities. All in all, a sense of uncertainty and change pervaded the area.

Analysts also could see changes in U.S. policy as a result of the reduced Soviet role in the region. The endgame of the Reagan administration began and ended with reinvigorated attempts to solve the ongoing Israeli–Arab conflict, including the previously unheard-of dialogue with the PLO. The first year of the Bush administration began and ended with attempts to restart negotiations between Israel, her Arab neighbors, and the PLO.

Despite unsuccessful attempts to jump-start the peace process in the Middle East, early 1990 was a time of international optimism. The cumulative effects of the transition from the old order to the new put statesmen in a mellow mood. Many dangerous maneuvers in Eastern Europe and the former Soviet Union had been accomplished without disaster. A "peace dividend" near at hand provided some economic and political relief to states that had been strained in capacity for some four prior decades. The Iran–Iraq war had sputtered to a halt. The world seemed to be in for a period of relative progress and prosperity.

The news in August 1990 that Iraq had invaded its neighbor Kuwait was received in the halls of government with anger and frustration. This act and its subsequent denouement demonstrated many of the points emphasized earlier in this chapter. Depending on one's point of view, the crisis constituted the last response of the old order or represented the first response of the new. In any event, Iraq's invasion of Kuwait and the world community's response to it constituted the primary international event of the early 1990s. Other regional events—the continuation of the intifadah, the release of hostages, and attempts to begin peace negotiations between Israel and the Arabs—were overshadowed by this single event. The conflict was certainly architectonic to the conduct of international relations in the Middle East and, at the minimum, evidence of the new international politics. It must be looked at and analyzed with care if we are to draw appropriate inferences.

Iraq–Kuwait Crisis

The background to the Iraqi invasion of Kuwait in August 1990 is complex. There is a long history of conflict between the two states, and this was not the first time that Iraqi troops had rolled down the Basra highway toward Kuwait. There are claims and counterclaims. Iraq has long claimed Kuwait as its own, an area severed from it by the arbitrary act of the previous colonial power; by contrast, the al-Sabah family claims to the region are old and long-standing. Kuwait and Iraq were only more recently defined as independent nations, emerging from the interaction of two colonial administrations, Ottoman and English.

There was much geographic uncertainty and strain as well. Because of the nature of the desert terrain, the borders between Kuwait and her neighbors have never been clear or well defined. Areas of disputed ownership predate this conflict, and the presence of petroleum in some of the disputed areas has resulted in areas of joint exploitation or administration or both. Nomadic herders crossed these porous borders with impunity for decades, further complicating the problems of national definition. Kuwaiti control of key areas at the top of

the Gulf frustrated Iraq, whose access to the Gulf through the Shatt al-Arab was all but destroyed by the war with Iran. The result was a landlocked Iraq, making import and export difficult. Kuwait evinced little concern over these Iraqi difficulties.

These historical and geographic conflicts were exacerbated by the long-running war between Iraq and Iran. As one of the states backing Iraq in that war, Kuwait had extended loans and credits to Iraq. Now, as the war ended, Iraq sought further help and the forgiveness of the loans. Kuwait responded by demanding payment. Iraq was outraged, and this outrage was fueled by its belief that Kuwait had pumped unfair amounts of petroleum from the Rumeilah oil fields, fields that dip slightly into Kuwait but whose bulk lies in Iraq. Kuwait played a key role in OPEC decisions in the summer of 1990 not to increase the price for petroleum. Iraq, counting on a substantial increase in price to offset the costs of the war with Iran, believed that it had been "whip-sawed" by Kuwait, which opposed price increases and deliberately exceeded its production quotas.

These charges of unfair profiteering were given some credence by the reputation of Kuwaitis before the invasion. It is no exaggeration to suggest that Kuwaiti prestige was fairly low in the Middle East at the time, particularly in countries without substantial petroleum resources. Wealthy Kuwaitis vacationing in London, Cairo, Damascus, and Baghdad did for the Kuwaiti public image what earlier generations of "ugly Americans," "ugly Germans," and "ugly Japanese" had done for their own countries' reputations. Public sympathy for the plight of the wealthy Kuwaiti minority was relatively scarce outside of Saudi Arabia, the Gulf States, and the European West.

The U.S. restraint on Iraq evaporated shortly before the invasion of Kuwait. In a much-publicized conversation with Saddam Hussein, the American ambassador in Baghdad, April Glaspie, observed to the Iraqi leader that the United States had no mutual defense treaty with Kuwait. The interpretation of this remark was apparently critical to Saddam Hussein's appraisal of probable U.S. reaction to his planned invasion. Inadvertent or not, a green light of sorts was presented to Iraq in the prosecution of its dispute with Kuwait. The Soviet Union, long a supporter of Iraq, was not a major partner in these discussions.

The Iraqi invasion was swift, brutal, and massive when it occurred. More than 150,000 heavily armored Iraqi troops flooded into Kuwait. In 24 hours, the nominal defenders of Kuwait were routed, and less than a day later Iraqi troops were digging in on the borders with Saudi Arabia. Iraqi troops took up reinforced positions along the Saudi Arabian border, a presence that prompted fear in that country and in its customers for petroleum. The concentration of Iraqi forces on the border went far beyond that needed for the mere defense of the captured territory, raising speculation about the ultimate intentions of Iraq. At the peak, Iraqi forces in the Kuwaiti theater numbered more than 250,000 (during the hostilities these force numbers were greatly exaggerated in the coalition press and briefings). The ambiguity raised by such great concentrations of Iraqi power quickly forced reaction from interested parties, particularly Saudi Arabia, the Gulf States, the United States, and Western Europe. Within a week an initial force of U.S. and Gulf area troops took up positions on the Saudi side of the Kuwaiti border and Desert Shield/Desert Storm began.[2]

Events within occupied Kuwait did little to reassure Iraq's neighbors. One-third of Kuwait's native population fled, including most of the government and armed forces; people who remained behind were subjected to repressive occupation. Hundreds of thousands of guest workers from Jordan, Egypt, India, Bangladesh, and the Philippines also fled the area, becoming instant refugees and straining neighboring states' ability to provide for them.

A puppet regime was quickly established by Iraq, and the reorganization of Kuwait proceeded. As the occupation continued, reports of torture, rape, murder, and looting became regular features in the outside press. Sensationalism and exaggeration make objective appraisal of the occupation difficult, even long after the events in question. But it is clear that the occupation was brutal, if uneven in its administration and effect.

Iraqi objectives in this invasion were unclear, as mentioned. If Iraq's ultimate aim was the limited one of embarrassing Kuwait, securing the Rumeilah fields, and opening a water route to the Gulf, Iraq overcommitted in its efforts and prompted a stronger response from the international community than was necessary. If Iraq's ultimate objectives included the annexation of Kuwait or even the seizure of the major Saudi oil fields in its eastern province, its decision to take up defensive positions along the Saudi border signaled either a strategic miscalculation or a failure of nerve. Either way, the levels of force involved in the Iraqi invasion of Kuwait convinced the major world powers that Iraq was involved in a dangerous game that demanded a full and effective response.

The response to the invasion was not long in coming. Economic embargoes against Iraq were quickly put in place by the United States, the European Economic Community, and Japan. On August 6, the United Nations Security Council ordered a worldwide embargo on trade with Iraq. These actions were initially symbolic because economic processes are relatively slow to respond to changes in rules. In the long run, however, the economic punishment of Iraq took a great toll, particularly on the nonmilitary populations. By August 9, one week after Iraq's invasion, troops from the United States and other Saudi allies began to materialize on the border with Kuwait.

---

[2] Desert Shield was the name of the defensive phase of the operation. It was succeeded by Desert Storm as the coalition forces went on the offensive.

The United States took the leading role in confronting the Iraqi threat. President Bush, working chiefly through the United Nations, orchestrated a multinational response. The number of foreign troops in Saudi Arabia rose steadily in fall of 1990, until they could credibly contain an Iraqi attack. Desert Shield, as the exercise was named, built quickly, reaching a level of roughly one-half million men by December 1990. By the time of the offensive against Iraq, their number had grown to greater than 715,000 troops. Approximately, one-half of the troops were from U.S. forces, with the remainder drawn from Saudi Arabia, the U.A.E., Britain, France, Egypt, Syria, Italy, Morocco, Bangladesh, and a symbolically important contingent of Kuwaiti troops in exile.

Iraq, during this period, continued to reinforce its positions along the Kuwaiti and Saudi borders, substantially hardening its placements with extensive earthworks, minefields, and modern trench facilities. The elite Republican Guards were placed to the north, along the Iraqi-Kuwaiti border, in position to maneuver against invading forces. Diplomatic initiatives from a variety of sources, including France and the Soviet Union, failed to persuade Saddam Hussein of the seriousness of the coalition facing him, and as the new year dawned, "Desert Shield" changed into "Desert Storm."

The coalition facing Iraq broke new ground in Middle Eastern coalition building. Working under the legitimizing mandate of a series of U.N. resolutions, President Bush assembled a group of most unlikely partners. Any political coalition including Syria and the conservative monarchies of the region previously would have been considered unthinkable. For that matter, for the United States and Syria to be working partners would have stretched credibility even further, given persistent efforts by the United States to brand Syria a "terrorist state" and Syria's ongoing attempts to portray the United States as a "colonialist-Zionist" state.

For all of these states to work harmoniously with Egypt, Algeria, and Turkey further stretched

political credibility. For these former colonial states to consider military cooperation with France, Great Britain, and Italy against another Arab-Muslim state also seemed far-fetched. But such a coalition was assembled and did indeed endure—for no nation in that coalition was prepared to countenance Saddam Hussein's Iraq as the dominant military and economic power of the region. Ultimately, 16 nations contributed ground forces to the war (see Table 14.1).

The absence of Israel from the U.S.-led coalition was crucial to its stability. The Bush administration recognized from the start the symbolic importance of Israeli nonparticipation in this unprecedented coalition. This necessitated a diplomatic high-wire act as the United States moved to reassure Israel and its enemies simultaneously. This diplomacy was accomplished with mixed success, particularly within Israel, where calls for direct action against Iraq increased geometrically with each SCUD

Table 14.1 Coalition Members with Forces Committed at the Start of Desert Storm

United States	Bangladesh
Britain	Morocco
France	Oman
Saudi Arabia	Niger
Egypt	Pakistan
Syria	Qatar
Kuwait	Senegal
Bahrain	United Arab Emirates

Among the key U.N. initiatives were the following resolutions:

660 (August 2, 1990): calls on Iraq to withdraw immediately from Kuwait

661 (August 6, 1990): reminds all member states of their obligation to deny financial or economic resources to Iraq (embargo)

662 (August 9, 1990): rejects Iraq's annexation of Kuwait as illegal

665 (August 25, 1990): invites member states to implement embargo and engage in necessary military action using Military Staff Committee of the United Nations

missile launched against Israel. Although the SCUDs did little actual damage, the psychological impact was great. The government of Israel paid a relatively high price domestically for its perceived passivity in this conflict.

Multinational Actors in the Conflict

As alluded to earlier in this discussion, international organizations were major actors in the confrontation. The United Nations, acting under the guidance of the Security Council, took an active role in confronting Iraq's hostile action. The United States, careful to ensure that its actions were either anticipated or approved by U.N. resolution, clearly legitimized its military and diplomatic response to Iraq.

These resolutions and the others that followed internationally legitimized the coalition response to Iraq's aggression. Other international organizations also provided legitimation and support to the effort. NATO provided key logistical and political support, although informally, from the opening days of the crisis.[3] Other organizations joined in the chorus of condemnation: the Organization of African Unity, August 3; Gulf Cooperation Council (GCC), August 3; Organization of the Islamic Conference, August 5; League of Arab States, August 10. These organizations, representing the opinions of various Arab, Muslim, and third-world states, contributed immeasurably to the legitimacy of the U.S.-led opposition and greatly reduced the value of Iraq's invocations of Muslim and Arab unity.[4] Finally, the United States and the Soviet Union proclaimed joint resolutions condemning the attack, showing a commonality of purpose among the world's two superpowers. The Soviet government

followed these statements with diplomatic missions to Baghdad attempting to dissuade Iraq from staying in Kuwait. The government of Iraq rejected numerous efforts to arrange a nonviolent withdrawal from Kuwait.

Iraq was able to muster formal support only from Libya and the PLO. Jordan, caught in the middle between its two most important economic partners, attempted to play the role of mediator and failed in this attempt. Branded a collaborator by the coalition leadership, Jordan paid an extremely high economic and political price for its attempted neutrality. Iran, officially opposed to the annexation of Kuwait, waited to take advantage of the coming storm. The isolation of Iraq was complete.

Desert Storm

The coalition against Iraq went on the offensive in January 1991. Under the U.N. resolutions, the allies were justified in forcibly ejecting Iraq from Kuwait and restoring the previous government. They were even required to do so. Hostilities began with an air campaign on January 16, 1991, using the latest technologies in "smart" weaponry and some of the heaviest concentrations of "dumb" technology since World War II. Air supremacy was established quickly over Iraq, and what followed was a "turkey shoot" of unprecedented intensity. In the first week of the air war, more than 10,000 sorties were flown, punishing Iraq day and night. More than 80,000 tons of munitions were dropped.

The air war was covered from Baghdad by the surviving staffs of U.S. news networks, most notably CNN. This time the world was privy to war from the perspective of the pilot and his targets. The viewing public was shown the thorough destruction of Iraqi infrastructure, particularly in communication and transportation. Careful censorship in the coalition staging areas kept the official images technical and clinical, while the images streaming from Baghdad and other media sources supplemented this with endless footage of death and destruction.

---

[3] It is unlikely that U.S. forces could have moved into the region in such a short time without the logistical support of NATO, or without NATO's willingness to allow great reductions in its forces and supplies in Europe.

[4] For example, Saddam Hussein's repeated attempts to invoke jihad were blunted by the refusal of other Islamic authorities to recognize the legitimacy of his claim.

As the air assaults continued and Iraqi antiaircraft capability was suppressed, B-52 raids were initiated, targeted against major economic and military targets, including power plants and suspected military production facilities, and increasingly against the dug-in troops on the Saudi border. The unknowns regarding Iraq's rumored chemical, biological, and nuclear programs prompted an ever-broadening range of targets. The result, as inevitable as it was distasteful, was increasing loss of life among the civilians in Iraq. The totals of noncombatant losses in the air war probably will never be known, but certainly number in the tens of thousands. When combined with the people who died in the coming land war, and from the effects of the war on water, food, and sanitation facilities, total Iraqi losses may have been 200,000.

The duration and savagery of the five-and-one-half-week air campaign were conditioned by expectations that the following air–land battle would be long and bloody. Many analysts expected the land war to run for weeks and to generate high casualties on both sides. The Iraqi army, supposedly seasoned by a decade of high-intensity war with Iran, was considered a formidable adversary, particularly the elite Republic Guards held in the theater rear. Another factor for caution was based on Iraq's previous use of chemical weapons in the war with Iran. Iraq also possessed numerous tanks and impressive numbers of long-range artillery, along with sophisticated munitions for both of these systems. Further pause was given by Iraq's mining of most of the Kuwaiti oil fields and wellheads and its progressive firing of those charges as attack became imminent.

Given these expectations, the land phase of the battle for Kuwait was something of a disappointment. Begun on February 24, coalition forces were able in short order to breach the vaunted Iraqi defenses. The heavily dug-in Iraqi forces were not able to maneuver and were systematically destroyed by highly mobile forces using more sophisticated technology.

Most U.S. losses in the land phase of the battle came from "friendly fire." At any rate, the Iraqi forces were quickly surrounded, and a major rout of the Iraqi army ensued. Within only four days of battle, Kuwait was rid of its occupying army and was in the process of restoring its government and civil services. Iraqi troops streamed north, using whatever transport was available. The slaughter along the highway north was so complete that it was called a "turkey shoot" by knowledgeable military analysts. The Iraqi army in Kuwait was in danger of annihilation.

With the southern quarter of Iraq occupied, a cease-fire was negotiated permitting the withdrawal of the defeated Iraqi troops. Desert Storm had succeeded in expelling Iraq from Kuwait and in reestablishing Kuwait's legal government. There was great optimism in the West and considerable chaos and despair in Baghdad. Kurdish rebels in the north of Iraq and Shia groups in the south began secessionist struggles. Informed opinion awaited the inevitable coup deposing Saddam Hussein and the establishment of a government that would attempt to negotiate with the coalition leadership.

The endgame of Desert Storm was disappointing to those who expected and wanted a thoroughgoing destruction of Iraq's military establishment and the leadership of Saddam Hussein. The expulsion of Iraq from Kuwait and the reestablishment of the al-Sabah government satisfied the letter of the U.N. resolutions. The coalition itself had not defined its role further, and it is unclear that the political will existed for the final action against Iraq. What was a clear and signal military victory eventually transformed itself into a typical political quagmire.

The Middle East at the End of Desert Storm

As Desert Storm blew itself out over the deserts of the Middle East, the political, economic, and military contours of the region had changed.

Iraq was no longer the dominant military power in the region, although its military plant had by no means been eliminated. Although still ruled by Saddam Hussein and the Baath Party, Iraq had been profoundly damaged in the conflict. Disease and famine began to take its toll of the weakest in the country, mostly the children and elderly across all groups and ethnic spectra. It is estimated that 100,000 Iraqis may have died from the war and its direct and indirect effects. Reliable figures probably will never be known.

Economically, Iraq and Kuwait were exhausted. Neither country was pumping significant amounts of oil, and in Kuwait more than 700 burning oil wells created a nightmarish ecological disaster. The long-term effects on the atmosphere are unknown, as is the long-term effect of the intentional oil spill on the northern Gulf. The short-term effects were obvious: Life in Kuwait was a bronchial nightmare for the first six months following the war. If the prevailing winds did not clear the air, Kuwait was darkened at noon, with a reddish sun barely able to penetrate the rising plumes of smoke and gas. Great lakes of pooling oil and petroleum by-products dotted the landscape. Fires ringed the capital city, stretching out to the horizon. Kuwaiti nationals returned to a country transformed by the events of the war, changed from a center of leisure and luxury to a country where the basic necessities could not be guaranteed. It is estimated that 10,000 Kuwaitis may have died in the war of direct and indirect effects. Many Kuwaitis had been tortured and executed in a short but brutal occupation.

Political life in Iraq at the end of the war was dogged by uncertainties. The cease-fire agreement did not incorporate domestic political changes into its terms. Air and land surveillance by the coalition and by the United Nations proceeded in fits and starts, with agreements often negotiated on the scene on an ad hoc basis. The search for Iraq's "weapons of mass destruction" turned up development programs of impressive size and complexity.

As the government of Iraq attempted to implement a "shell game," hiding basic facilities from the inspectors, coalition leaders threatened the renewal of hostilities unless a measure of cooperation was extended. Coalition forces were forced to offer support and supplies to the Kurdish refugees fleeing in the north of Iraq and through narrow mountain passes into Iran and Turkey. Iran and Saudi Arabia were forced to give similar support to the Shia rebels in the south. In the long run, it would seem, the coalition allies had little stomach for the creation of independent Kurdish or Shia states on their own borders. In this situation, the plight of many refugees became desperate.

An elegantly executed military confrontation against a clear danger succeeded, only to produce an outcome of great ambiguity and frustration. Many of these factors were embedded in the very nature of the new international order.

Desert Storm as Indicator of New International Realities

To what degree did the Iraq–Kuwait crisis demonstrate the emergence of a new international system? Let us apply our observations from earlier in this discussion.

First, did the event show the disappearance of the old bipolar order and the emergence of a multipolar world? It did so in the absence of an influential role for the former Soviet Union. The U.S.S.R. clearly responded to the initiatives of the United States and its coalition partners. Soviet military power was not engaged in the conflict and never became an important factor in the strategic or tactical implementation of Desert Storm. The minimum standards of bipolar interest or confrontation were not demonstrated in the diplomacy or the military phase of the conflict. Only in the waning months of the century did Russia speak again in favor of its old ally, Iraq, calling for an end to economic sanctions and an end to U.N.-sponsored inspections of its military facilities. This support, although significant, and augmented by European concerns for the future of Iraq, did nothing to change the overall situation facing the Iraqis.

Second, the multipolar nature of international power was demonstrated. States from a variety of alliances and regions were involved directly and indirectly in Desert Storm. The U.S. leadership found it expedient and desirable to maintain a coalition of disparate members. It would be a distortion to call the operation a "U.S. effort." Members of the coalition showed political independence during the crisis, often at the displeasure of the United States. The roles of France, Germany, and the U.S.S.R. in last-minute attempts to persuade a peaceful Iraqi withdrawal are cases in point.

By 1998, the United States was joined only by Great Britain in its efforts to penalize Iraq for expelling the U.N. weapons inspectors (Operation Desert Fox, December 1998). From 1998 on, the United States engaged in a lonely war of attrition against Iraq with daily flyovers and weekly limited bombing of Iraqi facilities—a quiet war of attrition against Iraq with declining international support and even less international visibility.

Third, the role of international organizations in Desert Storm was crucial. The United Nations played an indispensable role in legitimizing the use of force against Iraq. Without U.N. sanctions, the presence of U.S., British, French, and Italian troops in the Middle East would have precipitated powerful denunciations of neocolonial imperialism. The domestic consequences of participation for the Egyptian, Syrian, and North African governments might have been disastrous. As it developed, however, their participation in the coalition did not result in widespread or effective domestic opposition.

In a different way, NATO played a key role. It is unlikely that the United States could have managed the concentration of troops and materials in the Gulf in such a short time on its own. Although it acted unofficially, NATO not only released large quantities of munitions and supplies from storage, but also coordinated the transportation of these supplies to the region. NATO staffers worked hard to identify the location of key technical equipment (e.g., chemical "sniffer" tanks) and make them available to U.S. procurement officers.

NATO was supportive in other ways as well. NATO staff provided much-needed intelligence to the coalition forces. NATO command, communication, and control procedures were used to coordinate the naval blockade of Iraq and Jordan and the tremendous complexity of the air campaign, allowing fighters and bombers of six nations to fly in and out of Iraqi air space without mishap 2,000 times (sorties) a day. NATO's indirect experiences in the Iraqi campaign were important precursors of NATO's subsequent interventions in Bosnia (1996) and Kosovo (1999), both under the legitimizing umbrella of the United Nations.

Other international organizations were important to the effort. The Islamic Conference was an important element in keeping the confrontation secular and in discrediting Saddam Hussein's efforts to link the conflict to religious issues. The Organization of African Unity was important in defusing the charge of yet another neocolonial intrusion into the area. The Arab League effectively kept the issue of Arab unity out of the conflict. From the start of the conflict, international organizations were fully involved, and their activities were responsible for much of the color and texture of Desert Shield–Desert Storm.

Regional actors also were important factors in the crisis. The response of the GCC to the Iraqi invasion was the key in catalyzing the initial response to Iraq's invasion. The GCC forces sent to the Saudi border were important beyond the significance of the troops. They also signaled the marshaling of significant international financial resources in the conflict, resources that underwrote U.S. expenses and promised political and economic support to Egypt and Syria. The crisis tested the commitment of the United Arab Emirates, Bahrain, Qatar, and Oman to the GCC and in the final result raised it to a new level of importance in political and economic coordination of these states. The GCC has expanded its role since Desert Storm, embracing solutions for regional disputes among its neighbors and beginning the first steps toward economic integration, particularly in the establishment of a GCC customs union.

The European Community was important in its early boycott against Iraq and in its tacit approval of NATO's informal but key role in logistical support for the coalition. Proposals for a European-led rapid deployment force within NATO got a real head of steam from the crisis, and the European Union is now engaged in the development of a multilateral military force. This force would contribute substantially to the political independence of this new regional international actor.

The regional integration of the United States and Canada should not be overlooked. Working largely through its NATO force commitments, Canada was shoulder to shoulder with the coalition in the crisis, particularly politically and in the naval blockade. Cooperation between Canada and the United States is nothing new, but the vitality of this regional integration deserves some emphasis, particularly as Mexico moves into alignment with the two. At any rate, regional actors were conspicuous in the crisis.

Nongovernmental international actors also were present and involved. The International Red Cross–Red Crescent worked both sides in the conflict, handling international relief efforts and the exchange of hostages and military captives. Amnesty International documented the outrages committed in the occupation of Kuwait. American Friends of the Middle East provided emergency relief to refugees occasioned by the war and to the endangered public in Iraq at the end of the war. Nongovernmental international agencies proliferated in the last two decades of the twentieth century. Governments increasingly rely on these agencies for back-door channels to opposing powers. These agencies may be more capable

of providing relief to endangered populations than their own governments. The Kurds have received as much help in their plight from these nongovernmental actors as from their own governments. Many analysts see these institutions as key actors in the future we all face.

Global interdependence was demonstrated in the Gulf crisis in numerous ways. First, the vulnerability of the world to disruption in petroleum supplies was obvious. To many analysts, the crisis was simply another manifestation of the world's dependence on a shrinking supply of petroleum. Second, the environmental effects of the war on the atmosphere and on the Gulf itself suggest our interdependence and vulnerability. The long-term effects of the environmental damage will not be known for some time, although it seems clear enough that the predictions of environmental catastrophe at the global level did not occur. Global environmental systems are complex and poorly understood. It is likely that some effect was occasioned by the burning of many billions of barrels of oil and cubic feet of gas, and there was real damage to the fisheries of the Gulf.

The type and quality of weaponry on both sides demonstrate the inexorable diffusion of technology around the world. The acquisition of "weapons of mass destruction" has been democratized. No longer must a nation be a superpower to pretend to chemical, biological, nuclear, or high-tech weaponry. The postwar documentation of Iraq's nuclear development program showed efforts of great sophistication—"world class physics," in the words of one U.N. inspector. Iraq was possibly less than a year or two away from the assembly of a workable atomic weapon. Iraq had a credible armory of other high-tech weapons, including cluster bombs and fuel-air bombs. It had independently modified the primitive Soviet SCUD missiles for longer range and larger warheads. It is a mystery of the war why these weapons were not deployed or used to better effect. In the larger scheme of things, Iraq's armory suggests that technological diffusion is a prominent reality of the new world order. Only multilateral international initiatives have the muscle to deal with such a reality.

The U.N.-sanctioned boycott against Iraqi oil sales and ongoing U.N. investigations of Iraqi efforts to acquire weapons of mass destruction kept Iraq and its regime on the defensive many years after Desert Storm. Although some neighboring Gulf States have supported a reduction in the sanctions on humanitarian grounds, joined by Russia, France, and China, Iraq continues to be a subject of multinational international intervention. Combined with the U.N. roles in Haiti, Bosnia, and Kosovo, it would be difficult to argue that multinational influence in world politics has declined.

The crisis demonstrated the phenomenon of instantaneous international communication. Saddam Hussein and President Bush were able to engage in an international game of name-calling in "real time." Negotiations in Geneva were presented to the world as they occurred (and failed). The conduct of the war itself was presented in the most complete detail, despite the efforts of both sides to control and censor the flow of information. Charges of treason against CNN for its continuing coverage of events from Iraq only demonstrate the significance of that coverage. *Time Magazine* anointed CNN founder Ted Turner as its "1991 Man of the Year" in recognition of these new realities. Consider also the emergence of Middle East Broadcasting Center, a new non-national cable news organization that is broadcasting all over the Arab world. Known to its viewers as MBC and owned principally by Saudi investors, the service seeks to imitate the success of U.S. networks in providing relatively unbiased news coverage. It now broadcasts to more than 300 million potential Arab viewers without government censorship or control. Finally, Al-Jazeerah, a satellite service based in Qatar, has set new standards for independent journalism in the Arab world.

Many alternative news sources and technologies (specialized news services using satellite transmission, fax, phone, VCR, audio cassettes, and even print) exist now. The images they produce, whether of the whimsy of a smart bomb pursuing a fleeing truck into its garage or of the horror of men, women, and children incinerated together in a concrete shelter, all affect our worldview. It is conceivable that without the goad of international televised reports of their difficulties, the coalition partners would not have come to the aid of the Kurds or the Shia, or, for that matter, Bosnians or Kosovars. As many governments have found, it is difficult to prosecute war in the light of television cameras. Russian attempts to limit or control coverage of the suppression of the Chechen rebels in 1995 and 2000 are a case in point, and Russia lost an element of independence from the widespread knowledge of what was transpiring in Grozny. A state can assume the luxury of privacy in fewer and fewer places.

Regional conflicts did not go away as a consequence of Desert Storm. There are still points of conflict between many of the coalition partners. Syria and Turkey have problems along their mutual borders that include people (Kurds) and resources (in particular, water). Turkey and Iran continue to compete for economic and political advantage in the Muslim republics of central Asia. Saudi Arabia is still engaged in a hostile relationship with Yemen. Bahrain claims evidence of Iranian encouragement of its domestic dissidents. The United Arab Emirates has lost two small islands in the Gulf to Iranian seizure. Qatar continued in its efforts to change its borders with Bahrain and Saudi Arabia. Egypt was outraged over the 1995 attempt by Sudanese extremists to assassinate President Mubarak on a trip to Ethiopia. Most Arab states still find themselves in disagreement with Israel over the future of Jerusalem and the meaning of "autonomy" for the Palestinians.

Regional conflicts have been exaggerated in the wake of the 1991 Gulf crisis, as Iraq was taken out of the regional military equation. At any rate, although we may see new axes of regional conflict, conflict itself has not declined. The world is still a dangerous place. In 2000 more than 30 "small" wars smoldered on around the world.

The conflict of rich against poor also is not solved in the region. In many ways, the conflict may have been intensified. The oil-rich states of the Gulf are under continued pressure to share their wealth with their poorer and more populous neighbors. One can make a point that the political stability of Egypt, Syria, and Jordan, all with few natural resources and fast-growing populations, can only be assured with substantial subsidies from the rich and developed nations. Failure to provide this aid most likely will result in increasing demands for a more equitable world order. The recovery of international petroleum prices at the turn of the twenty-first century has done much to aggravate the sense of distance between the haves and have-nots of the region.

Finally, is there an apparent "domestication of the international" in the postcrisis Middle East? Whether new or not, all governments seem to have international policies complicated by domestic concerns. Can a Muslim political leader sign an accord that would leave Jerusalem in Israeli hands? Can any government of Israel surrender most of the West Bank to Palestinian control, evacuate Jewish settlers from Hebron, or return the Golan to Syria without consequence? Can the successors of Prime Minister Rabin avoid continued domestic violence? Can the United States, for any reason, countenance a dramatic reduction in the supply of Middle East petroleum to the Western industrial system? Can any country in the region countenance the surrender of its water resources to an international or regional water authority, no matter how independent or scrupulously fair it might be? The answer, superficially at least, is a resounding "no." Domestic opposition would be fierce in any of these cases.

Yet there are examples of leaders and governments ignoring these consequences and plunging ahead. Foreign policy may be severely constrained by domestic considerations, and vice versa. But the stakes are too high to allow such simplification. Leaders must live with these constraints and work around them as well. The Gulf crisis resolved the question of Iraq's attempted annexation of Kuwait, but it left most other regional conflicts alive and kicking. How they are dealt with will be a crucial indicator of the real direction of life in the changing international system.

This rough survey suggests that events are moving in the direction of a new world order and increased global interdependence as we have loosely defined it. If this is true, these new realities should have manifested themselves in the most intractable of Middle East conflicts: the five-decade-old dispute between Israel and the Arabs. In fact, it has.

THE ARABS AND THE ISRAELIS

One of the most telling criticisms of the U.S.-led coalition in Desert Storm was its inability or unwillingness to spell out its ultimate objectives. One analyst of the crisis catalogued no less than 15 major reasons for the effort, as articulated by President Bush. These justifications ranged from ensuring international oil supplies through the protection of American jobs to the "definition of the Bush presidency." Ultimately, the coalition limited its objectives to the narrow goals of ejecting Iraq from Kuwait and reestablishing the al-Sabah government. This left many regional questions unanswered.

Chief of these questions concerned Israel and its occupation of Gaza, the West Bank, southern Lebanon, and the Golan Heights and the very human question of the future of the Palestinians in Israel and in diaspora. Saddam Hussein, early in the conflict, attempted to link his action to the liberation of the Palestinians. Although the linkage was enthusiastically accepted by the PLO, it was universally rejected by the governments of the coalition. Nonetheless, a widespread public expectation existed in the area that the same principles that invalidated Iraq's annexation of Kuwait also applied to Israel. In other words, many in the Arab republics expected the coalition to apply similar pressure and energy to the solution of the Israeli–Palestinian question. To do less would be to endorse publicly a double standard, one for Arab states, the other for Israel.

Analysts have long considered the Arab–Israeli conflict to be primary in the Middle Eastern system. No other important issues could be settled without or before progress on this issue. And, in fact, the issue has been remarkably persistent and pervasive. For this reason, it was deemed very important when President Bush in his March 1991 address to Congress included "justice for the Palestinian people" in his list of objectives for the postcrisis Middle East.

President Bush soon acted on this new initiative, sending Secretary of State Baker to the Middle East to enlist the coalition partners in a new effort to resolve the Arab–Israeli conflict. Between April and October, Secretary Baker formally visited the region at least eight times, shuttling patiently between Israel, Syria, Jordan, and Egypt. Ultimately, Syria and Israel proved to be the most intransigent of the principals involved; the shadow of the PLO hovered over most of these discussions and negotiations.

President Bush eventually prevailed in his efforts to convene a multilateral Middle Eastern Peace Conference. The first session of the conference was held in Madrid in November 1991. The mere convening of such a conference indicated international diplomacy of a high and intensive nature. How was the United States able to bring these adversaries to the table, despite their bitter history and long memories?

It is clear in retrospect that President Bush interpreted the success of Desert Storm as a mandate to go further in solving Middle Eastern problems. Bush and Baker took advantage of this postwar environment by embarking on a series of high-level diplomatic conversations,

conversations so private that even the upper-level bureaucrats of the foreign policy establishments were in the dark as to what was agreed on. One meeting between Secretary Baker and President Assad reportedly continued for eight hours with no breaks for relief or refreshment. At the end of the marathon, letters were exchanged between Baker and Assad, the contents and assurances therein known only to their most loyal and intimate advisors. In this way, domestic reaction to the negotiated points was minimized.

The most serious problem—the unwillingness of Israel to sit at any table populated in any way by the PLO—was overcome by a two-track approach. On one level, Jordan agreed to include a Palestinian component in its delegation to the conference. This met historical Israeli preferences. On the other track, the United States identified and encouraged the creation of an indigenous Palestinian leadership independent of the PLO. Although in fact such an indigenous elite already existed in the occupied territories, they were for the most part contaminated in Israeli eyes by their association with Arafat and the PLO. The fiction of an independent Palestinian negotiating team was accomplished by the expedient of selecting Palestinians of high educational and humanitarian accomplishments. The head of the Palestinian segment of the Jordanian delegation was the distinguished and long-term head of the Gaza Red Cross–Red Crescent, Dr. Haider abdul-Shafi. One by one, a delegation acceptable to even the most hardline Israeli official was assembled. It is also clear that the legitimacy of the delegation in the Palestinian community in the occupied territories was based on their support of the intifadah, a revolution that occurred beyond the direct control of the PLO.

We should not minimize the significance of this accomplishment. Much of the sympathy in Israel for the plight of the Palestinians had evaporated as Palestinian support for Iraq became apparent. Palestinians cheering the SCUDs from their rooftops effectively destroyed the Israeli peace movement. The Gulf crisis also provided the government of Israel with a pretext to clamp down tightly on the Palestinian community with a brutal six-week curfew. Both of these actions greatly increased the tension and distrust between the Israeli and the Palestinian communities.

It is also clear in hindsight that the United States was willing to use the carrot and the stick in motivating conference participants. Syria was exonerated in the bombing of Pan Am Flight 103, a boost to Syrian prestige, and financial incentives flowed from the Gulf States to Damascus. Israel received compensation for SCUD damage received in the war and an increased flow of U.S. weapons to the Israeli Defense Forces. The Soviet Union extended formal diplomatic relations to Israel, improving the prospects of emigration for many Soviet Jews. These carrots were important in Israeli and Syrian calculations.

Among the sticks applied were these. For Syria, there would be no postwar subsidies if it failed to come to the table and the end of a warming relationship with Washington. In the case of Israel, the Bush administration successfully withheld U.S. loans in the amount of $10 billion, dedicated to the settlement and housing of Soviet refugees in Israel, subject to Israeli participation in a peace conference. The Israeli lobby in the United States raised a furious objection to this linkage, but the Bush administration held firm and prevailed. In the opinion of many analysts,[5] this was the first and only example of an American president since 1948 successfully standing up to the Israeli lobby.

Another important carrot presented to Israel was the possible revocation of United Nations Assembly Resolution 3379 (1975), which equated Zionism with racism. This resolution had long poisoned Israel's relationship with the United Nations, and its promised removal would constitute a considerable gain in prestige for the government of Israel, both at home and abroad. After Israeli participation in two early phases of the peace conference, in Madrid and Washington, the resolution was revoked under U.S. leadership. Although most Middle Eastern and Muslim governments voted against revocation, the motion passed easily. Although the measure in both instances was largely symbolic, the symbolism was important. The aggressive role of the United States in its revocation was an important article of faith between the United States and Israel at a time when many other issues divided them.

It also is important to realize that certain positions were not abandoned. Israel not only refused to slow down or cease its settlement policy in the West Bank and Gaza, but also it seemed to time the announcement of new settlements to coincide with Secretary Baker's visits. Prime Minister Shamir never retrenched on his refusal to concede the "land for peace" formula that implicitly undergirded the conference premise and refused in any way to discuss the future status of Jerusalem or to countenance any withdrawal from the Golan. Syria, for its part, insisted that Israeli withdrawal from the Golan was a prerequisite to peace and continued its support of Palestinian movements independent of and opposed to the PLO. It also continued to press its case that Yitzhak Shamir was himself a terrorist, involved in the assassination of U.N. peacekeeping officials and the murder of Palestinian noncombatants in the 1948 war. For the Palestinians, the intifadah did not end, although its intensity was reduced. The independent Palestinian delegation publicly voiced its sympathy for the PLO as the appropriate representative of the Palestinian nation. By and large, U.S. diplomats ignored these reservations and obstructions. Even a few gratuitous acts of terror by Israeli and Palestinian extremists failed to derail the opening session in Madrid.

U.S. hopes for the conference were practical and visionary. In the most practical sense, U.S. decision makers placed great hope in the

---

[5] See the article by Tom Friedman, *New York Times*, October 6, 1991, p. E3.

process of negotiation, in and of itself. The momentum of the conference itself, undergirded by the privately assured carrots and sticks, would be hard to overcome. Once the principals came to the table, they would find it increasingly difficult to leave. International pressure, domestic public opinion, and the hopes of finding real solutions to intractable problems also would provide incentive to stay with the process.

In terms of idealism and vision, the conference structure suggested coming to terms with a wide variety of regional issues. While highly ceremonial conferences on the big issues of peace and war took place, lower level bilateral discussions and negotiations between Israel and Lebanon, Syria, Jordan, and the Palestinians, respectively, were to consider many important specific questions. Among them were regional arms control, nuclear proliferation and reduction, the return of occupied territories for guarantees of peace, land and autonomy for the Palestinians, water rights and distribution, regional environmental problems (of which there are many), and possible economic cooperation.

There was a frustrating aspect to these "successful" postwar peace conferences. In particular, this frustration was based on the realization that successful negotiations would be played out over a long time. Months, even years, would denominate the success of the effort. Early agreements often turned out to be difficult to implement. Consider the widely heralded Camp David Accords of 1978. By the late 1980s, it was widely conceded that the accords had produced a "cold peace," a reduction of conflict but not the hoped-for developments economically, culturally, or politically. For in the compressed and crucial space that is the Middle East, finding common solutions to long-standing problems involves the development of common trust. This rarely comes quickly, and sometimes not at all. History is full of failed peace efforts.

On a more positive note, it is almost always better to talk than to make war. If an emergent consensus on the desirability of peace in the Middle East is one of the factors in the emerging international order, the nations, international organizations, nongovernmental organizations, and information media will continue to keep pressure on the principals in the conflict, and progress may in fact occur. The progress made through 1992 would have been unthinkable in the depths of the preceding bipolar world order. So some optimism was justified. In the fits and starts of discussions between old enemies, there was some room for hope. A report of the United States Institute of Peace put the situation succinctly:

> Arab and Israeli leaders will finally sign if and when they become persuaded that they have more to lose if agreement slips away. They then demand a panoply of extra "side" benefits to help justify to their domestic constituencies the concessions they have made. Only a major power, in fact only the United States can now meet this need, which helps to explain why the United States remains uniquely acceptable as the essential third-party mediator for the Arab-Israeli conflict.[6]

The authors of the preceding quote got it both right and wrong. The Israelis and Palestinians subsequently did begin a process of substantive negotiations. However, the United States was less a player in this process than the authors anticipated.

From Jerusalem to Oslo

The dramatic signing of the peace accords in Washington in 1993 was less a confirmation of

---

[6] Kenneth W. Stein and Samuel W. Lewis, with Sheryl J. Brown, *Making Peace Among Arabs and Israelis* (Washington, DC: U.S. Institute of Peace, 1991), p. 31.

U.S. international influence and more a testimony to the growing influence of smaller states and nongovernmental organizations and a graphic demonstration of the changing international system. Frustration with the idea of the United States as an honest broker between the parties led Itzhak Rabin and Yasir Arafat to engage in secret negotiations in Oslo, Norway, in the spring of 1993. In retrospect, it seems that a common recognition between the antagonists that the United States could not be counted on to provide the incentives for an evenhanded solution led the leadership to accept the previously unacceptable.

For Prime Minister Rabin, the unacceptable meant face-to-face meetings with the PLO and its leadership, with the notion of some measure of autonomy for the Palestinian people. For the Palestinian leadership and Chairman Arafat, the unthinkable was the end of military resistance toward Israel, the elimination of the goal of the destruction of Israel from the Palestinian National Charter, and the acceptance of a status considerably removed from independent statehood. Facing a situation threatening the survival of Israel as a Jewish state and the possible elimination of any future state for the people of Palestine, two hardened players in the toughest international game glared at each other across the negotiating table. The master of the game, the dealer so to speak, was not the United States but tiny Norway, a Scandinavian state with little direct interest in the Middle East. In this effort, Norway was assisted by representatives of numerous international nongovernmental organizations and other peace-committed groups. The negotiations came as quite a surprise to the great powers of the world.

The product of the first Oslo negotiations in 1993 (Oslo 1) and a second set of negotiations in 1995 (Oslo 2) was a set of fuzzy objectives accompanied by broad timetables for their completion. Few of the objectives were implemented as originally conceived, and only a few met the original deadlines. That said, in a general way, however, the objectives agreed on in Oslo and symbolically ratified in Washington have been implemented. Chairman Arafat and his government in exile did return to Gaza and Jericho. Palestinian policemen, trained in Jordan and subsidized by great-power donors, deployed progressively over about 30 percent of the West Bank and Gaza. Palestinian principals took over the management of schools. Palestinian physicians took responsibility for Palestinian health care. And Israeli and Palestinian extremists did their best to undermine the implementation of the agreements.

Some actions carried more symbolic weight than others. Bus bombings and political murders combined with public demonstrations and political resistance to polarize the polities of Israel and Palestine. Two events merit mention because they both had the potential to set the process back considerably. The first was the assassination of Prime Minister Rabin in November 1995, by a young Jewish extremist. The subsequent investigation of the murder revealed the extent to which this murder occurred in a context of political extremism, including secret and violent organizations among Israel's settler groups. It demonstrated the implacable opposition of some groups in Israel to the very idea of returning land for peace, the key formula in the Oslo agreements.

Many observers of these events expected this act to slow the peace process as Israel sorted out the political implications of the event. In effect, the peace process seems to have gained momentum in the aftermath, as Shimon Peres succeeded to Rabin's position and used the opportunity to confirm the integrity of the peace process. Public opinion polls showed a considerable change in Israeli public opinion, in favor of continuing the process. There was also evident a deepening cleavage between people supporting the process and people opposing it. Unseemly celebrations of Rabin's assassination by extremist settlers and American Zionist radicals contributed to this polarization. Most significantly, Palestinian elections, previously scheduled for January 1996, went forward.

The Palestinian elections of 1996 elected 88 members of a new Palestinian National Council and ratified Yasir Arafat as president of the Palestinian National Authority. The election, monitored closely by representatives from interested foreign governments and international nongovernmental organizations (e.g., President Jimmy Carter), was an important step in the transformation of Arafat and the PLO into something other than a simple opponent of Israel. It conferred not only a small measure of real political power on the new institutions of Palestinian governance, but, more important, it symbolically placed Arafat and the other Palestinian leaders in the role of government officials, a reality not assumed in the original accords.

Any hopes that the Israeli election of May 1996 would provide more impetus to the evolving peace process were dashed with the narrow election of Binyamin Netanyahu as the prime minister and an even narrower victory for the Likud bloc in the Knesset. Netanyahu ran on a platform calling for greater Israeli security assurances in a dramatically slowed peace process and on a private reputation embedded in many speeches and articles expressing an uncompromising opposition to the return of any land for peace: The election of Netanyahu energized the domestic opposition to the peace process and greatly exaggerated the importance of the religious right in the Israeli government.

In the early days of his administration, Netanyahu reimposed many of the most oppressive of his predecessors' restrictions on the Palestinians in the West Bank and Gaza. The government took many steps that seem in retrospect intentional efforts to marginalize the Palestinian leadership. The most controversial of these acts involved the opening of a tunnel beneath the ancient walls of the Temple Mount, bringing Israeli tourists within meters of the

Al Aqsa Mosque and the Dome of the Rock. Prime Minister Rabin had declined to open this tunnel on the grounds that it would be extremely provocative to do so. The decision did turn out to be provocative and became symbolic of many similar affronts to the Palestinians particularly and the peace process in general. Deadline after deadline, all agreed on in international treaties by previous Israeli governments, was postponed.

To those most involved in the conflict, inside and outside of Israel, the question of Hebron and the scheduled Israeli withdrawal from it was the most controversial issue. Hebron, claimed by Jews and Palestinians as the burial place of their patriarch, Abraham (or Ibrahim), carries great symbolism for both sides. Both sides have experienced ethnic violence there, and both sides see it as a historically important place in the development of their respective ethnic and religious identities. Neither side, whether Palestinian Arab or Jewish settler, wants to see the site fall into the other's hands. This is particularly true of the 400-odd Jewish settlers living in the heart of Hebron, with the intention of reclaiming the city as Jewish. These settlers, among the most rigid and intransigent of Israel's radical religious right, became the living symbols of the Israelis rejecting the basic formula of "land for peace."

Hebron and Israel's treaty obligations there became the focus for intense domestic and international politics. The intersection of the domestic political system with the international system is clearly evident in the Hebron crises of 1996 and 1997. As such, the crises serve as evidence of the changing nature of the international system and the prospects and dangers these changes bring.

Nine months after the beginning of the new government, Israeli troops began a "redeployment," turning over 80 percent of Hebron to the control of the Palestinian Authority. Israel retained security responsibility for the area of the city containing its settler compounds and the Tomb of the Patriarchs.

Numerous amendments to the original accords were agreed on, most of which increased the rights of the Israeli government in the West Bank. These gains were offset by Israel's agreements to a more definite schedule of withdrawal from other areas. Both sides claimed victory in the negotiations, and both sides still had failed to satisfy their most vehement domestic critics.

In agreeing to the substance of these renegotiations, Prime Minister Netanyahu bowed to numerous international realities. First, he bowed to the pressure of the great powers (particularly the United States) insistent on the continuation of the peace process and the observance of treaty obligations. He also bowed to the domestic security needs of Israel's nominal allies in the region, most notably Egypt and Jordan, whose domestic politics would not have received news of a peace collapse well. Finally, the prime minister bowed to the interests of his own political center, a large bloc of Israeli voters concerned for increased security and for the continuation of the peace process.

President Arafat of the Palestinian Authority also bowed to many international realities. In accepting a deferred schedule of Israeli withdrawals from the West Bank, he compromised his legitimate legal position in the interests of accommodation with his long-time enemies in Israel. In many ways, he has allowed the second-class status of his government to be ratified in international agreements. He has made little or no formal progress toward recognition as an independent Palestine. For this, and for other reasons, he will continue to reap a harvest of invective and opposition from his own domestic opposition, most of whom accuse him of settling for too little in his negotiations with Israel.

Ironically, Arafat shared with Prime Minister Netanyahu the dubious honor of becoming the focus of anger among his right-wing religious constituencies. If there is one thing that ties Hamas to Gush Emunim, it is their mutual hatred

for the peace process and accommodation between Israeli and Palestinian.

The peace process had transformed the conflict between Israel and Palestine. It had in effect been institutionalized and transferred to the physical arena of Israel itself. Critics of the process on both sides pointed to large unanswered questions. It was still left to decide whether independent statehood was the ultimate status for the Palestinians, or whether Israel would insist on some dependent autonomous condition. The important question of the right of return for Palestinians in the diaspora must be dealt with, a question of great importance to the some six million Palestinians living outside of Palestine. The status of Jerusalem, a city holy to nearly two billion religious faithful of Jewish, Christian, and Islamic belief, has yet to be clarified.

The Israeli opposition to the peace process declared the surrender of land to the Palestinians a price too high to pay. The Palestinian opposition accused Arafat of taking a bad deal, one that continued Israeli domination of Palestine and penalized the Palestinian people. Arafat and Peres had the unenviable task of creating a silk purse.

The May 1999 Israeli elections swept Netanyahu and the Likud from power. In their stead, a Labor-led coalition brought former Israeli Defense Forces General Ehud Barak to power as prime minister. Barak moved quickly to reassure his constituencies of his intention to reinvigorate the peace negotiations with the Palestinians and his willingness to re-engage Syria over the question of the Golan and the ultimate withdrawal of Israeli forces from the "security zone" established in southern Lebanon. Prime Minister Barak made uneven progress on all fronts in the first year of his administration.

During Barak's first year as prime minister, Israel completed most of the military withdrawals agreed on in the Wye Plantation Accords of 1998 and suspended by the Netanyahu government. Some of the withdrawals were subject to continuing negotiations and maneuvers, but all in all, the large print in the accords was honored. The Barak government began, in early 2000, face-to-face negotiations with the government of Syria over the status of the Golan region seized from Syria during the 1967 war. Similar to the West Bank, the Golan negotiations are complicated by the strategic importance of the Golan Heights, with its commanding view of western Syria; by the presence of nearly 20,000 Israeli settlers in the province; and by the importance of the region as a source of fresh water for Israel and Syria. A land- for-peace agreement would be difficult to negotiate on the ground and still honor the security needs of both states. The United States is seen by both the Israeli and Syrian governments as a necessary presence in the negotiations, particularly because the final security arrangements undoubtedly would involve the presence of multilateral or U.S. forces on the site.

Barak, from the early days of his administration, attempted to move quickly toward the "final status" negotiations envisaged in Oslo and Wye. Here the questions of the status of Jerusalem, the right of return for Palestinian refugees, and the right of the Palestinians to declare a state on the West Bank and in Gaza would have to be engaged. These are sticky questions, and only the most foolhardy analyst would predict the contours of a "final" peace accord between the Israelis and the Palestinians.

SUPERPOWERS AND GREAT POWERS

As we have previously noted, recent events have radically changed the configuration of the international system. Nowhere is that more noticeable than in the change of status among the superpowers. Neither the C.I.S. nor Russia itself brings to bear on international events the power or prestige of its predecessor, the Soviet Union. That leaves the United States in a position as the only surviving superpower at the end of the bipolar era.

That position is less than enviable because the United States now confronts a world in which unknown risk replaces the known threat. To be successful as a global power, the United States has to make prudent judgments about just when and where its fundamental national interest is at risk. To do otherwise, to jump about the globe from crisis to crisis and conflict to conflict regardless of their importance, invites a fate similar to being bitten to death by ducks: a slow, inexorable, and painful decline.

U.S. policy, as defined originally by the Bush Administration and continued by the Clinton Administration, saw the world system as one in which decisive U.S. action, augmented and legitimized by multinational agreements and the actions of international organizations, could defend U.S. national interests and the larger system interests as well. In the Middle East, this apparently translated into a policy of a continued U.S. role in its regional conflicts.

In a less abstract formulation, this meant that the United States must try to have its cake and eat it too, finding and supporting solutions that would satisfy the security needs of its allies in the region and protect real U.S. interests. Those needs, as understood in the U.S. view, included continued security for Israel, restraint of Iraqi power and influence, the containment of Iran, and the continued stability of the oil-producing states in the Gulf. Added to this was the unknown potential of Islamic extremism, raising the possibility of internal instability in such important allies as Egypt, Saudi Arabia, and Turkey.

Internationally, Desert Storm provided an opportunity for the United States to strengthen its political and economic and military relationships with the states of the Gulf. New U.S. bases were established, forward supply depots were organized, and a steady flow of new weapons systems increased the capability of the Gulf military. These augmented previously established military relationships with Egypt and Oman. Economic cooperation, particularly with Saudi Arabia and Kuwait, is intimate and reciprocal. The Saudi decision to purchase Boeing airliners for its national airlines is a multi-billion-dollar example of the connections between the United States and its ally. The United States is now the full guarantor of the peace in the region of the Gulf. U.S. planes and warships regularly monitor activity in and around the Gulf, joint maneuvers are common, and the United States has demonstrated its ability to reinforce Kuwait when a threat from enfeebled Iraq seems possible.

The United States now presides over a grand alliance in the Middle East, composed of formerly hostile factions from the Arab system. It is anchored in the Gulf by the conservative states of Saudi Arabia, the United Arab Emirates, Bahrain, Oman, Qatar, and Kuwait. It is buttressed on the west by Egypt, the largest of the Arab states and the most influential politically, and it includes Syria in the Levant, now one of the strongest Arab military powers. Jordan has been rehabilitated, rewarded for its quick signing of a "warm" peace agreement with Israel and no longer doing penance for its unwillingness to join in the coalition against Iraq. Each of these states at one time or another has been at loggerheads with another state in the alliance. The alliance brings previously hostile nations together in a pragmatic relationship. Israel is also part of this grand alliance, based on its special relationship with the United States. Given the fundamental differences between members of the alliance and the historical strains between them, it will take a good deal of energy and diplomacy to keep the alliance intact.

There are, however, good reasons for doing so. The United States and the Western industrial states are still highly dependent on a regular and reasonably priced flow of petroleum from the area. Military interventions have proved costly, even when costs are shared by the beneficiaries, as in the Gulf crisis. The steady proliferation of weapons of mass destruction argues for a logic of mutual defense

rather than going it alone. Finally, intangible benefits accrue from reducing international stress and conflict.

Middle Eastern countries outside the alliance are for the most part objects of U.S. concern. Iraq, Iran, and Libya are all to an important degree isolated by the alliance. The strategic importance of Yemen also keeps it an object of U.S. attention. The Islamic government of the Sudan, strongly motivated by the desire to export political Islam, also has worried U.S. decision makers, particularly after the terrorist attacks on U.S. embassies in Kenya and Tanzania and the U.S. belief that the Sudan was a base and haven for its "terrorist de jour," Osama bin Laden.

Iraq, greatly weakened by the Gulf War, nonetheless showed signs of life. U.S. policy continued to try to keep Iraq from a major recovery, economically, politically, or militarily. The removal of Saddam Hussein and the Baath Party from power would continue to be a U.S. priority, and the relaxation of economic sanctions probably would not occur as long as the Baathist regime stayed in power. The alliance was fraying over the question of Iraq, and the European components of the alliance showed increasing signs of distress at U.S. insistence on maintaining the economic sanctions against Iraq and against Libya, as well.

Iran, now in the maturity of its revolution, was still viewed by the United States as a dangerous state. Even the release in late 1991 of all of the remaining U.S. hostages in Lebanon failed to erase U.S. suspicions completely. Iranian purchases of military equipment from Russia (submarines and nuclear technology) and China (missile components) also were alarming. The U.S. effort to discipline Iran by forbidding Conoco from contracting to produce oil in Iran was offset by the actions of U.S. allies allowing such contracts.

Extremist Islamic political movements drawing moral support and encouragement from Iran still exist in Egypt, Jordan, Syria, Turkey, Algeria, and Morocco. Tiny Bahrain complains that Iran has helped foment public discontent in that island state. As the independent republics of the former Soviet Union establish new relationships with the central Asian states of Turkey, Iran, and Afghanistan, the United States most likely will recognize growing priorities there as well. The United States will continue to place a high priority on frustrating the export of Iran's Islamic revolution to the rest of the Middle East. Efforts of the Khatami government to improve relations with the West are still embryonic, complicated by conservative opposition to normalization of such relations. Analysts agree, however, that there is a real possibility of a warming relationship between Iran and the United States if domestic trends toward liberalization continue to develop there.

Relations between the United States and Libya took a nosedive in 1991 as investigators finally placed the blame on Libyan diplomats for the 1988 bombing of a Pan American 747 over Scotland. U.S. demands for the extradition of two Libyan officials were rebuffed. Surprising many in the United States, Qadaffi in 1999 agreed to the extradition of the two officials to the International Court of Justice, presided over by a Scottish judge. Many U.S. allies, including the European Union, are now pushing for a wholesale rehabilitation of Libya and scrambling for lucrative contracts and trade agreements. U.S. resistance to this trend is unlikely to be effective in the long run.

Western Europe's relations with the Middle East are increasingly conditioned by its movement toward economic and political integration. The European Union is currently in the process of defining its common economic relationship with other world regions. Turkey, now approved for applicant status in the European Union, is unlikely to gain that status anytime soon, despite its European geography and millions of guest workers in Germany and Belgium. The states of North Africa (Morocco, Algeria, and Tunisia, mainly) have been given privileged access to the European Union as

a consequence of their previous colonial experience. They also have many guest workers, particularly in France and Belgium. GCC states also are engaged in discussions with the European Union. If these three relationships are indicative of future agreements, we can look forward to European Union's special relationships with other Middle Eastern states, including Iraq and Iran, currently enjoying rising sympathy and prestige in Europe.

European Union's political relationships with the region are changing. The European Union is now a much more tangible political entity, particularly following the successful introduction of the common currency, the euro, and the successful prosecution of the international intervention in Bosnia and Kosovo. The European Union's efforts to define and implement a common foreign policy are beginning to bear fruit. The fruit is clearly not simply a clone of U.S. policy preferences, as the EU efforts to establish political and economic relations with Libya, Iraq, and Iran showed. The EU interest in dropping or decreasing the severity of the existing sanctions against Iraq and support for new and different elements in Iraqi inspection teams produced strong U.S. objections. As the U.S. occupation of Iraq proceeded in 2003, the European actors actively positioned themselves for a role in the new Iraq and continued their efforts to increase economic and political relations with Libya and Iran.

Japan, as a dominant financial and industrial world power, continues to place strong emphasis on ensuring a regular supply of petroleum from the area. As in the past, Japan protects regular supply relationships with the Gulf States Saudi Arabia and Iran. Japan likely will continue its mutual trade relationships with the richest of the Middle Eastern states. It is unlikely that any dramatic increase in Japan's military capability will occur. Slow economic growth was a fact of Japanese life in the last decade of the twentieth century and will likely constrain any significant growth in Japanese commitments in the region. Japan most likely will continue to pursue the politics of prestige in the region. Nationally, Japan must contend regionally with a rapidly growing Chinese economy and political influence. Given that reality, it is likely that Japan will seek stronger political and economic ties with individual Middle Eastern states. As noted, Saudi Arabia and Iran are probable targets of Japanese initiative.

MIDDLE EASTERN STATES

Egypt

Egypt emerged from the period with enhanced prestige. Its early commitment to the coalition confronting Iraq was of immense importance to U.S. efforts, providing Arab and Muslim legitimacy. Egypt's long tradition of anticolonialism further legitimized the effort. It was able to commit substantial numbers of well-trained troops to the Saudi theater quickly. Its history of military cooperation with the United States, particularly its joint exercises in the 1980s and the 1990s and its adoption of the NATO munition and command and control standards, gave it the ability to coordinate command, control, and communication with the United States. By any measure, the Egyptian military contribution to the coalition was the most substantial of any Arab state.

Egypt remained close to the United States in the aftermath of the Gulf War. It became an important player in the convening of the Arab–Israeli peace conference, particularly in reassuring (and pressuring) Syria and Israel. Egypt was a critical voice when either the Israelis or the Palestinians threatened to withdraw from or slow the peace process. As a result, Egyptian prestige experienced yet another increase, and the flow of U.S. military and economic aid increased, as did the flow of aid from Saudi Arabia, Kuwait, and the United Arab Emirates. The election of Egyptian statesman Boutros Boutros-Ghali as Secretary General of the United Nations also enhanced Egyptian international prestige and reflected continued great-power approval of the Egyptian regime.

The road has not been completely smooth. Egypt has experienced increasing tension with the Sudan, its neighbor to the south. An attempt to assassinate Mubarak during a state visit to Ethiopia in 1995 was reputedly linked to a Sudanese political organization. Islamist opposition to the regime resulted in a series of attacks against tourists and Coptic communities in Upper Egypt and attendant strains on revenue from Egypt's important tourist industry. The increases in prestige and continued foreign aid notwithstanding, Egypt still faces a bleak economic and political scenario. A very high birth rate, declining revenues from overseas workers, and a relatively stagnant economy continue to put great strains on its political system. Efforts at regional economic cooperation and integration and accelerated foreign investment seem to be likely Egyptian strategies in the twenty-first century.

Saudi Arabia

Saudi Arabia took great risks in inviting the U.S. response to Iraq's invasion of Kuwait. No Arab state can routinely invite a foreign military presence, given the sensitivity in the region to its colonial and postcolonial past. Saudi Arabia, as custodian of the holiest of the shrines of Islam, has a special obligation to protect the purity of its land. The prospect of non-Muslim Western men and women tramping casually across the holy land of Arabia was distasteful to many people inside and outside of Saudi Arabia, but particularly to the religious elites and the most conservative elements in the political elite.

Saudi Arabia risked the exposure of its citizenry to the different social and political values of its guests. A country in which the most conservative of values prevail socially—including the public veiling of women, requirements of modest dress, and the prohibition of alcohol—theoretically could be scandalized or destabilized by the presence of large numbers of tank-topped, beer-swilling, Christ-worshiping foreign soldiers. Or at least so the argument went. The point was made by a rigorous segregation of foreign troops, even to the point of entertaining them on cruise ships anchored in the Gulf. In the postwar environment, the Saudi government reasserted its emphasis on its traditional social and political values.

Despite these efforts, the religious establishment in Saudi Arabia issued many public warnings to the Saudi government, indicating its dissatisfaction with the state of public morals and the policies of the government. The announcement by King Fahd in early 1992 that a consultative assembly would be formed was a response to increasing domestic pressure from its important religious allies. Such a concession failed to satisfy the conservative critics of the regime, however. Tensions increased in 1995–1996, punctuated by the bombing of an American training mission, evidence that the stakes in the internal conflicts in Saudi Arabia were rising. Osama bin Laden, a famous terrorist mastermind and former Saudi citizen, has significant support in some Saudi circles and reputedly still harvests substantial financial support from sympathetic parties. This is a source of embarrassment to the Saudi government.

Before and after the Gulf War, Saudi priorities remained basically the same. With a small native population spread out over a large and mainly uninhabited expanse, security concerns remain paramount externally and internally.

Saudi economic, political, and military relationships with the United States were enhanced by Desert Shield–Desert Storm. Saudi Arabia expanded its petroleum production to levels that ensured moderate prices globally. Its distribution presence in the U.S. market was allowed to expand, giving it a higher stake in the U.S. domestic economy. New discoveries of petroleum were acknowledged, increasing the Saudi percentage of known world petroleum

reserves. Military cooperation with the United States reached new heights, and there is little doubt as to the mutual assurances and guarantees existing between them. Dramatic increases in Saudi military capability were achieved, with most of the new systems coming from the United States. "Nativization" of the military and related security agencies was emphasized as well.

Regional relationships also intensified. The success of the GCC in coming to terms with the Iraqi crisis enhanced its attractiveness, and the GCC developed into a substantial tool for military and economic coordination among its member Gulf States. Saudi commitment to the GCC is tangible and growing. Military and political cooperation are understood as a high priority for countries with small populations and relatively modest military capacity. Saudi Arabia and the Gulf States have finally abandoned their long-standing policy against recognition of Israel and have attended the Arab-Israeli peace conferences as observers, further solidifying their joint relationships with the United States.

Saudi pragmatism continues to manifest itself internationally. It played a crucial formal and informal role in the attempts to settle the political questions in Lebanon, an initiative that brought it into intimate discussions and relationships with Syria. It continues diplomatic relations with Iran, exchanging visits between state ministers and the military, despite Saudi reservations about the regime in place there. It continues modest financial support to Lebanon and Jordan. The Saudis played a visible role in the relief efforts in Bosnia and Kosovo, both areas out of the traditional orbit of Saudi foreign policy. Saudi private investments in the new territories under Palestinian control continue and are likely to accelerate as Palestinian independence takes on more substance.

Saudi Arabia and its Gulf neighbors continue to live in a "bad neighborhood." Iran and Iraq are clearly perceived as potential threats. Bahrain continues to fear outside agitation of its restive Shia majority. Yemen has unresolved border disputes with Saudi Arabia and Oman. The deterioration of political and economic life in the nearby Horn of Africa (Somalia, the Sudan, and Ethiopia) presents potential threats as well. The introduction of nuclear capability into the India–Pakistan conflict in 1999 brings nuclear weapons closer to the neighborhood. Fluid and creative alliance politics will likely continue to be a major priority of the Saudi government and its Gulf allies for the indefinite future. The politics of prestige will continue to be a high priority, as Saudi Arabia continues to use its unique role in the history of Islam in its self-defense.

Other Gulf States

The foreign policies of the United Arab Emirates, Bahrain, Qatar, Kuwait, and Oman generally bear great similarities. The coordinating role of the GCC is particularly important for these small states. By and large, their foreign policies seek security through mutual cooperation and by extension of their military and economic relationships with the United States and their economic and political relationships with the European Union and in the surrounding region. Bahrain, Oman, and Kuwait have been the most aggressive in approving U.S. basing agreements and the prepositioning of military supplies. Bahrain continues to extend port facilities to the U.S. Navy as it patrols the Gulf, and U.S. sailors and aviators are common on the streets of Abu Dhabi and Dubai, even as the government continues to resist a formal defense arrangement with the United States. Similar to Saudi Arabia, the richer of these states—principally the United Arab Emirates, Qatar, and Kuwait—seek an additional measure of security by providing generous subsidies to the poorer neighboring states.

Kuwait has particular problems, occasioned by Iraq's invasion and occupation. Rebuilding has been a daunting task, although many of the earliest estimates of damage costs proved to be excessive. The extinguishing of some 700 oil well fires was accomplished in less than nine months, instead of the two to three years some experts had suggested. The damage to the Kuwaiti physical plant was very selective, also minimizing reconstruction costs. Even then, billions of dollars were needed. Kuwaiti oil production recovered faster than imagined, and Kuwait's substantial foreign investments provided income that was used in the reconstruction.

Kuwait wanted to reduce its population to roughly half of its prewar level, eliminating many of the foreign guest workers who dominated its economic and professional life and eliminating that point of vulnerability in its security. A "nativized" and expanded military is also progressing. These programs dispossessed permanently many foreign workers, particularly Palestinian, Jordanian, and Egyptian workers. This situation has exacerbated social pressure in Jordan and the West Bank. Grants in aid offset these effects in Egypt. Kuwait is not alone in reducing the number of Middle Eastern foreign workers—all of the neighboring Gulf States have pursued similar programs. The expatriate communities in these states now have higher proportions of Indian, Pakistani, Sri Lankan, and Philippine nationals, workers less politically engaged or significant than their Arab counterparts.

One measure of the changing realities for the Gulf States is apparent in Qatar, which is positioned to surpass the Sultanate of Brunei as the richest country in the world. Qatar, with a new leader and an expanding elite, is clearly working to settle most of the border disputes it has had with Bahrain and Saudi Arabia. It is positioning itself, along with the United Arab Emirates and Oman, as a long-term supplier of liquified natural gas to its traditional customers and to the Indian subcontinent. Qatar is a country in the midst of substantial change, domestically and in its relationships with the international system. The country's enthusiastic participation in the 2003 war with Iraq, including its hosting of the U.S. Central Command Headquarters in Doha, has confirmed its close relationship with the United States and, to a degree, distanced itself from its other Gulf neighbors.

Syria

Of all the states in the Middle East, Syria has made the biggest changes in its foreign policy. For years Syria was a close ally of the U.S.S.R., enjoying a wide range of subsidies and support. Syria's foreign policies opposing imperialism, Israel, the United States, and monarchism were supported in the main by Soviet economic and military subsidies. Its support for wars of national liberation (particularly in Israel by the Palestinians), pan-Arabism, Iran in its war with Iraq, and international socialism enjoyed similar advantage. But with the collapse of Soviet power, new international realities impinged on Syria's formula. As a result, Syria has changed many of its foreign policies to adjust to the emerging new world.

Syria's cooperation with the 1991 coalition forces against Iraq signaled a watershed in its foreign policy. Alignment with the United States, Saudi Arabia, Great Britain, and France against another Arab power would have been unthinkable in the Syria of the 1970s and 1980s. Even more unthinkable would be the current Syrian bilateral negotiations with Israel over the Golan. Syria earlier insisted on a comprehensive multilateral set of negotiations. That particular objective was undermined by direct Israeli-Palestinian negotiations, and Syria signaled its willingness to engage in direct negotiations with Israel in late 1999 and early 2000. These negotiations are important in the ultimate resolution of the Israeli-Arab conflict, and ultimately they reflect a change in worldview among Syrian leaders.

Recovery of the Golan region and Israeli withdrawal from southern Lebanon are high priorities for Syria. Fully normalized relations are a high priority for Israel, which still seeks to escape its relative isolation in the region.

President Assad previously considered Israeli withdrawal a precondition for negotiations, just as Israel considered a formal peace treaty a prerequisite to its withdrawal from the Golan. Both countries have backed down from these preconditions, and Syria and Israel have entered reluctantly into serious negotiations.

Syria for its part has not abandoned all its prior international agenda. Forces for pan-Arabism are still influential in its politics. Syria has not abandoned its dislike for monarchical regimes and remains committed to their replacement with democratic institutions. Its competition with Egypt for leadership of the Arab world continues. Syrian relations with Iran remain warm, introducing a note of disquiet into its new relations with the West. Syria shares a long common border with Turkey, and the water resources that flow across it are an important concern for Syria. Water policy generally is a high priority for Syrian decision makers and is the subject most likely to lead Syria into regional compacts and cooperation.

Syria still pursues military parity with Israel, albeit with fewer resources. Noting these apparent contradictions in its foreign policy, analysts suggest that Syrian policy is in the process of evolving. Given Syria's history, it would be foolhardy to predict its final contours.

Lebanon

Lebanon made progress toward reestablishing governmental legitimacy after the Taif Accords of 1989, only to relinquish that authority to growing Syrian influence. Syrian troops and administrators played key roles in suppressing the factional warfare that was the hallmark of the Lebanese civil war over the past decades. Lebanon's recent economic revitalization and relative political stability provide evidence that Lebanon is emerging from the worst of its difficulties.

Lebanese foreign policy priorities have largely revolved around recovering the "buffer zone" seized by Israel during its 1982 invasion.

The zone, which also contains the watershed of the Litani River, is important to the Lebanese government symbolically and substantively. This area, and the Bekaa Valley north of it, is the home ground of Hizbollah, Israel's most implacable foreign enemy and a considerable problem for the government of Lebanon.

The improvement of civil life in Lebanon is sufficient to have attracted real estate investment back to Beirut. The importance of establishing stable, representative government inclusive of the major factions and religious groups is still a pressing priority. Until that is accomplished, Lebanese foreign policy is destined to be at the bottom of the Lebanese priorities. A timely resolution of the Syrian-Israeli peace negotiations could have a profound effect on the substance and content of Lebanese foreign policy.

Iran

Iran gained much in the new politics of the Middle East. It was an interested bystander in the Gulf crisis, skillfully exploiting the difficulties of its old adversary, Iraq, without entangling itself in the actual conflict. Iraqi planes fled to sanctuary in Iran, only to find the planes first impounded and eventually integrated into the Iranian air force. The revolt of the Shia in southern Iraq benefited Iranian interests, but again Iran seemed content to reap such rewards indirectly. Iran did not move quickly to the establishment of an independent Shia state in the south of Iraq, although Iranian public opinion probably would have supported such a move. The Rafsanjani regime played its cards conservatively and cautiously during the crisis.

Iran emerged in retrospect as one of the primary beneficiaries of Desert Storm. The destruction of Iraqi military power directly increased the relative power of Iran. In concrete terms, Iran has used much of its increased oil revenues to increase its armaments substantially. Iran emerged from the Gulf crisis with enhanced military power. Its purchases of Russian submarines and nuclear equipment and Chinese missile components and other military equipment suggest that it has not abandoned its quest for military-based regional influence.

Iran has moved in recent years from a domestic climate of revolutionary intensity to a more moderate political climate. Under the leadership of President Khatami, moderate influences in Iran have competed successfully with the more conservative clerical groups, moving Iran toward a moderating domestic and international set of policies. Iran has moved to improve relations with its Gulf area neighbors and seeks improved economic relations with Europe and the United States. As noted in previous chapters, U.S. allies have been anxious to capitalize on new trade relations with Iran, often to express dissatisfaction of the U.S. administration.

Iran has reached out to the West in other ways. Cultural delegations were welcomed to Iran in the waning days of the twentieth century and into the new century. The country has sought opportunities to engage in wide-ranging discussions with Saudi Arabia, Oman, and the United Arab Emirates. Iranian leaders publicly call for improvement in the climate of its relationship with the West and the United States in particular. Finally, Iran's defusing of its targeting of author Salman Rushdie has reduced some of its tensions with the European states, particularly Great Britain. Iran seemed poised, at the turn of the twenty-first century, to reclaim some of its earlier international influence.

Regionally, Iran seems concerned about establishing good relations with the new independent republics of central Asia. It competes with Turkey in this process, and both countries have invested economically in the resource-rich Muslim republics, particularly Kazakhstan, Uzbekistan, and Azerbaijan. By 1996, Iran had established diplomatic relations with most of the 12 republics, including the Russian Federation. Relations with Turkey remained cool, although Turkey and Iran have a common interest in suppressing independence movements among the Kurds. Water resources are a recurring problem because Turkey disrupts the flow of water into the Tigris and Euphrates systems to fill the dams and reservoirs of its Grand Anatolia Project. Given all of these factors, it seems clear that Iran will continue to play a large role in the international politics of the region over the next decades.

Turkey

Turkey is an important member in the coalition suppression of Iraq, and it continues to play a key role in the efforts to punish Iraq for its refusal to accept U.N. weapons inspectors. U.S. and British aircraft continued to fly from Turkish bases in their periodic overflights of Iraq's "no-fly" zones. Turkey continues to be an important member of NATO and to pursue full membership in the European Union.

Turkish foreign policy is closely linked to the United States. In the waning days of the twentieth century, with the encouragement of the United States, Turkey engaged in a series of military training exercises with U.S. and Israeli defense forces. Unencumbered by Arab sentiment, Turkey accepted a de facto military alliance with the United States and Israel that greatly disconcerted its neighbors in Syria, Iraq, and Iran. Such a policy posture fits neatly with Turkish notions of its place on the globe.

As a nation astride the continents of Europe and Asia, Turkey has often identified itself with Europe. This has been evident in its attempts to achieve membership or associate status with the European Union. To qualify for membership, Turkey moved substantially in the direction of free market economics, accepting the economic and social costs of the attendant destabilization. Millions of Turkish workers continue to labor in Europe, and the Turkish army is the largest in NATO (except for the United States). Despite these political, economic, and military policies, Turkey has been excluded from membership in the European Union, although now Turkey has

been admitted to candidacy for membership. EU membership most likely will continue to be an important goal of any Turkish government, that is, if the Turkish domestic political equation stays constant.

Similar to Iran, Turkey saw opportunity in the dissolution of the U.S.S.R. and the emergence of independent states in Soviet central Asia. Turkey moved quickly to establish diplomatic relations with the Muslim and neighbor republics; foreign investments in communications, transportation, and resource development have taken place in Azerbaijan, Kazakhstan, Uzbekistan, and Turkmenistan. Turkey would like to be seen as a democratic role model for the emerging republics, a logical alternative to the Islamic republic model in Iran.

Relations with the Kurdish minorities continue to be problematic for Turkey and Iran, and both have had to contend militarily with independence movements in the area. Turkey's forceful attack on the Kurdish independence guerrillas in western Anatolia in 1995 was strongly supported by the United States, but it was roundly condemned in other quarters. All of this changed quickly when Turkey was able to capture the leader of the Kurdish independence movement (Abdullah Ocalan) and bring him to trial.

Turkish relations with Greece, Bulgaria, and Cyprus continue to smolder. A satisfactory resolution of its dispute over Aegean islands with Greece, its border problems with Bulgaria, and the continued Turkish occupation of half of Cyprus will have to precede any Turkish entry into the European Union.

Bulgaria forcibly expelled many Turkish nationals from its territory in 1991, creating great ill will between the two states and many refugees in European Turkey. Relations with both of these countries remain frigid. The civil war in Bosnia and Kosovo also raised concerns among the Turkish leadership, but NATO's successful intervention in both of these conflicts seems to have met Turkish concerns for the Muslim populations of this region.

Algeria, Morocco, and Tunisia

Algeria, Morocco, and Tunisia share some of the key difficulties facing Turkey. Similar to Turkey, they have been at pains to establish a working relationship with the European Union. In contrast to Turkey, they have been successful at establishing regional cooperation, particularly in the Saharan regions where boundaries are particularly permeable. Their governments in the main cooperated with the U.S.-led coalition against Iraq in the Gulf War. These states have enjoyed improving relations with the United States and the European Union.

Domestically, however, Algeria, Morocco, and Tunisia all face a growing tide of Islamic extremist dissatisfaction with their secular regimes. In Algeria and Tunisia, these actions have resulted in Islamic extremist success at the ballot box. The invalidation of the Algerian election by the losing government precipitated widespread, violent opposition. The military government of Algeria entered into negotiations with the Islamic opposition in 1995 and 1996, but no formal resolution of the dispute has been accomplished. The Islamist opposition in Algeria has initiated a horrifyingly brutal campaign against the government and its allies. As a result, Algeria is increasingly isolated internationally.

An organized Islamic opposition to the monarchy continues to grow slowly in Morocco. We can conclude that all three states face a rising tide of organized Islamic activism and political extremism. This tide threatens to change the political face of the Maghreb. The long-term implications of fundamentalist extremist rule are unclear, but most likely their policy preferences would run counter to those of the United States and the European Union.

Libya

Libya, since the U.S. raid in 1986, has adopted a fairly low profile internationally. The U.S.–Great Britain determination that Libyan diplomats orchestrated the Pan American flight 103 bombing reinvigorated Western demands for more punitive action against Libya. Libya's surprising decision to surrender the accused for trial in Europe seems to be part of a concerted effort to gain political rehabilitation with the West. The European Union seems anxious to seize this opportunity, much to the chagrin of the United States, which would prefer to maintain the program of sanctions and embargoes against Libya.

Muammar Qadaffi seems to have chosen a course designed to minimize the rationales for punitive action. As such, the foreign policy of Libya has become relatively conservative and quiet, seeking an economically based rapprochement with the European West. The earlier decline in world petroleum prices also had deprived Libya of the financial resources necessary for an expansive and aggressive foreign policy. Libya's current overtures toward the West demonstrate an economic and political pragmatism likely to find fertile ground in the emerging world system.

Israel

The emergence of the new world order has been especially important to Israel, which finds positive and negative implications. On the one hand, the collapse of the Soviet Union and the emergence of the Russian Federation allowed the continued emigration of Eastern European Jews to Israel. On the other hand, the collapse of the Soviet threat removed one of the key rationales for the privileged "special relationship" between Israel and the United States. The United States simply does not now need the Israeli military in the way it did during the dangerous confrontations of the bipolar cold war. This new fact was made clear during Desert Storm, when the United States formally kept Israel from participating in the coalition attacks on Iraq, going so far as to deny key communication codes to the Israeli air force. It seems clear that the nature of the relationship between Israel and the United

States changed dramatically under the Bush administration.

As indicated earlier in this chapter, Israel was more or less goaded into participation in the Arab-Israeli Peace Conference begun in 1991. The Shamir administration was unenthusiastic about multilateral negotiations under any circumstances, and it was ideologically committed to a policy of "no return of land" to the Palestinians under any circumstances. The nature of the coalition supporting the Likud government made any major deviation from this proposition unlikely, even in the improbable event that the government would see the negotiations in a positive light. These two attitudes put Israel on a collision course with the Bush administration, which saw the surrender of occupied territory in exchange for security guarantees as the most appropriate formula for settling the long-standing dispute.

Israeli policy after Desert Storm exhibited some fundamental inconsistencies. These inconsistencies have plagued Israel, the United States, and the Palestinians in the ensuing decade of negotiations and agreements, from Madrid, through Oslo I and II, through the Wye Plantation Accords in 1998, and up to and including Israeli–Palestinian negotiations in and around Washington. A series of Israeli governments (Shamir, Rabin, Peres, Netanyahu, and Barak) found themselves dependent on and resistant to the guarantees and influence of the U.S. administrations of George H. W. Bush, Bill Clinton, and George W. Bush. Unwilling to alienate a U.S. administration totally, the Israeli governments allowed themselves to be bullied into participation in the peace talks. They found themselves agreeing to concessions that would have been politically impossible without U.S. pressure or security guarantees. The result has been a peace process proceeding in fits and starts, with high risks and rewards for participants on both sides.

Israeli extremist groups and Palestinian extremists in and outside of Israel did their best to disrupt these negotiations. Israeli settlers, armed to the teeth and espousing the most nationalist of Zionist philosophy, established settlements illegally, seized Arab housing forcibly, even beat and murdered Palestinians. Palestinians outside the coalition involved in the peace talks also attempted to disrupt events. The complexity of the situation was underscored in one attack by Palestinian guerrillas on a bus transporting settlers, killing two. The Palestinians, attempting to disrupt the peace process, killed two settlers on their way to a rally to oppose the peace negotiations. Israelis and their Palestinian counterparts had to walk a very narrow ledge.

We have previously described and discussed the events that transformed Israel's relationship with the PLO. Although clearly an act in progress, the partial resolution of the conflict has changed the style and focus of Israel's relations with her neighbors, and with the United States and the other powers. Most of these changes have been mentioned previously in other contexts. Given their importance, however, they bear review again.

The conclusion of substantive peace agreements with its Palestinian foes has reaped some real, concrete rewards for Israel. Relations with the Clinton Administration continued on a positive note, and U.S. formal economic and military support for Israel has continued unabated. Israel's European relations also have been enhanced, particularly with Great Britain, France, and Germany, all of whom had been encouraging a rapprochement with the PLO. All of these sets of relationships are warmer in the twenty-first century than in the twentieth century.

This is not to suggest that tensions between Israel and the Palestinians have been eliminated, for they have not. Final status negotiations have yet to settle the question of settlements, the right of return for Palestinian refugees, the creation of a Palestinian state, or the final status of Jerusalem for both governments.

Relations with the United States also are problematic. Arafat frequently has called on the United States to pressure Israel to honor its agreements, leading to difficult conversations between the American presidents and the Israeli prime ministers. Prime ministers Netanyahu and Barak publicly called on the United States to become a silent partner in peace negotiations, to no particular effect. The repeated requests by Israeli prime ministers for the release of convicted Israeli spy Jonathan Pollard have done little to improve the tone of U.S.–Israeli conversations. Sometimes, disagreements between friends are the most troublesome. But nothing here should suggest any substantive decline in the U.S. preference for Israel in these foreign relations.

Relations within the Middle East also have improved. Israel's relationships with Jordan have become positively hot. Tourists pour across the Allenby Bridge, seeking Petra and Jerasch and Salt. Palestinians from Jordan visit their families in Israel with fewer obstacles and hindrances at the border. More important, Israeli and Jordanian businessmen search for investment opportunities. Foreign investors tour Amman in increasing numbers, looking for the pots of gold that follow in the wake of peace and the normalization of relations. Israeli progressives hope for a similar awakening in its relations with Egypt and Syria.

There are signs that the tense relations between the Gulf monarchies and Israel also are getting better. Symbolically, Gulf diplomats have ceased referring to Israel as "the Zionist entity," a phraseology emphasizing the lack of legitimacy of the state of Israel. Israel now is referred to as Israel. For its part, Israel supported Oman's appointment to the United Nations Security Council in 1995, an act unheard of in the earlier age. Trade with Israel now comes from the ports and trading centers of the Persian Gulf and the Red Sea. Ambitious plans that combine Palestinian labor and real estate with Israeli technology and Arab capital continue to float across the desert. Legions of nongovernmental organizations continue to provide relief and support for those unfortunates not yet swept up in the changes taking place. These are the surface signs of change, and many of them are encouraging. But difficult problems remain to be solved.

CONCLUSION

Questions abound. Is the old world order gone? Definitely. Is the new world order here? Maybe. Do we know the details and implications of this new system? Not yet. Does this new order complicate our understanding of and relations with the Middle East? Definitely. To what can we look forward?

If our description of the emerging international system is correct, we can look forward to a rapidly changing Middle East. We can confidently predict that the changes there will have an impact on much of the world. The industrialized world still depends on a regular flow of petroleum from the region to fuel its industrial economies. The concentration of financial resources in the hands of the petroleum producers will continue to make them important friends or foes in the world economy. That much has not changed. But the way in which we respond to risk and threat seems to have changed within and without the region.

It seems likely that the trend toward multinational responses to conflict will continue. The United Nations, in particular, seems destined to play a crucial role in the conflicts that emerge in the region in the near future. The European Community, using whatever military and diplomatic resources it creates in the coming years, also will likely play an important role. The influence of independent nations seems destined to relative decline, although the action of powers such as the United States, European Union, Japan, and Russia will continue to be important.

Within the region, alliance realignment and new concentrations of power seem likely.

Desert Storm increased the relative regional influence of Iran, Syria, and Egypt. Here, too, regional multinational organizations seem destined to play larger roles than in the past. The Arab League, the GCC, the Islamic Conference, and the U.S.-led coalitions have many substantive problems to address. Among them are arms control and the management of new arms technologies, particularly "instruments of mass destruction," the disposition of refugees, and the regional management of water resources.

Many of the problems confronting the region are manageable only with international cooperation. Declining water resources is one obvious problem. The problems of environmental degradation, dramatic increases in refugees, Palestinian and Kurdish aspirations for independence, population growth and attendant health and disease questions, and open access to religious sites also are complicated and persistent. There is no shortage of serious problems for these organizations to attack.

There is also the phenomenon of the rising tide of religious extremism, in and out of the region. No states in the Middle East are immune to the dynamics of religious extremism. The process unleashed in Iran has resonance throughout the Islamic and Christian world. The critique of government that nourishes Islamic activism, and, in some instances, political extremism, is based squarely on the public perception of policy failures by secular or monarchical government. Social justice, the principles of compassion and fairness that inspire the pious folk of Islam, has not been widely achieved, even as the technology of modern communication brings that failure to the attention of greater numbers in the public. The increasing gap between rich and poor nations and between the rich and poor within nations, the failure of governments to articulate a future other than the simple imitation of the industrial West, and the obvious materialism and hedonism of many officials and businessmen all fuel the fires of politics and extremism.

Governments inside and outside the Middle East are still "lagging participants" in the politics of this new age. They are still deeply mired in the assumptions, conflicts, and constraints of the old order.

The View from 2000

All in all, as the new millennium opened in 2000 C.E., there were reasonable grounds for cautious optimism. A new American president, George Walker Bush, proclaimed an era of "humbler" U.S. foreign policy, a policy less confrontational and less insistent on imposing American values abroad. Prime Minister Barak's administration in Israel removed Israeli troops from Lebanon and actively engaged the Palestinian Authority in peace negotiations, supported by an administration interested in an evenhanded role in the dispute. President Bush publicly endorsed the idea of an independent Palestinian state, living peacefully with its Israeli neighbor. Only later in the summer of 2000 would Israeli-Palestinian relations descend into Intifadah II, as General Ariel Sharon outmaneuvered Prime Minister Barak, regaining the government for Likud and initiating a bloody conflict that by late 2002 had taken more than 1,500 Palestinian lives and over 500 Israeli lives.

Oil supplies and prices seemed headed for relative stability. Nascent democratic institutions were emerging cautiously, even in the oil monarchies of the Gulf, long the most resistant to change. The region seemed on the cusp of important new relationships.

All of that optimism was to disappear in little less than an hour on September 11, 2001, as two hijacked airliners piloted by Islamist terrorists plunged into the World Trade Center in New York, initiating a new and frightening era in international relations. It is important to gain a systemic perspective on that event and the policy changes that followed it. We discuss this in Chapter 15.

15 | DID 9/11 CHANGE EVERYTHING?

There is no doubt that the events of September 11, 2001—specifically, the horrific terrorist attack on the World Trade Center in New York and the Pentagon in Washington, DC—resulted in major, important changes in the conduct of foreign policy by the United States. That is clear enough in the abrupt changes in rhetoric and policies that flowed from the attack. President George W. Bush, in the immediate aftermath of the attacks, found a new voice in his denunciation of the terrorists themselves, the states that supported them, directly and indirectly, and even those who sympathized in any way with them.

Departing from a foreign policy position that called for a "humbler" and more sensitive foreign policy, one respectful of the differences in beliefs and systems that existed around the world, President Bush headed in a new direction, calling for a war on terror and all its allies. Proclaiming a "line in the sand," pursuing Osama bin Laden and Al-Qaeda "dead or alive," declaring that states must choose to actively support the U.S. effort or embrace its enmity, the president loudly declared that the states of the world are either "with us or against us in this war." There was no room for moderation or indecision.

Within months of the attack, the administration put words into action, launching a major attack against Al-Qaeda in its camps, compounds, and caves in Afghanistan. In doing so, the administration took on the destruction of the Taliban, the extreme Islamist movement governing Afghanistan since 1996. In a series of asymmetric attacks against Taliban troops and installations, making effective use of U.S. special forces capabilities, the administration ran the Taliban out of power and pursued and killed many of its supporters.

Deprived of governmental support and patronage, the Al-Qaeda moved into the valleys and mountains of rural Afghanistan, dug in, and attempted to resist the U.S. forces pursuing them. The United States, its Afghan allies, and a small smattering of troops from Great Britain, Canada, and Australia began a slow and dogged pursuit of Al-Qaeda groups and operatives in some of the most remote regions of Afghanistan. Some of the Al-Qaeda fighters stayed to make a fight of it; others melted into the ill-defined border areas between Afghanistan and Pakistan, Iran, Uzbekistan, and other nearby countries. Osama bin Laden disappeared and no one was sure whether he was dead or alive.

A similar fate befell some of the other members of the Al-Qaeda "coalition." In the Philippines, U.S. special forces aided the Philippine military in attacking and destroying one of the guerrilla groups of Abu Sayyaf, on Basilan Island and in Northern Mindanao. Other successful raids were conducted in the Sudan and Yemen, and U.S. special forces teams were based in Djibouti and Eritrea. All in all, from a military point of view, the United States seemed to be successful in its initial attempts at suppressing the terrorist organizations attacking the United States and its allies.

By the spring of 2002, the Taliban and Al-Qaeda were effectively suppressed in Afghanistan, and a friendly government was established under the leadership of Mohammad Karzai. International promises of support for the new government led to high expectations that the Karzai government might garner the resources necessary to project its power out of Kabul and into the Afghani interior, creating the basis for a legitimate Afghan state with real pretensions to sovereignty. But only a small percentage of the pledged support materialized, and by the summer of 2002 it was apparent that the struggle for effective government in Afghanistan would be a long-term project.

THE REEMERGENCE OF IRAQ

The Bush foreign policy at that moment, the spring and summer of 2002, took a sudden change in direction. In one of President Bush's oratorical excesses during his 2002 State of the Union message, he had proclaimed the existence of an "axis of evil," composed of Iraq, Iran, and North Korea. All three states were conflated in this famous equation as states that broadly and infamously supported terrorists and their organizations. Despite scholars' and pundits' protests against this particular grouping of states, two of them long-standing mortal enemies themselves (Iran and Iraq), the administration decided to pursue the suppression of Iraq, moving the focus of U.S. policy away from Al-Qaeda and onto perpetual opponent and villain Saddam Hussein.

The administration presumed the existence of Iraqi weapons of mass destruction and the intent of Iraq to eventually use them against the United States, Israel, or Iraq's neighbors. Additionally, the U.S. accused Iraq of suppressing its own citizens, primarily Kurds and Shia, and of supporting Al-Qaeda and other terrorist groups. Evidence supporting the terrorist assertions was insubstantial and unpersuasive, particularly assertions that "secret evidence" documented an alliance of convenience between Saddam Hussein and Osama bin Laden, both understood conventionally as mortal enemies.

In the face of near-universal lack of international support for "regime change" in Iraq, in the summer of 2002 the United States threatened to "go it alone" if necessary and launch a unilateral attack on Iraq. U.S. forces in the region were increased, and nominal U.S. allies in the region were pressured to cooperate with them. In the end, only Great Britain and Israel were enthusiastic supporters of an American unilateral attack on Iraq; almost all of the 1991 Gulf War coalition partners refused to support or provide legitimacy for such an attack.

Both the lack of support for the war overseas and the growing domestic opposition to the war were given some momentum by the assertion that the United States had the right to launch a "preemptive" war against Iraq—that is, a war that would begin with a U.S. attack on Iraq with no presumptive *causus belli*. Such a war would in fact entail acceptance of a doctrine that has been anathema in most of American history, particularly since the sneak attack on Pearl Harbor by Japan in 1941, a "day that will live in infamy." Opposition and cultural antipathy toward such ideas aside, the administration pursued and promulgated a war-fighting doctrine that reserves the right of preemptive attacks and the use of chemical, biological, and nuclear "weapons of mass destruction."

Reactions within the U.S. polity and within the administration itself were divided. In spite of the loud and confrontational rhetoric emanating periodically from the White House, it became apparent that the administration itself was divided over the question of whether or not the United States would be well served by a diversion of its attention from Al-Qaeda to Iraq, and whether or not such an intervention could or should be attempted unilaterally. This largely boiled down to the question of whether the United States should seek U.N. approval for its proposed intervention, disarmament, and regime change in Iraq or simply proceed alone on a unilateral basis.

As is often the case, these questions and conflicts resulted in the appearance of personality conflicts. In this case, the internal White House divide was personalized in the leadership of Colin Powell, Secretary of State, former U.S. Army Chief of Staff, and an architect of the 1991 Gulf War, and Vice President Richard Cheney, former White House Chief of Staff and Secretary of Defense. In this case, Powell led those administration and professional military elements that emphasized a need for broad domestic support for the venture, a broadly based international coalition in support, and clear United Nations support for any military intervention—in short, a multilateral foreign policy strategy.

Vice President Cheney, joined by National Security Advisor Condoleeza Rice and Secretary of Defense Donald Rumsfeld, argued in favor of a muscular unilateralism, wherein the United States would exercise its military superiority without concern for the breadth of the international support or public reaction to it. To this coalition within the administration, the sooner the United States began its regime change in Iraq, the better, to this coalition within the administration.

The drums of war were pounding so hard by August of 2002 that most U.S. and foreign observers expected the United States to go to war with Iraq unilaterally in the fall. Material published by Robert Woodward (*Bush at War*) indicated that the administration was in fact deeply divided about the prospects of a unilateral war and was internally vacillating between the two policies. Ultimately, the administration decided to go to the United Nations to make its case against Iraq. But even at the very last minute, as reflected in the two dozen revisions of President Bush's speech, the administration was not clear about whether to simply present the U.S. case and then initiate hostilities (the Cheney position), or to pressure the U.N., more specifically the Security Council, for a resolution demanding the destruction of Iraq's weapons of mass destruction and invoking drastic penalties if it did not (the Powell multilateral strategy).

The Powell position prevailed and President Bush announced, before the United Nations, his intention to obtain a Security Council resolution on Iraq, specifying the demands and consequences for noncompliance. After tortured diplomacy within the Security Council, the U.N. complied and produced a resolution (SCR 1441) demanding the admission of U.N. weapons inspectors with unfettered access to Iraqi sites, programs, and personnel. The demand of such inspection used language threatening the strongest of responses if Iraq should fail to comply with the intent of the resolution. The final resolutions were remarkable in the breadth of support received, suggesting that the support for multilateral interventions was very much more palatable internationally than the muscular unilateralism of the world's remaining superpower.

As 2002 stumbled to a close, the world found the United States poised and prepared for an attack on Iraq, given a "material breach" of the U.N. resolutions. Saddam Hussein and his government met several key deadlines, including the acceptance of the U.N. Security Council resolution, and they delivered thousands of pages of documents to the U.N. detailing their weapons programs or lack of them. Teams of U.N. weapons inspectors doggedly pursued biological, chemical, and nuclear weapons of mass destruction across Iraq. Unimpeded access to Iraqi sites was allowed, including the vaunted "palaces" of Saddam Hussein. And in the ultimate irony, Saddam Hussein counseled the Iraqi public to cooperate with the U.N. inspectors as a way of refuting the U.S. claims about Iraq. In spite of its cooperation with the U.N. inspections regime, Iraq, for the most part, was isolated politically, economically, and militarily.

The ongoing U.S. preparations for war with Iraq inevitably detracted from the administration's pursuit of Al-Qaeda. Some critics of the administration's turn to the Iraqi front pointed out that the suppression of Al-Qaeda was incomplete and that the organization would reconstitute itself if the pressure were not continued on them. And the appearance of a controversial audiotape purporting to be the voice of Osama bin Laden himself in late November of 2002 added fuel to that fire.

More than the purported bin Laden tape, however, a series of attacks during the same period seemed to confirm the continued vitality of Al-Qaeda. Terrorist attacks on a tourist nightclub on the island of Bali, an Israeli-owned resort hotel in Mombasa, Kenya, a French oil tanker off the coast of the Arabian peninsula, and the assassination of an American aid official in Amman, Jordan, combined to remind the world that organized terror with a worldwide reach still existed and still required strenuous efforts to identify their supporters and root them out of the 60-plus countries in which Al-Qaeda is believed to work.

Another irony of American foreign policy in this period is that while there was apparent opposition to a unilateral U.S. attack on Iraq, substantial enthusiasm existed for the U.S. "war on terror." It was far easier to garner international support for coalition attacks against presumptive Al-Qaeda targets around the world than for a coalition of forces to punish Saddam Hussein.

Two Coalitions

It is instructive to compare the positions of those key states and international organizations that supported the U.S.-led Gulf War in 1990–1991 (refer to Table 15.1) and their positions on the Iraq question in 2002.

The prevailing international sentiment in favor of a program of inspections followed by a multilateral intervention if necessary seemed very clear and unlikely to change. From this it was argued that a U.S. insistence on a more-or-less unilateral attack without explicit Security Council approval would harm U.S. reputation and interests internationally. The "blowback" from the attack could be substantial and damage American international interests for some time, particularly in the Middle East.

For these and other reasons, the U.N. Security Council in the winter of 2002 refused to endorse an attack on Iraq, preferring to continue the regime of inspections that was in place. For American diplomats, French, German, and Russian opposition to the war, and Chinese ambivalence to it reduced the U.N. and the Security Council to "irrelevance." French and Russian threats to exercise their veto infuriated the U.S. administration and resulted in U.S. efforts to coordinate a "coalition of the willing" outside the U.N., relying mostly on the support of Great Britain, Spain, Italy, and Australia to legitimize a U.S. preemptive strike on Iraq. Ultimately, the United States was able to marshal over 40 states in its "coalition of the willing"— although the coalition lacked most of the international actors that could be described as influential or powerful.

This situation, moreover, raised many related questions. Among them are: Why did the coalition put together by the Bush Administration in 1991 fail to support another Bush Administration coalition in 2002? Are different issues in play at the international level? Can regional and local changes account for this dramatic shift? The answer(s) is

Table 15.1 Two U.S.-Led Coalitions: 1990 and 2003*

Country in 1990–1991 Coalition	Favors 2002 Unilateral U.S. Action	Favors Multilateral UN Action
United States	Yes	Yes
Britain	Yes	Yes
France	No	Yes
Saudi Arabia	No	Yes
Egypt	No	Yes
Syria	No	Yes
Kuwait	Yes	Yes
Bahrain	No	Yes
Bangladesh	No	Yes
Morocco	No	Yes
Oman	No	Yes
Pakistan	No	Yes
Qatar	Yes	Yes
U.A.E.	No	Yes
Turkey	No	Yes
Noncombatant States		
Russia	No	Yes
Germany	No	Yes
China	No	Uncertain
Japan	No	Yes
Israel	Yes	Yes
International Organizations		
United Nations	No	Yes
NATO	Uncertain	Yes

*Positions declared publicly by December 2002

problematically "yes," necessitating an examination of levels and points in the international system, a system that has certainly changed in the intervening years. Let us turn to a more detailed examination of the bases of support and opposition for U.S. unilateral action against Iraq.

THE MIDDLE EAST QUARTET

Although the United States is arguably the only remaining world superpower, that does not suggest that the United States should or could act unilaterally on the world stage without consequences. Other powers may not be as strong individually as the United States but, taken collectively in various constellations, they are capable of mustering enough military, economic, political, or social power to frustrate or punish the United States for simple-minded and/or nakedly self-interested independent actions.

To many international actors, Iraq is simply not the architectonic issue that must be solved before progress can be made on other issues. The ongoing conflict between Israel and the Palestinians, they argue, is a much more compelling issue, one more in need of solution than the come-again, go-again policies of Iraq. The same can be said for the war on terror, which threatens most states and shows no signs of going away. This point of view is true for many states active on the international scene and for a number of transnational international organizations.

One combination of states and organizations with a strong focus on the Israeli–Palestinian question is the so-called Middle East Quartet, a grouping of Russia, the European Union, the United Nations, and the United States. The United States has hoped that this group could provide some leadership on the Palestinian question. And in fact the group has advocated more aggressive efforts to settle the ongoing conflict.

The United States stands alone in this potent group of international players in its insistence that the situation in Iraq deserves a higher priority than the Israeli–Palestinian conflict. All members of the group are critical of the U.S. administration's largely one-sided support for Israel as the conflict slides into higher and higher levels of violence and intransigence. In fact, European Union diplomats played key roles in the protection of President Arafat on the several occasions in which his office was surrounded by Israeli soldiers and tanks, camping out in the few square feet of office space left after the deliberate destruction of the Palestinian Authority headquarters in Ramallah.

As the European Union moves slowly toward a unified foreign policy for its members, the EU leadership has found consensus on its call for more balanced and fair negotiations between Israel and the Palestinians. It is one of the few issues where the various EU populations share the perception that the Palestinians are the victims of a brutal occupation and repression, support the creation of a Palestinian state, and call for Israel to recognize and implement the key standing resolutions of the UN Security Council.

While the European Union continues to see the Israeli–Palestinian conflict as important and architectonic to Middle East politics, it also resisted the U.S. pressure for a military

incursion in Iraq. The issue of U.S. policy was important in recent elections in both Germany and France, and both Chancellor Schröder and President Chirac campaigned on a platform strongly critical of the Bush Administration's mideast policy. In some forums in Germany, U.S. foreign policy was compared to Hitler's. And in others, the United States was accused of nurturing imperialist aspirations. Neither of these allegations would have been raised a decade ago in public settings.

In another significant arena, the European Union began negotiations with Iran to normalize and expand trade relations with the union. These discussions, in the context of World Trade Organization rules and regulations, reflected another significant difference in policy between the EU and the United States. European enthusiasm for improved relations with Iran go contrary to the U.S. "dual containment" policy and vitiate the U.S. categorization of Iran as a "problem" state.

In Russia, President Vladimir Putin, in spite of a close working relationship with the United States and with President Bush personally, opposed the U.S. plans for military intervention in Iraq. Russia and Iraq have a long history of mutually beneficial economic and military relations, which has left Iraq with considerable debt to Russia, a debt that very well might be repudiated by a new government in Baghdad. Russia can ill afford to write off substantial foreign assets in a time of domestic economic stress. It thus opposed the U.S.-sponsored regime change in Iraq.

The final member of the Quartet, the United Nations, was also reluctant to see the United States–Iraq conflict go directly to war. Secretary General Kofi Annan skillfully worked to bring a new, vigorous inspections regime to Iraq, and he was important in the diplomatic maneuvers in the Security Council as the new resolution demanding Iraqi compliance and disarmament was hammered out. Consistent with the organization's charter, the UN was organizationally and principally committed to the peaceful resolution of disputes where possible. And in the eventuality of a clear and public Iraqi material breach of the U.N. Security Council Resolution 1441, there was little doubt that the U.N. would provide the legal rationale for military action against Iraq. In the meantime, however, it was preferable from the U.N. viewpoint to talk and talk and talk, and inspect, inspect, inspect, rather than to go immediately to war.

REGIONAL ACTORS

States within the Middle East were also suspicious of the proposed U.S. preemptive war against Iraq. In many cases, this reservation was predicated on fears of destabilization and disruption of the existing international system. This was particularly true of states immediately bordering on Iraq (Turkey, Iran, Syria, Jordan, Saudi Arabia, and Kuwait), and Egypt, Libya, Morocco, and Lebanon. Of these regionally situated actors, only Israel professed genuine public enthusiasm for a U.S. preemptive attack on Iraq, "the sooner the better," said Israeli leaders. But outside of Israel there is also a widespread belief that the military intervention has distracted the United States from its leadership role in the resolution of the Israeli–Palestinian conflict, a conflict with particular emotional power on the urban streets of the region. Should Israel, for whatever reason, engage in the "transfer" of Palestinians from the West Bank and Gaza, or expel or even assassinate senior Hamas or Fatah leaders, the resultant anger in the Arab street could threaten many governments in the area. It is clear that opposition or support for the U.S. policy has local, practical implications and ramifications.

Turkey had much at risk if the United States pursued its military agenda against Iraq. Turkey not only shares a long and porous border with Iraq, it also shares the two largest populations of Kurds, long a restless minority in both countries and historically bent on

gaining a country of their own. Although U.S. officials insisted that the United States would not sanction or encourage the creation of an independent Kurdish state in Iraq, on the borders of Turkey, the Turks were not sure that the United States could indeed dictate this particular outcome. Under the best of circumstances, an independent Kurdish state would create expectations among Turkish Kurds and nourish their own dreams for independence. This would endanger the ambitious development schemes that Turkey had begun in eastern Anatolia. And it could subtly or indirectly interfere with Turkish membership prospects in the European Union, the single-highest foreign policy priority for the Turkish state.

The electoral victory of an Islamic political party in the fall of 2002 Turkish elections also complicated the equation. It was clear that the new government of Turkey was more concerned with its prestige in the Muslim Middle East than the preceding government. It was less anxious for open conflict with other Muslim states. A compromise of sorts was produced. The result was Turkish willingness to allow key air force bases to be used in the U.S. effort, but an unwillingness to allow the stationing of U.S. troops in Turkey on the Iraqi border, as U.S. diplomats urged. Long-standing intimate relations with the United States notwithstanding, Turkey moved from uncritical support toward modest support for the U.S. policy.

Syria has long been at odds with Iraq, in spite of their geographical proximity, common ideological history (Baath Party), foreign policy alignments with the Soviet Union, and similar demographic characteristics. Syria did not hesitate to back Iran in the Iran–Iraq war in the 1980s and joined the U.S.-led coalition in 1991 to expel Iraq from Kuwait. It also voted in the fall of 2002, as a nonpermanent member of the U.N. Security Council, in favor of Resolution 1441. In addition, Syria cooperated in the hunt for terrorist organizations and was helpful in the search for Al-Qaeda links and allies.

In spite of this, Syria still ranked high on the U.S. list of "problem" states—states that encourage and support terrorism. In this case, the problem was the definition of the word *terror*. Syria saw some organizations that the U.S. classifies as "terrorist" as political resistance organizations. This explained Syrian support for Hizbollah and Hamas (two organizations fighting Israeli occupation in Gaza, the West Bank, the Golan Heights, and, until recently, in Lebanon). The Israeli classification of the groups was simply as "terrorist." In truth, there was more of a distinction here than was embraced in the simplistic rhetoric of "lines in the sand" and so on. For the reasons already enumerated, Syria was unlikely to reap any direct benefits from its support for the inspection regime in Iraq. In this case, the Israeli tail clearly wagged the U.S. dog.

One can also classify Iran as one of the major Middle Eastern states unsympathetic to Iraq. The Iran–Iraq war was a major drain on the Iranian economy and the cause of millions of Iranian deaths. Iran's political system, as an Islamic republic, is theoretically and operationally opposed to the secular republican notions of Iraqi Baathism. Nonetheless, Iran is reluctant to endorse even U.N.-mandated intervention as a dangerous precedent for the region. As the number two country on Israel's "hit list" of terror-sponsoring states, this home of Hizbollah and supporter of Hamas is not interested in legitimizing the intrusion of Western or European superpowers into the area.

Jordan was one of the few regional states that did not join the coalition in 1991. Jordan and Yemen, for different reasons, declined to contribute troops to the suppression of Iraq. For Yemen, the choice was mostly ideological. For Jordan, the problem was more complex, particularly since Jordan was one of the major trading partners of pre- and postwar Iraq, and since the Palestinian populations of Jordan to a large degree conflated their support of Palestinian independence with the Iraqi situation. Fear of anger on the street prompted a cautious reluctance in King Hussein.

Hussein's successor harbored fewer of these reservations and generally supported the multilateral approach to dealing with Iraq. And King Abdullah allowed joint military training exercises to take place with U.S. special forces. But Jordan was still reluctant to allow military operations to operate from its border facilities and air bases. The domestic political consequences were clearly just too high.

Egypt was a prominent member of the 1991 coalition against Iraq, providing a substantial number of troops and important intelligence to the coalition. Its presence to a large degree legitimized the operation and provided symbolic cover to the United States in much of the Arab world. By 2002, Egypt was less enthusiastic about the U.S. proposals for regime change and disarmament. Domestic critics of the war saw a resurgence of classic colonial politics in the U.S. attack on Iraq. Thus, the role of Egypt in the coalition fast became a domestic political issue that put serious pressure on President Mubarak and his government.

It can be argued that Saudi Arabia found itself in the most ironic circumstances of the original coalition members. One of the earliest supporters of the 1991 Gulf War, Saudi Arabia allowed its bases to be used by U.S. forces; contributed troops, material, and energy to the effort; and paid a large percentage of the costs of the war. It considered itself a loyal ally of the United States, in a mutually beneficial relationship based on perceived common interests: U.S. need for a regular and reasonably priced supply of petroleum and the Saudi need for military and political security in a dangerous neighborhood. This deal, they thought, was in good shape and standing. The attack on the World Trade Center brought these assumptions into question.

The first problem for the Saudi government was the embarrassment of discovering that 15 of the 19 hijackers in the attack were

Saudi citizens. In retrospect, this is not surprising, given the Al-Qaeda strategy of recruiting members from the mujahedeen soldiers of the Afghan war. Many of these men, supported then by the governments of Saudi Arabia and the United States in their efforts to drive the U.S.S.R. out of Afghanistan, had been socialized into a radical understanding of Islam and Islamic jihad. Moreover, bin Laden and his family had enjoyed a privileged life in Saudi Arabia, creating more opportunities for the recruitment of Saudi nationals into Al-Qaeda. Given these circumstances, it is not surprising that a substantial element of Al-Qaeda's membership would be Saudi by national origin.

The decision by Al-Qaeda's leadership to employ a disproportionate number of Saudis in the attack can also be explained. After the retreat of the U.S.S.R. from Afghanistan, Al-Qaeda turned to new projects, including the destruction of what they perceived as corrupt political regimes. Saudi Arabia topped that list, particularly given the important religious sites of Mecca and Medina in the country. And the United States, perceived by Al-Qaeda as the "great satan," was also high on the list of desirable targets. By using predominantly Saudi nationals in an attack on the World Trade Center, Al-Qaeda accomplished a twofold success: a demoralizing attack on the United States and the presumption of Saudi complicity.

Saudi Arabia's enemies in the United States, long angered by the privileged status of Saudi Arabia in U.S. foreign policy, launched a vigorous public relations attack against Saudi Arabia, accusing that state of being more of an enemy than a friend, of being a sponsor of the virulent variety of Islam that promoted international terrorism, and blaming a corrupt Saudi state for tolerating extremist religious leadership in exchange for their domestic political support. This attack was well coordinated and even resulted in public hearings conducted by Defense Department advisory panels.

The anti-Saudi argument gained momentum in the United States as the Saudi government rejected U.S. requests to use Saudi air bases in a future war against Iraq. Saudi Arabia essentially refused to recognize the U.S. raison d'être for a unilateral attack on Iraq. Ultimately, the Saudi government agreed that the bases could probably be used in the event of a U.N.-sanctioned attack on Iraq. But in the U.S. public and governmental view, this was less than satisfactory, and the United States turned to develop alternative sites for the war. Saudi prestige in the United States plunged to an unprecedented low and was unlikely to recover quickly. The relationship at the official level was still positive, but stress between the two governments was growing as the prospects of war with Iraq loomed larger.

If Saudi Arabia was a reluctant partner in the U.S. policy toward Iraq, the tiny state of Qatar expressed no such reluctance. Qatar enthusiastically endorsed the U.S. position on Iraq and permitted the construction of a large air base and command center on the Qatar peninsula that could easily serve as the nerve center of a U.S. attack on Iraq. Joint military exercises in December of 2002 included the movement of material and personnel from the U.S. Central Command in Tampa, Florida, to the base in Qatar. All in all, an intimate relationship developed between Qatar and the United States.

This relationship was uncharacteristic of the other Gulf states. Bahrain, a host port for the U.S. naval forces in the Gulf, refused to endorse the U.S. unilateral attack, as did the governments of the United Arab Emirates and Oman. This reduced regional support for a unilateral U.S. attack on Iraq to Israel, Kuwait, and Qatar. All three of these states have prepositioned U.S. military supplies on their territories, have cooperated with the United States in joint military maneuvers and exercises, and have accepted the U.S. reasoning behind its proposed military suppression of Iraq. Taken collectively, they represent a very small subset of the region and a marginal percent of the Arab world. This suggested that regional and world opinion had formed against the U.S. war on Iraq.

The proposed war on Iraq was enthusiastically endorsed by Israel. In fact, governmental and public opinion in Israel was and is supportive of a series of U.S. interventions, not only against Iraq but also against Iran, Syria, and Libya. Israel has publicly vowed to use its weapons of mass destruction, including its nuclear arsenal, against Iraq should Iraq venture an attack against it. It was unlikely in the event of actual war between Iraq and the United States that Israel would be noncombatant. The 1991 precedent, which kept Israel out of the conflict, was apparently over and the United States actively developed basing sites and coordinated strategies with the Israel Defense Forces. It seemed likely that in the event of a more or less unilateral U.S. attack on Iraq, Israel would take a key role. This was not well received in the rest of the Middle East.

Israel also assumed a green light from Washington in its dealing with the Palestinian intifadah. The Israeli reprisals to Palestinian attacks became larger in scale and intensity. Renewed emphasis on the destruction of Palestinian infrastructure, collective punishment, administrative detention, long-term general curfews, assassinations, and the construction of new settlements brought the conflict to new heights of violence, as increasing numbers of Israeli and Palestinian citizens died in the conflict.

Palestinian groups (Hamas and Hizbollah among them) responded with suicide bombings, ambushes, and attacks against settlements and military posts. As the conflict continued to spiral upward, Israeli politicians publicly contemplated the desirability of a mass expulsion of Palestinians (transfer), the exile or assassination of Yasir Arafat, and the final annexation of all of the occupied territories.

All of this convinced world public opinion that a major peace initiative, with the United States in the lead, was past due. This opinion did not prevail in the United States,

however, and it was unlikely that the United States would make any new attempt at an evenhanded resolution of the conflict.

WORLD PUBLIC OPINION

Domestic critics of the proposed war with Iraq often pointed to a deteriorating public regard for the United States abroad. In late 2002 and early 2003, a number of polls confirmed this belief. U.S. prestige, high and robust after the World Trade Center and Pentagon attacks and during the U.S. pursuit of Al-Qaeda and the Taliban, plummeted as the United States turned its attention from terrorism to Iraq.

Moreover, the deterioration in public regard for the United States proceeded not only among the usual suspects—countries traditionally suspicious or at odds with the United States—but among the populations of states long considered to be friendly and alliance partners. Decline in public support for the United States in Great Britain, France, Germany, and Canada was clear. In these states, the United States appeared to be viewed as increasingly arrogant, self-centered, and intransigent. In a world characterized by increasing complexity, the simple rhetorical flourishes of the U.S. government did not find a receptive international ear.

As the *International Herald Tribune* reported in December of 2002:

> While majorities in nearly every country supported the U.S.-led war on terrorism, U.S. threats of war against Iraq appear to have heightened concerns, recorded in earlier surveys, about an American foreign policy seen as overly aggressive and insufficiently concerned with the interests of friends and allies.[1]

---

[1]Brian Knowlton, "A Global Image on the Way Down." *International Herald Tribune,* December 5, 2002.

Is world public opinion important? Does it matter whether EU citizens develop a low regard for the United States and its citizens? Does our ability to travel as welcome guests weigh heavily in the equations of modern ideas of the good life? Should public opinion, at some important level, drive the foreign policies of states? Should governments be attentive to public opinion abroad in the same way they emphasize it at home?

In the short run, world public opinion can be discounted as an immediate concern for policymakers. Polls often register volatile results, and in the short run analysts and politicians can discount the variation. But in the long run, as trends and data consolidate, public opinion polling can register a reality that impinges on decision makers and political relationships. Were the United States to squander the decades of goodwill it generated as a positive force in the world by engaging in self-centered and muscular unilateralism, were it simply to see the world in terms of its own naked self-interest, then the tide of opinion could swell to a proportion that complicates U.S. foreign policy and leads to increasing isolation in its "fortress." If U.S. troops are unwelcome, if its diplomats are put at risk, if business leaders encounter boycotts of their goods and services, if travelers cannot presume their safety and a friendly welcome, then the world will be a more difficult place in which to live.

The world now presents a series of difficult and complicated choices. The choice between muscular unilateralism and international multilateralism is one such choice. If the United States insists on going it alone and ignores the wishes and policies of international organizations, there will be consequences. If the United States insists on a rule of law but seeks exemptions for its own officials in the new international criminal courts, there will be consequences.

WAR

In early March of 2003 it became very clear that the United States had reached the limit of its patience with the U.N. and Security Council

procedures. On March 17, in a televised address to the nation and the world, President Bush announced the end of diplomacy and the beginning of direct action against the Iraqi regime. After a general review of Iraq's previous violations of a series of U.N. resolutions and agreements, President Bush gave Saddam Hussein and his sons 48 hours to leave Baghdad for exile abroad. Precisely at the end of 48 hours, U.S. and British forces began a military campaign against Iraq, moving from bases in Kuwait into southern Iraq. Shortly after, air strikes began against Iraqi targets. The long-predicted war against Iraq had begun.

Substantial opposition to the war was apparent in the United States and overseas. U.S. efforts to characterize the war as the effort of a broad-based coalition were greeted with skepticism at home and abroad. The war was essentially a U.S. unilateral intervention, with approximately 200,000 U.S. troops joined by less than 30,000 troops from the "coalition" states. Muscular unilateralism prevailed over multilateralism and international consensus. The long-term consequences of the decision will mature over the coming decades.

In the short run, the U.S. war of "Shock and Awe," designed to demoralize the Iraqi opposition and decapitate the Iraqi government, worked well. Within two weeks of the invasion, U.S. and British forces had secured southern Iraq, including the major city of Basra, and were converging on the outskirts of Baghdad, over 200 miles north of the Kuwait staging areas. Within three short weeks the "Battle for Baghdad" had begun. All along the axis of conflict, Iraqi military formations collapsed and offered at the most token resistance. Superior U.S. airpower and land-based maneuvers destroyed Republican Guard divisions in their positions. No classic tank or infantry battle worthy of the name materialized and formal Iraqi military opposition literally melted away.

Such resistance to the U.S. advance as did materialize did so as the action of irregular Iraqi paramilitary troops (for example, the Fedayeen Saddam) engaged in guerrilla ambush tactics. While actions like this did distract and slow the relentless U.S. movement to Baghdad, it did less to hinder U.S. forces than did two to three days of intense sand storms in the Iraqi deserts.

The much-anticipated battle for Baghdad never materialized. The occupation of Baghdad was characterized mostly by the destruction of regime assets and Saddam Hussein iconography (statues, murals, palaces), and an orgy of looting set off by the sudden absence of police and other agents of political authority. The war in the north of Iraq progressed easily as well, as long-established Kurdish militias (Pesh Murgah, for example) came down from the hills and occupied important urban sites, cities such as Erbil, Dohuk, Kirkuk, and Mosul. The invasion of Tikrit, Saddam Hussein's birthplace and hometown, likewise turned out to be a non-event militarily. The expected "last stand" of Hussein loyalists never happened, allowing U.S. troops to move in without material opposition.

The war, by any American military expectation, went extraordinarily well. But this is not to suggest that the war was conducted without damage to Iraqi military personnel, Iraqi infrastructure, and Iraqi citizens. It seems clear that U.S. military ordinance was measurably more precise and deadly than the ordinance used only a decade before in the first Gulf War. The use of precision-guided munitions allowed the U.S. military to more precisely target its objectives. Deep-drilling "bunker buster" bombs were used to target the Iraqi command and control facilities and to attempt the destruction of Saddam Hussein himself and his leadership elite.

No military action, no war, can yet be characterized as "surgical" or "precise." During this war some munitions failed to reach their intended targets, others were improperly targeted (mistakes were made) and "collateral damage" ensued. The phrase *collateral damage* is one of the most objectionable linguistic misrepresentations of modern war. When it

occurs, civilians die but linguistically their deaths are sanitized and dismissed.

One of the most interesting aspects of the war was the incorporation of journalists from varying nationalities and organizations into the front line military units. Called journalistic *embedding,* journalists were trained to join combat units during the exercise of their missions. There were, of course, stringent limitations on what those embedded journalists could report, both as a consequence of security concerns and of the public relations concerns of the administration.

For example, embedded journalists were forbidden to broadcast the location of the troops with which they were operating. And it was considered a matter of policy not to broadcast images or descriptions of U.S. or British casualties or those killed in action. The resulting coverage offered 24/7 imagery of the war in progress, sanitized to a considerable degree and enthusiastic about the soldiers themselves.

And there were real casualties among the journalists so embedded. A few were killed by enemy fire, a smaller number killed by friendly fire or unfortunate health problems, as in the death of NBC reporter David Bloom. Peter Arnett, a veteran journalist stationed in Baghdad and reporting for MSNBC and the National Geographic Channel, was fired for giving to Iraqi national television an interview critical of the war's progress. Other independent journalists found themselves detained and removed from the area by both Iraqi and coalition forces. Journalistic objectivity, always a difficult standard to judge reportage by, apparently suffered at the gain in unprecedented images of the military operations in Operation Iraqi Freedom.

As American media, embedded with troops and otherwise, decided for one reason or another not to publicize or recognize the deaths of civilians in the conflict, the true costs of the conflict do not enter our public space. During the press coverage of this war, U.S.

media decided not to carry graphic images of dead soldiers or civilians. As a result, American media consumers saw a different surgical war than did their counterparts in Europe, Asia, and the Middle East, where media outlets carried explicit (and often horrifying) images of maimed and mangled soldiers and civilians and of the physical damage to buildings and historical sites. What resulted from such a difference in perspective led to a fundamental divergence in public opinion about the war. American public opinion coalesced in favor of the war (roughly 70 percent support), whereas public opinion abroad generally moved in the opposite direction (70 to 80 percent opposed). As might be expected, public opinion in neighboring Arab states achieved even higher levels of opposition.

Casualty figures for the war are imprecise, particularly on the Iraqi side of the equation. The figures that follow are for the most part estimates and should be taken as such. At any rate, by the end of the military campaign, four weeks into the war, U.S. and allied casualties totaled just less than 150. Of this figure, roughly half were the result of accidents or "friendly fire" incidents. In manpower terms, the invasion of Iraq was accomplished with very low levels of military casualties.

The same cannot be said of Iraq. The total number of Iraqi casualties may never be known, and it was not in the interests of either the coalition or the emerging Iraqi administration to emphasize them. Extrapolating from the number of military units that the coalition troops destroyed, one can easily project Iraqi military casualties to the tens of thousands and civilian noncombatant casualties in the thousands, from 3,000 to 4,000. There were no reliable estimates of civilian deaths due to environmental effects or infrastructure damage, such as water and electrical grids. And there are no reliable estimates of the extent of physical damage to Iraqi infrastructure such as roads, airports, buildings, hospitals, schools, and museums. Second-hand reports and anecdotes

suggest substantial physical damage requiring extensive reconstruction efforts. The overall costs are likely to be in the tens of billions of dollars. The coalition victors were quick to proclaim that Iraqi oil fields in the north and south were liberated without significant damage, leading to the conclusion that Iraq could afford to pay at least for part of the damage inflicted during the conflict.

There were other bothersome ambiguities in the early successes of the coalition. Saddam Hussein himself was still unaccounted for, his whereabouts unknown. Without a captured or killed Saddam, the war lacked a symbolic final moment. The destruction of numerous statues, murals, and representations of Saddam Hussein substituted for proof of his death. And a final symbolic moment of sorts was reached as American generals took over Saddam's largest Baghdad palace and smoked celebratory cigars in the dictator's own home.

Advocates of the war expected a joyous Iraqi welcome for the liberating troops. In fact, U.S. and British soldiers were met with a range of reactions and welcomes, including cheers, jeers, rocks, and rifle fire.

It is important to note one critical and unanticipated consequence of the war. Apparently, the invading forces underestimated the social disorder that would accompany the destruction of the Baathist regime. As a consequence, incalculable damage was done to Iraqi and world history as priceless artifacts in the Iraqi National Museum and other historical sites were broken or stolen. Artifacts as old as 7,000 years appeared for sale on the international art markets shortly after the looting. The losses are incalculable. Much of the evidence of the earliest days of human civilization is simply gone.

Coalition leaders denied responsibility for the looting and for failing to protect the artifacts, pleading military and security priorities. But critics outside those official circles were vociferous, leading to severe criticisms of the United States. For example, British journalist Robert Fisk filed this report from Baghdad in *The Independent:*

> U.S. troops have sat back and allowed mobs to wreck and then burn the Ministry of Planning, the Ministry of Education, the Ministry of Foreign Affairs, the Ministry of Culture and the Ministry of Information. They did nothing to prevent looters from destroying priceless treasures of Iraq's history in the Baghdad Archaeological Museum and in the museum in the northern city of Mosul, or from looting three hospitals.[2]

Fisk goes on to report with considerable indignation that U.S. troops did manage to protect two Iraqi ministries: Interior and Oil, both of which were apparently more important, in his estimation, than the others.

The looting and public disorder that followed the close of military hostilities did raise a significant issue, that of the transition from military intervention to occupation and administration. Having destroyed the regime of Saddam Hussein, the United States and its allies were now faced with the necessity of providing an alternative.

Within a week of the end of military operations, a U.S. management team, led by retired Lt. General Jay Garner, entered Iraq and began planning for an interim administration. Such an administration would, presumably, put basic services back on line while the Iraqi public and its leaders prepared for independence and a democratic form of government. A parallel administration, composed of senior coalition bureaucrats, would monitor and mentor a cadre of Iraqi managers, until Iraq was ready to resume independent governance.

The managers and designers of the new Iraqi government had to deal with numerous problems beyond the military damage to the country's infrastructure. Primary among the problems was the balance of power between the country's major ethnic and religious groups, primarily the majority Shia, the Arab Sunnis, and the Kurds. A number of Shia religious leaders presumed that the government would automatically reflect the majority status of the Shia community, and one Ayatollah announced his unelected mayorship of an eastern Iraqi city. In the north of Iraq, Kurds coming from the mountains clashed with the Sunni Arab administrators of important northern cities, and U.S. troops were pushed into uncomfortable mediation between the two groups. And at one point, U.S. soldiers opened fire on Iraqi demonstrators armed with stones and epithets. Upwards of a dozen Iraqi civilians were killed and scores wounded.

The pure fact of the situation is that the military destruction of Iraq was easy compared to the project of restoring public order and creating effective and legitimate government. There are no manuals and readily applicable paradigms for the transition from a brutal personal dictatorship (Saddam Hussein's government) to a Western-modeled electoral democracy. Such a project will likely be measured in years and months, not weeks and days.

One cannot deny the overwhelming military victory of the United States and its allies in Iraq. But the world was watching carefully how the United States implemented the postwar regime. In taking on the physical and political reconstruction of Iraq, the United States had the opportunity to show the world that its intervention was truly predicated on the greatest good to the Iraqi nation and to the international community, and not simply a self-interested grab for power, petroleum, and influence in a crucial region of the world. A quick transition to effective Iraqi government, accompanied by

[2]Robert Fisk, "Americans Defend Two Untouchable Ministries from the Hordes of Looters." *The Independent,* April 14, 2002.

a quick departure of U.S. troops, would reassure many critics of the United States around the world.

Similarly, an extended occupation, with the certainty of Iraqi resistance, accompanied by the self-serving exploitation of Iraq's petroleum resources by U.S. and British corporations, would bring the United States under increased suspicion and ultimately generate more political hostility. Great global stakes hinged on the ultimate perception of the war and its objectives. Particularly troublesome were those critics who saw in the war an assault on Islam.

Perceptions

The war and its aftermath are perceived differently in various parts of the world. In the United States, as the war ended, roughly 70 percent of the public supported the war. In coalition ally Great Britain, slightly less than 50 percent of the public supported the action. In Spain, another coalition state, nearly 90 percent of the public opposed the war. Why were there such different perceptions of the event?

One reason is the ubiquitous presence of the mass media, present as both embedded media and more politically independent media from both U.S. and non-U.S. sources. The ways in which these different media framed images and issues in the war go a long way to explaining U.S. public support for the effort and wide-ranging opposition outside of the United States.

Take, for example, the following widely circulated description of an incident. During the drive to Baghdad, U.S. forces encountered quasi-guerrilla attacks and suicide bombers. Both of these left U.S. troops edgy and fearful. In this context, an Iraqi van approached a U.S. checkpoint and failed to heed orders to stop. U.S. troops opened fire on the vehicle. After the shooting stopped, it was determined that the occupants of the van were Iraqi women and children fleeing the conflict.

U.S. and foreign media framed the event differently. American media, while acknowledging the loss of innocent life, chose to focus on the tearful reactions of the U.S. soldier who had opened fire on the vehicle. The soldier's reaction showed the personal agony that accompanied his decision. Moral soldier; amoral warfare. Many foreign media chose to focus on a surviving woman in the van, cradling her dead children in her arms and weeping inconsolably. In this case, an innocent parent was victimized by amoral warfare.

The two images, derived from the same event, prompted different reactions. Americans could take pride in their soldier, a man clearly bothered by the consequences of his caution and action. Others could feel indignation over the deaths of Iraqi children, an act accomplishing nothing for the conduct of the war or the suppression of Saddam Hussein. "Collateral damage," indeed.

Other observers differed over the advisability of appointing General Jay Garner, retired, as the U.S. administrator for postwar Iraq. Americans saw in General Garner a seasoned military official and administrator clearly capable of dealing with the postwar damage to Iraq and its infrastructure. They also saw in him an individual able to deal with the postwar militias and warlords likely to emerge in the ashes of the Baath regime, seasoned by his experience in the Kurdish north.

Observers in the Middle East and in Western Europe had different reactions to General Garner's appointment. They saw in this appointment the empowerment of an American general close to Prime Minister Ariel Sharon, a man publicly sympathetic to Israel and unsympathetic to the Palestinians. General Garner was well known for advocating a "get tough" policy for the West Bank and Gaza, an indicator of a repressive administration in Iraq.

General Garner was replaced within a month of his assignment by L. Paul Bremer, a highly regarded U.S. diplomat. This change reduced the most virulent criticisms of the post-war administration in Iraq.

Although public opinion moderated in a pro-American direction after the termination of the military phase of the conflict, overall majority public opinion abroad was generally critical of the United States and its deeper motives for the war. Certainly, the differing framing of the conflict complicated differences in perception of the war by a globally empowered media and its consumers.

Governmental opinion in the region also coalesced against a long-term role for the United States in Iraq. Shortly after the fourth week of the war, eight neighbors of Iraq met in Saudi Arabia to consult on a postwar Iraq. Representatives of Turkey, Iran, Jordan, Kuwait, Saudi Arabia, and Syria were joined by Egypt and Bahrain. The parties all agreed that an immediate withdrawal of U.S. troops and the involvement of the U.N. in the management and reconstruction of postwar Iraq would best serve the interests of the region. Needless to say, U.S. officials did not concur. Nor did they concur with the conference sentiment that U.S. political pressure on Syria, prominent as the war wound down, should be moderated.

Clearly, differences of opinion, globally distributed, accompanied the U.S. war against Iraq.

A New Decade

As the first decade of the twenty-first century staggered to a close, new actors and new realities emerged to affect the politics and conflicts of the Middle East. A transition toward major changes occurred in the United States in the fall of 2008 as national elections brought a new president to power: Barack Hussein Obama. Obama's election signaled major changes in the way in which the United States approached the international system. During the campaign, Obama had roundly criticized the Bush Administration's conduct of foreign policy, claiming that the muscular unilateralism of the

administration had alienated allies and placed the United States in a deteriorating international situation. Obama signaled intentions to replace unilterialism with multilateralism and engagement through international institutions such as the United Nations and NATO. Optimism was rampant that the election of Barack Obama would bring a new age of cooperative international relations to the fore, with predictable benefits for all parties in the conflicts of and in the Middle East.

It is clear that Obama inherited a difficult set of domestic and international problems. In one of its public relations announcements in 2010, the Chicago Council on Global Affairs, a prominent and well-regarded public affairs organization, characterized the Obama problem set in this way:

> At present, the Obama administration finds itself saddled with a tangle of foreign policy challenges, complex in character and long in the making: unfinished and unpopular wars in Iraq and Afghanistan, stalled peace talks in the Middle East, hostile states acquiring nuclear capabilities, an ongoing global economic recession, looming climate and environmental dangers, and growing "multipolar" worries brought on by an ascendant Asia.[3]

Considerable optimism in the Middle East attended President Obama's election. National polls across the region, notably excepting Israel, found high regard and expectations for this young president, based both on his public pronouncements and his personal history, particularly the facts of his parentage and his early life in Indonesia. Obama was quick to exploit this public predisposition, giving his first major

---

[3]From the June 29, 2010, webpage of the Chicago Council on Global Affairs.

international address (June 2009) to an audience at the University of Cairo. This presentation, which held an olive branch out to the Muslim world and promised greater respect for Islam in the conduct of U.S. foreign policy, resulted in very high levels of public approval in the Muslim world for President Obama, and less so for the United States generally. Nonetheless, Obama began his presidency riding a wave of international popularity.

It is significant that we are able to analyze the early years of the Obama Administration in terms of four critical and important elections: the 2008 presidential election in the United States; the February 2009 parliamentary elections in Israel; the June 2009 presidential elections in Iran; and the parliamentary elections in Iraq in March 2010. It is significant in that all three Middle Eastern states had conducted fair elections previously, in a region notorious for corrupt elections and regimes. And it is also significant that each of these elections produced important political results.

The immediate consequences of the U.S. elections were apparent early on. The new administration signaled its intentions early to approach international problems in a multilateral context, seeking cooperative policy initiatives with a wide range of states. The bellicose rhetoric of the previous administration was replaced with less bellicose formulations, dropping the "war on terror" and "with us or against us" formulas. And the personnel of international diplomacy was populated with persons of more cooperative approaches to international problems—for example, former Senator Hillary Clinton as Secretary of State and former Senator George Mitchell as special envoy to the Middle East, Israel and Palestine. The immediate impact of these changes were seen in the various multilateral approaches to such topics as the war in Afghanistan, the sanctions regime against Iran's nuclear program, and the response to Israel's punishing blockade of Gaza, policies in which wide ranges of international actors were engaged. Support for U.S.

international policy was evident from Russia, China, India, Brazil, Turkey, and the European Union. Coupled with the new president's previously mentioned Cairo speech, public expectations for progress were heightened.

ELECTIONS IN ISRAEL

The first discordant note for the new administration occurred in Israel where parliamentary elections brought an ultra-conservative government into power, with the conservative Likud block at its center. Headed by veteran prime minister Binyamin Netanyahu, the new government incorporated many of the most radical right-wing parties in Israeli politics. The result of this new political coalition dramatically increased the influence and importance of the most conservative religious parties (Shas, Ahi, Agudat Israel, and Degel HaTorah, for example).

The new government quickly took a more aggressive posture toward Hamas and the Gaza strip, putting in place a very restrictive boycott that quickly threatened economic and social viability in the area. International opinion was quite critical and the Obama administration was placed in a position of simultaenously calling for changes in Israeli policy while uncritically supporting the Israeli government. An important denouement occurred during Vice President Biden's (March 2010) visit to Israel, when the expansion of West Bank settlements were announced during his visit, a visible and dramatic slight to the U.S. government. Tensions continued to be strained between Israel and the Obama Administration. In the spring of 2010, Israeli IDF forces intercepted a flotilla of ships bringing relief items to Gaza. In the boarding of the vessels, at least nine peace activists were killed, the majority of them of Turkish nationality. International condemnation of the action was widespread, and a month later the Israeli government announced a reduction in the severity of the embargo, allowing foods and medicine into Gaza. The whole series of events damaged Israeli prestige abroad and risked the U.S./Israeli special relationship. Significantly, one of Prime Minister Netanyahu's subseqent vists to the United States occurred without a White House reception or visit, an unheard of situation in earlier administrations; and a second visit was cancelled without comment.

In a more practical perspective, the changes in Israeli policy are largely of intensity. Israel continues to confront and limit Hamas; to expand existing settlements in the West Bank; and to create the "facts on the ground" that will lead to a de facto annexation of most of the West Bank. Israeli foreign policy has recently damaged its alliance relationships with Turkey, Egypt, and Jordan. And it continues to threaten Syria and Iran with direct military action. The only likely credible opposition to these policies is in the domestic opposition in Israel proper.

Elections in Iran

In June of 2009, Iran held its most recent presidential elections. Iran has previously conducted a series of national elections that most international observers found fair and reasonable. In many analysts, perspectives, Iran was one of the most democratic polities in the Middle East, regularly changing leadership in national elections. The election of 2009 broke that mold. In an election that pitted incumbent president Mahmoud Ahmadinejad against several credible and more moderate candidates, including former president Mohammad Khatami and former prime minister Mir Hussein Mousavi. Eventually, Khatami withdrew, leaving the moderate position to Mousavi.

The election of 2009 turned out to be an electoral disaster, with Ahmadinejad "winning" an election that had clearly been rigged and manipulated by the incumbent government. Protests over the election were widespread and quickly turned violent as the supporters of Mousavi and reform poured into the streets of Tehran and other major Iranian cities, coordinated by the diffuse technologies of cell-

phones and Twitter. The government responded with intimidation, arrests, and outright violence, plunging the nation into weeks of protests and recriminations. The Iranian regime clearly lost some of its legitimacy in the aftermath of the election. Although President Ahmadinezad was able to retain his position, it was apparently with some costs to his standing and credibility. Of great importance was the defection of many senior clerics from the government coalition, evidence of conflicts within the ruling religious coalitions in Iran. The long-term impact of this failed election is unknown, but likely to be persistant. The irony here is that many observers feel that Ahmadinezad would have achieved relection without the government intervention in the election, although with a reduced majority. The price for this "victory" may be very high in the long run.

In the short run, Iran's government has continued to pursue some level of nuclear capability. In so doing, it defies the authority of the U.N. generally, and the International Agency for Atomic Energy (IAEA). And it defies the policy objectives in the International Non-Proliferation Treaty that seeks to deny states the technology to build nuclear weapons. Iranian objectives in this regard are not clear cut. It operates a large number of facilities producing low-grade enhanced uranium (20 percent enrichment) but claims these uraniam stocks are for energy fuels and medical research. And in truth, weaponizable uranium needs enrichment levels above 80 percent, and ideally above 93 percent, the threshold for technologically advanced nuclear weapons. There is no publicly credible evidence that Iran is attempting this level of enrichment. The United States and Israel both believe that Iran is on the brink of building nuclear weapons, but most other important international actors think that threshold is several years away at best.

The United States has been able to recruit many leading international actors into the effort to penalize Iran for its nuclear policies: punitive procedures against Iranian banks and trade in weaponizable products have been put in place through the United Nations. Significantly, Russia and China have both joined in this effort. Iran remains defiant, but at an increasing economic cost. Politically, it enjoys a fairly high prestige in the region, particularly in Shia majority states, with the major exceptions being the states of the Arabian Gulf and Israel. For its part, Israel continues to repeatedly threaten Iran with military action, an action that would require at least tacit cooperation from any of Turkey, Iraq, or Saudi Arabia. At this point, Turkey and Iraq have proven to be uncooperative and unwilling to open their airspace to such a project. The Saudi position is less clear. The United States continues to leave military action "on the table," but clearly prefers nonmilitary sanctions, at least in the short run.

One aspect of the Iranian situation remains quite clear. It is more than likely that a large-scale military attack on Iran and its nuclear facilities would result in an immediate suspension of Iranian oil exports, with predictable impacts on supply and price. Economists can debate the specific ranges of these effects, but it is hard to imagine the events not disrupting global commerce. It is also probable that Iran would seek to mobilize its regional allies in retaliation, bringing Hamas and Hizbollah into play again. Any of these regional ploys would be disruptive to the peace in the region, with consequences for all concerned.

Elections in Iraq

The fourth in this series of critical elections occurred in Iraq in March 2010. In an election that most international observers found fair and relatively nonviolent, the electors returned results that produced a difficult draw between the Sunni-dominated secular list led by Ayad Allawi, an occupation prime minister, and two Shia dominated lists, one led by current prime minister Nuri Al-Maliki and the the other by Moktada Al-Sadr, scion of an important

Shia clerical family. Only two or three seats separated the major contenders after the results were certified, although the manipulation of election rules disqualified a small number of Sunni candidates postelection. In these few cases, candidates were accused of having Ba'athist sympathies or membership and thus ineligible for elective office in the new Iraqi government. This maneuver effectively disenfranchised the Sunni opposition, and the dominant Shia party attempted to form a government. Months after the election, the attempts had yet to yield a new government, and the former government of prime minister Maliki continued in a caretaker capacity. In December 2010, the president asked Maliki to form a new government. Predictably, instances of communal violence began to rise, principally between Sunni and Shia groups, often targeting Shia groups in religious pilgrimage. The level of political violence rose but not nearly to the levels prior to the surge in 2007.

The uncertainty over the formation of an Iraqi government clearly irritated U.S. interests, and a variety of U.S. policymakers and influentials visited Iraq to put pressure on the government for a solution to the stalemate. The lack of a formal government could make the scheduled U.S. withdrawal from Iraq problematic over 2010–2011, a withdrawal devoutly hoped for by the administration.

REGIONAL POLITICS

For the most part, the formal international policy postures of the Middle Eastern states remained fairly stable over the decade. There were a couple of exceptions to this observation, and we shall begin there.

Turkey

Turkish foreign policy has made a couple of relatively sharp turns in the past decade. In the first instance, as Turkey unsuccessfully petitioned for membership in the European

Union, it turned its attention elsewhere, cultivating stronger relationships with states in the Middle East and the developing world generally. This was in keeping with the maturation of both the Turkish economy and the Turkish political system, the latter of which managed to accommodate a modest Islamist influence in its electoral and administrative institutions. The most prominent of these realignments involved an evolving relationship with Israel and India.

Turkey's "opening" toward Israel was severely compromised with the 2010 Israeli commando assault on the Turkish relief flotilla in the Mediterranean, an action killing nine Turkish nationals, an event for which Turkey demanded an apology, which the Netanyahu administration coldly refused. The result has been a further orientation of Turkey toward the Arab states of the Middle East, and further Turkish initiatives with partners as varied as China and Brazil. Many analysts see in these events the emergence of Turkey as a serious player in the international system, with higher levels of prestige and influence than before.

Saudi Arabia

Saudi Arabian foreign policy has remained for the most part stable. Two glaring exceptions are the Saudi attitude toward Iran, which has become more confrontational, and toward Israel, where Saudi efforts to relaunch an earlier-sponsored peace initiative have been largely ignored by the Netanyahu government. Consistent with past Saudi practice, much of the related diplomacy has been informal and behind the scenes. There are apparent instances of close consultation and cooperation between the United States and Saudi Arabia; and Saudi Arabia, alone among the Gulf Cooperation Council (GCC) states, has not publicly announced its denial of air rights to a possible U.S.-Israeli raid on Iran. It also seems the case that Saudi Arabia is more willing to credit the Iranian nuclear program as credible and near term, a possibility it strongly desires to avoid. In other areas of foreign policy, the Saudi

government continues its slow efforts at liberalization, for example, allowing and granting multiple entry visas to businessmen and tourists visiting the kingdom.

GCC

The remaining states of GCC—Kuwait, Bahrain, Qatar, the UAE, and Oman—remain wary and suspicious of Iran generally. They are also committed to the use of traditional tools of diplomacy to contain Iran and keep it from meddling in their internal affairs. Taken collectively, the GCC has the military capability to defend itself against any possible Iranian conventional military aggression. Indeed, a recent analysis by the highly respected scholar of Middle East military capabilities, Prof. Anthony Cordesman, of the Center for Strategic and International Studies, characterized the Iranian military equipment mix as dating from the 1970s and largely obsolete, offsetting Iran's clear advantage in manpower.[4] The GCC states continue to worry about Iran's ability to launch asymmetrical attacks against Gulf infrastructure, particularly those assets critical to the production and distribution of petroleum and natural gas. Collectively, the GCC states provide a number of platforms for the projection of U.S. military power in the region, particularly in Qatar and Oman. The international economic crisis has had predictable impact on the Gulf states, particularly on the UAE in Dubai, where an ambitious program of development has been slowed. All in all, however, the states of the GCC have contributed to the continued expansion and institutionalization of the GCC itself, a project that has "paid off" in terms of security cooperation.

Egypt

Egypt continues to be an important player in the international politics of the Middle East. Egypt's history, population, geography, and continuing

---

[4]Anthony Cordesman. "The Conventional Military Balance in the Gulf," SUSRIS Roundtable, July 2010.

role in the politics of the Arab League assure its prominence. It is also one of the Arab states in regular contact with Israel, managing the Egyptian side of the border with Gaza and often called up as an intermediary in the conflicts between Hamas, Fatah, and Israel. Relations with Israel can be termed correct and "cold." Relations with the United States, by contrast, are often characterized as "warm" and beneficial, particularly as the United States continues an annual subsidy designed to keep Egypt aligned with U.S. interests in the region. As Egyptian president Hosni Mubarak approaches the inevitable end of his rule, a leadership transition appears inevitable in the next couple of years. New leadership may bring new policy initiatives to Egypt and the region generally.

Syria

Syria has been traditionally seen by American policymakers as one of the "bad apples" in the Middle East barrel. President George W. Bush famously included Syria in his "axis of evil" with Iran and North Korea. In truth, Syria has traditionally championed causes seen as unfriendly to the United States and its allies, taking the lead in the support of Palestinian resistance organizations, opposition to what it perceived as imperialist foreign policy emanating from the United States and its European allies, allying itself with the former Soviet Union, and participating in two formal wars against Israel. In addition to the facts of these policy initiatives, Syria has also borne the brunt of efforts in the West to demonize Syria and isolate it politically. These efforts were to some degree successful over the postwar years.

In recent history, under the leadership of Bashaar Assad, Syria has taken steps to open and improve its relations with the United States and its allies. Ongoing backroom talks between Syria and Israel have continued for several years, accompanied by a mild thaw in U.S.-Syrian relations: A U.S. ambassador returned to Syria, and the public demonization of Syria was toned down in U.S. diplomatic rhetoric. Much of the

"thaw" is apparent in the somewhat trivial areas of policy.

For example, in 2009, Sr. NBC correspondent Andrea Mitchell accompanied Secretary of State Hillary Clinton on a diplomatic mission to the region. One leg of the flight was from the Persian Gulf to Beirut, a trip ordinarily made burdensome by the necessity of avoiding Syrian airspace, a trip that necessitated a much longer flight to the Eastern Mediterranean and an approach to Beirut from the west. Midway through the flight, Ms. Mitchell reported breathlessly that the plane was flying in Syrian airspace, an unanticipated privilege making for a shorter and more pleasant trip. It was diplomatically significant that an official U.S. aircraft carrying a high-ranking U.S. officer was allowed to transit Syrian airspace, suggesting that some of the petty restrictions and suspicions between the two states had relaxed. A small incident, surely, but it was evidence of increasing tolerance and cooperation between two old adversaries.

It should also be noted that in addition to diplomatic initiatives, there are numerous examples of U.S. businesses establishing offices in Syria. As Syria moves to modernize its antique economy, it is likely that a significant Western economic presence will be established.

Finally, we should note the circumstances regarding an Israeli air raid on Syria in 2007. On September 6 of that year, Israeli warplanes bombed a facility in Dayz Al-Zawar, a remote location near the Syrian border with Turkey. The facility bombed may have contained nuclear materials originating in North Korea, but the details and provenance of that account are not clear. What is surprising about the aftermath of the raid is the lack of a strong public outcry against the attack. Reactions were muted and the usual round of condemnations absent from diplomatic discourse and public media alike. Neither side in the event seemed interested in exploiting the matter. And in point of fact, Israel and Syria embarked on a series of "conversations" regarding the Golan and Palestine in the aftermath of the raid. All of these seemingly unrelated facts produce an impression of Syrian rehabilitation in diplomatic circles and a slow improvement in American-Syrian and Israeli-Syrian relations.

Jordan

The kingdom of Jordan, as noted in preceding chapters, is geographically and politically vulnerable to the vicissitudes of contemporary Middle Eastern politics. Lacking a strong economic base and possessed of a diverse population, located adjacent to the political hotbed of Israel and Palestine, Jordan has historically found it necessary to play the balance in regional politics. King Abdullah has managed to keep Jordan on this course of accommodation, playing both sides in the controversies over Israel and Palestine and being careful to maintain good relations with both regional and global centers of power—particularly the United States, the EU, Egypt, and Saudi Arabia. This theme of "good neighbors" is unlikely to change in the near term. One point of controversy has emerged over Jordanian plans to enrich uranium for nuclear power generation. This plan has not resulted in the storm of protest that has accompanied Iran's efforts in this arena, something of a testament to Jordan's good standing in the region. But it is a program that clearly makes Israel nervous, and anything that makes Israel nervous becomes a concern of the United States.

Iraq

As a closing note to this brief survey of international relations in the region, some mention should be made of Iraq and its foreign policy. First, it should be forthrightly recognized that Iraq is in no way at this time a sovereign power. As a result, its foreign policy is largely mediated by its occupier, the United States. In spite of this, a couple of observations can be made.

First and most important, we need to recognize the warm informal relationships between Iraq's leadership and the government of Iran. Officials of both governments frequently consult the other and just as frequently visit each other's countries. Much of this interchange is conditioned by or involved with the close connection

between the Shia institutions of the two countries, including important pilgrimages in both countries. But we should also realize that many common concerns are shared by Iraq and Iran, including such important issues as petroleum production and distribution; periodic Kurdish irruptions; the common hostility of radical terrorist organizations; and expatriate populations on both sides of the border. It is likely that the progressive withdrawal of U.S. forces from Iraq will allow Iraq a stronger hand in developing relationships with its Middle East neighbors.

A Clash of Civilizations?

There are political theorists who have predicted a clash of civilizations as the likely successor to the Cold War between Russia and the West. Samuel Huntington describes the relationship between the West and the Islamic world in these terms:

> The underlying problem for the West is not Islamic fundamentalism. It is Islam; a different civilization whose people are convinced of the superiority of their culture. . . . The problem for Islam is not the CIA or the U.S. Department of Defense. It is the West, a different civilization whose people are convinced of the universality of their culture.[5]

Although Huntington does not insist on the inevitability of civilizational war, he does insist on the probability of the same. In this, religious and political leaders in both the Western and Islamic worlds, who apparently wish to hasten the conflict to a higher, more-violent level, join him.

Prominent religious spokesmen in the United States have spoken out against Islam, in what has appeared to be a coordinated attack on the religion, widely reported in both the

---

[5]Samuel Huntington, *The Clash of Civilizations: The Remaking of World Order* (New York: Simon & Schuster, 1996), pp. 217–218.

Western and non-Western press. Reverend Jerry Falwell, for instance, pronounced the Prophet Muhammad a "terrorist." Reverend Franklin Graham denounced Islam as an "evil" and "wicked" religion. Reverend Jimmy Swaggart called for the expulsion of all Muslim foreign students from the United States, and a similar fate for those Muslim citizens who protested it. The Reverend Pat Robertson publicly criticized President Bush for his kind words on Islam on the occasion of Eid Al-Fitr, the conclusion of the Islamic holiday of Ramadan, suggesting that he leave theology to the theologians.

These tirades against Islam are registered and remembered in the Islamic world. And they are echoed by the Islamic equivalent of this demagogic quartet, mullahs and imams who use their privileged place in the madrasahs and mosques of the Islamic world to rail against the "heresy," materialism, hedonism, and excessive individualism of Christianity and the West in general. Collectively, they would increase the divide between East and West, between Christianity and Islam, to serve their own personal and religious needs.

These religious extremists appear to be in the minority in their respective countries. But the public appeal of apocalyptic imagery is strong: simple-minded charges of evil and wickedness are credible to a zealous religious community. In their zeal to bring about the "end times" of the apocalyptic prophesy, both Christian and Islamic extremists add fuel to the fire of international conflict.

Nothing in the individual theologies of Judaism, Christianity, and Islam necessitates such militant conflict between the faiths. They are, in fact, all Abrahamic religions, recognizing a common point of origin for all three faiths. And the faiths are all insistently monotheistic, a belief sanctioned by a series of prophets recognized by all three faiths. But history is nonetheless replete with horrifying examples of religious wars and conflicts: the Crusades, the Thirty-Years War, the persecution of the Huguenots, the Holocaust; the list can go on

and on. So, although there is no theological requirement of religious strife, there is every evidence of the probability of it.

CONCLUSION

The conflation of religion and politics adds measurably to the volatility of international politics. When one stirs into the mix extreme religious views, the sort associated with Islamic jihadists, Christian Zionists intent on hastening the apocalypse, Christian Identity organizations that racialize religion, and modern Jewish zealots intent on building a new temple on the site of the Haram Al-Sharif or recreating the "Promised Land" between the Euphrates and the Nile, then the brew becomes particularly unstable and amenable to the tactics of terrorism.

In their recent study of international terror, Daniel Benjamin and Steven Simon make the following observation:

> Time, as we have seen, is compressed for those in the thrall of apocalyptic ideas. Ancient dramas replay themselves in modern circumstances, and when the believer acts forcefully enough, a reversal in history occurs, wrongs are righted, and injustices avenged.[6]

If this view of sacred terror is accurate, the best corrective is a global system that takes the suffering of people seriously and attempts to ameliorate it. A "Fortress America" mentality or a "Europe First" mentality will only aggravate a growing trend augmented by demographic change. It is time for a major, coordinated assault on the causes of misery and pain in the world. Who is better prepared and positioned for such an effort than the only remaining superpower, the United States of America, aided by its allies?

---

[6]Daniel Benjamin and Steven Simon, *The Age of Sacred Terror* (New York: Random House, 2002), p. 445.

GLOSSARY

Abbasids   An important Hashemite Arab family descended from Abbas, which founded the Abbasid caliphate at Baghdad in 750 C.E. This dynasty saw the highest development of the caliphate during what is recognized as the golden age of Islam.

Afghani (al-Afghani)   Jemal al-Din al-Afghani. A nineteenth-century Egyptian schoolteacher who became one of the first modern nationalist writers and spokesmen. He traveled widely and was important in inspiring Middle Eastern opposition to European colonialism.

Alawites   A nonorthodox sect of Islam, found primarily in Lebanon and Syria. The Alawites dominate the Syrian government under President Assad, causing considerable internal resentment and tension among the Sunni majority.

AMAL (or Amal)   Acronym for a Lebanese faction favoring pragmatic, secular political strategies. They are often in conflict with Hizbollah for the loyalities of the Lebanese Shia.

Ashkenazim   The term generally used to describe Jews of European origin, specifically from north-central Europe.

As shura   A consultative assembly appointed by the king or emir.

Baath   The Arab Socialist Resurrection Party, a political party dedicated to Arab nationalism and socialism. Founded in Lebanon in the 1940s, the Baath Party controls Syria and controlled Iraq until the ouster of the Saddam Hussein government.

Bedouin   Refers generally to Arabic-speaking, camel-herding nomads in the Middle East and especially in the Arabian Peninsula.

Bida   Un-Islamic innovations or deviations from tradition.

Caliph   The title given to the successors of Muhammad as leaders of the Umma.

Diwan   Originally, a record listing those fighting for the Umma, used to determine shares of conquered valuable goods; later it became the rudimentary bureaucracy of the early Muslim state.

Djimmi   A religious community given special recognition in Islam, particularly Jews and Christians, the "People of the Book." Such communities enjoyed immunity from forced conversion but had to pay higher taxes than the Muslims. Also included, eventually, were Zoroastrians and Hindus.

Druze   Mystical, nonorthodox Muslim sect, located in Lebanon and Syria.

Fellahin (singular, fellah)   Peasants or occasionally manual laborers in an urban workforce.

Fiqh   Islamic jurisprudence; literally, an "understanding" of Sharia law. Different schools of fiqh were founded during the first centuries of Islam, most prominently the Shafi, Hanafi, Hanbali, and Maliki.

Ghazi   Defender of the faith, usually as a soldier.

Hadith   The collected reports about the life of the Prophet, which, along with the Koran, constitute the major authoritative sources of Islamic thought.

Hajj (Hajji)   The pilgrimage to Mecca, one of the five pillars of Islam and the once-in-a-lifetime obligation of the faithful, given adequate health and finances to undertake the journey. A successful pilgrim becomes known as "hajji" and enjoys significant prestige.

Hashemite   The family of the Quraish tribe to which Muhammad belonged and which subsequently became influential in Muslim affairs. Traditionally powerful in the Hijaz region of the Arabian Peninsula, Hashemites were established in power in Iraq and Transjordan after World War I.

Hijaz   A mountainous region of the Arabian Peninsula adjacent to the Red Sea coast, including the cities of Mecca and Medina; the region in which Islam originated.

Hijira   The migration of those faithful to Muhammad's preaching, from Mecca to Medina (then called Yathrib), in 622 C.E. At Medina the full fruition of the political and social aspects of Muhammad's revelation occurred.

Hizbollah   An Iranian-supported radical Shia group in Lebanon, often associated with terrorist activities; rival of the more moderate AMAL.

Imam   A religious teacher. Most often, the term refers to a leader of services in the mosque. In Shiism the term also refers to the leader of the Shia community.

Intifadah The uprising of Palestinians against Israeli occupation and rule in the Gaza Strip and the West Bank. The first rebellion began in December 1987.

Ismailis The followers of Ismail, the seventh imam of the Shia tradition. The sect is marked by a more esoteric and mystical emphasis than other branches of Shiism and includes the Qarmatians.

Jahiliyya The "time of wickedness" before Muhammad; also used by some fundamentalists to refer to the contemporary loss of Islamic moral guidance.

Janissaries The slave-soldiers who eventually became the core of the Ottoman bureaucracy. Highly trained in special schools, in the early years they were denied the right to have children, eliminating hereditary claims to administrative office.

Jihad "Striving" on behalf of Islam. Sometimes called the "Holy War," jihad refers to the obligation of the faithful to extend the Umma and protect it from its enemies, either by actual warfare or by spiritual struggle.

Kaaba A shrine dedicated to Allah, of great historical importance in Arabian history. Although of pre-Muslim origin, it was incorporated by Muhammad into the Islamic faith and associated with the prophet Abraham. Located in the Grand Mosque of Mecca, the Kaaba is the ultimate destination of the pilgrim (hajji). Maintenance of the Kaaba is important to the wider Islamic community and to the government of Saudi Arabia in particular.

Katib The scribes, or record keepers, employed by the traditional governments, especially under the caliphate.

Kharijite An early puritanical movement in Islam; initially allied with Ali, this radically democratic group eventually turned against him and assassinated him in 661 C.E.

Koran The written word of Allah as revealed through his Prophet, Muhammad.

Madrasah Schools of religion, sometimes independently supported by waqf endowments; often associated with a prominent urban mosque. I did not see this bolded in a chapter.

Mahdi The messiah or redeemer in Islam, expected to come to earth in the final days to lead the faithful in their war against the infidel.

Mameluks The slave dynasty of Circassians who ruled Egypt from 1250 to 1798. From 1517 until their destruction, they alone ruled Egypt, giving only nominal allegiance to the Ottoman sultan.

Maronites A Monophysite Christian sect located primarily in Lebanon and Syria.

Millets The religious groups given official status in the Ottoman Empire. In matters of civil conflict among members of the same millet, the conflict would be resolved by the traditional authorities and processes of the respective millet. A Christian was governed by Christian laws in his dealings with Christians, regardless of his physical location in the Ottoman Empire.

Miri sirf State ownership of land with specified rights to the tenant farmer.

Modernism (Islamic modernism) An interpretation of Islam that stresses its abstract spiritual values, rationality, and commitment to social justice rather than the accumulated details of Sharia law, and that argues that these basic Islamic ideas are compatible with modern social life. Modernist interpretations of Islam have been set forth by various Islamic scholars in the nineteenth and twentieth centuries.

Mosque An Islamic house of worship.

Muhammad Ali (Mehemet Ali) Ruler of Egypt from 1805 to 1849. He initiated major reforms in Egypt, many of which were blunted by a combination of European and Ottoman strategies. The economic and military power of Egypt was greatly increased by Muhammad Ali, who was also the first of the great modernizers in the Arab world.

Muharram A month of the lunar year, dedicated in the Islamic community to commemorating Hussein's martyrdom. The commemoration is an emotional event for the Shia faithful.

Mujtahid Religious leader, preacher, and scholar, the equivalent of the Sunni ulema.

Mulk Private ownership of land.

Mutawwa Semiofficial "religious police" in Saudi Arabia.

Muwahhidun "Unitarians"; the preferred designation for the fundamentalist sect that prevails in Saudi Arabia, founded in the eighteenth century by Abd al-Wahhab and popularly referred to as "Wahhabi."

Najd The extremely arid north-central region of the Arabian Peninsula.

Ottomans (Ottoman Empire) Founded by the Turkish leader Osman, the Ottoman state gave rise to the last great Islamic caliphate. Centered in Anatolia, the empire lasted from its founding in the thirteenth century to the second decade of the twentieth century.

Pir A recognized master in a sufi tariqah or order.

Qarmatians A long-lived communal movement within the Ismaili sect of Shiism.

Quraish An important and powerful Arab tribe, which controlled Mecca at the time of Muhammad. As descendants of the Prophet's tribe, the Quraish have always been accorded a special respect in Islam.

Ramadan One of the lunar months of the Muslim calendar. Fasting during the daylight hours of Ramadan is one of the five pillars or ritual obligations of Islam.

Riddah The Wars of Apostasy, fought soon after the death of Muhammad, forcing rebellious Arab tribes to continue their allegiance to Islam.

Sadaqa In Islam, a voluntary charitable contribution, bringing religious merit to the donor.

Sanussi A Sufi order that became influential in North Africa.

Sephardim Generally, the "Oriental" Jews of Spanish, African, Asian, or Middle Eastern origin. Specifically, the term refers to Jews from Spain.

Shahada The declaration of faith in Islam: "There is no God but Allah, and Muhammad is His prophet."

Sharia The Muslim legal code, founded on the Koran and hadith (traditions of the Prophet) and codified by various systems of interpretation or fiqh.

Sheikh A term that can apply to high-level political, local, communal, or religious leaders.

Shia Muslims following Caliph Ali and his successors, differing on various points of doctrine from the orthodox Sunni majority. Shiism, concentrated largely in Iraq and Iran, is divided into several different sects. Most Shia prefer this designation to the commonly used term, "Shiite."

Sufism A movement pervasive in Islam, based on mystical experience. The diverse Sufi orders, each with its own tradition of mystical teachings, have cultivated the inner, ecstatic aspect of Islam, and their appeal has greatly aided the spread of Islam in some parts of the world.

Sunni The largest, "orthodox" division of Islam.

Suq Bazaar; a place for commerce, composed of many merchants selling a limited variety of wares. An important setting for social interaction and commercial exchange.

Sura Chapter in the Koran.

Tanzimat Generally, a series of attempted reforms in the Ottoman Empire from 1839 to 1876; at least partially a response to growing European dominance at that time.

Tariqahs Specific orders of Sufism, with specified secret paths to mystical ecstasy. After the decline of the caliphate, tariqah lodges often filled many local social needs as well.

Taqiyyah Dissimulation, or the disguise of one's true religious feelings to avoid persecution. Widely used among the Shia in response to the many attempts to control or persecute the Shia community.

Tawhid The undivided unity of God and His authority over humankind; also refers to other, derivative concepts of unity, including social or political unity.

Ulema Muslim scholars who function as religious leaders in Islam. In contrast to Christian priests, the ulema are not organized into a clergy and claim no special powers of sanctity beyond their study of the documents of Islam.

Umayyad One of the most powerful and important of the Arabic families at the time of Muhammad. The Umayyad caliphate was founded at Damascus by Muawiya after his conflict of succession with Ali.

Umma The worldwide community of Islam, which ideally commands a Muslim's loyalty above all considerations of race, kinship, or nationality.

Wahhabi Another, less preferred, term for Muwahhidun.

Wajh Group honor, "face," a concept of great importance in the maintenance of group and individual prestige.

Waqf Religious endowments, usually made in perpetuity, that support a specific institution devoted to good works, such as a madrasah, a home for orphans, or a religious building. The institution of waqf sometimes became a device for avoiding taxation.

Zakat One of the five pillars of the Islamic faith, obligating the faithful to support the unfortunate and the needy.

INDEX

Note: The letters 't' and 'f' followed by the locators denotes 'tables' and 'figures'.